MATHEMATICS AS AN EDUCATIONAL TASK

MATHEMATICS AS
AN EDUCATIONAL TASK

by

HANS FREUDENTHAL

D. REIDEL PUBLISHING COMPANY / DORDRECHT-HOLLAND

Library of Congress Catalog Card Number 72–77874

ISBN 90 277 0322 1

Printed in The Netherlands by D. Reidel, Dordrecht

PREFACE

Like preludes, prefaces are usually composed last. Putting them in the front of the book is a feeble reflection of what, in the style of mathematics treatises and textbooks, I usually call the didactical inversion: to be fit to print, the way to the result should be the inverse of the order in which it was found; in particular the key definitions, which were the finishing touch to the structure, are put at the front. For many years I have contrasted the didactical inversion with the thought-experiment. It is true that you should not communicate your mathematics to other people in the way it occurred to you, but rather as it could have occurred to you if you had known then what you know now, and as it would occur to the student if his learning process is being guided. This in fact is the gist of the lesson Socrates taught Meno's slave. The thought-experiment tries to find out how a student could re-invent what he is expected to learn.

I said about the preface that it is a feeble reflection of the didactical inversion. Indeed, it is not a constituent part of the book. It can even be torn out. Yet it is useful. Firstly, to the reviewer who then need not read the whole work, and secondly to the author himself, who like the composer gets an opportunity to review the *Leitmotivs* of the book. Though I just did it with one of them, I would prefer not to continue this way. I would rather try to do justice to some of the features I seem to have neglected a little.

The present book is not a methodology of mathematics in the sense that I will systematically show how some teaching matter should be taught; it is not even a systematic analysis of subject matter. I hardly ever refer to well-organized classroom experiments evaluated by statistical methods, nor do I cite experimental results of developmental psychology or the psychology of learning. Maybe the most striking feature is that this book contains few quotations. I will try to justify all these features.

First, to take the psychological literature. To be honest I should say that I feel there is no need to embellish low-key education using high-brow psychology, in particular if the cited literature is far removed from educational preoccupations. If others prefer this procedure, then indeed, I feel the need to oppose it. Misusing Piaget's name has become quite a habit in didactical literature. This led me to discuss in passing, and finally in a more connected form in the Appendix, what Piaget's investigations could mean for mathematical education.

Perhaps in mathematics instruction one expects more from the psychology of learning, and in a more technical sense this expectation may certainly come true in detailed investigations. I found a lot of interesting and even exciting things in the psychology of learning though hardly anything I was looking for. When in an excellent modern book* I tried to find out what I should understand under learning and how I should subdivide it, I felt myself very far from what I had experienced myself and with others as *mathematical* learning. A feeling of loneliness seized me: is mathematics really so different? I wish that someone who profoundly understands both mathematics and psychology would show us the bridge.

Except for some general ideas I did not take my empirical material from psychology. My most direct sources are textbooks, didactical designs, actual lessons, as well as observations with individual children; indirectly my main sources were talks and discussions with teachers. With respect to the second kind of source one can find an acknowledgement of some of the influences at the end of this Preface. On the other hand I avoided all citations with respect to textbooks, designs and lessons wherever it was feasible. I believe I had a compelling reason to do so for this material was frequently subjected to criticism, which in fact was often negative. The material could be sharply divided into serious work and trash. Citations in footnotes would have meant tarring everything with the same brush. This I would hate to do. At the same time, it would have been too much an honour for trash to be quoted along with the serious literature. Therefore, I have made explicit quotations only in a few quite specific cases.

For a few other reasons I did not mention mathematical-didactical investigations. The main reason is that except for some generalities I did not use their results because I could not. I will explain why.

* R. M. Gagné, *The Conditions of Learning*, London 1965.

The first kind of investigations I have in mind are of the kind that intend to show that some particular subject matter is teachable. The author submits the subject matter to us; he tells us where and when it was tested, and gives, or does not give, statistical data about its success. Mostly there is no additional data relating to the teaching methods, and this makes the report worthless, because without any further experimentation it may be taken for granted that with the appropriate methods all you want to test can be crammed into the children's heads. Quite recently I saw a course for individual instruction (an excellent one, I should add), where, indoctrinated with a wrong recipe, the children obediently proved the same nonsense for quite a number of years and never protested – and this therefore proves that this subject matter was "teachable"!

There is still, however, a more serious reason why I do not believe in such investigations. At most they prove that the subject matter is learnable, not that it is teachable. It is not true that this means the same thing. That a subject matter is teachable by a few does not imply that a sufficiently large number of teachers can teach it. If it is mathematically wrong, or didactically mistaken or worthless, quite a few teachers may simply refuse to teach it or will do it with so much distaste that it ceases to be teachable. Further, some subjects can be so uncommon that they can only be taught if it is told in all details how it should be taught, but such details are usually lacking. I mean by this, indications on the form of instruction which is best adapted to the subject matter, rather than on didactic details. This is a point which has perhaps been a bit neglected in the present book. If we design teaching material and methods, we should not only weigh up what can be learned and is worth learning, we should also be concerned about what kind of subject matter the teacher can learn to teach, or rather what we can teach our teachers to teach their pupils – if I look back on my own activities and on this book, I am not prone to estimate my own capabilities too high in this regard.

I am going to continue discussing the kind of investigations I was not able to use fruitfully. A second kind are those where with respect to a particular subject matter two teaching methods or subject arrangements are compared, say, with the result that the author has inferred with a probabilistic certainty of 98% that one method is not as bad as the other. About thirty years ago was the first time that I saw such an investigation;

not in mathematics but in geography. The investigation was above reproach; the only thing that surprised me was that it was still the same geography which had been the most boring chapter of my own school career. Since then I have seen a lot of similar investigations, and as far as the authors described their teaching methods, I often could not believe that what I was reading was still possible today.

Maybe these were exceptions, but however technically perfect such investigations may be, they cannot answer the preliminary educational questions what, for which purpose, and to whom is a subject matter being taught. My criticism is aimed at the spirit behind such research. Embellishing it with a statistical analysis does not mean that the rigour of natural science has been transferred to educational research. The only thing that reminds one of (bad) natural science is the pretension that the seventh digit after the decimal point is correct while everything left of the point is wrong. Rather than from such experimental investigations, I learned a lot from my own and from reported classroom experiences, from textbooks and manuals, whether I liked them or not, and from honest analysis of subject matter and learning behaviour, as performed by experienced teachers.

True educational activity means tracing the right path to education, guided by one's own honest conviction. Educational science should, first of all, be the rational justification of this honest conviction. You may call it philosophy. But whatever it is called, it cannot be missed. Investigations on details cannot replace it, on the contrary, they can flourish only in the soil of a healthy educational philosophy.

In spite of all the detailed investigations in this work this book is above all a philosophy of mathematical education. I am not the first to have written such a book. The least one should have learned when studying his predecessors is that one has come to terms with their ideas. The scientific character of a book like the present one is not measured by the number of footnotes but by the thoroughness of this preliminary discussion.

I have often lectured and written about teaching. This book does not contain any essentially new material compared with my earlier papers; in a few places I have even reproduced texts that have already been published before. Here I have taken the opportunity of rearranging my old ideas. As a mathematician I did not feel that it was an easy job.

The problem was not the dialectic instead of the deductive style, and the local organization of the subject matter was not a problem either. But the *global* organization was the sore point. I could not use the formal organization of a mathematics course or treatise where the author says, or writes things like "because of theorem... (cp. p. ...), applied under the condition of corollary... (p. ...), it appears that the definitions of ... on p. ... and on p. ... are equivalent." I could not use this method nor could I invent another form of organization. Thus the present book is, from the viewpoint of a mathematician, badly organized. Numerous repetitions were unavoidable.

Though I cannot cite in detail how much I have learned from others, I am fully conscious about its importance and acknowledge my debt. The first suggestions to occupy myself theoretically with education came from my wife during the course of common educational studies. Among pedagogical psychologists I believe that I was most strongly influenced by O. Decroly. My educational interpretation of mathematics betrays the influence of L. E. J. Brouwer's view on mathematics (though not on education). From 1945 to 1963 I learned much of principal importance as well as many didactical details in the mathematical working group of the Dutch section of the New Education Fellowship; among its members to whom I owe so much, I need only mention the names of P. M. van Hiele and his late wife Dieke Geldof. More recently, thanks to activities in the international educational field, my circle of friends has been enlarged; I am grateful for all I learned at international meetings, and in particular my thanks extend to Emma Castelnuovo, Zofia Krygovska, and W. Servais, and more recently, to A. Revuz. My book is dedicated to all who are committed to mathematical instruction.

Utrecht, 27 December 1970

CONTENTS

LIST OF SYMBOLS

∨ or, ∧ and, ⋁ there is a..., ⋀ for all...,

→ if ... then, ¬ non-,

∪, ⋃ union, ∩, ⋂ intersection,

∈ adherence, ⊂ inclusion, ...\... without,

○ void set,

number of ...,

⌜a, b⌝ ordered pair a, b,

⌜A, B⌝ set of the ⌜a, b⌝ with $a \in A$, $b \in B$,

$A \rightsquigarrow B$ set of the mappings of A into B,

$\{x|...\}$ set of the x with the property ...,

$\curlyvee_x$..., ... as a function of x,

N set of the natural numbers,

Z set of the integers,

Q set of the rational numbers,

R set of the real numbers,

C set of the complex numbers,

with superscript +, ... positive ...

CHAPTER I

THE MATHEMATICAL TRADITION

Somebody once made the funny and effective remark mathematics was she
  who first is sneaking with a low frame, but soon raises her head to the heavens
  and walks on the earth   *Iliad* **IV**, 442–3, speaking of Eris

because it starts with the point and the line, but its investigations comprise heaven,
earth, and universe.
                                            Hero, *Definitiones*

Non igitur lector lacrimes? decepit utrosque
maxima mendacis fama mathematici.   (*CIL* **VI**, 27140)
Not for this reason weep – look to my parents, misled by the great renown of the
mendacious mathematician.

               From the epitaph of four year-old Telephus on the via Appia

If the army of the enemy sets out 6 days ago and is marching $3\frac{1}{2}$ miles* daily, and ours
starts today, how many miles should it march a day to catch up in a week?

                    From a German arithmetic book of 1799

Nobody knows what man invented first, writing or arithmetic. The alphabet is two millennia older than our present Indo-Arabian numerical system but this in itself proves nothing. Mathematics is much older than those numerals. The first exercises in writing and arithmetic are closely connected with each other. Whether, how, how much and how long before this time people counted orally or with counters, nobody can tell. It is a striking fact that the numerals up to 10 and that for 100 belong to the common stock of the Indo-European linguistic family. They were invented long before writing.

No matter how they developed, by the end of the third millennium B.C. well-groomed elementary arithmetic and algebra existed in Babylonia. It is not our formal algebra of x and y. The unknowns are indicated by the terms "length" and "width" (of a rectangle). It is said that science in Babylonia was the business of priests. But this term is a misleading one. What they called priests were in fact the intellectuals of that era, the clerks, the teachers, the librarians, the star-gazers, the

* A German mile equals about 5 statute miles.

augurs and haruspices, the soothsayers, the temple and palace architects, and the sorcerers. At the cradle of mathematics stood the calculator, the surveyor, the merchant, the money-changer, the banker, the book-keeper, the executor, the publican, and the builder of bridges, roads and cities. Yet their wants were quickly satisfied. The problems students had been solving in the temple schools of Babylonia for two millennia were not quite as practical. Teachers let them cover a road 100 km long and one mm wide with asphalt and then compute how many day's wages it cost. Or they posed the problem of inheritance of 65 gold coins, divided among five brothers such that the younger brother gets three coins fewer than his immediate older brother. Every generation solves these immortal problems anew – the stone that weighs one pound more than half its own weight, or the lance that towers one cubit above the wall against which it is vertically placed and which recedes three cubits if it leans against the wall without exceeding it.

Indeed, this is what they learned – useful multiplications and divisions with tables and counters. But with what purpose did they do so? To solve useless linear and quadratic equations? One wonders if they ever complained? And if they did, what did their fathers or their teachers answer?

Did they reply that students had been learning mathematics as early as the flood, that mathematics was a whetstone of wit, or simply that other topics were even more useless? For instance Sumerian, which was still being taught when it had already been extinct for two millennia, or Accadian, and the cuneiform script, when they spoke Aramaic in the streets of Babylon and when the alphabet had been in existence for the last thousand years. Or did their teachers answer – wait a few months, and next year you will be told how this mathematics can be applied to compute the calendar, the feasts, and the course of the sun, the moon and the stars?

Astronomy was the next science of mankind, and mathematical astronomy was two millenia younger than mathematics itself. This was indeed a practical science. You cannot conjure stars and planets out of a void just like cooking up mathematical problems. What was the use of astronomy? To foretell the calendar, feasts, eclipses, wars, pestilences, whirlwinds, storms, inundations, the fortune of nations, and finally even of individuals. Was it not a useful science, a useful application of mathematics that would live on for two millennia? In fact, even in these celestial applications, there was no use of quadratic equations. To apply these, one had to rely on problems like this one: "Length and width, I multiplied length and width and got the area; I added the excess of length over width to the area, 183; I added length and width, 27; asked for: length, width, area." Thousands of such problems have been preserved on clay tablets, though very little remains of the theoretical literature, the "teaching texts" with the rules for solving such problems.

Even less has been conserved of Egyptian mathematics, which was not entrusted to clay tablets, but to much less durable papyrus. But the principle is still the same: it was a mathematics that quickly and to a great extent surpassed practical needs. We can only too well understand why the calculator and the surveyor were fascinated by the figures and shapes they were familiar with, that they liked to play with these objects, to unravel their secrets, and to fathom their mysteries. Most books tell us that up till the time of the Greeks, mathematics was a collection of basic applications, but this is simply not true.

Certainly, Greek mathematics was different, and if the few sources that have survived are trustworthy, it was different from the very beginning. Some time in the sixth century B.C., the Greeks must have learned Babylonian mathematics and astronomy. In what is traditionally known about Thales, Babylonian influence is easily recognizable and Babylonian mathematics accounts for much that is told about Pythagoras and his School. Who does not know the so-called Pythagorean theorem? This theorem was known by the Babylonians some two millennia earlier than the Greeks. Was Pythagoras perhaps the first to prove it?* No, a theorem like this which is not obvious by mere sight, can only be discovered by proving it; it cannot be found empirically by measuring the sides of triangles. Yet most books will tell you that proving theorems was a Greek rather than a Babylonian invention.

What the Greeks actually did was to make demonstration a principle in mathematics. In Greek mathematics is outlined what is today called a deductive system. This indeed possibly started with Thales. He is said to have proved theorems, and a closer look at these propositions reveals they are not the kind of the Pythagorean theorem but like that

* Contrary to modern tradition, there is no indication that the ancient Egyptians ever knew it.

of the equality of angles in an isosceles triangle, that is, theorems which are obvious by sight alone. When people start proving such propositions, they betray they have discovered a new game, namely demonstrating for demonstrating's sake. From the fact that they were able to prove such propositions, we may conclude that they had constructed a system in which demonstrating is a meaningful activity. If such a system and such a method of demonstrating ever existed in Babylonia, all traces of it have vanished. Aristotle expounds what a deductive system is more clearly than has ever been done up to modern times. Every true science, according to Aristotle, starts with "archai", principles, on which it rests by its very nature and from which it can be derived. Euclid's Elements start with Definitions, Postulates and Axioms; other authors use other terms, but this custom of starting geometry with such principles was at least one century older than Euclid's Elements. Probably Hippocrates of Chios, the first author of Elements, already knew it. We do not know the origin of this custom, whether it sprang from philosophy or from the discussion techniques of public meetings. One can imagine that such a stock of principles was a means of fighting chicanery and litigation.

Euclid did not explicitly account for all the axioms he used but blaming Euclid for this incompleteness is too modern a stand-point. A science rests on principles but nobody asks you to enumerate all of them; how far to go is open to dicussion.

There are parts of Euclid that look like modern mathematics, for example, the theory of proportions and similarity in the 5th and 6th books. It is ascribed to Eudoxus; it plays the part which we today allot to the theory of real numbers. There are, on the other hand, parts which have an extremely weak deductive structure. Euclid's work was essentially a compilation. Nevertheless, for well on twenty centuries it excited admiration and invited imitation. This admiration was justified, but imitations were not usually very successful. Of course, people like Archimedes and Christiaan Huygens have been as great axiomaticians as Eudoxus, but the axiomatic efforts of Spinoza's philosophy more geometrico, Leibniz' example of axiomatic jurisprudence and politicology, Whiston's axiomatic cosmology, and whatever else produced in this field, all were not truly convincing. What axiomatics means and how its axioms should be formulated was not shown until the end of the 19th century, in Pasch's work – he taught it to the Italian geometers – and Hilbert's.

Deductivity and the germ of axiomatics are in our view the most striking, and in fact the most modern, feature of Greek mathematics. Another great feat of Greek mathematics was the discovery of the irrational, the incommensurability of diagonal and side of a square. There are few things that look more obvious than that every ratio of magnitudes can be expressed by natural numbers. The discovery that this was not true should have caused a crisis in the foundations of mathematics according to modern historians, but this is probably too modern a view. It is true that it did not fit into the Pythagorean doctrine that all was number, but the mathematicians among the Pythagoreans tried to find a way out. A fresh definition of ratio was required, though not by natural numbers. It was first done by infinite approximations, which finally were again eliminated. The definitive solution in antiquity was something like Dedekind's cuts. It is presented in the 5th and 6th books of the Elements, along with the antique version of epsilontics. Greek doctrine took a further step: not only infinite processes, but also Babylonian algebra were eliminated. Since numbers did not suffice to explain geometrical ratios, they were banished from geometry; real numbers were unknown, and rational numbers forbidden – in exact science that is. Merchants and craftsmen continued to use fractions. To the mathematician, as to Pythagoras, number, that is, the natural number was sacrosanct. Plato reacted with irritation to attempts "to divide the unit".

Was algebra thrown away? No, not completely, for a surrogate was invented, a geometrical algebra, a system of geometrical mummery of algebraic operations, of linear and quadratic equations, and of solving procedures. This system was expounded in Euclid's 2nd book and, was applied in the 10th in particular, in the classification of irrationalities – a paragon of unreadable mathematics.

Geometrical algebra, this impractical product of methodical dogmatism and fanatical rigourism was the disease which killed Greek mathematics. As long as the heuristic methods of algebra and infinitesimals were still taught orally alongside the official Euclidean-Archimedean rigorous mathematics, students could learn to work within the official straitjacket. As soon as this tradition was interrupted, all was lost. As late as the 3rd century A.D. the Babylonian tradition seems to have survived – this is proved by the existence of Diophantus, who was a genuine algebraist – but this, then, was the last flare. Algebra was re-invented in the Arabian world, and both the Indians and the Christian Middle Ages contributed to its revival though Greek rigour still dazzled the heirs of Greek culture. The first to cut free from the Greek tradition was Descartes, the challenger of all tradition. He put the cart before the horse: rather than geometrizing algebra, he algebraized geometry. The result was what in school and university instruction used to be called analytic geometry. Meanwhile, limit procedures and infinitesimal methods had come into vogue and finally led to the invention of calculus (Newton's fluxions and Leibniz's differential and integral calculus). Nobody actually realized what scruples had led the Greeks to reject algebra; Eudoxus' epsilontics was not understood, or if it was, it was rejected. Euclidean-Archimedean rigour was still admired, but there were scarcely any who really understood it, and after Christiaan Huygens there was nobody left to imitate it. Not until rigour was recaptured in the 19th century did people understand the essence of Greek mathematics. Maybe this course of events was a historic necessity: Eudoxus' strait-jacket that choked Greek mathematics, the non-mathematical millennium, the liberation when the good was cast away with the bad, the laborious reconstruction of rigour (which lasted longer than in antiquity) and finally the rediscovery of the Greeks who long ago already knew so much – perhaps each link was historically indispensable.

So much about the tradition of mathematical rigour. Once more I must warn against exaggerated ideas on antique rigour. Elementary geometry in Euclid in particular shows gaps, and even sham arguments. On the other hand, the modern reader is struck by the care that was bestowed on the theory of parallels. The postulate on parallels, such as it is found in Euclid, was in antiquity the final solution of a problem that must have preoccupied Greek mathmaticians for a long period before Euclid. From rare allusions to other views on parallels one can guess that the Greeks knew more about it than what has been handed down in the Elements, and that they were nearer to the historically still remote non-Euclidean geometrics than straight historical data would seem to allow. Yet again, as in the case of mathematical rigour, the content of tradition in foundations of geometry was fixed for two millennia by Euclid's Elements. The same is true of the geometrical method, the well-known auxiliary lines by which figures are parcelled out into sequences of congruent triangles which permit a systematic walk from one to the next to forge a chain of congruence relations between two magnitudes which are to be proved equal – a methodical madness. Take, for instance, such a classical problem of school mathematics as proving that in a cube, given a vertex A, the plane through three vertices that are joined with A by edges, is orthogonal to the space diagonal through A. How many congruent triangles are needed to prove it, whereas mere sight shows that the rotation through 120° with a space diagonal as an axis, leaves the cube and the aforesaid plane invariant, which proves the assertion immediately! A decennium or two ago such a proof would have been considered improper. Fortunately today mappings like reflections, translations, and rotations are *dernier cri* in school instruction. In creative geometry, mappings emerged in the 19th century; they are a principle of modern geometry, but the Euclidean tradition of congruent triangles was still in this century so coercive that even as great an authority as Felix Klein did not succeed in introducing mappings into German school instruction. Up to the last "Elements" before Euclid, mappings seem to have been an admissible argument; though some relics have survived in Euclid's Elements, it is a fact that Euclid weeded out geometrical mappings and that this revision decided their fate up to the 19th century. Why were mappings outlawed? Probably because their kinematic undertone was out of tune with the lofty static character of geometry; geometry's detachment from the material world did not tally with the variability which is characteristic of motion – such philosophical dogmas, which are still heard in more modern times, may have been the afterthought when mappings were rejected. So strong was the Greek tradition that even the kinematically-motivated modern concept of function did not modify geometrical habits.

Pythagoras, according to ancient tale, raised geometry from an artisan's business to a liberal art, that is, to an occupation of a free man who does not soil his hands. Together with Arithmetic, Music and Astronomy, Geometry belongs to the four 'non-trivial' arts of the medieval quadrivium. All of them were ascribed to Pythagoras; it is a fact that they were at least taught by his first disciples. The term "mathematics" sprang from that circle. Among Pythagoras' adepts there was a group that called themselves mathematicians, since they cultivated the four "mathemata", that is geometry, arithmetic, musical theory and astronomy.

The claim that these were liberal arts and that their subjects were detached from the sublunar world, was put forward by Plato and his School, and it has been accepted by tradition.

This, at least, was their theory, though it did not prevent Greek mathematicians from trying to apply mathematics. Some even practiced technical mechanics, the greatest among them being no less a mathematician than Archimedes. In fact, in Greece as in Babylonia mathematics was far ahead of its applications – how far ahead is shown by the theory of conics, which was not applied until two millennia after their discovery when Kepler described the planetary motions by ellipses. Mathematics has always been ahead of its applications; it is the way of mathematics – to look for patterns of thought from which the appliers make their choice.

No doubt the scientific performances of the Greeks reached their peak in mathematics; they did better in the theoretical than in the empirical sciences. This is not hard to understand. Babylonia was not much different. Whoever has grasped the power of thinking, will continue to exercise it. Sensual perception is delusive, again and again this is stressed by philosophers. From a distance objects look smaller, square towers seem to be round, the oar appears to be broken by the water. Only a clear head can outwit nature and can find out nature's tricks.

Rationalism plays a great part in Greek thought. But if some maintain and many do, that the Greeks did not observe nature, they are exaggerating tremendously. As a warning, they usually quote Zeno of Elea, who ventured to prove that Achilles could not catch up with the tortoise, though everybody knows that this is contradicted by normal experience. Of course, Zeno knew this, but his paradoxes did not aim to refute reality but inconsistent theories on reality. People also quote Aristotle as a rationalist who preferred deduction from principles above experience. This characterization in general is not true either. What strikes us about Aristotle is that he interprets nature in a psychological-biological rather than in a mathematical-mechanical frame of thought, which sometimes makes his arguments look magical. Modern mechanics did not evolve because Galileo, Huygens, Newton were better observers than the Greeks, but rather because they analyzed nature in a more logical and more penetrating way. Aristotle's proof that the world is finite should primarily be rejected not because such statements cannot be proved, but because his proofs contain serious blunders. On the other hand, Galileo established his thesis of the equal velocity of falling bodies *in vacuo*, not on observations but on a profound and surprising analysis. Astronomy testifies that the Greeks knew what observation meant. The astronomers exerted themselves to "save the phenomena", that is, to adjust the parameters of their model of the planetary system, with all its excentres and epicycles, to the astronomical data. Of course they had to do so, since the goodness of fit was a criterion of truth which could easily be checked. Yet, even outside astronomy, there subsisted a kind of practical mathematics besides the pure science, examples of which have come down to us in Hero's compendia. Today there is an almost continuous transition between the manifestations of extreme theoretical and extreme practical mathematics. Whenever science of the past is under discussion, it should not be forgotten that the stimuli mathematics received and could receive from the applications were not too numerous. This alone could have decided the fate of ancient mathematics were it not that it carried with itself the germ of paralysis since its structure made it almost impossible to take up the thread over a gap in the tradition. It was a consequence of the style of the Elements, a paragon of ready-made science, an open text if a good teacher was available, but a sealed book to the autodidact. We shall come back to this point.

When the Indians, Arabs and mediaeval monks restored mathematics, it was a new science that arose, a science without the touch of a Pythagoras, who would have raised it to a liberal art. The renovations were mostly practical. From India, the Arabs learned a new way to write numbers, which they in turn handed down to the Europeans. This is our decimal position system, which is much superior to Greek literal and to Roman numerals. Indeed, it is much superior, but its superiority should not be exaggerated. How did the Greeks calculate, people ask, and how did the Romans, with their impractical number indications? It must have been torture. How could they ever be so impractical? In astronomy, the Greeks accepted the Babylonian sexagesimal position system. If they knew how this worked, why did not they write their numbers in a positional system (and then in the decimal version)?

In fact, the question as to how the Greeks and the Romans managed to calculate with their impractical numerals is quickly answered. The answer is: not at all. Ancient nations calculated, not as we do on paper, but with counters on an abacus, which has been a positional instrument from the start. This was the way numbers were handled from antiquity to modern times, and it is still common in the Far East. In spite of a few inconveniences, it is as fast as pencil and paper. Indo-Arabian computing, that is, computing with written numerals, progressed together with the use of the dust-plank, on which figures are written in dust or fine sand, and later innovations in computing methods depended on the availability of cheap paper.

Nevertheless, the Indo-Arabian system was quite an achievement, but progress was still slow. It is strange that decimal fractions had to wait for Stevin in the 16th century, while sexagesimal ones had existed from Babylonian times.

Common fractions are a still stranger chapter. It took a long time before they were accepted. What is 2 divided by 7? To answer "two sevenths" sounds like a subterfuge. The true calculator calculates as long as there is something to be calculated. $\frac{2}{7}$ can be written $\frac{1}{4}$ plus $\frac{1}{28}$, and this looks much nicer. It was the Egyptian custom of displaying fractions in a sum of fractions with a numerator 1. The Greek imitated this. Even mathematicians and astronomers did so, if their philosophical scruples allowed them to accept fractions at all. Not until the Indian period were fractions really accepted. Indians indicated fractions by numerator and denominator as we do, except that they did not write a horizontal stroke. Admitting common fractions (and later negative numbers, too) is a characteristic algebraic idea which surpasses plain computing. It is an algebraic idea to demand the unrestricted possibility of all operations and to fulfil it by introducing new objects. Another algebraic idea is symbolism, the use of signs which do not belong to everyday language, to indicate variables. "Think of a number" is how the problems are introduced in old narrative algebra. In Diophantus' work the word "number" becomes more and more a computation symbol. This continues in Indian and Arabian mathematics. The "*cossists*" of the late Middle Ages had a whole system of symbols for the unknown and its powers, even beyond the third to which geometers would have limited the system. An important step in the progress of symbolic algebra is the appearance in the 15th century of formal fractions with polynomials of the unknown in numerator and denominator. Algebra as we use it started at the end of the 16th century when Vieta indicated by literal symbols, not only as we would say, the unknowns, but also the indeterminates. The next important step is Descartes' algebraization of geometry. Descartes overcame the restriction that to be algebraically added terms should be of the same dimension. In Descartes, the Greek tradition in algebra is definitely brought to an end.

At the same time Descartes created a new tradition in algebra. It is often overlooked how strong it became. Huygens fought Descartes in physics, while Leibniz did the same in mathematics. The great mathematicians devoted themselves to infinitesimal calculus and promoted it – Newton, Leibniz, the Bernoullis, Euler, Lagrange and Laplace. Certainly there were even more who learned and understood the new methods, but how many were there in all? It is true, numerous popular Euclid adaptions and algebra textbooks in the vernacular are proof of the spread of geometrical and algebraic knowledge, even at the universities. But how about infinitesimal calculus that by that time had surpassed algebra. Where was it being taught? If I am not mistaken, during the whole 18th century there was no place where people could learn calculus. This is a most astonishing feature, with no precedent in history. How could this happen? Was it so difficult to sell calculus to the universities that had just with much pain converted to Cartesianism and even accepted the Copernican system?

Universities in the 18th century were in fact fairly inert. Moreover, almost no leading mathematicians taught at the universities. Science was the concern of academies and learned societies, which had no business in teaching. But there was more to it than that. The art of printing had led the tradition of science onto new tracks. Oral teaching, though still important, was no longer indispensable. If calculus had been invented a few centuries earlier, it would have vanished without any trace if there had not been schools where it was taught. Things had changed, there were now books from which one could learn calculus and since calculus was at least needed in astronomy after Newton, a few people tried to read those books. They were probably not many. To understand what was published in calculus, the reader had to be congenial to the writer. So it happened that much fewer people learned calculus than algebra – a tradition that still subsists. The art of printing freed the leading scientists from the need to establish schools. Quite a few of them enjoyed this liberty, but at the same time the tradition of science was seriously obstructed by the lack of schools. We will see later how this was repaired in the 19th century.

The return of active science to the universities is marked by the founding of the *École Polytechnique* in France and the Humboldt reforms in Germany. The pace was not as equally quick everywhere and in all branches of teaching. In Königsberg and Berlin, Jacobi with his seminars, gave the keynote, while in Göttingen, under Gauss, only the most elementary mathematics was taught. New traditions were formed: from France came those of the *Cours d'analyse*, of the Mécanique rationnelle, of descriptive geometry; and from Germany, that of the course in elliptic functions. The classical structure of the *Cours d'analyse* has meanwhile disintegrated under the influence of set theory, topology and algebra; it became a victim of the restructuration of mathematics that was initiated by Cantor and continued by Fréchet, Hausdorff, Steinitz, and Emmy Noether. The tradition of theoretical mechanics died when this application of mathematics was understood in an even broader sense. The most absurd phenomonen was the tyranny of descriptive geometry that lasted more than a century. Nobody now understands how this technique could have been exercised and admired as a paragon of applied mathematics, though it is rather the paragon of a completely isolated field of mathematics, a domain with no relations to other parts of mathematics or to the applications of mathematics, a discipline that was nowhere and never applied because it was much too rigid to be applied. The historical importance of elliptic functions is better understood; they were, indeed, the first break-through of function theory after the well-known "elementary" functions, and they were the indispensable cross-roads to new fields. That they survived themselves for decades is one of the expressions of the inertia law of tradition.

Another 19th century fashion was the algebraic theory of invariants. Anyone who has become familiar with the charms of the so-called symbolic method, can understand this state of mind. It is astonishing how this discipline died. Hilbert terminated it by showing implicitly and unintentionally how petty its problems looked under a more comprehensive point of view. With Hilbert's discoveries, the algebraic theory of invariants passed into the algebra of polynomial rings. The fate of broad fields of geometry in the 19th century was similar. They vanished into a part of algebra which got the unsatisfactory name of algebraic

THE MATHEMATICAL TRADITION

geometry. Likewise was born and died in the 20th century a kind of complex function theory of one variable which was extensively and profoundly developed in Germany. Another instance is analytic number theory that started with Euler and flourished in the first third of the present century; it has now come to a relative standstill, though its great problems are still open. A certain kind of differential geometry that was quite popular in the twenties and thirties of our century soon turned into a rigid and infertile formalism. Throughout history, tradition and renovation alternate with each other. Today the resistance of the old lasts no longer than one generation. Achievements have a convincing power, in particular in mathematics where achievements can be more objectively evaluated than elsewhere. Neglected geniuses are rare in mathematics. The sentimental stories told about Abel are pure invention. Abel's significance was immediately acknowledged by his contemporaries, even by those who did not read his work as soon as it was published. Abel did not starve, indeed he received comfortable scholarships which enabled him to travel around; it is also sheer gossip that Cauchy lost one of Abel's treatises. Nevertheless it is true that Abel died too young to see himself become famous. The same is true of Galois – if he had lived longer, his theory would perhaps have spread faster. According to the story-tellers, starvation was also Riemann's fate. Like Abel, he died of tuberculosis, but older than Abel and at the height of his fame. Cantor is remembered as the victim of the indifference of his contemporaries, but this was not the cause of his illness, and it is not true either that people were indifferent or hostile to Cantor's ideas. His point set theory was immediately accepted, though abstract set theory needed a longer time of incubation. By a slow process, set theory penetrated other parts of mathematics; they had to mature to need set theory, and in order of maturation, they were imbued with it. This development will be sketched in the next chapter.

It is at the same time an exaggeration to reckon Boole among the misunderstood geniuses. It is no use overestimating the merit of isolated and hollow formalisms which proved valuable much later; as long as they were not filled with a substantial content, contemporaries cannot be accused of neglecting them. Logicians usually consider Frege as a genius, which is again an enormous overestimation. Frege lived in his own cosy corner of mathematics; his ignorance and hardly intelligent appreciation of what was happening in contemporary mathematics around him are not testimony in his favour.

In the beginning of this chapter, we spoke much about useful mathematics. The further we progressed in history of tradition, the less we came back to this subject. As early as ancient Babylonia, the mathematics of the common man, of merchants, craftsmen and surveyors was complemented by that of the astronomer; in Greece it reached new peaks and besides the astrologers it could count on navigators as its clients. Greco-Roman technology certainly required more mathematics than that of Babylon and Egypt, but it was still a poorly applied mathematics and this again hampered the development of pure mathematics. It was not only because of this that mathematics lacked stimuli, but even more because a socially useless discipline is not fitted to enlist many adepts in any society. Characteristically when a Roman speaks about a mathematician he means an astrologer – also called a Chaldean, because astrology came from the East. How could a mathematician make a living? Law, rhetoric, art, philology, even poetry were more promising. In the Christian Middle Ages, though, there were monasteries that could afford to promote sciences, but in them mathematics played a modest part.

What caused the seemingly sudden growth of mathematics and sciences in the 16th century, which in the 17th century gave us Galileo, Descartes, Kepler, Huygens, Newton, Leibniz? History is usually written by scholars in the humanities, who view the growth of mathematics and sciences through the prism of the renaissance of the arts and humanities. For these new developments, however, the rebirth of antiquity was less crucial than people usually think. Technology as a motor driving history is usually overlooked because it is outside the scope of most historians. They do not notice that in technology this development starts three full centuries earlier. Between 1200 and 1500 more things were invented than ever before in human history – a chain of very fundamental inventions in which the art of printing is the last link. It is this technology that prepared the seemingly sudden growth of mathematics and sciences. Not because it immediately required a much more profound science but rather because it is the same attitude of mind which concocts inventions, plays tricks on nature, and searches for the secrets in numbers and figures.

There can be no doubt either that mathematics was used more and more. The great number of textbooks with often a practical touch were of course written for people who wished to use mathematics. Newton made the step from celestial kinematics to celestial dynamics, and for this had invented fluxions. The Bernoullis were already trying out mechanical problems which could be of some technical use. Yet the really great influence of applications on the problems of mathematics dates from the beginning of the 19th century. The background to this sudden growth in applied mathematics in the 19th century has been little noticed till now.

The names Fourier, Poisson, Cauchy indicate the key role that French scientists played in it. Suddenly it became a great honour to occupy oneself with applied mathematics since this made you worthy of the *École Polytechnique*, the new school of the Revolution which contemptuously looked down on the old calcified universities. This, again, was an exaggeration. The overestimation of applied and underestimation of pure mathematics did much harm to mathematics as a whole in 19th century France. But this phenomenon was secondary. In the main, the shift towards applications was enormously beneficial and to a high degree programmatic for the development of mathematics in the 19th century.

By applications we mean neither astronomy (which after thousands of years reached a peak with Laplace) nor other traditional uses, nor even probability, which still tended to grow more on the surface than sink deep roots. By applications we mean the broad field, from which future mathematics received strong stimuli, the field that is today called mathematical physics. In spite of Euler, Lagrange and Laplace it started properly with Fourier, Poisson, and Cauchy.

Textbooks may evoke the idea that mechanics was in principle established by Newton and that nothing more remained to do than to elaborate some details. This idea is entirely wrong. Already the mechanics of systems required new principles, not to mention the mechanics of deformable media, heat conduction, elasticity, and vibrations in solids, fluids and gases. These were the problems which were tackled in the 19th century. Guided by physical ideas, the searchers developed methods which now have become paradigmatic for the analysis of partial differential equations and integral equations, and for functional analysis.

The profusion of impulses which were brought forth by these problems has even today not ceased to act.

It is striking that this mathematical physics was theoretically developed by people with a sure feeling for physical significance, but with a poor empirical background and far removed from actual experimentation. The mathematical methods developed for elasticity were first really applied and tested in electromagnetism and optics, which proved to give an unpredictable yet magnificent reward. Once again, in this century, mathematics got a similar enormously stimulating injection from applications; not until it is guided by quantum mechanics does functional analysis blaze new trails. How much mathematical statistics is indebted to the problems of statistical praxis is well-known. How much mathematics may expect in the future from numerical analysis and computers, nobody can tell.

Enthusiasm for number theory, algebraic geometry and categories should not prevent anybody from acknowledging how much poorer mathematics would be without the impulse it received from the applications. Mathematics started as a useful activity, and today it is more useful than it ever was. This is, however, an understatement. One should say: if it were not useful, mathematics would not exist.

Why this stress on the use of mathematics? Because nothing is as easily forgotten as a truism. Even the people responsible for instruction and education often forget this. I do not claim that they could or would deny it. Yet teaching and educating is acting-out, and what is readily acknowledged in speech, usually takes a long time before it influences actions.

CHAPTER II

MATHEMATICS TODAY

Sir,
It is sometimes a matter of wonder to us in Hades, that what we had believed to be our best work remains buried under thick layers of dust in your libraries, while the very talented young men in the mathematical world of the present day strive manfully against problems which are by no means as novel as they think... Unfortunately, it appears that there is now in your world a race of vampires, called referees, who clamp down mercilessly upon mathematicians unless they know the right passwords. I shall do my best to modernize my language, but I am well aware of my shortcomings in that respect; I can assure you, at any rate, that my intentions are honourable and my results invariant, probably canonical, perhaps even functorial. But please allow me to suppose that the characteristic is not 2.

R. Lipschitz, Letter to the Editor
Annals of Mathematics **69** (1959), 247–251

Sous prétexte de mesurer un degré du méridien, si bien déterminé par les Anciens, ils (les charlatans académiques) se sont fait accorder par le ministre 100,000 écus pour les frais de l'opération, petit gâteau qu'ils se partageront en frères.

Marat, *l'Ami du Peuple*

Among the worst barbarisms is that of introducing symbols which are quite new in mathematical, but perfectly understood in common language. Writers have borrowed from the Germans the abbreviation $n!$ to signify $1 \cdot 2 \cdot 3 \cdot \ldots \cdot (n-1) \cdot n$, which gives their pages the appearance of expressing surprise and admiration that 2, 3, 4 etc., should be found in mathematical results...

A. de Morgan: Penny Cyclopedia (1842), in voce Symbols.

WHAT IS TODAY?

It is never easy to tell when "today" began. Historians set the point where *Historia hodierna* starts at their own coming of age. This is, indeed, the turning point in history. As for mathematicians, a questionaire would probably yield a majority for the answer "with Bourbaki", though the people around Bourbaki would presumably be the last to admit it. Another popular date is 1870, characterized by modern theories on real numbers, and by Jordan's *Traité des Substitutions*, the first codification of group theory. 1870 however has the disadvantage that it cuts off half a century off the genesis of group theory; even worse, a mathematician as modern as Riemann would then have died yesterday.

Not long ago, at a mathematical colloquium, a young colleague said in his lecture "from this it follows by a theorem of the Stone Age..." If I am not mistaken, the theorem he meant was about 20 years old. One of the very few older listeners interrupted him, "you mean the Neolithic Age, don't you?" The end of the Stone Age was apparently different in various regions of the earth, as it seems that there are still people living in the Stone Age. Likewise, in mathematics many ages coexist, the day before yesterday with today and tomorrow. The news hits the one earlier than the other. Young people are closer than the old to the new things.

According to an oft-quoted sentence, domains like abstract algebra, topology, measure theory, functional analysis and Hilbert space were nowhere taught before the Second World War. This, of course, is incredibly exaggerated. The author of this sentence clearly meant only the university he knew, but the people who quote him, generalized it. I took my Ph.D. degree in 1930, and on all these subjects except abstract algebra, I followed courses given by prominent mathematicians. In 1930, I also learned abstract algebra when I visited another university, where on the other hand functional analysis did not appear in the curriculum. At that time, measure theory and topology were already represented by printed courses and textbooks.

It is, however, true that before 1930 these modern subjects were not taught at all, not even in the majority of universities, not to mention subjects like foundations of mathematics and Lie groups which were, in fact, represented at my own university. This, however, is not the point. It does not matter whether, but how these modern subjects were taught. When did these types of courses come into being as witnessed today by numerous, more or less identical, textbooks – linear algebra instead of old analytic geometry and determinants, *abstract* algebra instead of the traditional one over the complex field, a calculus course influenced by functional analysis, and so on? Giving a small margin each way, I would say 1935. It is difficult to say when the new ideas got the upper hand in university education. But I would say that in 1950, or at the latest in 1955, the new style prevailed in the universities.

THE CHANGE OF STYLE

It should be clear that the basic mathematical knowledge that a mathematics and physics student acquires in the first university year is not at all new as regards the subject matter. The new thing is the style. To understand how mathematical style has changed within a few decades, take a book or a paper written at the beginning of this century, read its sentences one after the other and try to formulate them in the language of today. In fact there are books of that era which you can read almost as though they had been written yesterday like for instance, Hausdorff's *Mengenlehre* of 1914 but these were the trail-blazers of the new style. How far ahead Hausdorff was becomes clear when his book is compared with A. Schoenflies' *Berichte* on the same subject. Certainly, we have not yet reached the end of this history of changes of style. Maybe formalizing, as the new trend is called, has just started its course; maybe at the end of our century the mathematical literature of its beginning will sound much like *Beowulf* now does to the modern English ear.

Very few who have experienced or created mathematics in this period have been conscious of undergoing this change of style, but if they compare their own notes or publications of the past with their present ones, they will notice a great change. I recall from a course in number theory I followed as a student, the remark of an listener who wanted some theorems interpreted in group theory and proved by group theory methods, whereupon the teacher shook his head and said "These are unrelated things". Today nobody would try to prove these properties without group theory. Not until after my study did I understand that *Galois-Felder* – this is how they named finite fields – were *Körper*. In my first year, I learned linear dependence and related notions in three different courses, with three different subjects and under three different terminologies. It struck me, but I dared not believe it, that it could be the same. Like in a nightmare, I remember coordinate transformations, which for mysterious reasons sometimes turned "contragredient".

THE CHANGE OF STYLE – VARIABLES

I cannot remember when I first grasped such fundamental facts as that variables in propositional forms must be bound to yield propositions, that there is existential and universal binding, and that you should always explicitly state which kind you mean. I do not believe that when I started studying mathematics there was one teacher who gave more than *oral* explications on how the various variables on the blackboard should be bound, and since students like to assiduously copy from the blackboard and to ignore the narratives, my notes looked bad. In the vernacular, people do not care about the kind of binding. It is clear from the context that in "I have got a car" the "a" means existential binding (there is a car I have got) and in "a car is expensive" a universal binding (for all cars, a car is expensive) because nobody would believe that I own all cars, or that I was maintaining that there was only one expensive car. Yet if a poor student has diligently copied what has been written on the blackboard, but not the bindings the teacher was preaching to the winds, then the context from which they could be inferred is non-existent. When I started teaching calculus I bestowed pains on writing the literal definition of limit and continuity on the blackboard, but not until much later did I understand that whenever the convergence of a sequence or the continuity of a function was used or proved, I should write on the blackboard the litany "to each... there is a... such that for all..., whenever..., then...". Of course, this pattern had been familiar to mathematicians for half a century. But can you tell me where in the whole of the mathematical literature up to the last 40 years this pattern is clearly outlined?

Not only here, but everywhere in mathematics, the explicit formulation marks only the end of a sometimes long period of non-formulated operativeness, and in such a period the student must read in the teachers' face what his mind knows only semiconsciously.

The change of style implies that such patterns are now made conscious. In my calculus course in 1938, I suddenly hit upon the idea to work out in all detail the negation of continuity, once with the ε–δ-definition and once with the limit definition, in order to prove their equivalence. I remember this fact as if it had happened yesterday because it was the first time I grasped the didactic value of emphasizing thought patterns. I suppose that quite a few mathematicians from that time onwards must have harboured the same feelings as I did; they too were probably convinced of the value of logical symbols in abridging boring writing on the blackboard, but did not venture in a mathematical course to put on the airs of a *mad* logician. Present style requires not only making the logical patterns explicit, but also using logical symbols though I should add that most of this logical stuff displayed on the blackboard is hardly fit to print (which is not bad at all).

Since we have just discussed the change of style in binding variables, it is perhaps the right moment to mention a terminology that was fairly general up to the thirties yet disappeared within a few decades. Assume a paper began with the words "Let R be a topological space", or "let G be a group", or "let f be a continuous function", or "let P be a point of the projective plane". Then, a little later, the author would speak about an "R", if he meant a topological space, a "G", if he meant a group, an "f" if he meant a continuous function, or a "P" if he meant a point of the projective plane. It could even happen that he continued "Let S be an R" or "Let $R_1, ..., R_p$ be certain R's. R had metamorphized from space into the species of spaces, and likewise the other things too. This is a quite natural influence of the vernacular, where "man" means both a variable and its domain species. It is maybe also an influence of traditional logic with its propositions like "all S are P", but from another point of view it is slovenliness which creeps in as long as people are too lazy to introduce short names or good abbreviations for important substrate entities as the class of topological spaces, of groups, of continuous functions, of the projective plane as set of its points. Even today this slovenliness still exists orally but it did not strike me in print for quite a few years.

THE CHANGE OF STYLE – FUNCTIONS

I do not remember when I first became aware that a function should not be called $f(x)$ but f. I estimate it was 1935. But even after I had grasped it, I did not dare conform to it consequently. For a while, I remember, I even wrote 'the mapping $f X \subset Y$, if I meant a mapping f of X into Y – anything else would have looked like affectation. Wen for years I had condemned "the function $f(x)$" and forbidden it to my students, I still wrote "the sequence a_n".

The obstinate ones who finally converted themselves can now witness how inevitable such renovations were. Why shouldn't you write 'f' or '$f(x)$' for a function if you wish as long as it does not really matter. And as long as you stay in a field where it does not matter, you will look down on the acriby of others as if it were some kind of acrobatics. As long as the subject is one function at a time or two functions or a system of explicitly given functions, it does not matter. But how can we indicate that a function belongs to a set A of functions? Would $f(x) \in A$ do it? No, this means something different. It asserts something about the belonging to A not of the function but of the function values. Of course, it may be clear from the context what we mean, but this is not a thing to rely on.

If this is admitted, we are no longer allowed to write

$$S(f(x)) = \int_0^1 K(x, y) f(y) \, dy$$

or

$$T_a(f(x)) = f(x + a).$$

to define an integral operator S or the translation operator T_a.
It should be

$$(Sf)(x) = \int_0^1 K(x, y) f(y) \, dy$$

and

$$(T_a f)(x) = f(x + a).$$

As a matter of fact, these are no trifles. Functional analysis has contributed much to clarifying notations. If sets and spaces of functions are a major concern, with mappings of such sets on each other, which again may be collected in spaces, which once more are mapped upon each other, and so on, then it is naive to trust that the context will explain what you mean. With the increasing abstractness of the objects being discussed, the necessity of exact expression becomes more and more imperative.

THE CHANGE OF STYLE – ANACOLUTHA

There are even greater subtleties. Let us analyze the proof of a well-known theorem.

THEOREM: $\sqrt{2}$ is irrational.

PROOF:

(1)   Supposition (to be refuted): there are integrers p, q such that $p/q = \sqrt{2}$.

(2) p, q may be supposed relative prime.

(3)   Squaring (1) one gets $p^2/q^2 = 2$, thus

(4) $p^2 = 2q^2$,

(5) $2q^2$ is even and so is p^2, hence p,

(6) $p = 2p'$ for some integer p',

(7) $2q^2 = 4p'^2$,

(8) $q^2 = 2p'^2$,

(9) q^2 is even, and so is q, which is contradictory.

In (1) the variables p, q were bound by an existential quantifier. In (2) they occur free, but it is clear that they shall be subjected to the condition of (1). This does not appear from the text. In the text the 'p', 'q' of (1) and (2) are unrelated. In (1) where 'p', 'q' are bound, they can be replaced by two different letters, and if we take the liberty of doing this, the nonsense becomes obvious. A situation like this is met in (6). The variable p' is bound, its occurrence in (8) is therefore unrelated to that in (6).

This is hair-splitting, isn't it? Yes, at present, it still is. Tomorrow people will ask the same question the other way round. Even today, there are already people who blush whenever they write down proofs like our example above. Yet they will continue in the old style as long as others do so; most people do not like to show off. Ten or twenty years from now nobody will dare to write such obscurities. It is strange that style absurdities like this are so tenacious even though they can be as easily redressed as the present one. The only thing we need is an ornament like "and we call them p, q" added to the end of (1) to sleep the sleep of the just. We should do likewise in (6).

Another earlier mentioned slovenliness that has disappeared is "the mapping $fR \subset S$" if a mapping f of R into S was meant. Today the style is: "the mapping $f: R \to S$". This is more satisfactory but it only shows that people still did not realize what was wrong with the old notation. Otherwise the cleaning up would have been more radical. A few examples will show what I mean.

Let A, B, C, D, E, be points in general position; the plane $\alpha = ABC$ intersects the line $l = DE$ in $\alpha \times l = F$.

I choose $x \notin M$.

$Z = X \otimes Y$ is called the tensor product of X and Y.

The series of the $a_n = 1/(n^2 + 1)$ converges.

What is the matter? '$fR \subset S$', '$\alpha = ABC$', '$l = DE$', '$\alpha \times l = F$', '$\alpha \notin M$', '$A_n = 1/(n^2 + 1)$' are what is called in grammar, sentences, or in logic, propositions. If it is spoken about "the mapping..." "the plane...," "the line...," one expects at the place indicated by the three dots the name of the mapping, the plane, the line; after "I choose", one expects an object. But in all cases, what follows is a sentence. Of course, the meaning is obvious: after the f, the α, the l, the x, a punctuation should be thought of, or the sentence within brackets. Thus:

"the mapping $f(fR \subset S)$",
"the plane $\alpha(= ABC)$", or "the plane $\alpha(\alpha = ABC)$",
"the line $l(= DE)$", or "the line $l(l = DE)$",
"I choose an $x(\notin M)$",

and likewise in the other instances.

Whereas in the case of mappings a neater notation has carried the floor, in other cases slovenliness still reigns. I am sure most people know this, but do not wish to make a fuss. Ten or twenty years from now this mess will have been cleaned up.

I have just quoted examples where modern trends have not yet conquered the older forms. There are too many people who speak about "modern mathematics" with a self-assurance as if now all problems have been settled up to the Day of Judgement. *Panta rhei*, all is always in full swing, and linguistic formulations of mathematics are not exempt.

Thirty years ago, it was a good style to write:

Let R and S be compact spaces, and let R be one-to-one continuously mappable upon S. Then R and S are homeomorphic.

Of course, this is true, but it is less than the writer has proved or really means. Of course R and S are homeomorphic, but they are so even by means of that continuous mapping of R onto S, the existence of which was assumed.

Thus:

Let R and S be compact spaces, and f a continuous 1-1 mapping of R upon S. Then f is an homeomorphism.

This is what the author meant. It comes out when he quotes the theorem and applies what he meant rather than what he formulated.

THE CHANGE OF STYLE – A DOG IS IF IT BARKS

A group used to be defined such as
"*a* set G in which a multiplication is defined such that

(1) $(ab) c = a(bc)$,
(2) $ae = ea$ for a certain e,
(3)   for every a there exists an a^{-1} with $aa^{-1} = a^{-1}a = e$."

It is a bit disturbing that this definition twice contains the word "defined" both with different meanings. It sounds strange that a definition should be a tool of a definition. In fact, objectively, the second "defined" does not mean any more than that there exists in G a multiplication but the use of "defined" should evoke the feeling that this multiplication may be chosen arbitrarily. Therefore let us say:

"*a* set G, in which a multiplication exists such that ...". Now it becomes much clearer what is unsatisfactory here. "Multiplication" occurs as a bound variable, but how to call upon it if need be? Fine, let us call it M.

"*A* set G with a multiplication M".

However, what is a multiplication? Obviously, a mapping of the ordered pairs from G to the elements of G,

$$M \in \ulcorner G, G \urcorner \rightsquigarrow G,$$

as I like to write. A group consists of two things, a set G and a multiplication M, hence a group is a pair $\ulcorner G, M \urcorner$. After this, we must honestly express the product by M, so that the definition reads:

"*A* group is a pair $\ulcorner G, M \urcorner$ of a set G and a mapping $M \in \ulcorner G, G \urcorner \rightsquigarrow G$ such that

(1) $M \ulcorner M \ulcorner a, b, \urcorner c \urcorner = M \ulcorner a, M \ulcorner b, c \urcorner \urcorner$.
(2)   There is $e \in G$ with $M \ulcorner a, e \urcorner = M \ulcorner e, a \urcorner = a$.
(3)   For every $a \in G$ there is an $a^{-1} \in G$ with $M \ulcorner a, a^{-1} \urcorner = M \ulcorner a^{-1}, a \urcorner = e$."

It is still wrong. Again there emerges an existentially bound variable, viz. 'e' in (2) which plays the role of a constant in (3), and which will be quoted again and again. And what about the strange a^{-1}? What kind or symbol is the '$- 1$' in the exponent?

The simplest way to redress this is to include the special element e and the function "inverse of..." in the primary group data. The group definition now becomes:

"A group is a quadruple $\ulcorner G, M, e, I \urcorner$ of a set G, a mapping M ($\in \ulcorner G, G \urcorner \rightarrow G$), an $e(\in G)$, a mapping $I(\in G \rightarrow G)$ such that ,if $a, b, c \in G$ then:

(1) $M \ulcorner M \ulcorner a, b, \urcorner c \urcorner = M \ulcorner a, M \ulcorner b, c \urcorner \urcorner$,
(2) $M \ulcorner a, e \urcorner = M \ulcorner e, a \urcorner = a$,
(3) $M \ulcorner a, Ia \urcorner = M \ulcorner Ia, a \urcorner = e$.

Once this has been done, all scruples are gone. You may cheerfully write "the group G", $(ab)c$ and so on, and do everything in the old-fashioned way. It is a good thing, though, to have once thoroughly analyzed the situation and to give at least the definitions of many mathematical entities according to this pattern.

The vernacular cannot do justice to the subtleties of mathematics. For instance, "commutative group" and "topological group" is the same grammatical pattern, a noun explained by an adjective. But both explanations are of an entirely different character. A commutative group is a group that also fulfils $ab = ba$, the class of commutative groups is contained in that of groups. A topological group, however, is not a group but a pair consisting of a group on G and a topology on G, which moreover, should be compatible, that is, M and I should be continuous in the topology of G. From a topological group I come to a group by forgetting something, namely, the topology. If I forget the other half, I get a topological space.

Likewise, a finite field is a field, though an ordered field is not a field but a pair, consisting of a field and an order on the set underlying the field. An Archimedean ordered field, though, is a ordered field. A Euclidean vector space is not a special case of vector space, but a vector space with a Euclidean metric. An oriented Euclidean vector space is again not a special Euclidean vector space, but one with an orientation added. The predicate n-dimensional, however, is in any case restrictive. It is not easy to find analogies in the vernacular for this, seemingly subtle, but in any case fundamental, distinction in mathematical language.

An analogous feature that has for a long time not been explicitly understood is the following. Real numbers may be considered as complex ones, but not conversely. However, a complex vector space is at the same time a real one, but not the other way round. Indeed, a vector space that admits the multiplications with complex numbers, also admits those with real numbers but (in general) not conversely. If R is finite-dimensional as a complex vector space, it has a double dimension as a real one. If, however, a basis is distinguished in the real vector space R, then R can be extended in a natural way to a complex vector space (or rather, the pair consisting of R and the basis can); the only thing to be done is to admit all complex linear combinations of the basis elements.

There is a simple fact in the background of this phenomenon. A function from M to the real numbers is also one to the complex numbers but not the other way round. However, a function from the complex numbers to M can be considered as one from the real numbers, namely by restriction, but not conversely.

From about 1930 abstract structures that had originated and grown independently were systematically amalgamated. There arose topological groups, rings, fields, i.e. sets that bore a topology on the one hand, and an algebraic structure on the other, which should be compatible, that is, the algebraic operations should be continuous in the sense of the topology. There arose metric groups, rings, fields, groups with a measure, ordered groups, rings, fields, topological vector spaces, and so on. The technique of amalgamating developed about 1930; its linguistic expression such as has been explained here dates from the last twenty years.

There were amusing features in this development. Take one example, for decades a topological space was defined as a set R in which certain subsets were indicated as open such that the empty set and R itself are open and that the intersection of two open sets and the union of an arbitrary set of open sets are open. If a topological space was given, people used to say that on the underlying set a topology was defined. But what is a topology? It is what should be added to transform a set into a topological space.

Now the definition of topological space reads as follows: a topological space is a pair $\ulcorner R, \mathbf{T} \urcorner$ where R is a set, and $\mathbf{T}$ a set of subsets of R such that $\bigcirc \in \mathbf{T}$, $R \in \mathbf{T}$, $P, Q \in \mathbf{T} \rightarrow P \cap Q \in \mathbf{T}$, $\mathbf{T}' \subset \mathbf{T} \rightarrow \bigcup_{P \in \mathbf{T}'} P \in \mathbf{T}$. (Of course, $\mathbf{T}$ consists of the sets which in the earlier definition were called open.) Of the topological space $\ulcorner R, \mathbf{T}, \urcorner$ R is the set. But what is $\mathbf{T}$? Its topology, of course. Indeed, the topology should just be the thing that is to be added to transform the set R into a topological space. But this thing is just **T**, the set of open sets. Once "the topology of a space" was a vague thing, now it is simply the set of its open sets.

The example of geometric axiomatics shows how long tradition can last. Both ancient and modern axiomatics originated in geometry, and for this reason geometry conserved certain archaic features longer than other axiomatized domains did. An axiomatics of projective geometry may still start in the Hilbert style:

The axioms deal with certain things called points and lines. Axiom I: Through two different points there is one line and only one. Axiom II: Two different lines have one and only one intersection point. Axiom III: and so on.

Compare this with the definition of a group. It is as if we coin a definition without using the word "group": "We are given things which can be multiplied, such that...".

How should we express the above geometrical axiomatics properly?

A projective plane is a triple $\ulcorner P, G, I \urcorner$, consisting of two disjoints sets P, G, and a relation I between them, such that.... The elements of P are also called points, the elements of G, lines; I is called the incidence relation; instead of $I(x, y)$ one can also say "x lies on y" or "y passes through x".

THE CHANGE OF STYLE: THE BUSINESS OF FORMALIZING

Our examples of the change in mathematical style were restricted to linguistic phenomena. They may seem to be motivated by a craving for hair-splitting. The charge of hair-splitting, if applied to mathematicians, is not totally unfounded, so it is a strange thing that it sometimes lasts a generation until the result of such a hair-splitting procedure is accepted. In spite of all hair-splitting, I predict that some contemporary slovenly habits will still persist for decennia. What is the reason? Well, mathematicians are as conservative as any other people. Innovations have to overcome resistance. They are eventually accepted because and when they can no longer be avoided. As long as ideas can be illustrated intuitively, slipshod language is accepted; the more abstract, that is the further away from intuition, a subject matter is, the more is careful linguistic expression required. In a retrospective view on my own university studies, I believe I can truthfully say that my present colleagues have succeeded better in explaining to students the fundamentals of analysis than the teachers of the past were able to do, and they have done so, I believe, through the use of better linguistic means which have developed meanwhile by many single steps. These same means extend the possibilities of passive and active information at higher levels as well as in research.

I have stressed that perfecting mathematical language is a continuous process. The final stage could be a language that is so exact as can be handled by a computer. Symbolic logic shows globally what such a language looks like. But it is not at all certain that in a few decades mathematicians will write their textbooks and scientific papers in the language of symbolic logic. Computers shall have to be addressed in a very special way – some say because computers are dull – I would say because their intelligence is different from ours. Thanks to our general life experience, which they have not acquired, we consider as obvious many things which sound strange to them. If we wish to communicate something to somebody, it helps a lot if we can count on his benevolent understanding. To the man who programmes a machine, we can speak in quite another language than we use with the machine.

Language is an elastic tool. To express mathematical facts in the vernacular, one has to adapt it to the requirements of mathematics. This process still continues, and though it would not be wise to predict a final stage, we seem to be heading for a version of the vernacular which will have strongly been modified by logistical elements but will not be wholly formalized, or rather there will be a family of versions with different degrees of formalization, each adapted to a special aim and a special communicational environment.

The conscious occupation with language as a tool of exact expression is called formalizing. It is one of the means of organizing modern mathematics. As will be expounded more fully later, modern mathematics shows a strong tendency to organization, and formalizing is one of its means. Meanwhile, I dare to predict that in future formalizing, which is now mostly exercised within mathematics, will prove one of the most efficient transferable activities of mathematicians. Indeed, there is no tendency which is shared to such a high degree by all fields of human activity as is that of linguistic expression; the conscious analysis of linguistic possibilities as exercised by mathematicians is due to exert a strong influence everywhere.

THE EXTENSIONAL ABSTRACTION

In characterizing modern mathematics, I first turned to its most modern features, the re-creation of mathematical expression, and the activity of formalizing. But the time has come to uncover older sources which are still providing fresh impetus. I mentioned earlier that according to some reviewers modern mathematics started about 1870, that is, with Cantor and Dedekind. According to a well-known witticism of Kronecker "God created the integers, the rest is a human contraption". Kronecker forgot about sets – intentionally I imagine. Sets were created by Cantor. Since we do not know who, under God, invented number, it comes out that Cantor is the only mathematician of whom the layman with no mathematical education can be told what he did, and believe me, people do so. Yes, it is too bad. They will say that it was his greatest merit that he invented the term "set". (Actually "set" (Menge) was a later invention, initially Cantor called it "variety" (Mannigfaltigkeit)).

Of course, it was not the word "set", neither was it the idea of calling some objects sets, which is usually presented to non-mathematicians as the main thing. It was neither the empty set, which is Zermelo's, nor was it the forming of subsets, union, or intersections of given sets, nor was it that sets could be mapped on other sets – quite other features of set theory profoundly influenced mathematics.

I mentioned Kronecker's saying that integers were created by God. Before Cantor, the natural numbers were unanalyzed and unanalyzable presuppositions of mathematics. With Cantor the natural number becomes a special case of the more general concept of potency. Sets which can be mapped one-to-one upon each other are called equipotent, and potency of sets is the thing common to equipotents sets. Potencies can be added by adding the (supposedly disjoint) sets which represent them. Of course, it should be shown that the result does not depend on the choice of the representative. According to the same pattern, products and powers of potencies are defined. The products of a set Φ of sets consists of the mappings f of Φ into the union of the X of Φ such that $fX \in X$ for all $X \in \Phi$, and likewise one defines powers. Finally arise the integers (≥ 0) and the operations with them from the potencies of the finite sets. *.

* A misinterpretation of this theory is the most spectacular show piece of modern school texts.

At one point, Cantor's definition of potency is not "modern". Potency should be what is common to all equipotent sets – this is a vague concept. Today people say that "equipotent" is an equivalence relation, and potencies are the equivalence classes of this relation, that is, the potency of M is the class of all sets equipotent with M. (Cautiously I said "class"; the collection of the sets equipotent with M is "too" big; if the usual set theory tricks are played on it, paradoxes like that of the set of sets turn up.)

The artifice of describing a concept by its "extension", that is, as the totality of the objects that fall within the concept, is a pivot of concept-building in modern mathematics. Such formulae as "what is common to…" or "I consider… as equal" are called intentional because they represent the notion as an intention, as it were, of the concept creator; the description of a concept by its extension is called extensional, and the tendency of extensional concept description which started from Cantor's set theory or, at least, was strongly suggested and promoted by set theory, is called extensionalism. (For instance, the expression "mapping of A into B" seems to indicate the intention of mapping; its extensionalist formulation reads: "A mapping of A into B is a subset f of the pairs set $\ulcorner A, B \urcorner$ such that to every $a \in A$ there is one and only one $b \in B$ with $\ulcorner a, b \urcorner \in f$.)

We delay the answer to the question as to whether it is better to define integers as potencies of finite sets or by means of Peano's axioms. It does not matter here because we would rather stress the just explained pattern of concept building which has become paradigmatic for modern mathematics and which is now a commonplace in mathematics. I mention a few other examples. From the integers, the rational numbers are reconstructed as fractions (or ordered pairs of numbers) by considering such fractions as $\frac{2}{3}$ and $\frac{4}{6}$ as the same, more generally a/b and a'/b' are considered as identical if $ab' = ba'$. The rules are old hat: behave as if a/b and a/b' are the same; define addition of a/b and c/d by $(ad + bc)/bd$, multiplication by ac/bd; it does not matter, as can be easily seen, whether a term is replaced by another that by convention represents the same thing. The modern extensionalist formulation, however, runs: define a relation $\sim$ by $a/b \sim c/d \leftrightarrow ad = bc$. This is an equivalence relation. By definition the rational numbers are its equivalence classes, that is, the maximal sets of pairwise equivalent pairs. Rather than saying "I consider equivalent a/b, c/d as identical", I introduce the new object, which is shared by all equivalent pairs, namely their equivalence class, and I call it a rational number. Addition and multiplication of equivalence classes are derived from those for the pairs a/b; of course, it should be shown that equivalent plus (times) equivalent is equivalent.

With this kind of artifice, computing with integers mod m is justified. The intentional version "a and b are considered equal if they differ by a multiple of m" is extensionally transformed into "a and b are called equivalent if $a - b$ is divisible by m; the equivalence classes are the integers mod m." Again one has to make sure that addition and multiplication, defined by representatives of integers, transfer to integers mod m, that is, sums and products do not depend on the choice of the representatives.

Another example is computations mod an irreducible polynomial $f(x)$ in polynomial rings $P[x]$ over a field P, which are carried out to adjoin a root of $f(x)$ to P. Still another is the extension of the rational field $\mathbf{Q}$ to the real field: in the set Ω of Cauchy sequences from $\mathbf{Q}$ an equivalence concept is defined, and its equivalence classes are called real numbers; addition and multiplication are extended from $\mathbf{Q}$ to Ω and it is again shown that equivalent plus (times) equivalent is equivalent.

I could continue this way but I would not be saying anything essentially new. The same pattern of extensional concept-building is repeated; from a class Ω with an equivalence relation $\sim$ one gets the class $\Omega/\sim$ of the equivalence classes; a given structure on Ω (whether determined by relations or operations) can be transferred to $\Omega/\sim$ as soon as it is known to be compatible with the equivalence. In fact, this is an important principle of concept-building outside mathematics, too. With the relations "equally heavy", "equally long", "equally coloured", objects can be distributed over weight classes, length classes, colour classes (such as 3 kg, 5 m, light red) to which order relations may apply (more or less) and in which additions may be possible. Yet this is not, in everyday life, the only principle of concept-building. A concept such as "chair", is fixed by a number of criteria of use. This kind of concept-building turns up in mathematics is we consider another tool among its modern features.

THE AXIOMATIC ABSTRACTION

Not only does set theory start about 1870, so also does modern axiomatics. Of course this happened in geometry, where from antiquity onwards the construction of a deductive system based on fundamental hypotheses, axioms, has been a well-understood task. Non-Euclidean geometry, which could have started modern axiomatics, was discovered about 1830 but hardly noticed until 1870. In the eighteen-forties and eighteen-fifties Chr. K. G. von Staudt had attempted axiomatics of projective and of complex projective geometry. Pasch became the builder of the first irreproachable axiomatics of Euclidean geometry. He taught mathematicians how to formulate axioms. His work was soon overshadowed by D. Hilbert's profound *Foundations of Geometry* (1899). What is meant today, in particular since Hilbert, by "axiom" and "axiomatics" is a new idea. From the Greeks up to the philosophical literature of the beginning of the 20th century, "axiom" means a kind of proposition which cannot be proved, but which needs no proof either, because it is the foundation and presupposition of any proof, and of greater distinctness, necessity, evidence and generality than everything which is derived from it. It is true that statements like the postulate on parallels, which people would have liked to prove for centuries, is neither in Euclid nor usually later on found among the axioms. Even Pasch does not speak of axioms if he means the fundamental statements of geometry, and in the French and English literature of the beginning of this century it is still the custom to call such statements "postulates". It seems that Helmholtz was the first to term the geometrical postulates axioms, maybe as a consequence of his wrong interpretation of Kant. Helmholtz was followed by Poincaré, and by Hilbert, who by his *Foundations of Geometry* sanctified the present use of "axiom" and "axiomatics".

Hilbert's *Foundations of Geometry* starts according to the following pattern: "We imagine three different kinds of things, ...*points*, ...*lines*, ...*planes*,.... We imagine the points, lines, planes in certain mutual relations, such as "lying on", "between", "parallel", "congruent", "continuous", ...the precise and complete descriptions of these relations being contained in the *axioms of geometry*.

Those who expect descriptions like Euclid's "a point is what has no part" will be disappointed. There are no explicit descriptions in Hilbert's axioms. They describe implicitly by postulating certain properties of the points, lines, planes and the relations prevailing between them.

For instance: "To two points there is one line that contains them." Frege castigated Hilbert's system because it did not allow him to verify what a point is, in particular whether his watch was a point. Hilbert is said to have stressed against Frege and others that it is the essence of axiomatics that instead of points, lines, and planes one could speak of tables, chairs, and steins as well. Only those properties mentioned explicitly in the axioms are relevant to deductive reasoning. It is like playing chess, where the men are not defined by their shape, but by the rules of the game, which they have to obey.

This recognition of the implicit definition was an important step, which has become paradigmatic for the modern methodology of science in general. The importance of the implicit definition was first stressed by the geometer *Gergonne* (1818). This was a decisive step on the road away from Aristotle's theory of science. From Aristotle to Gergonne, it had been a hardly questioned though never even approximately realized ideal to derive the sciences from explicitly formulated principles.

No sooner had Hilbert succeeded in founding Euclidean geometry axiomatically, and by this way defining the concepts of geometry implicitly, than axiomatics took a turn in another direction, which in fact was already anticipated in Hilbert's *Foundations*. It was the most important aim of Hilbert to investigate the bearing of his various axioms – what happens if this or that axiom is dismissed? If nothing happens, the axiom could be dispensed with. If it is indispensable, then the poorer axiomatic system that arises from its omission does not define Euclidean geometry, but a class of, in general, weaker geometries which fulfil the truncated axiomatic system. After Hilbert such axiomatic systems which have many, non-isomorphic "models", gained momentum. Properly said, such axiomatic systems were known of before, but up to that time nobody referred to axiomatics if he meant them. Today the postulates which are imposed to a set to make it a group are also called axioms – group axioms. It is a big step from what traditionally had been called an axiom.

How such axiomatic systems can arise is marvellously shown by the history of the group concept. In the renaissance of geometry in the 19th century, transformations were the keynote. The projective, affine, equiform, and other mappings were discovered as well as their composition and the fact that they form groups, long before the word "group" was earmarked for this concept and even before people knew and could tell what a group was. Other groups which were investigated while the group concept still resided in the realm of the ideas were the permutation groups. When, about 1870, the group concept is formulated, there is not only a large stock of groups accumulated, but also a vast experience in group theory, though all theory was formulated in terms of special cases. Group theory arises as a means of organizing this conglomerate of special results by the procedure that the properties which are shared by all "groups" and which are relevant are explicitly formulated. These together – associative multiplication with existence of the one and the inverse – are what were later called the "group axioms". What is meant by a group is fixed by certain postulates – that is the same as with geometry. But the axioms of geometry are realized by essentially one model, whereas the group axioms are satisfied by many models. In fact, this was just the rationale of the group axioms: to work with one instrument in many situations, which makes life a lot easier.

What happened here with groups is paradigmatic for a kind of concept-building which can be opposed to the extensionalist method. The group concept has not been produced by collecting in one class everything that one would like to consider as a group, but by stressing common features in the variety of known groups and then calling "groups" all objects with these features. This is postulational or axiomatic concept-building. Of course, it is older than the example I have just given, but not until the present century do the examples of axiomatic concept-building multiply to such a degree that there would be no use in trying to account for all of them.

The field concept has an analogous history. For centuries people were familiar with the system of rational numbers and its four operations: addition, subtraction, multiplication and division, which are known to obey certain laws. The system of real numbers, with the same kind of operations and laws, was known as well, though it was less familiar and less formalized. Then came complex numbers, which except for the lacking order property, were not much different from the earlier ones. Complex numbers were also the substratum of algebra, in which the algebraic operations were carried out; algebraic equations, too, could be solved in this domain. As a matter of fact, this domain was much too large for algebra as exercised in the 19th century; what mattered in algebraic investigations, were smaller number systems, characterized by the fact that they allowed the four operations, and these systems were called *Körper* (fields) by Dedekind – you must not believe the story that Dedekind invented the modern concept of field, he knew number fields only, that is, subfields of complex numbers, and in the same way his "rings" are number systems in which the first three of the four operations work. It is true that the extension of the field notion to function fields belongs to the 19th century (Weber, 1893). Moreover, in number theory, the finite fields were known, though under the name "Galois fields" (in German, *Galoisfelder*, as opposed to *Zahlkörper*). But this was still not enough to instigate the discovery of the field concept. Not until p-adic number fields emerged as a new example had the time come to bring all those examples under one heading – the general field concept of Steinitz (1910). What is called abstract or modern algebra actually starts here. In a set, an addition and a multiplication are postulated by such properties as were familiar from the old fields, and such a system is called a field, an *abstract* field as compared with the old ones, which were more "concrete" because they had been known longer.

The story of other algebraic notions is not much different. I will mention only one of them, the first that finally also covered material outside algebra. It is the algebraic concept of module (over a number ring or field) that is in modern terms, an additive subgroup which allows multiplications with the ring (or field) elements; usually only finitely-generated modules were considered. About 1914, analysts invented the linear space as a heading under which they could bring all familiar function spaces. In the thirties, a didactic renovation of analytic geometry took place to define the usual geometric vector spaces in general and axiomatic terms. It is always the same concept, but even today the terminology has not yet been unified. Algebraists speak of modules, geometers of vector spaces (which is adopted by algebraists if the underlying ring is a field), analysts of linear spaces. It would be desirable if the last terminology supplanted the others.

The first mathematical domains which were axiomatized after Hilbert, were algebra, from which we took our examples, and topology (Fréchet, Hausdorff). It is the same phenomenon: the tendency to bring subsets of Euclidean space, Riemann surfaces, manifolds, and function sets under one heading, first that of metric then of topological space. Whereas abstract algebra could reasonably continue with the concepts of old algebra, topology started conceptually from scratch; as by necessity new fundamental concepts arose which could never have been noticed in the older, too singular approaches – concepts like completeness, compactness, and separability, or concepts which could only be understood in a broader approach, such as connectedness, dimension, and product of spaces. Of course as time went on algebra too was enriched by new concepts.

The "abstract" view was perhaps even more decisive for analysis, because the abstract way led to a great many results which were concrete in the sense that they could be expressed by means of old analysis, though they would never have been obtained by the old methods. I vividly remember that I was struck as by a bolt from the blue by the example of the theory of almost periodic functions. H. Bohr had called a continuous function f of one real variable almost periodic, if for every $\varepsilon > 0$ there was an $l(\varepsilon)$ and in every interval of length $l(\varepsilon)$ an "almost period" $\tau(\varepsilon)$ such that $|f(x + \tau(\varepsilon)) - f(x)| < \varepsilon$ for all x. It is a marvellous invention, if you can understand it, though I should confess that when as a student I participated in a seminar on almost periodic functions, I did not really grasp what an almost periodic function was. One day I read S. Bochner's abstract reformulation of this concept. Consider the linear space Φ of bounded continuous functions with the sup-norm, and in there, the translations T_a (that is $(T_a f)(x) = f(x + a)$); an f of Φ is called almost periodic, if the space of the $T_a f$ has a compact closure. The scales fell from my eyes. Suddenly I understood the essentials of *Bohr's* definition and proofs. *Bochner's* abstract translation of *Bohr's* definition is in my experience the most convincing proof of the power of the abstract method. As a matter of fact, it led much further than Bohr's definition, to the almost periodic functions on arbitrary groups, generalizing those on the translation group of the real line.

Up to the end of the twenties, the axiomatic efforts in algebra, topology and analysis had expressed themselves rather independently. Analysis, which included both algebraical and topological elements, provided the suggestion to combine structures. Known entities as the field of real numbers are considered as a topological field, or as an ordered field, or as a metric field. It is amalgamating two or more structures which should be compatible in a suitable way. A topological field is a field with a topology such that, in this topology, the field operations are continuous.

For an ordered field it requires an order that is invariant under addition and under multiplication by a positive element. A metric field has a norm $|...|$ such that $|a+b| \leq |a| + |b|$ and $|ab| = |a| \cdot |b|$. The same way one gets topological groups, groups with a measure, topological linear spaces, and metric linear spaces. By analyzing and classing the properties of the objects, the axiomatic abstraction creates more perspicuity and more profound understanding. Even in the most elementary theory of real numbers it pays to know which properties depend on the ring axioms, which on the field axioms, which on the commutativity of multiplication, which on completeness, which on local compactness and so on.

WHAT HAPPENEND TO GEOMETRY?

Viewing the present structure of mathematics, it looks as though geometry had had its day. For centuries, even after the successes of algebra and analysis, geometry was esteemed as the only true mathematics, as the paragon of mathematical rigour. Not until the second half of the 19th century, after algebra and analysis had been put on rigorous foundations independent of geometry, did it come out that traditional geometry was not as rigorous as people had believed, and this of course eroded the firm position of geometry. In fact, since antiquity up to the end of the 18th century, geometry had hardly progressed and had hardly contributed anything to the growth of mathematics. Then, at the beginning of the 19th century, geometry awoke to a new life and by its flourishing it contributed greatly to the development of group theory and to many chapters of algebra, and helped prepare the shape of modern axiomatics.

What is now left of geometry? In Bourbaki's system of mathematics it does not appear, in review periodicals what is called geometry hardly fills five percent of the space, in university curricula geometry is just mentioned, and people who could call themselves geometers do not do so because the name sounds outmoded. But on closer examination things look different. From one paragraph of a paper I have chosen at random, which according to its title belongs to analysis, I have picked out the words "Hilbert space", "vector space", "dimension", "eigen vector", "similarity", "mapping", "convex", "reflection", "neighbourhood", "number line", "centre", "cube", "linear", "translation", "envelope", "projection" – all geometrical undertones of a seemingly ungeometric theme. Apart from these, I have not yet mentioned the most conspicuous example, the word axiom, which was given its modern meaning by Hilbert in his *Foundations of Geometry*.

Words cover notions. The geometrical terminology in modern algebra and analysis points to a pervasion of all mathematics by geometrical intuition, which can be explained by a few examples.

One of them is the tempestuous development of complex function theory in the 19th century which was started by an invasion of geometry into analysis, by Gauss' representation of complex numbers as points of a plane. The algebraic import of the equation $x^n = 1$ became clear by its geometrical meaning, its close relation to the construction of the regular n-gon in the Gauss plane. The double periodicity of elliptic functions became interesting and perspicuous through its geometrical interpretation. In spite of the seemingly definitive victory which in the last third of the 19th century Weierstrass' algebraization of function theory carried on geometrical intuition, the great problems which were solved about 1900 descended from Riemann, from the geometrical ideas of the Riemann surface, of conformal mapping, and of uniformization − concepts originally formulated solely by geometrical means and ever since dealt with by intuitive methods.

Another example is the new life in the number concept since the 1870's. Numbers as numbers of something, as cardinal numbers, are of intuitive origin; in the history of mankind and individual man adding and multiplying started from operations on fingers and pebbles. Soon, however, and especially as a consequence of extensions of the number domain, the number concept is frozen in algorithmic rules, both in the development of the species and of the individual; the number as a number of something is a matter of the crudest application, and in mathematics proper it is not at all relevant. At least until G. Cantor, who first made conscious the unconscious intuitive process of abstraction which leads from an intuitive origin to a formal number concept. We already mentioned it: the sets, the mappings, the one-to-one mappings and the equivalence classes that they determine.

Set theory appeared to be more abstract and more rigorous than any mathematics up till then. For the same reasons geometrical intuition was never before, and in no other domain, as important as an organizing means and as a stimulating force in preventing set theory from degenerating into sheer algorithm. From the geometry of the number line, Cantor took the abstraction of order and the point set theory. Another enrichment of set theory in the beginning of this century, was the measure concept which descended from the geometrical notion of area and caused a revolutionary revision of the classical notion of the integral which had become a dead algorithmic tool. At the same time point set theory developed into a new geometric discipline, topology, studying geometrical shapes by specifying intuitive ideas on connexion. The most powerful algebraic methods of topology originated in the study of the intuitively most elementary shapes, the polyhedra, as instigated by L. E. J. Brouwer, whereas the highest demands upon geometrical intuition were made in the construction of all those pathologically-looking counter-examples which are favourites of the more abstract set theoretical topology. Topological methods of algebraic and set theory origin have strongly influenced modern algebra and analysis. Meanwhile geometrical intuition seems to have vanished in topology itself. This, however, is a superficial impression. Most of the ideas and problems, emerging at such and such a time out of the topology mill, have a strong geometrical background, and in the last few years old problems have been solved by straight forward geometrical methods, which do not depend on the apparatus of algebraic topology.

Under the influence of algebra the naive space notion underwent a momentous sophistication during the 19th century. In analytic geometry, plane curves and surfaces in space are being described by equations with two or three unknowns. Conversely it is possible to elucidate algebraic properties of equations by interpreting them as properties of curves and surfaces. Could geometry not be of some use in the study of equations with n unknowns, provided the geometer would look and think in n-dimensional space? Could n-way determinants not be better understood when interpreted as volumes in n-dimensional space, even for $n > 3$? By the end of the 19th century n-dimensional space was a matter of course to the geometer. Its algebraic origin, however, is still palpable; it is built up in an algebraic way, starting with coordinates. The new approach in the twenties was stimulated by the abstract algebraists who at this point proved to be more genuine geometers than the geometers proper. They urged that in defining and dealing with n-space the geometrical elements, points or vectors, should be primordial, leaving the coordinates with a derived title. Today the concept of linear or vector space is the property of all mathematicians.

Much in linear algebra only became clear in its geometrical interpretation. A striking example is the method of least squares, invented about 1800, an algebraic thicket which cannot be cleared unless the sums of squares are understood as distance squares in a Pythagorean metric.

Meanwhile the space concept had been extended to infinities of dimensions. The innovators were the analysts who needed abstract function spaces for their new methods. Together with the term 'space' they seized upon the whole geometric terminology, geometric ways of thought and intuition.

As mentioned previously the term and the concept 'axiomatic' started conquering mathematics from geometry. Geometry had been a philosophical problem for centuries, the problem of how pure reason, as it were with closed eyes, could make statements about reality (was space with its triangles, parallel lines, spheres and so on, not part of reality?), statements which turned out to be true, as soon as man opened his eyes, drew lines, gauged and measured angles. A slow process of ripening in the 19th century led to the famous solution in Hilbert's foundations of geometry, which later on was given a pithy formulation by Einstein:

'Insofar as the mathematical theorems refer to reality, they are not certain, and insofar as they are certain, they do not refer to reality ... The progress made by axiomatics consists in the sharp separation of the logic form and realistic and intuitive contents... The axioms are free creations of human mind ...'

Hilbert's system did not start with definitions, as Euclid's had, but with axioms, *i.e.* statements involving undefined notions like point, line, between, and congruent – the meaning of these terms is settled by the axioms in an implicit way. As rules of a game axioms are arbitrary, though for practical use they have to answer some purpose. From a *logical* point of view it does not make sense asking whether an axiomatic system is true, but rather whether it is consistent.

The logical status of geometry was clarified by the concepts of axiom and axiomatics. The impact of its explanation in Hilbert's foundations was first felt in topology where Hausdorff axiomatized topological space, and in algebra which was rebuilt on the axiomatically-defined entities of group, ring, field and so on. Today the axiomatic method pervades all mathematics. Originally creative geometry was not greatly influenced by the new approach. As late as the thirties geometers remembered the freedom of the human mind to create axioms – a freedom to be checked by the judicious intuition of the geometer as well as by the requirement of consistency. Hilbert's way of proving an axiomatic system of geometry to be consistent by means of an algebraic system fulfilling the axioms (an analytic geometry) may lead to the discovery of new important algebraic systems, as in fact it did in the thirties when geometry gave birth to the new and momentous algebraic concept of alternative field (a field with some restricted associativity of multiplication).

This is but one example out of a host. In group theory where objects are not much more structurated than in abstract set theory, geometrical questions often show the way to interesting problems. It might be true that 'algebraic geometry' has ceased to be geometry in spite of its geometrical terminology; however, its development is often influenced by truly geometric questions. 'Geometrical number theory' on the other hand is genuine geometry in its problems and methods.

Fading frontiers between classical domains are a feature of modern mathematics. Geometry as a connected domain is hardly distinguishable nowadays. But the method of geometry crops up again and again. Why does geometrical intuition, often pronounced dead, still stay vigorous, even in domains that seemingly have nothing to do with geometry? Clearly because geometrical intuition may tell us what could be important, interesting and accessible, and save us the trouble of going astray in the huge desert of problems, ideas, and methods. To say it with a variation on a saying of Kant's: Intuitions without concepts are void, concepts without intuitions are blind.

CONCEPTUAL AND ALGORITHMIC MATHEMATICS

You are given a glass of white wine and a glass of red wine, both containing the same amount. Put a spoonful of the white wine into the red wine, mix it, and put a spoonful of the mixture back into the white wine. Is there now more red wine in the glass of white wine than white wine in the glass of red wine, or is it the other way round?

It is the same. Let the content of a glass be a and that of a spoon b. After the first action there is…. You understand how to solve it. But one-third of those who attempt to solve this became stranded on mistakes in the calculation. There are very few who reason as follows: both glasses finally contain the same amount of fluid; imagine that in each glass the white and the red wine were separated. The red wine in the white wine glass is lacking in the red wine glass, it is replaced by white wine. Thus there is as much red wine in the glass of white wine, as white wine in the glass of red wine.

The first attempt was an algorithmic solution, the second a conceptual one. This is one example out of a host, though it is a typical one. We shall meet more of them. Just for the moment this example should clarify the difference between algorithmic and conceptual mathematics. Its pedagogical importance shall be indicated later. At this stage I will put it within its historical framework.

The term "algorithm" immortalizes the name of Al Huwârizmî (Muhammad ibn Mûsâ, 8th century) who codified the Indo-Arabic method of computing. Computing methods, or if you prefer, computing recipes, are now called algorithms. Vieta's algebra, Descartes' analytic geometry, and Leibniz's calculus are such algorithms and their inventors were quite conscious of this fact. Vieta stresses it in the introduction of his work, Descartes proposed his *Géométrie* as a first example of his method in his *Discours de la méthode*, and Leibniz was obsessed by the quest for algorithms; in fact he only once succeeded, though admittedly so marvellously that his algorithm eclipsed Newton's materially equivalent work. Nowhere is the power of an algorithm so clearly demonstrated as in Calculus. Problems that once required the genius of an Archimedes or a Huygens are solved mechanically by every mediocre mathematician after Leibniz.

Operating an algorithm can increase one's self-confidence, it can satisfy one's instinct for play. This may be the reason why so many algorithms of restricted import have flourished for a time: descriptive geometry, the symbolic method in the theory of invariants, Schubert's calculus of enumerative geometry – those who have never played with these tools cannot imagine how fascinating they are. Fourier series, and more generally, series of orthogonal functions, the Fourier integral, residues, the Gauss–Green–Stokes integral formulae, the Heaviside calculus and the Laplace integral – these terms recall well-known algorithms which came down from the 19th century. From our century I mention only the most striking examples, like the homology theory, which, invented in topology, is still developing, and also closely connected to the homology theory, the method of "diagrams" of morphisms.

It is often asserted that modern mathematics is distinguished from the old by the stress on the conceptual component as opposed to algorithms. I agree that this is true and several times I have mentioned that the most striking innovations that start the process of modernizing – set theory, abstract algebra and analysis, topology – were eruptions of conceptual thinking, which burst through the petrified crust of algorithmic tradition. But all lava petrifies eventually. Each conceptual innovation encloses in itself the germ of algorithmization – this is the way of mathematics. Once computing was a science; not until it was mechanized, could number theory thrive. Without the algorithm of calculus, analysis would never have flourished. Algorithmizing means consolidating, starting from a platform to jump even higher. Algorithms provide the technical means of fathoming greater conceptual depth. It is not fair to confront algorithmic and conceptual mathematics with one another as though one is the lofty tower from which you may look down on the other, and we certainly cannot identify this opposition with that between new and old.

ORGANIZING AND MATHEMATIZING

As soon as science outgrows mere collecting, it becomes involved in the organization of experiences. It is not difficult to indicate the experiences that should be organized in arithmetic and geometry. Organizing the reality with mathematical means is today called mathematizing. The mathematician, however, is inclined to disregard reality as soon as the *logical* connection promises faster progress. A stock of mathematical experience is formed; it asks for its part to be organized. What kind of means will serve this purpose? Of course, mathematical means again. This starts the mathematizing of mathematics itself; first locally – what to choose as a definition, and what to derive as a theorem? Should this support that or should it rather be the other way round? Should I prove this as a special case of that, or would I be better starting with the special case and generalize it? As time goes on, mathematizing applies globally, as the conscious building of theories, of explicit or axiomatic nature.

This is an old story. The Greeks knew that certain quadratic equations could be interpreted as plane curves, which were identified by Menaichmos with the plane sections of a cone. Apollonius, however, started just with the conics to arrive at their equations. In modern times the tables were again turned to start with the quadratic equations. But in projective geometry one succeeded in defining conics as the loci of intersections of corresponding lines of projectively-related pencils. The elliptic functions were discovered as the inverses of elliptic integrals; they were doubly periodic and fulfilled certain functional equations. Later on people contrived to use these functional equations or the double periodicity to define the elliptic functions.

Today, mathematizing mathematics is one of the main concerns of mathematicians. In no other science has the habit of recasting become second nature as it has in mathematics. Mathematicians sometimes behave as if repetition and copying was forbidden by law. Anybody who gives a course remodels the subject matter to his own satisfaction – and why not, if it is really new and original and better than the old stuff?

This craving for formal innovation is not indulged as much in other sciences. I am inclined to deplore this when I see certain chapters of theoretical physics copied from one textbook to the next for decades, even centuries, by authors who are not even aware of the formal and material contradictions between parts which have come down from different stages in the development of physics. In textbooks on mechanics, it is quite normal that on the one hand orthogonal transformations are dealt with according to Euler without eigen values, while symmetric transformations are treated according to Laplace, using eigen values – and both of them with methods which have long since become obsolete in mathematics! How strange it looks indeed in statistical mechanics when theories which replaced each other historically are nevertheless expounded as equals, each of them with its contingent apparatus of concepts and formulae with which it had been created long ago?

A mathematician who did not follow step by step the continuous reorganization of mathematics could get into trouble if suddenly he were to jump over a whole chain in its evolution. A non-mathematician who is used to applying the mathematics of his apprenticeship in his own domain, tends to reject modern mathematics. It is well-known how physicists often keep aloof from a new mathematics that causes no difficulties to economists, psychologists, linguists – simply because the physicists have always applied mathematics, whereas the others are relative newcomers. It is not likely, however, that in the long run physicists can afford to nurse their own mathematics, alongside that which students now learn at the university, and which before long will be taught at school, too.

It has been stressed that continuous refashioning is not a whim but a necessity. Everybody knows how fast science develops. To master aquired knowledge, it must be organized. This is just as true for mathematics as it is for all sciences. The only difference is that mathematicians are committed to organizing more consciously and on a higher level because in mathematics organizing is itself a mathematical activity. No doubt a mathematician today surveys an essentially larger part of the field of mathematics than his colleague of half a century ago was able to, in spite of the growth of mathematics on the one hand and thanks to the new organizational forms on the other. In the long run others will profit by the organizing experience of mathematicians, and mathematicians will be able to help them. In the not too far distant future, organizing of experience and even of domains of investigation will be an applied concern of mathematicians, where they can put to good use among other things their experiences in formalizing, that is, in linguistic organization.

The most spectacular example of organizing mathematics is, of course, Bourbaki. How convincing this organization of mathematics is! So convincing that Piaget could rediscover Bourbaki's system in developmental psychology. Poor Piaget! He did not fare much better than Kant, who had barely consecrated Euclidean space as "a pure intuition" when non-Euclidean geometry was discovered! Piaget is not a mathematician, so he could not know how unreliable mathematical system builders are. Bourbaki's system of mathematics was not yet accomplished when the importance of categories was discovered. There can be little doubt that categories will be a new organizing principle and that rebuilding of Bourbaki's structure in categorical style will leave no stone left on top of another. If a leading development psychologist could then convince us of the categorizing genesis of all mathematical concepts – which will certainly eventually happen – then it will just be in time to see the categorical style mathematics, before it is ready, being pulled down in favour of some new principle, which will certainly have its day. Mathematics is never finished – anyone who worships a certain system of mathematics should take heed of this advice.

Meanwhile categories are a wonderful means of organizing mathematics. If the reader does not know what categories are, he should not worry too much, since the writer of the present book is not quite convinced that he knows what they are either, among other reasons because it is still in full swing. He could make himself and others believe that he knew what categories are, if he was able to teach them, but in spite of a few attempts he has never succeeded.* Some day somebody will grasp how to do it by finding an approach, and somebody else will improve it, and it may just happen that after twenty years, or even less, first year students will learn categories.

If, for all that, I cannot yet expound what categories are, I will tell you a story about a mathematics professor and a man who had brought him his completed thesis on some modern subject – it was not one of his own students, and not even a mathematician but an engineer. He carried a 30-page manuscript, which he hoped would be accepted as a thesis. The professor was in a hurry, he just glanced through the paper and said "This cries out for categories, you know about categories, don't you?". "No", replied the man, and went away to learn about categories. This does not take much time today, because the more modern mathematics is the simpler it becomes. It appeared that the thirty pages could be reduced to three. Three pages is a poor thesis, but after a short delay, it had again grown to thirty, with ten times the original contents.

This story reminds me of a poem by Christian Morgenstern, which I quote in German and will interpret afterwards in English – which is not very easy.

> Korf liest gerne schnell und viel;
> darum widert ihn das Spiel
> all des zwölfmal Unerbetnen
> Ausgewalzten, Breitgetretnen.

* Meanwhile he succeeded – only to understand better the limitations of categories as an organizing power.

> Meistes ist in sechs bis acht
> Wörten völlig abgemacht,
> und in ebensoviel Sätzen
> lässt sich Bandwurmweisheit schwätzen.
>
> Es erfindet drum sein Geist
> etwas, was ihn dem entreisst:
> Brillen, deren Energien
> ihm den Text – zusammenziehen!
>
> Beispielsweise dies Gedicht
> läse so bebrillt man – nicht!
> Dreiunddreissig seinesgleichen
> gäben erst – Ein – – Fragezeichen!!

(Korf likes reading much and fast so that he is sickened by all that unwanted, ground-out, spun-out stuff. Most of it could be said in six to eight words, and in as many sentences "tapeworm wisdom" can be told. Therefore his mind invents something to save himself, spectacles to shrink the text. For instance, this poem seen through such glasses he would read – not at all! Thirty-three of these poems would only give a question mark.)

THE APPLICATIONS

Reading this chapter one could believe that modern mathematics is only a formal version of the old. Nothing is less true. Not only have many old problems been solved in this century, but mathematics has also been enriched by brand-new disciplines. I have stressed the formal element so much because it is decisive for mathematics instruction at school level. As for the content, I believe that in the near future school mathematics will not yet cross the threshold of the 19th century.

As a matter of fact, I should make one exception, and this in regard to what is usually called applied mathematics. It is possible that at school the most modern examples of applied mathematics will overtake the older ones – later in this chapter the reason for this will become clear.

I began the first chapter with applied mathematics, or rather with directly useful mathematics, because this was the first mathematics of all, and I tended to stress the continuous interaction between mathematics and its applications. Did the change of mathematics in modern times influence its relations to the applications? Not so much, the lion's share of mathematics in natural sciences and technology is still claimed by the classic domains: algebra, special functions, integrals, differential and integral equations, variations calculus problems of a quite "concrete" kind. Only modern computing techniques have made them still more important because many approaches which in the past were sublime theory have now become accessible to more earthly numerical treatment. This should be stressed against the tendency to neglect analysis in school and university education.

It should, however, also be stressed that among the users of mathematics, modern mathematics has not had an easy time with the physicists. This resistance goes as far back as 1930, when group representations and hermitean operators in Hilbert space entered theoretical physics. Modern physics depends on this kind of mathematics, which, however, has never been wholeheartedly accepted by physicists – group theory is reduced to classical algebra and all advantages of genuine group theory methods are forsaken, likewise the abstract component of abstract analysis is avoided as much as possible. There can be little doubt that the physicists will obstruct themselves if they try to avoid modern mathematics by using *ad hoc* methods, or trying to reduce it to classical matter. Confronting physicists with modern mathematics means essentially acting in their own interests.

One of the modern domains of applications of mathematics is statistics. It started in its present form about 1930. Compared with what is called mathematical physics, statistics mostly applies quite elementary mathematics. So it is no wonder that statistics is a field for all sorts of people with no proper mathematical education; scientists and engineers of all professions work in this field. The number of statisticians increased rapidly after 1945; the rate of growth has slowed down but statistics still is an important application of mathematics and it will remain so in the future.

The most striking apparition among the applying disciplines, however, is one that is not easily described in one word. The most general description is by means of the expression "operational research". This then includes the theory of automata, the logic of switching circuits and computers, the system analysis of computers, game theory, mathematics of communication techniques and information theory, mathematics of data processing and information retrieval, linear programming, cybernetics, and much material from graph theory. Rather than throwing words about, I will give a few examples of problems from this field – it doesn't matter if a few of them look trivial or too vaguely formulated, if only they display essential features.

What is the fastest way to find the largest member in a number sequence, or to arrange it according to magnitude? By which method can a linear equations system with 100 unknowns be solved, and what about the precision of the result? What is the best switching circuit for a prescribed aim? How large should a telephone exchange be to reduce queues (or telephone call losses)? What size of stock allows a shop keeper to sail safely between the Scylla of "out of stock" and the Charybdis of too much dead stock? When playing poker, does bluffing pay? What is the shortest way for a commercial traveller to visit fifty given places in a particular country? What is the fastest way of finding among a set of balls of otherwise equal weight the one that is too light? What is the cheapest coding of texts that have to be telegraphed? What about decoding cryptographs? How can one protect number sequences against errors in telegraphing? How can we eliminate noise from messages? How can hidden periodicities be discovered in noise? How can we compose a jigsaw puzzle?

I trust these examples will explain more about operational mathematics than the earlier catalogue of subdomains. Often these are problems for which classical mathematics does not mean much, problems which each ask for its own particular mathematical theory, especially "finite" problems, that is, problems which possess a theoretical solution in a finite number of steps, which, however, is practically meaningful only if there is an appropriate solving strategy, and in fact, this strategy is the only thing that matters.

This leads us to the big computers, for which such solving strategies are invented, and which themselves are sources of problems that require solving strategies. From the oldest times numerical methods were important in astronomy, where the trigonometric and logarithmic computation methods have been developed. The next group of numerical practicians were the geodesians and the insurance mathematicians, who in the 19th century constructed their numerical apparatus. Towards the end of the 19th century many of the current numerical methods were developed. With the rise of the computers the logarithmic era drew to a close. The proper revolution in computing began after 1945 with the automatic computers. Their enormously increased speed blazed the trail for solving numerically numerous problems. As a consequence the proper content of numerical mathematics grew enormously. Nowhere are the different levels of mathematics so clearly outlined as in numerics – how differently can it be exercised: by the person who is mathematizing a problem, by the person who is understanding the formulae and making them accessible to numerical evaluation, by the person who can read the formulae and translate them in behalf of the machine, and by the machine processing the formulae. And along another line: by the creator of computers, of strategies, of processing languages, of programmes. It is indeed a many-sided mathematics which is being pursued in the computer centres.

The number of domains where mathematics is applied has increased. I need not enumerate where computers are put to use. Likewise mathematical methods have carried the day wherever statistical material is processed. In general it is neither the classical analysis nor the "methods of mathematical physics" which satisfy the needs of the new domains of application. The matter proposed by the new users often consists of combinatorial problems, extremalizations, logical problems, and organizational problems – problems for which no ready recipes are found in the literature. Some sciences have been revolutionized by the computer. The problem of how to use computers to read and to translate linguistic texts is far from being solved but it has presented a new challenge for linguists to study the structure of languages from new, mathematically-influenced viewpoints. If computers are to be used in medical diagnostics, the stock of symptoms must be organized in a logical way. The economists use mathematical models of prognostics to propose macro-economic measures.

Who does not recognize the familiar bugbear of those computers which may one day be our rulers? Is it just our imagination, or is that what the world of tomorrow will really look like? No doubt, the answer to this question is as true mathematics as solving a differential equation.

CHAPTER III

TRADITION AND EDUCATION

It becomes the disciple to listen... during the lesson he shall not speak. For otherwise he prevents both master and disciples from finishing the lesson on time. If he need ask something, he shall note it down. After the lesson there is time enough.

> Ratke, *Artickel auf welchen fürnehmlich die Ratichiansche Lehrkunst beruht*, Leipzig, 1617.

On my bookshelves is a seventeenth century parchment-bound booklet "True description to explain who were the authors and inventors of the various crafts, discoveries, and professions"*. It answers many questions: who invented weights and measures, arithmetic and time-reckoning, who the first sorcerer was, who the first potter was, who invented weapons, and neither horseback-riding nor fornication are forgotten. Gods, heroes, and sages from the Bible and mythology taught man the arts, science, and wisdom, and respectful tradition tells their names. The author of the booklet admits that he is not omniscient. He cannot tell us who invented gunpowder, the compass-needle, or the clockwork mechanism. Indeed, these inventions came fairly late on in history, too late perhaps to invent besides these inventions the people who were supposed to have invented them!

Technical progress is as old as mankind. But if names and dates are the backbone of history, then the whole technique before the fifteenth century belongs to pre-history. All we know about earlier inventors is legend. The plough and the wheel, arithmetic and geometry were as important discoveries as the steam-engine and electricity. Why have the inventors of olden times remained anonymous, and why did our ancestors ascribe their inventions to godly or mythological benefactors?

During the last few centuries patterns of thought have changed; it becomes more and more difficult for us to understand the way of thinking of our fathers. From the oldest times tradition was the cement of the human society. Laws and classes, customs and habits were superhuman

---

* I have translated the Dutch title.

institutions; indeed it was dangerous to rebel against tradition. As every-body knew, history once started with a Golden Age, and development since was nothing but decay and regression. Our ancestors were our superiors in body and mind, in wisdom and virtue, and our children will never be what we have been. This is an inalienable law, and all we can do is to try to administer our heritage as good sons and heirs. Mankind will grow old and weak. Progress is a fancy of the meddlers and the godless. This is the old philosophy of history, which still lives on in some places. You can read it in Lucretius, in Simon Stevin, and in our own century in the books of Ortega y Gasset.

In spite of all this kind of philosophy, human history has been a history of progress. Lawgivers, inventors and artists, however, were cautious people, who knew what they were doing. It was risky to be an innovator. Thus they never claimed to innovate. Their apparent concern always was rather to restore patriarchal customs, to save old wisdom from oblivion and to revive old crafts. Whoever made an invention obliterated all traces that would betray its author; maybe even he himself created the legend of a benefactor who bestowed these gifts from heaven on mankind. Scientists were bolder; what inventors did not dare, they ventured one day regardless to assume. The first we know by name was Thales. Was not Miletus a great city, this place where a man could dare predict an eclipse and boast to have discovered mathematical theorems and yet not run the risk of dying on the gallows as a sorcerer?

Yet tradition generally was an iron law. Such as algebra and geometry were created in Babylonia in the third millennium B.C. – maybe by one single man – they were handed down for twenty to thirty centuries with practically no supplement and no progress, until they were taken over by the Greeks. There in Greece the Babylonian tragedy was staged anew. Short eruptions of creativity and genius were followed by long periods of fossilization. Masters were succeeded by disciples who them-selves never became masters. Masterpieces did not breed masterpieces but commentaries. Not the sacred fire of creativity but the mild glow of reverence burned in the torch the disciples carried ahead.

When Greek science was disseminated in Indian and Arabian soil, the same story repeated itself, and when the spell of ancient civilizations was cast on Medieval Europe nothing indicated a new pattern, the pattern of non-stop cultural development, which is supposed to characterize

European history. The reception of foreign cultural assets was even slower and the reverence greater than ever.

The Renaissance looks like an eruption of creativity compared to the centuries of incubation that had preceded it. I have already mentioned that professional historians generally tend to underestimate the import of the accelerated technical development from the twelfth century onwards – a cornucopia of technical inventions which are topped by that of the art of printing.

It is this art that prevented the vicious circle from closing once again. Manuscripts could never spread knowledge and science as easily as printing could do. *"Ceci vaincra ceça"* – says Victor Hugo in *Notre Dame de Paris 1482* when his look slips from the cathedral to the printing-office. The schoolmaster's authority was taken over by the book. Disciples left their teachers. The autodidact began to play the first fiddle. Science was transformed into research, and scholars became investigators. There has been a Holy Writ, but never will there be a "holy print". What is printed is secular, and is in itself a challenge to criticism, and it becomes still more secular yet in our century of tape and xerox.

Aristotle had asserted that the heavier bodies are the faster they fill and for two millennia learned scholars had repeated this. What conceited person would dare be wiser than Aristotle? Galileo dared. He weighed up Aristotle's doctrine in his mind, and concluded that it could not be true. He made experiments and indeed proved it to be wrong.

Prejudgments can survive a surprisingly long time. When Röntgen discovered his famous rays, everybody was convinced that the wave character of these rays could not be checked with man-made grids, because their wavelength must be much shorter than that of visible light. Therefore Laue took natural crystal grids, and in all the books and courses students were told that Laue's method was the only possible one, because man-made grids were too coarse. That is, until after a quarter of a century somebody tried it with man-made grids and it worked.

Until a few years ago it was an established truth that physical laws were invariant under spatial reflections, that is, until Lee and Yang doubted it. And indeed, it was not true. It is very often the younger generation which kicks against the pricks, which doubts what the older people repeat one after the other, and what they copy from one another. For them, nothing is sacred. In only a few centuries the whole social look of academic school practice and of research has been totally changed. No more is the master's doctrine sacrosanct, nor are students merely disciples who preach their master's message. In our laboratories students are the collaborators of the professors. In the team authority cannot be ordained, it springs only from the awareness that the most mature should be the *primus inter pares*. If one last tradition still flourishes at our universities, it is the tradition of no tradition, of non-conformism. The printing press still spreads ready-made science but the university laboratory has even higher pretensions: to prove that science is not taught and learned but created.

Am I painting the picture of modern higher education in too glowing colours? Have I exaggerated? Surely I have. I would not maintain that science at university looks like this in all its aspects and branches. I am even sure that it is not the same everywhere. For just as the ethnologists tell us, there are still contemporaries of us who live in the Stone Age. Recently I discussed the task of the university with a bunch of students, mostly from the humanities. Its task is to provide information, they said, and if they challenged the university, then it was because the university did not provide enough information, or provided the wrong information, or biased information, or because it suppressed information. The university should offer its disciples all information available, and from this stock they would choose what they liked. Projects would be still better, they said, and by projects they meant pools of information collected by united effort.

Maybe this was just the look of the disciplines they studied (if they studied at all and were not referring to information about studying). Anyhow they seriously believed that elsewhere studies were being conducted according to such a medieval system of didactics. They believed that the future physician was being told by his professors how to cure illness, the engineer how to build bridges, and the mathematician how to calculate. In fact, this was once the practice, till about one and a half centuries ago. Today, I told them, scientific attitudes are taught in hospital wards, laboratories, and practice rooms, and for the advanced student participation in research is part and parcel of his curriculum. While they agreed that cycling, swimming, and skiing cannot be learned from a textbook, I could not convince them that science was also an activity that could be better learned not in lectures and books but rather by acting it out. When I told them what students do in a laboratory, and how a science is learned by solving its problems, they reacted as though I was making fun of them. Students as scientific collaborators of their teachers – this they would not believe, this must be a fairy tale.

Is it a fairy tale? I often remember an incident that happened about thirty years ago: a lecture of a famous scholar in one of the humanities, and the club meeting afterwards. The guest of honour had just come from an international congress where – and I will never forget his anger – all kinds of young people had presumed to lecture rather than listen to what the old guard had to teach. I felt embarrassed. At that time I was about thirty, and I also had returned from a congress where I had lectured on a subject that I would now consider as one of the least trifling chapters of my own work. Of course, I did not give myself away. I was afraid of his wrath, and maybe I even felt guilty.

Today I cannot imagine a discipline where a young man must keep silent and lend his ear to the wisdom of the old. In mathematics and almost all the natural sciences that era is long gone. Yet I am not entirely sure whether that image of the university and scientific trade does not still live on in the mind of outsiders and young students, and whether this might not explain many features of the rebellion of this young university generation. The idea of a science which is not exercised but taught and learned still lives on in the mind of the general public. It is most certainly wrong as regards the natural sciences and their laboratories. With regard to mathematics at university I am not so sure. A younger colleague told me that when turning to research after a successful study of mathematics, he had believed that mathematical papers are invented in the style in which they are written, and that for a long time he had attempted to carry out his research in that way, of course to no avail. Fortunately he finally learned how it is really done – a thing that nobody can really tell you. During his study my colleague had never been compelled to solve problems that required more than a routine performance of his skills though this would have been the only proper way for research. Finally he grasped how to do mathematics. I am convinced that he is applying this knowledge in his own teaching.

The kind of mathematical instruction my colleague has suffered from may be exceptional today, I mean, at university. Yet in spite of all the theory little is known about actual teaching itself. I am afraid that passive learning still means too much in many schools. For many years we have had the practice of interviewing our first-year students. One of the questions we asked them was aimed at evaluating their mathematics teachers at school. With almost all students the quality in their teacher they appreciated most was that the teacher "could explain things well". They liked an active teacher who tells a lot, who is easy to listen to, who works out an example of each type of problem, and who would not for the world ask you to exert yourself. (These, of course, were not our worst students, but rather our future mathematicians!) Though I honestly believe that the great majority of our teachers do not give in to this love of ease in their students, I think it is worth-while knowing what a student thinks a teacher should be. Another interpretation of the role of the teacher by the student is only found where the entire school system has been changed to favour pupils' activity, where the class system has been abolished, where work is done individually or in small groups, and where the teacher, rather than dominating learning activities, guides them from the background.

Our first-year students would often complain that we did not "explain" enough in our courses, that in the practical exercises they were confronted with problems that have not been preceded by an example of the same type and that they were supposed to develop more and different initiatives than they were used to in school. Rather than students being tempted by the prospect of greater self-reliance, this must often be imposed on them! All this is true for a short transition period although even up to the end of the second year we find that we must firmly resist the desire of our students for more lecture hours. We are absolutely certain we have to do so because several times we experienced that with more lecture hours, leading to more explaining, the curve of students' achievement drops quite sharply; a broader treatment of the subject matter immediately reduces tension in practical work. These are things we explain to students if it is discussed; they may not believe it in the beginning, but they will come to understand that the system of a short supply of explanatory courses with relatively broad exercises under the guidance of assistants is not arbitrary but has been intentionally so designed.

Maybe the reader thinks that I have mixed up two quite different things. I started this chapter with the belief in tradition and the gradual deliverance from this constraint, and continued it with the development of instruction from passive listening to active acquisition. How are they connected to each other? They are connected through what is called education. For this reason I entirely dismiss the question whether people learn better by actively building up the subject than by the passive reception of ready-made matter – in fact much depends on the kind of subject matter, whether it is more adapted to the one than the other method. For this moment I am not interested in the didactical consequences. It does not matter whether an authoritarian method is bad or wrong or inappropriate in the learning process. It goes much further than this: this method is simply impossible because it does not agree with the character of modern society. The authority of the old cannot be maintained in the learning processes of emancipating youth. Our cultural assets are too dangerous to be offered to youth as ready-made material. Our instruction should create the opportunity for youth to acquire the cultural heritage by their own activity, and they should learn that the self-reliance they claim elsewhere extends to their own role in the learning process.

In numerous witty verses in his "Faust" Goethe ridiculed tradition. At the same time he also expressed this feeling in a positive way: *"Was du ererbt von deinen Vätern hast, erwirb es, um es zu besitzen".* (What you have inherited from your fathers, acquire so as to possess it.) In the static cultures of the past no rupture between heritage and possession existed. Sons were minors as long as their father lived, and when he died, they continued his life and work. Today everybody is heir to the whole world and for none is a special plot reserved – and if this is not yet true today it will be so tomorrow. Possession is no longer a state but is the continuous activity of taking possession. Educating is guiding this process rather than filling hands and brains with well-intentioned gifts.

Babies are immune to infection for a few months. After their first year their bodies learn to defend themselves. The immunity acquired in the womb is lost; childhood diseases attack them, the body is activated, and its reactions are tested. It is the doctor's art to excite the body to form antidotes.

Youth can be poisoned mentally. Worthless products of art and literature fabricated by the advertising and pleasure industry are a menace to youth, not because they poison the natural sources of morals and taste but because their consumption requires no activity. There is one defence against it – to excite the mind into activity – it does not matter perhaps in which field. A child that has discovered science, art or morals by its own activity is protected against mental infection just as it is against physical infection.

No creature is born as helpless as man. Therefore philosophers believed that the mind starts out with a tabula rasa. This, of course, is not true. It *is* true, however, that man must learn numerous physical and mental activities which other creatures are gifted with by instinct. Learning is a slow process. It is slow, and it cannot be forced, not even with patent methods. This distinguishes man from other animals. The lack of instinct and the need for learning lead him into the characteristically human situation of the freedom of choice between accepting and rejecting. Nature that gifted animals with the immediate necessities gave man the opportunity and the task to acquire his heritage in order to possess it.

In our society the path from cultural heritage to cultural possession is long, while property has become a dubious concept. At the beginning of this century, a boy who had been taught arithmetic, had learned just enough for a human life to eke out a scanty livelihood as a bookkeeper, at least as long as the old firm he worked for did not flounder. Business has converted itself so gradually to mechanical and electronic computers that meanwhile the cheaper, human computers could die out. If our instruction today consists in drubbing things in children's heads that in ten or twenty years will be better done by computers, we are asking for trouble. To be honest, we cannot know whether the subject matter we are teaching our children will be what they need in the future. Instead of a particular subject matter, however, we can teach children a more precious thing, namely how to master subject matter.

No astrologer is needed to read the writing on the wall. The students I told of who could understand the learning process only as an information flow are the same who reproached the university with providing wrong information and who would use the information channels of the university to funnel what they consider as true information. If this were the point, they could even be right. The only answer they should be given is that learning is a quite different thing from receiving information.

To what degree has the practice of instruction been pervaded by this idea? Once when I confronted passive learning with active acquisition, somebody said: "This is as old a story as good Comenius." With regard to Comenius I am not sure but I know at least that Pestalozzi urged it again and again. This means that "once" is not enough. If somebody proves a mathematical theorem, it is proved; if somebody shows the invariance of the velocity of light, much will have to happen before another person denies it. Once invented, calculus conquered because it was objectively better. If we say "this was already known to Pascal", we probably mean that he knew something before Leibniz rather than that he was in the possession of some mathematical truth which up to now has been opposed by many.

Of course it is not true that nothing has happened in education since Comenius. In the *Orbis pictus*, or as we would say, the picture book, the horse and cart were successively superseded by the train, the automobile, the plane, and the rocket. This is not said tongue in cheek. If Comenius or Pestalozzi had already said this or that, their words in another age did not have the same meaning. Do not believe that the great pedagogues did not achieve anything worthwhile because their desires have not been fulfilled. Meanwhile society, too, has changed. When education had done no more than keep pace, we were relatively speaking no step further forward than in Comenius' and Pestalozzi's time. I do not believe that things are as bad as that. The mistake is to consider ideal conceptions as realities. If we take a closer look at how Pestalozzi himself interpreted his ideal conceptions in practice, we are bitterly disappointed, and this same disappointment befalls us if we look at the practicians who tried to realize Herbart's or Dewey's conceptions. On the other hand it is true that the gap between ideal and reality is not an irrefutable law as is shown by the examples of Fröbel, Montessori, and Decroly.

I cannot judge to which degree today educational practice fulfils these demands for active learning. Is it old hat or breaking new ground to repeat such demands? In the last few years some experiences I had really startled me. I recount here some of them: a native language lesson for the 7th grade of a model school with a teacher who for one hour lectured on some kind of linguistics, with no interruptions, no questions, and no answers. Then mathematics lessons in another model school (7th and 8th grades) where teachers lecture so brilliantly that there is hardly any time left for questions, though I admit that in the first ten minutes a pupil was allowed to repeat the contents of the preceding lesson, which attempt, not being brilliant enough, was interrupted several times by the teacher. Next I saw demonstration lessons in mathematics for the 5th, 7th, and 10th grades where teachers of the highest quality lectured unswervingly for three quarters of an hour to an audience which did not even dare to swallow, followed by written exercises where the students applied the theorems proved by the teacher by filling in numerical values for the parameters occurring in the theorems.

What depresses me most is the crowd of pedagogues attending such demonstrations, who clearly consider such procedures as didactically normal. Enraptured by the high qualities of the lecturer, they do not seem to be aware that this is the kind of school Wilhelm Busch characterized: *"Wenn alles schläft und einer spricht, den Zustand nennt man Unterricht"*. (When everyone is sleeping and one is speaking, this state is called instruction.)

I do not believe that at school or university I ever had as brilliant teachers as those I have just mentioned, and I go down on my knees and bless myself for my good luck. I congratulate myself, too, because of the good pedagogues I more often met in the classroom than the good lecturers. Model lessons like those I just mentioned could not possibly exist at that time. I think it is an achievement of the last few years. They were model lessons as on the T.V. screen, and I would not be at all surprised if some of those lecturers are used to staging T.V.-style lessons with their classes. In such a lesson nothing can be left to chance. Imagine if a student would pose a silly question which the teacher cannot answer! Or a discussion would develop and the goal of the lesson would not be reached. T.V. is much too expensive to allow for such hazards. For many weeks I daily saw a kindergarten teacher one hour a day on the screen, one who chattered on for an hour like a waterfall; after a fortnight she had reached a point that none of the children dared to interrupt her. Then, however, she got a new group to test her power on. Obviously this is staged on T.V. because it is a model, and it becomes a model because it is staged on T.V. Meanwhile I do not any more believe that I am breaking open doors.

There is an important factor that should be acknowledged. Does the traditional classroom not prevent active learning, does the chair with the blackboard behind it to which the students' eyes are turned not invite lecturing from one side and passive learning from the other? As a matter of fact, I believe that most schools need a reorganization of instruction that aims at making active learning possible and passive learning impossible.

The part of the teacher in the learning process asks for a revision in still another respect. The student who exchanges the small school class for the modern mass university is often struck by the lack of a personal bond between teacher and student. In olden times this would have existed they believe. I do not know how old those olden times would have to be – some would go back to the Middle Ages, but perhaps paradise is a more plausible time. I readily believe this is felt as a lack, in particular by those students who rise against the authority of the university, because it is a natural need of rebels to be seen by the people they challenge. Is it too much if students want to meet their professors face to face? Even the speaker on T.V. looks at you out of his box, why does the professor not?

The longing for a personalized university is romantic. Future instruction will become even more impersonal, and not only in the universities. If instruction is to reach ever broader social layers, it has to be sold as a mass product. Large parts of mathematics are already suitable for programmed implementation in learning processes. It is an unnecessary luxury to teach such parts in personal intercourse. Personal interventions should take place where they are strictly needed, for instance in checking the learning process as far as self-checking does not suffice. Programming instruction is a task for the near future; in a few decades personal instruction will have touched its quantitative limits. The major question now is how active and even creative learning can be programmed. We will pose it more than once in this book.

Rationalizing education is an urgent need. Education is becoming a mass product. Even before Ortega y Gasset there were people who complained about the masses. I do not agree with them. But even if you do agree, you cannot refuse the masses the education they ask for.

Mass production has been the secret of our expanding society and economy for one and a half centuries. Till about a quarter of a century ago there was a general belief that a "hand-made" article was better than a mass article. Even then it was a wrong generalization. Today most people will agree that in almost all industries individual manufacture can never reach the quality of mass production; therefore we try to restrict individual labour to producing objects of a more or less artistic character.

It is a much greater problem how to produce education as a mass article; we cannot afford to ignore it, because we simply cannot refuse education to those who ask for it. I am afraid this problem is hardly understood. In particular in Western Europe, if at colloquia and congresses we talk about mathematical education, we usually mean the education of an often socially determined élite, and we do not care about the others. The differentiation of education in élite and mass is a tradition canonized by the names of kinds of schools – names like the German *Gymnasium* and the French *Lycée*. Dutch legislation in the early sixties refined this differentiation even further. Ten years is a long time. People must be blind with their eyes open, they must have forgotten everything and learned nothing, if they still believe that differentation according to types of school can be maintained for any considerable time. Or should one become more noisy in order to rouse people from their sleep? Not only at school is the abolition of status differentiation in education long overdue. It is also true of education above the age of eighteen. On the other hand we may expect from the future school more differentiation according to talent, interest and learning attitudes.

Up till now education in Western Europe has been élite education, that is to say education of an élite or at least for an élite. This tendency alas has been reinforced by most of the innovation movements. As for mathematics, I am afraid that its educational programmes and methods are influenced by a belief which is natural for every mathematician, that mathematical education is education to become a mathematician – those who cannot keep pace are left behind. And for those who were left behind or who never even embarked, they serve up a second infusion of this mathematics for the élite. Even the United States with its vaster experience in mathematics for all, mass mathematical education is still in the experimental stage, with no convincing image of a new mathematics for all. There is one thing we need most badly, whether it be mathematics for an élite or for all – an image of mathematics for the totality of education.

CHAPTER IV

USE AND AIM OF MATHEMATICS INSTRUCTION

Der Wert einer mathematischen Disziplin ist nach ihrer Anwendbarkeit auf empirische Wissenschaften zu schätzen.
                                         C. Runge, Doctorthese Berlin 23.6.1880

Der Wert einer mathematischen Disziplin kann nicht nach ihrer Anwendbarkeit auf empirische Wissenschaften bemessen werden.
                                         F. Rudio, Doctorthese Berlin 23.6.1880

Horse trail. Horses not admitted.
                                         Notice-board in the Ozark Mountains

The use and aim of mathematics instruction have been discussed so long, from so many standpoints and by so many people that there is little reasonable left to say on this theme. To demonstrate this, indeed, is the purpose of this chapter.

The great problem of mathematics education is the gap between use and aim; in no other field of instruction is the distance between useless aim and aimless use so great. Is not use only the nearby aim, and aim any far-off projected use, and is there not a continuous scale of transition so that nobody can tell where the immediate use ends and the indirect aim begins? The problem does not arise because use and aim are fundamentally different but because it is a long way from one to the other. Maybe when the child starts learning to read and write it is not conscious of the aims behind this, but at least the teacher can tell of every line he teaches what it means with respect to its aim. The aim is clear – the art of reading and writing. In fact, this art begins when the child reads or writes its first line and everything that follows ia a perfecting process. Of course there is a didactic order, there is good and bad material but on the whole it is not presuming too much to claim that every exercise in reading and writing brings the pupil nearer the goal. This goal is not to read this or write that, but to read and write without further restriction. The invention of the alphabet has made it possible for people to read and write both known and unknown words, and to be able after the first reader to move on, to newspapers and encyclopedias.

Arithmetic is not much different though there are divergences, and the more arithmetic approaches true mathematics the more doubtful it becomes. Everybody knows what the use of reading and writing is – to read and write things. But what is the purpose of learning arithmetic? The use of $2+2$ may be taken for granted but what about long divisions, fractions with fractions in numerator and denominator, word problems, and interest computations? As a matter of fact, what does it mean to know arithmetic? Whoever has learned reading and writing can read and write everything he wants. But even if you have done arithmetic for years and years, there is still much left you have not done yet. The most elementary arithmetic may still be an aim, its bearing is well defined: the numerical problems of everyday life. But the higher the aim is, the looser its grip becomes. People have become more and more sceptical towards plain arithmetic as a subject matter, because if problems grow involved they trust machine computers more than even the most skilled human "computers". Formerly – I mean just half a century ago, it was different. At that time a schoolmaster who had drilled his pupils to solve problems in arithmetic could still believe this was an everlasting gift, and he was proud of it. In a way he was even right, for then a skilled calculator could earn a livelihood. These schoolmasters who feel it is their life's work to drill children in arithmetic still exist. If the wind blows you into such a classroom you will probably not believe your eyes and ears, when faced by this class of computing prodigies. Does not its master merit our admiration? What is shown there is not witchcraft but honest achievement. The man who manages to do this with an average class is an artist. On closer inspection the visitor reacts more thoughtfully. Children are fairly malleable, an educational artist can mould them. Experiments show that almost anything can be taught if only it is done well and incisively. In such a class of computing prodigies the visitor who is not dazzled by this asks himself: "Is it all worthwhile?" For the computing fanatics among the schoolmasters arithmetic is an end-goal; they believe in computing and also in its educational value. Likewise there are believers in calligraphy, in gymnastics, and in grammar and syntax. Yet those who believe in arithmetic are the most capable and therefore the most dangerous. The arithmetic they teach is the summit and the limit of their own ability. But it is always wrong if an educator does not know more than he teaches. If he knows no vantage point to look down on his subject matter, he extols it to the skies, making a creed of it. This is just as dangerous with arithmetic as with anything else. Mathematicians who design mathematical programmes for schools they do not know and who never dreamt of anything else to be taught at schools than mathematics are of course just as narrow-minded as the computing fanatics.

In the most modern terminology which comes from the United States, arithmetic is comprised in mathematics. This is a good terminology if it is more than a terminology, that is, if mathematics from $1+1$ onwards is taught as a unit. But I cannot see many symptoms of this in modern schoolbooks, and still less in the training of the present teachers. Soon "mathematics" will be taught in the lower grades of the schools of quite a few countries by people, I am afraid, who do not even know what mathematics is.

I pointed out that there was a time when people could, with some right, consider arithmetic as an educational aim in itself; in every class there was some clever boy who promised to make his way in the world with his computational skill. But the brilliant performance by that arithmetic class was an optical delusion. The observer notices mental arithmetic performed fast and almost flawlessly. Of course he does not count the mistakes to make the judgement of flawlessness more precise. One mistake out of one hundred elementary additions and multiplications looks like a brilliant achievement. Such a percentage, however, means that out of three average written multiplications or divisions one is wrong – in fact, this is approximately the average result of ordinary primary instruction in arithmetic. There is little if any need to argue that in practice this result is not only unsatisfactory but at the same time rather worthless. A thousand times this precision is probably not yet good enough, and as regards the speed nobody can compete with modern computers.

Besides pure computing problems, traditional arithmetic instruction knew structured problems (fractions and brackets) and word problems. By this kind of science, arithmetic crowned itself. A wall against true mathematics was built to defend an arithmetic which had become deadlocked. The worst abscesses were meanwhile cut out but I am not sure whether real mathematics has already penetrated into low-level arithmetic.

THE SYSTEM

There is no way of telling positively what the aim of mathematical instruction is. All of us understand that mathematics admits of numerous applications and that more pupils than ever will have to apply mathematics. We would be fortunate if we could tell of each of them which mathematical concepts and techniques he would need in the future. It is not as simple, on the contrary we are sure it is just the opposite: mathematics is so flexible that neither individually nor collectively can we give sharper contours to a bunch of generalities as regards its application and applicability.

Does this mean complete liberty in prescribing curricula? If we do not know what kind of mathematics the pupil will finally apply, can we not afford to teach him what we like? Some answer "yes" aloud, and a good many as an afterthought.

At any rate, there is one restraint – the capacity of students. This is not as serious as people would believe because much depends on how the subject matter is organized. Moreover there is no genuine criterion of success. Experiments are undertaken with some subject (or at least, they call them experiments) by teaching the subject and checking whether the pupils have understood it. A judgement like this may mean many things: e.g. that they consented to all details, or that they could solve problems in which special values were given to parameters in the general propositions of the subject. I agree that this judgment can also mean more essential features and I can confirm this by examples. These, however, are always local criteria. A teaching success with an isolated subject may be claimed but it is a cheap success, because any isolated matter can be taught successfully if it is done forcefully, in particular if the subject matter is neither unusually extensive nor profound. Little can be performed, however, with such local achievements. What really matters is to know how the subject fits into the whole corpus of mathematics teaching, whether it can be integrated into the whole, or whether it is so eccentric or isolated that it finally would not leave any trace in the whole of education.

It sometimes happens that the conclusions drawn from such experiments are so exaggerated that it is quite terrifying. For instance, it is often stated that such-like experiments have shown that it is possible to teach group theory – say at primary school. Actually the experiments alluded to did not involve anything more than having children operate with some special groups (which may be an extremely useful activity);

that perhaps these objects have been called a group; or on a higher level, that a group definition was given. This is group theory according to the same standard as computing would be number theory, dealing with functions would be function theory, and weighing and measuring would be physics! That is, by no reasonable criterion is it group theory. It is dangerous to call it so, because people could actually make themselves believe that it is group theory and that dealing with it would mean that one has fulfilled one's duty towards group theory. I admit there have been genuine attempts to teach group theory in school. I think they really proved it was possible though neither at primary level nor in the lower grades of the secondary school.

At the same time, if some subject can be taught this does not imply that it *should* be taught. Even in mathematics instruction with no a priori deliminations there are priorities that cannot be ignored. This subject may be more or less important than that, though if isolated both are teachable. Finally this subject must yield to that if, for instance, it fits better into the whole than the other subject. There is a much more doubtful argument which is not all that rare in reports on experiments: that the subject matter was fun. This is a hypocritical argument because we are not used to choosing subjects according to the criterion of students' pleasure. In fact, even pleasure knows a scale of values, and it is the educator's task to inculcate a sense of taste, too. The true schoolmaster can make computing fun. Children like to solve computing problems, in particular divisions that come out. Computing mechanically, copying, and tracing can be fun. But a teacher who abuses this is no educator but a demagogue. We do not spoil our children with sweets, do we? Of course, I do not claim that the worse food tastes the more healthy it is. I simply say that taste, too, should be educated.

I discussed the – often implicit – opinion that it does not matter which kind of mathematics is taught since nobody can predict which one children will need. It is, however, not true that the average pupil's future career lies in absolute darkness. One thing can be predicted with near certainty, that is, that he probably will not become a mathematician. This certainty decreases a little when the pupil passes from the primary to the grammar school, and yet again if in the higher grades he selects a science branch, and once more if, at university, he turns to some field of study that presupposes some mathematical instruction. Again and again we should stress this one point that is so easily forgotten: that besides the future mathematician a great many others must learn mathematics, that those who finally apply a relatively sophisticated mathematics are a minority among those who will apply mathematics at all, and that even those who never will apply mathematics should learn mathematics because they need it as one aspect of their being human beings.

A mathematician's natural inclination is to train mathematicians. To design a methematics lesson the teacher imagines a pupil he would like to teach, and it is quite probable that this imaginary scholar looks a bit like the teacher himself; since the teacher is a mathematician he cannot easily avoid the temptation to design mathematics instruction for future mathematicians. To explain this habit does not mean to approve of it. A mathematician should never forget that mathematics is too important to frame its instruction to suit more or less the needs of future mathematicians. It has happened in discussions that boasts such as the following were made – "We are mathematicians, we know what good mathematics is, this is our business, and everything else is humbug." Such reactions tend to be exceptional. But the inclination to teach mathematics with no regard to anything else is deeply rooted in the mind of mathematicians, and it remains active even though it is often suppressed. Much rationalization is needed to recast it. The mathematical mind expresses itself in the trend to mathematize mathematics. Of course students should learn to mathematize – I mean to mathematize real situations, to begin with; mathematizing mathematical situations may be the end but not the start. For quite a few it is the aim of mathematics teaching to introduce children into a system of mathematics, a system that irradiates undeniably aesthetic charm, which, however, cannot be apprehended by people who have no profound knowledge of mathematics. The system of mathematics as a final aim is an aim for future mathematicians – I do not claim for all of them, because quite a few do not at all feel happy with the system. But it never can be the aim of a general mathematical education, for many reasons. If the vaguely intended system determines the subject matter, it invariably determines the inclusion of worthless and the exclusion of worthwhile matter (examples of the first case, stressing relations and hairsplitting number concepts; examples of the second, the cutting-off of all geometry that does not fit into the system, the gradual outmanoeuvring of analysis which is too far away, at the last branchings of the system, to be reached in due course). If the system is well constructed in the view of the author it may enchant the author by its logical rigour, and if other mathematicians share this view (which is rare) it may enchant others, too. But if teaching follows the system, it is anti-didactical (for instance the anticipation of the affine against the metric view, dictated by systematism).

The system constraint is the most conspicuous expression of the tendency to educate pupils to become mathematicians. Rather than predicting it to be a successful attempt, I believe it contradicts natural inclinations to such a degree that it can only stimulate an aversion to mathematics. This is a point I will have to argue more carefully. Meanwhile I must deal once more with the argument that we do not know which mathematics the student would use in the future and therefore we are allowed to teach what we like. Of course, it is true that we cannot predict too much in every particular case, yet the guess that the student will not become a mathematician is statistically rather trustworthy, and for that reason we should better not try to educate him to become a mathematician. I agree that it is a natural inclination to try it against all odds, but such inclinations are not just the privilege of mathematicians. Geographers tend to educate all people to become geographers, and calligraphers, to become calligraphers. As soon as somebody proposes to put mathematical statistics or computer mathematics on the curriculum, you may be pretty sure that this will result in a course for future statisticians or programmers, with all attendant professional sophistication. This is the way we are, either narrow-minded or fanatic, and sometimes both. (And please remember if I say "we", I mean "we"; if people are criticized, I am both proud and ashamed to be included.)

Often it is narrow-mindedness. If somebody says that he does not know how the student will finally apply mathematics, it can be modesty, or it can be a subterfuge to conceal that he himself does not know how mathematics is applied at all. Examples of sets in many modern textbooks and in almost all films convincingly show that the author did not know what the use of sets was; it is improbable that otherwise they would have invented such horrifying examples, as I will sum up later. The obstinate attempts of some authors to avoid infinity in sets and mappings is one more sympton of the isolation of this domain, and its sterilization *in usum Delphini*. The way in which some authors introduce general functions and avoid special ones shows that they have not grasped the meaning and importance of functions wherever they are applied. But not all awkward phenomena can be explained by ignorance. It is improbable that the author of a probability theory for schools who deals with probability as pure measure theory has never heard about applications of probability. To cut probability off from all reality can only be the work of a fanatic, the work of a man who has set out to protect pure mathematics against all applied infections. Let us be honest, this fanatic is slumbering at least in all of us. Imagine a well-balanced structure of probability, an architectonic miracle, where all is arranged according to rigorous laws. Examples could only disturb this grand unity, like flower-pots and plants in the windows of a lofty concrete structure. Should we adapt such a course to the needs of appliers? Should we start with real problems to design the ground-plan? Should we dismiss a fundamental theorem which never applies in favour of a less fundamental one? Never, because this would lead to complete chaos. This is just not possible, and even if we belong to those mathematicians who are more enchanted by beautiful problems than by the system, we still do not like to abandon the system.

THE APPLICATIONS

Recent developments in elementary arithmetic raise disturbing fears. Whatever one has reproached traditional arithmetic books with, at least they expressed the clear consciousness of the applicability of mathematics and provided a knowledge of the multifarious possibilities of application. Certainly there were serious flaws: pursuing needless complications, inventing irrealistic problems, prescribing *ad hoc* solving methods within the frame of elementary arithmetics where a bit more profound mathematics would have been the proper tool. It is a bad thing that in the last few years didactics of arithmetic has fallen out of step with social reality, that it has not accounted for the increasing possibilities of application, presumably because they are badly known. Instead, in the past few years formal transformations were carried out or tried by people who could not resist the dazzling fascination of the formal aspect. Too many traditional experiences have simply been thrown away. An example is the overstressing of the potency aspect of natural numbers, which in number's multifarious entanglements with reality plays an insignificant role. I am afraid these tendencies, if they continue, will seriously damage arithmetic instruction, not with regard to computing skill that is near to the heart of some people but rather with regard to its applicability. In my opinion there is no doubt that traditional instruction prepared students not only for practising computing routines, but also for applying elementary arithmetic to a great variety of problems (I exclude fractions from this which were a sore point). I fear serious disappointments in this field in the future, and I am sure that modern mathematics, though innocent, will be held responsible.

Functions and mappings are generally introduced with no relation to earlier mathematical experiences and to reality, or if there are relations they are not illustrative. I conclude that such relations are in general unknown. It would be worthwhile once to demonstrate their great variety. So far as they are dealt with at school, functions, mappings, and also elementary algebra admit of many applications to science. This brings us to another alarming phenomenon. Physics and chemistry teachers consider it as a task of mathematics instruction to prepare the applicability of mathematics in their own teaching, but they never trusted this uncontrolled resource. Therefore they have tried to do it with as little mathematics as possible. In this regard miracles have been wrought in scientific instruction from the elementary level up to university – miracles of demathematized science. It is astonishing to see how little mathematics the physics teacher needs in the secondary school, how he succeeds in avoiding functions, how he tries to reduce all mathematics to substituting numerical values for the parameters in given formulae. This demathematization of science hurts both mathematics and science education. It results in cultivating a sterile mathematics and a depraved science. Neither mathematics nor science could have developed to its present stage if mathematics had not assisted science and if mathematicians had not learned from this assistance which problems are important. Of course, the pupil's development does not reflect that of science. History knows of no system while education can and should be systematic. If we wish to teach the pupil to apply mathematics, we should it make easier for him to apply it. We should break the barriers surrounding mathematics. We should apply mathematics as much as is needed in other sciences, in order to teach how it is applied. We must not teach a lack of relations if we wish him to learn about relations. If I blame the physicists for teaching a demathematized physics, it is fair to turn again to the mathematicians who have isolated mathematics. The general view of the mathematics teacher is as follows: I teach the mathematics which I understand. As for the applications, I do not know them, and the few I know are not reasonable mathematics, they are not rigorous and I do not know to make them rigorous, and if I accepted them, they would break the logical structure of mathematics to pieces. Or if it was not the mathematics teacher himself who weighed the extraneous subject matter and found it too light, it was done for him by the man who wrote the textbook the teacher uses. Among all the arguments against teaching mathematics that is not isolated from applications, I can understand that of incompetence, and if it is no affectation, I can appreciate it. The mathematics teacher does not know how mathematics is applied, and we cannot blame him for this ignorance. Where should he have learned it? In the mathematics teacher training of many countries scientific minor subjects have become rare, and in a good many cases mathematics is taught by people who even at school never attended a physics lesson. And even if they learned physics, it was a demathematized physics. Though this is well known, organizers of courses of further training for mathematics teachers in many countries accept the fact that their courses lack any relation to applications. Somebody who once organized such courses told me: "If we teach our teachers useful mathematics, industry will buy them up as soon as they are ready. We can only teach them a mathematics which they can never use outside school". This is an honest remark but I cannot believe things are that bad. Anyhow, this is certainly not the reason why relations to applications are avoided in such courses. It is the organizers who have no idea what to do about these relations.

This reminds me of an international conference on further teacher training. When the curriculum of such courses was discussed, somebody criticized the fact that computers were not even mentioned. A mathematics teacher should be expected, he said, to know how to answer questions on computers. The reaction was stony silence. This was pure accident. If a few computer people had been present at the conference, they would have hooked in on the subject and proposed a complete course in numerical mathematics, the successful followers of which would indeed have better gone into industry than stay on at school. Neither did a non-mathematician attend the conference; he would have also been stirred up, because for outsiders it is quite obvious that a mathematician should know about the most sensational subject mathematics can offer, the miracle of computers. Of course nobody would ask this from a university mathematician. This man would recommend people interested in computers to his numerical colleague who is a better expert in this field. But what about the poor teacher who is asked a question about computers? Or is it perverse to assume today that pupils would ask such questions? Of course, a good teacher is never at a loss for an answer. He may say that it does not belong to the curriculum, which might provoke the next question: "Why not?" Another subterfuge would be to answer that: "Science is tremendously specialized today" – an answer which certainly was already in use in Šumerian schools when the teacher was not familiar with the subject. The easiest way out is to say "it is the 11th grade curriculum", hoping that by that time all will be forgiven and forgotten.

But what can we do? Though you have designed a sterilized course of further training in abstract mathematics, you cannot deny that mathematics plays a role in our society, that the classroom where mathematics is taught does not float in empty space, but with its past, present and future pupils belongs to society. If you have just made efforts to banish geometry because it is not exact enough, and analysis because it could not be taught in exact terms at school, would you then admit computers which nowhere fit into the programme? You have designed a course as it should be, one piece of the same mould, from sets and relations up to vector spaces. Is there any place where one can put computers? It might be useful but it is a foreign body.

Maybe somebody will find the solution – here at this point we can deal with the dual number system, and this means computers. Yes, it means computers, just as answering a question on a sexual matter with stories about stamens and pistils can be called sex instruction. Some people still believe that the dual system is the most profound secret of computers. Probability and statistics can fare as badly: stuck somewhere on the general measure concept to be treated as part of measure theory. Likewise it can happen that analysis is disposed of as an offshoot of topology.

FRAUGHT WITH RELATIONS

In principle it is a healthy idea not to teach isolated pieces but coherent material. Connected matter is faster learned and longer retained. But

there is more than one kind of connection. There is one which is understood by the teacher, and another which is only understood by the
textbook author. Both of them are of little use but unfortunately most
connections constructed in a logically coherent school programme are
of this kind. They are connections *within* mathematics, constructed in
order to teach a unified mathematics, which is constructed at the expense
of the outside connections of mathematics which are possibly more
natural and more important. This is a point for later discussion.

With a view to the use and aim of mathematics instruction I mentioned
applied mathematics. Among applied mathematicians one finds people
who do not like this term. There is but one mathematics, they claim, of
which some parts are more and others are less closely related to outside
matter. They are right in saying so, though this characterization is readily
taken up by people who abuse it to justify teaching mathematics with no
outside relations. Here the past passive participle "applied" is probably a
literal translation of French "appliqué" which has an unusual meaning
in this context (as in *anatomie comparée*, where it means "comparing"
rather than "compared" anatomy). Likewise applying or applicable
mathematics would be better. Anyhow I hope nobody has concluded
from the discussion that I would like to have applied mathematics taught
at school – I do not advocate computer mathematics at school in order
to train programmers, nor probability to bring up statisticians, nor any
applied mathematics whatever it might mean. The greatest virtue of
mathematics is its flexibility. A mathematics tailored to some applications
is beside the mark, it fossilizes. While I do not urge that the pupil learns
applied mathematics, I do wish that he learns how to apply mathematics.
This does not mean utilitarism. Therefore instead of applied mathematics,
I would prefer to speak of *multi-related* mathematics. It was again old
Comenius who urged that everything people learned should be fraught
with relations. But the point is to know which relations should be cultivated and reinforced. Under the influence of the Herbart school the
postulate of relatedness has been interpreted in the sense that the instruction in a single discipline should form a connected chain. I still remember
my old German language teacher and grammar school principal; if in
the last lesson he had dealt with, say, Wieland and if in the next lesson
he was going to commemorate, say, Eichendorff's birthday, he would
construct a long and ingenious chain from the one to the other. Of course,

we soon got to know this trick, and everybody was in keen expectation to know where the old chap was going to move to next. It is remarkable that we appreciated not the continuity but rather the discontinuity, the surprise.

In any case these are not the relations I have in view. I do not aim at the relations within the discipline, inside mathematics. If they are natural, they arise naturally, and whether they are so or not should be decided from the viewpoint of the pupil. The most perfect expression of the inside relations is the system. Where all pieces are so well balanced that none can be withdrawn, everything is fraught with relations. The question, however, is whether a pupil can understand the system. Or is it a valid question? In fact, it is improbable that the student can, and it is still more improbable if the whole system is a delusion. The bad thing, however, is that the inside relations are bought at the expense of the outside ones.

For instance, it cannot be avoided that at the beginning instruction in arithmetic, geometry, and set theory lacks the essential relations between these domains. From a higher vantage point, on a higher level, they can be constructed, but they must not be anticipated even though the teacher may hate not to indulge his logical-aesthetic passions in the classroom. Even within those domains the conception of essential logical connections must be delayed, as for instance those between the different aspects of natural number, between different ideas of the algebraical operations, and between order, affine and metric properties of the geometrical shapes. What primarily matters are the relations of the arithmetical, geometrical, and set theory concepts with reality.

Of course, strong relations are important but the point is to know where. The mathematical matter should be interconnected but the connections need not be direct and intra-mathematical. Indeed there exist stronger relations. Anyone starting to learn his own mother tongue starts with narrow bonds between the linguistic expressions and reality, that is, the situations designated by those expressions. The lived-through reality is the framework that guarantees the connection, and linguistic expressions are here and there attached to this framework. Between these appendices connections grow, primarily to reflect the connections within the framework, and only gradually will they grow more formal as is required by the proper structure of the language. This complex of relations strives for an ever greater autonomy and an autonomous system. It can finally rise to an autonomous structure, free from the framework of reality, but this is a singular and extra-ordinary phenomenon. Without lasting relations to reality, language becomes ghostly and unreal.

Certainly, mathematics is not only a language, but even language is not only a language (where the second "language" means the formal system). Nevertheless I think the analogy is not too bad. To teach connected mathematics it is not wise to start looking for direct connections; they should rather be found between the contact points where mathematics is attached to the lived-through reality of the learner. Reality is the framework to which mathematics attaches itself, and though these are initially seemingly unrelated elements of mathematics, in due process of maturation connections will develop. Let the mathematicians enjoy the free-wheeling system of mathematics – for the non-mathematician the relations with the lived-through reality are incomparably more momentous.

I stress this for practical reasons. Why does a pupil learn to speak his mother tongue but not mathematics? In the mother tongue he is living the whole day, maybe even in his dreams too. Mathematics can only claim 4 to 5 hours a week. What is learned unrelatedly does not last long. Is it not a disappointment familiar to every teacher that subjects taught a few weeks ago seem to have disappeared out of the pupils' minds, with no trace left unless they have been retrained in the meantime? It is not of much use whether a logical path leads from the subject of a few weeks ago to the present, because it is not the pupil but the teacher or rather the textbook author who has constructed this contraption, convinced that such constructions are, in some mysterious way, still active in the pupils' mind. The pieces of mathematics that the student has exercised in those weeks were foreign substance in his lived-through reality; as fast as possible they were eliminated. Everybody can check with himself to see how fast unrelated subjects are forgotten. I mentioned earlier the statements of experimenters who claimed to have proved that this or that is teachable; this is no wonder, I answered, children can learn all you want. It is another fact that they can forget it just as completely. A teaching experiment is irrelevant if it does not tell how deeply the taught material has settled, and how long it remains active. The depth of settling is nothing else than the connectedness to lived-through reality, and its persistence can be guaranteed by the strength of these relations.

Of course this does not exclude cultivating internal mathematical relations as far as they are effective. But this condition should not be interpreted too narrowly; it is not restricted to deductive relations. Analogy, for instance, can be much more efficient a relation – Emma Castelnuovo's didactics* strongly depends on them. Inside and outside analogies to mathematical situations are highly efficient tools. They can involve great educational values: the motivating surprise, the convincing force, and the abstract imagery, because each of the analogies may illustrate the other.

Certainly words like analogy give the rigorous systematician the creeps. They are so vague, they lack rigour. If only they were at least "isomorphisms" or "models of axiomatic systems". Then indeed it is formal mathematics. But nobody can recognize isomorphisms and construct models of axiomatic systems unless he has noticed analogies leading to such discoveries. The student learns more if he sees an analogy which is not formalized in the language of isomorphism, than if isomorphisms which he cannot grasp are forced upon him.

The analogy is such an effective means of building inside and outside mathematical relations because it is the most natural and primitive means of all with which the organization of the world is attempted, a means which nevertheless remains vigorous at higher levels too. The student knows it even before he learns mathematics. Its overestimation is dangerous, in particular in mathematics, but to weigh it up correctly one has to learn its application consciously.

I mentioned the anlogy by the way, though much more could be told about it. I mentioned it to fight against too narrow an interpretation of what I would call mathematics fraught with relations.

When speaking about mathematics fraught with relations, I stressed the relations with a lived-through reality rather than with a dead mock reality that has been invented with the only purpose of serving as an example of application. This is what often happens even in arithmetic teaching. I do not repudiate play realities. At a low level games may be useful means of motivation. But it is dangerous to rely too much on games. Ephemeral games are no substitutes for lived-through reality. The

---

* I only mention the analogy between addition of even and odd numbers, multiplication of positive and negative numbers, composition of the linguistic assertion and negation. – Emma Castelnuovo, *Didaktik der Mathematik* (1968), Frankfurt a.M. Akademische Verlagsgesellschaft.

rules of games that are not daily exercised are as easily forgotten as mathematics or even faster. The lived-through reality should be the backbone which joins mathematical experiences together. However motivating and charming games may be, they can never fill this place.

The richness of relations should warrant that mathematics, once learned, is not easily forgotten. Yet it would obviously be nonsense to propose that it is the aim of mathematics not to be forgotten. With a well-organized mnemonics such an aim could be reached with any subject whatsoever. Rather than a benefit memorized matter can be a burden. But as a mind matures, its stock of knowledge becomes more and more interrelated, which entails that it depends less and less on intentional memorizing: closer acquaintance with a foreign language makes versified grammar rules and rhytmic conjugations more and more dispensable; with a more profound knowledge of history, dates and years can be missed as structurating elements. They are not needed so they will be forgotten. This does not mean that one should not have learned them. For they were the ladder kicked away by him who has reached the top. This is true in the life of the individual as in that of mankind. Though maybe 90% of all mathematics a mathematician learned in a lifetime can finally be ruled out as redundant, it was indispensable, because it was its role and destiny to be replaced by better mathematics. Thus, not being forgotten is not only no sufficient criterion of the mathematics that should be learned, it is not even necessary. The criteria of retaining and forgetting are too rough and ready, indeed. Retaining in the sense of identical reproduction and forgetting in the sense of complete blackout are singular border cases. It is the operativity that matters, and this is again true in individual life as it is in history. Hundreds of abortive attempts of the trisection of the angle, of elastic light theories, of models of benzol were necessary to prepare the way for the Galois theory, the electromagnetic light theory, and the knowledge of cyclic compounds. These were not simply dead ends, but operative attempts. What matters is not that the mathematics one learned is not forgotten, but that it has been, and still is, operative. To attain this, mathematics fraught with relations should be taught.

To conclude, it seems that it does not matter what kind of mathematics is offered to be learned if it is mathematics fraught with relations. In a sense, this is true. It is an old belief that learning is a value in itself whatever one learns; it is a formal value. In fact, nobody asserts it this way; formal values may differ according to the disciplines. Latin used to be in high esteem as a formal discipline; it was said to train logical thought. This claim may be not unreasonable; the regularity of Latin must have some formal value. Linguistic analysis can, indeed, be an activity with strong outside relations. This may be true but it is also true that most of what is done at schools in this field is a dreary pseudo-science.

DISCIPLINA MENTIS

Among the seven medieval liberal arts of ancient Pythagorean tradition the trivium of the linguistic arts (grammar, rhetoric, and dialectic) stood lower than the quadrivium of the mathematical arts (arithmetic, geometry, music, and astronomy) though all of them were still below philosophy which itself was the hand-servant of theology. The high esteem in which mathematics was held as a teaching discipline was partly due to its illustrious pedigree. It is not to be wondered at that the humanistic renovation favoured mathematics, too. Indeed humanities then included mathematics – who would believe it today – since at that time the "human" science was still the stepsister of the "godly" one, and the controversy between the sciences of nature and the sciences of the mind had not yet been invented.

Mathematics, however, was more than of noble birth. Mathematics was, people believed, a whetstone of wit, a discipline of mind, *disciplina mentis*, and so it was dear to all who believed in education. Disciplinarians who could exercise this discipline of mind were wanted, and so were the professors who would train such teachers, and when the idea gained ground to choose the professors among those who cultivated mathematics as a science, mathematical research migrated from the academies to the universities.

There was more to it. Not only arguments of cultural tradition and education helped to restore to mathematics some of the dignity it had enjoyed in Platonic education. In France, the only country where in the 18th century mathematics had been promoted systematically though not just high-mindedly, mathematics got a new chance through the revolution. The rationalist mentality of the revolutionaries, and later Napoleon's interest in mathematics broke new and fertile ground for mathematical training and research. The *Grandes Ecoles* which were established in those days can be characterized as military schools with a mathematical background or, if you prefer, as mathematical schools with a military background. If people wanted to explain Napoleon's military sucesses, it was quite natural to stress the mathematical education of his officers, and this was actually done, in France and abroad. It was an old experience that mathematics could be useful to the military art: a general had to be able to work out when he would meet the approaching enemy, and a fortress builder had to know how to construct regular polygons. But mathematics as a means of military education was another story; there it was a discipline of the mind. After the French successes the others did not hesitate. They, too, created schools after the French image, and by doing so they contributed to the preconditions of the accelerated development of mathematics in the 19th century.

I am not sure whether mathematics really merited this renown. If there was any relation between the reliance on mathematics and the military performance of the French officers corps of about 1800, then it certainly was not of such a simplicity that a good knowledge of mathematics determined its successes. It was not the mathematical *education* that raised the French military above those of other nations but rather the *selection by means of mathematics*, which apparently was more to the point than that by patents of nobility or juridicial or philological abilities.

Whatever the reason might have been, it is a fact that the renown of mathematics as a discipline of mind was a historically important factor. A host of unfortunate pupils were to learn a lot of mathematics to justify the existence of their teachers who, for their part, had to study mathematics to justify the existence of their professors, who, for their part, created that mathematics which when technology needed it, proved to be available. Today, of course, mathematics is an enormously useful science, which, however, in order to attain this status has had to cross a desert of uselessness where mathematics was to be nursed tenderly, by a spiritual aristocracy that was borne on the mass that had to learn mathematics, a useless mathematics as a discipline of mind.

Isn't history a strange guide? Columbus discovered America which he believed to be India. If the story of the discipline of mind is a fake and the belief in mathematics as a whetstone of wit is an illusion, then it was an illusion pregnant with reality. A will-o'-the-wisp lured us up the right path.

Is there a discipline of mind, and is mathematics one of them, or even the keenest? How can one answer such a question? The current methods by which teaching results are rigorously tested do not mean anything for such a general and vague question. All those methods are of local validity; to follow learning processes globally, we lack all methods. From olden times educators always answered this question in the positive, and I doubt whether there are many sceptics who would revert this answer into an unconditional "no". Of course, it does not prove much that good mathematicians perform better than average in other fields, too. Possibly the mathematical gift is universal in the sense that it is a sympton of more general gifts. It is not convincing either that mathematicians feel their general mental behaviour is strongly determined by mathematics, because nobody knows how they would have behaved if rather than mathematics they had studied something else. Even statistics cannot help us. Against the statistical proofs of the bond between smoking cigarettes and cancer some people objected that the inclination to smoke and the susceptibility to cancer could be connected not by the category of cause and effect but by a common factor. Everybody feels this is a far-fetched argument. But is it far-fetched to reject a causal relation between the study of mathematics and a general exact intelligence and to assume instead a common factor in the preference for mathematics and that general intelligence?

THE MEANS OF SELECTION

Every teacher will confirm it: the person who is good in mathematics is ususally good in other fields, too. This may be true but nobody knows whether he would not have been as good in the other fields if he had never studied mathematics. But the remark tells its own tale. I wonder whether people who praise mathematics as a discipline of mind, do not in fact mean that from one's mathematical achievements, they can tell whether he is intelligent, that is, whether they do not mean that mathematics is a good selection test. Actually this is the only thing about the general value of mathematics that is fairly certain. As a means of selection in intellectual functions mathematics is more trustworthy than any other school discipline (maybe even than intelligence tests), and it is also more easily applied. For this reason mathematics is indeed used as an instrument of selection in a vast field, for all scientific, technical, and medical education it is a shibboleth, and a certain doubtful minimum of non-elementary

mathematics is even required of students in most humanities subjects.
May we conclude that it is the aim of mathematics teaching to select
students on the ground of their reaction to mathematics teaching? In
other words, the goal of mathematics teaching is the examination? All
our feelings struggle against this conclusion, which, however, states a
certain reality, the fact that mathematics is held in high esteem as an
instrument of selection. We struggle against this as educators who refuse
to accept selection as a goal of education, and as mathematicians who
believe that mathematics is too good to be used for this end.

The stairs that lead to the upper floors of society are narrow; to stave
off crowds, they sell tickets, the admission examinations. Today the upper
floor has been extended somewhat, the stairs are more comfortable, maybe one day the distinction of floors will disappear. Up to that day there
will be selection, and educators would be fools if they would refuse to co-
operate in selection procedures. The only question is: how? "If there were
no admission examinations, everybody would try to study medicine, phar-
macy, or law, and this must be prevented." A lottery would be simpler,
but who would accept it? On the other hand, can an educator allow
some subject to be taught to be used eventually as an instrument of
selection? The argument that mathematics is an excellent instrument for
predicting general abilities is no longer conclusive. As soon as a discipline
is admitted to be taught in order to be an examination subject, it is obvious that the things taught are the things that can be most easily examined. And is it not too far-fetched to doubt whether mathematics as a
discipline of mind is adequately represented by those mathematical subjects that are the readiest to be examined? I need not substantiate this
doubt; at school every discipline is in danger of degenerating into the
instruction of examinable matter.

Examining is a meaningful activity. The teacher should be able to
check the influence of the teaching process, at least in order to know how
to improve it. The student has the right to know whether he has really
learned something, whether his learning attitude is appropriate, and
whether he is capable of learning what is required. Finally there are
others who are interested in knowing what somebody has learned. Earlier
I pointed out that our examination and test methods are attuned to
ascertain local study successes. It is absolutely possible to test the study
results globally, and it is easier in mathematics than in any other disci-

pline. From our mathematics instruction at university we know that it is more informative to observe a student during his mathematical activity than to grade his papers; I suppose any educator will confirm this experience. I shall come back to this point and expound it in more detail, but meanwhile I claim that this should be the point of departure for any global appreciation of teaching results. I know everywhere there are laws and regulations that prescribe another kind of examination. In many countries the universities are the only institutions where programme, instruction, and examinations are all under one roof. If it is useful, they adapt the programme to the instruction, and they need not separate instruction and examinations from each other. Since they are empowered to, they should set a good example and take away from the examination the acuity of an instrument of selection. Maybe others will be allowed to follow suit.

This remark has to do with, I would say, instruction policy. I cannot dwell upon this point. It may or may not be regretted but it is a fact that society is not very much interested in how profoundly some student has fathomed mathematics if it cannot be specified by a grade which together with others build up a criterion of selection. Teacher and students must acknowledge this fact – the student who seeks recompense by a grade for every single achievement, and the teacher whose professional duty is the golden mean between leniency and rigour. The examination becomes a goal, the examinable a programme, and teaching examinable matter a method.

Or must it? It is a pity that this too often reflects reality. This should not be the case even if the realities of society are duly acknowledged. This I will show later.*

LOGICAL THINKING

Meanwhile the question whether mathematics is a discipline of mind stays open. It is a painful question. We of course want the answer to be "yes". But does it pay to lie to oneself?

From olden times it was of course logical thinking that had to be trained by mathematics. What the adjective "logic" means here is difficult to tell. Why not simply "thinking"? As a matter of fact, there exists a so-called logic of Aristotelian workmanship, but it is not the logic of "logical

* See Chapters VI and X.

thinking", because it does not have much to do with thinking. There are other thinking patterns besides the famous "All men are mortal, Socrates is a man, thus Socrates is mortal". This pattern cannot suffice because there is not much thought that can be expressed in the subject-predicate pattern. Relational patterns and quantifier sequences are indispensable. Moreover thinking is more than the exercise of formal methods. It often proceeds informally, e.g. by analogy:

"If you invite Black, you should invite White, too."

"Why?"

"They are friends".

"When the other day we were at Miller's, they had invited White but not Black. So ..."

"So ... That is quite another thing. We can invite White without Black, but not the other way around".

"Why not the other way around? If they are friends then White is as much Black's friend as Black is White's."

"But if you invite Black, Mrs. Black will tell Mrs. White, and Mrs. White resents it, but Mrs. Black is not as touchy".

"The womenfolk are no concern of mine."

"Excuse me, aren't you married?"

"I am, but not to Mrs. White."

"She is lucky, isn't she?"

"The fat is in the fire. That is female logic."

I think this is a good example of what people call logical thinking. I mean it seriously. The talk contains few formal elements like the argument of symmetry between Black and White, but it differs from a mathematical discussion in that the formal elements remain implicit and the discussion proceeds in concreteness. (It should be noticed that the first "illogical" argument, that is, which breaks the formal frame, is the husband's "but not to Mrs. White"; so he is not entitled to blame his wife's bad logic.)

If it is true that mathematics instruction is a training in logical thinking, then it may be taken for granted that logical thinking *in mathematics* will be the first thing to be trained. Whether this training can be transfered to something else may well be the next question. Let us ask by which means such a transfer of highly formalized thought might be possible. If something is transferred, then it would be in the way of analogy, more or less consciously, or maybe unconsciously and nevertheless efficiently. I mentioned certain formal elements in what is usually called logical thinking; in the present example, symmetry was such an element, or to be more precise, there was a situation which was claimed to be symmetric with respect to two parameters and in which therefore a symmetric action should be taken. Symmetry arguments play a role in mathematics, too, though in traditional mathematics (or rather in school mathematics) they are hardly recognized or even obscured, being eliminated or replaced by irrelevant algorithms – compar ethe suppression of symmetry arguments in geometry by the algorithmic use of congruence theorems, and in algebra by algorithmic computations. If formal arguments like symmetry are considered so useful that they should be spread from mathematics, it would be reasonable to train them in mathematics itself, first unconciously and implicitly, and then finally exhibited in an explicit way. Making formal elements conscious is nowhere else as easy as in mathematics and nowhere can it be performed as efficiently.

It is conceivable that recognizing and handling certain mathematical structures is a discipline of mind. But this presupposes that it is taught as a discipline of mind, that is, the recognizing and handling of such structures is exercised and is made conscious in mathematics education itself, and that this is done in a related way, that is, that these abilities are exercised with non-mathematical examples, too. What is operative as a discipline of mind is the mathematical method rather than the subject matter; the method should be stressed, and made as explicit as possible. How this can be done shall be discussed latter.

For many years I have observed, not too systematically but with continuing interest, a change of attitude in mathematics and physics students in the course of their first university year; I do not presume that these observations prove anything, and I also admit that mathematics and physics students are not a random selection among the youth of their age-group. I observed these students only in their mathematical development though I also looked for features that pointed to more than mathematics. I will enumerate a number of questions I usually like to ask first-year students during their first weeks at university to compare them with older students of the second university year. Except one, they have never been used in a formal test; rather they were asked in informal talks:

(1) Is the greatest painter among the poets, and the greatest poet among the painters the same person?

(2) Is the oldest painter among the poets, and the oldest poet among the painters the same person?

(3) If among the poets there is only one painter, is there then among the painters only one poet, and are they the same person?

(4) In a town there are houses, and in the houses there are tables. It happens that for every $n = 1, 2, 3, \ldots$ the following is true: if in a house there are tables with n legs, there are no tables with more than n legs. What about the statement ($n = 1, 2, 3, \ldots$): If in a house there are tables with n legs, there are no tables with less than n legs?

(5) In a basket are various objects of different colours and different shapes. Are there then necessarily two objects in the basket which differ both as regards colour and shape?

Such questions cause enormous difficulties for our first-year students, though after one year even average students laugh at me for posing such childish questions (except for the last which seems to be the most difficult). I cannot but conclude that the mathematics they have learned meanwhile has helped them to make this progress, and I am certain that the stress which is laid in mathematical education on the mathematical *method* has not been useless.

The fourth question, which I had asked to no avail of 80 mathematics first-year students in a course, was afterwards given as a written test to 23 pupils of the highest scientific grade of a grammar school by a teacher who pays much attention to the logical training of his students. Of 23 students only 2 gave an answer that was somehow related to the question, one answer was wrong, and the other was totally wrong.

After one year of mathematical instruction at the university this question is considered ridiculous.

LANGUAGE

These five questions, which can hardly be termed mathematics, are characterized by certain formal elements which are familiar features of mathematical structures. Do my experiences prove that recognizing such structures has been exercised in the first university year? They do so indeed, provided I can eliminate one factor: I am not sure whether the students did understand linguistically the questions I   asked them. In some cases I am even sure they did not. I would readily posit that in the majority of cases linguistic understanding may be taken for granted if I were not afraid to make the same mistake that characterizes much of Piaget's work: in almost all of his experiments where he wants to prove that at such and such an age the child is not able to perform this or that action correctly, it is absolutely certain that the child did not linguistically understand the task it was expected to perform; thus Piaget's experiences are related not to the cognitive but to the linguistic development.

But this does not matter here. Certainly by means of mathematics our university students improve their command of language during their first year *. Whenever mathematics is considered a discipline of mind, the influence of mathematics on the command of linguistic means is usually explicitly mentioned. The universalist character of language, which connects all our mental expression and activity, makes it plausible that the peculiarities of mathematical language can be operative far beyond mathematics.

The language of scientists and the relation between science and language varies considerably through the family of sciences. Poets and novelists are once again a different chapter though that which characterizes their language is not entirely unheard of in some of the humanities – I mean a tendency to linguistic autarchy or even a dominance of the linguistic form over the material content, sometimes with the magical undertone of discovering secrets in the melody or etymology of words. There is a broad spectrum of linguistic practice from there to the language of the mathematician, who handles his vocabulary arbitrarily and whose words, free from undertones, just mean what he wants them to mean. Of course no other scientist can take it as easy as the mathematician, no other scientist can afford this arbitrary policy because in no other system besides mathematics can one reduce by definition all things to notions which are so simple that they do not allow any disagreement. Already the physicist has to rely more on the vernacular with all its uncertainties.

In the past there have been sporadic influences of mathematical ter-

* The study of three modern foreign languages, and in our "gymnasiums" Greek and Latin also, does not seem to contribute much to the formal command of linguistic means, since too little time is left for the mother tongue. I would not be astonished if in countries where the mother tongue is more cultivated, experiments with our questions, which require quite a bit of formal linguistic means, would be more successful, even in the lower grades of the secondary school.

minology on the vernacular. An expression which has been conserved in all languages is the "centre of gravity"; for a long time a favourite term in politics was the "parallelogram of forces", which perhaps disappeared because in politics today all forces seem to act in opposite directions; the term "resultant", however, is still in use*. The inclination to call unknown factors x seems to have ceased, but a new fashion is the word "set" from set theory, which is nearly always used in a wrong way. As soon as the mathematical term "information" is abused, we may be sure that it is sheer charlatanism. When people use mathematical terms without being aware what these words can mean, mathematicians are perplexed: what kind of mathematical instruction has this man received! I remember a journalist who after the dedication of a big computer reported in his newspaper that the new instrument calculated with two thirds of the speed of light; a biologist who was concluding a list of the speed of propagation of different animal species with the comparative data of the speed of propagation of sound and light; and the cultural philosopher Oswald Spengler, who made great boast of mathematical terms and who, for instance, sketched the progress of group theory to greater abstraction approximately as follows: initially only groups of permutations were known, later they were joined by groups of transformations, and the summit finally was groups of differential equations**. Recently I got into a collision with a kind of language philosopher, who juxtaposed Abelian and Galois groups†. Discussions are entirely useless in such cases. At the best it ends with the doubt: "But then the name would be wrong." The 250th commemoration of Leibniz' death was a great opportunity for solemn misrepresentation. Because Leibniz coined the word "Analysis situs" he was celebrated as the prophet of topology; it did not matter that by this term Leibniz meant an entirely different thing; he was still the prophet. Another philosopher celebrated him as the discoverer of the irrational; he had intermixed "irrational" and "infinitesimal", and if you would call his attention to this mistake, he would

---

* All these terms seem to derive from A. Comte's knowledge of Laplace's mechanics.
** In the first two cases" of" means "consisting of", in the third "belonging to". Hessenberg paraphrased it nicely: coffee, wind, and water mills.
† An analogous error. "A group is abelian" means: $ab = ba$ for all $a, b \in G$. "A group is Galois" means nothing. A Galois group is the Galois group of something, namely of one field relatively to a subfield, that is, a group of relative automorphisms.

prove that both were the same*. With such an attitude towards language people are indeed far from mathematics.

Among the humanities a discipline with a highly developed exact language is law – but its exactness is restricted to the vocabulary, while its syntax is as old-fashioned as it could possibly be. After the inaugural address of a mathematician in which the still unproved Riemann hypothesis ("vermoeden") was mentioned, one of our colleagues from the faculty of law asked me: "This is a contradiction, is it not, a hypothesis *is* a proof?" I gave him long-winded explications which did not help a jet; suddenly on the way home I understood what the background of this remark was. If, for instance, a father and a son have been the victims of a fatal accident in the mountains without witnesses being present and if it matters in the division of their estates who died first, then the law (of certain countries) prescribes the hypothesis ("vermoeden") that the older died first, and in a process such a "hypothesis" has the vigour of a "proof". For the lawyer the term "proof" has a well-defined meaning, viz. a series of arguments by which a judge can be convinced; the only thing my colleague can be blamed for is that he did not realize that in mathematics such a term could have a different, more objective meaning. Or rather, if anybody was to be blamed, it would be those responsible for his mathematics education, which means not so much his mathematics teachers, but the slaves of tradition who design programmes for such instruction and write textbooks for it.

If I proposed that mathematics could be a discipline of mind, in particular with regard to the command of language, I did not, of course, believe that by mathematics one could learn how to understand and to use certain words. Rather can mathematics teach one how to manage to establish the meaning of words, how to avoid circular definitions, and how to construct statements linguistically as to exclude misunderstandings. I restrict myself to a few examples to explain this. I earlier** mentioned the curious distinctions between the adjectives in "abelian groups" and "ordered groups", to which I can add the "Galois group" and "Weyl group". An abelian group is a group (viz. with the commutation property

---

* To be more precise, he wrote in Dutch; rather than "irrational" he said "onmeetbaar" (= incommensurable = irrational); since infinitesimals are "onmeetbaar klein" (immeasurably small), the confusion is not too farfetched in Dutch, and the proof of synonymy would not be too difficult.
** p. 26.

$ab=ba$), an ordered group is not a group, but a pair consisting of a group and an order (on a set), with certain compatibilities. A "Galois group", however, is a functor that assigns to certain pairs of fields a group, and a 'Weyl group" is one which assigns a finite group to a Lie group.

These are seemingly high-brow examples. There are more elementary ones. For instance: an equilateral triangle is a special triangle; but what about an isosceles triangle? It is certainly not a special triangle. For in theorems an isosceles triangle has an apex and a base, but if by chance such a triangle is equilateral, I would not know what its apex and its base are if they are not included in the definition. Thus an isosceles triangle is a pair consisting of a triangle and a vertex of that triangle such that the sides at this vertex are equal. To an equilateral triangle belong three isosceles ones, depending on which vertex has been distinguished. A right triangle is fortunately a triangle. But again congruent triangles are not special triangles though this happens for other reasons than with the isosceles ones; they are triangles of special subsets of the sets of triangles. A three-sided pyramid is a special pyramid, but it is not the same as a tetrahedron, because otherwise a regular three-sided pyramid would be a regular tetrahedron, which is not true. It is, however, true that a three-sided pyramid is the same as a pair consisting of a tetrahedron and one of its vertices.

I admit that conventional geometry is not as sophisticated; its language has been fixed by a two thousand year-old tradition which looks inviolable. If someone believes that good linguistic habits constitute a discipline of mind within mathematics itself, he is going to be disappointed; not even within mathematics does linguistic analysis as it has arisen in modern structures stain the language of another domain, that of geometry. Indeed, nothing is a discipline of mind if it is not taught as such. If linguistically conscious people saddle you with a group definition which does not hurt ears and eyes educated in modern ways of expression ("a group is a quadruple consisting of a set, a multiplication, a one, and an inversion, such that...") before you have noticed what is wrong with the old one, they will not evoke the need to apply such artifices in places where linguistic expression suffers from the same evils. And if rather than re-inventing it, you have echoed it like a parrot, any presupposition for self-reliant application will be absent. The heritage that the heirs of culture must acquire, includes language. The learner should be given the opportunity to acquire it, but he will not get it if the smoothened technical language of mathematics is forced on him as an unproblematic heritage. It is, however, possible and even probable, that the technical language of mathematics, if acquired in a self-reliant way and in a multi-related context, is a discipline of mind.

The above examples depended on a kind of concept-building that is today formalized by pair-forming, triple-forming, and so on. It may be useful also to mention quantifiers; making them explicit has been one of the great progresses of the mathematical language in the past decades. Strangely enough this instrument is almost completely disregarded in the professional analysis of language. A flourishing chapter in this literature are paradoxes in the vernacular which arise because people are not familiar with the technique of quantifiers; one does not notice that the difference between

$$\text{Always somebody was here,}$$

and

$$\text{Somebody was always here,}$$

is explained by the interchange of quantifiers:

$$\bigwedge_t \bigvee_x \; x \text{ was here at time } t,$$
$$\bigvee_x \bigwedge_t \; x \text{ was here at time } t.$$

This gap in understanding is a consequence of the procedures of instruction in mathematical logic. If quantifiers are to be illustrated by examples from everyday language, both teachers and textbooks are satisfied with phrases similar to "all men are mortal", and "there is an immortal man". It pays much more to illustrate successions of quantifiers by examples, but this is usually omitted or restricted to mathematical examples. Since in everyday language the quantifiers are often hidden in definite or indefinite articles, in words like "always", "everywhere", "sometimes", "here" and "there" it is not usually noticed that our vernaculars know quantifier sequences of considerable depth, as does mathematics. To grasp such structures more firmly, mathematics, in particular mathematical logic, could be a discipline of mind, supposing that it is taught as such.

Mathematicians discovered the almost self-evident fact that logic cannot do with the subject-predicate-structure, but badly needs relation-

and quantifier-structure, but professional analysis of language does not yet betray much influence of this knowledge. Compare definitions in explanatory dictionaries like the following:

brother: a male human being considered in this relation to another person having the same parents ...

In spite of the complications it is hardly correct since the position of the quantifier, hidden in "another" is not clear; it would be correct to say

brother of x: a male human being that has the same parents as x.

ratio: the quotient of one quantity divided by another ...

the correct version would be:

ratio of x and y: the quotient of x and y.

random number: a number whose likelihood of occurrence is equal for all numbers of the set of numbers to which it belongs. (Remark: defined in singular.)

The "Remark" belongs to the text; it is not an ironic addition of mine. It reminds me of the old theatre joke behind the curtain: "People are flocking into the house – look, there is another one who is flocking". Any kind of criticism would spoil this beautiful example. But allow me to quote the well-known Orwellian phrase

All animals are equal, but some are more equal than others*.

And Hessenberg's:

Mrs. Johnson, your twins are so similar, are they not, and in particular the one on the left.

Such sayings can become accepted language. In a students' election campaign I saw on a poster with a list of three candidates:

The independents that think as one.

It would be a statistical miracle if the like-minded were independent, but the term "independence" has here developed from a relation into a – meaningless – property.

The influence of mathematical language on the vernacular is almost non-existent – I need not repeat why.

* Orwell, *Animal Farm*.

SOLVING PROBLEMS

Mathematics is held in high esteem because it is a means of solving many problems; this faith into mathematics has more than one source. First, there is the charm of numbers. Secondly, there are reminiscences of arithmetic instruction, for instance on the subject of interest which allows one not only to calculate interest but, if need be, capital, rate of interest, or time. Is this not miraculous? If some data to solve a certain problem are lacking, people turn to the mathematician, firmly convinced that in spite of everything he can work it out. In such cases I tell the story of "How old is the captain?" (Of an oceansteamer you give the length, width, height, displacement, speed, year of construction and a few other data, and then you ask the question "How old is the captain?". If people cannot answer it, you say "thirty-four"; if they then ask "how do you know?", you reply "he told me".) It is not easy to shake this simple faith in mathematics; people suspect you of hiding secrets. They do not believe that you cannot calculate how to win at Monte Carlo; the explanation that no gambling system exists is not believed. In fact, if somebody displays a gambling system for the stock exchange, even mathematicians may feel in doubt – Gauss and John Maynard Keynes earned a lot of money this way, did they not? There were mathematicians, though, who lost their money on the stock exchange. That is the gap between theory and practice – or so the honest man will explain.

This faith in mathematics is today enhanced by a faith (or superstition) in computers; one day computers will take over – in fact, in America they are already replacing humans as programmers; and super-computers are learning to programme computers. A sociologist, with whom I participated in a public discussion, had read this in an American book. When I replied that even the super-computers had to be programmed somehow, he answered with a wink which meant "please cook up a more original joke", and the public laughed at me. When I advised the sociologist to take a fortnight's course in programming to learn what computers can do, this was felt to be an ill-natured remark by the man who had lost the game.

To this faith in mathematics is connected a disappointment with mathematicians who clearly do not know or will not betray what can be done with mathematics. In this context situations with which mathematics can cope are not recognized as such. People do not guess how far mathematics can help if the electricity bill looks too high or if the electricity meter is suspected to be faulty. Nobody appeals to mathematics to check whether an income tax tariff admits that you keep less if you earn more. The following occurrence surprised me very much.

At a party of intellectuals somebody demonstrated a card trick. 27 cards were laid out in three columns and nine rows, a bystander had to choose a card, keep it in mind, and tell in which column it was lying. The cards were picked up in columns, again laid out by rows and again the bystander had to tell the column of the card. Again the cards were picked up by columns and laid out in rows, and a third time the bystander had to tell the column. Now the performer played the cards one after the other face down upon the table and turned one over, which was indeed the original card chosen.

Most of the onlookers reacted as if the trick were witchcraft or prestidigitation. One of them, closely connected with mathematics, immediately explained the trick. When he said that the card was number 14, the others and the performer believed that he "knew" the trick*. They believed that the trick was an empirical fact and were unable to imagine that it could be completely analyzed and understood by mathematics.

Of course, the analysis of such a problem can hardly be called mathematics. Mathematics starts with generalizing the problem and understanding it more profoundly in the frame of information theory. I shall come back to the didactic uses of such problems*. Yet it is not our aim to deal with it from so high a vantage point. What matters here is something else. From a non-mathematician I would not demand that he should solve this trick without help. But it is disappointing if intellectuals who learned a bit of mathematics at school look upon this trick as if it were juggling or an empirical fact.

It proves that school mathematics did not prepare their minds to recognize which kind of problems are accessible to mathematical methods. This, of course, does not testify for mathematics as a discipline of the mind. But how could it do so if people never experience mathematics as an activity of solving problems, except according to fixed rules?

---

* Each time the cards were picked up so that the column with the chosen card was between the other two columns.

Even solving problems is only one aspect of mathematical activity, which should not be overestimated. I repeatedly pointed out that after solving a problem, the mathematician will turn it around and inside-out, reconsidering it from many viewpoints. How many symmetry axes does a regular n-gon in the plane possess? Anyone can see it by intuition, and anybody, even though he has never learned geometry can supply the answer. It is a fact that he will make the distinction between even and odd n. For odd n he notices one symmetry axis through every vertex, which meets the opposite side in its midpoint; for even n he finds two types, either through each pair of opposite vertices, or through the midpoints of each pair of opposite sides. But in both cases there are finally n symmetry axes.

That is where the non-mathematician stops. The mathematician, however, asks: Is there not a unitary way? Of course, he notices that the axis of a symmetry S passes through the center of the n-gon and is determined if the S-image of another point p, given in advance, is known. If p is taken to be one of the vertices of the n-gon, Sp is necessarily also a vertix. This leads to n symmetry axes.

The idea of unifying a proof with case distinctions is pronouncedly mathematical; a non-mathematician does not hit on it so easily. In fact this idea has not been exercised in mathematics since olden times, or in any case, not as intensively as at present. Gradually it has progressed, it has proved to be fertile and it has generally been accepted. It should be a discipline of mind. But to make it so, it should be taught as such, which means that rather than being confronted with meticulously trimmed proofs, the student has to invent rough proofs and to trim them himself. By such an activity he would be taking the first step beyond local problem-solving to self-reliant system-building in mathematics.

Mathematicians are prone to simplifying problems and solutions. Take the following example*: An early customer in a bookshop buys a book worth 10/–: he pays with a £1 note. The shopkeeper has no change, and goes to his neighbour, the shoemaker, who indeed can change it. At the same time the shoemaker gives him a pair of shoes which he has

---

* This example was formulated in British currency before it was decimalized. Each pound sterling was divided into twenty shillings.

repaired, keeps 16/- for the shoe repair minus 2/- which he owed the bookseller. As a consequence the bookseller only receives 6/-. He adds 4/- from his pocket and gives the customer 10/- and the book that he had bought. In the afternoon the shoemaker enters the bookshop with the bad news that the £1 note was false. How much does the bookseller owe the shoemaker, and how much did he lose?

Settlements of this kind, in particular between husband and wife, or among friends if one pays for all in a restaurant, are a hotbed of confusion. The safest way is to cut off all fringes, but in order to do so, it is indispensable to see through the problem and know what is fringe and what is body. It would be untrue to say that only mathematicians can do this, but it is a fact that strangers to mathematics are suspicious of simplifications, and fight them tooth and nail. I still remember from one meeting of mathematicians such a settlement after dinner, and the on-looking waiter who shook his head as if to say: I see, the gentlemen are mathematicians.

I could not tell where in mathematics one learns the ability that is expressed here. Another experience was still more perplexing: in a commission contract between a commercial firm and a salesman the commission was fixed at 5% for sales up to 400 Dutch florins and the square root of the amount for sales above 400 florins. There was no provision in the contract whether the square root could be taken on the basis of the single sales or of the monthly or yearly totals. Fortunately the salesman died before this affair was decided.

NUMBERS

If mathematics instruction is to achieve anything, we would expect it to be that people learn what numbers mean. The understanding of numbers that exceed the limits of direct comprehension leaves much to be desired. Three zeros more or less is a sophistication people do not care about. Whether there are milliards or billions* of people in the world is all the same to them; whether a country's budget consists of milliards or billions, whether the world is millions or milliards of years old is beyond comprehension. Newspapers told about a plane holding 20,000 tons of

---

* I take this in the European rather than the American sense; the difference itself is a source of much confusion.

fuel in its tanks, or about an ice-floe on the Rhine with an estimated weight of 100,000 kg extending from Bonn to Cologne. Even the heights of mountains and aeroplanes are readily transformed from metres into kilometres; millimetres of rainfall often become centimetres. "A light year is 300,000 times longer than a calendar year, whereas a light second is a 300,000th part of an ordinary second." The information that 40% of the Dutch national budget was marked down for "Research and Development" appeared in many publications and newspapers and was repeated in discussions inside and outside parliament, until a mathematician who did not believe it checked the figures and found that a clerical mistake had been made. It should have been 4%.

Percentages are a sore point. If, according to the newspapers a party won 5% since the last elections, it can mean, that the party increased its share of the popular vote from 15% to 20%. "10% of the participants were unmarried women" can mean that 10% of the female participants were unmarried. "The percentage of illiterates in Portugal is higher than in all other Western European countries together." When in 1969, France brought the gold price from 16 to 18 francs a gram, newspapers from San Francisco to Tokyo, from Rekjavik to Cape Town told their readers that France had devalued its currency by a rate of $12^1/_2\%$ (instead of $11^1/_9\%$). The analog happened the other way round a few months later with the German revaluation.

Conversions are another sore point. Rounded-off data in feet and miles are converted into metres and kilometres, with several decimal places. On the other hand in the news that the Mt. Everest was 50 metres lower than hitherto believed, the new improved height was given as a few hundred metres higher than the old one found on maps and in encyclopedias, since the newspaperman had made a rough conversion with a foot of one-third of a metre. For temperatures there are conversion tables to convert Fahrenheit degrees to Centigrade degrees, which if need be, can also used to convert longitudes and latitudes. Once I was happy prevent an even worse conversion when I was called by a newspaper office, who wanted to know the value of π in America.

After the high-flown examples of the possible uses of mathematics I feel the need to come back to more solid ground. For this reason I have ended this chapter with these trivialities.

CHAPTER V

THE SOCRATIC METHOD

Socrates (to the slave): Then tell me: is this our quadrupedal square? Do you understand?
Slave: Yes.
Socrates: We can add here an equal one?
Slave: Yes.
Socrates: And to both of them a third?
Slave: Yes.
Socrates: And finally to complete in the angle this one?
Slave: Sure.
Socrates: Then these would be four squares?
Slave: Yes.
Socrates: How many times is the whole now of the original?
Slave: Four times.
Socrates: Though it should be the double, do you not remember?
Slave: Certainly, I do.
Socrates: Does not a line of this kind, from corner to corner, divide the square in two equal parts?

Plato, *Meno*

Socrates (to Meno): What do you think about it, dear Meno. Has he uttered any opinion that was not his own?
Meno: No, his own only.

Plato, *Meno*

Plato's Meno is famous as paradigm of the Socratic method, an elaborated lesson where the master pre-thinks all thoughts, both false and correct, and the discipline shows by a "yes" or a "no", and perhaps by a "by Jove" or "God forbid" that he is receiving the lesson. It is a variant of the Socratic method to have the pupil say more essential, but of course well-prepared things. Arithmetic textbooks or teacher manuals of the past century contain elaborate examples of such lessons, for instance on proportion- and distribution-division. I suppose they were staged with parts assigned to two or more children. This version of the Socratic method must be well-prepared, whereas the original always works provided the teacher is well-trained and the student does not sleep.

Maybe the reader would not believe it but I am absolutely sincere.

The Socratic method is still one of the fundamentals of teaching, or rather it should be – a good many of our contemporaries are still pre-Socratic. If a lecturer lifts his voice to say "Dear audience, we will discuss tonight the question whether ..." he is announcing the Socratic method. Maybe they are empty words, maybe after the first few sentences he draws a manuscript out of his pocket to read what *he* had thought about it at home without the public. Yet the introduction may be serious but pronounced on the wrong place. It stems from the preparation at home, and there it was to the point. There, in his study, he said "Dear audience" and he looked at the audience that he had called up in his mind. He addressed them and they lent him their ears; he glanced at one of them who answered, somebody in the imaginary audience cut in on him and he discussed with the interruptor, people agreed with him and attacked him and he defended himself. All this he wrote down or memorized, even mistakes which he had corrected in time – he marked the place where they should arise, and he did not forget also to mark the right moment for a witty pun. Finally he gave his lecture, and when he said "I will discuss with you tonight the question whether ...", he made a slight mistake as though he would say "the wind is whizzing over the roofs" because it was stormy when he prepared his talk. Later when his listeners go home, they say that "he expressed my innermost thoughts" or "he refuted me point by point as though he knew what I would have said" or "now I know why I disagree'.

I like such lectures, such lessons. One person is speaking, but it is not just a one-man-band, the other party is heard too. When he has finished, everybody has decided on his own what is right. The lecturer (let us be grateful) was only our midwife – and this is what Socrates pretended to be. He has delivered us of our own thoughts rather than his.

That is the Socratic method, or dialectics, or as I would prefer to say, the method of the thought-experiment. The latter expression comes from Mach, who described it as a method of theoretical physics, the central method from Galileo to Einstein (and maybe still today). In didactics I mean by thought-experiment the attitude of a teacher or textbook author of imagining a student or a group of students and teaching them in his thoughts while reacting in advance to their probable reactions. The imaginary students are active, and their activity allows the teacher to determine his way. In the narrower sense I will suppose as Socrates did that the teaching matter is re-invented or re-discovered in the course of teaching. Rather than being dogmatically presented, the subject matter originates before the students' eyes. Though the students' own activity is a fiction in the Socratic method, the students should be left with the feeling that the teaching matter arose while teaching, that it was born during the lesson, and the teacher was in effect only a midwife.

The opposite of this method is what French call *parachuter*: like parachutes thoughts come out of the blue. Mathematicians easily yield to the temptation of the latter method. Mathematics is logically inter-related. From an ordained definition it follows a theorem which is not ordained but proved, though the fact that and the way it is proved is again ordained. That is the way to pass through a rigorous logical system which somebody has designed and then ordained. It is difficult to change the mind of the teacher who has invented the system; he loves the system that he has constructed with so much pain, and he likes to climb up and down its fabric. In fact, there is no weak point in it to attack him, since all he does is mathematically meticulous; it is logical, and the person who does not understand logic should better learn no mathematics. Such teachers can hardly understand that there are other viewpoints besides that of the logical system. Theoretical physicists often think like mathematicians. I learned electromagnetism from a professor who put the Maxwell equations on the blackboard to derive all electromagnetism from them. Physicists call such procedure axiomatics, and they defend it by the argument: "It would be boring to try to arrive at the Maxwell equations step by step, it goes much faster with axiomatics." They are probably right, it would be a bad thing if the professor becomes bored!

Urging that ideas are taught genetically does not mean that they should be presented in the order in which they arose, not even with all the deadlocks closed and all the detours cut out. What the blind invented and discovered, the sighted afterwards can tell how it should have been discovered if there had been teachers who had known what we know now. It is too bad that Clio was not a master of the Socratic method and that the teachers of mankind hardly ever saw more than a noselength further than their disciples. For a long time people believed nature was wicked. Nature deludes one to believe that objects at a distance become smaller, and that the river breaks the oar. Was the good Lord (of whom

Einstein said that he was sophisticated but not wicked) laughing up His sleeve, when Planck, by the sweat of his brow, hatched the quantum out of statistical formulae, while a few years later, with no trouble at all, Einstein was to extract it easily from the photo-effect?

Genetically – this means neither "according to Bourbaki" nor how Clio put the riddles of the Sphinx and their solutions on record. It is neither a logical nor a historical concept, and it is not psychological either. If a psychologist explains that Bourbaki's system is confirmed by developmental psychology, I am warned thereby not to trust him. Moreover, it does not matter how mathematics develops spontaneously in an individual. This is what psychologists look for. Yet as an educator I like to know how mathematics originates under the guidance of a good *teacher*, and since I would *teach* according to just this method, the obligatory circle is closed. It is not a vicious circle, however, since the stress is on ":originating" which is contrary to "imposing".

It did not truthfully report what Socrates claimed. Socrates did not believe that true knowledge is really invented. Inventing stories is the business of adventurers, poets, and sophists. From its pre-existence the soul possesses all true knowledge; the disciple has only to recall it, and it is the master's duty to help him. The teaching process consists in leading the student to remember what he has forgotten. To acquire knowledge is re-discovering not what others knew before me but rather what I myself knew when my soul stayed in the realm of the ideas. We need not devour Socrates to the last morsel and we need not share his belief in pre-existence. What then remains is learning by re-discovery, where now the "re" does not mean the learner's pre-history but the history of mankind. It may seem as though the learner is repeating the development of his ancestors in rediscovering what they knew. Therefore I would prefer to call it re-invention, but this is an unimportant point of terminology.

In the Socratic method "re-invention" was not understood literally; it is simulated rather than true re-invention. It could not be otherwise, could it? The teacher's authority was still dominant, and as far as it had been slightly shaken by the sophists, Socrates was just the man to consilidate it again. The initiative is only on the part of the teacher. Not only does he lead the student, he also shows him how rediscovery works, he rediscovers on behalf of the student. In the thought-experiment, he has already found out how to do so.

There exists another quite different method. Its philosophy is that instruction should be systematic, and that the system should be the result of a logical analysis of the subject matter or rather the inverse of this result. So if analysis shows that language consists of sentences, sentences consist of words, words of syllables, syllables of sounds, then reading one's own or another language was to be taught by starting with letters and sounds, which have to be joined together, to proceed by steps to syllables, words, sentences and eventually whole stories. If analysis shows the existence of ten classes of words, then grammar has to be taught according to these ten classes, starting with a chapter on the article (which can be omitted if the language has no article) and ending with a catalogue of interjections*. If the analysis of mathematics shows that mathematics has a deductive structure, then mathematics has to be implemented according to that structure, and more precisely, according to that special deductive system which the teacher or textbook author believes in.

This is what I called the antididactic inversion. The only didactically relevant element, the analysis of the subject matter, is dropped; the student is confronted with the result of the analysis and may watch the teacher who knows the result, putting the things analyzed together again.

This is the way we write our mathematical papers. We conceal the train of thought which led us to the result. We would not even know how to express this; if we did, it would be like exhibiting dirty linen in public. As mathematicians we are used to objectivate, which in itself is a good habit. The way we got a particular idea is nobody's business. It is true that we are writing a mathematical paper and not our "confessions". Some didactically-gifted authors, however, appreciate another kind of acknowledgement. They reveal how they would have invented the results if they would have been as clever before inventing them as they were afterwards. These authors exercise what I called the thought-experiment. They imagine a somewhat cleverer *Alter Ego* and have him invent the subject matter anew by a more convincing, more useful, and more intelligent method than the real *Ego* used. It is not the historical footprints of the inventor we should follow but an improved and better guided course of history.

This method is not very popular. Mathematical papers are written for

---

* Such textbooks were still published fifteen years ago; perhaps they even exist today.

experts who know the tricks, who are well trained to read in the completed paper how it could have been invented. Authors of school manuals who attire themselves in this style forget that they are not writing for mathematicians, and that the student has probably not the slightest inkling of what to do with the text. I quoted* earlier a mathematician who at the end of his university studies still believed that mathematical papers are invented in the way they are finally edited. He eventually though finished his studies with flying colours. Who cares about the poor people who are stranded at university or already even at school?

There is a continuous production of textbooks for schools, in particular, for what is called "New Mathematics". There are good ones and there are bad ones. The bad ones can be detected by their gross errors; it is easy to warn against them. And the good ones? There it is obvious that the author thought about each detail and that he left nothing to chance. But again he concealed all he did, not in a mathematical but in a didactical respect. He profoundly analyzed why he should arrange the subject matter as he did rather than by other criteria; why he choose one definition rather than another, why he put the theorem before the example rather than the other way round. Maybe he performed thought-experiments before writing the text, but if he did so, any trace whatsoever has faded away. It could be a help if some background information can be extracted from the author in a personal talk. It can then become clear that every step in the design had been maturely considered. But what difference does this make for the teacher, who does not know of these considerations?

It is the same with the numerous programmes of modern mathematics which have been produced and published in the last 15 years. They offer little new to teachers who know what set theory, modern algebra, linear algebra are; to those who do not know, they offer too little, both with respect to understanding of the subject matter and with elaborations, which are not adapted for teaching. As a matter of fact such programmes used to serve as a basis of discussion. But even in this respect they are not much to the point. It can be a point on the agenda how much set theory, modern algebra, linear algebra should be taught at school. Then all decisive arguments should be of didactic nature, but those programmes provide no opportunity for a didactical

* p. 56.

discussion, since all the didactical arguments which have led to the programme have been concealed by the author. Again the mathematician has outstripped the educator. As mentioned before, a mathematician is used to objectivate. Rather than giving his course of thought he edits an objective elaboration: definition, theorem, and proof. If he had to publish some of the ideas that led him to the result, he would feel as if he had been put out on the street in his underclothes. He remains faithful to this objectivating attitude in his didactic publications. He communicates the result while concealing the way he reached it. But what now comes out is not objective but dogmatic. An elaboration of a mathematical investigation, if fit to print, does not show how the author arrived at the result but it at least shows in the form of a mathematical proof how some objective mind could achieve it. In the programmes I just mentioned, any argumentation is lacking; everything that could instigate a discussion is dropped; their style is dogmatic.

A cross-examination can be helpful. It can appear that every step was well considered and can be didactically motivated. It can also appear – and this is what mostly happens – that didactical arguments played no role at all or that they were subordinated to the author's philosophy of the subject matter. Why did you arrange this that way? – the author of a geometrical axiomatics is asked, and he answers: Because in this way I can delay the introduction of orthogonality and up to that point restrict it to affine notions." The next question would be "Is orthogonality too difficult for 12 and 13 year-olds?" And he would continue by saying that his affine conscience forbids him to use right angles as long as he can do without. He did not reveal this reason to the pupil because then he would be betraying the fact that there are right angles, which he was trying to avoid. Does he believe that this affine conscience of his is transferred in some mysterious way from the designer of the method to the teacher and finally to the pupil? A thought-experiment would show whether this could possibly happen, or he could at least have searched in his own past for the origins of that conscience. If he had done so, he would have noticed how much knowledge of geometry is needed to feel such scruples, and he would have been able to estimate at which stage in geometrical instruction the method he proposed would work.

Why do you do it this way? Because it improves the systematics of the field. Because that way I can easily get a lemma which I can use later.

Because the student ought to have heard about ... Because congruence should be dealt with before similarity.

Why did you omit this? Because it follows later on as a special case from ... Because it cannot be dealt with rigorously with this class ... .

These are answers which all depart from the basic assumption that pupils are taught a ready-made mathematics, a mathematics which is pre-fabricated by the adult mathematician who knows how the parts fit together and what is the use of each of them but a meaningless pile of isolated bricks for the pupil who is not being introduced to this esoteric knowledge. So many secrets can be stowed away in such a system that even the expert mathematician can be perplexed. Why? Because the author is seeking full aesthetic enjoyment in mathematics, or because he is haunted by scruples of mathematical rigour and systematism. The rigour, then, is just the level which the author considers to be the true faith while the systematics is that which grants him the clearest understanding.

This kind of didactics is simply pre-Socratic. The concepts of rigour and systematics that prompted the author cannot affect the pupil because all presuppositions are lacking with him. Should the pupil, if he echoes the teacher, also simulate the scruples of the teacher (or rather of the textbook author)? He is not haunted, or is he?

I am far from believing that this kind of programme and this kind of textbook are characteristic of actual education. I got other answers, too, if I asked mathematicians (most of them school teachers) the question: "Why do you do this that way?" If I had not got other answers, I would never have written this book. All it contains on teaching practices I have learned from practical educators. They knew how to motivate didactically what they did. A few among them wrote textbooks, good textbooks, though I believe they did it rather like tightrope-walkers, and sometimes is led to complete disaster. The classical example is Prings-heim, a brilliant university teacher and the author of textbooks which read as pleasantly as an emetic.

It is good thing to place oneself in the situation of a man who is writing such a book. I am looking at it from the point of view of a university teacher but it would not be too different from the standpoint of the school teacher – it could perhaps be depicted in even more vivid colours:

I define a concept, I prove a theorem. The theorem suggests that the definition was not good so I change it and I reformulate the theorem. Is this not what you do in a course? But do you put this into a book? You would not even publish it if you believed that the student cannot understand the new definition if he has not yet grasped why the old one has failed, would you?

I explain the axioms of vector space, that is, over the field of real or complex numbers, because others are not available. Later, when the students become familiar with other fields, I must extend the concept. This is too bad. Why not invert the order? No, this would be didactical capitulation. If I consider vector space as the methodic point of departure, any other appraoch would be betrayal, it would be an anti-didactical solution. But who would define vector spaces on page 1 of a book to admit on page 100 that the definition was too narrow?

I produce an incomplete proof to ask "what is wrong?" Nobody dares to print it. He would not find a publisher.

Look how this reckless lecturer quite happily makes computations mod m on the blackboard by acting as if numbers are equal if their difference is a multiple of m. A few months later he reveals how this is made more precise with equivalence classes. Now let someone write a book this way. People would believe he was drunk when he wrote it, even those who would act in a classroom as he did. Even his own students tend to censure him. "Why did you first give such a provisional definition, without rigour?" "Why did not you then protest?" "Then I was just a stupid first-year student". "For me this is a reason to be glad that I did not tell you everything at that time. Take it easy, if once you say «now I know everything definitively», you are senile."

This is the curse of the art of printing. There is, though, besides Holy Scripture, a "Holy Print"*. What is printed has to be definitive. You cannot recant on p. 112 what you asserted on p. 12. Nor can you prove on p. 12 what must be generalized a little on p. 112 to be applied on p. 114, but prove the whole thing already on p. 12, hoping that the reader will not have forgotten it on p. 114. Otherwise a reviewer could remark: "The author did not notice that the proposition on p. 112 is a slight generalization of that on p. 12 which could have been proved there without much difficulty."

* See Chapter III.

In fact, this curse of the printing art has today been alleviated by less presuming polycopying methods. Nevertheless, the book has become the major enemy of the Socratic method. It need not be like this! Someone ought to write a book in the same way he teaches a course. Yet who dares to do so? At school level there have been a few attempts of this kind. Such books are often rejected as too chaotic. Yes, they will always be so if viewed by the systematician rather than by the educator.

I believe that many teachers teach according to more reasonable methods than those reflected by textbooks. But what do teachers do, if they are not as self-reliant as this, if they depend on their textbooks? Let us not deceive ourselves. They read aloud from the books. I have seen this. Fortunately textbooks contain problems too. One problem is shown by the teacher and the students do the others. Once the teacher is used to this, he does not even bother to read the intermediate text. The only thing, indeed, that is required in examinations is to solve problems.

What should replace the textbook? How can we study methods, how can one teacher learn from another how to teach? By publishing experiments? Yes, but then I mean lessons as they were *really* taught. Till now it has not often been done. By publishing thought-experiments? The most striking example in this field are Polya's books, where old Polya lets the boy Polya invent mathematics. You may object that very few children are Polyas. If this is left out of consideration, one ought to admit that Polya's books show and illustrate principles of methodical-didactical research, and for this reason they are superior to methodical-didactical literature with no principles.

RE-INVENTION

The best way to teach an activity is to show it.

Comenius, *Did. anal.* **42**

Once I observed Laplace one hour busy recovering a chain of reasoning he had hidden in his *Mécanique Céleste* under this mysterious symbol: It is easily seen.

Biot, *Mélanges scient. et litt.* **1**, Paris, 1858, 3

Joyfully he jumped out of the bathtub and naked he ran home, announcing aloud that he had found what he had searched for. Indeed while running he exclaimed: Eureka! Eureka!

Vitruvius on Archimedes in *De architectura*

COMENIUS

No doubt there were pedagogues between Socrates and Comenius, but whatever they have done, Comenius is the first who attracts our attention, who wrote more on pedagogics than anybody before him and who has hardly been outstripped in productivity by anyone since.

In Plato's dialogues the main conversant needs somebody to address himself to and to answer "yes" and "no". Quite a few among Comenius' contemporaries had not gone as far as even this. The pedagogue Ratke says in his 13th article*: "It becomes the disciple to listen ... during the lesson he shall not speak. For otherwise he prevents both master and disciples from finishing the lesson on time. If he need ask something, he shall note it down. After the lesson there is time enough."

Comenius rejects this, both for theoretical and for practical reasons. The teacher should rather stir up the students' activity by cross-questioning, to make sure if for no other reason that they did not go to sleep as we would say today.

It is Comenius' main principle that the pupil learns by taking in not only words but the whole sensual reality. To this end he created among

* Artickel, auf welchen fürnehmlich die Ratichiansche Lehrkunst beruht, Leipzig, 1617.

others his famous "Orbis pictus". Opening the sense-organs means a new activity for the pupil, new at least compared with the passive taking-in of words. Example, prescription, and imitation – these are the three stages of Comenius' teaching method. Is the student passive before the third stage? No, Comenius discovered that seeing, hearing, feeling, tasting and smelling can be activities, if they are as such consciously inserted into teaching. The "example" is followed by the "prescription"; the teacher draws the theoretical consequence from the experience. This is indispensable lest we would act as unreasonable beasts. Theory extracted from sensual experiences precedes practice. Practice is the imitation of the example by means of the prescription. It is the teacher's task to show and explain the example and to tell how to imitate it. It is the pupil's task to experience, to understand, and to imitate. If writing is taught, it is not enough to tell the pupil "do it this way". It should be shown to him, and this should be done in such a way that he can follow the moving hand with his eyes, and then imitation sets in. He should not be told how a clock is composed, but it should be shown to him: a clock should be taken to bits and put together again before his eyes, and it should be compared with other clocks. Comenius' "example" is not static, it is itself a process. The pupil learns not only to regard but to act, on the injunctions of the teacher who shows him the right actions ("right" in the moral sense, too). The principle of Comenius' didactics is:

The best way to teach an activity is to show it*.

It is useful to quote such a sentence and to consider how we would say it today. I myself think:

The best way to learn an activity is to perform it.

Perhaps it is not too much different from what Comenius aspired to, but the stress is shifted from teaching to learning, from the teacher's action to the pupil's, and from the sensory to the motor effects. To teach cycling, swimming, and driving there is not much use in example and theory. The pupil must perform the action, but this should be done under conditions which favour success. In teaching motor abilities this is the way to do it today; but let us refrain for the moment from discussing how far it has pervaded the teaching of mental abilities, or whether we still live in Comenius' or pre-Comenian times in this regard.

* *Did. anal.* **42.**

Between the example and the imitation, where the student is fully active, Comenius places the theory, where the student is passive. Could it have been otherwise? It is the teacher who knows the theory, who can communicate it to the pupil. The theory, that is: the names of the categories of words, the genus rules, the division of plants and animals, the knowledge how to add and to multiply, under which conditions the balance is in equilibrium, how to behave in the classroom, in the street, among people, and under God.

THINKING AND ACTING

Meanwhile everything has become more complex, the sensible world larger, the opportunities of imitation vaster, but, above all, the theory has grown so much and its character has changed so profoundly that Comenius' division of the teaching process is no longer suitable. Or rather we should say that what people call theory has become so much more relevant for so many, as an implicit background and as the explicit act.

Anyone learning to swim needs neither examples nor a theory of swimming, but a theory is operating or should be so in the mind of the person who is teaching him to swim; he should know the conditions under which someone thrown into the water makes the right swimming movements. A farmer today must theorize much more than a farmer of Comenius' time, an electrical engineer more than a blacksmith. Theory is not restricted to the study, it is acted out in the field and in the workshop where it is nothing else but extended action.

I need not tell in detail how padagogy developed after Comenius. The stress shifted more and more from the teacher's to the student's activity. The student is allowed ever increasing self-reliance – from another viewpoint I exhibited this development in Chapter III. But there is more to it than that. The alleged frontiers between sensual experience, theory and praxis faded away: before becoming conscious, sensual experience has been theoretically edited, thinking is only a mentally continued action. What becomes conscious in the sensual experience contains so much explanation that necessarily the teacher can no longer monopolize the explanation; likewise his monopoly of prescribing the actions expires if acting itself starts earlier in the midst of theory.

How odd a world having artificial frontiers between thinking and acting appears! A striking example of this is Euclid's Elements. It contains two kinds of mathematical exposition: theorems and construction problems. The theorems are proved, while the constructions are made. A theorem closes with "what had to be proved", a construction with "what had to be made". Commentators usually tell us that constructions, too, are proofs, viz. existence proofs – by this means they try to save the static character of geometry at any price. There can be little doubt, however, that the Euclidean constructions are stylized acting and therefore one of the most beautiful demonstrations of the conceptual unity of thinking and acting. The didacticians of older times could not stand this. If constructions were an activity, a practice, which could be left to pupils, it should be preceded by a theory, because practice without a theory does not become reasonable human beings. Therefore to prepare Euclidean constructions they invented analysis. With an analysis figure the construction is, in a more or less stylized way, discovered. The analysis of constructions became the Socratic part of mathematical instruction. It would have been quite natural to have the proof of a theorem, too, preceded by an analysis by means of which the proof was invented, would it not? No, only practice should be preceded by theory (that is by an analysis), therefore constructions should also, while proofs should not. This absurdity is a consequence of the separation of thinking and acting. Of course, everybody who tries to prove something new starts with an analysis, but after the draft stage it vanishes, and the definitive proof is the inversion of the analysis. In the case of constructions both the analysis and the construction belong to the definitive text, because otherwise the construction would be a practice without theory. Is it not strange?

From a sociological point of view, too, the relation between thinking and acting changed. It is not so long ago that labour was only called what required a certain minimum of physical effort. The workshop of the scientist and technician is therefore still called laboratory (though this is etymologically not too far from "labour"), that of the learned man is his study, and the merchant has his office. They do not go to a workshop, but to their institute, to their office. A distinction was made between brain and manual work. But where does one begin and the other end? From the construction worker trundling bricks in a wheelbarrow, to the crane-operator who presses a button to insert a concrete block, to the engineer who anticipated that at this moment this concrete block would be fixed into position, to the architect who designed the building, is a long chain with many links. Where does the planning end and where does the execution start?

It is not a metaphor to say that thinking and planning is acting. If the chemist analyzes or synthesizes a protein, where does acting begin? At the test-tube or on the paper? And where does it end? In the computer or if the analysis or synthesis is described, on paper? In the spring of 1938 a theoretical physicist described a thought-experiment to me in my garden: "Supposing we could pile up somewhere in the Sahara desert so many kilograms of Uranium U-235". It was a thought-experiment, because such a quantity of Uranium U-235 did not exist anywhere in the world at that time, but nevertheless he was careful enough to perform it in the desert because there was no doubt about what he described as the outcome of this experiment, as little as one could doubt about that a projectile launched with a speed of 8 km/sec would move around the earth. Seven years after our talk the thought-experiment had become a reality, though not in the Sahara but in the desert near Los Alamos, and a little later above Hiroshima. Where in this chain, I asked myself in August 1945, did thinking end and acting start? Where did the nuclear era begin? With the formula $E = mc^2$, or with the balance of the neutron production of U-235, or with the nuclear bomb, and who among us can say he has not been present at its birth?"

Some time in the late twenties together with a friend I had to solve a differential geometry problem for an anonymous principal; thirty years later I discovered that it had been the Wankel motor. This does not mean that somebody who works in algebraic geometry or topology can hope that what he finds out today will be applied in the very near future. But it would be as wrong to think that the world he lives in is much more abstract than that of butterflies is to the lepidopterologist, that of cyclic compounds is to the chemist, or that of archaic artifacts is to the archeologist. Adepts of the humanities claim a scientific method of their own, the *Einfühlung*. Their concern is, they say, humans and human expressions, which can be grasped by *Einfühlung* only. They cannot imagine that the objects studied by mathematicians and natural scientists are closely related to human nature, that they are conceptual systems created by humans like a fabric which covers the one nature including man. They consider the mathematician to be a computer, rigorous and without initiative, and in this age of automation they believe, like the earlier-mentioned sociologist that everything that is being done by mathematicians and theoretical scientists can also be done by computers as soon as they are programmed to do so. Their own work, that of humanities on the other hand requires human initiative and *Einfühlung* – they believe. Yet anybody engaged in creative mathematics knows that in any kind of problem related to mathematics, *Einfühlung* plays a more important part than logically rigorous procedures. John von Neumann once said: "A fortnight before proving a theorem, you should know that it holds; then it suffices to verify it, which is easier than proving." Yet outsiders have great difficulties in seeing mathematics and natural sciences as a human activity.

READY-MADE AND ACTED-OUT MATHEMATICS

It is true that words as mathematics, language, and art have a double meaning. In the case of art it is obvious. There is a finished art studied by the historian of art, and there is an art exercised by the artist. It seems to be less obvious that it is the same with language; in fact linguists stress it and call it a discovery of de Saussure's. Every mathematician knows at least unconsciously that besides ready-made mathematics there exists mathematics as an activity. But this fact is almost never stressed, and non-mathematicians are not at all aware of it.

Up-to-date mathematics has in general only been analyzed as a ready-made product, and if the analysis was followed by a formalized synthesis, the result was presented as ready-made mathematics. Look at a work like Russell and Whitehead's "Principia Mathematica." The only thing that reminds one of the fact that mathematics is an activity in time, is the arrangement of the theorems which implies that to prove Theorem 87 it is allowed to use Theorem 43 though not Theorem 141. That the system is dead as a door-nail is proved by the fact that all its sentences are propositions. There are no questions, no problems, and it lacks all linguistic means of formulating questions and problems. Linguistic analysts struggle past hope with paradoxes that arise from the static interpretation of linguistic expressions. A classical example is the following. Since Walter Scott is the author of "Quentin Durward", it is in any instance allowed to replace 'the author of "Quentin Durward"' by

'Walter Scott'; since $\frac{1001}{11} = 91$, it is allowed to replace $\frac{1001}{11}$ everywhere by 91. But what about statements like "It is a fact (I know, I have discovered, I ask whether, I have dreamt) that Walter Scott is the author of 'Quentin Durward'; that $\frac{1001}{11} = 91$"? Painful efforts are made to explain why the substitution here changes the meaning. In fact what is wrong here is the static interpretation of linguistic expression. Logistic analysts of language have grown up with this interpretation of language as a ready-made product and cannot get rid of it. It is an interpretation that may easily seduce mathematicians. Of course they know that mathematics is created, but once it has been created, it is ready, it is a clean copy. Of course, a genuine mathematician will never respect the other's ready-made mathematics as such. The only mathematician I can tell precisely of how he reads mathematical papers, am I myself. I never read mathematical papers from the first to the last word. I start with the results. I appreciate them being neatly exhibited. Then I think about them. If I cannot confirm them, I look through the paper for some indication how they can be proved. Maybe I then succeed in confirming the results. Otherwise I look for lemmas I understand and try to derive the main theorems from them. Maybe I have to take a closer look at some proof; if an earlier result is referred to, I go back to it. If finally by my own means and a bit of cribbing I have confirmed the results, that is, if I master all the connections, I am likely to read the papers through once again systematically. Others have told me that they also read papers written by others in approximately the same way. There are people who can read papers systematically, page by page, line by line, letter by letter. To do so testifies to a strong discipline of mind which is not everybody's attribute. I think it is the rule that in trying to understand papers written by others, people behave as if they are making original investigations. They try to re-invent the contents of the paper; this is a bit easier than brand-new inventions because you can crib as much as you want.

Is it hypocrisy to offer on one hand the world our mathematics as a ready-made product, and on the other to transform the ready-made mathematics we are offered into acted-out mathematics? We know, indeed, that nobody can understand the ready-made product, or do we not? In fact, it is not as simple as that. We present the ready-made mathematics with shades of acting-out. Instead of "there is a δ" we say "I find a δ", instead "from p follows q" we prefer "from p I conclude q". We say

"I make the substitution ..." and "we will show that ...". Even if these are superficial phrases, they show that we cannot maintain the fiction of ready-made mathematics. We should not forget either that there have always been gifted mathematicians who wrote in a style that gave their readers the illusion of a mathematics created under their very eyes. Their work is so good that it can be read from the first to the last letter. Such reactions were evoked by C. Neumann's *Abelsche Funktionen* at the end of the century. From my own studies I think of Heffter and Koehler's *Analytische Geometrie* as such a pedagogically excellent work. Van der Waerden's *Moderne Algebra* also belongs in this class, and most of H. Hopf's work. I do not know modern textbooks in higher mathematics well enough from the viewpoint of the learner to tell whether this kind of literature still exists to day.

I earlier showed how in a few centuries the centre of gravity has shifted from ready-made to active science, from the scholar to the investigator. This process also led to the shaping and the secession of what was accepted as school science, in particular school mathematics. It differed so much from true mathematics that as early as the beginning of our century a double break in mathematical education was noticed, involving discontinuities in the training of the mathematics teacher, who first on passing from school to university had to forget school mathematics, while a few years later when he returned to school as a teacher he had to forget university mathematics and tie the threads he had broken a few years before. This double break was noticed but was not repaired when it could have been effected with little effort. Fundamentally the antagonism was one between an active science under the competitive responsibility of its adepts (though beyond the range of a *misera plebs*) and a ready-made science, a collection of algorithms *in usu Delphini*, a weak concoction of the first, a fairy tale for schoolchildren. Of course to be taught science should be adapted to the level of pupils, but what happened here was that the fairy tale version of mathematics developed independently from true mathematics. After a century of autonomy school mathematics had reached an impasse that led nowhere, neither to higher mathematics nor to life. With regard to school mathematics in my own country I can truthfully assert that this applied to two-thirds of the subject matter and to all of the method.

This development was a consequence of the collision of two badly compatible efforts. The first, with respect to subject matter, was to teach mathematics, and since it ought to be mathematics, to teach a deductive system, a ready-made science. The second with respect to pedagogics, was to stimulate active learning. Since the proper mathematics was taught as a ready-made product, the only opportunity left for students' activity was in so-called applications, that is, problems. It could not involve true mathematics as this opportunity had been cut off when mathematics was introduced as a ready-made science. What remained for problems was a mock mathematics, which has been nursed with much dedication for a century. The lowest level of this mock mathematics was substituting special values for the parameters in the general statements or thinking patterns of the theory. This was called applications. Thus the pupil left school with a perverse image of mathematics which had been built up in his mind for many years.

There would not be much need to once more trace this wrong track of history, if we were not threatened by the danger of history repeating itself. This fear is not unfounded; history already has repeated itself. Much faster than the old mathematics, the new one, once it had been introduced at school, developed into an autonomous school mathematics, with a long appendage of problems which compete successfully in absurdity with the traditional problems. The cause is the same – the only thing the pupil can do with the ready-made mathematics which he is offered is to reproduce it. Therefore to activate him, this stuff must be complemented by so-called applications which either grow out above the theory to allow one to dispense with it, or consist of simple substitutions of parameters of the general theory. I will come back to this point again later.

The activity of the pupil is desirable not only for pedagogical reasons but also with regard to school organization. It is a major problem of organization in all kinds of education how the teacher tests the progress of his pupils. The pupil can be taught to parrot the ready-made mathematics he learned, but of course, this is unsatisfactory. So the problems develop into exercise and test material and finally become the goal of instruction. A century of exam problems testifies against the dreary mock mathematics that has been taught for so long – a worthless rather than valid mathematics.

The increasing importance of mathematics has increased the urgency of the didactic problem. If mathematics is to be applied, applying mathematics should be taught and learned. Applying is often interpreted, as mentioned above, as substituting numerical values for parameters in general theorems and theories. This is a misleading terminology. Mathematics is applied by creating it anew each time – I will expound this in more detail too. This activity can never be exercised by learning mathematics as a ready-made product. Drilling algorithms may be indispensable, but inventing problems to drill algorithms does not create opportunities to teach applying mathematics. This so-called applied mathematics lacks the flexibility of good mathematics. The most serious flaw in old school mathematics was its uselessness. Let us make the new mathematics become more useful.

The opposite of ready-made mathematics is mathematics *in statu nascendi*. This is what Socrates taught. Today we urge that it be a real birth rather than a stylized one; the pupil himself should re-invent mathematics. It is the generally acknowledged right of the adult mathematician as far as he is a learner, to learn by re-inventing. Can we not treat both mathematician and pupil alike? Alas there are mathematicians who would deny it to him. *Quod licet Jovi, non licet bovi.* I, Jupiter, organized the world mathematically for the student, why should he, the ox, start anew? There are not many left who hold this view. But to grant the student the right of re-invention, yet in practice abstain from everything that can make this right effective is perhaps even worse. This is easily said, and I do not say it to cast a blame on teachers. I am fully conscious of the major problems that have to be solved here.

Today, I believe, most people would agree that no teaching matter should be imposed upon the student as a ready-made product. Most presentday educators look on teaching as initiation into certain activities. Science at its summit has always been creative invention, and today it is even so at levels lower than that of the masters. The learning process has to include phases of directed invention, that is, of invention not in the objective but in the subjective sense, seen from the perspective of the student. It is believed that knowledge and ability acquired by re-invention are better understood and more easily preserved than if acquired in a less active way. I do not know whether this thesis has been formally tested but there are many indications which make it probable. I earlier*

* p. 103.

explained that the static interpretations of, say, language and mathematics lead to an analysis of the teaching matter as a ready-made product; the analyzed matter is then presented to the pupil to be synthesized in the teaching process. I noticed that as a consequence, the native or foreign language is taught as a synthesis of sounds or of the word categories, of main and subordinate clauses, and mathematics is taught according to a pre-established deductive system. This fits excellently into the static interpretation of language and mathematics, though the Socratic method at least shows how to have the student participating in the basic analysis in order to let him know what should finally be built from the bricks. Such teaching as characterized above, however, is far away from any interpretation of language and mathematics as an activity.

THE ANALYSIS OF AN ACTIVITY

This interpretation first of all requires that the teaching matter is analyzed as an activity. Language teaching has today progressed farther in this direction than mathematics teaching – I have still to explain* in which respect language teaching can be easier than mathematics teaching. Little has been done to analyze mathematics as an activity. Maybe this is caused by the competition and the high quality of the analysis of ready-made mathematics, which is classical and acknowledged by systems like *Principia Mathematica* and Bourbaki and many textbooks. I mentioned Polya's books as one example of the very few contributions to the analysis of acted-out mathematics. Anyone who really looks around will find more of them, because every good teacher will at least once or even quite a number of times have tried such an analysis by means of thought-experiments. A beautiful older example is T. Ehrenfest-Afanasjewa's *Übungensammlung zu einer geometrischen Propädeuse***; in its background the analysis of active geometry is clearly distinguished though, in fact, it is misleadingly presented as an epistemological analysis. Among Dutch teachers the late Mrs. Ehrenfest strongly influenced the van Hieles; in the background of their textbooks the analysis of acted-out mathematics has been operative and in their theses it is explicitly exercised. In fact, they have analyzed two kinds of mathematics, both of the teach-

* Chapter IX.
** Den Haag 1931.

ing and of the learning process – I will come back to this complication.*

I stated that little has been done to more systematically analyze mathematics as an activity, in particular as the activity of a learner. Does not the work of Piaget and his School represent such an analysis? Here I would say, no. There is no real interpretation of mathematics to which Piaget's research can be related. Though the subjects of his experiments are set mathematical tasks, he almost never tests whether they understood the language in which the task was formulated. It is rather the *linguistic* than the mathematical content of the task which is object of the investigation. In other cases, rather than testing the reaction of the child to a mathematical problem, the leader of the experiment tests how the child manages to disentangle irrelevant complications of the problem, or whether you can cheat the child by misleading suggestions. A still sadder sight is the attempt by the experiment leader to induce the experiment subject, who might hesitate between a right and a wrong answer, to choose the wrong one. Even worse are the manifest blunders of the experiment leader who marks correct answers as wrong. Yet if quite aside from these gross errors, there are more profound reasons why the sole construction of Piaget's experiments does not promise to reveal essential features of learning mathematics. This will be dealt with later.**

RE-INVENTION AND DISCOVERY

I termed the teaching method that is built on interpreting and analyzing mathematics as an activity the method of re-invention. It dawned upon me when I was studying the work of T. Ehrenfest and her disciples, both in their classrooms and in discussions with them. The same ideas developed in many places, independently of one another, both earlier and later. Today the method of re-invention seems to be generally accepted in principle. It can easily be understood why not much has been realized in practice. In education it is a long, hesitating course from ideal to reality, from demand to fulfilment, and there are good reasons why this is so.

What I have called re-invention, is often known as discovery or re-discovery. I have also used these terms a few times, and it would not really matter which are used, were it not for the fact that the word

* p. 121.
** See Appendix.

"discovery" is often pronounced with undertones of the unexpected, the sensational, the surprising, or the striking. Yielding to these suggestions means a radical restriction of the re-invention method. Series of experiments indeed exist which clearly show this application of re-invention to what is considered as striking. A few justify the method of re-invention by the force of motivation they ascribe to it – again a restriction of this method according to criteria that are irrelevant.

What troubles me most is that quite a few start from a much too narrow, because too superficial, interpretation of re-invention. I feel that the van Hieles' interpretation of re-invention is more deeply rooted. To explain this statement I must expound what they meant by the levels of the learning process. Readers who are accustomed to a certain meaning of the term "level" in learning processes, are asked to forgive me for using it in another sense, a sense which I have preferred for many years. I must also apologize for the lengthy digression which follows.

THE LEVELS OF THE LEARNING PROCESS

When the van Hieles started teaching they were just as unprepared as many other young teachers; nobody had told them how to do it. Of course they had passively undergone teaching, maybe even observed their teachers' performing, but this was not enough. As time went on, they got the opportunity of discussing their teaching with each other and with others. They subjected their own actions to reflection. They observed themselves when teaching, recalled what they had done, and analyzed it. Thinking is continued acting, indeed, but there are relative levels. At the higher level the acting of the lower becomes an object of analysis. This is what the van Hieles recognized as a remarkable feature of a learning process, namely of that in which they learned teaching. They transferred this feature to the learning process that was the goal of their teaching, to the learning processes of pupils who were learning mathematics. There they discovered similar levels. To me this seems an important discovery.

What these levels are, I can only locally explain here with a few examples. Let us consider complete induction, a principle that can be looked on by somebody as important enough to be re-invented up to definitive formulation by pupils. It is obvious that inventing complete induction presupposes the acquaintance with nontrivial, or at least non-trivially-looking examples of complete induction. In history the binomial coefficients and the binomial theorem were such examples, and in a similar stock of previous knowledge they are perhaps still the best examples though a few others are not much worse. Textbooks usually present the binomial theorem as a consequence of the principle of complete induction. In the course of mathematical invention this would be a vicious circle. A principle like complete induction cannot be formulated unless it has been experienced, and the binomial theorem is the decisive experience that leads to this principle. It is a similar didactic circle if a formal theory of natural numbers as Peano's axiom system is presented so as to derive complete induction from it. It may be taken for granted that nobody can invent Peano's axioms unless he can formulate the complete induction. To formulate complete induction, it is indispensable to know what complete induction is, and to be known it should have been exercised, for instance with the binomial theorem. The deductive course is to derive from Peano's axioms the principle of complete induction as a theorem, and to apply it afterwards on various examples. This is a striking example of the antididactic inversion. Indeed, the analysis of the learning process shows that the didactic course is precisely the opposite. First, there must be examples which compel the student to invent complete induction; in these examples he recognizes the common principle; he then applies it to more complicated cases. If he has grasped the principle, the teacher tries to have him formulate it; in this he probably needs considerable help; and finally he could be set on the track of Peano's axioms, provided he has had earlier experience in axiomatizing. Almost all modern textbook authors seem to believe that a formal theory of natural numbers can be based on cardinality, which is mathematically and didactically wrong, as we shall explain later*. On the contrary, every more or less formal theory of natural numbers presupposes acquaintance with the principle of complete induction. This sets a lower limit for such a theory. It certainly belongs to an advanced stage of school instruction; other considerations may even raise this limit.

Here the levels of the learning process stand out in bold relief. On the lowest of the levels under consideration complete induction is acted out. On the next level it is made conscious as an organizing principle and can

* Chapter XI.

become a subject matter of reflection. On the same or on a higher level it is put into a linguistic pattern. From here to the Peano axiom system the path is not any longer locally determined. Now the data is not a bunch of mathematical derivations in which a common principle (like the complete induction) is hidden; it is rather the organization of an entire field, in which linguistic formulations (as that of the complete induction) among other mathematical activities become the subject matter of reflection; the complete induction then undergoes a re-interpretation; rather than describing a mathematical principle it is now interpreted as postulating a property which, with others, should characterize the natural numbers.

History moved according to these levels. The complete induction was exercised since antiquity; the "side-and-diagonal-numbers" are a profound application of this principle. The first man who grasped the principle consciously and formulated it was Pascal. The formulation, a noteworthy feat, required quite new linguistic means. This explains why Pascal's successors just arrived at the cognition though not at the linguistic formulation of the principle. Much later, in the course of axiomatization, Dedekind and Peano managed to reinterpret the principle as a definition. I recall that the group concept has had a similar history: in the first half of the 19th century instinctive operations with groups, in some cases up to a high degree of consciousness of principles, then the explicit formulation of the relevant group properties, and finally the axiomatic abstraction.

Mathematical activity is, as we will see later, an activity of organizing fields of experience – this alone does not characterize mathematics, since its fields of experiences and means of organization are quite specific. How levels stratify this activity has been shown by an example: the means of organization of the lower level become a subject matter on the higher level. Which phases the learning process passes from one to the next level is a pedagogical question, which should be answered in specific cases by pedagogical experience. The relation, however, between one level and the next is overwhelmingly logical and accessible to logical analysis. Often the level-raising tools are heavy quantifiers, as in the case of complete induction, that over all properties of natural numbers – this is a point we will come back to later*.

* Chapter XIX.

Operations with integers such that multiples of a certain m are neglected may be unproblematic activities on a certain level. On the next level they can become a subject of scrutinizing, and their rules can be formulated. Likewise fractions can be intuitively operated on on a certain level, and on the next they can be formalized by subjecting simplifying of fractions and operating with them to certain rules. Formulating such rules for both integers mod m and for fractions can be subjected to a discussion on a still higher level and further formalized within the frame of the extensional abstraction. The example of fractions shows that none of these levels can be dispensed with, though it is a habit in this field to pass over the first level, or at least to pass to the next too early. Even if the pupil masters the operations on a lower level, it is no use pressing him to pass to the next as long as the need, which is the motor of re-invention, is not felt. A closer investigation will later show, in the case of fractions*, where the need for algorithmic rather than intuitive fractions comes from.

The example of level structure the van Hieles started with was geometry instruction. Geometry will be dealt with later as a separate subject but meanwhile we can try to outline the levels in geometry. Geometry starts with mathematically organizing the phenomena in space, by which activity *gestalts* become geometrical figures. At least, geometry should start this way. On the contrary almost all courses starts with a mathematically organized matter. The student is deprived of the finest opportunity that exists in mathematics to learn to mathematize a non-mathematical subject matter; an important connection between pure and applied mathematics is bluntly obstructed. If, then, the student has grasped the geometrical figures as context of geometry, he could start organizing their variety. Once he has been shown a number of parallelograms, he will be able to grasp what a parallelogram is. This is no more mysterious an abstraction than that which leads him to call some objects chairs. But the usual procedure is that the teacher now gives a formal definition of a parallelogram. Again a level is passed by, and the student is deprived of the opportunity to invent that definition. It is even worse. It is utterly improbable that at this stage the student understands the meaning and the aim of a formal definition or even would be able to understand it. (I know of textbooks which at this point even explain what a definition is, which means that yet another level is passed over.)

* p. 278.

How would a student proceed if he is allowed to re-invent geometry? If he is given a number of parallelograms, he would discover a great many common properties, parallelism of opposite sides, equality of opposite angles, supplementarity of adjacent angles, mutual bisecting of diagonals, congruency of certain triangles into which the figure is divided by diagonals, the possibility of paving the plane with congruent parallelograms, and so on. This is a host of properties, each just as important as the other. The student discovers connections between these properties; paving the plane is the most efficient way leading to these discoveries. Logical organization starts. The connections are registered by a pedigree with implication arrows, in which he finally discovers one property among them from which all others can be derived. Maybe different students choose different fundamental properties. By the fact of these choices the student has grasped the meaning of the formal definition, its relativity, and the concept of equivalence of definitions. He has learned the act of defining rather than having some definition imposed upon him.

Of course to the authentic mathematician such instruction is quite loathsome. Indeed, the student has presumed to prove, when he did not even know what a definition was! Is the correct order not – definition, supposition, statement, proof? The authentic mathematician simply forgets that if this is a shocking mistake, then he himself becomes guilty of the same kind of mistake as soon as he begins to investigate a new domain as a research subject. But then his modest answer would be: *Quod licet Jovi, non licet bovi.*

The learning process is structured by levels. The activity of the lower level, that is the organizing activity by the means of this level, becomes an object of analysis on the higher level; the operational matter of the lower level becomes a subject matter on the next level. The pupil learns organizing by mathematical means, he learns to mathematize his spontaneous activities. Or rather, it would be desirable that he should be taught this way. How to proceed to skip levels in the learning process has has also been described by the van Hieles. "To a certain extent it is possible to disregard these levels. It is possible to teach a skilful pupil abilities above his actual level, like one can train young children in the arithmetic of fractions without telling them what fractions mean, or older children in differentiating and integrating though they do not know what differential quotients and integrals are. If a pupil is to be taught proficiencies above his actual level, one has to describe the actions he has to perform by means of plain rules (algorithms) which can be managed without any reference to the sense of the actions. It is true that a pupil, who has acquired the above-mentioned faculties in this algorithmic way, will not be able to apply them, but this can be prevented by teaching a good deal of application patterns, too. There is the danger that patterns are confounded or spoiled in another way, but this can be prevented again by an able mnemonics. In many cases this will be sufficient, especially if there is no necessity whatsoever to retain the acquired knowledge longer than a fixed date, e.g. of a test or an examination. But even in these cases it is not certain whether reduction of the subject matter to a lower level is not a clumsier didactic method than it would be to raise the pupil to the higher level. It can even happen that a learning process will be hampered and definitely stopped because the pupil is not given the opportunity to advance to a higher level." *

I knew a teacher – this may illustrate the last remark – who taught his students two forms of the Pythagorean theorem to solve geometric problems, $a^2 = b^2 + c^2$ and $a^2 = b^2 - c^2$, with mnemonic rules to know which one had to be used in a specific case; to this end he had classified all known problems in which the Pythagorean theorem was used according to types, to arrive at a list like those for the determination of plants; he taught no proof of the theorem.

The van Hieles noticed the discontinuity of the learning process. "The discontinuities are as it were jumps in the learning curve. These jumps reveal the presence of levels. The learning process has stopped. Later on it will start itself as it were. In the meantime the pupil seems to have "matured". The teacher does not succeed in explaining the teaching subject. He (and also the other pupils who have reached the new level) seem to speak a language which cannot be understood by the pupils who have not yet reached the new level. They might accept the explanations of the teacher, but the subject taught will not sink into their minds. The pupil himself feels helpless, perhaps he can imitate certain actions, but he has no view of his own activity until he has reached the new level. The learning process will get a more continuous character then. Valencies (routines) will be formed and an algorithmic skill will be ac-

* *Report on Methods of Initiation into Geometry,* (ed. by H. Freudenthal), J. B. Wolters, Groningen, 1958, p. 76.

quired, as the presuppositions to a new jump which may lead towards a still higher level.*

THE BOTTOM LEVEL

I had to deal with the levels of the learning process in general to explain why I consider the part attributed nowadays to "discovery" in mathematical education as entirely unsatisfactory. In general the laboratory experiment on which didactical opinions are usually based can survey learning processes by statistic means, rather than individually via classroom experiences: discontinuities in the learning process that strike the observing teachers are very likely to be ignored in the laboratory. The laboratory experiment moves on a fixed level; in spite of all petty *Aha-Erlebnisse* the only feature that can be noticed is a continuous development of algorithmic techniques the progress of which can be traced back to an aimful and trustworthy application of the discovery method. A well-known example is Z. Dienes' experiments where the subjects, 6–12 year-olds, handle quadratic equations, finite groups, isomorphism, modules as though this were mere child's play. Seen as a demonstration, this is impressive, and it is rightly so. What really impresses is the performance of both the experiment leader and the children, which clearly conceal much greater abilities than traditional instruction can extort from them.

I already indicated the natural limits of this method. Everything develops on a fixed level of the learning process which in the present case is the bottom level. I do not claim that this level could be disregarded. On the contrary, I stressed that passing it over is one of the mistakes of traditional mathematical instruction. It is the investigation of this level that has recently been taken up by a few people (among them Dienes). But to make it entirely clear, it should also be stressed that this is the bottom, the pre-mathematic level. If this is not explicitly stated, I am afraid that the whole activity will be judged to be unmathematical and, consequently, rejected as being irrelevant. In fact, the activity is not unmathematical, but pre-mathematical, and therefore relevant to a high degree.

What children perform in this kind of experiment is not mathematics.

* *Ibid.*, p. 75–76.

It is true that the onlooker can interpret it as mathematics; because of his training in adult mathematics he knows what the children's actions mean in the mind of the experiment leader. But the child does not know it. The child is playing a game. He is playing this game with mathematical concepts excellently and purposefully as it manipulates the concepts (where by manipulating I mean literally operating them with one's hands). The game is enormously important – in a similar way the children in the van Hieles' classrooms played geometry – but it is the bottom level, which means indispensable and transitory.

On the next level the child would reflect on what he did on the bottom level; the organizational means of the bottom level would be objects of analysis; mathematics would begin; to say it in a trifling fashion, it would no longer be a joking matter. On the bottom level, the child operates the concepts by manipulation but he does not know what he is doing. We know this from our higher level. On the next level the child, too, will know what he has done before and what another child is doing on the bottom level. To call what a child is performing at this level set theory, group theory, or linear algebra, is the same as to claim that a child who is singing is learning music theory, that a child who is tinkering is doing mechanics, that a child who is looking at the sky is doing astronomy, and that a child who is speaking is doing linguistics. Of course mathematics is different. People can perform superbly in singing with no idea of musical theory, they can acquire astonishing skills in crafts and physical experimentation without learning mechanics, know the sky without any grasp of the simplest facts of astronomy, and speak a language fluently and never reflect on language. Mathematics means that students are driven on to ever higher levels, if not along the whole front, then at least in certain sectors. It is a pity that many of them have never moved on the bottom level. It is of great importance that this level is now investigated. It is just as important to realize honestly that this is not the last word. Otherwise people would believe it is irrelevant, and that the method of discovery works only on the bottom level and is not adapted to raise the level and to progress on the higher level.

Erroneous conceptions have already taken root. This is proved by J. Brunner's much-quoted sentence: *

* J. Brunner, *The Process of Education*, Harvard University Press 1960, p. 33.

We begin with the hypothesis that every subject can be taught effectively and in some intellectually honest form to any child at any stage of development.

Clearly this has been suggested by a similar remark of B. Inhelder at the same place, with a important qualification that had not been included by Brunner:

... provided they are divorced from their mathematical expression and studied through material that the child can handle himself.

Indeed, children can be taught an astonishing amount of mathematical matter as soon as all mathematics has been eliminated from the matter. It is possible to have the child acting as an automatic computer in a way which from the viewpoint of the adult admits of the interpretation of performing mathematics. It is possible but if people try this experiment, they should be asked: for what purpose are they doing this?

From the preceding the answer is obvious: because it is bottom level, the precursor of mathematics. But the mathematics that these precursory exercises are to prepare should follow them closely or, in any case, such that the intensive stream of preparations does not ooze away. The child should not be directed to train its mathematical abilities on the bottom level, unless it is, in principle, able to progress to the next level, which means able to reflect on its bottom level mathematical activities. I cannot tell at which age this would be possible, it obviously depends on the individual. At the age of 6 or 7 we can have a child computing but we can also ask him how he solves simple computation problems. It is always striking that at the age of 8 or 9 children can solve a somewhat involved word problem while the question "how do you know" is answered by "I just felt it"; when a little older they cannot solve such problems any more without help. Several times I tried the problem:

Anne is double the age Mary was when Anne was as old as Mary is now. Anne is 24 years old. How old is Mary?

Adults posit Mary's age x, and so on. Children, who usually calculate more visually than adults, seem to have the course of time before their eyes; they somehow "see" how old Mary is. Their capabilities of expression, however, are still unequal to the task of explaining what they did.

Anyone who has observed children doing arithmetic, has experienced this phenomenon: the shrug of the shoulders if the onlooker asks "How did you do it?". If mathematics should be taught as re-invention, this reaction sets a lower bound to the maturity. As long as the child is not able to reflect on its own activity, the higher level remains inaccessible. The higher level operation can then, of course, be taught as algorithm though with little lasting consequences. This has been proved by the failure of teaching fractions. (I admit it is an aggravating circumstance that teachers and textbook writers have no sound ideas how to progress from intuitive to algorithmic fractions, and finally to the rules for fractions.)

To summarize, the activity stimulated by re-invention on the bottom level is a necessity. It is meaningful as long as it takes place under conditions where it is preparatory rather than an unessential game. Re-invention that is a didactic principle on research level, should be the principle of all mathematical education not only on the bottom level where it is too near to manual playing to show pronounced mathematical features.

CHAPTER VII

ORGANIZATION OF A FIELD
BY MATHEMATIZING

In the history of forestry science one knew the period of the mathematicians, yet today foresters are glad to know that this era of aberration has gone... These people would calculate the most incredible things, and the problems of forestry they could not force into the mathematical jacket were simply omitted as "not fit for scientific treatment".

P. von Lossow, Zeitschrift d. Ver. d. Ing. 43 (1899), 360

He says "mathematical training is almost purely deductive. The mathematician starts with a few simple propositions, the proof of which is so obvious that they are called self-evident, and the rest of his work consists of subtle deductions from them. The teaching of languages, at any rate as ordinarily practised, is of the the same general nature – authority and tradition furnish the data, and the mental operations are deductive." It would seem from the above somewhat singularly juxtaposed paragraphs that, according to Prof. Huxley, the business of the mathematical student is from a limited number of propositions (bottled up and labelled ready for future use) to deduce any required result by a process of the same general nature as a student of language employs in declining and conjugating his nouns and verbs – that to make out a mathematical proposition and to construe or parse a sentence are equivalent or identical mental operations. Such an opinion scarcely seems to need serious refutation. The passage is taken from an article in *Macmillan's Magazine* for June last, entitled "Scientific Education – Notes of an After-dinner Speech", and I cannot but think would have been couched in more guarded terms by my distinguished friend had his speech been made *before* dinner instead of *after*.

The notion that mathematical truth rests on the narrow basis of a limited number of elementary propositions from which all others are to be derived by a process of logical inference and verbal deduction, has been stated still more strongly and explicitly by the same eminent writer in an article of even date with the preceding in the *Fortnightly Review*, where we are told that "Mathematics is that study which knows nothing of observation, nothing of experiment, nothing of induction, nothing of causation." I think no statement could have been made more opposite to the undoubted facts of the case, that mathematical analysis is constantly invoking the aid of new principles, new ideas, and new methods, not capable of being defined by any form of words, but springing direct from the inherent powers and activity of the human mind, and from continually renewed introspection of that inner world of thought of which the phenomena are as varied and require as close attention to discern as those of the outer physical world (to which the inner one in each individual man may, I think, be conceived to stand in somewhat the same general relation of correspondence as a shadow to the object from which it is projected, or as the hollow palm of one hand to the closed fist which it grasps of the other), that it is unceasingly calling forth the faculties of observation and comparison, that one of its principal weapons is induction, that it has frequent recourse to experimental trial and verification, and that it affords a boundless scope for the exercise of the highest efforts of imagination and invention.

J. J. Sylvester, *The collected math. papers*, II, 654

Up to now our didactical analysis has been mainly local. No global structure of mathematics to be taught was visible – it would have been otherwise if mathematics were supposed to be taught as a pre-established deductive system, as an inverse pyramid as it were, but it is now obvious that this would never fit the didactics of re-invention. Earlier analysis, however, shows how the global structure of mathematics to be taught should be understood: it is not a rigid skeleton, but it rises and perishes with the mathematics that develops in the learning process. Is it not the same with the adult mathematician's mathematics? Its structure is not exhibited on a bookshelf by a collection of Bourbaki volumes that he has never read, nor by any other work written by other authors or by himself; it is changing every day. Why should students learn a mummified mathematics?

The globally structuring force, as we called it, should be lived through reality. Only this way can we teach mathematics fraught with relations, can we be sure that the student integrates the mathematics he learned, and can we guarantee the applicability of learned mathematics. This way they taught arithmetic from olden times, and indeed, the majority of those who learned it can apply it. The import of opportunities for applying arithmetic should not be underestimated; people are inclined to judge too lightly the difficulty and the importance of what they have learned well and solidly. Beyond elementary arithmetic there is no field of mathematics which can be applied by an appreciable fraction of those who learned it, and this holds up to the university. Such mathematics is learned in an unrelated manner, far from lived-through reality and therefore soon forgotten.

If in traditional mathematical instruction the applications of mathematics are touched upon, it is always done according to the pattern of didactical inversion. Rather than departing from the concrete problem and investigating it by mathematical means, the mathematics comes first, while the concrete problem comes later as an "application". This is still the lesser evil. What people usually call applications are routines of specializing, that is, substituting special values for the parameters in a general formula or a system of formulae. By these trifles the applications of mathematics are so completely discredited that in the recent spring-cleaning the relations of mathematics to reality were put up for sale or put out for the dustman. It is felt as another advantage of this clean-out that the paramount simplicity and quiet grandeur of the deductive system is not spoiled any more by application.

Arithmetic instruction shows us the correct way. If mathematics fraught with relations should be taught, it should be tied to the other member of the relation, to start with and again and again, whether the other part of the relation be mathematics, physics or everyday life. Negative numbers should start at the lever if they should be applied to the lever, logarithms should start with the slide rule or with air pressure, or with the hyperbola if it should be applied there, the inner product should start with mechanical work, the derivative with velocity, density, and acceleration, and the linear function with all those proportionalities in nature and society that everybody must become acquainted with.

Today many would agree that the student should also learn mathematizing unmathematical (or insufficiently mathematical) matters, that is, to learn to organize it into a structure that is accessible to mathematical refinements. Grasping spatial *gestalts* as figures is mathematizing space. Arranging the properties of a parallelogram such that a particular one pops up to base the others on it in order to arrive at a definition of parallelogram, that is mathematizing the conceptual field of the parallelogram. Arranging the geometrical theorems to get all of them from a few, that is mathematizing (or axiomatizing) geometry. Organizing this system by linguistic means is again mathematizing of a subject, now called formalizing. The story repeats itself – each general statement on parallelograms is a mathematical statement but the whole of these statements is in itself a jumbled-up mess, it becomes mathematics if it is structured by logical relations, and that is mathematizing. The geometrical theorems are a mess, and even if they are related locally, they are still a mess of geometrical chapters. By axiomatic mathematization this conglomeration is mathematized. Linguistically this is again a mess like all that is expressed in the vernacular; here linguistic organizing leads to a formal system.

I already alluded to the higher levels of the process of mathematizing, where the material is locally mathematical and has to be organized globally. Anybody who has written a mathematical paper, has had the same experience: if the results and their proofs are assured, it is still necessary to organize them mathematically, a process which, of course, can have started on the way to the results. Establishing a definition can be an essential feat, more essential than finding a proposition or a proof. It can hardly be understood why mathematicians would prescribe the exclusion of mathematizing from instruction, because it is considered as a scribbler's activity. Mathematizing should be the business of the adult mathematician they claim, not of the learner. Contrary to this tendency there is no doubt that pupils should learn mathematizing, too, and certainly on the lowest level where it applies to unmathematical matter, to guarantee the applicability of mathematics, but not much less on the next level where mathematical matter is organized at least locally. How far this should go is a question we must discuss later. If, however, axiomatics and formalism are taught at all, axiomatizing and formalizing cannot be passed by. There is no mathematics without mathematizing, in particular, no axiomatics without axiomatizing, and no formalism without formalizing. And if so, one should at least observe Comenius' advice that an activity is the best taught by showing it, unless one is convinced that it is the best learned by performing it. This means teaching or even learning mathematics as mathematization, axiomatics as axiomatization, formalism as formalization. This is what follows from the interpretation of mathematics as an activity.

Today quite a few people demand this from mathematical instruction, though, I fear, in too narrow a framework. Often mathematization is only meant as an activity on the bottom level, that is, when it is applied to entirely unmathematical matter. In this case it has become fashionable to speak of mathematical models to be constructed to a situation in reality. On the other hand the term "situation" reveals that small, isolated fragments of reality are intended to be mathematized, that is, provided with a mathematical model.

Others speak of "problem-solving" if they think of instruction oriented towards mathematization. This, indeed, can be problems on any level. Beside the local restriction which has been met in the "situation" subjected to mathematization, I object against the "problem" that, in general, it describes the nucleus of a situation in too abstract a manner. The problem should grow out of the situation, and the child should learn to recognize the problem in the situation. Raising a problem is mathematics, too.

After these preliminaries it is clear, I hope, what I mean by organization of a field by mathematizing. It is the broad approach that must guarantee the global structure, rather than the pyramid on the top, which is the tendency of mathematical instruction. Situations and models, problems and solving activities are important as indispensable local means, which, however, should be subordinated to the method.

What I mean by a field to be organized by mathematizing should have been understood by earlier examples. If mathematics is dealt with according to subjects, we will get more of them. The most convincing are from geometry – kinds of quadrangles (in order to arrive at discriminating definitions), symmetry, paving the plane with congruent figures, the concept of angle, and the algebraization of geometry. From other domains: the laws of the lever and the barycentre with the resulting algebra, the relatedness of natural magnitudes according to laws, in particular by functions, mathematizing a micro-economy (a particularly attractive subject, which to my knowledge has never been tried at school), building up analysis with numerical methods as a starting point, wave propagation and oscillations. At this point a dry enumeration may suffice.

Some of the subjects I mentioned are generally counted as being part of physics. Consequently I should say a few words on what today is called integration of disciplines. In any case I would prevent the identification of what I have called organization of a field with the so-called project method.

There are noteworthy arguments why scientific education, at least in the beginning, should better not be differentiated according to disciplines; as in mathematics, if instruction is to be related to reality, the broad approach should be preferred. How long an integrated science education can be continued is another question. An effective means of integrated science education is the "project"; examples of projects as developed here and there, are "The Earth", "Space", "Water", "Nutrition". They are quite appropriate to phenomenological exploration, but less to exercise science more theoretically. Many claim that not until the age of 14 can the theoretical attitude supersede the phenomenological one. I should say I do not believe the psychologists who say they have proved it. But if it is true, integrated science instruction could be recommended up to 14 years; after this age well-organized coordination would be better than integration.

Including mathematics in integrating projects has been attempted. Now and then there is something to be added or multiplied and often percentages are figured out. It goes without saying that this does not do justice to mathematics. Even 8–9 year-olds usually do more profound mathematics than the 14 year-olds in those projects. Mathematics has a very long head start on sciences proper. This is a fact in our instruction system. Whether it is justified is another thing. In history, too, mathematics started earlier than the others. This, of course, proves nothing, and, as I stressed before, it is doubtful whether psychologists can prove that sciences must start much later than mathematics. I have not been struck by attempts at starting theoretical science earlier. In the next future, we must still take into account that at the moment when natural sciences instruction starts using mathematical tools, mathematics has already developed too far to be integrated educationally in science, or at least in physics education.

This should not prevent us from coordination, in particular with physics. Physics needs mathematics as an auxiliary discipline, but physics can also belong to the lived-through reality from which mathematics is provided with subject matters and suggestions for mathematical organization. Coordination patterns for mathematics and physics have been designed, but it seems to me that they are not radical enough. An example: in physics at a certain stage the refraction law is found though it could not be formulated mathematically because the mathematical tradition does not allow sines until two years later. Does this not prove that sines should be dealt with earlier? It is impossible, the mathematician objects, trigonometry takes such and such a number of weeks, which I cannot spare because trigonometry cannot start unless algebra has been finished. This is a reaction characteristic of system fanaticism. It is asked that sines be introduced earlier, but sines according to the system come into trigonometry and therefore must be taught in trigonometry. To sines belong cosines, tangents, cotangents, duplication and addition formulae, the sine theorem, the cosine theorem (maybe even Mollweide and Neper), as long as you are reluctant to swallow this whole drugstore, you will not get sines either. All or nothing. Could the sine not be a wonderful example of a mathematical function that is introduced graphically, from the circle, rather than algebraically? I would even say it is one of the first examples of a function the student ought to learn.

Another example – in physical music theory emerge arithmetical and geometrical sequences related to each other. Mathematics has not got as far, simply because the system says it should not. But why not deal with this subject earlier? Is it not a beautiful example of functional connection?

Calculus always comes too late for the physicist. Yet what the physicist needs from calculus, the concepts of differential quotient and integral, and the derivatives and integral of a few functions, need not come all that late, unless the mathematician ties introducing these concepts to swallowing immediately all of calculus, or what is called all of calculus at school. Mathematical concepts that are strongly motivated by their applications in the physics lesson, the gradient and the line integral, are not mentioned at all in the mathematics classroom because by definition analysis of more variables does not belong to the curriculum.

In the other encampment, physicists are just as much hypnotized by the system. Laws of the mass effect type such as the law of gravitation and Coulomb's law, which mathematically belong together, are dealt with separately, because they stem from different domains. All the "specific" magnitudes (specific weight, heat, resistance, and so on), which could help the mathematician to motivate and illustrate the linear function come much too late in physics. The laws of the lever could be a valuable motivation and illustration in early algebra but then physics has hardly, if at all, started.

If mathematics and physics instruction are to be really coordinated, both mathematicians and physicists will have to abjure the system. Algebra, trigonometry, analytic geometry, infinite series, calculus should not be any longer considered as closed units. Mathematics on the one hand and physics on the other should be seen as a whole; they should be articulated according to degrees of difficulty and according to what belongs together.

But is it wise to complicate the task of modernizing mathematical instruction by coordinating it with physics? I would advise it to be done in countries where there is a personal union of mathematics and physics instruction as in Germany. In other countries it would require serious measures in teacher training.

Another question – is the coordination of mathematics and physics instruction really necessary? Does the physicist really use as much mathematics as he claims to, and can mathematics really appeal as much to physics as he ought to if he intends to teach a mathematics fraught with relations? A closer inspection of physics textbooks to find out how much mathematics they use is highly disappointing. It mainly means that the physicist demands that his students can read formulae where letters occur and that they can substitute numerical values for these parameters. Maybe the physics teacher figures out a few more or less easy mathematical formulae and proofs which are relevant for physics, and maybe he even mentions differential quotients in mechanics. But in general he avoids all the really more profound mathematics; physics has been thoroughly de-mathematized, and as far as mathematics is applied, it occurs on a much too low level. From textbooks I have taken a few astounding examples: specific weight is defined as the weight of the volume unit, without even mentioning the proportionality of volume and weight, thus disregarding linear functions and proportionality coefficients; the laws of the lever are from the start formulated with moments without mentioning anti-proportionality, since this dispenses with a lot of mathematics; in general, whether it is about specific magnitudes or about the lever, the concepts of proportionality and anti-proportionality, and in a broader context, the concept of function is circumvented, in order to impose ready-made formulae on the student.

One can understand that the physicist does not wish to rely on his students being well acquainted with the mathematics they are expected to apply. So it is quite natural that he reduces the mathematical level of his physics instruction. So the mathematician need not make efforts to please the physicist. So he does not bother any more about physics. So the physicist is right to expect nothing from the mathematician and be content with the use of the poorest mathematics he can think up. It is a vicious circle of indifference. If this continues, it is bound to end with the complete mutual isolation of mathematics and physics instruction. There are countries where the situation is not as bad as this. But in my country there is hardly any mathematics teacher left who knows more physics than he has retained since his final school examination, and the only mathematics applicable in physics, the physics teacher knows of is the mathematics he was confronted with as a schoolboy in the physics class.

The reason is that applying an *ad hoc* trivialized mathematics continues up to physics instruction at the university, again joined with the evil of mathematicians indifferent to physical applications. I feel obliged to stress this, because at university level it could most easily be remedied. There is no authority there prescribing our programmes and schedules, and regular contact between the teachers of the first-year courses could effect quite a lot.

But meanwhile it remains a sad fact that physicists in their instruction use degraded mathematics. For the student this means that he learns de-mathematized physics, that he is not introduced to understanding how mathematics applies in physics, and that he experiences mathematics and physics as unrelated. May he expect that the mathematician will offer him what the physicst has refused to?

I would answer, yes – for it is the mathematician's task. It is not to be expected that the physicist take the effort in his instruction of demonstrating to students the applicability of mathematics. This is more the interest of the mathematician. But then he should be interested in making sure that the student not only learns mathematics, but also how to apply it. And not only on physics. I did not mention chemistry, where things are even worse. Though it is a very elementary mathematics that is used in chemistry lessons, the failure of mathematics there is complete, since chemists are pleased to apply a mathematics of their own.

I think integration should be understood in a different way from the side of mathematics, since the case of mathematics is so different from others. This uniqueness is at most equalled by that of instruction in one's mother tongue. I would recommend integration or coordination of mathematics not *with* other disciplines but integration *around* mathematics, that is with mathematics as a nuclear discipline that attracts subject matter of other disciplines to have them worked on by the student as fields of mathematical organization. This does not make other disciplines dispensable nor are they devalued in any way, but at least the student would learn what he can do with mathematics.

Properly said this is the way mathematics starts. Elementary arithmetic instruction is integrated, not with the sciences which have not yet emerged on the child's horizon but with the various life activities of the child. This integrated state should be maintained, as long as possible, in particular when the child becomes accessible and susceptible to the concepts of science. In fact, there is an intermediate stage which is neither physics nor chemistry nor biology and which scientists are likely to concede with the greatest of pleasure to mathematics. I mean the connections in a world that has not yet been analyzed by natural sciences, and which are described mathematically by functions.

The connections cultivated by traditional arithmetic instruction are those with social life – connections which, if it is about redemption of loans or mixing two sorts of prunes of different quality and price, can hardly be fitted into the child's lived-through reality. There is little doubt that such problems embody sound ideas, as do the taps filling a basin and the meeting and overtaking columns of route. The proportionality factor of the linear function as price of the unit, specific weight, or velocity, the growth laws, periodicities – these are phenomena springing from a primitive analysis of reality which can hardly be called scientific though it precedes and facilitates scientific analysis. They fit very well into early mathematical instruction.

ALGORITHMS

The analysis that leads to the first arithmetical ideas is still more primitive. It nevertheless leads to the first algorithms. The word "algorithm" is here particularly well chosen, because ciphering according to a pattern that is not too different from the present one was invented, or at least first described by a certain Al Ḥuwârizmî whose name was gradually transformed into Algorithm. Before him, and in some places even centuries after him, people calculated with calculi, that is, pebbles, on the abacus. Computing on the abacus is an intuitive activity with concrete material. A mathematician who observes the calculator knows which laws he is applying (e.g. in the transfer of fives or tens); the calculator himself does not need know it. He is on the bottom level; and while he can rise to the next, this is not a must. This changes as soon as counters are superseded by ciphers, which originally, before paper was invented, were written in fine sand. First of all, ciphers are not as concrete as the sets of counters on the abacus, thus to translate his actions on the abacus into written calculations, the calculator must understand what he is doing. He creates written arithmetic on a higher level by recognizing its rules. In the long run this can be automatized to such an extent that even these rules disappear from one's consciousness, just like with people switching a light off and on, without knowing how the switch works. People, however, who do know this can repair the switch if it does not work properly. Likewise calculation errors can be repaired by people who know how ciphering works. The child learns to work out $8 + 5$ intuitively, and with appropriate material it even constructs the splitting $(8 + 2) + 3$. Maybe this is at first an unconscious artifice; as soon as it becomes conscious, the child attains the next level where it can develop the algorithm of written additions; if finally he formulates this algorithm he has again climbed to a higher level. Of course, the child can be bluntly confronted with a ready-made algorithm in order to make him jump the intermediate levels. This can accelerate the learning process or can slow it down or even stop it. Not until the child has justified the splitting $(8 + 2) + 3$ and felt its need, can he apply it algorithmically. The best way to understand the trick is to discover it. Nothing is as quite as convincing as self-reliant discovery. If the child is not given the time it needs, and if the algorithm is bluntly dictated, a bad reaction is bound to follow. Algorithms should be applied as routines; this is their rationale and for this end they were created. But unless they work properly it is no use applying them as routines. If a child below this level is taught the algorithm as a set of rules, it will not work. The child will make stupid mistakes and will confuse and mix up different algorithms.

Algorithms are of the greatest importance for mathematics. They exist in algebra, in calculus, in probability. In today mathematics strong tendencies to algorithmize prevail. The algorithms of homology and co-homology, of diagrams, and of categories are recent creations. Algorithmizing a domain is the way to pass beyond it with greater ease. Algorithms are not in themselves automatisms, though by means of routines they make automatisms possible. This is their rationale, but is also the reason why they may endanger instruction. They tempt both teachers and pupils: teachers who rather than teaching mathematics teach algorithms which the pupils are not allowed to re-invent and which they are compelled to learn, maybe even before they were able to re-invent them; pupils who are as easily captivated by a well-functioning algorithm as they would be by a game. Taking a terrifying example, are there not the division problems which aim at nothing but terminating without remainder and which have nothing to do with dividing one number by the other? Are there not the awful fractions and bracket expressions which were invented as aims in themselves? Is there not the algorithm of algebra drubbed into the children's heads, which never works?

I stress it once more: algorithms are fine, and routine is inescapable in mathematics. Certain algorithms must be learned, with due account to the levels, by re-invention. Automatisms are necessary; they are acquired by drill, and drill is part of the training. In the past the training that fixes automatisms was often exaggerated. Innovators tend to stress free exploration, in particular on the bottom level, but I would not say that they exaggerate. I have already* expressed the wish that more attention should be paid to the transition to higher levels, and to exploration on higher levels. Drilling automatisms is also a serious task; I will come back to it when the language of algebra is dealt with.

Besides the algorithms one knows what I would call patterns, tactics, strategies – all of which being less appropriate to automatic use than algorithms. A pattern: if it is about items bought in a shop apply addition. A more general pattern: the rule of three. A tactic: I put the unknown x (to apply algorithms of algebra). A strategy: to solve a problem, generalize it.

To one of my sons, then 6 years old, I gave the following problem:

"In the window of the shop there are books for 50 cents, dolls for 25 cents, and spinning tops for 10 cents. Mary has a florin. She makes a choice, walks into the shop, and buys what she wanted. She leaves the shop with 50 cents. What did she buy?" Without any hesitation, my son answered: "A doll". On being asked why, he answered: "Mary is a girl, isn't she?" One year later I gave him the same problem, and he answered: "One florin 85 cents."

It is an unusual problem, because rather than a number the solution requires a decision among three possibilities. It is easily understood that at that time the patterns did not yet function; the situation was unusual. Unfortunately I did not investigate what my son would have answered if "Mary" had been replaced by "a child", as the name and sex is mis-

* p. 127.

leading. I believe that at that age he would have motivated a correct and correctly-found result, but also in an inadequate way. At his age he knew some patterns of arithmetic, but he had not yet grasped the tactics that "in word problems the names of persons are irrelevant". (In parentheses: Why? In everyday life names are relevant. With more advanced students the use of such data should be exercised, for example by problems which numerically admit of two solutions one of which is eliminated by a datum on age or sex.)

What occurred with my son in the intervening year is obvious. He had been taught systematic arithmetic, and became familiar with routines too early, and then applied tactics like the following: "If a problem contains more than two numbers, they are added." This kind of tactics can still be met with at the highest level. In a course on group theory where I had defined groups and automorphisms and introduced inner automorphisms as an example, the question whether there exist other automorphisms besides inner automorphisms was answered by a student: "Yes, because otherwise you would not have distinguished inner ones".

Of course patterns, tactics, and strategies are important, just as algorithms are. They should be exercised, but not too early on and not until the pupil is able to reinvent them himself.

SINGULARITIES

A counterpart of algorithms, patterns, tactics, and strategies is the singular experience, the individual one, the *hapax legomenon* like they call in Greek language instruction the rare words: those that are only said once. History consists of such singular events, though one tries not to teach it this way. Only once did Caesar cross over the Rubicon, but what happened once is often interesting as a historical paradigm. Conjugations and declinations are learned by paradigms as are mathematical activities. To be sure, there is much in mathematics which could, would, and ought to be learned for its own sake, for instance out of curiosity rather than as a paradigm. What is this matter worth? I mean, not for the teacher, nor for the future mathematician who could appreciate it as mathematics fraught with relations, but what is it worth for the average student who is compelled to learn it? What is the value of such a matter to him? To occur once and then to be forgotten?

You know what I mean – all those proofs of geometrical theorems and trigonometric formulae, which are learned, maybe repeated in the next lesson, and then forgotten. It would be possible to learn such things paradigmatically, but this requires a lot of re-interpretation. In a series of textbooks I saw set theory in the second grade, which was not applied until the ninth grade. I saw a formal introduction of rational numbers as equivalence classes of integers with no other aim than to satisfy the teacher's (or the textbook author's) longing for exactness, and entirely isolated within the whole. I saw formal axiom systems of real numbers the essential part of which (the existence of the upper bound of bounded sets, or Dedekind's cut) never became operational. It is easy to multiply these examples: a definition of continuity that is never applied because all functions considered are continuous, or the Riemann integral that never works since in practice integrating is the inverse of differentiating.

Another type of *hapax legomena* are the plums in the mathematical pudding, the showpieces of the demonstration lessons. For instance, Socrates' heritage, doubling the square, the irrationality of $\sqrt{2}$, or from Euclid, the existence of an infinity of prime numbers. With such problems public success is warranted, in Socratic and even in re-invention instruction. After such a lesson the mathematics teacher goes home asking himself the question: "Does it help teaching the solution of the quadratic equation?"

It looks like teasing but it is not far off the mark. Only I would re-formulate the objection. Show lessons are misleading because they are show lessons. To pick the plums out of the mathematical pudding is *a priori* unrealistic instruction. Even if it is not done for show, the local access is insufficient. It is desirable and indispensable to know how a subject fits into mathematical instruction as a whole. I certainly do not assert that splendid pieces as the ones mentioned must remain isolated. Since they are splendid, they even merit our efforts to integrate them more profoundly into mathematical instruction rather than to have them blooming as *hapax legomena*. This requires that teachers must scrutinize them again more closely. With those three examples, I will show how their didactics suffers from faith in a two-millenia-old tradition.

I learned how to approach Meno's problem from one of my sons (then 10 years old). He was telling me about some tinkering he would do and casually said: "I am going to make a square hole of 2 square millimeters".* Instantly I slipped into Socrates' toga and asked him: "How would you fix it?" Of course, I expected the trivial wrong answer, but he gave another: "A square with a side of $1\frac{1}{2}$ mm." I was perplexed and asked "Why?" I was sure to answer it he would square $1\frac{1}{2}$. No, the boy, who was an eidetic, answered: "I take two squares of 1 mm in length, cut one of them into four equal strips and stick them on the sides of the other." I pulled a long face, and he hesitated. Indeed, it did not fit; in the corners there was something missing. I told him he should have cut the square in another way into equal pieces though not rectangles. It is not easy to have the learner find cutting by diagonals. At any rate this pasting method is much more natural than Meno's.

The exploration could be continued in two directions towards Pythagoras' theorem and a systematic study of content with splitting and complementing, or into algebra, with systematic approximations of $\sqrt{2}$ of which $1\frac{1}{2}$ is the roughest, and continued fractions, side and diagonal numbers, and numerical solutions of algebraic equations. This can save Meno's problem from isolation.

The irrationality of $\sqrt{2}$ can be handled with the old methods, putting $\sqrt{2} = p/q$ (simplified), squaring to $p^2 = 2q^2$, going after the divisibility by 2 to arrive at a contradiction. But the formulation of the problem is didactically wrong, at least if this should be the first appearance of an irrational number in the course of instruction. Already a level has been passed over in the formulation. Formulated on the right level, the problem reads: work out $\sqrt{2}$. The insight that this is not possible with the means available should be the result of an experiment rather than the gist of a pre-established statement. But even the problem is not right. It is a local problem where a field should be explored. Moreover, what does it mean to work out $\sqrt{2}$? Has it not already been worked out? It has got the algorithmic expression '$\sqrt{2}$'.

It is better to proceed as follows. One writes an equation like $x^3 + 3x^2 + x - 4 = 0$, which should be solved. The graphic shows there is a solution, which, however, cannot be integral. (In the case of $\sqrt{2}$ the existence of a solution and the non-existence of an integral one is much more obvious, which is a disadvantage.) One tries, for instance, $\frac{9}{10}$. A

---

* Millimeters indeed, the construction was entirely imaginary.

bit too large. Maybe $\frac{8}{10}$? No, this is much too small. It is instructive to look for fractions near $\frac{9}{10}$ which are not too involved. The best we can find, is $\frac{8}{9}$. It is a little too small. After such like preparations p/q (simplified) is tried. Does it do it? Multiplication by q^3 leads to $p^3 + 3p^2q + pq^2 - 4q^3 = 0$. The divisibility by 2 used in the classical proof of the irrationality of $\sqrt{2}$ was in fact quite irrelevant. To arrive at a contradiction a prime contained in q must be considered. This leads to $q = 1$. From here there is a way to systematically find the integral p which fulfil such equations. On the other hand one can continue to systematical approximations, Horner's scheme and so on. This is exploring a field.

Finally the existence of an infinity of prime numbers. The classical approach is well known. The teacher heads straight to $p_1 \ldots p_k + 1$ where $p_1, \ldots, p_k$ are all *known* prime numbers. In experiments I never got this solution, but lot of others instead. First of all, the question was badly formulated. It should be instead: systematically find prime numbers. Whether there is an infinity, this can only be formulated on a higher level. The start is, of course, the sequence of natural numbers, which is sieved out according to Eratosthenes. 2 is a prime. It is noted down, and all its multiples are crossed out. What remains? The numbers of the kind $2n + 1$. The next prime, 3 is noted down, and its multiples are crossed out. What remains? The $2 \cdot 3 \cdot m + 1$ and $2 \cdot 3 \cdot m + 5$. Which of them are not divisible by 5 either? The $2 \cdot 3 \cdot m + 5$, where m is no multiple of 5, is grist to our mill. From here it is a smooth path to numbers like $p_1 \ldots p_j + p_{j+1} \ldots p_k$, which are not divisible by $p_1, \ldots, p_k$. Such numbers have new prime factors, and this finally yields infinitely many. $p_1 \ldots p_k + 1$ is not as obvious. A more systematic approach opens still other perspectives:

How can we find all numbers not divisible by 2, 3, 5? They are of the form $2 \cdot 3 \cdot 5 \cdot m + r$, with $r = 1, 7, 11, 13, 17, 19, 23, 29$, that is $1 \leqslant r < 30$ and r relative prime to 30. The concept of relative prime remainders mod 30 emerges. How many? This leads to Euler's function. The original problem is embedded in a field, that of divisibility problems.

A lesson can be drawn from this, namely that didactically fertile problems should not be too simple, should not be too special, and should not be too sharply formulated.

CHAPTER VIII

MATHEMATICAL RIGOUR

Would it be believable that the logicians always proceeded from the general to the particular, as the rules of formal logic seemed to prescribe? By this way they would never have been able to extend the frontiers of science; scientific conquests are only made by generalization.

H. Poincaré, *C.R. 2ème Congrès Int. des math.* Paris, 1900, 127

When mathematical science becomes rigorous it assumes an artificial character which cannot be overlooked. It forgets about its historic origin: it shows how problems can be solved but not how and why they are posed.

This shows that logic does not suffice; the science of proofs is not the whole science, intuition is assigned a complementary part, I would say, as counterpart or antidote of logic.

H. Poincaré, *C.R. 2ème Congrès Int. des math.* Paris 1900, 123–4

LEVELS OF RIGOUR

Above all other mental exercises, mathematics has the advantage that with each statement you can decide whether it is right or wrong. Whether a mathematical paper is good or bad, important or unimportant, original or trifling, is not as easy to decide but there can be no doubt about it being right or wrong. Already in physics it is more difficult to tell this, unless it is a kind of physics that is practically mathematics. A physical theory is expected to be confirmed in reality but even if it is not confirmed it need not be wrong but can have been applied less appropriately. In all sciences except mathematics the criterion of usefulness is often more relevant than a criterion of truth that actually nobody knows for sure how to handle. The reason is that on no other science can be imposed so strong a deductive structure as on mathematics. In mathematics it is not only certain whether the result is correct but even – or actually solely – whether it has been founded correctly. This is what is called mathematical rigour. It is the measuring-rod of mathematics, and if we teach mathematics we use it also.

Who judges whether the mathematics taught is rigorous or not? The teacher, of course, perhaps by using red ink. The student would not be able to, he must first learn what rigour is. He learns just like a mouse is trained by electrical shocks to jump over a hurdle if a bell rings. I admit this is a rather lame comparison. The teacher distributes red ink not arbitrarily but according to laws which some way suit the pupil, who is a *homo sapiens* too, and their efficacy is reinforced by red ink. When one of my former students gave his first lesson to a school class, they asked him whether it was his rule, too, that expressions moved from one side of the equal-sign to the other should change their sign, as it had been with the former teacher. New teachers are always interviewed about their rules – so why not mathematics teachers?

Red ink is a means of teaching mathematical rigour to a student who keeps staying on the bottom level. Not only is education more human than drill, it is more efficient, too. One of the characteristics of education is freedom. There can be no doubt that the student cannot learn mathematical rigour in any other way than mathematics at all, that is by re-invention. This, too, should happen on different levels. Rigour can be acted out without knowing what it is. Rigour can be a conscious criterion that is applied to isolated arguments, and finally there is a global notion of rigour that can be applied to mathematics as a whole.

This, however, is not so easy to do, and many divergences in the appreciation of rigour are caused by the fact that quite a few people have never grasped that it is not as easy as they thought. In the course of history mathematical rigour has not been the same in the mind of all mathematicians, and unless people are blind, they will agree that it is still not the same. Up to a century ago people operated intuitively with infinitesimal concepts, and it worked excellently because it was intuitive. Then criticism grew stronger, and people put their faith in epsilontics. Now epsilontics is losing ground, and after one or two decennia we can expect the "great discovery" that, properly understood, the infinitesimal methods of a century ago are completely rigorous. Algorithms with differentials are already modern.

When I studied at university a rigorous course in calculus for first-year students started with a foundation of number theory: natural numbers, integers, rationals, and real numbers. Today it is no crime to start with an axiomatic definition of the real number system as an ordered or a topological field with certain properties. Forty years ago they would have stoned you to death: "How do you know that such a field exists?"

The answer today would be: "If you start with integers or with sets, how are you sure that they exist?" Of course, in an advanced course the "existence proof" (notice, a *relative* existence proof) may be added, but even this arrangement betrays a conscious didactic choice. Even more astonishing is the fact that today textbook authors, apparently worried by scruples of being exact, are trying to teach at schools what for didactic reasons has been delayed from freshmen to more advanced courses: formal theories with existence proofs for natural numbers, integers, rationals, and real numbers. The faith in the system prescribes that to make it rigorous, you have to go back to integers or even to sets. Asserting however, that this is the summit of rigour is not modern at all – it is old hat, and it is wrong. Truly modern mathematicians could tell those innovators that integers are more problematic than real numbers, just as sets are more problematic than integers. In a certain sense it is consoling that these attempts at formal number theories at school level are both mathematical and didactical failures to such a degree that they will hardly convince anybody. I will come back to this point.

This is by way of parenthesis. What matters didactically is quite another thing. It is whether the learner can understand why rigour dictates reducing reals to rationals, rationals to integers, integers to natural numbers, and natural numbers to sets or whether rigour does not allow him to abstain from it. As long as you cannot explain to the learner what this decision means, it is not fair to impose on him a theory nobody has asked for.

Some of our contemporaries believe that there is no rigorous mathematics outside axiomatic systems. Yet there is no reason for stopping at axiomatics. One step further would mean urging full formalization, that is, communicating in a language with all its links with reality cut. This would be pretending even more, but already the axiomatic postulate excludes a great part of that mathematics which ought to be taught to non-mathematicians. Advocates of axiomatics at school know and admit this undeniable fact and allow non-axiomatic mathematics to be taught as so-called experimental mathematics because it is indispensable, while meanwhile washing their mathematical hands of it. This is the mathematical dualism we characterized earlier, the doctrine of two mathematics, one for Jupiter, and one for the ox. Experimental mathematics, that is, the mathematics of free discovery, is much more important than that which is confined to axioms imposed by the teacher or textbook author, and there is no reason to claim that it is any less rigorous. There are levels of rigour and for each subject matter there is a level of rigour adapted to it; the learner should pass through the levels and acquire their rigour. The adult mathematician, too, operates according to various levels of rigour; it is blindness to assert there is only one rigour (which, of course, happens to be that exercised by the person who is asserting it) and any others below are fake and all above are hair-splitting!

If a six year-old works out $8 + 5$ on his fingers or with counters, it is perhaps not mathematics, but at that level it is a rigorous proof. As he advances, rigour demands that $8 + 5$ is computed according to splitting $8 + 2 + 3$, because at this level it is an implicit rule that memorized tables are only used for additions $a + b = c$ with $1 \leqslant a < 10$, $1 \leqslant b < 10$, $2 \leqslant c < 10$. Somewhat later it is rigorous to use $8 + 5 = 13$ without computing it, that is, using memorized tables $a + b = c$ with $1 \leqslant a \leqslant 10$, $1 \leqslant b \leqslant 10$, $2 \leqslant c \leqslant 20$. Teacher and pupils are here playing a game according to unconscious rules and obeying these rules in rigour. They are rules that nobody invented *ad hoc*; they resulted from the inter-action of the players; nobody, not even the teacher, could formulate them explicitly. The transition from one rule system to the next is discontinuous though natural: one day the pupil will refuse to continue the old game.

To the problem on p. 142 my son's argument (is she not a girl?) was not rigorous. Of course, even the solution was wrong, but if Mary had left the shop with 75 cents rather than 50 cents, it still would not have been rigorous, because there are some girls who do not play with dolls. It is, moreover, non-rigorous in another sense. It sins against the implicit rules of the game that in such problems personal names do not matter, that rather than Mary the person could have been named John. (It is not a must; on a higher level there could be problems where realistic details as the names can be essential.)

LOCAL ORGANIZATION

If the pupil constructively discovers that along the circumference of a circle its radius can be stepped exactly six times to form a regular hexagon, and if he explains this experience by noticing that the angles of an equilateral triangle are 60°, then this is rigorous. To the thorough-bred mathematician this argument is, of course, shocking. Indeed, how many tacit presuppositions do not lie hidden within this argument? How many axioms are there not required to reach this, whether it is done according to Euclid or Hilbert or by linear algebra? He is right, it is a long way to come to this point in this or that system, and the pupil has to learn this fact, but he will never learn it if an axiomatic system is imposed on him. Didactically this would be a wrong procedure. It is the task of rigour to convince, but ready-made mathematics never convinces. To progress in rigour, the first step is to doubt the rigour one believes in at this moment. Without this doubt there is little learned by letting other people prescribe oneself new criteria of rigour.

Of course with a problem like that of the regular hexagon the pupil should ask himself: "What did I actually presuppose?" We know that if he asks this question again and again, he will finally go astray in vagueness and circular arguments. We know it. The pupil does not know this yet. He has to experience this, too. Without such experiences he cannot grasp the meaning of axiomatics.

Up to that moment he will exercise what can be called the local organizing of a field. This is a concept that will be important in particular for the didactical understanding of geometry instruction. Geometrical concepts and relations are always analyzed up to a certain rather arbitrary frontier, let us say up to the point where the naked eye as it were, distinguishes what notions mean, and whether propositions are true. This is the way everybody reasons in the geometry of experienced space; never from axioms which are much too far away, but from the hazy and shifting horizon of facts which happen to be assumed as true. The field is organized to a larger or smaller extent piecewise, rather than as a whole. This is the way it is done in physics, too, and in any field where mathematics is applied.

LOGICAL RIGOUR

Nobody is entitled to reject this procedure as not being rigorous. Local organizing knows its own rigour. What distinguishes a theorem from its converse, what a circular argument is, or the difference between "necessary" and "sufficient", or between existence and universality – this is as clear in local as it is in global organizing. I would even claim some aspects of rigour are clearer in acted-out than in ready-made mathematics, in particular knowing what is relevant and irrelevant. In ready-made mathematics such statements as "if a triangle has four vertices, it is equilateral" are true though in active mathematics they are absurd. In ready-made mathematics the question why $(a + b)(a - b) = a^2 - b^2$ is true (if at all it allows of any question) may be answered by "because the earth is round", since logicians tell us that $p \rightarrow q$ is true as soon as q is true. Operative mathematics cultivates a different concept of rigour: the answer to a "why" is rigorous mathematics if it is relevant. Thus the rules of formal logic are not even sufficient to tell us what rigour is. Oral examination questions like "why did you define this that way?" or "can you prove this by means of that?" or "where did you apply that method before?" cannot be asked within the framework of formal logic, though it should be stressed again and again that they belong to mathematics as firmly as computing an integral or proving a formula. This, however, is easily forgotten in all ready-made mathematics. To answer this kind of questions a different sort of rigour is required. What rigour means here nobody has attempted to formulate up till now. As for the logic of operated science all mankind is still at the bottom level. I do not regret this. On the contrary, it prevents us from teaching the logic of acted-out mathematics as a ready-made subject. But here and there we should realize that this, too, is mathematics.

CUTTING MATHEMATICS OFF FROM REALITY

In discussions people have protested to me: "Eventually the pupil will have to learn the clear and rigorous difference between mathematics and the real world". I answered: "You are as right as you are wrong. You are right if you aim at teaching mathematical rigour, and wrong if you are defending teaching unrelated mathematics. You are right if you stress "learning", but wrong if you advocate teaching ready-made axiomatics".

Separating mathematical theory and the real world already starts when the pupil learns to calculate, I mean when he learns unrelated arithmetic. Yes, this is worth training. Drill implies that the pupil can sometimes forget that in the real world 7 consists of seven units. The pupil learns to put a mathematics into brackets lest it should be spoiled by the touch of reality and in order to function more safely. It is worthwhile also to understand that there is truth that depends neither on the weather nor on goodwill. But fortunately the student also learns to do away with the brackets protecting pure mathematics, if everyday problems of arithmetic are to be solved or if the way a computer works is to be understood.

This is not what we meant – my opponents reply. We intended that the pupil should finally learn an axiomatical theory that is separated from the world by waterproof compartments. Why – I would ask? The separation of mathematical theory and real world can better be experienced at an earlier stage and with simple examples than later on with highly sophisticated ones. But simple examples like integers – they reply – are too closely knitted to the real world; the 7 cannot be cut off from the seven days of the week or the seven dwarfs. My answer to this is: Is it easier cutting sets and mappings and logical connectives off from the real world?

Certainly the pupil should learn putting mathematics into brackets within the real world – this is the essence of mathematical rigour – but he should also learn that it is an illusion to believe there are waterproof brackets, because otherwise he will not learn how to improve the waterproofness of the brackets. I pointed out that axiomatics formulated in the vernacular is not the summit of rigour; is the vernacular not like blotting-paper? Though, nobody would try bringing completely formal mathematics into the classroom. Moreover, acted-out mathematics does not stand within brackets and cannot be put between brackets, and as soon as something has to be performed with mathematics confined within brackets, the brackets have to be dissolved, and this, too, ought to be learned.

Our students like it – is the reply. They are so used to axiomatic systems that they do not like anything else. They reject this half-rigour, they like to move within systems where there is no doubt, where every Yea is yea and every Nay is nay. That is your own fault – I say. Think about what you are doing! Maybe one out of a hundred of your students will become a mathematician, ninety-nine will apply mathematics and they will do so in a world where there is no system, where there *is* doubt, and where a clear "Yea" or "Nay" are rare. You are misleading your students with false hopes. Your students like it, don't they? They love it, they love the long divisions with no remainder, the formidable fractions, differentiating mechanically if you teach it to them. Education teaches true love.

A PROBLEM

The phone rings and I put down my pen. Last night in light-hearted company I had posed a problem. The caller was one of those present. He has solved it. This is the problem:

A finite oriented graph (a "lattice") with *one* highest and one lowest node is given, both of them different. Two players play a game. Alternating they put pawns on the nodes of the graph. If a node is occupied, all lower ones (according to the orientation) are forbidden. The player who is compelled to put a pawn on the highest node loses.

Prove that the beginner has a winning strategy.

When I set the problem last night, somebody checked with me what an oriented graph is, and another what I meant by "forbidden". There was no question about the meaning of "highest" and "lowest", of "game" and "alternating", about "beginning", "putting", "winning" and "loosing", and about what a winning strategy was. It is no problem within brackets, though. We can really play it with any real graph, or can't we? In fact, if we solve the problem, we are playing the game, living within the game situation. To solve it, no axiomatics can help us, neither can bracketing. On the contrary, only in the real world can we understand it. You can solve it so rigorously that it can be one of the most convincing instances to show what mathematical rigour is.

Please ring me up if you are the teacher who says: these are the problems my pupils love.

CHAPTER IX

INSTRUCTION

Wenn alles schläft und einer spricht,
Den Zustand nennt man Unterricht.*

Wilhelm Busch

THE AUTHORITY OF THE THEORETICIAN

Most educators have formulated their philosophies as demands. They used to tell others how they ought to teach. Some also showed how it should be done. As early as the 17th century some of them travelled around evoking admiration by their demonstrations. They complemented their practice with various theories. We often do not know how one matched the other. Whatever may have been the case, nobody can deny that they were capable men. But were they for this reason entitled to prescribe to others what they should do in teaching?

At any rate they have exerted some influence though perhaps not enough. But could it have been much more? Are there not limits? First of all, the limit of understanding: how far were they understood? Secondly, of human nature: did they not urge more from the educators than they were capable of as human beings? Thirdly, of society: was the education they strove for possible in the society they lived in?

This is one of the many variations on the theme "ideal and reality", to put it into traditional terminology. But do not forget that ideals are a reality too, the reality seen by people who look a bit farther than their contemporaries.

I lack the proper credentials to prescribe to others their instruction methods. In the school classroom I sat as a pupil and spectator, and not in the teacher's chair. Learning how to teach university students gave me great diffiulty – but maybe this has been a positive factor. My longest experiences and greatest difficulties were caused by the worst student I have ever taught – I mean myself. If, however, somebody claims that the

---

* If all are sleeping and one is talking,
  that is called instruction.

Socratic method or the method of re-invention are unrealistic and impossible, I can assure him that I have seen them work in the classroom; what I have added to this experience is nothing but a logical analysis. I have even seen examples of what I have called organization of a field in the classroom and in the literature; but I agree that many more analyses of teaching matter are indispensable before this viewpoint can be generalized.

This is by the way. I do not believe that it is the essence of this book and of what I used to advocate in teaching theory that I should prescribe to practising educators their teaching methods. But it certainly has been, and still is, my philosophy to fight any attempts at influencing school instruction in an anti-didactical way. In particular I oppose all purely content-oriented instruction, and all dogmatic views on mathematics which neglect all the psychological pre-suppositions and social implications of mathematical instruction. Such dogmatic efforts are often made by university professors, who by their very nature are prone to view school mathematics as subject matter and as a system. But sometimes even schoolteachers, too, if they plunge into the subject matter, can be more and more captured by the material aspect of teaching. University teachers lecturing on school mathematics will usually apologize that they restrict themselves to the subject matter aspect because they do not dare to judge the teaching possibilities. Often, unintentionally, simply through the choice of the subject matter and its presentation, they are making a didactic choice, namely in favour of teaching a ready-made, unrelated mathematics, and against teaching a kind of mathematics that the pupil would be able to apply. Schoolteachers will exert such influences if they produce textbooks; I explained earlier how, in writing a text, didactics can be killed.

It is easy to imagine how dogmatic influences work, and it can be illustrated by historical examples. If an authority declares that something is rigorous one way and slipshod another way, it may crucially affect instruction though it does not matter whether such a statement was properly understood or not. After such an authority had discovered that Euclid's proof of his first congruence theorem was not rigorous (which is quite correct) nobody who did not want to disgrace himself dared to motivate this theorem or to introduce it in any other way than by prescription. After a badly-understood remark by a university teacher on Hankel's permanence of algebraic laws, nobody dared to prepare decently the extensions of the number concept; instead the algebraic laws were introduced as unmotivated postulates. In Germany thoughtless re-echoing of Klein has blocked many a sound development. With pain I remember something similar that happened in the Netherlands in the nineteen-thirties. In 1937 a reform of mathematical curricula in Dutch academic high schools took place; the reform was the expression of the idealism of a few teachers who honestly relied on the imposing power of mathematical deductivity as a self-starting didactical agent, and who did not feel the need for any pedagogical and didactical argumentation and for any social background to justify their proposals. The programme advocated in those reports was frankly unrealistic if not quite fantastic. This has been proved by a few decades of actual teaching of it, if ever such proof was needed. But at that time almost no one dared to protest against these ideas. One of the very few exceptions was our greatly regretted friend D. van Dantzig, who with the most convincing arguments fought against this teaching philosophy which disregarded the psychological and social conditions and its implications for mathematical instruction. Van Dantzig's arguments however did not induce anybody to renounce those idealistic teaching theories. Good teachers who set their own standards may believe that they are carrying out such a programme, and they are wholly entitled to do so even if their standards do not quite match those of the programme they believe to be carrying out. Most teachers, however, do not wish to admit that they are not able to carry out an unrealistic programme which apparently enjoys such general agreement. The ideas underlying the 1937 reform were not being refuted, but were simply betrayed. There were a few textbook authors who honestly tried to realize a small part of this idealistic programme but their books were used in very few schools. The other group of authors did not understand what was meant, or if they understood, they paid merely lip service to the noble-minded programme in their textbooks. Topics which had been inserted into the programme in order to promote a more profound understanding of mathematics, were transformed by textbook authors into subject matter which had to be taught and learned without understanding or simply omitted.

I am telling this story not only to show the unreliability of programmes and curricula, but also because it looks paradigmatic, and because I fear that history will repeat itself. The part played in those days in propaganda and defence by the adjectives "rigorous" and "sloppy", is now taken over by "modern" and "old-fashioned". Sometimes it seems more like a ladies fashion shop than anything else. It has really happened that on the strength of authoritative sentences dating from 1955 something was rejected by someone who did not know that it was most modern style since 1965. There is nothing against this. But it demonstrates that in mathematics subject matter and methods are always being rethought. Whether something is new is not a decisive criterion for teaching. But of course nobody wants to disgrace himself by falling behind, and no teacher will readily admit that he cannot teach as rigorously as the university professor or the textbook author prescribe it to be done. I fear, indeed, that if teachers pay what seems to be lip service to "modern" mathematics in school teaching and "modern" rigour, it is not only a sign of respect but often of frustration, too: fearing the critical eye of authority, and fearing to be considered backward or old-fashioned if one admits that one deals with the limit concept a bit sloppy, or that geometrical axiomatics cannot possibly be taught in the ninth grade. As a matter of fact I cannot understand why school teachers almost never protest, not even against projects where all evidence shows that they are illusory. Do they think it is not worthwhile or are they afraid of looking silly by doubting whether something is really as simple as the author advertised it to be?

THE PRAXIS OF INSTRUCTION

If theoretical-programmatic literature is excluded, it is not easy to know how teachers actually teach. The bulk of material consists of

(1) curricula and programmes,
(2) textbooks and syllabi,
(3) examination papers,
(4) theoretical teaching research,
(5) experimental teaching research.

Curricula are mostly vague and usually admit of a great variety of interpretation. Programmes generally show more detail, but their main feature is to set goals and standards. They do not say whether these goals were reached or whether these standards were matched by the actual education. The earlier-mentioned reports which led to the 1937 reform in the mathematical curriculum of academic high schools in the Netherlands provide a striking example; this reform only took place on paper, because its underlying ideas were quite impossible.

Can teaching be judged by textbooks? Everywhere there are both good and bad ones. Which are most influential? Usually the good ones are used in a small minority of classes, but even this negative symptom does not prove anything. I do not believe mathematical education is as bad as the textbooks which are used. Education as a human activity is too involved a matter to be reflected in textbooks. It is the characteristic of a good textbook that its author has analyzed the subject matter logically, has arranged it deliberately according to his (implicit or explicit) teaching theory, and in some cases has even accounted for it with a comment. If a teacher hits upon such a book, his reaction can be two-fold. Either he does not understand the underlying teaching ideas; he only notes that the arrangement differs from what he learned himself at school and from what he is used to apply, and he bluntly states that the book is confused and confusing. Or he does understand the underlying teaching theory, but disapproves of it. In either case there is a great chance that he falls back upon one of those colourless textbooks written without any previous analysis of the subject matter and lacking any didactical background, mere catalogues of problems arranged in an arbitrary way, and for conscience's sake held together by tiny pieces of theory. It is not altogether impossible that even an average teacher using this kind of book and implementing a theory of his own does better than a good teacher who is bound to a textbook of a character that does not match the character of his own teaching.

The third source of information on actual instruction that we mentioned are examination papers. It is even quite a trustworthy source of information provided that it is used by someone who is well acquainted with the peculiarities of the drill in preparing for examinations and with the techniques for evaluating the results. A foreigner who happens to see our exam problems in solid geometry or our translation pieces in three foreign languages could seriously believe that our students are geniuses in geometry or languages, until he discovers that the performances in geometry are the result of highly specialized training and that the linguistic performances are evaluated according to pretty poor standards.

Theoretical teaching research often has the character of telling other people how they have to teach. Then it is programmatic, and often even unrealistic. It is backed by firm belief or by the actual teaching experience of the man who is presenting his ideas. He claims that his method has proved successful, though others may doubt whether his success is not due more to his personal qualities rather than to the method itself. Experimental teaching research often suffers from the unrealistic situation in which it is carried out. Experiments with test classes are particularly suspect if they have taken place under conditions which differ from ordinary conditions in schools. The laboratory of the pedagogical psychologist is an even less suitable environment for experiments which can in any way be called representative. Verbatim records of mathematics classes are still exceptional achievements in didactical research.

My personal experience as a visitor in school classrooms shows two extremes: on the one hand an instruction that realizes to a high degree what I have called re-invention, on the other hand an authoritative instruction with passive listeners, such as I never knew as a schoolboy; even at university it was not often as bad as this. I must also confess that there was a very high positive correlation between the most pretentious modern mathematics and the most archaic pedagogics.

This can be due to chance. What is midway between the extremes is never as striking, and I believe there is a lot in between. As I explained earlier, instruction is probably better than its textbooks.

THE ORGANIZATION OF INSTRUCTION

To be sure, truly modern mathematics education is not possible unless instruction is organized in a radically different way. The method of re-invention cannot develop freely in the traditional classroom. It requires a laboratory, where students work individually, or rather in small groups while the teacher observes their activity in order to intervene if intervention is needed. In still another respect the classroom should be abolished: the teacher should not teach alone, but in a team of two or three where one observes the other, each learning from the other. This means combining classes, of equal or unequal age. Of course the laboratory work is to be complemented by a dialogue of larger size, where the teacher separates a larger group from the rest.

There are examples of instruction material which can be used in such instruction in place of textbooks. It would even be possible to give re-inventive instruction with books, and the germs of such an approach exist. There is, however, a still more advanced stage which is conceivable: programmed re-invention instruction.

In European countries today about 1% of the population work in education. The demand for education will certainly double in the next few decades, maybe even treble, and this will to a great extent happen in sectors where today the number of students per teacher is small. This means that with the present methods of instruction the number of workers in education would have to multiply by a factor five to ten. This indicates that our present methods are sure to fail. Instruction of higher age brackets by individual teachers will shortly be as outdated as handwritten books. This should be stressed to today's romantic and radical youth when they ask for more personalized instruction. In the same way as adult mathematicians have learned to accommodate the reading of literature to the liberty of re-invention, so we should teach this attitude to our adolescents, and the way to do it would be by programming re-invention in the learning process.

CHAPTER X

THE MATHEMATICS TEACHER

Wanted a swimming-teacher who can swim himself.
Advertisement in a French provincial newspaper.

Was sie gestern gelernt, das wollen sie heute schon lehren;
Ach, was haben die Herrn doch für ein kurzes Gedärm!*
Schiller

Whoever put the above advertisement in the paper obviously took it for granted that a swimming-teacher was able to teach swimming. For reasons unknown he even demanded that possible applicants should be able to put into practice what they were expected to teach others. Besides this the teacher could have been required to master rescue swimming, to be trained in first aid, to know something about the anatomy and physiology of arm and leg muscles, and to have studied history of swimming – I do not know what they teach swimming-teachers today.

From the memoirs of a successful American – I do not recall whether he became a professor or a millionaire or both – I remember an anecdote. Once as a young man when he had no money, he replied to an advertisement which asked for a teacher in the Czech language. Actually he did not know a single word of Czech himself but this was no problem. He took lessons himself for half the money and saw to it that as a student he always was one lesson ahead of himself as a teacher. It serves its purpose if the teacher masters one lesson more than the subject he is teaching. Schiller already knew and appreciated this as can be seen from the above quotation.

All are agreed on this point. The person who is teaching should know *more* than he is teaching, and he should know it not just at the moment when he has to teach it, but somewhat earlier. But how much should it be, this "more" and this "earlier"? There is no agreement on this

---

* What they learned yesterday, today they would teach;
  how short their digestion tract is!

point, neither among experts nor among laymen, neither within nor between the nations.

Not only in teacher training, but everywhere in instruction, this problem arises. A Papuan child learns from his parents exactly what he needs in life, in his own life that is not too much different from that of his parents. This is, in fact, the big difference between developed and developing countries, that our children and adolescents must learn so much more than they properly need. The excess can always be justified by the alleged formal value of the learned matter, and in mathematics it is justified as a discipline of mind, but let us not dwell on this point now.

What should the teacher know about the discipline he has to teach? The indispensable minimum is in any case what he has to teach himself. If this were the essential condition, a clever boy who passed the high school with high grades in French or mathematics could teach French or mathematics just like one of the people with short bowels, according to Schiller. I mean he could do so with regard to the subject matter, but of course in order to teach he should also know *how* to teach, though whatever this may be it is not taught properly at university.

It is more obvious in French than in mathematics that such a training is not even sufficient with respect to the subject matter. Just as a swimming-teacher is required to be able to swim so a French language teacher should be expected to be able to speak, read and write French. But these are capabilities that do not belong to the aims of language teaching at school and are not acknowledged by a high grade in French. For a modern language the limit of strict necessity is consequently much higher than that of the teaching matter. Fortunately we need not investigate at this moment how much should be added to this minimum, how much Sanscrit, Latin, historical grammar and literature.

For mathematics it is not as simple. A student who got a straight A in the final school examinations, may have acquired a much too modest vocabulary to be able to translate an unseen text as read in the classroom without a dictionary. But with such a grade in mathematics, a clear brain can tell whether an argument in school mathematics is valid or not, and can set problems to be solved and graded. Nevertheless just as long as there have been mathematics teacher exminations, candidates have been required to know more mathematics than they would have to teach afterwards. The "more" then indicated not only a gradual difference but even a qualitative distinction between school and higher mathematics. We mentioned this philosophy of two mathematics before, one a fairy tale version of the other. F. Klein coined the term of "double-forgetting", first forgetting school mathematics on going to university and then having to forget higher mathematics on going back to school as a teacher. After Klein, up to a few years ago, the gap continuously widened. For a long time school mathematics had hardly changed whereas at university some teachers even aspired to lead their students towards the ever-moving frontiers of research, before they return to school as teachers.

What is the use of this period of study at university, which is bracketed in between the first and the second forgetting? Of course, there are sound arguments why secondary schools should not be left to the mercy of "people with short bowel tracts". For good reasons we appreciate that there must be a certain interval between somebody learning mathematics in the classroom and teaching it to a class, and if this interval has to be filled somehow it is not too strange a demand that it be filled with a serious study of mathematics. Even on the ground of these presuppositions there is no way of telling how long this "bowel" period should be – 4 or 8 years. When the social ladder was narrower than it is now, stringent conditions for the ascent were perhaps of some use. The weight of examinations was, to a certain extent, determined by supply and demand.

Sometimes in spoken and written texts the most important part stands between brackets. Maybe the same applies to the university studies bracketed in the teacher's life. It should exert influence across the brackets. Does it matter then what the future teacher learns at university? Of course, it does. But what should be between the brackets? Or can we do away with them?

In the last few years efforts have been made to cement the breach of the "first forgetting" between school and university mathematics. Taking giant steps school mathematics should catch up on the backlog of a century. If it succeeds then in mathematics and its applications the step from the last school examination to the universtiy classroom should not be wider than that from one school grade to the next. Of course, quite a number of conditions must be fulfilled in order to guarantee success.

It is a striking feature of this reform that it gives us one important criterion that teacher training should satisfy: that the teacher should also be able to teach according to a programme that vastly differs from the programme that was in vogue when he went to school. The experience we have had in the Netherlands with background courses for further teacher training shows that the mathematical training of academic high schoolteachers in the past roughly fulfilled this criterion. This, however, can hardly be said of the initial training of the other secondary schoolteachers, and not at all of primary schoolteachers.

Obviously the criterion that every training must contain within itself the susceptibility for fast change, applies in our society not only to the training of mathematics teachers. According to American estimates I came across in a newspaper, a university graduate who leaves university now will serve in an average of five professions three of which do not as yet exist at present. (I cannot check whether this is true or whether I have remembered the data correctly.)

Why has the cementing of the breach between school and university mathematics been so long delayed? Why is something now being attempted which has been demanded as long ago as half a century or even longer? With the growing social importance of mathematics the need to bridge the gap has grown stronger. But mathematics itself also grew. Mathematics grew on all sides, not only away from school mathematics, but also towards school mathematics. Several times I pointed out that restructuring mathematics often means that by preference its most elementary ideas are questioned anew, and often these ideas lie precisely in that plane which today from a breakage plane between school and university mathematics readily transforms into a contact plane. The breach is being filled thanks to the growth of mathematics from both sides towards one another.

What exactly has changed since F. Klein's abortive attempts to heal the fracture becomes clear by an analysis of his *"Elementarmathematik, vom höheren Standpunkt"*. There are quite a few phenomena of elementary mathematics which can only be profoundly understood within the frame of theories which are not at all elementary. It was Klein's idea to provide a scientific background to the teacher's everyday classroom activity. Without a doubt this meant for a few a mitigation of the breach. But Klein's background was rather a Sunday landscape for the teacher to stroll in than side-wings to be moved into the classroom. The background, therefore, did not influence school mathematics. For instance

F. Klein expounded Galois theory as a background to solving quadratic and cubic equations at school, but Galois theory in fact hovered at too elevated a level above school mathematics. The *Erlanger Programm* could have had didactical effects provided the tendency of school mathematics entirely reverted, but as this was far from everybody's mind, the *Erlanger Programm* remained a background science.

Today anyone who would wish to resume Klein's attempt to teach "elementary mathematics from a higher vantage point" would have to do so on a much lower level, nearer school mathematics. Via abstract algebra such dry concepts as field and group have blossomed so as to impregnate school mathematics, to which they are so near that they can even be included in teaching; by the new turn to abstractness the examples by which the concepts are introduced and illustrated have grown so much simpler that applications as profound as Galois theory are not needed to create the higher scientific background. Characteristically ideas like axiomatics and domains like set theory were not even mentioned by Klein. That the most fundamental is close to the most elementary is an insight that needed half a century to mature.

While our understanding of the structure of mathematics has in that period improved so much that it can influence school mathematics, we can tackle the other question how mathematics is applied by crude empirical means only. There is no answer to this because nobody has ever considered the problem seriously. Therefore we can answer the question of how to teach mathematics to be applied only with much hesitation and many reservations.

On the ground of the preceding considerations I tried some time ago to formulate minimum demands for the mathematical training of the mathematics teachers such as I see it:

(1) that it enables the teacher to employ self-reliantly the fundamental methods of today's mathematics,

(2) that it provides the fundamental knowledge that is needed to understand the structure of today's mathematics,

(3) that it develops certain notions on how mathematics is applied,

(4) and that it gives a first look at how mathematicians do research.

Some explanations are perhaps useful. In points 1 and 2 I restricted myself to fundamentals. This means that I included non-fundamentals only as far as they lead to fundamentals or help to illustrate them. In point (1) I stressed self-reliance of the activity, while in point (2) I omitted this. I explained several times why point (3) is indispensable; I formulated this point in a way to avoid the training of the teacher as an applied mathematician. Point (3) obviously includes computer mathematics. I doubt whether point (3) can be realized by having the future teacher studying a minor subject; in any case training in the minor subject should be entrusted to those who have mastered the mathematics of the minor subject and do not try to eliminate it. I added point (4) to give the teachers not only a view on global organization of fields but to have them also participating therein. This could be realized by seminars.

This minimum programme is meant for mathematics teachers in all kinds of secondary education, with of course higher demands for the upper grades of secondary school. Teacher training based on such a programme would take less time than it does today. This need not be a loss. I do not support demagogic cries for shorter studies. Curriculum restriction would in any case not be an adequate means to bring about shorter studies. Students would simply study less in the same time, at least this is what would happen in my country. I would rather break with the present fiction that by the examination which opens the road to an academic career, the student has learned enough for a lifetime. I think his studies should be spread over a longer period: a short first training, complemented by regular repetitions that allow him to refresh his knowledge and to adapt it to new developments. I will come back to the character of such courses, which have become widespread in the last few years.

Up to now I have not accounted for the pedagogical training of the mathematics teacher. Obviously teaching also belongs to the activities people learn by doing, and obviously in pedagogics, too, it is no good staying on this bottom level. This implies that the first study at university can contribute only to a modest extent to pedagogical-didactical training. If, deviating from Comenius, we urge today that the theory should be re-invented (and therefore cannot precede practice) there is only a small amount of teaching theory left to be learned before a teacher starts teaching, namely to learn from one's own and others example to analyze the instruction one is attempting to give, is giving, and has been giving. The future teacher should learn the method of the thought-experiment and how to report on it. This prepares for the theoretical activity that in this profession should be connected to the practice of teaching. In my experience there are not many teachers who consider their own teaching and that of others as a matter for investigation; most of them are greatly surprised when told about such activities.

Besides professional literature, continued teacher training in many countries up to a few years ago was restricted to listening to casual lectures, mostly on the subject matter science though maybe discussion groups also existed here and there. Teachers initially participated in the innovation movement as listeners; perplexed or frightened they listened to revolutionary expositions of new subject matter; didactics though nearest to the teacher's heart was then hardly discussed. With new programmes pending in the near future the retraining of teachers had to be considered. This led in many countries to refresher courses. Designed as an emergency measure they will probably acquire a permanent status; I have just explained why such a dosage of teacher training is desirable in itself.

These courses showed great variations in character. Regarding the subject matter there were examples of both extremes: to teach the teacher precisely what he should teach himself within a few years – with the catastrophic consequence that he would teach exactly that – or to provide him with a background science, which he cannot apply in teaching. The method of such courses developed towards ever greater activity of their participants; it was not unusual if they took the form of seminars. There were, however, big national differences. There are countries or regions where seminars are impossible because "well-bred" people leave discussing to politicians.

I can go into more detail with regard to our own experience in the Netherlands. For a few years adaptation courses have been organized two weeks a year; these courses gravitated around practical exercises, that is in the activity of individual problem-solving. These courses were attended by half of all academic high schoolteachers; the great majority were able to participate actively in the practical exercises. On a lower level the other secondary teachers got evening courses; the results were satisfactory. For both groups didactical courses were organized. In these courses, too, one abstained from telling the teacher what and how they should teach. The task of these courses were group discussions on didactical experiences and analyses. When it appeared that the discussions were too vague on such an abstract basis, audio-video material about classroom teaching was prepared as a subject of discussion.

The big problem is still that of the primary schoolteacher (there are six years of primary school in our country). Since mathematics has been abolished as an obligatory subject in the training of the primary schoolteacher, it can happen that a teacher is allowed to teach arithmetic and mathematics in the primary school and in some cases beyond, even if the last insufficient mark he or she can boast of in mathematics was related to linear equations of one unknown and numerical applications of the Pythagorean theorem. The number of primary schoolteachers is about 50 times that of academic high schoolteachers. Though the problem of their retraining looks insoluble, we are going to launch a large-scale project to come to grips with the problem.

The above-mentioned adaptation courses were organized within the framework of modernizing mathematical education. In 1970 the Dutch Ministry of Education decided to raise development of subject matter and teacher retraining in mathematics to the status of a permanent institution.

CHAPTER XI

THE NUMBER CONCEPT – OBJECTIVE ACCESSES

His mathematics stemmed from Piaget, and his developmental psychology from Bourbaki. He did not like complete induction so he preferred complete intimidation.

From the biography of a didactician.

The singular "number concept" is misleading. There are many number concepts, both as regards content and form, from methodological, genetic, and didactic viewpoints.

Regarding content, there are natural numbers, integers, real numbers, and complex numbers. I passed over algebraic and transcendent numbers and it would not be too far-fetched to consider also the elements of certain other fields as numbers (e.g. finite or certain simple non-Archimedean fields). The sorts of numbers I mentioned are connected to each other by embeddings; adjunctions lead to larger, and restrictions to smaller systems.

The content of the number concept will be dealt with throughout the following chapters, and this means that it will be done fairly unsystematically, with the formal elements as their natural companions. Here we will approach the number concept more systematically with respect to its methodology, that is, we will discuss the question of its accesses. How do numbers emerge, and how are their domains and and operations extended and restricted? The genetic aspect can hardly be neglected here, but we will try to put the individual development of the number concept within brackets to reserve it and its didactical implications for the next chapter.

A rough distinction of the accesses to the number concept would be: counting number, numerosity number, measuring number, and reckoning number. I shall briefly indicate what I mean by these terms.

Counting number. To begin with, this is the reeling off in time of the sequence of natural numbers, the first steps of which are as arduous for children as learning the names of colours and letters, until they suddenly grasp the whole unlimitedly continuing sequence – a conceptual seizure that has no analogue in learning the names of colours and letters. The counting number becomes the irreplaceable object of the calculating activity. Soon the need is felt to count back into the past, that is, by negative numbers. The counting number, mathematically called the *ordinal number*, is formalized in the complete induction, and further in the Peano axioms, its apotheosis are the transfinite ordinals.

Numerosity number. Perhaps the numerosity number is genetically earlier than the counting number. Animals recognize small numerosities though they certainly cannot count. The child, however, learns to count so early on that initially it does not notice that counting can serve to determine the numerosity of a set. At the same time, however, as anybody can easily verify, it identifies small numerosities independently of counting, in particular if they are arranged according to distinct patterns. The numerosity number is formalized by the potency or cardinality of sets; its apotheosis is the infinite cardinals.

Measuring number. If a magnitude is measured, it is exhausted or tried to be exhausted by means of copies of a unit, like a vessel is emptied with a scoop. As in weighing or handling money multiples of the unit can assist in the measuring process. As on a ruler copies of the unit can be marked in advance, but a linear arrangement is not essential for measuring; an area can be exhausted in varying order by area units.

Incomplete exhaustion leads to division with the remainder on the one hand, and if the unit is divided, to fractions on the other. The measuring number is formalized in the field of rationals from which by infinitary processes the real numbers are obtained. A counterpart of the magnitudes that can be measured by each other is found in the non-Archimedean fields.

Reckoning number. This is the algorithmic aspect. The number is operationally comprehended, by the rules according to which the user plays with it. It is formalized in the axiomatic approach. The numbers appear as elements of rings and fields that are axiomatically fixed.

Linguistic forms like "seven times", "one-seventh" conceal more refined approaches to numbers; they will be fitted into the above rough pattern.

COUNTING NUMBER

The number sequence is the foundation-stone of mathematics, historically, genetically, and systematically. Without the number sequence there is no mathematics. If some modern mathematical texts suggest another view, the reason is that their authors misinterpreted mathematics. Even little children are better informed than they are. Counting soon becomes a theoretical need. The child soon counts further than its practical need for counting implies. Primitive peoples often lack words for numbers but never signs and symbols to express numbers. Language families have in common the number-words up to 10, the structure of the multiples of ten, the words for 100, while at 1000 they branch off. Could the ancestors of these families not count further? Cunning or intelligent people maybe invented more number names but they did not broadcast them. Was there then actually any need for new designations for yet higher powers of ten? Maybe if numbers had to be written such a need would have existed, but not if numbers were objects of calculation on the abacus. To climb to even higher powers, columns could be added to the abacus, though they needed no names. With the written decimal position system this became still more obvious. The spoken and written number words up to 20 are in most languages irregular. Just the start of the number sequence causes unnecessary trouble to the learner. On the abacus and with ciphers it is much more regular. It is a simple principle, the positional system: if a 1 is added to a 9, a 0 arises and a 1 is added to the next position.

From olden times it has been a rule to teach the first grade the numbers up to 20, the second up to 100, the third the unlimited number sequence – or something like this. But the child grasps unlimited counting as early as the first grade, and this is a great event. This is how it happened in a Montessori school, in a kindergarten: At a certain stage children are told to write numbers below each other on a long wound-up tape: 1, 2, ..., 10, 11, ... Maybe after 19 the teacher has to help, perhaps again after 29, while maybe after 39 no help is needed, until perhaps when 99 is reached the child again asks for help. The girl of my story was deeply absorbed in that activity. New pieces were continually been stuck on the ever-lengthening tape. On the third day she passed 1000. At 1024 she obstinately refused to go further. "So it goes on", she said, "does it not?" The game was over, at least I mean *this* game was over. In an old-style school the teacher would have said: "Be good and count even further, up to 2000." Fortunately her teacher knew new games to play. I do not

THE NUMBER CONCEPT – OBJECTIVE ACCESSES

know which ones. Perhaps counting by twos, or threes or by triangular numbers, or by squares. Or – I do not know. Because – so it goes on – up to the power series, well ordering types, and recursive functions.

The number sequence belongs to mathematics, and therefore some people call mathematics what the little girl was doing, namely writing down the number sequence. I have already explained why I do not use this terminology. But whatever you think about it, the exclamation "so it goes on" *is* mathematics, it is the first mathematics mankind produced and individuals are producing. It is great and important mathematics, it is first and last mathematics; it is the loftiest and the most profound mathematics. Is it ridiculous to stress it? There are people who do not know this – that is my excuse.

The girl was disappointed when she became aware that "so it went on". The observer was perhaps too enthusiastic about the child's discovery. He ought to have asked her what in fact was going on. It is not, indeed, the number sequence the going on of which is being proved on the tape, though it looks like it, but it is rather the number notation. Suddenly there are principles available to write down all numbers. There are very few principles: 0 followed by 1, 1 followed by 2, and so on, 9 followed by 0, with a transfer to the left. It is so simple that it can be taught both to children and to machines. The positional notation is a simple model of the abstract mechanism of the number sequence.

Would the girl have been able to formulate the principles? I doubt it, and in this respect she was not yet mature enough for mathematics. But even to handle such principles and to have grasped their illimited applicability is a noteworthy performance. The child has discovered infinity, which is the alpha and omega of mathematics.

Counting is soon followed by the most elementary arithmetic. Adding is counting continued, subtracting is counting back. This is a fundamental principle of old didactics. It is a sound principle inspired by the counting number aspect though it is badly neglected by the didacticians of the new mathematics. Of course, counting should not be a dull chore. If on the abacus the child adds 3 to 6 old-style schoolmasters saw to it that the child did not count the 6 anew but that he counted further with 3 steps: plus 1 makes 7, plus 1 makes 8, plus 1 makes 9. Further counting and backward counting as well as other kinds of systematic counting such as counting by twos, threes, and so on, filling up tens, and so on, have been intensely exercised in traditional arithmetic; it can be nicely connected to working on the number line, which will be dealt with later. It prepares mental arithmetic with imagined further and backward counting rather than that concretely represented, and it prepares the path to the algorithmization of counting and written arithmetic.

Besides this, pure counting remains an activity, not only if marbles, years, street-lamps, railway-carriages are counted where the counting number yields a cardinal number, but also counting that is just a rhythmic activity in time, such as counting out "who is it" or counting to mark a time period in a game of hide-and-seek. Seats, houses, and telephone numbers are numbered in order, and to operate this system one must know its principles. The knowledge "so it goes on" is operative in the whole of arithmetic instruction, in all the rules one learns, and in infinite decimal fractions. Whether it is an infinity of time or space, it is grasped according to the principle "so it goes on" of the number sequence. $\sqrt{2}$ is computed up to a certain decimal, and then three dots are set as a sign of the unlimited continuability. Infinite series and limit signs enter, to the circle is inscribed an infinite sequence of polygons with an unlimited number of sides. Do not forget that in this stage all infinite processes, from the generation of the number sequence to the convergence of infinite function series, are imagined as reeling off in time. It is the same, as we will see, with continuous changes.

It is also the same if the Pascal triangle is built up following to the prescription that every row starts and finishes with a 1, and that every later place bears the sum of the numbers left and right above this place

$$\begin{array}{ccccccccccc}
& & & & & 1 & & & & & \\
& & & & 1 & & 1 & & & & \\
& & & 1 & & 2 & & 1 & & & \\
& & 1 & & 3 & & 3 & & 1 & & \\
& 1 & & 4 & & 6 & & 4 & & 1 & \\
1 & & 5 & & 10 & & 10 & & 5 & & 1 \\
\end{array}$$

$$\cdot \ \cdot \ \cdot \ \cdot \ \cdot \ \cdot \ \cdot \ \cdot \ \cdot \ \cdot \ \cdot \ \cdot$$

The dots in the last row mean an "and so on" that is obvious to everybody. Indeed, so it goes on. There is, in fact, a closed formula; on the k-th place in the n-th row from above, counting from 0 on in every row, the number is $\binom{n}{k}$, a binomial coefficient. It is easily proved that

$$(*) \qquad \binom{n}{k} = \frac{n!}{k!(n-k)!},$$

which is indeed a closed expression, that is to say, a ready-made one. Or is it? What does $n!$ mean, what $k!$, the factorials? It is

$$n! = 1 \cdot 2 \cdot \ldots \cdot n,$$

and likewise $k!$ Again the three dots which should be, and are, understood by the reader as "and so on". It is not a closed form. Again it is a product to be formed in a temporal run-off.

Can we not eliminate this definition process projected into time? Yes, we can.

DEFINITION: $0! = 1$, and whenever $n!$ is already defined, then

$$(n+1)! = (n+1) \cdot n!$$

Did we succeed? No, besides the monstrous "is defined" within a definition, it hurts that "whenever" still suggests a time process. It would look more neutral so:

DEFINITION: $0! = 1 \wedge \bigwedge_{n \in \mathbb{N}} (n+1)! = (n+1) \cdot n!$.

This suffices. '$\wedge$' is the strict neutral logical 'all'. Now, indeed, $n!$ is defined in one blow. I mean, logically, not for the calculator who, to compute $1000!$, should again perform the calculations as a process in time.

We are discussing the recursion or the principle of complete induction, which serve to encapsulate infinite processes; it is the milkmaid on the cocoa-tin with an image of the same cocoa-tin in her hand. It is the seizure of infinity by induction, as formulated by Zeno at the end of one of his paradoxes of plurality: "It is the same to say it once or again and again."

We were led in a natural way to the definition by means of complete induction. It happened when we asked for the meaning of $n!$ But the Pascal triangle itself is defined by complete induction, namely

$$(**) \qquad \binom{n}{0} = 1, \quad \binom{n+1}{k+1} = \binom{n}{k} + \binom{n}{k+1}.$$

To connect the definition (*) of $\binom{n}{k}$ to the formula (**), that is to prove (*), complete induction must again be applied in the proof.

Complete induction, however, starts earlier; everything done with natural numbers, if it is to hold for all of them, needs complete induction. For instance, to define addition and multiplication, one first defines the addition of 1 by urging that for every $n \in \mathbb{N}$ by $1 + n$ is meant its successor in the number sequence, and then one sets

$$0 + a = a \land \bigwedge_n [(1 + n) + a = 1 + (n + a)],$$
$$0 \cdot a = 0 \land \bigwedge_n (1 + n) \cdot a = a + na,$$

which then defines addition and multiplication throughout all $\mathbb{N}$. The laws of associativity, commutativity, distributivity, etc., of the operations can now be proved, again by induction. If in the above definition of addition and multiplication the process in time is restored, it reads

$0 + a = a$ and whenever $n + a$ is already defined,
put $(1 + n) + a = 1 + (n + a)$,
$\quad\quad 0 \cdot a = 0$ and whenever $n \cdot a$ is already defined,
put $(1 + n) a = a + na$.

It is an astonishing feature of this definition of addition and multiplication that it exactly reflects what the teacher tells the pupil when he is teaching arithmetic: $6 + 1 = 7$, $6 + 2$ is 1 more, that is 8, $6 + 3$ is still 1 more, that is 9, and so on. Multiplication is still more convincing: $1 \cdot 3 = 3$, $2 \cdot 3$ is 3 more, thus 6, $3 \cdot 3$ is again 3 more, thus 9, and so on. Addition is counting further by induction, and multiplication counting further in intervals by induction. In the principle of complete induction the "and so on" is formalized, infinity is tamed, caught in a small space as on the cocoa-tin.

The principle of complete induction was mentioned here, but has not yet been formulated. The classical formulation reads:

$\mathscr{P}$: Let E be a property of natural numbers.* Suppose

$$E(0) \land \bigwedge_{n \in \mathbb{N}} (E(n) \to E(1 + n)).$$

Then

$$\bigwedge_{n \in \mathbb{N}} E(n).$$

That is, 0 should have the property E, and as soon as the natural number n has the property E, then its successor $1 + n$, too, should have

---

* Originally natural numbers were considered to start with 1; now people like to include 0 in the natural numbers.

the property E. Under this condition, the principle affirms, E is true for all natural numbers.

This, then, is applied to all kind of properties E. For instance it is applied to the statement (*) if it should be proved that it is true for all natural numbers n. We applied complete induction in defining, too. This has to be done carefully. "$n + a$ is defined" cannot be properly considered as a property of n. An involved reformulation is required to meet this criticism, but we abstain from tackling this here.

The principle of complete induction can alternatively be expressed, if E is replaced by the set M of those elements of $\mathbf{N}$ that share the property E. Then it reads

$\mathscr{P}'$: Let $M \subset \mathbf{N}$. Let $0 \in M$ and $\bigwedge_{n \in \mathbf{N}} (n \in M) \to (1 + n \in M)$.
Then $M = \mathbf{N}$.

How do we know that $\mathscr{P}$ (or $\mathscr{P}'$) is true? This is a silly question. Indeed $0 \in M$, whence $1 = 1 + 0 \in M$, whence $2 = 1 + 1 \in M$, whence $3 = 1 + 2 \in M$ and so on. That is, to prove $\mathscr{P}'$, the can must be opened and the all-quantifier must be replaced by the induction in time, and by the "and so on".

This is one way. The other way is to tell that $\mathscr{P}'$ is an axiom, and that $\mathbf{N}$ is characterized by $\mathscr{P}'$. More precisely, it is done as follows:

$\mathscr{P}''$: Let $\mathbf{N}$ be a set with an element 0 and a mapping f into itself (fx being called the successor of x) such that:

f is one-to-one,
$f\mathbf{N} = \mathbf{N} \backslash \{0\}$

(that is, every element of $\mathbf{N}$ has one successor, and every element has one precursor, except 0, which has none),

$$(0 \in M \subset \mathbf{N} \wedge fM \subset M) \to (M = \mathbf{N})$$

(that is if 0 belongs to M and of every element of M the successor belongs to M, then M exhausts $\mathbf{N}$).

The last is, as it were, a minimality property: no true subset of $\mathbf{N}$ has the property that 0 is in it and with any element its successor. This requirement is indispensable. If, for instance, after $\mathbf{N}$ is placed a copy of $\mathbf{Z}$, thus

$$0, 1, 2, ..., ..., -3', -2', -1', 0', 1', 2', ...,$$

then you get a set K with a one-to-one successor function f, such that

$fK = K\backslash\{0\}$, though it possesses a true subset (namely **N**) that already has the same properties.

What we have exhibited here is essentially Peano's axiomatization of the sequence of natural numbers. From the most primitive number concept, which does not yet include infinity, to naive counting, to naive acting out of complete induction, to its conscious cognition, to its formalizing, and finally to its axiomatic embedding in set theory, ever more sophisticated number concepts have emerged. Without asserting that they just correspond to levels in the learning process, it is not far-fetched to wonder about dogmatists who believe they can teach mathematics on one level of the number concept. In fact, there are even more shades of the concept of counting number than I have just mentioned. In Peano's axiomatic system an arbitrary subset (M) occurred (in the original formulation it was an arbitrary property). This is not as harmless as it looks and as naive set theory would make you believe. Foundationalists therefore investigated how far weaker formulations than $\mathscr{P}''$ lead. It is their general idea not to admit arbitrary subsets M but only such that have been produced in a well-determined retraceable way, for instance, by addition and multiplication; addition and multiplication then are defined inductively, and induction is only applied in the frame of this definition. I mention it only to illustrate the rich variety in the spectrum of the number concept. This richness makes a certain relativism recommendable.

To believe that by complete induction and Peano's axioms infinity has been encapsulated is nothing but pious self-delusion. Encapsulated infinity is not really tamed, it fights back. As Gödel has shown, it can never completely describe free infinity unravelling in time. Peano's axiomatic system and any axiomatic system whatsoever that admits defining natural numbers, also admits, besides the ordinary model, so-called non-standard models; it is incomplete in principle.

Moreover, in every practical use of mathematics the encapsulated infinity must be pulled out of its capsule. Infinite processes by which some result should be obtained, or something is to be calculated, should again be performed in time, and step by step, and even the time needed for every single step should be estimated.

Several times I stressed that there is more than one level of rigour. In teaching and in research the counting number concept presents itself on various levels to be applied on each with the rigour that corresponds to it. There can be little doubt that most often this will be the number concept of freely developing, non-encapsulated infinity, with or without explicit use of complete induction. This I would like to stress, not because in present-day education the counting number is implemented at too high a level, but on the contrary, because people are prone to disregard it. I will return to this point.

NUMEROSITY NUMBER

The number of elements of a set is usually obtained by counting, but this need not be the only way. Can the concept of number of elements of a set not be found independently of counting? The numerosity number is, indeed, mathematically formalized as potency or cardinal.

The potencies of sets were G. Cantor's discovery. Two sets are called equipotent if they can be mapped one-to-one on each other. The set of fingers of the left hand is equipotent to that of the right hand: the mapping is performed by matching the hands to each other. The set of integers is equipotent with that of even numbers: map n on $2n$. Non-equipotent sets can also be compared with each other. A is called more potent than B if B can be mapped one-to-one into A though not conversely.

To Cantor the potency or cardinal of a set was that which is common to that set and all its equipotent sets.* Today it is more usual to say that the potency of A is the class of all sets equipotent with A. What matters is that under the viewpoint of potency equipotent sets are not essentially different.

Potencies α and β can be compared as to magnitude: $\alpha > \beta$ if a set of potency α is more potent than a set of potency β (according to the earlier definition of more and less potent). Potencies α and β can be added and multiplied. Take a set A of potency α and a set B of potency β. To form $\alpha + \beta$, arrange that A and B are disjoint; then $\alpha + \beta$ is the potency of $A \cup B$. Further, $\alpha\beta$ is the potency of $\ulcorner A, B \urcorner$, that is of the set of ordered pairs $\ulcorner a, b \urcorner$ with $a \in A$ and $b \in B$. Even α^β can be defined; it is the potency of the set of mappings of B into A. In any case it should be verified that these are decent definitions, that is, that the validity of

---

* Actually Cantor's definition is even more vague than this.

$\alpha > \beta$, and the values of $\alpha + \beta$, $\alpha\beta$, α^β do not depend on the choices of A as a set of potency α, and B as a set of potency β.

Infinite sets have the noteworthy property that they can be equipotent with proper subsets. This phenomenon disturbed mathematicians before Cantor. It prevented many from considering infinite sets as ready-made, closed subjects.

This property can be used to define what should be a finite set: a set that is equipotent with no proper subset. This includes the void set, with the potency called 0; every set with one element – potency called 1; every set with two elements – potency called 2; and so on. Sum, product, and the power of potencies such as defined in general yield the usual definitions in the case of finite sets: if A and B have m and n elements, then the union $A \cup B$ (if they are disjoint) has $m + n$, the ordered pairs set $\ulcorner A, B \urcorner$ has $m \cdot n$, and there are m^n mappings from B into A because such a mapping is determined if for each of the n elements of B one of the m possibilities of elements of A is chosen. Likewise in the finite case the comparison of potencies boils down to the usual one of natural numbers according to order. Moreover the different laws (commutativity, associativity, and distributivity) are rather obvious.

Is this not wonderfully simple and convincing? Compare it with the traditional concept and introduction of the counting number as shown above. There it starts piece by piece with *ad hoc*-invented number words, an artificial and even a foggy system. The question "how much?" is answered there by counting the elements of the given set. To compare two sets, one must count both of them; if they yield the same number, they are equipotent, and if counting finishes earlier with A than B, then A is less potent than B. Is it not an unnecessary complication? Are not the essentials obscured by the introduction of the number sequence whereas from the viewpoint of potency sets are compared directly, and the natural numbers are defined *ab ovo*. Moreover sum and product now emerge easily and in one stroke, whereas with the counting they are obtained by the troublesome procedure of counting further. And finally, if natural numbers are defined as potencies, children can be given a clear piece of deductive mathematics at an early stage. With the counting number, however, one must wait for the complete induction, which is a rather advanced study, to offer a deductive treatment of the number concept.

It is obvious that this is the way it should be done at school: introducing the numbers as potencies, that is, having children operating with the numbers as if it were potencies.when they begin at school, they know the number as counting number, that is, they can recite the number sequence like a verse without knowing what numbers mean. The number as measure of numerosity then is an excellent mean of restructuring childrens' minds. Pedagogues have never liked counting. On a higher level the children can become acquainted with the mathematical theory on which this didactics rests, that is with a conscious construction of natural numbers as potencies of finite sets.

Is it not wonderful what can be done thanks to Cantor, and how mathematics can be renewed according to Cantor's ideas? No, it is not. I have been pulling my reader's legs. But in doing so I am in good company, and so are the readers who are being fooled. How a wave of mystification has descended upon mathematical didactics is shown by the present textbook literature-arithmetic books under the influence of potencies, textbooks on a higher level where the theory of natural number seems to be developed rigorously from potencies. I will now show that: —

(1) the opinion that the numerosity number, that is the potency, suffices as a foundation of natural numbers, is mathematically wrong – at least if mathematics is understood in the usual sense,

(2) the numerosity aspect of natural numbers is irrelevant if compared with the counting aspect,

(3) the numerosity aspect is insufficient for the didactics of natural numbers.

NUMEROSITY NUMBER – MATHEMATICALLY INSUFFICIENT

Maybe the reader noticed in my exposition of the potency of finite sets that after the potency 2 I did not continue but just said "and so on". I took French leave. Of course I could have continued up to 3,426,789 or could have at least mentioned such a number (as happens in some textbooks). In principle this would not have made any difference. If the natural numbers should be subordinated to the general potency concept, one is obliged to define what the finite potencies are. The way it is done is to define 0, 1, 2 and maybe a few more. Of course this is not enough; somehow you should catch hold of all finite potencies. Why, this is done by saying "and so on", and everybody knows what it means: by adding a new element to a set of n elements, it is understood that I get one of $1 + n$. It is a reasonable and entirely acceptable definition that, indeed, yields the finite potencies. But it is a pity that the whole procedure can only be applied if the natural numbers are already available. Since N is supposed to be fully known, the definition of what potency n is can be stated even simpler:

$$\{1, ..., n\}$$

is a finite set, namely of potency n. The set N itself becomes a representative of the countably infinite potency.

Well, one could say: we, indeed, use N, but we do so only to define what a finite potency is, what sets of potencies 0, 1, 2, ... are. The only thing we rely on is the number sequence N with no more profound relations in it, no operations as addition and multiplication; these operations are independently defined as operations on potencies. It may look promising, but it is dead wrong. To conjure up from N the finite sets and their properties, the most profound that can be told about N is needed: complete induction.

First one must show that every $n \in N$ uniquely represents a potency, that is

if $\{1, ..., m\}$ is equipotent with $\{1, ..., n\}$

then necessarily $m = n$. Try to prove it. You cannot do it without complete induction. In textbooks that stress the numerosity aspect of numbers, it is either tacitly assumed, or explititly suggested to the student to be true, or quasi-proved by "and so on" methods.

This, however, is only the beginning. Potencies must be added, multiplied, powers of potencies must be formed, and in any case it should be proved that the union of two finite sets is finite, that the pairs set of two finite sets is finite, and that the mappings of a finite set into a finite set from a finite set. Textbooks that stress the cardinal aspect often show gaps at this point; the need to prove such propositions is not even mentioned, while others do it with casual "and so on" methods. To prove really these facts, complete induction is indispensable.

It is as bad with the usual proofs that the countable potency is the smallest infinite potency, that is, that any infinite set contains a countably infinite one. It would be conceivable to introduce the finite potencies one after the other without formulating any general principle. Yet if a countably infinite set shall be counted out of a given infinite set M, one needs the totality of $\mathbf{N}$. There is no way of avoiding it; even an "and so on" does not suffice:

Let M be the given set. Either it is void, and then its potency is 0, or it has an element, say a_1. Either $M = \{a_1\}$, then its potency is 1, or M is properly larger and has an element a_2, $\neq a_1$. Either $M = \{a_1, a_2\}$, and then M is of potency 2, or M is larger and has an element a_3, $\neq a_1$, $\neq a_2$, and so on.

This is absolutely rigorous, I think, on the level on which it is formulated. With a naive concept of $\mathbf{N}$ that has not yet been formalized by complete induction it is entirely acceptable. It ceases to be so as soon as it is mixed up with the pretension that $\mathbf{N}$ can be defined in the frame of pure potencies. It is inacceptable if around sets and potencies a formal apparatus is developed, with axioms of set theory and many other rites and if the only procedure that, as it were, screams for formalization or at least explanation is again and again stepped over with the comfortable phrase "and so on".

Counting a countably infinite set out of a given infinite set M as it has been shown here, really happens in time; spinning off $\mathbf{N}$ as a temporal activity is indispensable in this context. Even complete induction does not suffice to eliminate it. Complete induction applies to the construction of a sequence $\{a_n\}$ if by some recipe to every element of the sequence the next is given. To get encapsulated rather than free infinity here, more is needed, namely explicitly the principle of choice or one of its equivalents. The principle of choice allows, in particular, to find to every finite subset X of M an element $x \in M \backslash X$, or more precisely, it postulates a mapping f of the set of finite subsets of M into M, such that $fX \in M \backslash X$. After this the path is free for induction: It is defined $A_0 = \bigcirc$ and $A_{1+n} = A_n \cup \{fA_n\}$ to finally get $A = \bigcup_{n=1}^{\infty} A_n$ as a countably infinite subset of M. Now the construction of A is encapsulated, of course, with the use of complete induction.

Can complete induction be thrown out here, can finite potencies be defined independently of complete induction in $\mathbf{N}$? I mentioned the characteristic property of finite sets that they are not equipotent with any proper subset. In fact, Dedekind departed from this property to define finiteness of sets; in this context sets are infinite if they are equipotent with certain proper subsets. So being infinite implies the existence of a one-to-one mapping φ of M into itself such that $\varphi M \neq M$. With such a φ a countably infinite subset of M can be constructed without the principle of choice, namely by $a_0 = M \backslash \varphi (M)$ and $a_{n+1} = \varphi a_n$, or, if infinity should be encapsulated, as the smallest set that contains a_0 and with any x also φx.

The difficulty is now shifted to the sets that are finite in the sense of Dedekind. It is easily seen that the finite sets in the usual sense are Dedekind finite. To prove the converse that any set M which is equipotent to no proper subset is equipotent with a piece of $\mathbf{N}$, one needs either counting a countable subset out of M in a temporal process, or again the principle of choice.

Moreover in the Dedekind approach, to get a countable infinite set such as $\mathbf{N}$, it is indispensable to have some infinite set available, and a closer look at how Dedekind gets such a set shows that it boils down to assuming $\mathbf{N}$ itself.

Russell and Whitehead proceeded in approximately the same way. They defined the finite potencies inductively and produced at the same time $\mathbf{N}$: 0 is the potency of the void set, and if m is the potency of M, then $1 + m$ is that of $M \cup \{c\}$ with $c \notin M$. The smallest set containing 0 and with x also $1 + x$ is, by definition, $\mathbf{N}$. They could not avoid a postulate of the existence of infinite sets, either.

This is the moral of the matter, and its reason is clear. We can indeed imagine a set theory with finite sets only; all customary operations with sets can be performed in this domain. In a mathematics built on such a theory every single natural number can be defined, but since there is no set of natural numbers in this mathematics, no theorem on all natural numbers can be stated in it, and no operation with natural numbers can be generally defined in it. It is very primitive mathematics if it can be called mathematics at all, remaining on a level where infinity has not yet emerged.

In some of the textbooks alluded to it is stressed that $\mathbf{N}$ should be a set, or it is even formulated as an axiom. This, however, is not sufficient for building mathematics. One also should know that every countable sequence $\{a_n\}$ generates a set.

Still other complications can be noticed in textbooks stressing the numerosity aspect of number; for simplicity's sake I did not mention them till now. Today the potency

$\#(M)$ of M is defined as the class of sets equipotent with M. I said that this is a class to be as careful with as with the set of all sets, which easily can lead us astray into all kinds of paradoxes. This danger can be avoided though there is something to say for a policy that avoids these classes as such. With an artifice due to J. von Neumann (used by him for the types of well-ordered sets) it can be done as follows:

To every potency of sets a standard set of that potency is chosen and potency of M is by definition the standard set equipotent with M. Thus $\#(M)$ is a set itself, and in particular in the case of a set M consisting of n elements, it can be arranged that

$$n = \#(M) = \{0, 1, 2, ..., n-1\},$$

where $0, 1, 2, ..., n-1$ are themselves potencies. To reach this goal, one puts by definition

$$\#(M) = \text{set of potencies } \#X, \text{ such that } X \text{ is less potent than } M.$$

Though it looks like it this is not circular. The defining conditions contain not the notion of potency but of comparing potencies, that is of X being less potent than M. (The definition works for finite M, as it were inductively. It still holds for countable M but from $\aleph_1$ the next potency beyond the countable, it fails because the set of potencies below $\aleph_1$ is countable. If there are higher potencies which the definition fits, they must be very high; it is not known whether they exist.)

I put the last two sentences between brackets. I mentioned this whole idea because in some school texts for 11–12 year-olds I had noticed what seems to be an intention to introduce finite potencies by this artifice of von Neumann's. If this was meant, and I cannot tell what else it could be, they erred. In the above definition they wrote one '$\#$' too much, namely

$$\#(M) = \#(\text{set of potencies } \#X, \text{ such that } X \text{ is less potent than } M),$$

and this makes the artifice useless and in effect blows up the whole project.

I would be glad to apologize for plunging the reader of a didactical exposition into such profound set theory. It is not however my fault. The textbooks whose methods I have analyzed here are not the first I took from the shelf; on the contrary, they belong to the choicest that have ever existed in textbook literature. If I claim that the method they advocate is wrong I have to argue it in detail. I add, however, that it is a minor point in my argument that their method is wrong. The main point is that as educators, the authors of these books are aiming much too high with their mathematical methods. If ever proof was needed that this kind of set theory and of introducing natural numbers is not suitable for school (except perhaps in the highest grade), then it has been proved by these textbooks, which are themselves much superior to many others.

Readers of these textbooks are left with the idea that natural numbers have been introduced as potencies, which is simply not true. They will not notice that essential theorems have been tacitly assumed and proofs have been omitted, or formulated with a casual "and so on". This is not the way to create a proper understanding of mathematics. Everything that is essential in natural numbers, complete induction, is obscured. I admit that complete induction may be too difficult for children of a certain age, but this is no reason to impose on them a quite illusive theory.

It has allegedly been proved that set theory, though by tradition notoriously difficult, can be taught even to little children. I earlier gave my opinion about such statements in general, and I will specify later what on a much lower level is often taught as set theory to youngsters. Here we are confronted with such a pretentious example. The reader, even if he has only superficially read the preceding argument must have noticed that set theory is not so simple, and that even on the level that people would like to consider as suitable for school, there are sophisticated questions and stumbling blocks which would even be obstacles for excellent mathematicians. They are not at all far-fetched, that is, I did not fetch them. I only analyzed what is being offered to 11–12 year-olds as foundations of natural numbers, and I frankly confess that before starting this analysis even my own ideas on this subject were not too clear and distinct. Things are not as easy, and I would advise anybody who could not follow my exposition or, rather, could not think it anew, not to teach this subject matter. The pupils would not lose anything, and the teacher would not either. A matter that has been proven to cause enormous difficulties to expert mathematicians cannot but uncritically be re-echoed by pupils with no mathematical experience. I do not say that it would be too difficult to attain this; pupils are most cooperative if it is rewarded by a high mark. What, however, should a teacher do with such a subject matter? If he is so uncritical as to accept it from the textbook writer, then maybe he can teach it, though he should not. If he is critical enough, then he could teach it, too, but he would not.

How is it possible that such subject matter could ever find its way into school teaching? I imagine that the authors of these textbooks, like everybody else, were hypnotized by the numerosity aspect of natural number; maybe they were also influenced by Piaget, who conducted investigations on the numerosity aspect of natural number, which we will inspect more closely later. But unlike Piaget they should have known as mathematicians that the numerosity aspect does not suffice for natural number to be founded on it, and certainly they knew it before they even started. What they probably did not realize was that the numerosity aspect yields so little, and that the gaps would be so large. When these appeared it was too late. The system was designed, and a system it had to be. At university we take the liberty of delaying the teaching of a formal theory of natural number; we are not slaves of the system. They tried to do better than the universities. "If you build a house, you have to start with the foundations" – some remonstrated at my objections to their faith in the system. I answered: "No, if you are going to build a house, you start on paper, and you do not work out the foundations until you know how high the building is going to be."

What is actually possible at school? I mean not just with 11–12 year-olds? Equipotencies and potency comparison, I daresay, are quite simple things. As examples finite and countably finite sets are acceptable provided it is made absolutely clear that the natural numbers and N are admitted as given concepts and provided they are not falsely represented as being founded on set theory. I am not able to say how old a pupil must be to understand that

$$\#\{1, ..., m\} \neq \#\{1, ..., n\} \quad \text{for } m \neq n$$

needs a proof, and which age he must be to understand such a proof; the authors of those textbooks did not investigate it either. With regard to the necessity and possibility of a proof for the finiteness of the union and the product of two finite sets I am utterly sceptical, since its necessity had even escaped the notice of textbook authors. The sum and product of natural numbers are algorithmically experienced by young pupils, and such experience should first be questioned in order to grasp whether it might be a problem. But let us assume that the teacher succeeds in convincing the pupil that proofs are needed here. How can he prove such facts? I suppose by a "and so on". If this is the case, it should be honestly admitted that this is unsatisfactory, because amidst a flood of formalizing, the one thing that is really essential has not been touched by formalization.

I see much more perspective in founding the natural numbers and the operations with them on the counting number by complete induction, which need not include Peano's axioms or even explicit formulation of complete induction. This is an honest, neat, exemplary and pregnant method; moreover, as we noticed, the inductive definition of addition and multiplication are close to that of elementary arithmetics. Such a founding of natural number as counting number is a possibility, which does not mean that it is a necessity. The other way, I think, has now convincingly been demonstrated to be impossible.

NUMEROSITY NUMBER – MATHEMATICALLY UNIMPORTANT

Though the numerosity aspect is not sufficient to describe natural number, it looks so simple and important that it is to be wondered at why mathematics had to wait till Cantor discovered it.

In fact, it is distorting Cantor's image to stress his achievement at this point. His achievement was rather than interpreting natural numbers and their operations in this way, he dared to apply this interpretation, which was natural for numbers, on infinite sets. Those who are anxious to avoid infinite sets in teaching and restrict the potency concept to finite sets, should remember this. The potency concept does not become pregnant until it is applied to infinite sets. The learner is fooled if on the one hand potencies are introduced formally while on the other hand it is played as though all sets were finite.

We have not yet answered why the numerosity aspect of natural number was discovered so late on in history. It is dead simple: because up to Cantor's era it had been entirely irrelevant. To this explanation may be added that it remained so even after Cantor for the greater part of mathematics. Numerosity number is an utterly primitive number concept that in human history was soon superseded by more refined ones, and this is what repeats itself, as we shall see, in the individual's development. Some animals possess, at least small, numerosity numbers, some birds know how many eggs they have in their nest. Beyond this, man possesses rather early on another number concept: he can count.

There is an old problem: are there two persons with the same number of hairs on their heads? The answer is: yes, there are millions of people, and the hairiest certainly has not more than a million hairs. So the mapping that assigns to every man the number of his hairs cannot be one-to-one.

This problem is at least four centuries old. It had always been looked at as a mathematical curiosity until Dirichlet first applied its underlying principle in serious mathematics. It is called the drawer principle: if a set of n elements is distributed over $m(<n)$ drawers, there is at least one drawer with more than one element in it. Dirichlet was the first in history to apply the cardinal aspect of number comparison in non-trivial mathematics. There are more applications today though hardly one in the domain of school mathematics. The safest way to find one is to look for cases when an infinite set is divided in a finite number of parts with the aim that at least one of the parts must be infinite.

Infinite potencies are an important mathematical instrument, or rather, they were so up to 1940. Abstract algebra, topology, and abstract analysis operated much with transfinite cardinals. Since then they have gradually withdrawn. The so-called Zorn lemma has been the key to a mathematics that is to a very high degree free from potency distinctions. Stressing cardinal concepts too much is not as modern as the people who advocate it seem to believe. This reminds me again of what happens with ladies' fashion.

When does the numerosity aspect play an effective role in school mathematics? First, on a very low level where the general concept of natural number is still foggy. Further, and this should certainly not be ignored, in combinatorial problems. It is a well-known fact that if disjoint sets are united it is their cardinals that are added. The fact that in element-wise pairing of two sets the cardinals are multiplied is, though not just an opportunity to define products, certainly one of the aspects of multiplication that has not been duly accounted for in old didactics. Present attention to this approach is in fact due to set theory. In the didactics of multiplication we will come back to the importance of the rectangular pattern for visualizing multiplication.

How badly this domain has been analyzed till now is shown by the fact that in combinatorial argumentations the set theory background is often obscured. Often the definition of multiplication by element-wise pairing is adduced as an argument, where in fact the situation is much more sophisticated. If with 5 girls and 4 boys all "boy-girl" pairs must be formed, the set of pairs is indeed the correct model, and this principle gives us 20 pairs. In most cases, however, the set of pairs does not fit as a model. Such problems are still neglected at school, even at secondary school; the consequences can still be noticed at university. Let us take the question: "There are 5 cats, each with 4 paws; how many paws are there?" No doubt multiplication will do the job. The little word "each" is a 100% guarantee. But is it proved by the set of pairs? Are there 5 cats to be combined with 4 paws as in the other problem the boys with the girls? Of course not, though there is a way to save this model, namely by numbering the paws of each cat arbitrarily by 1, 2, 3, 4, and then pair cats with numbers rather than with paws. But now we come to the question: "At a meeting of 5 people a chairman and a secretary are elected; in how many ways is this possible?" Let us see, 5 possibilities for the chairman, and then 4 for the secretary, 9 together – that is the answer you can still get at university.

Without tackling the didactics now, I venture to draw the conclusion that something was wrong in elementary arithmetic education. The model of the set of pairs does not work, and it is obvious why. The number 4 does not correspond to something that could be interpreted as a fixed set. It is a proof of insufficient conceptual analysis if in combinatorial problems like this the pairs set is relied on as a general model. The situation is rather as follows: Let P be the set of all pairs $\ulcorner$chairman, secretary$\urcorner$. There is the "forget-mapping" of these pairs that forgets the secretary and hence maps an element of P on its first component. The image of f has 5 elements, and the original of every image element consists of 4 elements. Then P must have $5 \cdot 4 = 20$ elements. The teaching theorists of mathematics should pay heed to this phenomenon. Here indeed the set theory formulation and the numerosity aspect can clear up the situation, and it is, unlike the flood of worthless ones, a valuable application of set theory. In a general formulation the principle reads: If P is mapped upon Q, such that every element of Q has its original consisting of r elements, and Q itself has q elements, then P has qr elements. It can be seen intuitively with small cardinals, but the numerosity aspect is again not sufficient to prove it generally, as the reader may experience by his own attempts.

In spite of the negative title of this section, I have included material in favour of the importance of the numerosity aspect of number. As compared with that of other aspects it is not much.

Justice is properly done to the importance of the numerosity aspect if the number as numerosity is dealt with in a context where it belongs according to its applications, that is, with combinatorial problems, rather than supporting misunderstood and ineffective foundations of the number concept.

NUMEROSITY NUMBER – DIDACTICALLY INSUFFICIENT

What about the aspects of the number concept in individual development? I already mentioned that children learn counting rather early. Mostly they can count further than they can recognize numerosities. It has often been noticed that though children can count, they need not know the connexion between counted number and numerosity. This may be quite right but it need not be relevant. I am going to tell you about an experience with a granddaughter of mine (5; 3). There were six of us at table. Suddenly she said: "12 eyes." She had silently counted. I asked: "How many ears are there?" She counted 1, 2... up to 12. "How many feet are there?" She counted the invisible feet. "How many arms?" She burst out laughing while she counted. "How many legs?" She counted and almost died with laughing. A few days later I asked her how many fingers I had on my (left) hand. 1, 2, 3, 4, 5. I matched the fingers of both of my hands, and asked: "How many on this hand?" She counted. I repeated it with her own hands. She always counted anew. Is it not quite natural to conclude that she still lacked the true number concept, the connection between counting and cardinal number? I do not believe this at all. It simply was the rule of the game that she always counted anew. At this stage this is the rigorous proof. Counting is fun, and it is even better fun if the outcome is always the same. At this age children like being told the same story again and again and if they play at hide and seek they always hide in the same place. Actually, the adults play it the same way: they ask children things they know themselves. By indirect means I ascertained that the girl correctly identified cardinals of sets up to five elements, but as soon as she heard the question "how much", the counting game started automatically. I later on tested on one of my grandsons (4; 11) with the sequence of questions, "how many eyes are there?" and so on, and as early as the second question he answered indifferently – "it is just the same". But this is a child who had developed quite different playing habits. For a long while it is exciting if always the same things happen, then it becomes boring and the counting game is over. Then counting 12 eyes proves rigorously there are 12 ears, too.

In the genesis of the number concept the counting number plays the first and most pregnant role. This should be recognized rather than ignored by developmental psychology and pedagogics. In this context numerosity is only one further aspect, corresponding to the fact that the counting number is invariant under one-to-one mappings. Nothing indicates that the child constitutes number from this fact of invariance. This interpretation would be a construction of the abstractive way of thought of the rationalizing mathematician. The child has acquired the counting number and at a certain moment states among others its invariance under one-to-one mappings, e.g. permutations. In no way does the child constitute the single number as a class of mutually equivalent sets, not even unconsciously. It is a self-deceit of adult optics to stress the invariance under one-to-one mappings; this is the mental attitude of an adult mathematician who cannot forget his own theory of natural numbers. The child learns this one invariance in a much broader context, not that the number is invariant under one-to-one mappings, but that even if I count again tomorrow I still get five fingers, that all men have the same number of certain things, and that the number of marbles under the handkerchief does not change if I say "abracadabra". The invariance under one-to-one mappings is a cosy corner in this large complex, the hobby of adults who sell it as the numerosity aspect.

How many invariances a child must learn, I noticed with my eldest boy (2; 4) when I took the first of our daily walks to a level crossing with turnpikes, to see the trains go past. The first time there we came by chance – I call it chance – upon a limping dog. Next time at the same spot my son asked: "Where is the funny little dog?" He had still to learn that limping dogs are not an invariant part of such a neighborhood.

Among the invariance properties of the counting number the invariance under one-to-one mappings is a special case; it is stressed in that analysis which is influenced by the set theory structuring of mathematics. It is the only invariance of the counting number that can be formulated *within* mathematics; having as many fingers tomorrow as today and knowing the number of other people's fingers from my own, is extra-mathematical. But the fact that the one-to-one mappings invariance is the only that can be formulated within mathematics is no reason to believe that it should be the criterion to test whether the child has grasped the number concept. No doubt the stress in psychology on the numerosity aspect is due to Piaget. Impressed by Cantor's analysis he turned to studying the development of the number concept under this aspect. In doing so he very much ignored the others. It is true he mentioned the ordinal number, but what he deals with under this heading has nothing to do with the ordinal aspect and the counting number. His indifference with regard to the counting aspect is so deeply rooted that he mostly tacitly assumes that his test children can count and he never mentions how far they can count. In fact, it is quite astonishing that a great many of them seem to be able to count far or even without restriction.

Clearly Piaget believed that the concept of natural number could be entirely derived from potencies. On the mathematical level of the subjects of Piaget's experiments, it may be even mathematically true, because on this level natural numbers exist only as individuals and have not yet been integrated in a totality. This may have seduced him to believe that it is also psychologically true; it was one of his ideas to trace in developmental psychology the system of mathematics he happened to be acquainted with.

For his part Piaget influenced mathematicians who should have known that Piaget was on a wrong track in mathematics, and who should have seen that the numerosity aspect of natural number was even insufficient mathematically. I already expounded that those who claim to create natural number out of potencies, tacitly and often unconsciously, presuppose the counting number. They are so familiar with this aspect that they often overlook the gaps in the system or simply disregard them; through this attitude they add strong though unintentional arguments to the psychological priority and the greater relevance of the counting aspect. It is a sad story to see didacticians founding their practice on theories they learned from a psychologist; what they borrow from Piaget are not the *results* of his experiments but the wrong, or at least misunderstood, mathematical *presuppositions*.

Piaget is even credited with the discovery that children constitute a natural number as a class of equipotent sets. This is too much. Piaget overstressed numerosity but this is no reason to blame him for something he did not do. Piaget could never have made such statements because he did not even know this abstract formulation of the potency definition. It is a fact that he could have read it in the mathematical literature he consulted, and he probably did read it but he did not interpret it this way. How Piaget understood it can be described as follows. Rather than "5 is the class of sets *equivalent* with a certain standard set" he understood "5 is a class consisting of 5 *equivalent* units", and with this equivalence he meant that the units may be arbitrarily interchanged with themselves or others. Obviously Piaget's sources used the colorless "equivalent" instead of "equipotent", and this may have contributed to the misunderstanding. *

I do not object to Piaget's idea what a natural number is. The formulation is quite natural and looks a bit like Cantor's original one. But there is no reason to credit Piaget with, or blame him for something he did not do, and there is still less reason to believe that children proceed according to a formal procedure which is not even understood by scientists who are not mathematically trained.

It would be rash to conclude that I reject the numerosity aspect of the natural number. Certainly the child must learn that the counting number is invariant under one-to-one mappings; certainly, if asked "how many marbles do they have together?", the child must perform the uniting of two sets, even if the result is obtained by further counting; certainly he must perform multiplication by pairing; and certainly, on a higher level these actions must become conscious and finally subjected to formalization. The tendency I oppose is to restrict the natural number to its numerosity aspect, which would be an impossible undertaking, or to overstress this aspect, which would be dangerous. As soon as the number concept is to be linked to the practice of number use, the numerosity aspect becomes irrelevant. Maybe the five on the die still reminds one of a potency, but nobody connects a numerosity idea with a 5-dollar bill, with 5 o'clock, with 5 minutes, with grade 5, with platform 5, with the age of five, or the point 5 on the number line. All these examples are quite different number concepts from the numerosity number. It is true that with a few among them the addition and multiplication of potencies may be meaningfully re-interpreted. This is an important fact, and it is part of the universality that explains the power of number.

BOTH ASPECTS IN TEACHING

Maybe the cardinal aspect of natural numbers has been a bit neglected by the older didacticians, and certainly it was so on the higher levels. Today it is overstressed as early as the lowest level though it is re-

* Un nombre cardinal est une classe dont les éléments sont conçus comme des "unités" équivalentes les unes aux autres... (avec Aline Szeminska, *La génèse du nombre chez l'enfant*, Paris, 1941, p. 195).

assuring that all good didacticians prefer the broad approach. Later when numbers are objects of a theory, overstressing the cardinal aspect becomes quite general.

It can be even worse than this. Strange things are shown on both the lower and the higher level: Venn diagrams with three pencils, two pencil cases, and one eraser, and, maybe, a flag attached with a '6' that makes the diagram a representative of the number 6. This Venn diagram may be followed by a union or plus sign, and a second Venn diagram with two pencils, two erasers, and a flag '4'. Then follows an equality sign, and all the rest can be safely left to the imagination of my reader. I guess that the problem will later be repeated with a minus sign. I wonder what the answer is.

I took it philosophically and smiled. But not for long. The smile turned into laughter when I saw television mathematics, where a house which had a flag on its roof, and on the flag a '6', indicating the house as the set of five windows and a door, was added to another house, by moving the houses together and confounding the two flags in one.

Even ghosts that I believed damned in the deepest pit of hell celebrate their joyful resurrection, thanks to the believers in numerosity number: Venn diagrams, one of three apples and another of two pears added, with five fruits as a result. I shut such books so terrified that I do not know whether two apples plus three pears are also five fruits, and whether the author draws such profound conclusions as the non-commutativity of the equality sign.

The reader can testify that I am not a faithful believer in tradition. But I deeply regret serious innovators behaving as if there had not been any didactics of arithmetic before the advent of the New Mathematics. This wild tribe of charlatans take it as their licence to indulge in all manifestations of insanity. While there has been noteworthy progress in instruction of arithmetic during the past decades, there has never been a true break with the past. Comparing arithmetic textbooks it is easy to prove that more happened between 1920 and 1940 than after 1940. By this I intend to say that centuries-old experience in the most sophisticated field of school didactics cannot be disregarded in favour of some modern dogma.

I compared a few modern methods of arithmetic; I noticed that the really good ones, which are easily identifiable, stress the counting number even if they make concessions to the prevailing fashion. Of course, it does not mean that according to these methods the child learns to calculate by stupid counting. The child should count *systematically*, and, moreover, work with countable *gestalts*. This aim is served by homogeneous structured material – the terrifying examples I quoted sin against both the principles of structure and of homogeneity. If the child is given Venn diagrams with 8 and 5 arbitrary and arbitrarily-arranged objects to be added, it may be good for the sacred belief in numerosity, but is it good for the child? The poor child cannot but rely on dull counting. This way he will never learn to add 8 and 5 *intuitively*. To learn this, he should structure the 8 and 5, maybe on two horizontal lines or on the abacus. Computing is learned with intuitive, palpable material. Representations of natural numbers by arbitrary sets cannot intuitively be handled. This has been known from the oldest times. On the abacus homogeneous structured sets, say of counters or beads, are operated on. Whenever I look into good arithmetic books I see this principle confirmed, and all the more recent material for teaching arithmetic, which has been invented by good educators shows intentional homogeneity and structuration. Of course unstructured and inhomogeneous examples should not be neglected as has sometimes happened in earlier times. They also exist in the world.

Good arithmetic books are probably in the minority. Most, I have noticed, disregard the counting number completely. I saw a few that do not even teach counting. The advices to the teachers rarely mention counting games. Due to the exaggerated stress on the numerosity aspect the only counting the children learn is dull counting; systematic counting, a favourite subject of traditional didactics, is either absent as a topic or it is badly neglected in this literature. Such an important link between mental and written arithmetic as interpreting additions as counting further and subtraction as counting backwards is simply missing. I saw a class using modern material where after a year only a few bright ones had discovered that to add 3 to 6 you need not count the total set anew but you can continue counting from 7 onwards.

On a higher level, where the number concept is made conscious and is even maybe formalized, even good textbooks completely forget about the counting number though the numerosity aspect does not suffice mathematically to found number, as I expounded. Again this does not

mean that it should be neglected. To what degree it should be acknowledged is another question. It can be posed more generally, and if this
is done, an earlier-formulated criterion can be applied. It does make
sense to create awareness of foundations of the number concept, whatever
this may be, until the content of this awareness is operational rather than
a *hapax legomenon*. Making conscious the numerosity character of the
natural number is a good thing if the student can do more with it than
proving formulae like $a + b = b + a$ or $a \leqslant b \wedge b \leqslant c \to a \leqslant c$, which are
long since familiar to him; it must be required that with such a theory
he can make progress that he otherwise would not be allowed to make.
This follows from a general criterion that has been argued from several
viewpoints. Most modern textbooks do not do justice to such a principle.
It is true there are not many opportunities to put the numerosity aspect
of the natural number into an operational context, but as we showed
with combinatorics, there are not so few either. If the numerosity aspect
is to be made conscious at a higher level, it can be done in the combinatorial context, as well as complete induction is the context for the counting
number aspect.

MEASURING NUMBER

In everyday life no number concept is as important as the measuring
number. The numerosity number is a measure for sets but otherwise
things to be measured are almost never sets. They are quantities or
magnitudes. A day is not a set of hours or minutes though if need be
it can be interpreted that way, a bag of peas or flour is not a set of peas
or flour particles, and it cannot be so interpreted so either. Five dollars
is quite a different thing to a set of five dollar-bills.

To count people and eggs there are natural units. To measure quantities, one needs gauges; the result of the measuring procedure is a
number, which measures the quantity. (I restrict myself to scalar magnitudes.) There is a variety of gauges, because there is a variety of
magnitudes; length, area, volume, height, mass, work, current intensity,
air pressure, and monetary value are notions that become magnitudes by
measuring procedures. Sometimes it is not clear why some magnitudes
need different gauges. Why are length and width measured by the same
unit, and area with another? Why was in the past air pressure measured
by millimetres or inches? Do we not measure distances in flight hours

and light years, as our ancestors did in walking hours and day's journeys. Why do they sell petrol by gallons, natural gas by cubic measures, electricity by kilowatt-hours, and heat by some other mysterious unit? A few of these gauges are learned in arithmetic instruction, and as far as he needs it, the physicist develops a rational measure system. In between a large domain is no man's land. This is the fault of the mathematician. To put it bluntly: ought students to wait for a scientifically sophisticated theory of electricity in order to learn what a kilowatt-hour is, and in general, to learn what is the thing one pays for in the various forms of purchasable work? Ought students wait for the physicist who may define force to learn what directed magnitude is?

The mathematician is inclined to treat all scalar magnitudes as being one idea. It is, indeed, the great virtue of mathematics that all magnitudes can be measured by the same kind of numbers as soon as a gauge is fixed. But if this is an important thing, the student must learn it, since mathematics should also be applied, and then the various origins and characters of the magnitudes are to be recalled and their interrelatedness must be understood. This, or at least a system of understanding it, is mathematics, too.

If didacticians ask what is measure mathematically, pure mathematicians will show them measure theory. I have heard that answer so many times in the last 15 years. I am ashamed to say that I have never protested. But so it happens: a celebrity is invited by a group of schoolteachers who would like to know the secret about what to do with measures in the classroom. Then he expounds measure theory, that is:

A system M, $\mathbf{B}$, μ consisting of a set M, a set $\mathbf{B}$ of subsets of M, a mapping μ of $\mathbf{B}$ into the set of real numbers, such that

(1) $M_1, M_2 \in \mathbf{B} \to M_1 \cup M_2 \in \mathbf{B} \wedge M_1 \cap M_2 \in \mathbf{B} \wedge M_1 \backslash M_2 \in \mathbf{B}$,

(2) $M \in \mathbf{B} \to \mu(M) \geqslant 0$,

(3) $M_1, M_2 \in \mathbf{B} \wedge M_1 \cap M_2 = \bigcirc \to \mu(M_1 \cup M_2) = \mu(M_1) + \mu(M_2)$

and perhaps a bit more.

This definition is followed by a few more or less trivial theorems and examples, as potencies, areas, and volumes. The listeners marvel at this great wisdom, and at the next meeting with no celebrity among them, they discuss what 3 kg means and what is the meaning of equations like 3 kg = 3000 g, whether kg is a factor like the letters used in algebra and whether the above equation follows from 1 kg = 1000 g by distributivity of multiplication. As late as 1969 I still took part in this kind of discussion. If you tell it to other university mathematicians they shrug their shoulders – "You can do it by measure theory."

But measure theory has nothing to do with these questions. For teachers and students it is stones instead of bread. Fortunately in the last few years a few didacticians have studied these questions. Though their explanations are neither new nor profound, they must be made explicit because they have continuously been obscured by references to measure theory.

MAGNITUDES

A magnitude is a non-void set with an order relation ($<$) and an addition ($+$) such that ($a, b, c \in G$):

(1) $a < b$ or $a = b$ or $b < a$ (exclusive "or"),
(2) $a < b \wedge b < c \rightarrow a < c$,
(3) $(a + b) + c = a + (b + c)$,
(4) $a + b = b + a$,
(5) $a + c = b + c \rightarrow a = b$,
(6) $a < b \leftrightarrow \bigvee_c (a + c = b)$.

(This c is easily shown to be unique.) From the addition is derived a multiplication with positive integers:

$$1 \cdot a = a, \quad (1 + n) \cdot a = a + na \quad \text{for } n \in \mathbf{N}^+,$$

that is $n \cdot a = a + \cdots + a$ with n summands.

The next thing that is usually required is divisibility, that is

(7) $\bigwedge_{a \in G} \bigwedge_{n \in \mathbf{N}^+} \bigvee_{b \in G} a = n \cdot b$.

(Here, too, b as the n-th part of a is uniquely determined.)

Thus G admits the multiplication and division by positive integers and, consequently, by positive rational numbers (elements of $\mathbf{Q}^+$).

Before continuing this exposition, we give an example for G. Let G be the system of weights. It is obtained as follows. In the system of objects a relation "equally heavy" is introduced, which is checked by means of a balance, and likewise a relation "lighter than"; moreover it is imagined that two objects can be joined to form a third. "Equally heavy" is an

equivalence relation, which leads to equivalence classes. These classes
are what is usually called weights. We prefer to call them weight classes
and to reserve the term weight to their totality, the set G. To compare
weight classes and to add them, we transfer the relation "lighter than"
as '$<$' and the joining as '$+$' from the objects to the weight classes. It
is in the sense of an idealizing description of empirical facts that the
above axioms then are fulfilled.

Other examples would be the linear, plane and spatial shapes, measured
according to length, area, and volume, maybe even united into one
system where lines come in order before surfaces and surfaces before
spatial contents.

We continue with our general exposition. We choose in G a unit or
gauge e. The rational multiples of e form a set $\mathbf{Q}^+ \cdot e$, which need not
exhaust G. To show this, no irrational weights, lengths and so on are
needed. The last paragraph contains another counter example: when
adding lengths, you never get surfaces, when adding surfaces you never
get spatial content.

As a principle it is thinkable that G has elements that are smaller than
all of $\mathbf{Q}^+ \cdot e$ or, likewise, larger than all of $\mathbf{Q}^+ \cdot e$, as it were infinitesimals
or infinitely large compared with e. Magnitudes G with this property
are called non-Archimedean. On the other hand G is called Archimedean
if the following is true:

(8)   For c in G there is no element of G that is smaller than and
none that is larger than all of $\mathbf{Q}^+c$.

This can also be worded as follows:
For $c, d \in G$ there is an $r \in \mathbf{Q}^+$ and $s \in \mathbf{Q}^+$ such that

$$d < r \cdot c \quad \text{and} \quad d > s \cdot c.$$

Then, of course r can be chosen as an integer and s as the reciprocal
of an integer, and we can say:
For $c, d \in G$ there are natural m, n such that

$$d < m \cdot c \quad \text{and} \quad d > \frac{1}{n} \cdot c.$$

Interchanging c and d shows that it even suffices to postulate:

(8') $\bigwedge_{c,d} \bigvee_{n \in \mathbf{N}} d < n \cdot c.$

This is the common form of the Archimedean axiom. Textbooks generally start with this form to derive 8 from it. We departed from 8 and tried to simplify it. This is what you do in active mathematics. The usual order is its antididactical inversion. Because this inversion was made more than two millennia ago nobody questions it. This is one reason. The other is that if you start with 8 everything looks dead simple; but to perplex the learner, 8′ is better to start with.

G is now supposed Archimedean. As above we choose an $e \in G$. Every $a \in G$ divides $\mathbf{Q}^+ \cdot e$ according to order in two parts. By this it determines a division of $\mathbf{Q}^+$, namely in the two sets

$$\{\tau \in \mathbf{Q}^+ \mid \tau e \leqslant a\},$$
$$\{\tau \in \mathbf{Q}^+ \mid \tau e > a\}.$$

This is what is called a cut in $\mathbf{Q}^+$; in the usual way it determines a real number $\alpha \in \mathbf{R}^+$. In other words

$$\alpha = \sup\{\tau \in \mathbf{Q}^+ \mid \tau \cdot e \leqslant a\}.$$

By definition α measures a with respect to e. It is a positive real number. We put $a = \alpha e$. In this way every $a \in G$ can be obtained as a real multiple e. It does not, however, follow from the preceding that every positive real number plays such a role. One could add another axiom:

(9) $G \supset \mathbf{R}^+ \cdot e.$

Then even

$$G = \mathbf{R}^+ \cdot e.$$

It is easily shown that for $\alpha, \beta \in \mathbf{R}^+$,

$$\alpha < \beta \to \alpha e < \beta e,$$
$$(\alpha + \beta) \cdot e = \alpha \cdot e + \beta \cdot e.$$

Let us call the measure of a with respect to e: $v(a)$. Then we obtained:

(I) v maps G into $\mathbf{R}^+$ (upon, if 9 is assumed).
(II) $a < b \to v(a) < v(b).$
(III) $v(a + b) = v(a) + v(b),$
(IV) $v(e) = 1,$
(V) $v(ta) = tv(a)$ for $t \in \mathbf{Q}^+,$

which follows easily from III.

The properties I–IV characterize v. There is one and only one function that has these properties, and this is the measure $v(a)$ of a with respect to e. If e is replaced with $e' = \alpha e$, a new measure $v'(a)$ of a is obtained, now with respect to e'. The two are related by

$$v'(a) = \alpha^{-1}v(a).$$

All this sounds obvious and it is hardly worthwhile to expound it with such emphasis. I did it only to prove that the theory of magnitudes has not anything to do with the set theory measure. To be sure, there are analogies, between the system $\mathbf{B}$ of sets with the measure μ on the one hand, and the magnitude G on the other. Among sets there is a union, among magnitude classes there is an addition, and both are additive with respect to μ and v, respectively. However what corresponds to the addition in G is the union of *disjoint* sets in $\mathbf{B}$. So arbitrary sets cannot be added in the sense of G. On the other hand the set operations of union and intersection are not meaningful for magnitudes. Changing gauges is unimportant in measure theory and a key notion in magnitudes. We noticed in earlier examples that the set model does not fit situations where magnitudes are usually considered. Set measure and magnitude theory are quite different things, though there are generalizations possible which cover both. In any case it is no use refering the teacher who is trying to understand magnitudes to set measure theory.

To inform the teacher, I analyzed magnitudes. To which degree the pupil should become acquainted with such a theory is another question that may be postponed. Meanwhile I must add a few things to the preceding exposition for it does not describe the measuring process adequately. Up to the choice of e everything is correct. Maybe it is still correct that the next thing to do after this is to look whether e is contained in a a finite number of times. If this is not true, then according to the theoretical prescription one should try all integral parts $(1/n) \cdot e$ of e and check for which integers m the $(m/n) \cdot a$ are smaller and for which larger than a, to divide $\mathbf{Q}^+ \cdot e$ in two parts that form the cut corresponding to a. (Of course if for integers m, n it happens that $(m/n) \cdot e = a$, we need not continue.)

Actually this is not what people do in measuring. Throughout history various ways were attempted. If two magnitudes a_0, a_1 are given, it can be tried to find a common gauge, by which they can be expressed with integers. This is the aim of the Euclidean algorithm:

$$a_0 = q_1 a_1 + a_2 \qquad (0 \leqslant a_2 < a_1)$$
$$a_1 = q_1 a_2 + a_3 \qquad (0 \leqslant a_3 < a_2)$$
$$\vdots$$

That is, a_1 is subtracted from a_0 as many times as it can; then the remainder may be o, in any case it is less than a_1. Then a_2 is subtracted from a_1 as often as it can, and so on. If the process stops with a remainder o in

$$a_{n-1} = q_n a_n,$$

then a_0, a_1 are easily seen to be expressed in a_n with integral factors; a_n is a common gauge of a_0 and a_1, and it is even the largest possible. The q_i are the continued fraction denominators in the development of a_0/a_1. Yet the process need not stop, and then an infinite continued fraction develops.

This idea is interesting under many aspects, but for the magnitude theory it is not relevant. Another solution of historical interest, but unimportant for other reasons, is the old Egyptian fraction system where the results of divisions which do not come out are represented as sums of fractions with the numerators 1.

The natural and practical method of measuring was developed in ancient Babylonia. If the $a \in G$ cannot be measured integrally by the gauge e, take a smaller gauge. For the magnitudes of everyday life there used to be so many gauges – for distances the day-journey, the mile, the fathom, the foot, and the inch. The Babylonians soon brought gauges of the same kind into fixed relations, with a preference for the factor 60. Once such a system has been adopted, it is not too far-fetched to divide the smallest available gauge by 60 if need be, and to continue this way *ad lib*. Today we prefer the 10; our languages and the abaci of our ancestors have always favored the decimal position system, though not until Simon Stevin (1585) has the old Babylonian idea of a continuing division of the unit been translated into the decimal system. This, then, is how we measure; if the available unit e is too coarse, it is subdivided according to powers of 10. Measuring results are decimally noted down before the decimal point, and if need be, after it. Certain larger steps can be marked by prefixes such as milli-, micro-, nano-, kilo-, mega-, and giga- to be attached to certain gauges like second, ton, and metre. In fact, numerals as a million and a billion behave linguistically as new units.

If decimal subdivision only is admitted, then the divisibility axiom 7 is not used to its full extent. For practical measuring 7 may read

$$\bigwedge_{a \in G} \bigvee_{b \in G} a = 10 \cdot b.$$

Then common fractions disappear from the scene. Only finite decimal fractions occur as measuring results, though by idealizing the measuring process infinite decimal fractions come in. In this system $\frac{1}{3}$ is represented by an infinite decimal fraction, and so are the rational numbers in general. To interpret common fractions as measuring results is no adequate interpretation of the measuring process. To the didactical consequences of this appreciation we will come back later. The source of the common fractions is dividing rather than measuring. I should have distinguished the multiplier and the divisor as specific aspects of number since in many languages there are even specific words for the particular multipliers and divisors. In the concept of magnitude which I analyzed they occur as operators to which correspond rational numbers, and as such they play a constituting role. However, to discover the measure of elements of G, a restricted divisibility suffices. I postulated that by 10. Mathematicians are more sympathetic to 2, but any other basis is allowed as well, and there is no objection to changing divisors with every step, as they do in the British system.

MEASURE INDICATIONS AS FUNCTION SYMBOLS

I come back to the old question of what 3 kg means and how the equation 3 kg = 3000 g should be interpreted. As a gauge e for the weight one can choose the kilogram, that is the equivalence class a certain object in Sèvres belongs to. This weight class is $e = 1$ kg. The measure v with respect to this e takes the value

$$v(a \text{ kg}) = a$$

for the objects in the weight class a kg. Or, the other way round: a kg is the original of a under v. Or, v^{-1} is a mapping of Q^+ that assigns magnitude classes to real numbers, in our special case the number a to the weight class a kg,

$$v^{-1}(a) = a \text{ kg}.$$

'kg' means the same as the function symbol 'v^{-1}' – only it stands on the right rather than left side of the argument. Would it not be advisable to put this function symbol left of the argument, as people have long done with currency notations, thus instead of 3 kg = 3000 g,

$$\text{kg } 3 = \text{g } 3000?$$

No brackets have been put around the argument, but this is not an unusual feature.

So measure symbols can be considered as function symbols. $, cm, sec, g are functions that map numbers on monetary values, lengths, durations, and weights. The connection between kg and g is expressed by

$$\text{kg } x = 1000 \cdot \text{g } x;$$

"kg is 1000 times as much as g".

It is so obvious an interpretation that it is incredible that up to now almost nobody has acknowledged it. This strange fact can only be explained by the force of tradition and by the continuous references to set theory measure.

THE RULE OF THREE

There is much more to the theory of magnitude. To show this I must go into more detail. As a matter of fact, we do more with magnitude than add classes of the same magnitude. Magnitudes are related in various manners to each other, and from given magnitudes new ones are built up.

A most natural relation between magnitudes is the homomorphism, that is a mapping f of one magnitude G into a magnitude G_1 that preserves the structure:

$$a < b \rightarrow fa < fb,$$
$$f(a + b) = f(a) + f(b).$$

From this postulate it follows that also

$$f(\tau a) = \tau f(a) \quad \text{for} \quad \tau \in \mathbf{Q}^+.$$

With respect to Archimedean magnitudes, as considered by us, such a mapping is also one-to-one, and as soon as (9) is required, it maps G on G_1. A homomorphism f is fixed, as soon as the image fa of one single

$a \in G$ is given, and if (9) is fulfilled fa may even arbitrarily be prescribed in G_1. Just as the magnitudes G and G_1 can completely be described by the measures v and v_1, respectively, so can f be expressed by a mapping g of $\mathbf{R}^+$ onto itself, namely

$$g = v_1 f v^{-1},$$

or, in other words,

$$gva = v_1 fa$$

which states that g assigns to the measure of a that of fa. g is the restriction of a linear mapping of $\mathbf{R}$ to $\mathbf{R}$, so g has the form

$$g\tau = \alpha\tau \qquad (\tau \in \mathbf{R}^+)$$

with a fixed $\alpha \in \mathbf{R}^+$.

This is the mathematical background of the rule of three. Likewise the inverse rule of three can be founded on anti-homomorphisms. By this term we mean an f such that

$$a < b \rightarrow fa > fb,$$

$$f(na) = \frac{1}{n} fa \quad \text{for} \quad n \in \mathbf{N}^+.$$

Then also

$$f(\tau a) = \frac{1}{\tau} f(a) \quad \text{for} \quad \tau \in \mathbf{Q}^+.$$

Anti-homomorphisms can be derived from homomorphisms since by the use of measures they can be expressed in the form

$$\varphi(\tau) = \alpha\tau^{-1}.$$

Examples of homomorphisms of magnitudes are well known: the mapping f that assigns to a weight class of a utility a monetary value; that assigns to the volume of a substance its weight; that assigns to the time the path travelled by a uniformly moving object.

It is an anti-homomorphism that assigns width to length of the area if the rectangle is given, or the number of workers at an enterprise to the time needed (with all relevant reservations).

MULTIPLICATION AND DIVISION OF MAGNITUDES

Not only by comparing are magnitudes related, they are also multiplied and divided by each other. By such operations one obtains the magnitude price/weight, with the possible gauge $/pd., weight/volume with the gauge $g \cdot cm^{-3}$, path/time with $cm \cdot sec^{-1}$ or mile/hour; the measure of such a magnitude is known as price per unit, specific weight, and velocity respectively. In the first two examples people are careful to write... $ a kg, ... miles an hour, but specific weight appears as an absolute number since it is introduced by the strange definition: weight of one cm^3 of the substance. Traditional teaching of arithmetic may haphazardly touch on some of these notions and part of this terminology. The pure mathematician, of course, detests concrete numbers and leaves them ungrudgingly to the mercy of the physicist. Are not divisions like

$$150 \text{ km}:3 \text{ h} = 50 \text{ km/h}$$

shocking? Let him retire to his ivory tower if it is against his nature to teach children something that belongs to everyday life.

The argument of rigour against computations with concrete numbers is completely mistaken. Concrete numbers are absolutely rigorous, and the resistance of some mathematicians against them is sheer dogmatism. I have already explained how to understand

$$\$ 7.50 = \cent 750 \, .$$

$ is a function, $\cent$ is another. So are m, kg, and so on. New ones can be formed by multiplication and division. Maybe mathematicians would admit, since they cannot forbid it, that the measures of magnitudes with respect to certain gauges are multiplied and divided by each other. The physicist is correct in understanding it in a different way, and if he were better acquainted with modern mathematics, he would tell a stubborn mathematician that the product of magnitudes is nothing but what in mathematics is called the tensor product, and that inverse magnitudes are, mathematically, duals of each other.

I cannot explain here the whole theory; the following is only a quick summary.

From two given magnitudes G and H, a formal product can be constructed according to rules which are a straight translation of those of tensor products of modules and linear spaces. $G \cdot H$ consists of the formal products ab with $a \in G$, $b \in H$, under the provision that

$$(\alpha a)\, b = a\,(\alpha b) \quad \text{for} \quad \alpha \in \mathbf{R}^+ .$$

From this it follows that with the gauges $e \in G$, $f \in H$,

$$(\alpha e)\,(\beta f)$$

depends on $\alpha\beta$ only. If now

$$a = \alpha e, \quad b = \beta f ,$$

then $\alpha\beta$ may be anticipated as the measure of ab with respect to the gauge ef, and the addition and comparison of elements of $G \cdot H$ can be defined a posteriori by means of that of their measures. (There is a more abstract approach that does not use gauges and measures.)

Take as an example

$$\text{work} = \text{force} \cdot \text{path},$$

with the fact from experience that half the force over the double path produces the same work. Or, taking an example from mathematics, for rectangles

$$\text{area} = \text{length} \cdot \text{width}.$$

It is here meaningful to write

$$\text{kg }\alpha \cdot \text{m}\beta = \text{kg} \cdot \text{m }\alpha\beta ,$$

where $\text{kg} \cdot m$ is the function constituted from the functions kg and m that maps numbers on work. Or

$$\text{cm }\alpha \cdot \text{cm }\beta = \text{cm}^2\, \alpha\beta$$

where cm^2 maps numbers on areas.

(Be careful – kg·m is not a function that arises by composition of the functions m and kg, nor is cm^2 a function that arises from iterating the function cm.)

To tackle the division of magnitudes we start with their inverses. Do they meaningfully exist? Dividing path by time or area by length is meaningful, but are there meaningful reciprocal times and lengths? Yes, reciprocal lengths are well known in optics as dioptrics (a dioptric is

m^{-1}); in acoustics the so-called frequency (e.g. $\sec^{-1}$ 425 for the concert pitch) is a reciprocal time, as is the k Hertz of radio waves. In each of these magnitudes meaningful addition, or at least a meaningful arithmetical mean, exists. (Remember the law of dioptrics that says that the sum of the reciprocal object and image distances equals the reciprocal focal distance.)

What is now the operational meaning of such reciprocal magnitudes? Let us look to the frequency. There it holds that

$$\text{frequency} \cdot \text{duration} = \text{number of oscillations}.$$

If I multiply the frequency of oscillations (per second) by the duration (in seconds), I get the total number of oscillations.

If a magnitude G and its reciprocal G^* are given, their interrelatedness is described by means of their product

$$G \cdot G^* = \mathbf{R}^+,$$

that is, for any $a \in G$, $a^* \in G^*$ is

$$a \cdot a^* \text{ meaningful as an element of } \mathbf{R}^+, \text{ and bilinear in } a, a^*.$$

Such G and G^* are called duals of each other according to the terminology for modules and vector spaces. Gauges e, e^* will be chosen in G and G^*, respectively, such that

$$e \cdot e^* = 1$$

(e.g. sec and $\sec^{-1}$ if it is about duration and its reciprocal). With the measures v, v^* of $a \in G$ and $a^* \in G^*$ one gets

$$a \cdot a^* = v(a) \cdot v^*(a^*).$$

In particular, if a and a^* are such that

$$a \cdot a^* = 1,$$

then $v(a)$ and $v^*(a^*)$ become reciprocals of each other. This is the reason why dual magnitudes look like reciprocals.

Often reciprocal magnitudes appear as factors in products, as we already mentioned:

$$\text{specific price} = \text{price/weight},$$
$$\text{specific weight} = \text{weight/volume},$$
$$\text{velocity} = \text{path/time}.$$

Computing with such measures is self-explanatory:

$$\$\alpha\cdot(\text{kg }\beta)^{-1} = \$ \text{ kg}^{-1}\,\alpha\beta^{-1},$$
$$g\alpha\cdot(\text{cm}^3\ \beta)^{-1} = g\cdot\text{cm}^{-3}\,\alpha\beta^{-1}$$
$$m\alpha\cdot(\text{sec }\beta)^{-1} = m\text{ sec}^{-1}\,\alpha\beta^{-1},$$

(Again do not confuse $\sec^{-1}$ with the inverse of the function that maps numbers on times; $\sec^{-1}$ instead maps numbers on reciprocal times.)

It would be useful to stick consequently to such principles in computations with concrete numbers. The everyday term for dividing by concrete numbers is the little word "per"; km/sec is kilometres per second. It is also part of "percent"; 5% is 5/100, or in interest computations $ 5/$ 100. As an interest rate it should be denoted by 5%/year, or $\frac{5}{12}$%/month, or 35%/7 years if need be. This is an absolutely exact notational system. Perhaps because a university professor might frown at it, teachers shrink from employing it at school, where it may be of great help. They should not; any disapproval is mistaken, since concrete numbers can axiomatically be systematized as magnitudes. I stress once more this does not mean burdening students with its axiomatics unless they have reached a very advanced level. I shall come back to this point.

LOGARITHMIZING OF MAGNITUDES

We have multiplied and divided magnitudes. If the reader believes that this is all that can happen with magnitudes, he is mistaken, though I admit what I am going to tell about now is more a curiosity than anything else. A measure that is obtained by logarithmizing magnitudes is known under the name of decibel. Technicians, even if they apply it in profusion, do not usually understand its logical status. Decibels are mostly used to describe sound intensity levels; a sound intensity is measured in watt/cm^{-2} and then the $10\cdot\log^{10}$ is taken of the measure number. It would be better to interpret it as a magnitude, though with an additive rather than multiplicative measure indication. Then a sound intensity of 1000 watt/sec^{-1} would in the decibel scale be denoted by

$$10\cdot\log^{10}\text{ watt/cm}^{-2} + 30,$$

as has several times been proposed. *

* R. A. J. Bosschart and H. Freudenthal: 'De decibel', *Begripsvorming en dimensieleer* **63** (1951), A. 203–208. 'De decibel als fundamenteel begrip', *De Ingenieur* **63** (1951), A. 246–247.

THE NUMBER LINE

I saved the most attractive aspect of the measuring number till the end. Certainly, the student should learn to work with magnitudes, and to transmit background knowledge to the teacher, I indulged in detailed expositions of this subject. In teaching, however, from an early up to an advanced level, one model of magnitude should be outstanding. According to our axioms all magnitudes are isomorphic; indeed knowing one means knowing all of them provided they are recognized as such. This means exercizing the magnitude concept with one model, but exercizing the recognition with many of them, in order to become acquainted with a variety of magnitudes and their mutual relations.

Among all magnitudes the most mathematical one is length; in fact it is one of the fundamental concepts of geometry. It is more palpable than duration; all length classes can be simultaneously localized on one, though infinite, ruler, whereas it is hardly possible to realize weight by a box with a continuously varying series of weight classes. The obvious model of magnitude is length; its realization on the infinite ruler, the number ray, fulfils high demands of concreteness. Well, once the number ray is accepted, it is a small step to the number line. On this line we can also localize one-dimensional vector magnitudes we did not mention till now.

I said "the number line" in singular, but as any model of numbers, it is known by many copies. Its usual image is horizontal or vertical, but most often the first which we will see later is not the best way of realization. Sometimes both the horizontal and the vertical number line are united in one figure to design graphics. In such a graphic they may be models of different magnitudes, such as quantity and value of a utility, while the graphic visualizes a price list, which may be, according to the rule of three, a linear function.

As a means of visualization the scope of the number line will be dealt with later, but I anticipate that, used appropriately, it can be an excellent means of vizualizing the four main arithmetical operations. Addition and subtraction of a number are interpreted as shifts of the number line, subtraction from a number as a reflection, multiplications and divisions as dilatations and shrinkages; computation rules become intuitively clear. I consider the number line as the most valuable tool which modern didactic of arithmetic has borrowed from modern mathematics.

In the literature I found three kinds of use of the number line which I shall investigate later on in more detail. First, the number line, as it were as a ruler, the points of which are solidly and invariably *identified* with the real numbers; second, the line on which an arbitrary origin and scale have been assumed to *name* points by numbers, without identifying both of them; third, the line as a rigid substratum acted on by the numbers as operators, *effecting* translations or dilatations. No doubt the second is the most systematic and the third the most elegant interpretation; we will see, however, that they rest on didactically wrong suppositions and cause didactical complications. For this reason, speaking of the number line in the present chapter, I wish it to be understood that I mean the first interpretation. That is, the numbers, and in particular 0 and 1, thus the gauge too, are fixed on the line. I admit that this fixed gauge is less adapted to the interpretation of the number line as a model of magnitude and to its aspect of measuring number, but it is a great didactical advantage.

The number line should be used from the start of arithmetic, or at least, very early on. In the beginning only the natural numbers are noticed and marked on it; then with subtractions negative integers show up and are marked too; with dividing and shrinking the common fractions appear, and with measuring the decimal fractions, first only the finite, and then the infinite ones. Gradually the number line is filled, not with numbers and points, but rather with numerically-seized points. This is not a procedure of introducing numbers, it is no genuine extension of the number domain, but a lasting growth of an "investigated domain". The real numbers are pre-existent by their intuitive images, and so are the operations, the addition as shift, the multiplication as dilatation, and the algebraical laws, as obvious or easily visualized phenomena.

To be justified, this approach requires a fundamental discussion which regards not only the number concept but all mathematical concepts in their teaching context, though for this discussion the number concept is the most appropriate point of departure.

DESCRIBING OR CREATING CONCEPTS – ANALYSIS OR SYNTHESIS?

The number line suggests the existence and internal structure first of the natural numbers, then of the integers, the rational, and the real numbers, or rather it should give the student the feeling of exercising his computations and operations in a given domain, the existence of which is neither questioned nor discussed. The domain he is confronted with is, indeed, so intuitive that such questions are not likely to arise. To be sure, the domain is ever closer analyzed and described; first only the places of the integers are indicated, it is shown how they are added, which ones are greater and smaller; divisions lead to the fractions, and finally, passing beyond, every real number is shown to its place between the rationals. Maybe it is still an imperfect description. In the first year at university the gaps can be smoothed out; using algebra, real numbers are told to form an ordered field, with a topological property added, such as the realizability of Dedekind cuts, or the existence of the upper bound of a bounded set. It means that the stress is shifted from the measuring to the computing number – a feature that is to be dealt with later on. This is all you need for calculus over the field of the reals as a substratum. Of course as with the number line, so also with the Dedekind ordered field the problem arises whether such a thing exists at all and if so how many different models there are. Well, if there is one field of this kind, there are more of them and all are isomorphic, including the topology. Their existence the professor says will be proved later, in this or that course (which usually is attended by mathematicians only, not by physicists). When I was a first-year student at university, I was confronted with the existence proof in the very first weeks, and as a young university teacher I taught it to my students as I had learned it a few years earlier.

The present approach is mathematically and didactically entirely legal and superior to the old one. Indeed, what does it mean to prove the existence of what is called today the field of real numbers? The real numbers are derived from the rational numbers as Dedekind cuts in the ordered field of the rational numbers, or by Cauchy sequences of rational numbers. To find the means of doing so, we have to dig down deep into our set theory baggage for subsets or subsequences, for equivalence classes, for algebraic operations with sets or equivalence classes, for an isomorphic embedding of the old into the new field, and finally for the most difficult task of all: showing that the new field does possess the required topological properties, for instance, that in the new field every

Cauchy sequence converges. What I just described is a most important procedure not because it leads from the rational field to that of the reals that everybody knows, but because it is a paradigm for many similar procedures and because it applies in exactly the same way to completing metric spaces, topological groups, rings, fields, thus creating a host of new structures. This is then the natural context of this procedure; rather than at the start of analysis, where it is doomed to the state of a *hapax legomenon*, its place is there where brand-new mathematical structures are to be created. Even at university motivation cannot be dispensed with, and a complicated logical construction that does not yield more than a derivation of the good old field of real numbers from the rationals is hardly motivated if it does not offer any perspective.

But what is our net gain if we succeed in building the field of the reals upon that of the rationals? Well, we have to start earlier, to derive the rational numbers from the integers by means of number pairs. This is again an important method, not because it shows how to proceed from the integers to the rational numbers, which are known from early childhood, but because by the same method any commutative ring with no zero divisors is embedded into its quotients field. This then is the natural context in which such a method is to be developed, for the same reasons I adduced above.

Again we have the question: what do we gain, if anything? From the integers where we stay now, it goes back to the natural numbers. And the natural numbers? They are reduced to set theory as classes of equipotent sets. But be careful here. I explained that this is not easy if you would not commit yourself, as many school texts do, to pious or impious fraud.

One thing is clear: always one existence is explained by another; nothing sprouts from nothing, but even if it were possible to underpin the last something by a nothing, it would exceed a beginner's comprehension.

This is no less true at school level. One cannot but start with some substratum such as the number line, which is given as it were by nature, and try to analyze and describe it more or less completely. It does not make much sense to exhibit this object as a free creation of the human mind unless the learner can somehow understand why this should be done. The reason can be that it looks unsatisfactory assuming the existence of the thing described and that it seems more desirable to derive it from the existence of something that looks more elementary. I would not consider this as a compelling reason. It would be didactically more convincing if this reduction of two existences to each other were no isolated act, but paradigmatic for the genuine creation of new entities.

REAL NUMBERS

If the number line is used, the real numbers do exist as early as the rationals. But whichever device is used, they announce their existence as early. The unit square has a diagonal, and this diagonal has a length, whether real numbers have been defined or not. Long before formulating generally the Pythagorean theorem, it is obvious that the diagonal of the unit square has length $\sqrt{2}$. Before proving $\sqrt{2}$ to be irrational, which is not difficult, the behaviour of $\sqrt{2}$ with respect to the rational numbers can nicely be illustrated. To the integral plane lattice (Figure 1) the point

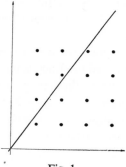

Fig. 1.

$\lceil\sqrt{2}, 1\rceil$ is constructed and joined to the origin to show how the lattice points are lying around this straight line. If there were a lattice point $\lceil a, b\rceil$ on it, then $t\lceil\sqrt{2}, 1\rceil = \lceil a, b\rceil$ would be solvable with integral a, b, hence $\sqrt{2}=b/a$ would be rational. Actually there are only better and better approximations of $\sqrt{2}$ by rational numbers.

There are irrational numbers, that is, numbers that cannot be obtained as fractions of integers. This is a fact, in spite of the disapproving mathematician, who cultivates sound ideas on rigour. According to him one should say that $(?x)$ $x^2=2$ has no solution in rational numbers, and that first the number domain should be extended to give the equation a solution. Such cannot be our position. It is true that up to this moment rationals were the only numbers we know face to face, but this does not mean there are no others. They exist; rather than being created, they have to be discovered. That is no philosophical Platonism. It simply is a consequence of the didactical behaviour as characterized in the last chapter.

$\sqrt{2}$ does exist. It is my business to compute it. I cannot write $\sqrt{2}$ as p/q with integral p, q, but there are other means available. If I am measuring with a ruler, I do not write the result as a common fraction, either; I use decimal fractions. With decimal fractions it is a common experience that a number can happen to require an infinity of symbols, as does $\frac{1}{3}$, which is 0.333... Of course, $\frac{1}{3}$ and $\sqrt{2}$ are different cases. $\frac{1}{3}$ is rational and it behaves in an obstinate way only on the Procrustean bed of the decimal system, whereas $\sqrt{2}$ is irrational and requires an infinity of symbols in any number system. You can measure or compute $\sqrt{2}$ as a decimal fraction as far as you like. Of course, this is not a thing the pupil should be told. He should see it, and it is not difficult to show it. But this should not be done with the classical square root algorithm, which my generation learned at school.

The Greeks possessed two good methods to conquer such irrationalities as $\sqrt{2}$. One is what is now called the Euclidean algorithm or development by continued fractions. If the method of p. 203 is applied to $a_0 = \sqrt{2}$, $a_1 = 1$, one gets $q_1 = 1, a_2 = \sqrt{2} - 1, q_2 = 2, a_3 = (\sqrt{2} - 1)^2, q_3 = 2, \ldots$. Cutting off the remainder at some a_n, which is put 0, and computing back, the following successive approximations of $\sqrt{2}$ are obtained:

$$\frac{3}{2}, \quad \frac{7}{5}, \quad \frac{17}{12}, \quad \frac{41}{29}, \ldots.$$

A more efficient procedure, which was already known to the old Babylonian mathematicians, is the following. Computing $\sqrt{2}$ means finding a square with the area 2, and approximating $\sqrt{2}$ means looking for a rectangle of area 2 with sides that do not differ much from each other. Let us start with one side

$$a_1 = 1,$$

then the other would be

$$b_1 = 2.$$

That is a bad approximation. No take the arithmetical mean of both sides and assume as new sides

$$a_2 = \tfrac{1}{2}(a_1 + b_1) = \tfrac{3}{2},$$

$$b_2 = \frac{2}{a_2} = \tfrac{4}{3}.$$

That is a bit better. The procedure is repeated,

$$a_3 = \tfrac{1}{2}(a_2 + b_2) = \tfrac{17}{12},$$

$$b_3 = \frac{2}{a_3} = \tfrac{24}{17}.$$

The difference of both sides is now a small as $\frac{1}{204}$. Once more,

$$a_4 = \tfrac{1}{2}(a_3 + b_3) = \tfrac{577}{408},$$

$$b_4 = \frac{2}{a_4} = \tfrac{816}{577}.$$

The difference is now $\frac{1}{235416}$. One can continue this at leisure, and it is even easily shown that the procedure converges and approximates $\sqrt{2}$.*

Common fractions crept in, and certainly some very ugly ones, but there is no need to do it with common fractions. The arithmetical mean $(\tfrac{1}{2}(a_n + b_n))$ and the reciprocal (a_{n+1}^{-1}) can be calculated as rounded-off decimal fractions, maybe with the use of a computer. Then the process stops if the last decimal stops changing. This is the way the Babylonians applied the method in the sexagesimal system.

The real numbers here occur as infinite decimal fractions, which is the most unproblematic way that can be thought of. They look almost less problematic than even the negative and the rational numbers, whereas the usual opinion is that the general real number ought to be the most difficult of all. In fact, an arbitrary real number is nothing but an infinite decimal fraction. To be sure, one should be careful. The representation is not unique, since

$$2.3000\ldots \quad \text{and} \quad 2.2999\ldots$$

are equal. Indeed up to the n-th decimal they differ by 10^{-n} which for large n is arbitrarily small. Thus, with this restriction that an infinite tail of nines can be replaced by zeros provided the last digit different from

* Hans Freudenthal, *Mathematics Observed*, London, New York, 1967.

9 is augmented by a unit, real numbers are given by infinite decimal fractions. These infinite decimal fractions are operated on by naive procedures, at least in the beginning. Later it may be worthwhile to analyze and scrutinize these naive relations and operations. For instance,

$$2.37894\ldots < 2.37901\ldots$$

is decided on account of the first differing decimal places. If two such fractions are to be added they are provisionally stopped at some place and then added as it is the use with finite decimal fractions. Of course, it is not as simple as it appears on the surface. If you stop at the n-th decimal, you are not sure how much the cut-off decimals may contribute to the decimal transfer. It is reassuring that it cannot be more than one unit of the last preserved decimal, but even this can be annoying. For instance, in

$$0.2354\ldots$$
$$+\,0.1645\ldots$$

it is doubtful whether finally the result will be

$$0.3999\ldots \quad \text{or} \quad 0.4000\ldots.$$

That means that even the first decimal is not certain, though the uncertainty in the value of the sum gets smaller and smaller if the number of preserved decimals increases. This then is the unavoidable consequence of the ambiguity of the representation by decimal fractions. Similar problems arise with the other operations. Division requires still more precautions. No more than by 0, one can divide by a number which has not declared itself to 0 or $\neq 0$. So division cannot start unless the divisor has been developed so far that it shows its first position different from 0.

Nevertheless it seems as though synthesizing the domain of real numbers is not a harder task than analyzing. A real number is a finite or an infinite decimal fraction, with the above identification of certain developments, it is easily definable whether some decimal fraction is larger than the other, and as we sketched in the last paragraph the arithmetical operations can be defined, and their laws can be derived. Finally it can be shown that this system fulfils the topological condition that becomes the field of real numbers, e.g. that a bounded set has a least upper bound.* This then proves that the set of decimal fractions with the defined relations and operations is essentially the field of real numbers.

Would it be worthwhile to develop these simple ideas in all detail? I am pretty sure that simple as this strategy looks, its final realisation will be tedious, or even worse, boring. I looked it up in a modern school textbook that is again and again quoted as the example of a synthethetic construction of real numbers by means of decimal fractions, in order to know how it was done. Careful analysis shows that the author took it fairly easy. To be sure he defined real numbers as infinite decimal or dual fractions, and he also defined the order relation, but he omitted any autonomous definition of arithmetical operations, and even worse, kept silent about the necessity of defining the operations, of verifying the field laws, and the topological condition.

Nevertheless I agree that an existence proof for the field of real numbers by means of the example of decimal fractions is possible at school (but of course not in the instruction of 12 year-olds) provided the students can be satisfied with a sketchy definition of the operations and a not too serious verification of the arithmetical laws (the field axioms). Such a theory would even harmonize very well with an introduction in the use of computers. Of course, this does not mean that it should be done. In examinations I always feel slightly irritated by memorized formulae like "it is easily shown" and "the proof may be omitted".

There is still one question left – if real numbers are as easy by means of decimal fractions, why were sophisticated Cauchy sequences, Dedekind cuts, interval nests, etc. invented? The infinite decimal fractions are special Cauchy sequences: stopping the decimal fraction a successively at the p-th position, one gets a sequence $\{a_p\}$ with the property that $|a_m - a_n| < \varepsilon$ as soon as $m, n > N(\varepsilon)$, where $N(\varepsilon)$ is chosen such that $10^{-N(\varepsilon)} < \varepsilon$. This sequence obviously converges to a. So these special Cauchy sequences already suffice to get all real numbers. The convergence of these special Cauchy sequences in the real field readily implies that of all Cauchy sequences. Therefore to define real numbers one can be

---

* This is not difficult. Let A be the set, let us say, situated between 0 and 1. Sieve out of A the subset A_1 consisting of those elements of A the first decimal of which is maximal. Then take in A_1 the elements with maximal second decimal which form the subset A_2, and continue in this way. The intersection of all those A_n consists of one real number, which is the least upper bound of A.

satisfied with these special Cauchy sequences. It is just enough to postulate that infinite decimal fractions represent numbers.

Why are we not content with this simple method? The answer is – it is not elegant. First of all the decimal system; this is a practical tool stemming from the decimal construction of our numerals, for which our ten fingers are responsible. This preferential role of the number 10 should cease to be respected as soon as higher mathematics begins. In electronic computers the 2 has beaten the 10. But the binary system does not match the mathematical situation either. If it is about infinite decimal fractions, then the point of departure is finite decimal fractions; in the binary case it is finite binary fractions, but both of them are unreasonable systems. The "correct" point of departure is obviously rational numbers. Within the set of rational numbers both the decimal fractions and the binary ones are a crazy choice.

The construction of real numbers on the basis of decimal or binary fractions is less elegant but it is practical. It just formalizes the procedures of practical computations. It appeals to that mental representation of the real number which after the geometrical image is the most efficient. Numbers ask to be calculated. Real numbers are tapeworms of digits that creep out of the computer. They are so concrete that everybody can understand their relations, operations and laws thoroughly on the bottom level, that is, without putting them into involved linguistic formulae.

It is a theoretical luxury to define the real number by Cauchy sequences or Dedekind cuts. If we could afford this luxury at school, I would not object against it. But I doubt whether we can. In any case wherever something like this has been tried, it is a fact that once the definition of real number is dished up, however it was formulated, explicitly or implicitly, it may immediately afterwards be forgotten. Its main function is beguiling the textbook author's conscience. The teacher is already expected to pass over it in his teaching. Between the world wars a group of exactness fanatics among Dutch teachers got the Dedekind cut inserted in school textbooks. I mean the bare Dedekind cut without any consequence, not even the addition of real numbers defined by Dedekind cuts. The teachers simply left it out, and they were right. Textbooks of this kind still exist today. Usually the least upper bound of bounded sets rather than Dedekind's cut is their topological axiom.

There are, however, also didacticians who draw the opposite consequence. They do not believe that what they call a rigorous introduction of real numbers at school is possible and for this reason they forbid analysis to be taught at school. "Rigorous" then means: Dedekind cut, Cauchy sequence, or suchlike. But others consider it already just as rigorous to mention such tools without using them.

These are misinterpretations of the concept of rigour. A student who is mentally fully aware of the real number as a point on the number line, or as an infinite decimal fraction, and who operates on it, is nearer to mathematical rigour than one who has made the acquaintance of some definition of real number that during the whole instruction never or seldom becomes operational. There is hardly anything in mathematics that is more operational than infinite decimal fractions, and the interpretation of real numbers as decimal fractions is as rigorous as it can be.

Of course I would not abolish general Cauchy sequences of rational numbers to establish real numbers upon them. But whoever advocates teaching them at some level should first investigate what their use can be, and at which point in mathematics they first become useful. I already pointed out that criteria of elegance speak out against decimal fractions. These criteria are absolutely legitimate. Elegance is fine if you can afford it and if others can appreciate it. The theory of divisibility in Z is more elegant if it is formulated with ideals; the linear dependence and independence of vectors becomes more elegant with Steinitz' exchange theorem. On a higher level much becomes more elegant, in particular, if you have once been allowed to stay on the lower level.

There is more to it than this. It is not just for the sake of elegance. The idea of completing structures by means of Cauchy sequences has a much wider scope than the one example of the transition from rational to real numbers. In those generalizations there is nothing like special Cauchy sequences of decimal or binary fractions. If the point is reached that the method of Cauchy sequences is used to generate quite different objects, it is indeed ridiculous to restrict the generation of real numbers to the use of decimal or binary fractions. But "the point" I alluded to is only reached by those who go to the university to study mathematics. At school, if there is any need to create the real numbers, understanding and interpreting them as decimal or binary fractions is the most adequate procedure.

I have propagated this approach for more than twenty years. Practicians probably always did it this way. But as theoreticians and textbook authors they seem to detest it. Perhaps decimal fractions are considered as unbecoming. Fortunately in many countries the teacher is free to omit chapters of the textbook he considers to be irrelevant. A theory of real numbers that, out of a deep-rooted prejudice or dogmatism, goes beyond what is relevant in real numbers is in itself irrelevant.

To resume, let us consider the real numbers as a datum on the number line, with its characteristic operations. This datum is analyzed by means of decimal fractions. From this representation the topological properties of real numbers are derived as soon as they are really used. If more should be done, then the real numbers may be re-created, but then it should be done by decimal fractions.

THE COMPUTING NUMBER

Counting and computing undergo their first systematization in the place value system. It should be stressed that the place value system is older than Indo-Arabic numbers. Long before the latter were invented people counted and calculated using the place value system. In fact, this is the essence of the abacus with its columns (or rows) for the successive places. To represent 762, one put or drew 2 counters or signs in the column of the ones, 6 counters or signs in the column of the tens, 7 in the columns of the hundreds, and in these representations the numbers were subjected to operations. In the Indo-Arabic system this place value representation of numbers was given a written form, by means of the digits 0, 1,..., 9. An essential step was the introduction of the zero, an explicit renounce or place-holder sign that as it were translates what the empty set is on the abacus.

I just mentioned the abacus to point out that positional computations were exercised for a long time with concrete material close to intuitive arithmetic. So it is not to be wondered at that modern didacticians come back to variants of the abacus. Its most recent progeny, the non-automatic computer, is as concrete a material as the old abacus and just as close to intuitive arithmetic. We will come back to the didactical consequences of this remark.

In the decimal place value system all calculations are reduced to the tables of additions and multiplications below 10. The rules of this reduction arise from actual calculating in so natural a fashion that calculators can work with them without explicit formulations. I do not believe that such formulations are ever given in all detail at school. In fact, these rules are not that simple, and this becomes clear as soon as they have to be formulated to explain them to an automatic computer.

To be sure, the algorithms of written arithmetic and machine arithmetic (I mean non-automatic computers) differ considerably from each other. In written arithmetic multiplication is reduced to the multiplication tables, while machine multiplication with a one-digit-number k is performed as an addition of k equal summands. Obviously it would be too much to insert the tables into the memory of a little machine, whereas the human memory readily accepts this charge. It is a compensating feature that the machine can add on all places in one turn, which would be too much for most human beings. Divisions are performed by the machine as iterated subtractions; the written algorithm of division is, as everybody knows, much more involved, and this is one of the reasons why it easily fails.

Computers based on the binary system may profit by the extremely simple tables of addition and multiplication; it is doubtful whether it would be advantageous to have men computing with such a system.

In the realm of naive arithmetic the place value system reflects the whole truth of numbers, and there is little use shaking this faith until algorithmic arithmetic is mastered. Choosing another base but 10 can hardly shake this faith; on the contrary, it is apt to reinforce it. I am not sure whether outside mathematically-interested circles a number concept detached from the positional system exists at all. The textbooks do little to promote it, even those that introduce number in the set theory context of potencies, because with no delay the finite potencies are identified with the numbers written in an algorithmic system. To be sure, the decimally-written numbers can be converted into their binary equivalents, but this is merely a new algorithm with no number concept detached from the representation system on the background. Such a number concept can hardly be grasped without the idea of complete induction, but this idea is not a favorite of textbook authors, who clearly did not yet grasp its mathematical and didactical importance.

School programmes in some countries used to contain a theory of the place value system. In other countries it has long since been abandoned

as a futile exercise. It is strange that in the countries where it was cultivated it seems to have survived all attempts at renovation. I admit that
today there is one context in which a theory of the place value system
is meaningful. I mean non-automatic computers provided that they did
not already accompany the building up of place value arithmetic at
primary school. The first steps of the theories of mechanical computing
and of the place value system are equivalent.

THE ALGEBRAICAL PRINCIPLE

Our former access to fractions was by dividing and measuring; it still
aimed at intuitive fractions. In teaching fractions it is the custom to
pass on to the algorithm as soon as possible. The rules for simplifying,
extending, and for the operations are formulated and applied. Later on
I will inspect more closely this didactics which is predestinated to flounder. I explained earlier that measuring leads to decimal rather than
to common fractions. The common fractions have been invented to
satisfy the need for unrestricted division. In this they are like the negative
numbers, which are easily motivated by counting backwards, though
their true origin is the need for unrestricted subtraction. For reasons
which still have to be expounded, it can be argued that algorithmic
fractions should better be introduced from this point of view, that is
by a strategy of extending the validity of the operations.

   If this should be our point of departure, that is, that fractions serve to
lift the restrictions from division, then $\frac{7}{3}$ would appear as the solution of
the division problem of "how much is $7:3$?" Once this $\frac{7}{3}$ has been accepted, it is dealt with in computations as though it were the result of such a
division. Mathematically it is more satisfactory to express it by saying:
$\frac{7}{3}$ is understood to be the solution of

$$(1) \qquad (?x)\, 3x = 7,$$

which is indicated by an x that in computations behaves as though it
satisfies the equation. This formulation shifts fractions from elementary
arithmetic to algebra. It is clearly based upon a fundamental algebraic
principle, which is met with wherever in algebra a number domain or
an operation is extended. Departing from the natural numbers it is a
natural explanation to introduce -3 as a number that fulfils

THE NUMBER CONCEPT – OBJECTIVE ACCESSES

$$(-3) + 3 = 0,$$

$\sqrt{2}$ as the positive number that fulfils

$$(\sqrt{2})^2 = 2,$$

and more general, $a^{p/q}$ as the number that fulfils

$$(a^{p/q})^q = a^p,$$

i as one that fulfils

$$i^2 = -1,$$

and on the strength of that definition to work with such an expression in formulae as though it fulfilled the imposed condition. For example, from (1) it follows by multiplication by 5,

$$15x = 35,$$

which shows that $\frac{35}{15}$ and $\frac{7}{3}$ are to be identified. This is the technique of simplifying and extending fractions, though now in a meaningful context rather than as the prescription that above and below the dash equal factors may be added and omitted. If two rational numbers, say $\frac{7}{3}$ and $\frac{3}{5}$, are to be added, the one shall be called x, and the other y, and from the defining equations

$$3x = 7, \qquad 5y = 3,$$

an equation for $x + y$ shall be derived. This is done by adjusting

$$15x = 35, \qquad 15y = 9,$$

from which follows

$$15(x + y) = 44.$$

Formally, this is nothing other than the usual addition of fractions, but again it has been put into a meaningful mathematical context. Other operations can be dealt with likewise. The method follows a clear pattern, and at the same time they are meaningful processes. There is not any question whether numerators or denominators are equalized, whether fractions are inverted or not. The step to fractions with indeterminate numerators and denominators is as obvious. One may regret that the intuitivity of fractions has been lost though it is doubtful whether this ever existed. The computations now take place according to a general pattern, which, to be sure, cannot be really understood without considerable algebra practice. The same idea could have been applied as early as negative numbers if intuitive methods were not available in that case.

Against this approach it can be objected that it is unknown whether an x solving the equation (?x) $3x = 7$ exists in such a way that the algebraic operations with all their laws apply to it in the way we tactily assumed. I will answer this objection on more fundamental grounds, but meanwhile I must remark that the traditional arithmetic of fractions does not yield this existence either. If the existence is to be the aim then the same technique should be presented in a different version, which would be essentially the method of equivalent number pairs. One defines $\ulcorner a, b \urcorner$ and $\ulcorner a', b' \urcorner$ ($b, b' \neq 0$) as equivalent as soon as $ab' = ba'$, and this definition is motivated by the fact that on the strength of the usual arithmetical laws the equations

$$(?x) \; bx = a \quad \text{and} \quad (?y) \; b'y = a'$$

lead via

$$(?x) \; a'bx = a'a \quad \text{and} \quad (?y) \; ab'y = aa'$$

to the same solution. Likewise the addition of number pairs is motivated by the kind of addition we obtained earlier for the solutions of (?x) $bx = a$ and (?y) $dy = c$ by applying the usual laws; and in an analogous way for the other operations. Finally the rational numbers are obtained as equivalence classes of numbers pairs, and the operations on rational numbers are got by transfer from those for number pairs.

At the moment I will not discuss the question whether and on which level rational numbers should be defined as equivalence classes. I earlier pointed out that the didactical value of the abstraction by class-forming is rather problematic. Rather than introducing equivalence classes, it is natural to behave with fractions as though $a/b = a'/b'$ whenever $ab' = ba'$. From the lowest to the highest level it is the practice of the arithmetic of fractions even if exercized by the most severe mathematicians, while the idea of equivalence classes hovers over the calculator like a guardian angel who allows him to work with representatives of the equivalence classes as though they were the equivalence classes themselves, and to speak of equal pairs where from the rigorous viewpoint of equivalence classes they should be termed equivalent. In the present case this means that we venture to say that

$$(?x)\ ax = b \quad \text{and} \quad (?y)\ a'y = b'$$

have the *same* solution as soon as $ab' = ba'$. If there is a need to check whether equals added to equals yield equals, it can easily be checked without mentioning equivalence classes.

I admit that my didactical objection against the equivalence classes of number pairs has not the same weight as against such uncomfortable classes as those of equipotent sets. The equivalence class of a fraction can be shown element by element, e.g.

$$\ldots, \frac{-14}{-6}, \frac{-7}{-3}, \frac{7}{3}, \frac{14}{6}, \frac{21}{9}, \ldots$$

Such comfort is in principle not allowed with potency classes. Therefore to define potencies one can safely adhere to Cantor's definition of assigning the same potency or cardinal to sets which are equipotent, that is, those which can be one-to-one mapped upon each other. Equivalence classes that define the rational numbers, however, as the above for $\frac{7}{3}$, can even be visualized nicely if the pairs are mapped into the plane according the Cartesian pattern; in this image an equivalence class of pairs is found on a straight line through the origin, and all straight lines through the origin that bear one more point with integral coordinates (except the vertical line) play a part in this representation. The rational numbers can even be defined by these lines. This would be an unusually suggestive introduction to rational numbers, though I have nowhere seen a systematic elaboration of this idea. It looks that suggestive because it seems to also produce the real numbers with the same ease; as soon as in this image all straight lines through the origin (except the vertical one) are admitted. Of course, since no other integral points are lying on these lines, these are ghost lines, though strongly related to the concrete world of integral points, which come closer and closer to such a ghost line. If more carefully inspected, this image loses much of its attractiveness. To be sure, the straight lines nicely represent the equivalence classes, but that is all they do. They do not betray how to add and to multiply rational numbers. The representation sheds light on simplifying and extending fractions but not on the algebraical operations. For the transition from rational to real numbers the image is better suited. I would not say that real numbers should be defined by suchlike ghost lines, but if the real numbers are supposed to exist, this image nicely visualizes their approximation by rational numbers.

This was a long digression. The question whether the rational numbers should be defined as equivalence classes of pairs of rational numbers should not be decided on the strength of such arguments. It does not matter too much whether this procedure is simply intuitive or convincing as long as it is unrelated and unoperational. If such a introduction of rational numbers remains a *hapax legomenon*, it can safely be dropped. If it can be exemplary, it is acceptable. In which context can the introduction of rational numbers as equivalence classes of number pairs become exemplary? As I earlier pointed out, the only context it fits in is the extension of a general integrity domain to a field. It is a general theorem that an integrity domain, that is a commutative ring without zero divisors, can be extended to a field, its quotients field, and this is again proved with equivalence classes of element pairs. It is a theorem with important applications, the first after the generation of rational numbers being that of rational functions, as fractions of polynomials, over a field. It is questionable whether this subject of abstract algebra still belongs to what can be considered as a school mathematics programme. In any case, the construction of quotient fields is not adapted to the level on which some school textsbooks teach the generation of rational numbers. It is a subject to be taught at the end rather than at the beginning of school mathematics.

Anyhow such a formal introduction or rather re-introduction should have been preceded by a less formal one such as I sketched above: a/b is introduced as the thing that in calculations behaves as if

$$\frac{a}{b} \cdot b = a.$$

I already mentioned that this can be done with negative numbers too: defining -3 as the thing that behaves as if

$$(-3) + 3 = 0,$$

and deriving arithmetics of negative numbers from such definitions in a similar way as shown above for rationals. For instance, from

$$(-3) + 3 = 0 \quad \text{and} \quad (-4) + 4 = 0$$

it follows by addition that

$$((-3) + (-4)) + (3 + 4) = 0,$$

whence

$$(-3) + (-4) = -(3 + 4),$$

or by multiplication of the first equation by 4 and the second with -3 that

$$4 \cdot (-3) + 4 \cdot 3 = 0 \quad \text{and} \quad (-4) \cdot (-3) + 4 \cdot (-3) = 0,$$

whence

$$(-4) \cdot (-3) = 4 \cdot 3.$$

Another example is roots. $\sqrt{a}$ (for positive rational a) is that which behaves as though its square were a. So e.g.

$$\sqrt{a}\sqrt{b} = \sqrt{ab}$$

because from

$$x^2 = a, \qquad y^2 = b$$

it follows by multiplication and using the old arithmetical laws

$$(xy)^2 = x^2 y^2 = ab.$$

This is an algebraical, that is, a mere formal argument. Whether something like $\sqrt{a}$ exists and if so in a unique way is another question, and as we shall see, an independent one. In fact, we already showed how it is dealt with.

It works the same way if the operations rather than the number domain are extended. $a^n (a > 0)$ has been defined for natural n, and the definition should be extended to rational n. The freedom of extending is restricted by the requirement that the usual laws for the arithmetic of powers remain valid, e.g.

$$(a^{1/n})^n = a^{(1/n)n} = a^1 = a$$

should hold, which defines $a^{1/n}$ as the number the n-th power of which should yield a. So $a^{1/n}$ must be the n-root of a, possibly up to a sign, and the only supplementary convention is that for even n, where there is a choice, $a^{1/n}$ is defined to be positive. Likewise a^{-n} is defined such that

$$a^{-n}a^n = a^0 = 1$$

whence

$$a^n = 1/a^n.$$

Finally for rational $r = m/n$ $(m \in \mathbf{Z}, n \in \mathbf{N})$, it is defined that

$$a^r = a^{m/n} = (a^{1/n})^m;$$

here it has to be checked, whether this does not depend on the special representation of r as m/n. Finally the usual laws have to be verified.

Similar things happen when complex numbers are introduced. Obviously $i^2 = -1$ has no real solution so i is convened to be a new number which behaves such that $i^2 = -1$.

From the start of algebra this is a familiar principle. In the subsection title I called it the algebraic principle. What I consider as the computing aspect of number expresses itself first in algorithmic arithmetic: certain symbols that each represent a specific number are operated on by certain fixed rules. Symbols of algorithmic algebra can be of different origin; they indicate an object implicitly rather than explicitly; at least in the beginning their sole meaning is that one knows how to operate on them. $\frac{7}{4}$ is completely determined by the rule that multiplied by 4 it yields 7, $\sqrt{2}$ by the rule that squared it yields 2. In my algebraic activity I may forget whether I met $\frac{7}{4}$ elsewhere, as the real number 1.75, or as an equivalence class of number pairs, and whether $\sqrt{2}$ can be located among real numbers. The number aspect I view here is that of computing number, in particular in algorithmic algebra. It is a highly efficient aspect as everybody knows from his own algebraic activity. It dominates not only such fundamental activities as extending the number concept and its operations, but, in general, setting and solving of equations. It is well known how it works there. Put the unknown quantity x, fix the suppositions it observes, and make calculations with this x according to the usual laws and as if it fulfils the stated conditions, in order to simplify them, that is to transform them from implicit into explicit ones.

With fractions and negative numbers it is a bit different. There are again equations like

$$x + 3 = 0, \qquad 4x = 7, \qquad x^2 = 2, \qquad x^2 = -1,$$

though they are not solved in the given number domain, where they do not have a solution, but by introducing new symbols for new kinds of number, the symbols $-3, \frac{7}{4}, \sqrt{2}, i$.

Yet there is little need, if any at all, to consider this as a true extension of the number domain. It is rather extending the algorithmically ascertained numbers. The treasure of explicit algorithmic means starts with the natural numbers up to 9, extends with the same degree of explicitness to the entire place value system and even to finite and infinite decimal fractions. Negative numbers are almost as explicit. Fractions, numerical root and logarithmic expressions are initially fixed in an implicit way, the way in which they are handled, but the more they are used the more explicit the status they acquire becomes; and finally $\sqrt{2}$ becomes a number as others rather than a computing token.

It should be realized that this is a natural and didactically sound development. First the natural numbers only and the operations on them are a familiar matter. Then the negative numbers arise as solutions of certain equations and undergo the usual operations. Such routines are used to prove things like

$$(-4)\cdot(-3) = 12.$$

The rational numbers appear as solutions of a certain kind of equation, the old operations are extended under certain conditions, which make that, e.g.

$$7/3 + 3/5 = 44/15.$$

It is similar with roots where it is proved that, e.g.,

$$\sqrt{a}\sqrt{b} = \sqrt{ab}$$

and with fractional exponents; it is proved that

$$a^{\frac{1}{2}} = \sqrt{a}$$

This is a characteristic algebraic way of interpolation and extrapolation, or as I would say, the formal or axiomatic extrapolation. Certain laws have been recognized in certain operations and in extending these operations it is demanded that those laws remain valid. The "permanence of computing laws" is a natural requirement, and it is a fact that in history such extending problems were decided by permanence arguments, and that extending into the complex domain has mainly been hampered by the non-permanence of certain laws (the order properties) under such an extension.

The "permanence of laws" is in bad odour. In particular, in Germany it has been banished by frowning rigorous university professors who declared that nothing is proved with the "permanence of laws". We will see that this statement is simply wrong; the principle proves a lot.

CRITICISM OF THE ALGEBRAIC PRINCIPLE

University criticism forbad the "permanence of arithmetic laws", so the safest thing left to a schoolteacher was to simply decree that

$$(-4) \cdot (-3) = 12,$$
$$\sqrt{a}\sqrt{b} = \sqrt{ab},$$
$$a^{\frac{1}{2}} = \sqrt{a},$$

This, moreover, was a kind of compliance to the usual view that algebra is a meaningless activity. Even today there are textbooks that decree such rules. Didacticians, however, found a way to save the rational motivation of such rules on the one hand, and on the other to save themselves from the severe censure of rigorous university mathematicians. They recommended a story like this:

«Extending procedures like the above are purely conventional. To be sure, we can make plausible why we put

$$(-4) \cdot (-3) = 12$$

and

$$9^{\frac{1}{2}} = 3,$$

but we cannot prove it. They are arbitrary conventions, which could be replaced by different ones.»

If you ask students in the final high school examination what they mean by this explanation, their answers show that they do not have an opinion of their own, but are simply re-echoing what their teachers have told them. On that level replacing one definition by another or one axiom by another is not a meaningful operation, unless it is performed. If this has never been done, talking about it is pure verbalism. In traditional algebra there is not, as far as I know, any opportunity to exercize the replacement of conventions; a field of such an activity would be more advanced abstract algebra or a piece of non-Euclidean, I would propose, spherical, geometry.

If negative numbers and operations on them are meaningfully introduced, they are uniquely determined. They cannot be changed *ad lib.* But even if the question of existence of a new number domain is raised or a more formal theory is aspired for, it is mathematically wrong to assert that the choice of the extending procedure has been made on the ground of mere plausibility arguments. This does in no way characterize what we did.

A teacher who has justified

$$(-4)\cdot(-3) = 12$$

according to the method on p. 229, would tell his pupils afterwards – of course, this was no proof, it was a mere plausibility argument, because in our so-called proof we have been so reckless as to use the distributive law for negative numbers which we never proved – to be sure, he did not prove it for positive numbers either.

The teacher denies that what he has done was a mathematical activity though the pupil must have received the impression that it was rather profound mathematics. The pupil is right. In denying it, the teacher causes harmful confusion.

The teacher has to know what axiomatics is, even if he never teaches it, and he has to apply this knowledge wherever it is useful. If he had done so in the present case, he would have described what he had done in quite another way. He would have said:

We want to introduce new numbers $-2, -3, \ldots$ by the requirement that $2 + (-2) = 0, 3 + (-3) = 0, \ldots$, and that the usual laws (commutativity and so on) remain valid. If this can be done, then we also can prove

$$(-2)\cdot(-3) = 6,$$

and so on.

Then he would continue as above.

The method by which this teacher has shown that $(-2)\cdot(-3) = 6$, is of the highest mathematical importance. It is not a plausibility argumentation, but it shows that if it is possible to extend the number notion from natural numbers to integers, such that the usual laws remain valid, the result is essentially unique. There is at most one extension like that.

It is the same way with fractions, with fractional exponents, with logarithms and so on. If the integers are supposed to be embedded in a field, than the field (the so-called quotients field) is *uniquely* determined up to inessential isomorphisms, which means that the arithmetical laws are fixed by the requirement of permanence. The *existence* of the quotient fields, say by equivalence classes of number pairs, is a second question. I literally mean: a second question, and I mean it both as regards the temporal succession, and as regards the importance. It is fundamentally important but operationally it is secondary. Clearly the first thing to be shown is what the extension (the quotients field) looks like if it is assumed to exist. Once this has been achieved, it can be verified whether the discovered structure really is the wanted extension – a field in which the integers are embedded. This is a liberty we take in research and in good university lectures. Why should it be refused to pupils at school?

It is much the same way with fractional exponents. First it is shown what the extension of the function

$$\Upsilon_{x \in N} a^x$$

to

$$\Upsilon_{x \in Q} a^x$$

would look like if certain laws on powers are to remain valid. Afterwards it can be examined if need be whether this candidate of extension really fulfils the necessary conditions.

Notice that it is the same as in solving equations. First the equations are dealt with as necessary conditions for the unknowns, to find out which values of the unknown are at most admissible; only afterwards is it checked whether they really suffice.

In all cases of extending the number concept or operations on numbers, the first part of the extending procedure is possible on a low level of the learning process. For the other part, the existence of the extension, the pupil should at least be on a level to understand as meaningful the mathematical question whether something exists – I mean not within the data but as a new creation. We already dealt with this condition from a general point of view: should the line of real numbers be accepted as a datum that is to be described by mathematical means, or should it be created with, say the integers, as a point of departure?

All that can be done formally in extension problems on a low level, points definitely to a unique result of the extension procedure if reasonable requirements have to be fulfilled. It is a paradoxical situation that textbook authors instead of proving the uniqueness which would be feasible, try to prove the existence which attempt must result in a complete failure, didactically and mathematically.

All the symptoms which can be understood at a low level denounce the statement that extensions be conventional. I pointed out before that without any indication of what could be changed, the claim of conventionality does not make much sense. The student might understand that driving on the right side of the road is conventional because he knows that there are countries where cars drive on the left, or at least because he can imagine such a situation. He can understand that names and measures are conventional, because he has experienced situations in which names or measures have arbitrarily been changed. Probably he could be taught that the arrangement of positions in our decimal system is conventional by making him write the digits in the opposite order and making him operate with this new kind of material. Similar examples of increasing profundity would be indispensable if we had to implement the idea of the conventional character of extensions of the number notion. But sound teaching requires that before doing so, we just stress the uniqueness of the extension procedure. Before claiming conventionality we have to understand that this claim tends to violate fundamental laws of operating with the material.

THE FORMAL ADJUNCTION

$\sqrt{2}$ is a computing object which behaves as if its square is 2. To assure the existence of such an object, I can identify it with a point of the number line or put it into the context in which I have happened to define real numbers. But how about sticking to the first definition? Can it not be justified to compute with $\sqrt{2}$ as if its square were 2? Does this method of operating with $\sqrt{2}$ not work to our satisfaction? Why should we always recall that $\sqrt{2}$ is a real number?

Whatever the answer may be, you have to be careful. Try to work with an x as if

$$0 \cdot x = 1$$

or

$$x^2 + 1 = 0$$

or

$$10^x = -1.$$

It does not work properly. It leads to contradictions; by the usual arithmetical laws the first equation is transformed into $0 = 1$; the second and the third equations flounder because according to the usual laws of order the left-hand expression should be positive, whereas the right-hand one is $\leqslant 0$. If the order laws are dropped the second is solved by complex numbers, while in the third case it should be discussed how to extend 10^x from real to complex x in a reasonable way such that it can take negative values.

Thus you can get inconsistencies if you try to calculate with an x, restricted by certain equations, as though it obeys certain arithmetical laws. This is why we have to be cautious. How do we know whether we can operate with -3, $7/4$, $\sqrt{2}$, i in that way, and consistently? We know in any case that internal contradictions have not shown up till now. But we can be more specific: if such an inconsistency did show up, we would be able to translate it into one in the arithmetic of natural numbers – we will come back to this point immediately. As soon as mathematics consists of more than counting beans, consistency proofs are merely relative: the consistency of one domain is reduced to that of another. One can try to bring everything back to sets and natural numbers, but one can also presuppose the number line, on which -3, $7/4$, $\sqrt{2}$ get their place (for i the geometrical picture of the complex numbers in the plane should be used). It is the method we analyzed earlier. There is, however, another more algebraic method, that of formal adjunction.

What does operating with $\sqrt{2}$ mean? We start with the rational numbers (**Q**). $\sqrt{2}$ is introduced. What can happen then? We get expressions like $a + b\sqrt{2}$ ($a, b \in$ **Q**). Such expressions can be readily added, subtracted and multiplied according to the rules

$$(a + b\sqrt{2}) \pm (c + d\sqrt{2}) = (a \pm c) + (b \pm d)\sqrt{2}$$
$$(a + b\sqrt{2}) \cdot (c + d\sqrt{2}) = (ac + 2bd) + (ad + bc)\sqrt{2}.$$

Even a division can be supplied:

$$\frac{1}{a + b\sqrt{2}} = \frac{a - b\sqrt{2}}{(a + b\sqrt{2})(a - b\sqrt{2})} = \frac{a}{a^2 - 2b^2} + \frac{-b}{a^2 - 2b^2}\sqrt{2}$$

is again of the same kind as we started with. (Note that the denominator does not vanish, since $\sqrt{2}$ is not rational.) The usual arithmetical laws hold among the expressions $a + b\sqrt{2}$ $(a, b \in \mathbf{Q})$; they form what is called a field, the field $\mathbf{Q}(\sqrt{2})$.

In all these computations the only thing I need know about $\sqrt{2}$ is that $(\sqrt{2})^2 = 2$; it does not matter where $\sqrt{2}$ as a real number is localized between the rational numbers. Is it only this localization that guarantees the existence of $\sqrt{2}$ and $\mathbf{Q}(\sqrt{2})$? No, there is a much simpler way. Rather than the $a + b\sqrt{2}$ consider the ordered pairs $\ulcorner a, b \urcorner$ from $\mathbf{Q}$ and work with them according to the recipe

$$\ulcorner a, b \urcorner + \ulcorner c, d \urcorner = \ulcorner a + c, b + d \urcorner$$
$$\ulcorner a, b \urcorner \cdot \ulcorner c, d \urcorner = \ulcorner ab + 2cd, ad + bc \urcorner$$

that is, as though it were $a + b\sqrt{2}$ and $c + d\sqrt{2}$. It is easily verified that these pairs fulfil the field axioms, and hence form a field. In this field the $a \in \mathbf{Q}$ can be recovered in the form $\ulcorner a, 0 \urcorner$, and moreover $\ulcorner 0, 1 \urcorner$ is a place-holder of $\sqrt{2}$ since

$$\ulcorner 0, 1 \urcorner \cdot \ulcorner 0, 1 \urcorner = \ulcorner 2, 0 \urcorner.$$

This happens to be abstract algebra and those who have pledged themselves to a belief in a system will separate it sharply from introducing $\sqrt{2}$ as a real number. In fact, however, as soon as roots appear and are algebraically operated on, it *is* abstract algebra. The reader may be surprised to learn that as early as the 8th grade, even before Bourbaki, he should have exercized abstract algebra. It is the same surprise as experienced by Molière's Bourgeois Gentilhomme Jourdain who gets excited when he learns that he has been speaking prose throughout his whole life. Of course such an activity as operating on roots does not become abstract algebra unless you think about it. In fact, as early as in ancient Babylonia, the formal adjunction was exercized, and since Lagrange, two centuries ago, this procedure has quite consciously been cultivated. What modern algebra since Steinitz has added to it, was to justify in set theory terminology that which has long since been in use. This will be substantiated later on.

I dealt with that aspect of number which I called computing number. "Behave in computations with $\sqrt{2}$ as if its square is 2." "Behaving as if" has been represented and justified here by means of number pairs.

Would this be a possible theme for school mathematics? I believe it would. Not at the moment when $\sqrt{2}$ occurs for the first time. Then it occurs naively, as something the square of which is 2. But later, if the old irrationalities are viewed from a higher vantage-point, it would not be a bad idea to let the pupil experience how he can interpret his naive activity with $a + b\sqrt{2}$ as computations with number pairs. It is so natural an idea that it is to be wondered at why it has never been realized at school. In school texts I have never seen any allusion to the formal adjunction. This is a strange thing. Many of them introduce the field concept, but with what purpose do they do so? I would say, for no purpose at all, whereas the formal adjunction would be an attractive opportunity to show what is the use of the whole abstract algebraic apparatus and how elementary algebra looks from a higher vantage-point.

I would go one step beyond this. Why restrict ourselves to such simple equations? Those things are better learned and more profoundly understood through more complex examples. Take an equation like

$$x^3 - x - 1 = 0.$$

It is easily shown not to be solvable by rational x. What can we do? We introduce something new, simply say x, that should solve the equation, and start operating with it as algebra has taught us, but of course such that $x^3 - x - 1 = 0$. This means wherever we meet an x^3, replacing it by $x + 1$; x^4 is replaced by $x^2 + x$, x^5 by $x^3 + x^2$, hence by $x^2 + x + 1$, and so on. All what we come across by applying the four operations can be reduced to $ax^2 + bx + c$ with rational a, b, c. This is obvious for addition, subtraction, and multiplication; for the division it must explicitly be proved. It goes as follows. Rather than dividing by a polynominal expression $f(x)$, which of course must not be divisible by $x^3 - x - 1$, because then it would be put 0, I can multiply with a polynomial $g(x)$ that should have the property

$$f(x)\, g(x) = 1 \quad \text{up to a multiple of} \quad x^3 - x - 1.$$

Such a $g(x)$ is found by solving

$$f(x)\, g(x) + (x^3 - x - 1)\, h(x) = 1.$$

that is looking for polynomials $g(x)$ and $h(x)$ that fulfil the equation. They can indeed be found, since $x^3 - x - 1$ does not split into factors with rational coefficients. It is done by practically the same method as used in number theory to find the greatest common divisor. For $f(x) = = x^2 + 1$, as an example, one would obtain

$$f(x)\left(-\tfrac{2}{5}x^2 + \tfrac{1}{5}x + \tfrac{4}{5}\right) + (x^3 - x - 1)\left(\tfrac{2}{5}x - \tfrac{1}{5}\right) = 1,$$

which means that

$$g(x) = -\tfrac{2}{5}x^2 + \tfrac{1}{5}x + \tfrac{4}{5}.$$

As in the case of $\sqrt{2}$ this can be interpreted as a calculus with number triples $\ulcorner a, b, c,\urcorner$ where

$$\ulcorner a, b, c\urcorner + \ulcorner u, v, w\urcorner = \ulcorner a + u, b + v, c + w\urcorner,$$
$$\ulcorner a, b, c\urcorner \cdot \ulcorner u, v, w\urcorner = \ulcorner au + aw + bv + cu, au + av$$
$$+ bu + bw + cv, av + bw + cu\urcorner.$$

What we have exhibited here is the field extension by formal adjunction. In textbooks on abstract algebra this is most often done from so high a vantage-point that no contact can be made with school algebra. It is, however, a good exercise to look into such a textbook in order to verify that what I have done here is the elementary source of what happens there.

It is already formal adjunction if computations are made with polynomials in one indeterminate (or in more of them). A polynomial

$$f(x) = a_0 + a_1 x + \cdots + a_n x^n \qquad (a_i \in \mathbf{Q})$$

is not meant as a function f of x, but rather as a formal expression which is associatively and distributively operated on. Everybody readily accepts that this works, and it requires a sophisticated criticism to analyze this naive expectation and to justify it by first writing $f(x)$ as

$$\ulcorner a_0, a_1, ..., a_n \urcorner$$

and then decreeing complicated computation rules according to which such $(n + 1)$-tuples should be added and multiplied. This, too, is abstract algebra. The existence of the polynomials is even less obvious than that of expressions like $a + b\sqrt{2}$, or $a + b\vartheta + c\vartheta^2$ with $\vartheta^3 - \vartheta - 1 = 0$. In abstract algebra the adjunction of, say, ϑ is formulated as follows. Form the ring $\mathbf{Q}[x]$ of the polynomials in x with rational coefficients, and in this ring the ideal I of the multiples of $x^3 - x - 1$, thus $I =$

$= (x^3 - x - 1) \, \mathbf{Q} \, [x]$. Behave now as if this ideal were 0, that is pass to $\mathbf{Q} \, [x]$ mod I, or, in set theory terms, consider the classes $g(x) + I$. They form a field, in which $\mathbf{Q}$ can be recovered as a subfield, namely if for $g(x)$ all polynomials of degree $\leqslant 0$ are allowed. In the new field $x^3 - x - 1 = 0$ has the solution $x + I$, or, for short, x.

This is a modern, as it were, static disguise of the above operational procedure, which was already known to Lagrange. To assure constructively the existence of such a field, the method is the same as with $\sqrt{2}$ – operating with triples $\ulcorner a, b, c \urcorner$ as though it were the expressions $ax^2 + bx + c$ mod $x^3 - x - 1$. It does not matter at all that from another viewpoint the elements of such a field are real or complex numbers.

If one root ϑ of the equation $x^3 - x - 1 = 0$ has been formally introduced, $x^3 - x - 1$ can be formally divided by $x - \vartheta$, to get a quadratic polynomial, viz. $x^2 + \vartheta x + (\vartheta^2 - 1)$. This has formally a new root ϑ_1, which is a root of $x^3 - x - 1$, too, and finally there is a third, ϑ_2, which can be expressed by ϑ and ϑ_1. It is a quite meaningless question to ask for the real or complex numbers to which they correspond. Algebraically the roots cannot be distinguished; Galois' theory was just created to interpret this kind of symmetry phenomena. Only if transplanted into the number continuum are the three roots individualized. Then it appears that one of them is real and the others are complex (which shows that they cannot be expressed by only one of them). Up to this moment it makes no sense to ask which one is real.

School mathematics accounts for such ambiguities by defining $\sqrt{m}$ as the positive solution of $x^2 = m$ $(m > 0)$. From the formal algebraic viewpoint $\sqrt{m}$ and $-\sqrt{m}$ are indistinguishable; they are defined as the solutions of $x^2 = m$. The utmost care is needed to avoid mistakes at this point.

Formal adjunction is rightly exercized in traditional instruction but it remains as it were unconscious, and only in one case is it duly acknowledged, namely in the transition from the real to the complex field. Again i and $-i$ are algebraically indistinguishable, but here they remain so, even under order properties that help to distinguish with $\sqrt{2}$ and $-\sqrt{2}$. One root of $x^2 + 1$ is called i, and the other necessarily becomes $-i$; it does not make sense to ask which one is now truly i. To be certain there also exists a geometrical representation of complex numbers. If they are mapped upon a previously-oriented plane (that is a plane provided with a "positive" sense of circulation) such as the real numbers were mapped upon an oriented line, then it is the custom to place i such that $1, i, -1$ in this succession are lying in the positive sense. Then i and $-i$ can be distinguished.

CHAPTER XII

DEVELOPING THE NUMBER CONCEPT
FROM INTUITIVE METHODS TO
ALGORITHMIZING AND RATIONALIZING

καὶ μὴν ἀριθμον ἔξοχον σοφισμάτων ἐξεῦρον αὐτοις ...

Number, the first science, I invented for them   Aischylos, *Prometheus*

In the development of the number concept I would distinguish the following phases of the learning process, which are not necessarily identical with what I earlier called levels:
    Intuitive operation,
    Algorithmic operation,
    Algebraic operation,
    Global organization (the field concept),
    Subordination to the system of mathematics.
The division into phases does not mean a temporal succession. With regard to different concepts the learner can be in different phases, and with regard to the same concept he can operate in two different phases at one time.

Moreover, after the intuitive phase I expressly mentioned the belonging algorithmic one, which consequently I should have repeated after the algebraic and the following phases.

INTUITIVE ARITHMETICS WITH STRUCTURED MATERIAL

We stressed the didactical priority of the counting number. From olden times the didactics of initial arithmetic has aimed at systematizing the counting process, and if I am not mistaken, it still does so with good teaching methods. The child should learn to add by counting further, to subtract by counting backwards, to articulate the counting by tens, to multiply by counting with other intervals but 1, and so on.

To teach systematic counting structured material played an important part from olden times, and there is no indication why this should have changed. It is one of the big disadvantages of Venn diagrams that they invite the textbook author and user to ignore the necessity of structuration. Of course, the pupil should learn to work with unstructured material, too, namely to learn how to structurate. To work with unstructured material as such or to destroy structure intentionally is a theoretical pleasure which has little to do with teaching arithmetic.

Venn diagrams are slowing down the learning of systematic counting. In the operation of adding they invite the pupil to count anew instead of counting further. No method has been discovered yet to teach subtraction by Venn diagrams. Apart from sheer nonsensical representations, I found many serious but no really convincing attempts. The cleverest I saw was of the following kind: five birds, three of them sitting, and two flying away, to illustrate the subtraction 5 − 2. Most of the representations of subtraction by Venn diagrams need clumsy verbal explications to be understood, even with adults. It is strange that after so many failures dogmatic belief in Venn diagrams is still unshaken.

Another requirement that calculating material had to fulfil from olden times was homogeneity. On the abacus they used stones, balls, counters which were considered as equivalent; on the abacus of my childhood beads of two colours were moveable. One should expect stress on homogeneity of the material as a consequence of the set theory viewpoint, since an element of a set is just an element, nothing else. The authors of most of today's arithmetic books, however, apparently make efforts to represent the sets with which children are expected to learn arithmetic as inhomogeneous as they can – Venn diagrams are a hotchpotch of letters, numbers, stars, crosses and other meaningless figures, all different. The background of this attitude is not a didactic principle but a mathematical error which will be analyzed later: two a's at different spots of the blackboard mean the same; so twice the same sign in one Venn diagram is not allowed, because it would indicate the same element instead of different ones – this seems to be the authors' course of thought. This is wrong. It presupposes that the Venn diagram is a meaningless collection of signs rather than a picture, which contains pictures, say of coins, which the child has to count. Some arithmetic textbooks even go as far as to make the child believe that the number of elements of a set can only be determined if all elements look different. Of course, the child should learn to work with inhomogeneous material, too. But this is less appropriate in training computing skills and inhomogeneous material as a principle is counter-sense.

As to the structuration of the material a logical (or conventional) and an intuitive view can be distinguished. Our number system is logical-conventionally structured by means of the place value; a similar structure exists in the systems of measures and, more concretely, in the monetary system. The place value structure is imitated on the abacus where a counter gets the 10-fold value if it is moved to the next column on the left (sometimes there are intermediate steps of 5). The abacus disappeared in our countries with the rise of written arithmetic. It was preserved in the Far East and in Russia. From there it spread again to the West in the beginning of the 19th century though in a trivializing interpretation. I mean the abacus of my childhood, with 10 rows of 10 moveable beads. This is *intuitively* strutured material; each bead means the same unit; there are no higher units as in the place value and the monetary system. Montessori reinterpreted this children's abacus in the place value sense to use it in teaching arithmetics.

PAPER-BOUND MATERIAL

Formerly operations with small numbers were learned by uniting and separating sets of concrete objects; in particular the fingers were familiar implements. There has been a tendency in the last few years to replace concrete and tangible objects by their pictures on paper. This is a reasonable idea if it is realized with common sense and imagination, which alas is apparently rare. Though sets are represented on the paper in a sometimes quite realistic way, a strange tendency prevails to envelop them up in unmotivated Venn diagrams. Later we will explain where this comes from – it is a long chain of errors, which ends up in a series of dull imitations. In spite of much better devices, the Venn diagram dominates the field. The excellent Hungarian arithmetic books, in my view the best textbook series in the world, avoid the Venn diagram completely. To represent sets they use natural groupings only, such as towers of blocks, books on a shelf, children on a bench, and in such contexts numbers are added and subtracted; e.g. $5 - 2$ by 2 blocks tumbling down from a tower of 5.

On the other hand with Venn diagrams such nonsense as Figure 2 is quite usual, maybe with the plus-sign instead of the ∪-sign, and in the sum diagram quite different objects but those of the summands. There

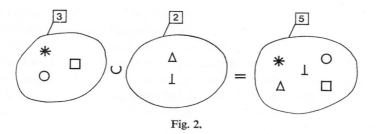

Fig. 2.

are, however, also correct representations like Figure 3 which is a faithful picture of what the child did in olden days when he had to add two heaps of counters – yet even this is artificial, abstract and dull compared to the Hungarian method. Less satisfactory is Figure 4. Subtraction is the stumbling block of all Venn diagrammatics. Concrete moveable material and the Hungarian method are quite superior.

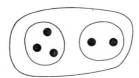

Fig. 3.

One may ask, what is the rationale of this material? Why cannot the child add counters on its desk, why should this be represented on the paper? Whenever practice material is replaced by consumption material, there is good reason for scepticism. With consumption material the teaching materials industry earns many times the amount they can get with practice material. Are there abuses? They produce a lot of bad consumption material, but in fact it is also the same situation as regards practice material and I am not left with the impression that the percentage of rubbish is any larger in the consumption than in the practice material. On the contrary, useless consumption material disappears faster from the market, if it ever reaches it, than textbooks and similar practice material.

Consumption material makes teaching more expensive. In the era of the slate writing, schools and pupils could not have afforded it. Do you get more value for this money? I think an experienced and imaginative teacher could make much better use of the opportunities provided by free rather than paper-bound material. Paper-bound material for teaching elementary arithmetic can, however, boast of two advantages, which must not be disregarded. First, the individual activity of the pupil can be easier checked; secondly, it imposes on the inexperienced teacher a well-designed didactics of concrete operations, which perhaps he would not have thought of otherwise. The second argument is particularly important – it can be advantageous to bind the teaching material as much as possible to paper to completely fix its order and didactics. This may even be true beyond the first stage of arithmetic teaching. Though it would be interesting to investigate in principle the pros and cons of paper-bound concrete consumption material, I must leave this problem where it is.

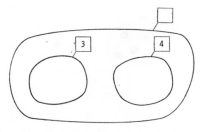

Fig. 4.

EXAMPLES OF STRUCTURED MATERIAL

Much modern material is quite intentionally structured. To represent numbers it is often an underlying principle that every unit fills the same volume, though the units are suitably arranged to form larger objects. This is the case with the material of Cuisenaire and of Stern with sticks built up from 1 to 10 elementary cubes. Cuisenaire has attached great value to binding the numbers to colours; this is defended by some as an article of faith, while others criticize it as the worst heresy, but both efforts are not really worthwhile. Stern has designed more material complementing the reckoning sticks.

Z. Dienes' material is more flexible. The elementary cubes are systematically arranged according to all dimensions, cubes, sticks of ten, plates of hundred, cubes of thousand, and maybe further in the same way. Other bases than 10 are also used. In demonstrations this material can very ably be used for other purposes than simple computing, e.g. for solving equations in algebra. It seems that children learn to work more easily with this material than mathematics teachers who are obviously too much attached to formal methods to be able to work as intuitively.

As stressed before, didacticians have never been prone to encouraging computing by pure counting. The last-mentioned materials favour *systematic* counting, structural addition and subtraction, which should finally lead to algorithmic computing. The intuitive material has sometimes been criticized. It is said that children remain attached too long to the material, which might retard the transition to algorithmic arithmetic, or even make it more difficult or even impossible. I can imagine that there is a real danger in counting with fingers, but I did not get the impression from modern material that it works in this wrong way. I think you can let the child play with the material as long as he likes to. The more sophisticated the material is, the sooner the child becomes fed up with it, once he has mastered it.

The sticks are also used in intuitive fractions arithmetic. More precisely, simple proportions are visualized with the aid of the sticks. This is going a bit too far, I think.

THE PAIRS SET

Under the numerosity aspect the product of two natural numbers is defined by means of the pairs set. If A is a set of a elements and B one of b elements, then $a \cdot b$ is the number of elements of the pairs set $\ulcorner A, B \urcorner$, that is the set of $\ulcorner a, b \urcorner$ with $a \in A$ and $b \in B$. The rectangular pattern of

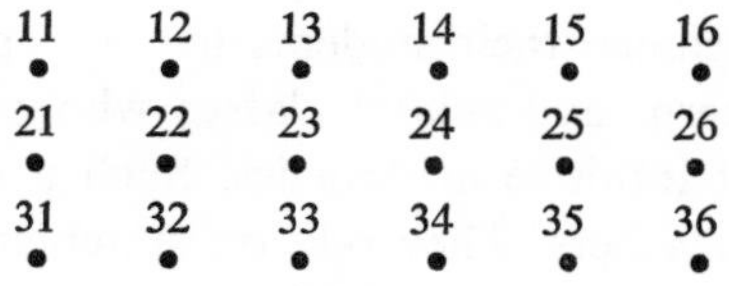

11	12	13	14	15	16
•	•	•	•	•	•
21	22	23	24	25	26
•	•	•	•	•	•
31	32	33	34	35	36
•	•	•	•	•	•

Fig. 5.

Figure 5 vizualizes the product $3 \cdot 6$. There can be no doubt that these rectangular patterns should be extensively used to visualize multiplication. In traditional arithmetic they were not neglected but they were not popular either; and it is obvious why – they are not much use in algorithmic computing. To see that $3 \cdot 6 = 18$ the pattern must be rearranged, which destroys its shape and symmetry. For this reason didacticians invented other devices. They trusted counting better, but used a sophisticated version of larger than unit steps. Systematic counting is, both in theory and practice, a useful instrument. Among modern arithmetic books there are some that completely disregard systematic counting.

In the present case systematic counting means the inductive build-up of the product, $3 \cdot 6$ as $6 + 2 \cdot 6$ and more generally $(1 + a) \cdot b$ as $b + a \cdot b$, with $0 \cdot b = 0$ or $1 \cdot b = b$ as a point of departure. Formerly this was *the* training principle for the tables of multiplication. Most desk computers build up products inductively by addition.

The inductive reduction of the multiplication to addition is the most efficient means of acquiring arithmetical skills. Through pure dogmatism it is rejected by some innovators. They contend that "later in the field concept it appears that multiplication is independent of addition, and this should be accounted for at an early stage". This argument is entirely wrong. In the general field concept the multiplication is *separated* from the addition. This is perfectly legitimate. But the general field concept is an empty box. To fill it, at least one example of a field is needed; at least once a set should have been provided with an addition and a multiplication, and unless one want to restrict oneself to finite fields, the field of rationals is the one that must have been produced before. But if in this field multiplication is to be defined no dogma can save you the trouble of reducing multiplication inductively to addition as it has always been done in elementary arithmetic.

But the rectangular pattern of multiplication should never be neglected. Stressing it has been a plus-point of the "New Mathematics" though overstressing it is not an entirely new feature. There have always been teachers who trained their students to "see" products like $7 \cdot 8$ in the rectangular pattern, and school classes who performed incredible feats in this kind of intuitive arithmetics. Such a degree of intuitivity does not suit most teachers. They rely on systematic counting, on the inductive generation of products and of tables. But again the rectangular pattern should not be forgotten. With the Dienes material it can nicely be supported; the sticks look less appropriate.

With respect to some overstressing of the rectangular pattern in the didactics of today, it is to be wondered at that applications in which the rectangular pattern could be operative are neglected. This attitude however can readily be understood, since in all applications the numerosity aspect of the natural number which is dear to many innovators is soon ground off; in applications the factors are soon real, even negative numbers to which the numerosity basis of the rectangular pattern does not seem to fit.

The usual applications, indeed, in elementary arithmetics are forming the pairs set $\ulcorner A, B \urcorner$ of two given finite sets A, with a, and B, with b, elements and stating that it has ab elements, for example: "how many boy-girl pairs can be formed from 5 boys and 4 girls?" The true applications, however, look much different. Then one is given a set that has still to be structured as a pairs set. I mean problems like the following. The school time is divided according to two criteria, the day of the week, and the class period, which yields a pattern of, say, 5 days and 4 periods, with 20 periods per week. The original set Ω of school time (if at all this is a set) is structured. Here A, B and $\ulcorner A, B \urcorner$ are to be understood as sets of subsets of Ω, viz. A the set of days of the week, B the set of periods, and $\ulcorner A, B \urcorner$ the set of pairs of days and periods.

A tremendous number of such examples are available. The most conspicuous is that of the rectangle that according to width is divided into 5 strips and according to height into 4 strips (which need not be equal) such that 20 subrectangles arise. This pattern serves area computation if the subsegments correspond to units, say 5 in the width and 4 in the height. I vividly remember my first mathematical experience in my pre-school childhood – the overwhelming bewilderment which came over me when I understood how the area of a rectangle is computed by dividing it horizontally and vertically. I am telling you this because adults forget only too readily what can astonish children. If I now understand that experience properly, then what mattered was not the fact that this set of five horizontal strips and four columns counted $5 \cdot 4 = 20$ objects. This I would already have known since I already knew about multiplication. The reason for my bewilderment must have been the constructive structuration of the structureless rectangle. My father drew it in the sand. A rectangle in a book with all auxiliary lines in it would never have matched the intuitive force of this structure *in statu nascendi.*

The potency of the pairs set as a product of the potencies of the factor sets can be memorized even by an idiot. It is entirely irrelevant. Just as irrelevant are problems where these general sets have to be replaced with special ones. The only relevant problems are those where the pairs set structure has still to be created by the pupil. In traditional arithmetic this is done with the rectangle though only to justify the area formula. Once this has been obtained, the pupil is allowed to forget about the structuration of the rectangle. Of course, to compute the area of a rectangle with the sides 23.46 cm and 17.89 cm nobody draws a rectangle of those measurements to subdivide it, in I do not know what. Thus the area formula does not become operative in arithmetic instruction. Of course, the schoolchild could imagine such subdividings. But to do this he has not exercised enough the structuration of a set as a pairs set. This should not be restricted to equidistant subdividings but the rectangle subdivided in two directions should be the application and the visualization of structuring a set according to two characteristics.

In spite of the stress I have laid here on the pairs sets as a means of structuring, I must also stress that it is entirely insufficient. It does not work in many cases in which it is wrongly quoted. I expounded this earlier.* If from 5 boys and 4 girls all pairs "boy-girl" are formed (which is a bit of a crazy problem), the set of pairs in the set theory sense is, indeed, the correct model. More often than not, however, the pairs set badly fits these multiplication problems. I recall the problem of the 5 cats each with 4 paws: "how many paws are there?" The "each" suggests multiplying, but as I explained earlier, the model on the background is not the pairs set. This model is even less adapted to the next problem – "at a meeting of 5 people a chairman and a secretary must be appointed; in how many different ways can it be done?" The mathematical model of such problems is the mapping of P into Q such that all elements of Q have the same number of originals. Likewise "m baskets with n eggs each" structures the set of eggs not as a pairs set but by means of a mapping f that maps every egg in its basket, and this is just a mapping

* See p. 189.

upon an image set of potency m, where every image has precisely n originals.

This model should be profoundly exercised in teaching. It would be a valuable application of set theory concepts instead of the host of worthless ones in which the newer textbooks abound.

THE RECTANGULAR MODEL GENERALIZED

Once the rectangular pattern has been exploited for intuitive multiplication of natural numbers, fractions announce themselves. By this model multiplying becomes the most intuitive operation with fractions. The unit square can be filled up with $5 \cdot 4$ rectangles with sides $\frac{1}{5}$ and$\frac{1}{4}$; thus such a rectangle is $\frac{1}{20}$ of the square, thus $\frac{1}{5} \cdot \frac{1}{4} = \frac{1}{20}$. As intuitively $\frac{2}{5} \cdot \frac{3}{4} = \frac{6}{20}$ is obtained.

From here, it is a small step (in particular along decimal fractions) to the interpretation of the rectangle, with respect to its area, as the product of its sidelengths, or conversely, to the interpretation of the product of two magnitudes as the rectangle with the given factors as sides. As is well known, in the geometrical algebra of the Greeks the product of two magnitudes is always called the rectangle; a vestige of this terminology is our reading a-square for a^2. But even today the interpretation of products as rectangles plays a great part, namely in the definition and application of the integral concepts. In the experiments of Emma Castelnuovo* it appears that children spontaneously view the moment of a force as a product of arm and force.

The rectangular visualization of the product should be further developed, that is, not only with length of sides and areas of rectangles, and not just with natural number factors. This is strongly suggested by the integral concept, but it can already be attempted at a much more elementary stage. One can map man-hours, kilogram-meters, kilowatt-hours and watts as unit squares, and magnitudes measured by such gauges as rectangles; for instance 100 man-hours (watt) as a rectangle of 5 men (ampère) and 20 hours (volt) or of 4 men (ampère) and 25 hours (volt), and so on. Earlier** I explained, how this multiplication of concrete numbers can be justified mathematically, and how important

---

* *Educational Studies in Mathematics* **2** (1970), 309.
** p. 207.

it is in applications and, consequently, as a teaching matter. The only thing I wish to emphasize here is its visualization.

The most momentous application of the rectangular pattern is in multiplying times by velocities to obtain paths (or volumes by densities to get masses and so on). I mention it here, though I do not believe that it can be done at an early stage. In fact, durations are already less intuitive than path lengths, and velocities, densities, and so on are merely derived magnitudes; to get them one has to divide path lengths by times, masses by volumes. As to the velocities one should start with the experience that there are different velocities; one should estimate their mutual relatedness, first by "more" and "less", then by "double" and "half", and the final task would be to find an exact measure of velocity. Such procedure can be repeated with weights (masses) and volumes, and with many other pairs of magnitudes. Out of these examples a general principle crystalizes, perhaps to be formulated explicitly. Of course the rules to compute velocities and similar magnitudes can also be dictated to the student, but this method has never been convincingly succesful.

Though it is not perhaps the proper place to discuss this, I mention it here to make clear that it is a rather long way before one comes to such notions as velocity. In an earlier stage of arithmetics teaching one should be content with logically similar though more intuitive notions as the price by unit obtained as the quotient of price and quantity. But once velocities have risen above the horizon of concepts, one should draw all consequences of intuitive representation. The rectangle "path" as a product of "time" and "velocity" should be exhibited. Variable velocities should be admitted, too, at least to prevent pupils from believing that velocities should be constant. With the uniformly accelerated motion, one should measure the path covered as the triangular area bounded by the graphic of the velocity and consciously prepare in this way the integral of a function as the area bounded by its graphic. I say this parenthetically to come back to it if graphics are dealt with as a means of visualization.

TWO KINDS OF DIVISION

After having strongly advocated intuitive models, I must warn against any kind of exaggeration of intuitivity.

The rectangle model of multiplication is rather symmetric with regard to the factors. This symmetry is lacking when concrete numbers are multiplied: if kilogrammes or piece numbers are multiplied by unit prices, hours by hour wages, numbers of months by 30, then there is a more or less pronounced distinction between multiplier and multiplicand; if amounts of money are multiplied by interest rates, contents by specific weights, volt by ampère, then multiplier and multiplicand can hardly be told apart, but there is still no symmetry between first and second factor. Nevertheless the model of the area of the rectangle fits very well in all cases. Models are expected to be useful for general purposes.

Strangely enough this asymmetry has strongly been felt by the older didacticians in the case of the division. The reason was, without doubt, that division itself was felt as a highly intuitive operation. Distributing 20 loaves of bread among 5 persons is intuitively a different thing from distributing 20 loaves of bread such that every person gets 4 and asking how many persons this is possible with. The first where 20 loaves of bread were distributed among 5 people was called the distribution division, the second, where 20 loaves of bread were divided by 4 loaves of bread was the ratio division. The pupil was committed to solving the two problems by different methods, in particular, long divisions looked different in both cases. I do not believe there were many teachers who understood and could implement what the textbooks committed them to do.

Obviously it is a devious course to translate the difference between the concrete problems into one between algorithms. It is the meaning of algorithms that they are universal. General patterns are to make life easier. Computers, too, know one division only, and what is good for the goose is good for the gander.

To be sure, there are differences in posing the problem; the teachers should know them consciously as should the pupil unconsciously. But the ways of posing the problem comprise a much greater variety than could be accounted for by the dichotomy of distribution and ratio division. Even in the distribution division it is not true, though the textbooks would make one believe it to be so, that the 20 loaves of bread are divided by an abstract number 5; it is rather 20 loaves of bread divided by 5 persons, which gives 4 loaves of bread/person (or 4 loaves of bread per person). Take further all the divisions where the area is divided by the length to get the width, kilogramme by volume to get

kg/cm^3, path by time to get velocity, and so on. To be consistent one should invent special kinds of division for all these problems. It cannot be held that two kinds of division are less absurd than a few hundred. It is, as has been pointed out several times before, a characteristic of mathematics that isomorphic procedures are reduced to one abstract scheme. If here an intuitive model is wanted, the rectangle model is ready to hand for both multiplication and division. The pupil should learn to interpret the multiplication of concrete numbers in the rectangular pattern to provide multiplication with a concrete meaning, not only if cardinals are multiplied, but even more so if they are numbers under the measuring aspect. If this model is used, a certain symmetry of factors is suggested, and as a consequence there is no need any more to distinguish divisions according to the factor that plays the role of divisor.

But again I would not like to be misinterpreted. The schoolchild should be trained to solve both problems as "by what should 4 be multiplied to get 20?" and "what should be multiplied by 4 to get 20?", and many others too, not to acquire a special routine in each case but to understand the common model so that one routine suffices.

I dealt with this subject because the twofold division, though long buried, rises up from the dead again and again, in every generation, if some didactician starts thinking about division on a less solid foundation than the theory of magnitude can offer.

THE NUMBER LINE – TWO MISTAKES

It is always drawn horizontally because that is the tradition to which we are attached. The most obvious number lines are, indeed, vertical: the thermometer, the floors, the instrument to measure body length. It is a fact that the horizontal number line does not work properly with young children. I learned this from a number of teachers, and I cannot believe that their classes were exceptions. It is probably generally known, or rather it should be. But it has not been changed. Tradition is much too authoritative.

It is with "positive-negative", or with "left-right" just as it is with many other concepts that arise by polarization, the poles are not properly distinguished. How long does it not take with some children before they can tell right from left, and even if they can do so, they still lack the applicability to turn right and turn left, to telling *b* from *d*, and 9 o'clock from 3 o'clock on the dial. I read in the newspapers that the inhabitants of Tristan da Cunha found difficulty in distinguishing the concepts right and left; instead they use East, West, North, and South, which caused them much trouble when they were evacuated to London. Adults often show a lack of comprehension in the polarisation difficulties of children. They consider it as self-evident that the right hand defines the right leg, the right eye, and the right turn, which for some reason does not hold for children who have difficulty with polarization. Whether the difficulty lies in kinesthesis or in the field of intuition, I do not know, and I do not know of any research on this subject either.

The natural numbers are first given as numerosity numbers or in the temporal reel-off as counting numbers. The temporal course also knows a polarization, that of past and future, which, however, is a natural and compelling polarization. A drawn straight line that should be interpreted as a number line, needs a direction; which of the two is preferred is convention. By the writing direction we prefer, we are led to direct horizontal or approximately horizontal lines from left to right, but vertical ones are usually directed from below to above though this contradicts the writing direction. What is below and above on the paper is, to be sure, again convention; it is strange that in all civilizations this has been settled by the same convention: below is the border that is next to the writer's chest. When children start drawing, this has often not yet been settled; but with all children books where people and animals are pictured "on their feet" the "below-above" indoctrination proceeds fast.

I believe if the number line is used with little children, it should be drawn vertically and directed below-above. Below-above is a polarization, too, but it is one that works much better than "left-right". Maybe an inclined number line would be even better, or an inclined ladder (do not use stairs) or a strip as in certain dice games. Of course such proposals have little chance of being adopted. The horizontal number line is too firmly rooted. Moreover vertical or even inclined number niels seriously hamper the smooth lay out of a printed text. Later on we will indicate other traditional conventions, which are as controversial as the horizontal number line though nobody dares to question them.

I must explicitly draw attention to another mistake I have found in books and films where the number line was represented. The number line is pictured as many rulers, with partition points or strokes, and at their left the numbers 1, 2,..., of course without a 0. This calls forth all the well-known mistakes children can make when using the ruler (measuring from 1 instead of 0). I even saw a number line, where the numbers 1, 2,... were exactly midway between the partition points. Obviously the author had the intention of numbering the intervals. In itself this is not so silly. We do so with the years A.D.: the year 1 is meant to be that in the beginning of which Jesus of Nazareth was born and at the end of which he was one year old, so his first birthday was the beginning of the year 2 (as it was of the second year of his life). What is impractical in this method shows up in the chronology B.C.: that at the end of which Jesus is meant to be born, is 1 B.C., and a year 0 does not exist. It is clear that the textbook author who numbered the intervals, got into difficulty when he continued exploring the number line in the negative region.

THE NUMBER LINE AS A MEANS OF VISUALIZATION

The natural number that was recognizable on the abacus as a numerosity of counters, with the sticks and plates as a numerosity of elementary cubes, is completely abandoned in the context of the number line. A sequence of equidistant points is numbered like the houses in a street, and soon the sequence is even continued beyond 0 to the left. All the textbooks I investigated show an abrupt and unmotivated passage to the number line after half a year, or one year's teaching of the numerosity number. One gets the impression that no textbook author is aware of this change. He simply starts using the numbers hitherto taught, in a context that has little to do with their numerosity definition. It is quite probable that neither teachers nor pupils will notice it or will be handicapped. In fact, the counting aspect that prevails on the number line though repressed by the numerosity approach has been for a long time a familiar one, even for children, who either knew it before they entered school or who met with it meanwhile in many contexts in arithmetic lessons, in other lessons, in numerous games, and outside school. It is on the contrary, quite improbable that the teacher for whom the counting aspect is the most vivid of the number concept, has refrained all the time from teaching it unconsciously in many instances while committed by a rigid textbook to teaching the official numerosity aspect only. With the number line arithmetic teaching which had been artificially isolated from the child's life, and cultivated as if in a hothouse, again becomes connected to it.

The intuitive character of the number line differs much from that of the earlier mentioned intuitive material. It neither exploits nor prepares the place value system, and as an access to algorithmic computing the number line is not useful. Quite a lot of other things are seen on the number line: The "less and more" is visualized by the direction in which the line is run through. Addition is visualized as a shift to the right, subtraction as one to the left, multiplication as a dilatation. The embedding of the natural numbers into the number line shows beyond natural numbers, it foreshadows extensions of number domains and operations. Moreover, mappings come on early, which no doubt can be an advantage. This makes the number line a valuable device, though as with all things, there is the danger that people might go too far and try to get from the number line more than it can yield. Compared with the other materials, it is definitive; unlike the sticks it is not abandoned after a while.

Whether the number line may be termed teaching material is a question of terminology. Properly said, something is teaching material if by selling it, one can earn money. But maybe there are already moveable pairs of rails as models of computing on the number line, or similar instruments, like sliderules. The principle is simple enough for multifarious concretization.

I have already mentioned that the number line is used didactically in three ways:

(1) The number line as it were a ruler, where the points are invariably *identified with* real numbers, for short, the ruler interpretation, or the object interpretation.

(2) The line on which a scale with an arbitrary origin, an arbitrary gauge, and an arbitrary direction have been marked, and the points are *labelled* by real numbers, in short, the coordinate interpretation.

(3) The line as a rigid substratum, on which the numbers act as operators (addition, multiplication) – the operator interpretation.

I will explain why the second and third interpretation should be didactically rejected, but before passing on to this discussion, I must explain how addition is represented in the object interpretation. In modern textbooks I saw two methods. In Figure 6 each single 3-addition to 0, 1, 2, ... is suggested by an arrow. In Figure 7 the number line is lifted as if it were a ruler and laid down three units further to the right. Both mappings can be imagined to have arisen from unit jumps. In this

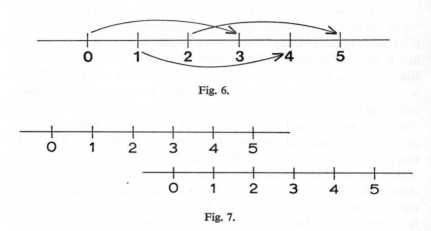

Fig. 6.

Fig. 7.

course of thought, shifts to the left are interpreted as additions to negative numbers. So negative numbers first appear only in the function sign; but this can lead immediately to their localization on the number line, hence to the extension of N to Z. Likewise are multiplications represented as dilatations.

Thus mappings are understood in this way that to an element of the number line is assigned an element of the number line, rather than that the labelling of the points is being changed. It is the way geometric transformations are understood today: points are assigned to points; it is the way motions of space are viewed as well as operators in function spaces. It is a universal method and didactically the most efficient through its direct appeal to the process of mapping. Its adversary is the next one.

COORDINATE INTERPRETATION

This is a method with very restricted scope and less clear since it divorces point and number from each other. In former times it was quite usual to interpret transformations as coordinate changes and physicists still adhere to this habit. Of course, as long as one sticks to one coordinate system and a realistic interpretation, it does not matter whether coordinates are used or not; it then is unnecessary duplication to divorce coordinates from points. But the adherents of the coordinate interpretation prefer to extend this interpretation to the transformations. This, however, can only be done in an artificial and badly motivated way, as we shall now see.

A new scale is introduced on the number line, with the origin at the old 3, though with the same direction and gauge. The old scale is coloured blue, the new one orange. The 3-addition is interpreted as a change of label: at the same point a new label x corresponds to an old label $x + 3$. Isn't it crazy that 3-addition leads from the new to the old labelling? To be sure this can be avoided by saying that the 3-addition is performed by a shift of the origin over 3 steps to the left (or if you prefer, of -3 to the right). This is quite confusing for pupils who struggle with the left-right polarity, and it looks absurd if the number line is drawn vertically.

With the multiplication it is the same. The multiplication by 3 is represented by introducing a new orange scale besides the old blue scale, and then assigning to the new label x of a point its old label $3x$, or by reducing the old gauge to a third of its size.

What grave sins have I committed to be plagued in my old days by the nightmares of my first year at university? Then they called it co- and contragredience. I did not understand it until to explain it myself in a first-year college course I put it into the frame of modern linear algebra. I dare to explain it to the present reader, though I would not dare to frighten undergraduates with such ghosts.

In a few words I will say what I mean: the n-dimensional vector space R is described by coordinates on an ordered basis $e_1, ..., e_n$. The coordinates of the point $x = \Sigma \xi_i e_i$ are $\xi_1, ..., \xi_m$. Another basis $f_1, ..., f_m$ is chosen,

$$f_j = \Sigma_i \alpha_{ij} e_i.$$

This provides the point x with new coordinates $\eta_1, ..., \eta_n$ such that

$$\Sigma_j \eta_j f_j = \Sigma_i \xi_i e_i,$$

hence

$$\xi_i = \Sigma_j \alpha_{ij} \eta_j.$$

This shows how coordinates transform themselves in a sense opposite to that of the bases. In today's terminology this is readily understood but it requires an advanced stage of study.

I think that the number line loses its proper character as a means of visualization if introducing the operations involves such complications. Of course at a certain moment the change of origin and gauge must also be exercised. This is a matter of coordinate transformations of analytic geometry or linear algebra. Teachers know this is a difficult chapter. It cannot be justified as a means of complicating the introduction and intuitive representation of the operations.

OPERATOR INTERPRETATION

In the operator interpretation the numbers are not identified with points of the line but with mappings of the line considered as a rigid stick. The line is a substratum; the mathematically essential thing is the operations with the line. 3 is not a point on the line, but the mapping that shifts each point through 3 units to the right. The sum of 3 and 5 is the mapping composed of the mapping 3 and the mapping 5, that is composed of the right shifts through 3 and through 5, and this results in a right shift through 8. Others formulate it as follows: 3 is an arrow of size 3 directed to the right which can be laid down everywhere on the line. Arrows are added by joining them point to tail.

It looks elegant. It is a method that is popular in higher mathematics and I think rightly so. The usual interpretation of the addition shows a lack of symmetry. A number is added *to* another, the one is a direct object of the operation, and the other an indirect one, to say it grammatically. On the number line it looks the same. If I add 3 to 5, the 5 is a point to which something happens, 3 is an operation, and the result 8 is again a point. By the operator interpretation this asymmetry looks removed. Later I will show that this feeling of asymmetry is not justified, it arises from a wrong interpretation of the method. Meanwhile I continue with the exposition of the operator interpretation.

According to this interpretation N consists of the right shifts over integral intervals of the number line, or moveable arrows. To get the multiplication one can consider the endomorphism of the addition-semigroup N, that is the mappings f such that

$$f(a+b) = fa + fb \quad \text{for} \quad a, b \in N.$$

Of course this is too abstract. To be operated on, N must be given more concrete substance. N should not consist of mappings, but it should be a substratum itself. One cannot but embedding N into the number line, and this is done by chaining up the arrows with their tails at an arbitrary but fixed origin. Now the addition in N has become an addition of points rather than arrows. Not until this has been done, can multiplication start. Multiplications are dilatations of the number line that respect its additive structure. The dilatation that maps 1 into a is called the multiplication by a. This again looks asymmetric. If the product $a \cdot b$ of a and b means the result of a multiplication of b by a, then a plays again the part of multiplier and b that of multiplicand. This is a new sin against elegance. It looks much nicer to define the product of two dilatations rather than considering dilatations as products. The product of the dilatations that map 1 into a and b is defined as the product of two mappings, and ab is defined as the 1-image of the product mapping. Afterwards the dilatation from 1 to a can again be identified with the point a of the number line, and then it appears that by operating the dilatation that carries 1 into a upon b, one gets again ab.

To resume, rather than defining the operations of addition and multiplication as mappings, certain mappings of the line are considered as elements of a group (or semigroup), and addition and multiplication are introduced as group operations, and only afterwards are the group elements identified with points on the number line. All this, the details as well as the principle, should be understood by the teacher and taught to the students.

The first who really fathomed these difficulties and successfully worked to overcome them has been Dienes. He grasped that the interpretation of numbers as operators cannot be maintained indefinitely. At a certain moment the operators of a certain domain must be reinterpreted as objects, if new operators should operate on the old domain. This re-interpretation should be done carefully and it cannot be performed until the student masters the first domain to such a degree that to work with it he can dispense of the intuitive bonds. How these demands can be satisfied has been shown by Dienes in a marvellous way. At the same time, I daresay, he showed that it is a task which should be left to didactical geniuses. Notwithstanding the didactic profit that can be gained from the operator interpretation of numbers, one should better not exaggerate. Rather than being made more complicated, things should be made easier, for both teachers and students. There cannot be the slightest doubt that the aim is numbers as objects. Numbers as operators can only block the view on this aim.

The operator interpretation of numbers is cultivated by some didacticians only in the case of multiplication, especially that by fractions. If the 3-dilatation of the number line is inverted as a mapping, one gets a 3-contraction, which is written as a multiplication by $\frac{1}{3}$. That is, this is the definition of $\frac{1}{3}$: the multiplicatively interpreted operator of the 3-contraction. A 5-dilatation composed with a 3-contraction yields by definition the multiplicative operator $\frac{5}{3}$. Multiplying such operators, say $\frac{5}{3}$ and $\frac{7}{4}$ in the sense of composing mappings, then, is an intuitive operation, and multiplication rules become obvious. The addition of operands and the distributive behaviour under multiplication are well motivated. But nobody can explain why these operators should not only be multiplied but also added. Adding distributive operators can mathematically be motivated but in an intuitive context it has not the slightest intuitive meaning. There has never been any didactic trouble with multiplying fractions; it is the easiest operation with fractions. Addition remains an obscure activity if fractions are interpreted as operators, and division is not at all accessible in this way.

OBJECT INTERPRETATION

Here everything is definitive from the very beginning. The numbers are objects rather than operators first, and then, by reinterpretation, objects. They are firmly attached to the number line, they neither stray, not get notice to move under changes of origin and gauge. Mappings assign objects to objects.

Many people do not like it: the 3-addition maps 5 on 8, where 5 and 8 are clearly objects, while 3 is an operator. It looks asymmetric, and that is ugly. This is how many people see it, but this view is due to a wrong interpretation. To explain this I first consider multiplication.

$3 \cdot 5$ is read in many European languages as three times five (or something like this). Strangely enough in most countries it was, and in a few it still is, a prescription, that 5 rather than 3 should be considered as the multiplier. I do not know what the reason is, perhaps it was the practice in written arithmetic to put the smaller number second, and a certain inclination to consider the smaller factor as the multiplier. Anyhow, in such school systems children learn tables in the order $3 \cdot 1$, $3 \cdot 2$, $3 \cdot 3$, $3 \cdot 4$, ... and to stress that in $3 \cdot 5$ the multiplier is 5, they are obliged to read this as "three five times". It is incredible that the trend towards modernization could leave such a tradition untouched. Consequently in many textbooks the 5-multiplication is indicated* by

$$x \to x \cdot 5 \quad \text{or} \quad \curlyvee_x x \cdot 5,$$

rather than by

$$x \to 5 \cdot x \quad \text{or} \quad \curlyvee_x 5 \cdot x$$

Because of the commutativity of the multiplication it in fact makes no difference, but it is not the same in practice. It is, indeed, very impractical, and that is the clue to the misinterpretation we are going to analyze.

As a matter of fact it is not true that in the 3-multiplication of 5 with the result 15 the numbers occur as asymmetrical as people would have us believe. It is not true that '3' is an operator here; this is an unnecessary and inadequate interpretation. 3 is a number, an object on the number line, as are 5 and 15. To be sure, 3 determines an operator (or a function), to wit the function thrice (or three times). This is the way we express it in everyday language, and there is no reason why we should abandon this comfort of everyday language, where there is a clear distinction between the number n and the operator n-times; why should we blot out such subtleties of everyday language?

The "why" is easily answered. Against all odds people try to have the second factor play the part of the multiplier, and one queer interpretation implies the other. As soon as it is written in the natural way,

$$x \to 3 \cdot x \quad \text{or} \quad \curlyvee_x 3 \cdot x,$$

the operation thrice is clearly indicated by '$3 \cdot$'. Thus the function sign is '$3 \cdot$'. To every $a \in \mathbf{N}$ (or, for that matter, $\in \mathbf{Z}$, or $\in \mathbf{R}$) belongs a function, indicated by $a \cdot$. It is dead simple:

$$a \cdot : x \to a \cdot x \quad \text{or} \quad a \cdot = \curlyvee_x a \cdot x.$$

---

* Of course these function notations are not meant to belong to the language of the learner; it is the language of the analyzing didactician.

It now becomes much easier to change over from the number a to the operator $a\cdot$, and conversely. There are different notations for both of them, and there is no reason left to bother oneself and children with an unnecessary identification of operand and operator.

Why should addition not enjoy the same facilities as multiplication? Why not interpret $3 + 5$ as indicating the result of an addition of 3 to 5? In Figure 6 I anticipated this interpretation. Here the operator

$$a + : x \rightarrow a + x \quad \text{or} \quad a + = Y_x \, a + x,$$

that is, the shift over a to the right, is indicated by '$a +$'. As to addition this is an extension of everyday language. As an analogue of 'three times' we introduce "three plus" to avoid that 3 is launched both as an operator and as an operand. In the operator '$3 +$' the number 3 occurs as an object that determines the operator. In '$3 + 5$' the 3 and the 5 are objects of the same kind, but the '3' rather than being a lone fellow is part of the function notation '$3 +$'.

Likewise the minus can be understood. One gets the functions

$$- : x \rightarrow - x \quad \text{or} \quad - = Y_x (- x),$$

which is visualized as a reflection at the origin, and, e.g.

$$7 - : x \rightarrow 7 - x \quad \text{or} \quad 7 - = Y_x (7 - x),$$

the subtraction from 7, which is the inversion of the number line, interchanging 0 and 7 (Figure 8). More general

$$a - : x \rightarrow a - x \quad \text{or} \quad a - = Y_x (a - x),$$

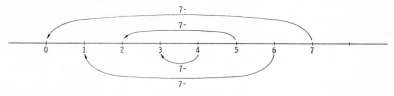

Fig. 8.

an inversion that interchanges 0 and a. Of course ' $-$ ' can be understood as a special case of '$a -$', that is, as a shorter notation for '$0 -$'.

Children handle this visualization of subtraction without any difficulty. Maybe the reader cannot believe it. At first I could not believe it either. Not until I had pulled off the straitjacket of my algorithmic habits did it dawn upon me that $7 - 3$ is easiest performed if the three is detached at "the end of the seven", and that is just the adequate description of what happens to 3 if it undergoes the reflection that interchanges 0 and 7. This is the reason why children are quicker in perceiving the result of $a-b$ than adults are.

OBJECTION AGAINST THE OBJECT INTERPRETATION

In fact, our interpretation of addition and multiplication only shifts the asymmetry, which some do not like. In $a + b$ and $a \cdot b$ the a and b are objects of the same kind, but unlike the second, the first is determination part of an operator. This shows up, when

$$(?x)\, 3 + x = 7 \quad \text{and} \quad (?x)\, x + 3 = 7$$

are intuitively understood. Indeed, then they mean different things: "which number passes into 7 under a 3-shift?" and "how much should 3 be shifted to get 7?" Before rejecting the use or the interpretation of the number line because of this asymmetry, one should consider that both inversions have to be exercized, if not on the number line, then certainly on the time axis, in problems of the kind "John is 7 years old; how old was he 3 years ago?" and "John is 7 years old; how long ago was he 3 years old?" The older didacticians knew that in practical problems one inversion does not guarantee the other; like many good customs in teaching arithmetics this one seems to be ignored too often today.

It should be the aim of teaching arithmetics finally to restrict to one model, and then to a symmetric one, and to attain this, the pupil should learn effacing the asymmetries of addition and multiplication. They cannot be effaced as long as addition and multiplication are viewed on as "addition to" and "multiplication by", that is as mappings of one variable, which has a great intuitive value. It is an aspect of addition and multiplication which is not transitory. It coexists with the symmetric aspect of viewing addition and multiplication as binary operations. But cultivating different algorithms for the two inversions as has been a tradition with the two kinds of division is untenable.

Likewise in the case of subtraction both inversions have to be exercised,

$$(?x)\,7 - x = 3 \quad \text{and} \quad (?x)\,x - 4 = 3,$$

if not in pure mathematics, then certainly in applications, and this too is often neglected.

STATE AND OPERATION SIGNS

By our interpretation of addition another problem of traditional didactics is overcome. Didacticians always complained about the double role of the plus and minus signs, as an operation sign and as a state sign. Notations like $\bar{1}, \bar{2}, \bar{3}, \ldots$ or $^{-}1, {}^{-}2, {}^{-}3, \ldots$ were invented to distinguish both meanings, while others prefered different colours. Non-definitive methods and notations should better be refrained from. They remind me of Latin language instruction, where in the first year's texts all nouns of the 3rd declination, which constitute the great majority, were replaced by synonyms of the first and second (e.g. urbs by oppidum), and all irregular verbs by regular ones (ire by ambulare); as we shall see later, arithmetic teaching also knows such tricks.

The sign trick, anyhow, is an unnecessary one: In '3 + (− 7)' the '−' is a state sign or pre-sign, as it is in '(− 3) + 7'; in the latter expression the '+' is no pre-sign to the '7' but a post sign to the (− 3). As to the pre- or state signs, '+ 7' is the same as 7. In other word, the '+' as a state sign is dispensable, whereas the '−' can occur as a pre-sign and as a post-sign, and if it happens it is absolutely clear what it is.

THE SYSTEMATICS OF THE NUMBER LINE

At the start the only points marked on the number line are the elements of N. The 3-addition is a right shift by 3 unit steps. If the 3-addition and 5-addition are composed, they produce the 8-addition. This leads to the associativity law in a more convincing way than the usual mock proofs. As far as possible in N, both inversions of the addition are exercised. The subtraction from 7 is the reflection that interchanges 0 and 7; its intuitive value has already been mentioned. $(a + b) - b$, and $(a + b) - a$ have different intuitive meanings.

The need for an unrestricted inversion of the addition causes the images of the negative numbers to emerge from limbo on the number line. Then (-3) can either be interpreted as the determination part of the addition operator $(-3) +$ which arises if $3 +$ is to be inverted as far as possible, or $-1, -2, -3, \ldots$ are first noticed on the number line when it is required to solve the problem $(?x)\, a + x = b$ with no restriction. In any case $(-a) +$ comes in as the inversion of $a +$. Moreover $b - x$ appears as the solution of $(?x)\, a + x = b$. It should be noticed that by the foregoing

$$7 - 3 = 7 - (+3)$$

is a triviality, that is a mere notational convention, whereas

$$7 - 3 = 7 + (-3)$$

is non-trivial.

The multiplication by a positive factor proves to be a dilatation of the line, namely, if the factor is a, that dilatation which maps 1 into a. How the multiplication with a negative factor should be interpreted, is not as obvious in this context. It is a point to which we will come back later. Like additions so can multiplications be composed and laws on them can be stated as a consequence. Finally one can try to invert the multiplication, say the 3-multiplication. Then fractions with denominator 3 arise from limbo, and $\frac{1}{3}\cdot$ announces itself as a new multiplication operator. Composing $\frac{1}{3}\cdot$ with $7\cdot$ one gets the $\frac{7}{3}\cdot$, and more general all rational multiplication operators $r\cdot$, where r is a rational (maybe negative) number.

Here, too, $\frac{1}{3}\cdot$ rather than $\frac{1}{3}$ is interpreted as an operator. Such an operator interpretation is satisfactorily intuitive. Quite a few who have thought about didactics of fractions found it attractive, and certainly it works well in the classroom. As I already explained, there are limits to this method. If fractions shall be interpreted in some way as multiplication operators, then multiplying fractions is as natural a procedure as composing mappings, though adding and subtracting such operators is badly motivated. There exist attractive intuitive methods to introduce fractions; they nicely cover multiplication and then flounder on addition, or keep silent about it.

If then the addition of fractions should be visualized, better than as operators are they imagined on the number line as they arise from limbo when the multiplication in **Z** is inverted. Subdividing the number line should be exercised, and addition and subtraction of fractions should also be viewed as shifts on the number line.

From the intuitive viewpoint there is a two-fold way of inverting the multiplication,

$$(?x)\, a \cdot x = 7 \quad \text{and} \quad (?x)\, x \cdot a = 7.$$

The first appeals to intuition as long as a is an integer; this appeal fades away if a is a fraction. The second inversion is hardly accessible to intuition even if a is an integer that is not a divisor or multiple of a.

Finally the division by other numbers than integers is a formal operation with no intuitive roots, whether the number line or other means of visualization are used or not. On the number line and in the rectangular pattern, the multiplication can still be seen as taking the multiple of something, but the division soon fails to reflect a process of dividing. Of course it can still be explained as the inversion of the multiplication, but this is a logical rather than an intuitive explanation; understanding such an operation requires quite different presuppositions than are usually made in elementary arithmetics.

We shall come back to the didactical problem of fractions. But even before fractions we noticed cases where the number line proved not entirely sufficient for an intuitive approach to the arithmetical operations. This is not be be wondered at. No single intuitive material or model can cover the whole domain but together they can complement each other. It is a natural inclination to overstress one material, but the didactician should test all possibilities in a thought experiment, and at the point where some method fails it should be cut off. In experimental sciences, if an experiment has failed, it is not saved by self-deceiving tricks. Why need teaching theory cultivate its own failures?

GRAPHICS AS A MEANS OF VISUALIZATION

Multiplying concrete numbers has several times been discussed here; one of its visualizations is the rectangle model. A quite different visualization is that by graphic representations of linear functions. A. Delessert* proposed a device of materializing the linear function by a transparent ruler that turns on a pivot over a chequered plate. It is a pity that the graphic representation is still too little used in the domain that was traditionally dominated by the rule of three. Of course pricelists that give the price of a commodity from 1 to 10 kg are practical but a graphic is more convincing. With the graphic of path as a function of time one should be more careful: motions need not be uniform. The technical term for what others call speed is mean velocity, but there are few people who actually know what it is. If you fly from London to Amsterdam, a distance of 350 km travelled in 55 minutes, you can listen to the purser telling the passengers that the plane is flying with a mean velocity of 850 km/h, where mean velocity probably means, as it often does, maximal velocity. Anyhow, graphics of non-uniform motions should not be neglected.

It is obvious, I think, that in this context the graphically represented function is not only a means of visualizing but also of solving. Even the ill-famed problems of meeting and overtaking cyclists, of sources and sinks that control the water economy of a lake, and of mixing wines and groceries, can be solved in a natural way by graphics. Of course this is no reason to deal with these problems. I rather mean the pattern, which can also be filled with reasonable subject matter.

What I have in mind is using graphics long before functions and their graphical representations are studied more systematically. As a first example I mention the "life lines" of a boy born 1 July 1962 and his father born 1 January 1937: "When will the boy be half the age of his father?" (Figure 9.) Or take the example in Figure 10, trains travelling from A and B in opposite directions with different velocities: "When will they meet?" Or in Figure 11 which shows how somebody transfers a monthly sum from his account to that of another, with the question when will the receiver's account be larger than the sender's. Finally we look at an example of graphical additions and subtraction as in Figure 12 where a ship moves with or against a current. Figure 13 shows the graphical representation of cyclical motions such as the hands of a clock that meet regularly. The earlier discussed functions

$$\bigvee_x a + x \quad \text{and} \quad \bigvee_x a \cdot x$$

* *Educational Studies in Mathematics* **1** (1969), 374.

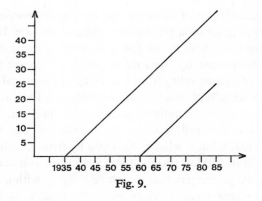

Fig. 9.

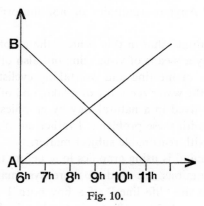

Fig. 10.

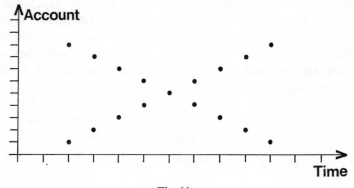

Fig. 11.

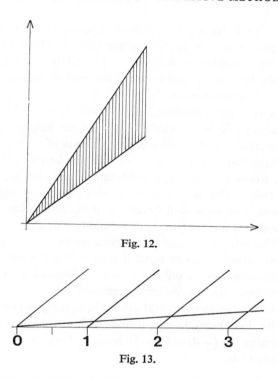

Fig. 12.

Fig. 13.

should not be forgotten either; in these examples the numerical variables
have a very concrete meaning.

THE LEVER

Several times I proposed the lever as a means of visualization, to show
not only negative numbers and certain operations but also the algebraic
laws. Afterwards, when trying to elaborate my proposals, I ran into
difficulties. The result was not satisfactory. Maybe others will learn
from this and try it with more success. The situation is as follows:

The integers (or even the rationals or reals) are represented on the
lever in two ways: firstly, as distances on the lever arm which are counted
from the axis as origin to the right positively and to the left negatively as
done on the horizontal number line, secondly, as forces (weights) that
act positively from above to below and negative from below to above – the

usual device to invert forces, is the pulley*. The product of two differently represented magnitudes is physically available as the moment (force times arm). The addition is realized by physically adding. It is well-known that the lever is in equilibrium if the sum of moments, that is, a certain sum of products vanishes.

This brings us to the difficulties I mentioned. How should the equality of two expressions be interpreted? If it were the balance, equilibrium should be the criterion of equality of the contents of both scales. But as soon as we count distances on one arm positive and on the other negative, we loose the freedom to do so. Equilibrium means that the sum of the moments vanishes. The only equations we can directly read from the lever are those that state equilibrium, that is, assert that the sum of certain expressions vanishes. Maybe one should try to identify the moment with an intuitive rotational effect and to consider two expressions realized by weights on various arms as equal if they exhibit the same rotational effect. But this would work only at a rather advanced level. Rotational action and moment are not elementary enough.

In a more concrete way one could define the equality of two expressions at the lever by their being in equilibrium with a fixed weight at a fixed arm; for instance, $3 \cdot (-4) = 4 \cdot (-3)$ because both are in equilibrium with $4 \cdot 3$ (Figure 14).

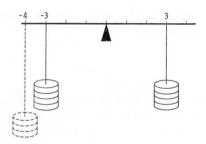

Fig. 14.

Let us suppose this problem solved; then a second arises – the representation at the lever yields sums of products. How should the sub-

* K. Orlov (*Educational Studies in Mathematics* **3** (1971), 192–205) uses another device. Since he prefers constant arms he cannot represent multiplication with his instrument.

traction be represented? Taking away does not work properly. Of course, if need be you can suspend the subtrahend on the "wrong side" of the lever, but this is an artificial interpretation.

Notwithstanding these problems, I believe the lever is a valuable device if rather than overburdening it with the whole of arithmetics, one uses it to illustrate algebraic ideas and to exhibit one of the most important applications of negative numbers. By means of the lever one can show whether some expressions should be considered as positive or negative. Positivity or negativity of expressions are recognized by looking whether they turn the lever right or left. What I called the rotational effect is not easy to comprehend if it should be a *quantitative* comprehension. But if it is the "quality" that matters, that is, if it should only be decided whether some force turns the lever right or left, it is more palpable. By this means it is easily decided with one of the expressions $5 \cdot 7$, $(-5) \cdot 7$, $5 \cdot (-7)$, $(-5) \cdot (-7)$ should be counted positive and which negative. In particular, the lever shows neatly that minus signs cancel each other in products. It should be mentioned that for this rule Emma Castelnuovo produced other nice justifications by analogy.

Why – you may ask – so many illustrations for $(-a) \cdot (-b) = ab$ if the most expedient way is to simply ordain it? And if there is really any need to illustrate it, why not restrict oneself to one example? To this I would answer, because formalizing opposite action by a minus sign is the thread that leads through all applications of negative numbers, and because to use multiplication is the test to know whether the application is relevant and profound. From arithmetic onwards mathematics should be fraught with relations. One cannot afford to miss even one. But of course one should refrain from squeezing out a model to the last drop. Before running into difficulties one should stop and delay more systematic treatment of the lever.

COMPUTERS

Several times I mentioned the abacus as intuitive material for teaching the decimal place value. Though it is unusual I would also count the computer among the intuitive materials – I mean the non-automatic desk computer with the crank, not a surrogate, nor an electric model. I discussed it quite a few times in lectures. I suppose it has been tried somewhere in classrooms but I know of no relevant publications. I would propose the use of the computer as soon as additions like $8 + 5$ are to be performed, though at this stage together with the abacus. What may we expect of this material?

First, it prepares the pupil for something he has to learn anyhow, that is the use of computers, but this aspect is rather unimportant. What matters now is that non-automatic computers can give excellent insight into the decimal place value system; it is an ocular demonstration of positional adding and subtracting, and of transfer; it shows how digits are put into columns, how multiplications and divisions are performed as iterated additions and subtractions, and what is a remainder; the position of the decimal point becomes clearer with computers. It is another advantage that the pupil can be confronted with realistic, and consequently numerically involved problems without being drowned by computing errors, and in particular in hopeless long divisions.

I know people object that after being spoiled with computers the student would not learn the tables of addition and multiplication any more. This, of course, should be prevented. An imaginative teacher can contrive many tricks. Let the student generate $1 \cdot 7, 2 \cdot 7, \ldots$ using the computer and note the results down in his exercise-book; it is more trustworthy than the old method of establishing the tables by his own means, and it serves the same aim. Let two or more students compete with each other in multiplications and divisions, one with the machine, and the others mentally. If it comes to doing it in full swing, the machine calculator will learn and never forget that $9 \cdot 9$ by computer takes quite a time.

Among the intuitive methods I have discussed, the computer leads most smoothly to written calculations. Of course, I would not abolish long written computations. If I do not discuss these techniques in the sequel, it only means that I would not know what to add to the didactics of this classical field of instruction, except its close connections with the use of the computer. No doubt the skill in mental and written arithmetic will diminish with the increasing use of the computer, but I do not believe this should be deplored; in fact this skill has never been in the past as good as people used to believe. For more than a century, each adult generation has complained about the decline of arithmetical skills in the younger generation.

There are, however, two algorithms I cannot avoid discussing – fractions and the rule of three. In traditional arithmetic these algorithms have a rational rather than intuitive basis. In this respect they differ from the algorithms of pure arithmetic with integers. But before dealing with these subjects, I must turn to a problem of a more fundamental character.

RATIONAL VERSUS INTUITIVE METHODS - RULE OF THREE, AND FRACTIONS

How far should the frame of elementary arithmetic extend? In teaching elementary arithmetic numbers and operations are originally intuitive data, and applications too have a quite intuitive character. To be sure, arithmetic gradually becomes more and more abstract; numbers out of the bounds of imagination are operated on, and the content of applied problems also exceeds the imaginable. Skilled didacticians try more sophisticated intuitive devices to pass these limits, and often with success. We mentioned the graphic of the linear function, which however fails if dependency on more than one variable is to be illustrated. The classical device for organizing this field is the rule of three; but this is far from intuition and logically surcharged. Everybody knows that such methods are beating about the bush. Those who have learned algebra solve such problems algebraically, or should do so; if the problems in this field are more involved, he will algebraicize them immediately by an explicit use of unknowns. Teachers and textbook authors who know algebra yet nevertheless have their pupils solving such problems with traditional methods from elementary arithmetics, are practising fraud; if they have not mastered algebra, they are leading their pupils gropingly through the dark. This is again double-standard pedagogy, the doctrine of the two truths, one for Jupiter and one for the ox. This is quite common in university education, too - eliminating from a function theory proof of the fundamental theorem of algebra all function theory, perhaps even complex numbers; replacing integrals by astounding sums; in short, elementarizing a subject in such a way that the elementary version can only be understood by those who have mastered the non-elementary one - these are quite common features of a reprehensible teaching philosophy. If algebra is the most adequate means to solve a problem, then the pupil has the same right as the teacher to solve it that way. If Paul Pry in the fourth grade asks whether you can do it with x, then answering "wait for the eighth grade" is a declaration of pedagogical bankruptcy. The answer is not truthful either because in the eighth grade with quadratic equations as a next goal you have to spend too much time in opening and closing brackets that there is no opportunity left to take up the problems of elementary arithmetic which in the fourth grade this teacher promised Paul Pry to be solved by algebra. For the majority of schoolchildren this means that they never learn what you can do with algebra.

What can we do with traditional word problems? I mean where out of three magnitudes a, b, c connected by the relation $ab = c$, two are given and the third is asked for, or from four magnitudes a, b, c, d connected by $abc = d$, three are given and the fourth is asked for (e.g. path = speed times time, or interest = capital times rate of interest times years, and so on. But I also mean the kind of problem like: "which number must be multiplied by... to get..." or "by which number must... be multiplied to get..."). These are questions which emerge within elementary arithmetic but point beyond. One should not banish them from elementary arithmetic but one should not cultivate them there either as was often done in the past. The pupil should learn to tackle such problems by intuitive means, even by *ad hoc* means, and he should do it in a diversified way. With respect to these concepts such intuitive methods are again bottom level pre-mathematics. The pupil should not stay at this level because he has to go on to learn mathematics. The first expression of mathematical trends in such a context is, indeed, to analyze and to understand one's actions. From olden times able didacticians of elementary arithmetic have tried this approach though with little success. They aspired to the hope that the schoolchild should analyze his activity logically, by linguistic means borrowed from everyday language or by an artificial version of everyday language – I mean formulations of the kind: "the quotient of a and b is the number by which b should be multiplied to get a." To be sure, it is simpler with x. The vernacular version is one of the artificial elementarizations I rejected above. It is an illusion to believe that a pupil who is not mature enough to use x can work with such formulations even though he is able to understand them.

The exercises I mentioned above can only be justified with a view as to what they are to foreshadow; they are only meaningful if they are a preparation for the corresponding mathematics, namely algebra. So they are meaningless if they come so early that access to a higher level is not yet possible, as well as with schoolchildren who are not capable of mathematical thought; but they should not last longer than is needed to prepare the schoolchild for algebra. On the other hand they cannot be missed as a preparation for algebra if the pupil is at all to learn algebra as something that should be applied.

Perhaps my remarks on the rule of three and its like are outdated. Maybe I am forcing open doors. I stressed this matter the way I did because in a similar case (I mean fractions) similar consequences have not yet been drawn, though I believe the same arguments as against the rule of three apply against traditional teaching of fractions. It can hardly be doubted that the teaching of fractions is a great didactic failure. I am convinced that it will remain so as long as fractions are confined to the present context, that is, of elementary arithmetic.

Children can work intuitively with intuitive fractions. This is the reason why the traditional intuitive introduction to fractions functions excellently. This success tempts the teacher after a short introduction to face algorithmic fractions and, soon afterwards, the inevitable catastrophe. Between the devil and the deep blue sea the child learns the rules of simplifying and of the four operations only to mix them up and modify them *ad lib*. In fact, it is a meaningless game. $\frac{2}{3}+\frac{1}{3}, \frac{2}{3}-\frac{1}{3}, \frac{2}{3}\cdot\frac{1}{3}, \frac{2}{3}:\frac{1}{3}$ – this is no problem; you can see it, if you open your eyes, on the number line. But what must be done with $\frac{127}{131}$ and $\frac{8}{47}$? To be sure, these numbers can be approximately located upon the number line; before working out expressions containing such fractions, the pupil should roughly estimate the result by eyesight to avoid disasters. The most meaningful and intuitive operation with fractions is multiplication. Simplifying is still meaningful but lacks intuitive support though it is well motivated; addition and subtraction may still be intuitively related but are poorly motivated and hardly meaningful. Division, even with intuitive fractions, is far from intuition in elementary arithmetic, unmotivated and meaningless. Operating on complicated fractions, except maybe simplifying, can hardly be motivated in elementary arithmetics.

The complicated fractions and the operations with them are school teacher's inventions, which can only be understood at a higher level. Van Hiele noticed and stressed the fact that the idea that pervades and motivates fractions is pronouncedly algebraic. Fractions and operations on fractions are introduced to enforce an unrestricted validity of the four fundamental operations and their laws. This idea of a domain closed under certain operations is entirely algebraical; it is the basis of all algebraic entities. So far as they are less intuitive, fractions and their operations should be motivated by this idea. I feel it is only honest to tell it this way – to explicitly urge the unrestricted validity of arithmetical operations. It is an abstract motivation, hardly influenced by practical needs; it is algebra *in optima forma*. I agree that negative integers, too, owe their existence to the desirability of an unrestricted operation, viz. subtraction, but besides this they are highly motivated by intuition, which is much less, if at all, the case with fractions.

Today one witnesses many efforts to improve teaching fractions in the frame of elementary arithmetic. Some of them are remarkable and I would be the first to welcome them if they did not divert attention from the real problem. If these efforts are didactically valuable they are at the same time especially dangerous, because they can only delay the actual solution, perhaps indefinitely. In my view the only acceptable solution is to deal with fractions in algebra.

This of course does not mean introducing them as equivalence classes of number pairs. Though I tackled this subject in Chapter XI*, I think it is worthwhile to repeat my analysis briefly. A fraction like $\frac{7}{3}$ is invented in order to solve the equation

$$(?x) \, 3x = 7 \,.$$

Thus, take an x and work with this x as though

$$3x = 7 \,.$$

I called this behaviour rule the "algebraic principle". Multiplying on both sides by 5 yields

$$15x = 35 \,,$$

which implies that $\frac{7}{3}$ and $\frac{35}{15}$ are the same. To add $\frac{7}{3}$ and $\frac{3}{5}$, one proceeds by deriving from

$$3x = 7 \quad \text{and} \quad 5y = 3$$

* p. 226.

an equation for $x + y$, to wit

$$15(x + y) = 44,$$

thus

$$x + y = \frac{44}{15}.$$

The other operations should be taught in a similar way. It means operating
with $x, y, \ldots$ as though they were solutions of certain equations, while
applying the usual arithmetical rules. I discussed the inevitable reproach
that this strategy presupposes the existence of sum, product, and so on.
The same remark can be reformulated in a positive version: supposing
the existence of sum, product, and so on, and the arithmetical laws in
the extended system, the algorithmic form of the sum, the product, etc.,
are rigorously proved. This is much more important than the existence,
because it is the very feature that is used again and again.

RATIONAL VERSUS INTUITIVE METHODS –
THE NEGATIVE NUMBERS

Regarding the rule of three and fractions I advocated passing from the
intuitive methods straight to algebra. As for negative numbers it looked
as if I believed that intuitive methods allow one to proceed indefinitely. I
would rather warn against uncaution. There *are* limits. In the long run
intuition can be a drag on the pupil. The aim of elementary arithmetic is
algorithmic skill – it is not by accident that the word algorithm is derived
from the name of the author of the first book on Indian-Arabian computing.

Experiments from the beginning of this century show feeble arithmetic
often connected to an obstinate primitive intuitivity of the number
concept, but I do not believe that such pathologies can prove much.
Normally intuitive components in mental activities are gradually ground
off. This does not mean that they have not been useful. If the pupil can
work out $7 + 5$ and apply it, the reason is that once he did it intuitively;
if he is adding with pencil and paper, it is the aftereffect of his abacus
experiences with this; and if finally he is able to apply arithmetic in the
way he has been drilled in, it may be decisive that he knows the intuitive
meaning of the operations in many versions.

But it is not recommended to rely too much on intuitivity as a didactic device. We mentioned that in fractions it eventually fails, though initial successes with it may tempt the teacher to premature algorithmization. We also admitted that by attractive artifices and deliberate didactics the validity of intuitivity in teaching fractions can be extended, but also that it does not lead far enough to pay off, and that fractions are definitively to be approached in another way. The rule of three is the same problem. Intuitive methods, however valuable they may be, do not yield enough. I concluded that a timely withdraw of intuitive methods in favor of rational ones is recommendable though it should be stressed that these rational methods should be genuine mathematics rather than surrogates.

Even at an earlier stage the question should be asked as to which degree intuitivity should be trusted. It should be asked as soon as arithmetical laws are formulated. Should they be borrowed from intuition or should the student learn to justify them by rational means? If I mention arithmetical laws I do not aim at addition. Commutativity and associativity look so evident that their evidence can be questioned at a high level only. Of course, they are implicitly applied, e.g. if $8 + 5$ is worked out via $8 + (2 + 3) = (8 + 2) + 3$. This, in fact, is an arithmetical law, but does it pay to motivate it explicitly? The connection between addition and subtraction looks different. But in order to motivate that $(?x) \, 8 + x = = 13$. is solved by $x = 13 - 8$ and the like, the intuitive meaning of addition and subtraction suffice. The law of distributivity governs algorithmic arithmetic to a high degree, but even here I do not see any reason for a more than intuitive justification. Laws like $a - (b + c) = = a - b - c$ are a bit different; though they are intuitively clear, one is inclined to verbalize the intuitive idea: instead of taking b and c away together, one can do it one after the other.

I think that the need for a rationalization exceeding intuitivity is first felt with negative numbers – I like to place negative numbers prior to fractions though by tradition fractions are arithmetic and negative numbers algebra. The negative integers and their operation can be intuitively tackled, for instance on the number line, and it is extremely useful to approach them this way. But I hesitate to rely on it. One of the reasons why I would be careful are the earlier-mentioned polarization disturbances, which can devaluate the number line.

I already discussed one rational dealing with negative numbers. An x is operated on as though

$$x + a = 0.$$

Such an x can be connected to an y, defined by

$$y + b = 0,$$

by addition and multiplication that should obey the usual rules. Then from

$$(x + y) + (a + b) = 0$$

it follows that

$$-(a + b) = -a - b;$$

from

$$b(x + a) = 0 \quad \text{and} \quad (y + b)x = 0$$

it follows that

$$xy - ab = 0,$$

whence

$$(-a) \cdot (-b) = ab.$$

We already discussed this kind of argument.

It should be perfectly clear that the difficulty of teaching negative numbers resides not in their introduction, nor in problems like $3 - 7$, $7 + (-3)$, $(-7) + 3$, $2 \cdot (-5)$, but in $3 - (-7)$, $10 - (-7)$, $(-3) \pm (-7)$, $(-2) \cdot (-5)$. If a new teaching method for negative numbers is demonstrated, it is worthwhile to check which kind of problems have been included and which ones have been skipped over. (With fractions this is a still more revealing criterion.)

For many years I have propagated the inductive-extrapolatory method. The pupil works out tables like the following:

$3 + 2 = 5$	$3 - 2 = 1$	$3 \cdot 2 = 6$	$(-3) \cdot 2 = -6$
$3 + 1 = 4$	$3 - 1 = 2$	$3 \cdot 1 = 3$	$(-3) \cdot 1 = -3$
$3 + 0 = 3$	$3 - 0 = 3$	$3 \cdot 0 = 0$	$(-3) \cdot 0 = 0$
$3 + (-1) = \ldots$	$3 - (-1) = \ldots$	$3 \cdot (-1) = \ldots$	$(-3) \cdot (-1) = \ldots$
$3 + (-2) = \ldots$	$3 - (-2) = \ldots$	$3 \cdot (-2) = \ldots$	$(-3) \cdot (-2) = \ldots$

I think I need not add any comment. It is an inductive extrapolation beyond 0. The method can be combined with the intuitive method; it is an active complement of the passive contemplation of the number line, since it is checked by computations and inferences. Even if the intuitive approach is preserved, it is a valuable complement, and if the number line is not used at all, it is the most natural approach. Moreover, because of the implicit, though not yet formalized induction it prepares for genuine mathematics. It reproduces what happens to the counting number in the counting process, and it forshadows what on a higher level becomes a rigorous proof.

APPLIED ARITHMETIC

Not until I have added a few words on applied arithmetic, can I say farewell to elementary arithmetic. This separate section does not mean that applications should be a separate chapter in teaching arithmetic. On the contrary I would rather stress its close connections with "pure" arithmetic. Is there a need to do so? It is an old tradition that teaching arithmetic starts from, and continuously comes back to, the applications. At least up to fractions this has been the practice. A superficial glance into arithmetic books reveals a rich variety of applications, I dare say, detailed with a systematic completeness. It often looks as though such an author has thoroughly analyzed all possibilities and necessities of applied arithmetic. In fact, what strikes us is a many-layered sediment of a long tradition, but its final result is not too bad. This statement includes the educational results. In the market-place and in shops one can see that arithmetic is mastered by quite a lot of people. In particular it is remarkable that arithmetic instruction has been successful in implementing not only arithmetic but also its applications. This distinguishes arithmetic instruction from algebra and geometry instruction. The subject matter of the latter, taught far from reality cannot be applied by people who have learned and mastered it for a while. It is not a valid argument to say that applications of arithmetic are simpler. They are only so because arithmetic has been taught better.

Recently I looked through a collection of texts which some of my children used from 1940 to 1945 to learn arithmetic. This was long before the New Maths. I opened one of the booklets – for the 5th grade. On p. 30 is a crude picture of a railway platform with a train; on p. 31 is half a page from a railway timetable; and below are a number of problems which can be asked by looking at the timetable. The first is: "On Sunday father is ready to depart at 8 o'clock. He is going to travel from Zwolle to Utrecht. Which train can he take? When does he arrive at Utrecht?" I fear that the New Maths shrugs its shoulders at this kind of banality. The question is not well formulated either. Should we not have asked for the greatest lower bound of the departures times of a certain set of trains? This would at least have been a decent formulation though it is not decent mathematics as long as it is not framed within an axiomatic system.

Turning a few leaves I find a telephone tariff. It is a treat to hear a bell ring in these problems, though it is a pity that I must confess that according to the marks in the booklet these pages were skipped over, maybe because it was wartime and people did not travel or phone very much. The next page has problems on percentages, of money and sick children.

I wonder whether people realize how much children must learn in arithmetic lessons, I mean, beyond arithmetic itself. In how many different wordings can the same computing problem appear? For instance:

(1) John is 16 years old. How long ago was he 10?

(2) John is 10 years old. In how many years will he be 16?

(3) John is 10 and Peter is 16. How much is Peter older than John?

(4) John is 10 and Peter is 16. How much is John younger than Peter?

(5) John is 10 and Peter is 16. How long ago was Peter as old as John is now?

(6) John is 10 and Peter is 16. In how many years will John be as old as Peter is now?

(7) In 1916 John was 10. When was he born?

(8) John was born in 1910. How old was he in 1916?

This is a very small choice of wordings in the problem 16–10. Or would you not venture to produce a thousand problems like these? The average citizen can solve them and many more besides. Or do you think they are ridiculous? If you think so, it proves that you learned your lessons well.

Is it not a miracle that so many people have learnt it? It is miraculous but it is not a miracle. It is only too easily explained. Arithmetic has been taught in such close connection with its applications that no problem of applicability could ever arise. Applied arithmetic was and still is its most intuitive chapter, close to the child's imagination.

If I am as satisfied with the results of teaching elementary arithmetic as it would appear, why have I spent so much time on it? Why? Because I am not at all satisfied. Did I not find quite a number of faults in it? Moreover it is a fact that I took my examples from the arithmetic instruction of the recent past and therefore I cannot check the social impact of today's teaching on little children as I can do today with regard to the instruction which adults received in the past. I can judge teaching today only from the current textbooks. If I leaf through the most recent ones, I notice with some anxiety a tendency away from applications. There is an obvious endeavour to enhance intuitivity – that is in itself gratifying – but there is also more stress on abstraction. Again, in itself, this is not bad. But abstraction usually comes in dangerous company – commitment to a system. It is dangerous because it requires the exclusion of all that does not fit into the system. In numbers the system is: natural number, integer, rational number, real number. And the principle of natural number is potency. Few applications fit into this straightjacket. Is the number indication in $ 0.57 a rational number? Is it a natural number in ¢ 57? Obviously these are void questions. And what about the numbers in the railway timetable? In a *system* of arithmetic there is no place for timetables. The older arithmetic books showed a clearly recognizable development from easy to difficult problems but showed little systematics. The same problems were again and again repeated with more complicated numerical data. If 16–10 was put into a word problem, the possible wordings were not taught at the same time but scattered over a long range. Among the problems of a new type the old ones were repeated. In fact, there used to be numerous repetitions. Such a textbook is of course an eyesore to every systematician and nobody likes an eyesore while every mathematician likes systematics.

The wide choice of word problems was, as I have characterized, the result of continual sedimentation. Maybe this is just the moment to clean up. Maybe more abstraction carries further than many concrete applications. But throughout I have noticed a distinct tendency towards exaggerations. I am afraid that if this tendency conquers, our children will learn even more mathematics they cannot apply. This in itself would merely be the happiest possible result. But there are side-effects which are much worse than this. As I shall show later, a part of the "New Maths" literature is written by charlatans, although the greatest part is written by honest people who simply lack sound ideas on the mathematical principles they propose to be taught by others.

The tendency away from applications is now obvious even in good textbooks. I admit that possibly more abstraction could be a valid substitute for an excess of applications. This should be seriously investigated. For instance the eight wordings of 16–10 I quoted are complements of each other pairwise. Four suffice, since it is four times with different wordings namely, the equivalent of "how much is a earlier than b?" and "how much is b later than a?". Moreover the four remaining patterns appear strongly related to each other. With a few logical structure patterns used, it would be one and the same problem. Of course the child should learn to interpret such wordings as models of the same logical pattern, and this can probably better be done with a stress on the logical structure than on its arithmetic.

It would be tremendously worthwhile to investigate such logical structures in arithmetic teaching. I do not see any evidence that innovators have attempted anything of this kind. Usually they limit the domain of logic so narrowly that it cannot serve teaching arithmetic or mathematics at all. A favorite subject is relations. The child learns to register them in pedigrees. Maybe he learns the transitivity of the relation "older than". For teaching arithmetic this is worthless. There it does not matter whether Peter is older than John, or whether in six years John is older than he is now. There one is confronted with the more subtle structure "so many years older", and there one faces the logical principle that "a is n years older than b" implies "b is n years younger than a".

Of course the child has always learned such principles in arithmetic instruction, but there it happened as an activity at the bottom level with no conscious apperception or at least without any explicit formulation. It should be required that at this point instruction aims at lifting the student to a higher level. Formulations like "if Peter is six years older than John, then John is six years younger than Peter" belong to elementary instruction, and this is even true of the more general pattern of such statements like "if... is... years older than..., then... is... years younger than...". Moreover this would be one of the first opportunities to convince the pupil of the need to replace the triple dots by letters.

This reminds one of algebra. There however, the situation is much worse. Even at the bottom level the pupil does not even learn to apply algebra whereas in arithmetic we complained that he is too long or even indefinitely committed to the bottom level. No doubt by a careful analysis of concrete situations much could be improved. But this can only be done if one seriously turns to concrete situations, and this means leaving the ivory tower of the closed system.

I have looked out for other systems to teach applied arithmetic. What I propose is no new idea in itself. It has sometimes been tried though often delayed till the 6th–8th grades, whereas it could be done much earlier with a reasonable chance of success. Applied arithmetics is atomized in traditional instruction. I would not advocate a separate subject called "applied arithmetic" instead. I would rather introduce problems of a more integrated character, and circumstantial situations that should be conceived numerically and interpreted arithmetically. In olden times such situations were known in commercial arithmetic. Those problems are today outmoded, and in any case they are not attractive. A domain in which such situations are natural is descriptive statistics. Astonishing results can be achieved in this field is shown by the good textbooks in this field*. It is refreshing to read such realistic books after the usual dry abstractions. The parable of bread and stones still applies.

---

* e.g., U. Pampallona and L. Ragusa Gilli, *Che cos'è la statistica*, Torino, Loescher, no year indication.

CHAPTER XIII

DEVELOPMENT OF THE NUMBER CONCEPT –
THE ALGEBRAIC METHOD

Die ganzen Zahlen hat der liebe Gott gemacht; alles andere is Menschenwerk.

L. Kronecker

I must apologize for the disposition of my subject matter and in particular for the titles. I have made a sharp break between elementary arithmetic and algebra. Properly said, it is the break between the six-year basic school and the secondary school in our Dutch school system. No doubt it is ridiculous to behave as though arithmetic finishes and algebra starts exactly after the sixth grade. Maybe I should admit that this is a matter of practice and it will remain so in the near future. According to our present programmes primary school teachers will not boast more mathematics in their baggage than corresponds to the level of the eigth grade, because it is with this background in mathematics that they go to teacher training college, where mathematics is a facultative subject.

I would trust the senior teachers among the present primary school teachers to incorporate the algebraic method into their teaching of arithmetic wherever need be. It is a handicap that reforming primary education is a dangerous thing. Once the locks are opened, teachers and pupils will both be left defenceless before that stream of degenerate mathematics that is flowing into the market under the slogan of New Maths.

There are sound reasons why algebra was separated from arithmetic. Elementary arithmetic is intuitive and close to reality or at least it should be so. Algebra, however, is typically characterized by its formal-symbolic methods. It cannot be denied, however, that the traditional teaching of elementary arithmetic long ago transgressed its frontiers and by pseudo-elementarization usurped domains more rightly owned by algebraic methods, such as fractions and all that is covered by the rule of three. These are points where the algebraic method should be applied earlier than it usually is.

The classical characteristic of the onset of algebra was the literal calculus (obviously an ugly term). The progress of modern mathematics in teaching tends to favor the earlier use of letters as mathematical symbols. Wherever sets get names, they are letters, and they may even play a role as names of elements of sets.

Up to a few years ago didacticians and textbook authors were very much aware what introducing letters meant. This is explicitly shown by the numerous warnings and more implicitly by the inherent didactics of the textbooks. Every teacher knew how fast algebra could, if he took no heed, degenerate into a meaningless game with 26 letters. Devices to prevent this have gradually been developed in an empirical fashion. Teachers knew it was a problem, that it was a key problem and a difficult one. When compared in their historic setting though, the textbooks showed clear symptoms of a slow progress. This development has come to a sudden end by the invasion of all that so-called New Maths propagated by commercially-minded or ignorant authors. At this point the didactics of mathematics has been put back a century. It is now as far as it was in an era when a (bad) mathematics reader started as follows: "Among the numbers there are integers, negative ones, fractions, Arabic, Roman numbers, constant and variable numbers." Hardly ten years ago a Dutch didactician warned against the inclination of pupils to conceive in algebra a set of letters besides the set of numbers (it was actually formulated in this way though we dealt with an instruction where the word "set" was still unheard of). A few weeks ago I happened to open a new textbook just on the page where the author introduced the function

$$\ulcorner n, a \urcorner \to na$$

explicitly as a mapping of the pairs set formed from the set Z of numbers and the set L of letters into the set, if I remember well, of the monomials. This happened during a train journey, and in exasperation I threw the book out of the window, which was a pretty irresponsible act. Burning it would have been much safer!

In almost all New Maths the set of letters or sets of letters occur. The reason is obvious. People do not know what sets are and what aim they serve in genuine mathematics so they have to somehow invent sets and applications of sets. Yet they cannot afford sets of numbers, since numbers must be introduced by means of sets. The only example left by this exclusion are sets of letters. The problems caused by this measure will be discussed in more detail later – for the moment the following suffices.

Sets of letters are of course quite legitimate. Sets can be formed from everything that exists in the world. For many reasons sets of poorly mathematized objects are less useful, but sets of letters are dangerous. They are so dangerous that the people who introduce them look like people shipwrecked in the Polar Sea jumping from one ice-floe to the next before finally ending up in the freezing water. I have great compassion for those poor teachers and students committed to imitating the acrobatics of the textbook authors.

The use of letters in mathematics was already settled in ancient times. For instance C may be a point in the plane, it does not matter which one, except if something has been required, for instance, that C is lying on the line AB; but even then it does not matter either which point is meant unless something else is required, let us say that C is different from the midpoint of AB. In 'a^2' it is understood that a is a whole number or a rational one or a real number, according to what was required. In $x^2 - 2x + 3 = 0$, if it is required to be true, the x can be 1 or 2 only. 'π', which happens to be a Greek letter, indicates a specific number.

By 'Immanuel Kant' or '3' a specific man and a specific number are meant. 'Man' and 'x' can mean many objects though obviously 'man' can mean men only, whereas the domain that is granted to x has to be fixed every time anew. According to the aim such an 'x' serves, it is called a constant or a variable, which is sloppy terminology as long as the set in which x is allowed to vary is not indicated.

Didacticians used to make great efforts to explain this to learners. For the boy who bursts into tears because he does not understand how $a = b$ can be possible (is not $a = a$ and $b = b$?)–they invented a problem:

a may be one of the numbers 2, 4, 7, 11,
b may be one of the numbers 2, 3, 7, 9;
under which circumstances will $a = b$ hold?

(Ask it, if you prefer, with sets.) Or: If a and b are allowed the above values, what is $3a$, $2a + 3b$, b^2, and so on?

With the utmost patience teachers have tried to engrave in their pupils' minds that letters in algebra mean something, that no formula is meaningful unless the meaning of its components is told, and that algebra is not a meaningless game with 26 letters.

It was to no avail. What kind of instruction has been bestowed on those people who invented New Maths and what kind of mathematics did they teach before they wrote such books? Were they so hypnotized by the perspectives of modern mathematics as to renounce their former existence or were they not aware of the slippery ground they were walking on? The most likely explanation is they did things which are unusual in mathematics in order to create a self-reliant school mathematics *in usum Delphini*. To find such things as $\{a, b, c\}$ one has to look around quite far in genuine mathematics. Maybe you find $\{1, 2, 3\}$. Or: Let $\{a, b, c\}$ be the solutions set of the equation.... Or even: Let a, b, c be three different real numbers (so that $\{a, b, c\}$ is a set of real numbers). Of course, if a, b, c are different letters, then $\{a, b, c\}$ is a set of three letters, but be careful: $\{a, b, c\}$ may be the set of the last letters of the alphabet if a, b, c happen to be the letters '*x*', '*y*', '*z*'.

This is a complicated situation. I would prefer not to be caught in it myself and I would never dare to push my students therein, though if you think about it, it is easily disentangled. In New Maths, however, everything is muddy and obscure. $\{a, b, c\}$ is the set of the letters a, b, c. It has three elements, which of course are all different. The student is asked to find the intersection of $\{a, b, c\}$ and $\{1, 2, 3\}$ and is obliged to say that it is void since one set consists of letters and the other of numbers – Arabic ones, of course. The Roman ones make up a different set.

Monstrosities like this are very common in the New Maths. I feel sick at heart if I think of those conscientious teachers who dedicated themselves to good teaching and who now see their work swept aside by the New Maths parasites. With anxiety I ask myself what our algebra teachers should undertake with children who were exposed to such nonsense in primary school. How can they teach their students that by chance a can equal b, that because of $(a+b)^2 = a^2 + 2ab + b^2$, it also holds that $(u+v)^2 = u^2 + 2uv + v^2$, and that algebra is *not* a meaningless game with 26 letters? And finally, will not our secondary teachers too become contaminated by such nonsense? The parasites of New Maths are forcing their way into the textbook market, in radio and television, and they get peals of applause when they accuse those schools and universities which do not bow before them, of reactionary behaviour.

These people are not (yet) the most dangerous. I am even more afraid of the sincere and serious textbooks that are at least mathematically correct. If charged with didactic monstrosities, their authors answer: "What do you want? The mathematics is correct."

From my shelf I take such a work which, though not faultless, is of a relatively high level. It is for the beginning of the secondary school mathematics instruction − for the sixth grade. Of course it starts with set theory. Almost all are finite sets, which hardly occur in genuine set theory, and these sets are always explicitly written down, with their elements between braces and almost always explicitly represented by Venn diagrams. Never does it become clear what the elements are; they are most often indicated by Latin letters, though sometimes also by digits or otherwise. The same letters as within the braces are also put arbitrarily into Venn diagrams. Probably the author meant sets of letters but the Venn diagrams evoke the idea that every letter indicates the place in the Venn diagram where it stands. It does not matter too much because every letter $a, b, c, \ldots$ always means one thing, this letter itself or its place in the Venn diagram. Of course, it would be reasonable to interpret the $a, b, c, \ldots$ as variables since they are arbitrarily located within the Venn diagram. But this was not what the author meant and the student cannot be expected to interpret it this way. Never does a genuine variable occur in this context. Let us take such a set $\{a, b, c\}$ with its Venn diagram

Fig. 15.

(Figure 15) and ask the question: Is $x \in \{a, b, c\}$? The answer mathematicians expect and students should learn to give, is

$$x \in \{a, b, c\} \leftrightarrow x = a \lor x = b \lor x = c,$$

x belongs to this set if and only if x is one of the elements a, b, c. But never does the author ask such a question! On the contrary, the student is brainwashed to accept that x is just another letter or another definite though not indicated spot in the Venn diagram, and certainly he will answer

$$x \notin \{a, b, c\}.$$

The technique of variables is completely lacking. For this reason every function indication is lacking, too, in spite of numerous pictures of mappings. This is the way the book continues for the greater part of an academic year. But then out of the blue comes the sentence "let a be a natural number." Later b and c follow, and distributive and other algebraic properties are expressed by means of a, b, c. But up to this point the letter 'a' meant nothing but a; never did it indicate a number or anything else nor could it be replaced by any other letter. If it was a name, it was a proper name. The idea of variable did not exist at all but all of a sudden it appears (mind, between brackets) as if no other use of letters has ever been intended. This is exercised for a while, but just as suddenly and without any notice the old use is reinstated. What can the student do about this, or even the teacher who has to teach it? There is little doubt that it leads to catastrophe. Pupils who for almost a year at secondary school, and maybe for quite a long time at primary school, have been trained to consider letters as representatives of themselves or of definite spots in the Venn diagram, are required to understand that all at once a letter means something entirely different, namely a number though not a determinate but an arbitrary one. Moreover they are expected to understand it tacitly without any explanation! I fear that those poor students will be lost beyond any hope of salvation. Never will they learn a jot of algebra; and even the tears in their eyes when they ask how a can be equal b will not relieve them. The only effective remedy would be a broom to sweep out such textbooks from the classrooms where they are being used.

Among the collection of textbooks on my shelf are a few good ones, too. But if I see texts like the one I have already mentioned, I feel as if the collapse of mathematics teaching is imminent, even though I know my fear is disproportionate. Are the authors of such books aware of their responsibility for the damage they are doing? I hope they will read this question and answer it truthfully to themselves.

Of course, the new mathematics in general will be blamed if things go wrong, though the most guilty in this respect is New Maths. The book I quoted is one of the *better* instances of the new tendency. Obviously its author has never noticed that things like variables exist in mathematics, that in texts variables are indicated by letters, and that it is, as a rule, the scope of letters in algebra to indicate variables. Whereas generations of didacticians made efforts to accustom the students to the use of letters, these authors did not even seem to notice the problem. In New Maths the break with the tradition is complete. The whole high-brow set theory is a meaningless game with 26 letters. This is the bitter consequence of fifteen years of an innovation movement that for many years only aimed at a renovation of the subject matter. People who warned against this narrow-minded approach were laughed at. Any didactic argument was ridiculed. Behold the sharks in the wake of innovation!

At the beginning of this chapter I should have explained why I first deal with algebra and afterwards with sets and mappings. My subject matter chapters indicate an order of subject matter according to analysis rather than to teaching. Today it is a matter of course (though not of reason) that set theory precedes all other subjects because everything is founded on set theory. Let us accept it for a moment, that is, that the building of mathematics has to start with set theory. Even then it would not be true that its design had to start from set theory. If mathematics is to serve some purpose, the student must learn algebra and analysis. Set theory can improve the teaching tremendously and under this viewpoint set theory should be taught, as a means to improve mathematics teaching. The first school texts of mathematics that contained set theory, looked like that: in the second year the pupil learned set theory only to forget it completely until the 9th or 10th year. In the Dubrovnik project mathematics was divided into watertight compartments, and one of them was set theory, which was nowhere used. Such schizophrenia was severely criticized. Just a few years ago a well-known mathematician published a Modern Algebra for schools the first half of which was the most modern (though rather objectionable) set theory whereas the second half, completely unrelated to the modern first, was rather old-fashioned analytic geometry with the use of vectors. It seems that mathematics teaching has recovered from this schizophrenia. But now it has been struck by another evil – the mathematics the pupil has to learn after set theory is both as regards contents and didactics determined by set theory rather than the other way round. This is especially awkward if set theory, as often happens, is taught in a way that afterwards makes any further mathematics teaching impossible. If only finite sets are considered, if sets are incessantly illustrated by (often wrong) Venn diagrams, if the teacher behaves as though letters do not mean anything but themselves or mean spots in a Venn diagram, then the way to understanding variables is blocked. This prevents pupils from learning that letters are used to indicate variables, and that, in particular, a letter in algebra can mean an integer, a rational number, or a real number.

Do not misunderstand me. I am not saying you should speak about variables or explain what a variable is. This would be nonsense if it were possible at all. What matters is that the student gets accustomed to explanations like "where a may be an arbitrary positive number", and that whenever the student reads or writes a letter in a mathematical expression, he follows the habit of asking himself what the letter means. The student must learn that mathematics is not a game with letters.

Let us describe systematically the part played by letters as mathematical symbols. It is twofold, firstly letters as proper names, like π for a well-determined number, or 'A' for the intersection of two lines on the paper (or like 'London' naming the spot on the map where the name is printed); secondly, letters as ambiguous names like the name 'man' in everyday language, a name which can be given to all men, or the name 'stone', which applies to stones.* Sometimes ambiguous names are forced upon us by ignorance, that is because no other or no more precise name is available, while sometimes we are satisfied with them because we

---

* The two cases are psychologically rather than logically separated. The point notations in geometry differ only seemingly in character from number indications in algebra. In history this has only gradually come clear. 'A' in geometry means an arbitrary point, as 'a' in algebra an arbitrary number. If the point A is mentioned I am expected to fix my eye upon a certain point in the plane and behave as if it were A. With numbers it looks different. To be sure, if somebody asks me "think of a number, add 3, multiply by 4, and so on", I should really take a certain number in my mind, say 17, and operate on it that way. Yet this is not what I mean if in algebra I speak of an arbitrary number. If in algebra I consider 'a' and 'b' in $(a+b)^2$ as specific numbers as I do in geometry with A and B as specific points, I spoil algebra. So geometry and algebra seem to behave differently in their use of letters. Actually the difference vanishes, if the situation is more profoundly analyzed. In geometry, to prove a general theorem, one can afford to view a specific triangle ABC provided it is "generally" chosen. Algebraic geometry explains why all what is true of a "general" triangle, also holds for any special one. But there is no "general" natural number in this sense.

need no further specification. The first case is in algebra that of *unknowns* in an equation, the second that of *indeterminates* in a general statement.

If a letter occurs as an ambiguous name for a number, why do we use so many $a, b, c, \ldots$? It is the same device as if we should speak of this man and that man, this stone and that stone. The pupil who does not understand how a comes to equal b, can be told "in fact, a and b need not be equal, but they can be so accidentally, just as by accident the man or the stone I imagined can be the same as that you imagined". It is most essential that the pupil learns that letters mean something and that different letters or expressions can mean the same, such as 'London' and 'the capital of England' mean the same. For this reason it is a didactic mistake if letters are used too often as proper names as happens in the above-mentioned textbooks. If time and again every letter is used to indicate itself or a fixed spot in a Venn diagram, the student is led far away from the idea of variable or ambiguous name. Of course, I would not ban letters as proper names, e.g. in such examples as "let A be the set $\{1, 2, 3\}$". But even here they can be circumvented. For instance, if is about problems on intersections, the binding of A to a fixed set can be avoided by formulations like "let A and B be two of the following sets (a list follows) – determine their intersection."

Obviously standard proper names are needed for special sets, but at least typography shows that 'Z', 'N' are extraordinary things, that they are not variables, and not ambiguous but fixed names. Geometry is a more difficult case. But in my view the teacher should stress that ABC are different triangles in the different notebooks of his students, and even on different pages of the same notebook. The student chooses one triangle ABC; then, indeed, it becomes *the* triangle ABC though mine for me and yours for you.

It cannot be stressed often enough that letters in mathematics mean something, and their interpretation as ambiguous names for objects of the same sort is so natural and so close to what everyday language does with appellatives that it is hard to understand why it does not tacitly work and just as naturally, for example, in the case of the above-mentioned textbook authors. To explain this one has to stress a certain difference between everyday language and mathematical language. In everyday language the ambiguous names distinguish the sorts of objects they name. 'Man' and 'stone' name men and stones only, whereas 'a', 'b', 'c', $\ldots$

can be charged with many other tasks than naming numbers. The didactically weak spot of the ambiguous algebraic names is that their meaning, that is the sort of things they name, must again and again be mentioned explicitly while for 'man' and 'stone' it is implicitly given. To bridge this gap, one can stress that 'a' is an abbreviation of 'the number a', 'A' an abbreviation of 'the point A'. For a while one can even require the student to read '$a^2 + 3b$' as "number a squared plus three times number b". Would it be practible? I mentioned earlier problems like this one:

a may be one of the numbers 1, 2, 3, 4,

b may be one of the numbers 1, 2, 3, 4, 5;

what can $2a$, $3b$, $2a + 3b$, $a + b$, $a - b$, $(a + b)(a - b)$, $a^2 - b^2$, ... be

Of course this can be formalized by means of sets; a can be said to vary in A and B respectively, and finally even more formal versions can be learned, such as

$$\text{the set of } a + b \quad \text{with} \quad a \in A \quad \text{and} \quad b \in B.$$

The one does not exclude the other, on the contrary, they complement each other. They are exercises that greatly differ as to character and aim from the old-style substitution routines.

Whether the use of letters would start with unknowns or indeterminates is an old controversy. If motivating material is compared (indeterminates in general algebraic, geometrical, physical and everyday life relations versus unknowns to solve problems), the odds seem to be in favour of equations and unknowns. On closer inspection this looks more doubtful. The motivating material generally consists of simple problems or riddles which have been so much exercised in elementary arithmetic that students can solve them without 'x'. I think that indeterminates are more apt for exemplifying ambiguous names than unknowns are. In an algebra that is exercised close to applications, the indeterminates emerge most naturally – they announce themselves in a number of formulae by which natural and social reality is interpreted. Moreover, the indeterminate is close to the concept of function. It is true that the $2a$, $3b$, ... of the above example are not functions but they can be interpreted as functions of $a \in A$ and $b \in B$. I will come back to this point later.

Properly understood, variables always occur in a bound fashion to make the expressions where they occur meaningful. It is, however, an open question as to what degree the sort of binding should be specified explicitly. In geometry it looks reasonable to state once and for all that capitals mean points though occasionally versions like "the point A" "the segment AB", "the triangle ABC" will creep in, which gives an opportunity to remind the student of the sets to which the variables are supposed to be bound. The explicit quantification, however, "for all A" will be rarely added except in such versions as "the set of all points which...". In algebra, at least in its beginnings, it can only do good if the meaning of the letters is often stressed. How explicitly quantification should be stated, is another thing. There are so many shades of formality:

(1) Let a, b, c be integers;
$$a(b + c) = ab + ac.$$

(2) Let a, b, c be integers. Then
$$a(b + c) = ab + ac.$$

(3) Let a, b, c be integers. Then always
$$a(b + c) = ab + ac.$$

(4) If a, b, c are integers, then
$$a(b + c) = ab + ac.$$

(5) $$a(b + c) = ab + ac$$
for all integers a, b, c.

(6) For all integers a, b, c,
$$a(b + c) = ab + ac.$$

(7) $$\wedge_{a \in \mathbf{Z},\, b \in \mathbf{Z},\, c \in \mathbf{Z}} \, a(b + c) = ab + ac.$$

Explicit quantification occurs in (5), (6), (7) only. I would not like to propagate premature quantification symbolism, but in any case I would stress that there is no need to stick to one formula. On the contrary it pays to profit from the synonymic opportunities of everyday language. But however it is stressed, the binding of variables can only improve the understanding of the idea of variable.

How about the existential binding? In the beginning of algebra, it hardly plays a part. At this level an existence is stated by showing the thing desired; a more sophisticated meaning of existence then is still far away. What is more important is to recognize what a conditional equation is and what the unknowns are with respect to which it is to be solved. It looks more important to formalize this kind of binding than quantification. The reader will probably have noticed how I am accustomed to write equations, e.g.

$$(?x)\, x^2 - 2x + 3 = 0$$

or

$$(?x)\, a + x = b.$$

I need not explain this notation though it cannot be easily described formally – this is a point to which I will come back later.

Though it goes beyond school mathematics, I cannot help but incidentally draw the reader's attention to a sophistication of the idea of the indeterminate in abstract algebra, or rather to a re-interpretation of the linguistic idea of the indeterminate as a mathematical concept. There a polynomial $a_0 + a_1 x + \ldots + a_n x^n$ is not understood in the sense that the $a_0, a_1, \ldots, a_n$ are real or complex numbers but rather in that they are "indeterminates" which then means that to a fixed ground–field P free transcendants $a_0, a_1, \ldots, a_n$ have been adjoined and the given expression is considered as a polynomial over the field extension $P(a_0, a_1, \ldots, a_n)$. Of course the substitution of elements of P for $a_0, a_1, \ldots, a_n$ is allowed, but this is another thing. In algebraic geometry it is an accepted custom to work as it were with open fields to which new indeterminates can be tacitly adjoined whenever need be. This then is the way to interpret statements in which the word "general" occurs. "The general 5th degree equation cannot be solved by radicals" means that $a_0 + a_1 x + \ldots + a_5 x^5 = 0$ cannot be solved by radicals over $\mathbf{Q}(a_0, a_1, \ldots, a_5)$ if $a_0, a_1, \ldots, a_5$ are free transcendents over $\mathbf{Q}$; a new "general point" of the plane has as coordinates free transcendents over the field in which the already present points have their coordinates.

I mention this because it can serve to justify certain quite familiar algebraic habits which will be analyzed later. I mean things like the following. It is not unusual to operate algebraically on expressions like 'a/b' without always mentioning anew that it requires $b \neq 0$. If a and b are considered as indeterminates in the sense of abstract algebra, then b

is a transcendent over the ground-field and as such it is certainly $\neq 0$, since it even differs from all elements of the ground-field. Not until something from the ground-field is substituted for b can things go wrong.

This is part of the algebraic method, though not of its didactic fundamentals. But the didactic questions I deal with from the beginning of this chapter are not intended as teaching matter – I stress this for safety's sake. I am trying to tell the didactician and the teacher what the use of letters in mathematics is and to explain to them that those letters occur as ambiguous names. It is not intended to be taught to schoolchildren. A child learning his mother tongue is not told what an adverb is though he is taught how to use adverbs. Likewise the student should be accustomed to experience algebraic expressions as meaningful and the letters in these expressions as ambiguous names rather than as elements of a set of letters. There will hardly be any need to use such terms as "ambiguous name" even if the existence of such names in everyday language is used as an example. Good habits are more efficiently spread by good examples than by rules of behaviour. It is true that at a higher level "good habits" can become an object of analysis or even of criticism; as a rule the educator is committed to understand them more consciously than his students. I really doubt whether terms like "ambiguous name" are needed at school. Under certain circumstances, however, they can be indispensable. If pupils have been spoiled by the wrong kind of teaching to master quite a lot of mathematics yet have never experienced letters in mathematical expressions as meaningful, it may be necessary to help them analyze the field consciously and even to lead them to paradoxes. If bad habits are to be stamped out, proving their inferiority is compulsory.

THE EQUALITY SIGN

In exercise books of arithmetic

$$2 + 7 = 9 + 7 = 16 + 7 = 23 + \ldots$$

is a well-known feature. We reject it. It is not because it cannot be justified – not without long hesitation has this notation been forbidden. There are still rudimentary traces of the mathematical style which would allow such formulae. It could be maintained with appropriate brackets such as

$$(((((2 + 7 = 9) + 7) = 16) + 7) = 23) + \ldots,$$

or by the convention that with no further comment every formula is read by progressing from left to right. In fact this is the rule with all expressions that contain additions and subtractions only. They are read as staves from left to right, such as for instance

$$7 + 3 - 2 + 5 + 6 - 7 + \ldots$$

Maybe someone would object that if something is to be added it can be done with numbers only, and that

$$(2 + 7 = 9),$$

to which something should be added is a statement rather than a number. This is true but it is no less true that this rule is not too faithfully observed, even in the most sublime mathematics. From a book famous for the universally acknowledged rigour of its style, I take such instances as

the sum $\mu(f) = \sum_{x \in X} \alpha(x) f(x) \ldots$,

the integral $I(f) = \displaystyle\int_{-\infty}^{\infty} f(x) \, dx$

the union $A = \bigcup_n A_n \ldots$

the function $f = \sum_{k=1}^{n} a_k f_k$ is integrable,

the set of the $x \in X$ with $\ldots$

a set $M \in \Phi \ldots$

the open set $G \subset X \ldots$.

What is wrong here? Why, after great hesitation it is generally agreed that patterns like

$$\ldots = \ldots , \quad \ldots \subset \ldots , \quad \ldots \in \ldots$$

indicate statements (which may be right or wrong). If, however, we read something like "the sum...", "the integral...", "the open set..." then at the spots indicated by three dots we would expect a sum, an integral, an open set, rather than a statement that is found in the actual text. This sloppiness is still fairly general (I, too, am guilty of doing this). Within a quarter of a century this will have died out. It could be repaired by a pair of brackets, the first before the equality, inclusion, and adherence sign, and the second after the mathematical expression.

The old and natural interpretation of

$$2 + 7 = 9$$

is: Given 2, I add 7, the result is 9. Finally this interpretation has been rejected. $2 + 7$ is viewed as a number; the total expression is read as a statement that pronounces two numbers to be equal.

The interpretation that makes $2 + 7$ a number is genuinely algebraic. It is closely connected to literal calculus. As long as $2 + 7$ is interpreted as an arithmetical problem, as we did above, expressions like $a + b$ cannot be understood. In fact, how can we compute $a + b$ if neither a nor b are known? We cannot interpret $a + b$ as a command to add a and b, but only as the sum of a and b, that is as a number if a and b are numbers. In the history of algebra this interpretation announces itself in fractions. People wrote $\frac{3\,7}{7\,1}$ and then decided that this was not a problem but a number. With algebraic expressions this step occurred about 1460 A.D. when someone wrote

$$\frac{2x^2 + 100 - 20x}{10x - x^2} = 25.$$

Here again a fraction is interpreted as a number. (This shows anew the close relation between fractions and the algebraic method.)

It is not too difficult to believe that what stands around '$\leqslant$', '$\in$', '$\subset$', is a statement. With '$=$', however, it is not as easy to believe this. What kind of statement should it be? Obviously that something *is* something else. But what kind of "is"? In "Socrates is a man" it is the $\in$; in "An ape is a mammal", it is $\subset$. What is it here? It is like "London *is* the capital of England" – the "is" of equality. But what is equality? Are not $2 + 7$ and 9 quite different things, one consisting of one sign, the other of three signs? Indeed, that is what happens with 'London', too. I can describe this city using one word, or if I prefer, using four words. (Of course then I have to know that London *is* the capital of England, just as to be able to express 9 by '$2 + 7$' I would have to master arithmetic.) '$a = b$' means that a and b are the same thing.

Usually people express this by saying that what stands to the left and to the right of the equality sign are names given to the same thing. This is correct. '$2 + 7$' and '9' are indeed expressions that designate the same thing, as well as 'London' and 'the capital of England'. It is correct but this does not involve one being obliged to express oneself in such a clumsy way. It is simpler to state (and it means the same) that a and b are the same thing. It is true that it is not a mathematical fact that a and b are the same thing; the words "thing" and "the same" do not belong to the mathematical context. But the expression "name of the same thing" is even less of a mathematical nature.

Unfortunately much confusion has been caused by this formula, "names of the same thing". A few people seem to have become alarmed: "computing $2 + 7$ is not a reasonable task; it is only another name for $2 + 7$ that is being asked for". Meanwhile timid textbook authors started providing such problems with the preambule "find another name for $2 + 7$"! This repeats itself indefinitely, sometimes, with the variation "find the standard name of...". This is a quite ridiculous procedure for nothing is gained by it. It is merely a display of pseudo-rigour. It would be just as ridiculous to claim that solving a problem simply boils down to finding another name for the thing asked for. In this way you can even reduce Riemann's hypothesis in size to only finding out another name for the set of the non-trivial zeros of the ζ-function outside the line $Re\ s = \frac{1}{2}$! If the detective Mr. Dupont sets out to solve the mystery of the murders in the rue Morgue, the thing to discover would be no more than another name for "the killer of the rue Morgue".

This complex of questions is closely related to what I called the antagonism between "ready-made" and "acted-out" mathematics. Computing $2 + 7$ does not make sense in ready-made mathematics, it is finished. A formalist could not even tell what should replace $2 + 7$. Why 9? $7 + 2$ is just as correct, $1 + (1 + 7)$ also, and so on. What is required if the problem reads "compute $(a + b)(a - b)$" or "resolve $a^2 - b^2$ into a product"? Whoever interprets mathematics as a ready-made product, or chooses a formalist point of view, cannot understand such problems, or at least would be committed to not understanding them. Of course they should be formulated in a way that the pupil who is asked to solve them knows what is meant. This is not difficult. The pupil knows very well that "how much are $7 + 2$" should not be answered by '$7 + 2$' or '$2 + 7$' and so on. (A method of formalizing the posing of such problems would be the multiple choice test – the pupil may choose from a few answers where all but one of them are even formally wrong.)

When I have explained to first-year students the axioms of vector space and drawn the first conclusions, it almost always happens that one of them objects to the way I used, say, the associative law $(a + b) + c = a + + (b + c)$, to replace $a + (b + c)$ by $(a + b) + c$ in some expression or other. My formulation, he claims, allows the replacement of the left-hand by the right-hand member rather than the other way round. Obviously the bad habits in mathematics learned at school motivate his objection. Certain equalities are always memorized in a fixed order of the terms. The solution of a linear equation is always written as $x = \ldots$ and never as $\ldots = x$. A quadratic equation may read $x^2 - 3x + 2 = 0$ but never $0 = x^2 - 3x + 2$. Normally one will meet $\frac{4}{6} = \frac{2}{3}$ though not $\frac{2}{3} = \frac{4}{6}$. If I inquire for the reason why I should not convert the associative law, I will get explanations like: "An ape is a mammal, but a mammal does not have to be an ape". Or, in an earlier-mentioned version: "3 apples plus 2 pears = 5 fruits, but not the other way round."

Of course, all rules known from the equivalence relation apply to the equality sign $(a = a, a = b \to b = a, a = b \land b = c \to a = c)$. This is a mere consequence of the interpretation of $a = b$ as "a and b are the same thing". In spite of this it is a sad fact that producers of axiom catalogues for equality are not willing to retire from business. I saw them again recently in a widespread algebra textbook for first-year college students. In defining what a field is the author was not satisfied with the field axioms he took from other textbooks. He explicitly required the axioms of the equivalence relation for the equality and moreover the exchangeability of equals for equals in the four operations, which entails quite a lot of axioms like $a = a' \to a + b = a' + b$. This is a ridiculous business because even if this point of view were accepted, the catalogue would still be tremendously incomplete. It justifies the exchangeability of equal a and a' in rational expressions only, though much more is needed. One should be able to replace a by a' in every function, statement, and relation as soon as $a = a'$, but this is not guaranteed by the above catalogue of axioms. In our interpretation, however, this exchangeability is assured by the mere fact that a and a' are the same thing. If more formalism is preferred, it can be stipulated that $a = a'$ as soon as each statement $E(\ldots a \ldots)$ implies $E(\ldots a' \ldots)$ (and conversely, but this is a mere consequence because then $\neg E(\ldots a \ldots) \to \neg E(\ldots a' \ldots)$, too). This is the famous definition of equality we owe to Leibniz – that two objects are identical if they have all properties in common and therefore different if they differ in respect of at least one property). It is not our intention to enter into more detail, and certainly not to recommend this kind of analysis in school mathematics. I do not know of any serious school textbook that would introduce equality in this way. If it looks different otherwise, it is almost certain that the author never pondered on the consequences.

THE LANGUAGE OF ALGEBRAIC FORMULAE

The pupil must learn to read and write algebraic formulae just as he reads texts in his mother tongue or staves. As every teacher knows it takes much trouble to attain this goal. Some textbooks very consciously stimulate the process of learning the language of algebraic formulae, whereas others behave as though the problem of this process did not exist at all. The latter are those that teach a ready-made system of mathematics, and then this neglect is only a logical consequence of their adherence to a system since there all didactics should be implicit in constructing the system; once the system has been fixed, there is no room left as regards didactics. In fact they often attempt to fill the gap by means of appendices of problems outside the system, which are supposed to train practical skills.

I would not, however, claim that the textbooks which pay more attention to the apprehension of the language of algebraic fromulae provide the didactical analyst with more material. I do not know of any systematic investigation on schoolchildren learning the language of algebraic formulae. My own material is empirical. I know what I remember from talks by teachers and what struck me in studying textbooks. Many teachers depicted the process of learning this language to me as a mystery. After a shorter or longer period of struggling the pupil finally masters this language though neither he nor the observing teacher knows what has happened. Nobody seems to know what the original obstacles were and how they have been overcome. Schoolchildren would have to be observed for a long period to understand this phenomenon, short experiments would not suffice.

Learning the language of algebraic formulae may be somewhat alike to learning one's own mother tongue. But the mother tongue is a permanent concern while the language of formulae is only rarely exercised.

In this respect staves would be a better means of comparison though this breaks down for other reasons. Learning staves requires no more than creating fixed and quite regular associations between optical images and motoric events; understanding them is a secondary matter. If someone says he cannot learn staves, it probably means that he does not take it seriously, and spends neither time nor trouble to learn it. The language of algebraic formulae differs greatly from our natural languages, and from staves or chemical symbolics. Very few realize this. In a philosophical thesis on symbolics delivered by a chemist, I was struck by the chapter on symbols in mathematics. Quite flabbergasted, I read how he interpreted mathematical formulae, for instance $2 + 7 = 9$ as though the 2 is reacting with the 7 to produce 9. (I cannot imagine how he would interpret $9 = 2 + 7$.) This, probably, was someone who could make something of mathematical formulae. Few can tell what worries pupils when they are initiated into this language. But a surprising number of textbooks treat this problem with an irritating indifference.

I dwelt upon the strange part letters play in algebra. Obviously this should be learned and all misleading procedures should be avoided. It cannot be often enough stressed that $a + b$ is a number if a and b are so. But the teacher should realize to which degree our algebraic conventions impede this understanding. Often if some '$a + b$' is substituted for some 'c', let us say in '$cd = dc$', the signs complex '$a + b$' is surrounded by brackets. If in 'ab' the 'a' is replaced by '$- a$', it becomes '$- ab$'. If, however, 'b' is replaced by '$-b$', it does not become $a - b$ but $a(-b)$. Isn't this crazy? The student must learn where to add brackets and where not. It is far from simple. Think what you should have to tell a computer about these tricks, and how much you would forget to tell when you are teaching human beings. It has been proposed always to bracket algebraic expressions which mean a number or something similar. '$a + b$' should mean the command to compute this sum, whereas '$(a + b)$' would be the sum itself. For instance one should write

$$((((2((ab)^2)) + (3c))$$

with a profusion of brackets which would have to be solved afterwards according to fixed rules. I am afraid that this is far too complicated.

Structuring algebraic expressions systematically by means of brackets and conventions is just what distinguishes algebraic language from the vernacular. In "hot chocolate and ice cream" it is as clear that the hotness does not extend to the ice cream as it is in "three days and nights" where the "three" counts both days and nights. Whether in "Dear Mary and John" one is as dear to the writer as the other is not clear without brackets, but it does not matter much either. In mathematics the brackets in $2 \cdot (3 + 4)$ *do* matter. By conscious bracketing the text is structured.

This is not the whole secret. The system is much more involved. In some countries students learn versified rules on the order of algebraic operations, which should be: raising to a power, multiplying, dividing, extracting roots, adding, and subtracting. The last pair are obviously wrong as appears from expressions like

$$3 - 7 + 6 - 8 + 4,$$

which according to this rule should be worked out as

$$3 - (7 + 6) - (8 + 4)$$

whereas the usual procedure leads to

$$(((3 - 7) + 6) - 8) + 4.$$

The verse does not explain either whether

$$3 - 5 - 8$$

should be understood as

$$(3 - 5) - 8 \quad \text{or} \quad 3 - (5 - 8)$$

In addition and multiplication it does not matter since they are associative, but in subtraction, division and powers it does matter. For addition and subtraction the language of algebraic formulae follows

Principle A: Proceed from the left to the right as it stands. In other words, put all opening brackets at the left-most place.

This is a quite natural principle. It is so natural that before brackets came into general use, deviations from this principle were indicated by infringing on the linear order, that is by arranging terms which belong together in a column. Fractions are the first example of this principle; there and in similar instances it still prevails. It is

Principle B: What, against the linear order, belongs together is arranged vertically.

There is also a quite singular

Principle C: A dash above a piece of text holds things together.

Before brackets people also used dashes to indicate connectedness. In very special expressions such as $\overline{n+1}$ this continued up to the beginning of the present century. We still preserve this method after the root sign, $\sqrt{a+b}$, and with the functional dash of the complex conjugation.

Principle D: Pairs of brackets include things belonging together.

Pairs of brackets first appear in Stiefel's work (1544). Leibniz propagated them but it was not until Euler that they were generally accepted.

Principle E: Some algebraic operations have a connecting force.

This is the oldest means of syntactic structuring of algebraic expressions, even older than the language of mathematical formulae as such. In a sense it can be traced back to cuneiform texts. It accounts, in particular, for the feature that multiplying is more closely connecting than adding and subtracting. This convention comes from a quite natural source, the same as that which leads some teachers to explain why $2a + 3a = 5a$: it is like 2 cows + 3 cows = 5 cows. The denomination is interpreted as a multiplication – "3 cows" is read as if it were "3 times cow", which is not far-fetched though today we would prefer to interpret the denomination as a function. If the tables are turned, multiplication is interpreted as denomination. In equations this is a natural view. From ancient times an equation like $x^2 + 21 = 10x$ was pronounced according to the pattern of "thingumajig-square plus 21 equals 10 thingumajigs". From the first appearance of algebraic formulae there has never been the slightest doubt that multiplication precedes addition and subtraction, in particular, in those formulae where multiplication is not indicated by a sign, but this habit extended to the case of explicitly indicated multiplication. The priority of raising to a power over other operations has been as self-evident since Descartes introduced exponents.

All punctuations we mentioned till now had a connecting character. In the vernacular, separating punctuations prevail. It should be realized what this contrast must mean for the learner. We now turn to

Principle F: Some punctuations are separating.

The equality sign has this property; in a certain sense this sign belongs to the vernacular; $\geqslant$, $\sim$, and so on can also be considered as separating signs. Skill in reading long formulae means looking first for such signs of structuring. To our mind the separating character of the equality sign is a most evident thing, though it may be doubted whether learners share this feeling; they are rather inclined to read every text from the left to the right, as they write it in

$$2 + 7 = 9 + 7 = 16 + 7 = 23 + \ldots$$

Connecting punctuations which like brackets occur pairwise, are rather uneconomical; in non-associative multiplication compound products are structured by dots, for instance to distinguish $a \cdot bc$ from $ab \cdot c$. Separating punctuations are more economical and distinctive. Russell and Whitehead, in *Principia Mathematica* fully adhered to the principle of separating punctuations. Then, of course, instead of brackets of various connecting powers separating punctuations of various separating powers are needed. The punctuations of P.M. consist of groups of dots; the more dots it contains the sharper it separates. Would not it be better to accept separating punctuations? It is a rational but vain desire.

The above enumeration was to show that the language of formulae is not as simple as people who master it believe. It is still complicated by a few absurdities we owe to history. There is, for instance, the fractional notation $2\frac{3}{7}$ which, older than the use of the plus sign, has been handed down the centuries to us from a time when addition was indicated by putting things one besides the other. Teachers know how easily students forget that this is no product. Is not it time to abolish such notations? In mathematics $\frac{17}{7}$ would be preferred anyhow, and if mixed fractions are needed at all, they can better be written with a plus sign, such as $2 + \frac{3}{7}$.

Another didactical affliction is the double meaning of plus and minus signs, as state signs and as operation signs. Earlier I gave an interpretation that reduces the disadvantages of the double meaning sharply. Other devices have been proposed: colored digits restricted to provisional use and illustrations, dashings ($\bar{3}$ instead of -3), and liftings ($^{-}3$ or 3^{-}). The device of dashing proves quite useful if decimal fractions are also used as labels on the number line, since $\bar{3}, 25$ is easier to be located than $-2,75$.

Apart from the strict, though often not explicitly formulated rules, we know of certain customs which can be looked on by students as strict rules. Why do we write $2a$ and not $a2$, $2ab$ and not $a2b$, ab and rarely ba? Students could easily believe that the "forbidden" expressions were wrong, and this taboo prevents them from understanding that the allowed and the forbidden expressions are equal! It is, in particular, dangerous if the taboo forbids all superfluous brackets. Forbidden expressions such as $2(ab)$ are so rare that the student does not learn they equal $2ab$. This didactical negligence accounts for mistakes like $2(ab) = (2a)(2b)$, in particular if a and b are represented by more involved expressions. In the past didacticians recognized these dangerous corners, but this knowledge seems to have very much faded away. Exercising the punctuation of algebraic formulae is not adequately organized. The student hardly understands the structuring task of punctuation devices. He is tempted to believe that brackets serve to be done with away, because where they can be missed they are systematically omitted.

All language instruction requires a vast and well-directed reading drill. Algebraic expressions are a linguistic matter with a peculiar structure, which can be much more complex than ordinary linguistic matter. Reading algebraic texts should not be left to haphazard learning. It should be guided by a well-designed plan which proceeds according to scales of increasing difficulty. Yet material which has been designed in this way is rarely found.

Much stress instead is usually laid on substituting. It is much exercised in the restricted way that letters are replaced by numbers. Problems where, say, a is replaced by $2a + 3b$ and b by $a - 4$ are rare or even absent. But the student should learn to come from

$$(a + b)(a - b) = a^2 - b^2$$

to

$$(2a + 3b + a - 4)(2a + 3b - a + 4) = (2a + 3b)^2 - (a - 4)^2$$

The student should explicitly exercise the substitution of $-a$ for a and $-b$ for b. Rather than disguised, such operations should be explicitly exhibited as substitutions. Patterns like

$$(\square + \bigcirc)(\square - \bigcirc) = \square^2 - \bigcirc^2$$

are a familiar and widespread didactical device. I fear they only obscure the fact that *each letter* as such is like a box into which you can put all you want.

A very important kind of substitution is almost never exercised in school mathematics because it is not formal enough. I mean substituting variables for constants to generalize numerical results.

The view that the language of algebraic formulae can be taught by haphazard methods still prevails. It is a dangerous belief. The use of this language should become an automatism. Didactic mistakes can fix wrong automatisms. They should be prevented, for remedy is not easy. The problem is to a great degree one of language instruction. The teacher should be highly conscious of the peculiarities of the language of formulae, and textbook authors should consciously use this knowledge.

Of course, this includes, besides the language of formulae, that around the formulae, which is mostly of logical character. I will deal with it later. Algebraic formulae are of two sorts, those which correspond to words and those which correspond to sentences.

Among the latter there can be different kinds – affirmative, conditional, and interrogative. Problems should clearly show what is required, whether a "word" is to be transformed and according to which principle, whether a conditional sentence should be completed into an affirmative one, or whether an interrogative sentence is to be answered. The least that should be indicated around an equation with more than one letter in it, is *what* is to be computed. Tradition requires that if there is a choice between x and a, then x is the unknown. Much can be improved here by better formalization. When asking for the unknown x I like to use the symbol

$$(?x) \ldots$$

I will come back to this question later.

While stressing the linguistic aspect of algebra, one should not overlook an important feature by which the instruction of the language of algebraic formulae is distinguished from other linguistic instruction. To a high degree the language of formulae can be handled autonomously, independently of the understanding of the content. Such an autonomy does not apply to everyday language. As in elementary arithmetic the training process in the language of algebraic formulae should never block the regress from the formal language to the content, and this regress should be performed as often as is needed. As long as they are not fool proof, the automatisms should not be cut off at the root. In teaching arithmetic this is attained by scattering applied problems among the purely arithmetical exercises. When teaching the language of algebraic formulae, one should prevent the algebraic matter from becoming a meaningless game. This can be reached by realistic problems as well as by problems that test not only whether the student can apply some formula or rule but rather whether he does so consciously and knows why he is applying it in this way rather than otherwise.

CHAPTER XIV

DEVELOPMENT OF THE NUMBER CONCEPT – FROM THE ALGEBRAIC PRINCIPLE TO THE GLOBAL ORGANIZATION OF ALGEBRA

With the introduction of the sign x^{12} for the 12th power of x the newer analysis started.

C. G. J. Jacobi (L. Koenigsberger, C. G. J. Jacobi, Leipzig, 1904, p. 390)

The method of the algebraic letter calculus is, indeed, not implicit to the objective-intuitive number theory.

D. Hilbert, *Über das Unendliche*, 1927

THE DEVELOPMENT OF THE ALGEBRAIC PRINCIPLE

From the static description in Chapter XI of what was called the algebraic principle, we now pass to its development.

It starts with the natural numbers. They are operated on by adding and multiplying, according to rules that arise spontaneously, maybe to be made explicit at a certain moment. These rules may be a wild heap. Somewhere at a higher level one arrives at viewing these rules as a whole to state that very few among them are sufficient. It should be clear that this idea of sufficiency is not at all self-evident. It does not indeed mean "sufficient for practical needs" or "sufficient for the next test" or "sufficient for passing on to the next grade". There are lists of formulae where such expressions as $(a + b)^2, (a - b)^2, (a + b)(a - b)$ have been collected; they contain formulae of major importance for practical use. We cannot blame the user if he interprets sufficiency in a practical sense, but we mean something different. $(a + b)(a - b)$ can be derived from simpler and more fundamental rules. Of course, one should know whether it pays to derive some formula, but this is again a question of practice.

I stress this yet again. It should be perfectly clear that sufficiency in the sense of deductive basis is not an obvious idea. It may be doubted whether the Babylonians or the Egyptians, who were not too bad mathematicians, ever knew it. In geometry the Greek mathematicians came close to it. Algebra had to wait till modern times before there too this idea of sufficiency was conceived.

Sufficiency thus should be understood in the sense of deductive basis. Some laws are wanted to derive all that are appreciated from these ones. To conceive this idea one should have once had the opportunity of deriving one law from another. I do not mean merely once either, but rather often. Logical connections between arithmetical laws must have become the most natural thing before they are organized under a deductive view. In the tought-experiment we can distinguish the bold relief of the levels in the learning process. First, operating with numbers, then noticing the laws which these operations fulfill, formulating those laws, organizing locally these laws according to local connections, and finally organizing them globally into a deductive system. I will not discuss here where and when these levels can be reached.

Meanwhile, in the learning process, other things may have happened. It is annoying that some operations cannot be performed without restrictions. New objects were introduced to repair this fault. It can have happened in an intuitive way and before any general laws were formulated for the old numbers, maybe even before they were noticed. The extension of the number domain can also, however, have been achieved by rational means, more or less explicitly by the "algebraic principle" as I have called it. To perform this, the arithmetical laws in the old domain should at least have been recognized, because the extension takes place along this guideline that one should operate on the new things as though the old laws remained valid. Notice that I use the term "extension", which is not strictly proper, since the new things need not be created out of empty space as in abstract algebra. As I explained earlier, it may rather be that the new objects have been present before on the number line, and have waited to be recognized and denominated.

In the preceding exposition I viewed the transition from the natural numbers to the integers or to the positive rational numbers or further to the rationals. They are similar patterns though not necessarily the same in all cases. The negative numbers can be introduced intuitively though it is hardly possible to conceive fractions before arithmetical laws have been recognized.

FROM POWERS TO LOGARITHMS

Meanwhile a new operation has come into practice – squaring. Terms like squaring and raising to a power sound old-fashioned. Indeed, these are not new operations. With the same right any new expression as a function of its variables could be raised to the dignity of an operation. Of course, this could be done. What matters, however, is that squaring and raising to powers are experienced as unary or binary operations, and that the arithmetical laws of these operations are to be recognized and formulated. All these laws together present a mess of bewildering confusion. Why

$$(xy)^z = x^z \cdot y^z \quad \text{though not} \quad (x + y)^z = x^z + y^z,$$

and

$$z^{x+y} = z^x \cdot z^y \quad \text{though} \quad z^{x \cdot y} = (z^x)^y?$$

At this point the old didactics has failed, and I am afraid the new will not fare must better, though for other reasons. The two-fold inversion of these operations is still more confusing.

Square roots can already have been brought in early, with attempts to solve quadratic equations. Square roots are not unrestrictedly possible in the rational domain. So it should again be extended. It cannot be avoided, indeed it is even desirable, that $\sqrt{2}$, say, shows its double face, both as an algebraic and as a real number, as a computing number and as a measuring number, as something that is operated on as though its square is 2, and as a something that can be computed with arbitrary precision while approaching it by common fractions or developing it as a decimal fraction. Both aspects are indispensable. Students should learn to work smoothly with $\sqrt{2}$ as a thing that if squared yields 2, but they should not forget either that $\sqrt{2}$ is located somewhere on the number line between the rational numbers.

With roots emerge a vast variety of new arithmetical laws, which strangely enough, yet fortunately look much alike those for powers. But for logarithms the laws look much different than those for powers. On principle some didacticians avoid the term logarithm and the notation log in logarithmic computations and do not introduce them until the students master the logarithmic computational technique. They interpret the so-called table of logarithms in the sense that it allows one to write a number a in the form 10^p. If ab is to be computed logarithmically, the students write down $a = 10^p$, $b = 10^q$ numerically, transform it into $ab = 10^{p+q}$ and look in the table what is 10^{p+q}. This method works excellently. It dispenses of learning laws for logarithms.

I have skipped over another detail. Long before logarithms the question of extending powers to negative, rational, and maybe even real exponents has become urgent. Again this extending is performed by the algebraic principle, though now there are no new objects to be introduced but operations to be interpolated and extrapolated with certain laws preserved. The need for a small list of laws from which the others follow is distinctly felt here. Real exponents also exist though they may provisionally be neglected since tables and numerical procedures know rational numbers only.

THE PROCESS OF ORGANIZING ALGEBRA

What I disclosed in the preceding section may look somewhat chaotic, yet in actual fact it is. Somehow it reflects the classical development of school algebra, which is poorly organized. School algebra is acquainted with a lot of arithmetical laws that suffice for examinations, but there is little deductive order according to sufficient arithmetical laws. The innovators present us with the opposite view – they begin with the deductive order. They choose the straightest path to arrive for example at the field axioms (or those of ordered fields), which, indeed, can be formulated as soon as students know about the four fundamental arithmetical operations, and they continue deductively, from the field axioms onwards. This works excellently a long way – I mean, to the benefit of the teacher who need not bother any more about a lot of classical obstacles.

The student is not allowed to globally organize the subject matter himself. He is not allowed to choose the right ones from the rich variety of emerging laws but gets them ready-made, to derive conversely from them the more involved ones (or rather to have them derived by the teacher). It can happen that the ready-made laws are imposed on him at a moment in time when he has not yet experienced what it means to derive laws from each other and still less to reduce a variety of laws to a few of them. The field axioms are an excellent drug the teacher can depend on to enable him to sleep quietly and never be disturbed by bad dreams.

This is the anti-didactical inversion *in optima forma*. The student is given no opportunity to organize the subject matter himself. It is *imposed* on him in an organized shape by the teacher. And what about the teacher – has it been organized by him? No, it was given to him by the textbook author. And the textbook author? He did not organize it either! He simply imitated what he could find in every algebra textbook at university level, starting algebra with the field concept. Now all textbooks at university level presuppose that the student is familiar with school algebra. But what should be done if thanks to the innovators the essentials of algebra have been embezzled from algebra instruction at school?

The organization of algebra by means of the field concept was borrowed from the algebra cultivated at university. There are profound reasons why at this level algebra has been based on the field concept. I prefer not to explain them now because it would merely be vain verbalism. But whatever the arguments may be, nothing authorizes us to assume without any proof whatsoever that at school also algebra should be organized with the view to the field concept (or rather the concept of ordered field), and that the field concept should be the only organizing principle even if it were agreed that it should be one of them. I would say it would be a wonder of wonders if it were as simple as this – that merely by diluting university algebra to a certain extent it would be transformed into school algebra. Not until it has been seriously investigated can we tell whether the field concept is an adequate principle of organization at school level. Whether this has been investigated I cannot tell, since almost all didactical publications are dogmatic. If somebody offers me a method of algebra instruction, he may have had profound reasons for arranging the subject matter as he did, though it is just possible that he did not have any reason at all but followed tradition or dogma. I simply cannot tell.

Let us compare the traditional construction of algebra with that around the field concept – what is the difference? Classical algebra knows seven operations: adding, subtracting, multiplying, dividing, raising to powers, taking roots, logarithmizing – all of them binary operations (except perhaps the last). In the modern view there are two binary operations, addition and multiplication, and two unary ones, opposite and reciprocal, and besides this the order (the "greater and smaller") plays a part that formerly was not taken too seriously. One feels a bit ashamed today of the seven good old operations; which nevertheless are still quite vital. The student should master fluently at least the laws of powers; he should know how to derive from them those for roots; the logarithmic rules can be dispensed with for a while but finally they will be badly needed.

Would it be wise to restrict school algebra to those operations that are considered essential according to the field concept, and if so, how can the others be eliminated?

A field K is with respect to addition a commutative group, as is $K\setminus\{0\}$ with respect to multiplication. The axioms which refer to addition in K and those for multiplication in $K\setminus\{0\}$ usually are the axioms for commutative groups. If the student has learned before to axiomatize groups, then these field axioms offer an enrichment rather than a new problem; after the old groups he meets new ones and he learns the important trick that, as it happens, the group operation can be interpreted as an addition or a multiplication. If the student has not yet become acquainted with groups, then the scrutinization of addition and multiplication in the rational field could be an opportunity to introduce him to the pattern of group axiomatics. With a view to later developments he should be confronted with the formal analogy between addition and multiplication:

$$a + b = b + a \qquad\qquad ab = ba$$
$$(a + b) + c = a + (b + c) \qquad (ab)\,c = a\,(bc)$$
$$a + 0 = a \qquad\qquad a \cdot 1 = a$$
$$a + (-a) = 0 \qquad\qquad a \cdot a^{-1} = 1$$
$$a - b = a + (-b) \qquad\qquad a/b = a \cdot b^{-1}$$
$$-(a + b) = -a - b \qquad (ab)^{-1} = a^{-1}b^{-1}$$
$$a + a = 2a \qquad\qquad a \cdot a = a^2$$
$$a + a + a = 3a \qquad\qquad a \cdot a \cdot a = a^3$$
$$(-a) + (-a) = -2a \qquad a^{-1} \cdot a^{-1} = a^{-2}.$$

At this moment the second half of the last line could be a new inductive discovery – definitions, too, can be discovered. The list of analogies can easily be extended though there is no need to do so at this moment. It could be one of the objectives of this exploration to show that the first four lines suffice, and in particular that the sixth follows from them, but I will not stress this now. What matters is to create an organization though not a pre-established one.

It pays to extend the above lines with two more, in which the analogy partially breaks down. It is still true that

$$a > 0 \rightarrow a + a > 0 \qquad a > 1 \rightarrow a^2 > 1$$

but in

$$a > 0 \to a + b > b \qquad a > 1 \to ab > b$$

the second half is only true if $b > 0$ is added to the assumptions.

The distributivity law connecting addition and multiplication is still lacking in this list. It is committed to neither of the columns. But if it must be written into one of them, then one is advised to put it in the left-hand one where both addition and multiplication have already been present. Thus

$$n(a + b) = na + nb \qquad (ab)^n = a^n \cdot b^n,$$
$$n(a - b) = na - nb \qquad (a/b)^n = a^n/b^n,$$

where the distributivity law on the right is necessarily restricted to integral n if other exponents are still unknown.

A well-known interpretation of the distributivity law says that

$$\curlyvee_x nx \quad \text{is an homomorphism}$$

of the additive group of the field K into itself, that is

$$n(x + y) = nx + ny, \quad \text{and} \quad n \cdot (-x) = -n \cdot x.$$

Likewise the right-hand column says that

$$\curlyvee_x x^n \quad \text{is an homomorphism}$$

of the multiplicative group of $K \backslash \{0\}$ into itself, thus
$$(x \cdot y)^n = x^n \cdot y^n.$$

The left-hand homomorphisms preserve the order or invert it:

$$a < b \wedge n > 0 \to na > nb \qquad 0 < a < b \wedge n > 0 \to a^n < b^n,$$
$$a < b \wedge n < 0 \to na < nb \qquad 0 < a < b \wedge n < 0 \to a^n > b^n,$$

where again the analogy is not perfect, because in the right-hand column a supplementary assumption $a > 0$ is needed. This leads to the convention in the second case of restricting homomorphisms to K^+, the positive part of K.

The homomorphism

$$\curlyvee_x nx$$

of the additive group of K maps K one-to-one upon itself if $n \neq 0$, since

$nx = ny$ implies $x = y$ and $(?x)\, nx = a$ is solved by $x = (1/n) \cdot a$. The homomorphisms with $n \neq 0$ are automorphisms of the additive group of K.

The homomorphism

$$\underset{x \in K^+}{\curlyvee} x^n$$

of the multiplicative group of $K/\{0\}$ is still one-to-one for $n \neq 0$, since $x^n = y^n$ implies $x = y$. Whether it maps $K\backslash\{0\}$ upon $K\backslash\{0\}$ depends on whether for $a \in K^+$

$$(?x)\, x^n = a$$

possesses a solution x in K^+, in other words, whether K^+ is closed with respect to taking roots of positive elements.

The field $\mathbf{Q}$ of rational numbers does not have this property; even the square root of an element of $\mathbf{Q}$ need not exist in $\mathbf{Q}$. The field $\mathbf{R}$ of reals, however, is closed in this respect. At this level this should be familiar to the student who is expected to have computed roots; in any case he should now grasp this feature consciously. In Chapter XI* I explained a procedure to "compute" square roots, that is to approximate them by rational or decimal numbers. Since it appears here in the context of the mapping

$$f = \underset{x \in K^+}{\curlyvee} x^n$$

an intuitive illustration of this statement is to be recommended: f preserves the order; if x is running over the number line from 0 to ∞, fx is running in the same direction, first behind x, to overtake x at 1 and to fall behind x from this point. It is an intuitive datum that in this course fx passes every point of the number line. Proving it at this stage can only mean reducing it to facts which should be intuitively more evident. As soon as such more evident facts are available to the student, he can try the reduction provided he doubts it first. I would not know where in the world more evident facts exist at this level. Of course the student can be given such topological axioms of the real field as imply the surjectivity of above f from $\mathbf{R}^+$ to $\mathbf{R}^+$; but it may be doubted whether they are more evident than what should be proved. What is more important is that at this level there is hardly any way to raise serious doubts on fx running through the whole positive number line.

* p. 216.

Whatever it may be, the closedness of K with respect to roots of positive elements emerges as a postulate in these organisatory explorations as had earlier been the case with the existence of rational numbers. For $n \in \mathbf{N}$

$$\curlyvee_{x \in \mathbf{R}} \, n \cdot x \qquad \curlyvee_{x \in \mathbf{R}^+} \, x^n$$

are now automorphisms of the additive group of $\mathbf{R}$ and the multiplicative of $\mathbf{R}^+$ that preserve order. They can be inverted;

$$\curlyvee_{x \in \mathbf{R}} \, 1/n \cdot x \qquad \curlyvee_{x \in \mathbf{R}^+} \, x^{1/n}$$

are again automorphisms, where the second notation is motivated by the first. The mapping can be composed with

$$\curlyvee_{x \in \mathbf{R}} \, m \cdot x \qquad \curlyvee_{x \in \mathbf{R}^+} \, x^m$$

($m \in \mathbf{Z}$), which leads to the automorphisms

$$\curlyvee_{x \in \mathbf{R}} \, m/n \cdot x \qquad \curlyvee_{x \in \mathbf{R}^+} \, x^{n/m} \, .$$

Dividing a number in n equal summands is parallelized by dividing it in n equal factors; the rational multiplier is parallelized by the rational exponent. The next step would be real multipliers and exponents,

$$\curlyvee_{x \in \mathbf{R}} \, \alpha \cdot x \qquad \curlyvee_{x \in \mathbf{R}^+} \, x^\alpha$$

as automorphisms for $\alpha \neq 0$. This is for the left column a well-known and unproblematic fact; in the right column it is an intuitive definition.

Both kind of automorphisms for $\alpha \neq 0$ preserve the order if $\alpha > 0$ and invert it if $\alpha < 0$. Finally it can be seen that these are all automorphisms of the additive group of $\mathbf{R}$ and likewise all of the multiplicative group of $\mathbf{R}^+$ that preserve or invert the order.

Subsequently the multipliers and exponents can be viewed as systems with compositions. In general, if G is an additive commutative group, its homomorphisms φ and ψ can be composed by means of the group operation to get a χ defined by

$$\chi(x) = \varphi(x) + \psi(x)$$

which by

$$
\begin{aligned}
\chi(x + y) &= \varphi(x + y) + \psi(x + y) \\
&= \varphi(x) + \varphi(y) + \psi(x) + \psi(y) \\
&= \varphi(x) + \psi(x) + \varphi(y) + \psi(y) \\
&= \chi(x) + \chi(y)
\end{aligned}
$$

yields an homomorphism; on the other hand homomorphisms of G can also be composed as mappings, that is θ can be defined by

$$\theta(x) = \varphi(\psi(x)),$$

and this is again an homomorphism (even for non-commutative G).

If this is applied, it appears that with respect to both multipliers and exponents one composition must be interpreted as an addition and the other as a multiplication, to account for well-known arithmetical laws:

$$\gamma \cdot x = \alpha \cdot x + \beta \cdot x \qquad x^\gamma = x^\alpha \cdot x^\beta$$
$$\rightarrow \gamma = \alpha + \beta \qquad\qquad \rightarrow \gamma = \alpha + \beta$$
$$\gamma \cdot x = \alpha \cdot (\beta \cdot x) \qquad x^\gamma = (x^\beta)^\alpha$$
$$\rightarrow \gamma = \alpha \cdot \beta \qquad\qquad \rightarrow \gamma = \alpha \cdot \beta$$

Far-reaching analogies between the addition group of $\mathbf{R}$ and the multiplication group of $\mathbf{R}^+$ have been obtained, not only as far as they are ordered commutative groups but also with respect to the homomorphisms of these groups, which show striking analogies. It is worthwhile to stress that in this parallelism between the additive and the multiplicative group the operation of raising to a power as a counterpart of multiplication indeed plays the individual role it is granted in traditional algebra and its applications, and the same is true with regard to division and root extraction.

The question arises whether there is more behind this parallelism. At a certain point the additive structure of K and the multiplicative one of K^+ will have been subordinated to the group concept; maybe examples of isomorphisms have been met so it may be asked whether some isomorphism could be constructed between the two ordered groups. In fact, for fixed $a > 1$

$$\curlyvee_{x \in \mathbf{R}} a^x$$

is such an isomorphism; with x running through $\mathbf{R}$ it happens that a^x runs through all of $\mathbf{R}^+$ in the same sense and such that

$$a^{x+y} = a^x \cdot a^y, \qquad a^{-x} = (a^x)^{-1}.$$

Likewise for $0 < a < 1$,

$$\curlywedge_{x \in \mathbf{R}} a^x$$

is an isomorphism that inverts the order.

By this isomorphism it is in fact possible to translate statements as written above in the left column into their right-hand counterparts. Depending on a they are isomorphisms or anti-isomorphisms of the additive group of $\mathbf{R}$ into the multiplicative group of $\mathbf{R}^+$; in the traditional terminology these isomorphisms and anti-isomorphisms are called exponential functions.

They are more directly obtained if the *a priori* question is raised to construct an isomorphism f from $\mathbf{R}$ to $\mathbf{R}^+$. Such an f must fulfill

$$f(x + y) = f(x) + f(y).$$

In particular f must map an arithmetic sequence

$$0, h, 2h, 3h, \ldots$$

into a geometrical one,

$$1, k, k^2, k^3, \ldots .$$

This is the way logarithm tables were invented in the 17th century. (A precursor was the use of trigonometrical tables to simplify computations.) Logarithms must allow to translate geometrical sequences into arithmetical ones and by this way multiplications and divisions into additions and subtractions. Initial choices* of h and k were $h = 10^{-7}$ and $k = 1 + 10^{-7}$, which meant that to $10^7 \cdot 10^{-7} = 1$ in the arithmetical sequence corresponded

$$(1 + 10^{-7})^{10^7} \sim e$$

in the geometrical sequence; thus the arithmetical sequence behaved as the natural logarithms of the geometrical sequence. Gradually the functional aspect of logarithms was stressed more and more, and in a more geometrical view the natural logarithm of x emerged as the integral

$$\int_1^x \frac{\mathrm{d}t}{t}.$$

Not until Euler was the logarithm clearly recognized as the inverse of an exponential function though vague ideas about this connection had existed much earlier.

---

* This is a simplified version of the actual history.

In our exposition the logarithm arose in a pronouncedly algebraic context. If square roots are counted as algebra, logarithms may claim the same right; no more topology or analysis is needed to get them. Like the roots of algebraic equations so also do the logarithms arise from an algebraic problem, namely from the problem of constructing an order preserving isomorphism between the addition group of R and the multiplication group of R^+. Such an isomorphism is uniquely determined as soon as it is settled which number should be mapped on 1 (it is 10 for decadic and e for natural logarithms). This is an idea of algebraic character.

I need not be told that it is old-fashioned to consider this as algebra. I do not care about names and subdivisions. We set out to organize a domain where besides the four fundamental operations, raising to powers extracting roots and logarithmizing are exercised. The devices of organization were till now of an algebraic nature though they did not lead to the field concept. Of course in the final redaction of the result of organization the field of reals will play a part but as the main tool of organization an exponential or logarithmic function has emerged. Compared with, say, the linear space concept, the field concept is much too colourless; in fact it is not much more than a verbal definition, since it is rather useless as long as its examples are very few. If one looks in higher mathematics to find out where the field concept becomes operational, then I believe the first instance is algebraic and transcendent adjunctions, which is simply not the most favorite school subject.

GLOBAL ORGANIZATION OF ALGEBRA —
THE SLIDE RULE AXIOM

Notwithstanding a few dissenters there is a consensus of opinion about the content of school algebra. This algebra that is met with everywhere and in all simple applications is too rich to be exhausted by the field concept, and this greater wealth cannot be subsumed under the heading of analysis, though in the higher grades the many-sided relations to analysis should not be neglected. As an illustration I would like to tell of experiences I have often met with at our final school examinations (which permit entrance to university). The question "what is $2^{\sqrt{2}}$?" was always answered by showing how this is computed by taking twice the logarithm. More often than not I succeeded in leading the candidate the long way, first to define 2^r for rational r and then to obtain $2^{\sqrt 2}$ as the limit of 2^r where r converges to $\sqrt 2$, but this was paper knowledge, a *hapax legomenon*, which soon after the examination will be forgotten; moreover, the students lack any feeling for the convergence of 2^r, for what it looks like and for how fast it may be.

The candidate's answer on the question "what is $2^{\sqrt 2}$?" was quite right. If such an expression is somehow living, it owes its life to the fact that it can be computed logarithmically. The logarithmic, or the exponential, function cannot be detached from algebra, and this fact should be accounted for if algebra is to be organized.

Let us now formulate our result synthetically, in an axiomatic disguise:

AXIOM 1. K is an ordered set with two binary operations, and with the constants $>$, $+$, $\cdot$, 0, 1 (greater than, plus, times, zero, one).

AXIOM 2. With respect to addition K is an ordered commutative group* with 0 as neutral element, that is, besides the axioms of ordered set and of commutative group it fulfills the compatibility condition

$$a < b \rightarrow a + c < b + c .$$

AXIOM 3. With respect to multiplication $K \backslash \{0\}$ is a commutative group, with neutral element 1, and K^+ $(= \{a \in K \mid a > 0\})$ is an ordered commutative group, that is, it fulfills besides the axioms of commutative group the compatibility condition

$$0 < a < b \wedge c > 0 \rightarrow 0 < ac < bc .$$

AXIOM 4. The multiplications $\curlyvee_{x \in K} ax$ are homomorphisms of the addition group of K (the distributivity law).

AXIOM 5. The multiplication group of K^+ possesses an ordered isomorphism, called log, on the addition group of K.

These axioms are intuitively convincing. The last, the *slide rule axiom* as I would call it, can be roughly pronounced as follows:

There is a slide rule.

Another suitable name would be "logarithm table axiom" but though the slide rule is less precise than the usual logarithm tables I feel that the slide rule better visualizes the continuously defined logarithmic function. So do the logarithmic scales which are extensively used for

---

* More precisely, an Archimedean group, but this does not matter now.

graphics in science. Though they are less important for mathematics, they should not be neglected in mathematics instruction. Examples to show how to use them can readily be found in science.

The slide rule axiom suffices to define the other operations which are usual in school algebra.

First of all, there are more isomorphism from K^+ to K. If I have got one of them, I can compose it with automorphisms of K^+ or of K to get new ones.

Let a be the original of 1 for the isomorphism provided by the slide rule axiom. Then this isomorphism will be denoted by $\log_a$, thus

$$\log_a a = 1 .$$

Now

$$\curlyvee_x \gamma \log_a x$$

is again an homomorphism of K^+ into K, which for $\gamma > 0$ preserves and for $\gamma < 0$ inverts the order. In particular, with $\gamma = (\log_a b)^{-1}$ we obtain one for which b has the image 1 and which we denote by $\log_b$. Thus

$$\log_a x / \log_a b = \log_b x .$$

By this procedure we get isomorphisms from K^+ to K with $c \in K^+ \backslash \{1\}$ prescribed as the original of 1. If K is the real field, this procedure delivers all of them.

In this axiomatic approach powers can be defined the way our candidate proposed, that is $u^v (u \in K^+)$ by putting

$$\log_a u^v = v \log_a u .$$

The definition does not depend on the choice of the logarithm (that is of a). For integral v it coincides with the elementary power definition, as follows immediately from the homomorphism property of log. The arithmetical laws are easily obtained. E.g.

$$(u_1 u_2)^w = u_1^w u_2^w$$

from

$$\log (u_1 u_2)^w = w \log (u_1 u_2) = w \log u_1 + w \log u_2 =$$
$$= \log u_1^w + \log u_2^w = \log u_1^w u_2^w ;$$
$$u^{w_1 + w_2} = u^{w_1} u^{w_2}$$

from

$$\log u^{w_1 + w_2} = (w_1 + w_2) \log u = w_1 \log u + w_2 \log u =$$
$$= \log u^{w_1} + \log u^{w_2} = \log u^{w_1} u^{w_2} \, ;$$
$$(u^{w_1})^{w_2} = u^{w_1 w_2}$$

from

$$\log (u^{w_1})^{w_2} = w_1 w_2 \log u = \log u^{w_1 w_2} \, .$$

If, however, the slide rule axiom has emerged as a consequence of the above attempts of organizing algebra, these laws are conceptually clear, without any computations. In fact, by definition,

$$\log_a a^x = x$$

which implies that

$$\curlyvee_x a^x \text{ is the inverse of } \log_a \, ;$$

this leads from the homomorphism properties of the log to those of the exponential functions.

It seems to me that the result of these organisatory attempts must be overpowering. The key axiom suffices to derive with almost no trouble all operations laws that before were just a mass of confusion.

RETROSPECT ON THE ORGANIZATION OF ALGEBRA

Are we really being granted the liberty to add such a slide rule axiom to the axioms of ordered field? I have often been asked this question and I think it is asked because the axiom is unusual. In any case, it is a fact that the axioms of ordered field are not sufficient. Something should be added. The definite additive would be a topological axiom, e.g. the existence of the least upper bound of bounded sets, or the realizability of Dedekind cuts, or the convergence of Cauchy sequences – all of a kind that is not easy to understand and, what is more important, not easy to apply, and which consequently in school texts is taught as a *hapax legomenon*, never to be used.

In its place we proposed an axiom of definitely algebraic character, which was a direct consequence of the organisatory attempts, and which is applied wherever power and logarithm computations are carried out.

It is true that the slide rule axiom does not suffice if, later, the first stages of analysis should be organized. But to arrive at the organizing topological principle of the real field, a quite different material should be available and should ask for organization; only if materially the boundaries of algebra are transgressed more exacting needs of organizing can be felt.

The fact that I proposed the slide rule axiom should not be interpreted in the sense that the pupil should necessarily tackle an axiomatic organization of school algebra. Whether the pupil can attain the level of global organization of algebra, depends first of all on whether he once stayed at an even lower level. Above I expounded a circumstantial analysis of the algebraic situation. It was meant as a source of information of the teacher. I do *not* claim that it should be done as circumstantially as this. I did not discuss how far the arithmetical laws for powers and their relations to the homomorphisms of the additive and the multiplicative group must have been dealt with and understood before an attempt of global organization can be made.

THE INTEGRAL DEFINITION OF THE LOGARITHM

I would rather like to stress that the logarithm, once introduced, should be experienced in an abundance of relations. There are many natural laws that lead to logarithmic and exponential functions but the most urgent is a relation within mathematics, which, however, is almost never dealt with in its natural context. I admit that the word "integral" in the title of this section also evokes a wrong context – what I would advocate is, in fact, that the integral definition of the logarithm is independent of integral calculus and that it is due long before integral calculus starts.

Let us consider the function

$$y = \frac{1}{x}.$$

Let us suppose the domain between the x-axis, the curve $y = 1/x$ and the lines $x = a$ and $x = b$ $(0 < a < b)$ has an area $F(a, b)$. Let us submit the $\ulcorner x, y \urcorner$-plane to a dilatation in the x-direction with the factor $u(> 0)$ and at the same time in the y-direction to a dilatation with the factor u^{-1}. Then the domain under consideration passes into that between the x-axis, the curve $y = 1/x$ and the lines $x = ua$ and $x = ub$, thus with the area $F(ua, ub)$. But obviously this transformation preserves area, thus

(1) $F(ua, ub) = F(a, b)$.

Moreover

$$F(a, b) + F(b, c) = F(a, c),$$

which by the previous formula can also be written as

$$F(1, a^{-1}b) + F(1, b^{-1}c) = F(1, a^{-1}c);$$

this after putting

$$F(1, x) = \varphi(x)$$

yields

$$\varphi(x) + \varphi(y) = \varphi(x \cdot y).$$

φ is a monotonous function with the characteristic property of the logarithm so it *is* a logarithm. The numerical value of its basis is not obtained in this way but geometrically the basis is well defined by the abscissa of a surface with unit area.

Is it not simple, convincing and beautiful? Of course it finds no favour in the sight of the rigorous mathematician. Is it not an offence to operate with areas of curvilinearly-bounded domains if area has not yet been defined? And since textbook authors are afraid of the disgrace of the rigorous mathematician, they stow away this subject into integral calculus, where they risk nothing. In fact, this reasoning is as exact as any reasoning can be. To deny it, you must be born with blinders. It is an example of what rigour means in local organization. Integral calculus puts this result into a broader context, but does it become clearer by the analytic approach? The lucidity of the geometrical approach can hardly be surpassed.

In which respect does integral calculus contribute more to this question? It defines the area of curvilinearly-bounded domains by step polygon approximation. The content of the rectangles, and consequently of the step polygon is invariant under the combined dilatation in the x- and y-directions with factors u and u^{-1}. This justifies formula (1) under the supposition that such a function F, that is the area as a limit of the areas of approximating polygons exists at all. In integral calculus this follows generally from the uniform continuity of continuous functions, which is hardly proved, let alone mentioned at school. In the present case the remainders can be estimated to prove that the polygonal areas form a Cauchy sequence; this is even relatively easy. With a few words the geometrical proof can be made as exact as integral calculus. Should it be added here? I would say, no. It is better done as an introduction to integral calculus. I come back to this point when I explain how integral calculus can be started unalgorithmically and how the premature algorithmization of the integral concept can be avoided.

THE PROTRACTOR AXIOM

The slide rule axiom has a counterpart, which should more closely be investigated when we tackle geometry. A protractor is a hemicircle or a circle with a scale that runs cyclically from 0° to 360°; the scale is proportional with the arc length; just as on the ruler with segments, so on the protractor arcs are congruent if the difference of scale values at the ends of the arcs is the same. In other words, a rotation of the circle expresses itself on the scale as an addition of a fixed amount. Here the angles must be counted mod 360°. Rather than this angular measure mathematicians use arc length on the unit circle; to the 360° corresponds the periphery of the unit circle, 2π. We will accept this convention: angle measures are real numbers mod 2π.

If this geometrical interpretation of angles were definitive, I would not have to add much. It is, however, a fact that angles are not only measured but also computed, e.g. if the angle of two vectors is asked for, or, in a more traditional setting, if the angles of a triangle must be obtained from its side lengths. These tasks can be brought back to the following: in the Euclidean coordinate-plane a point $\ulcorner x, y \urcorner$ is given on the unit circle around the origin; which angle is formed by the ray from $\ulcorner 0, 0 \urcorner$ to $\ulcorner x, y \urcorner$ and the x-axis ray; or, otherwise, what is the measure of the arc on the unit circle from $\ulcorner 1, 0 \urcorner$ to $\ulcorner x, y \urcorner$?

An angle- or arc-measure w mod 2π is then to be assigned to the point $\ulcorner x, y \urcorner$ in an additive way: if $\ulcorner x, y \urcorner$ and $\ulcorner x', y' \urcorner$ are two points on the unit circle and from $\ulcorner x, y \urcorner$ the arc $\ulcorner 1, 0 \urcorner \ulcorner x', y' \urcorner$ is transferred in a direct congruence to obtain the point $\ulcorner x'', y'' \urcorner$ on the unit circle, then it is required that

$$w \ulcorner x'', y'' \urcorner = w \ulcorner x, y \urcorner + w \ulcorner x', y' \urcorner.$$

Complex numbers $z = x + iy$ of absolute value 1 are better suited than pairs of real numbers. These complex numbers form a multiplicative group E. A rotation of the unit circle can then be represented as

$$\curlyvee_{z \in E} \alpha z \quad \text{with} \quad |\alpha| = 1.$$

This leads to assigning the number z_2/z_1 as a multiplicative angle measure to the angle $\ulcorner z_2, 0, z_1 \urcorner$; multiplicativity means that composition of angles results in a multiplication of their measures.

This shows how an additive angle measure can be obtained: it is a function ω from E to the real numbers mod 2π,

$$\omega \in E \rightsquigarrow \mathbf{R}_{\text{mod } 2\pi},$$

such that

$$\omega(z_1 z_2) = \omega(z_1) + \omega(z_2).$$

This thus is a sort of logarithm. Actually,

$$\omega(z) = 1/i \log_e z \bmod 2\pi,$$

which is a well-known fact. Or, if the univalent inverse is preferred,

$$\omega^{-1}(v) = e^{iv}.$$

We need not care here about these rather profound connexions with analysis. What matters is that ω is an isomorphism from the multiplicative group of E to the addition group of reals $\mathbf{R}_{\text{mod } 2\pi}$ that preserves the cyclic order of E. This can be resumed in an axiom that can be added to the former ones as number 6:

AXIOM 6. Let $K(i)$ be the complex extension of K with the norm $|a + ib| = (a^2 + b^2)^{\frac{1}{2}}$ for $a, b \in K$. Let E be the cyclically ordered group* of the elements of norm 1. Then there is an order preserving isomorphism from E to the additive group $K_{\text{mod } 2\pi}$.

This axiom also yields cosines and sines,

$$\cos \alpha = Re\, \omega^{-1}(\alpha), \qquad \sin \alpha = J\, \omega^{-1}(\alpha),$$

with their familiar properties and formulae.

The names slide rule axiom and protractor axiom testify the realistic

---

* I provisionally skip the definition of cyclic order.

content of these axioms. The question whether they should be formulated as axioms in school instruction is better delayed until it has been investigated what is required for teaching an axiomatics that becomes operational in instruction. Of course I would never propose delaying the intuitive mathematical idea of the additive angle measure till linear algebra has progressed far enough. It is a terrifying example of dogmatism to let a pre-established system determine the moment where such simple and fundamental ideas may be tackled. Models as the slide rule and the protractor should again and again be discussed, from an ever higher viewpoint. Their embedding in the axiomatic organization of algebra may be one aim; their place in analysis would be an nother. At any stage they can and may be valuable subjects of mathematical instruction.

There are mathematicians who would ban angles and logarithms from serious mathematical instruction at school because they are analysis and thus too difficult for school. Slide rule and protractor are close to reality. Only a mathematician who does not trust mathematics close to reality can advocate this kind of radicalism. But this is not all. It is simply not true that angles and logarithms are possible in analysis only. Our ancestors had a clearer judgment when they subdivided the subject matter differently. It is only reasonable to acknowledge this fact. Misunderstandings on this question have so widely been propagated and by such unfair methods that the circumstantiality of the above exposition was badly needed.

CHAPTER XV

SETS AND FUNCTIONS

Thus by the gigantic cooperation of Frege, Dedekind, Cantor the infinite was raised to the throne and enjoyed an era of great triumph... From the paradise created by Cantor, nobody may be allowed to evict us.

D. Hilbert, *Über das Unendliche*, 1927

Set theory knows no barrier of principle between the finite and the infinite. Under this view the infinite is even simpler.

H. Weyl, *Die heutige Erkenntnislage in der Mathematik*, 1925

The letter killeth but the spirit giveth life.

2 Cor. III, 6

I need hardly explain why I deal with sets after numbers. I hope I have made clear that both as regards content and as regards teaching, mathematics starts with number, with counting, and the greater part of mathematics that most people have to learn, centres around number. Set theory's voice in the last chapters was surprisingly soft, compared with the arrogant shouting of false set theory. It is good to start with the arrogant shouting of false set theory. It is good to start with the most important things; it is reassuring to know how much less important matter is needed to do the important ones right.

Should sets at least be second in line after numbers? I do not believe so. The second ought to be functions. How much did we not use them with the number concept? Functions pulled sets with them into the title of the chapter so it is not at all fair to concede first place in the title and in the chapter to sets, it is a concession rather than a principle.

WHAT IS A SET?

"Please tell us: what is a set?" That is what a group of teachers asked a university mathematician some years ago as they were frightened by the emergence of New Maths and the coming of the day when they should have to tell it to their students. I do not know what he told them and whether they were happy with it. If you hear and read what a set is in the opinion of teachers and textbooks, it is rather obvious that the mathematicians who for a few years have been telling educators what a set is, committed didactical mistakes of great dimensions. We will soon see which ones they made. If afterwards one reads the lectures and reports of conferences, it often strikes one that teachers were told quite a lot about sets, except what you do with sets in mathematics. So teachers had to improvise. I like learning by re-invention if it is well-guided, but here it was far from being the case.

Explanations of set theory concepts move between two extremes which are approximately as follows. One is a formal definition of what a set is. People who give such a definition even define what an element is. It reminds me of Euclid's definition: "Unit is that after which things are called one". This, of course, was what the worried teachers of the above story asked the professor. To be sure, in mathematics lessons it is defined what a parallelogram is, and what a definition is. How can you start set theory at school, if the pupils are not supposed memorize sentences of the kind – "A set is...", "An element is...", "An element is said to belong to a set if...".

Axioms and axiomatics are taught and learned today, but quite clearly many people do not know where they come from. Certainly, axioms and axiomatics serve to organize globally a domain but this is not the origin of axiomatics. As we explained this in detail earlier we can now restrict ourselves to a brief explanation. It is at present generally accepted that explicit definitions finally fail because to avoid being confined in a deductive circle, you should stop analyzing somewhere in order to start synthesizing, with some undefined material. This is how an axiomatic system, say of geometry, is interpreted today – a system of sentences involving undefined concepts like "point", "line", "lying on", which should be operated on according to these axioms.

Concepts such as "set", "element of..." mark a threshold you cannot transgress with fresh questions – it is the same with the concept of natural number though some people mistakenly believe they can define it by pure set theory. This does not mean that set theory should be started by axioms. Set theory like any other field cannot be conceived axiomatically unless you know it, which in the case of set theory includes knowing its traps and ambushes. In my view there cannot be any doubt that this is absolutely impossible at school. Examining the single axioms of the usual axiom systems of set theory, I cannot discover among these axioms one which I would be able to explain what purpose it serves to someone who knows so little mathematics as even a pupil of the higher grades at high school. There are, however, school texts for 11–12 year-olds that axiomatically introduce sets. Of course it is pseudo-axiomatics, like the traditional one of school geometry, with a few trivialities worded as axioms, while the decisive suppositions are not even mentioned, whether by axiomatic or any other means.

But if it is true that there is no way, explicitly or axiomatically, to tell what a set is, how can you start set theory? The answer is obvious – the same way as numbers and geometrical shapes are dealt with. Just as little as you need to explain to people what a number is and what the number two is, as little as you need a figure on the blackboard to explain what a point is, so is there just as little need to define what a set is. Are sets a different case because you can define numbers by sets as potencies? No, since this alleged reduction is wrong. Are sets a different case from points, because points are number pairs? No, because to identify points with number pairs you have first to learn quite a lot of geometry, which includes the knowledge of what is a point. Though nobody defines what breathing is, or walking, falling, and swimming, people learn doing or observing it, for example in order to live and to do physics. Presuming explicit definitions are a symptom of old-fashioned methodology and methodics.

This is one of the extremes of explaining set theory: the formal sham definition. The other is Venn-diagrams. Almost all textbooks are prone to make the readers believe that it is a set if a closed curve is drawn around a number of letters, figures or meaningless symbols. To be sure there are also sets between braces such as $\{a, b, c\}$ or $\{\S, <, \odot\}$. A teacher showed me on the blackboard how he explains to his pupils that Venn diagrams and braces are the same: by parallel lines below and above, the braces are joined and both points are smoothed away. I asked him what he did with the commas. Indeed, he answered, one comma can be missed since the elements of a set should be different.

To be sure there is another use of braces. The set of planets is written

$$\{x \mid x \text{ is a planet}\}.$$

It is a paradigm that pays a hundred-fold with pages of examples such as – note down... (or, more shrewdly, find another name for ...): The set of mounted policemen, the set of unfeathered bipeds, the set of all present Presidents of the United States, the set of children in the classroom with long hair and spectacles, and so on. If the parents of the present school generation or the television public are to be impressed with the great wisdom of New Maths, such examples serve very well. To reach even higher levels of amazement draw Venn diagrams of all those examples and stress that the horses of the mounted policemen stay outside the concerned Venn diagrams, as well as the spectacles and hair of the bespectacled long-haired children, that neither are Saturn's rings in the Venn diagram of the planets nor is the nose of the President of the United States in that of the presidents.

The highest degree of amazement, of course, is caused by the empty set. After it has been proved that there is only one empty set, you ask problems like – "give three more examples of empty sets!"

A ten year-old girl asked her father for help in New Maths. Rather than a mathematician he was a scientist who had learned mathematics though I must confess it was good old maths. The next day it came out that all the problems were wrong. The girl was clever enough to explain why. Two sets with the same cardinal (this was the word) need not be equal as sets. Two empty sets have the same cardinal, namely 0, although they are not equal. An empty refrigerator is not the same as an empty wastepaper basket, is it? (It reminds me a drugstore with different prices for coffee with milk, coffee with cream, and coffee without milk– why not for coffee without cream?) Dad, ignominiously beaten, told it to a colleague, a mathematician, who called on the teacher. She was much cleverer than he had anticipated. To be sure she maintained that two closed curves on the blackboard with nothing in it were different empty sets, but she did so with reasonable arguments. She said something like the following – let us suppose the discourse is about people, then the empty set is "no people". If it is about letters, then the empty set is "no letters", if it is about points, it is "no points". What the empty set is depends on the "universe of discourse". If, however, I am given two Venn diagrams, they mean two different universes of discourse, which, consequently can boast of different empty sets. The mathematician objected that intersection and unions are made up of such pairs of Venn diagrams, which involves that they are not different universes. She agreed though not without saying: "Sure, but then what do the ovals around the Venn diagrams mean?" She had put her finger on the sore spot!

BRACES

I write down

... is a set.

What can be put in place of the three dots? I do not yet require that the result should be true. I am content if it means something, even something wrong.

Let us make things easier. Take the pattern:

... is a donkey.

What may be put here in place of the dots? Thomas for example? It depends on circumstances whether it is true. "Thomas" could be the name of a donkey, maybe a donkey named Thomas was just mentioned. Maybe Thomas was a man, who nevertheless satisfies the assertion though not zoologically.

It could have been – the father of a donkey. The statement would still be true since the father of a donkey is a donkey. "The father of a horse is a donkey" is still meaningful. Inserting "when" for the three dots, however, would hardly be allowed, it is ungrammatical. Likewise I would not admit there 'le père d'un âne', because it is French. But what about

'x is a donkey?

I understand that 'x' is not the name of a donkey in the usual sense, at least because 'x' is not a capital. But maybe just before it was spoken of some x who balked. Could it also be

'A is a donkey'?

Why not provided somebody tells me what 'A' means. I would, however, be somewhat embarrassed by

∗ is a donkey,

but maybe it aims at a game where '∗' symbolizes a donkey.

But how about putting a real donkey in place of the three spots? Of course, this cannot possibly be done. Then, let us be satisfied with a picture of a donkey. To be sure, not 'a picture of a donkey' but a picture of a donkey. Thus, I do not mean:

'a picture of a donkey is a donkey',

which would not be too bad, but a clause in which in place of the subject a donkey is pictured.

Time and again one sees such funny texts printed, but I do not believe that anybody would consider this as grammatical, even if the picture shows a very particular donkey. Imagine "Cave" with the picture of a dog beneath; philologists would become ill if they saw this because by what means would you express the accusative 'canem' (maybe by some angle of the tail).

It is a custom in linguistic texts to quote things by names rather than by pictures. Maybe in the margin of such texts pictures are shown though then they are accompanied by captions like "Fig. 27: A donkey". Or you find a reference in the text like: "Fig. 27 pictures a donkey."

Certainly, I should be more careful. Actually, it can happen that a picture of something gets lost in the text. I mean cases like

A is a letter.

Obviously here 'A' does not name a certain object as it did in 'A is a donkey' but is simply a printed image of the letter A which is under discussion. More cautiously such statements are usually made as

The sign A is a letter,

or

'A' is a letter.

But this is not our main concern at the moment.

Let us come back to

... is a set.

Instead of the dots one can put: the union of two sets. Or **N**, or **Z**, if the reader knows what the letters mean. Likewise

$\{7, 9, 12\}$ is a set

is meaningful and correct. What about

'$\{a, b, c\}$ is a set'?

I can answer the question if I know what a, b, c should be. E.g.

If a, b, c are three different points, then $\{a, b, c\}$ is a set of points.

If a, b, c are three different thunderstorms, then $\{a, b, c\}$ is a set of thunderstorms.

In almost all school texts $\{a, b, c\}$ is dealt with as a set of letters. In fact, this can be perfectly reasonable.

If a, b, c are three different letters, then $\{a, b, c\}$ is a set of letters.

But then it should be perfectly clear that a, b, c can be the letters x, y, z. By no means can it be held that $\{a, b, c\}$ be the set of the letters a, b, c. If I wish to indicate this I would rather say:

Let x be the letter a, y be the letter b, z be the letter c. Then $\{x, y, z\}$ is the set of the letters a, b, c.

In fact, in '$\{a, b, c\}$' the signs under question are standing as names of some objects, which can be of various kinds, numbers, points, or thunderstorms. They may even be the names of letters, but then the things quoted by the signs a, b, c need not be the letters a, b, c unless this is explicitly required.

It is the custom in mathematics, and one cannot ignore it, that letters stand for something else and never for themselves. This is reasonable because if one does not pay heed to this rule, one gets into enormous difficulties. This is not hair-splitting. How can a pupil understand $a = b$, if 'a' and 'b' mean letters? How can you convince pupils that

$$x \in \{a, b, c\}$$

is perfectly possible (viz. if $x = a \lor x = b \lor x = c$), if just before he learned that $\{a, b, c\}$ is the set of the letters a, b, c, which, indeed, are all different from x? How can he learn that

$$\{a, b, c\} \cap \{1, 2, 3\}$$

can be non-empty, if he has been told that the one is a set of letters and the other a set of numbers?

Please do not object that this is high-brow sophistication. I would have preferred not to discuss questions like this in the first place. Ordinary mathematics does not know of letters as elements of sets. They are never needed, and the problem whether they should be avoided or with what precautions can they be admitted simply does not arise. The literature of New Maths is almost unanimous in admitting, if not cultivating, sets of letters. Where does all this come from? I am pretty certain that the authors of such textbooks have thought so little about it that they do not even guess that something could be wrong. Since they like to start with set theory before mathematics, they have not much choice. Since they feign to possess neither numbers nor points, they cannot speak of number and point sets; moreover the pupils are not yet acquainted with variables. So $\{a, b, c\}$ becomes the set of the meaningless letters a, b, c, which entails building up mathematics from the foundations as a meaningless activity. It is the old story of the two mathematics, with, alongside serious mathematics, a school mathematics, a kind of fairy tale mathematics. It is, however, a fairy tale which could prevent the growth of real mathematics. Writing this, I am afraid that the producers of the New Maths will brush away my arguments as mere demoded Old Maths.

I dealt with the sets of letters earlier. Many variants are possible, e.g.

$$\{\triangle, \bigcirc, \square\}$$

which according to the context should be a set though there is no explanation what its elements may be. Between the braces a lion, an elephant and a camel can stand. Does the author mean a set which consists of one of each of these species, or is it *the* set consisting of a definite lion, a definite elephant, and a definite camel, and if so, which ones are meant? Or does he mean the set of the three *species*, Lions, Elephants and Camels? The same questions can be asked about the triangle, the circle, and the square though in this case there is another explanation, which probably is what the author meant. He could have meant the set consisting of the one triangle, the one circle and the one square pictured between the braces. Of course then

$$\triangle \notin \{\triangle, \bigcirc, \square\}$$

since the triangles inside and outside the braces are not the same. A reasonable description of a set A as meant by the author would be as follows:

$$A = \{a, b, c\}$$

where a is the triangle, b the circle, c the square of Figure 16.

Of course this would not fit into the system of the author who uses letters as objects rather than as names of objects. He would interpret such A as the set of the letters a, b, c.

Maybe he is even committed to avoiding letters, perhaps he is writing a textbook for children who cannot read. Such books exist; they have been written by people who claim that little children can learn set theory! Modern parents will buy such books to teach set theory to their pre-school-age children, and though they studied mathematics themselves even they feel that they are not intelligent enough to understand

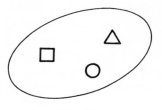

Fig. 16.

those books meant for little children. Perhaps a few of them would dare consult a university mathematician – who probably does not understand them either! From one of these books I have finally succeeded in finding out the principle: pictures of living objects that look alike apparently represent the same object; pictures of non-living objects mean the same object only if they are perfectly congruent. Yet I do not believe that the author was conscious of this principle – these books are written by people in a very naive state of mind.

It is perfectly legitimate and hardly at all objectionable to denote elements of a set within braces by pictures rather than by names. Those pictures are semi-linguistic, as ideograms can be. But then one should conscientiously analyze what one is doing. That is:

firstly, each picture should denote one object, and it should be clear which,

secondly, if an object is represented in different ways, it should be clearly shown that the different representations refer to the same object,

thirdly, it is recommended to avoid species of objects which cannot be represented with clearly distinguishable variations, to prevent the idea that in a set any species of objects could be present by one individual only.

These desiderata can be realized as follows. Page 1 of the book shows the whole universe, which can consist of a few children, elephants, balls, dolls, chairs, cherries, or anything else. To make it more attractive the same child could be pictured in different clothes, the same elephant in different attitudes and so on, but then a "vocabulary" on the first page should show by equality signs between pictures of the same objects, which ones are equal. Among the objects of the universe I would not choose a green Peugeot 404, nor a penny, nor a banana, because the members of these species are almost indistinguishable from each other.

It could be done this way. I did not say it should, and I would not do so. If objects are to be quoted, it is normal that it is done by using their names. I do not mean it to be dogma. It can happen in life that a picture must replace a name. But if objects were systematically quoted by their pictures, it should be done according to a reasonable system. I tried to explain above what such a system may look like.

VENN DIAGRAMS

We asked previously what can be put in

... is a set

in place of the dots. Though I have seen a great deal, I have never yet seen a Venn diagram in that place. It is true that people often behave as though a Venn diagram were a set (e.g. if they connect two Venn diagrams by a union symbol), but nobody dares to claim that it really is the name of a set. It is clear that the place of the three dots has to be filled by a linguistic something, which incidentally may be meaningless. $\{a, b, c\}$ is a linguistic something; this is shown at least by the commas. Animals between braces are no normal linguistic means of expression, but they are at least a linguistic surrogate, as are ideograms.

The Venn diagram is not a linguistic phenomenon; but what else can it be? Mathematical texts usually contain more than linguistic matter. You can meet there figures, pictures of a equilateral triangle, of the logarithmic function, of the Peano curve, and many more. A linguistic text *means* something, a picture *represents* an object. To be sure, a, picture can be said to mean something. Or rather, if it is not clear enough, one can say that I do not understand what it means. Or the picture on a traffic sign can mean "school", but then it is an ideogram, and thus of linguistic character.

Pictures are supposed to map something even if the thing mapped is pure fantasy. Mappings sometimes claim concrete, sometimes structural accuracy and faithfulness. An example of the first is a picture of St. Peter's in Rome, an example of the second is a ground-plan of this church; such pictures are also called diagrams. A picture can contain linguistic references, which are explained at the side, and sometimes even the names of some details. The streetnames on a map of a city can be considered as pictures of the street nameplates, but such an interpretation is hardly possible with the name of a river in the picture of the river.

A rather high degree of faithfulness is often attained with pictures of very abstract objects. A drawn triangle with the names A, B, C of the corners in it maps the intended image so faithfully that both of them are readily identified. A horizontal line with numbers at certain points excellently maps the set of real numbers. Graphic representations usually are good images of the function they are to represent. An open set is excellently pictured by an oval. A flow diagram may faithfully represent a particular process.

What should be didactically required of pictorial matter? I think first of all that it should map something. Secondly, that it easily and without long explanations shows what it intends to map. Thirdly, that the principle of mapping itself is clear and easy to grasp. I think that these are reasonable demands. I will now examine the usual Venn diagrams to see how far they fulfill these requirements.

The easiest case is what I would call natural Venn diagrams. By these I mean the picture of the interior of a simple closed plane curve which is obtained by drawing the image of such a plane curve, and perhaps hatching what on paper looks like its interior. These pictures obviously satisfy our criteria to the same degree as do the usual pictures of triangles and functions. They are simple and beyond questioning. For not-so-young children the principle of such a representation is well known from geographical maps. In this way Venn diagrams were applied in old mathematics courses at least from my own university years onwards. Using such ovals it was pictured what the intersection and the union of sets mean and how complements behave. If such notions had been introduced and one would check whether the listeners understood the definition, one would draw two intersecting ovals and ask: "If this were the set of adults and that the set of females, what would this be?" I never noticed in old mathematics that to ascertain what is the intersection of the sets of the adults and of the females, one drew Venn diagrams and meditated about their intersection. This, however, is how Venn diagrams are mostly applied today. In other words, formerly Venn diagrams did not serve to represent sets as they do now, but to represent inclusions and relations between sets and their unions and intersections, maybe also to represent analogous relations between logical statements, and this aim Venn diagrams can, indeed, serve very well. This use of Venn diagrams has been illustrated by the above example. Two ovals are drawn as images of two plane sets, but the idea to be illustrated is union and intersection of arbitrary sets, and in this context adults and females are only one example. It does not matter what the sets look like, if only they are situated to each other as it should be in the case under discussion, e.g. disjoint, non-disjoint, within each other, and so on. But relations such as one set being an element of another, or properties of a set of being finite or infinite or having a certain number of elements, were never represented by Venn diagrams simply because Venn diagrams cannot do it. Nor were Venn diagrams ever formerly used to represent what kind the elements of a set were.

What I have called natural Venn diagrams are hardly met with in school texts. I do not know what the reason is; maybe people are afraid of infinite sets and try to avoid them. In fact they cannot avoid the infinite set of natural numbers, which to intuition is much less a ready-made object than is the set of points in an oval held together by the oval.

Though natural Venn diagrams are lacking, there has been unanimity in preserving one of its features, namely the closed curve. It is so constant a part of the Venn diagram that it is identified by most users with the Venn diagram. The meaning and function of this curve are obscure; in particular, it is not clear what it is meant to map. I do not have the impression that anybody has really thought about it. It has simply been copied from old-style Venn diagrams where it really did mean a curve, and it is now continued by tradition. 10–20 year-old traditions can in many respects compete with thousand year-old ones.

I have the impression that the curve only serves to hold together non-connected things. A collection of meaningless figures such as crosses, stars, circles are drawn on the paper, and to neutralize this heterogeneity, a curve is drawn around them. It is an obvious question to ask why such heterogeneous material should be collected in a set. No doubt the pupil should become acquainted with heterogeneous material, too, but why should sets be systematically or even exclusively heterogeneous? This is unnatural.

There is a reason for the heterogeneity principle, and this reason rests on a misunderstanding. The set as it appears in the Venn diagram should consist of visibly different elements, so they conclude, two triangles in one Venn diagram are forbidden. But why? There are two and even more triangles in the world. They agree, but it does not solve their problem, which is how to indicate that two triangles drawn in the same Venn diagram, are different triangles. The set $\{\triangle, \triangle\}$, indeed, has only one element, namely $\triangle$. Well, the two triangles in the Venn diagram *are* different. They are obviously different since they are lying in different places just as two eggs and two coins are different even if they are in the same basket or pocket. What are standing between braces are not things but if it is to be at all meaningful, *names* of things. If in order to reach those who are illiterate, I now write '$\triangle$' instead of 'a triangle', it is unfortunate that by doing this I can indicate only one triangle. Everyday language is richer, it knows more names for triangles, such as "this triangle", "that triangle", "a third triangle", and so on. The usual mathematical device would be to say:

$$\{\triangle_1, ..., \triangle_m\}$$

where $\triangle_1, ..., \triangle_m$ are different triangles. A Venn diagram, however, could without objection look like Figure 17 though certainly not like Figure 18. It should, in fact, be a set of triangles rather than a set of names of triangles (even if it were a set of names, it would not be clear why such names should be arranged so irregularly).

Thus there is not the slightest reason why pictures of sets should have to show heterogeneous elements. The reason for the closed curve seems to be that it should collect the heterogeneous elements. Since hetrogeneity has been eliminated as a necessary feature of Venn diagrams, there is no reason left for the Venn diagram curve. To be sure it is a symptom of a terrifying lack of imagination. It is worthwhile to look at the earlier-mentioned Hungarian book series to see how natural and illustrative sets can be pictured. I am convinced that nobody who has once seen these books will understand any more why people are so keen on Venn diagrams. A set of blocks can be represented as a tower, or as a wall, or as a building. If this is done using coloured blocks, you

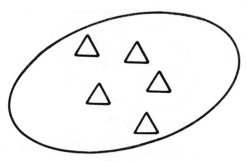

Fig. 17.

can consider the set of red blocks of the first floor as an intersection; you can have a tower leaning against a wall to compare their cardinalities. Is this not much more sensible than Venn diagrams? To post a set of children as points in a Venn diagram, is absurd and if there is anything even more absurd, it is asking where Mary's nose is and requiring it to

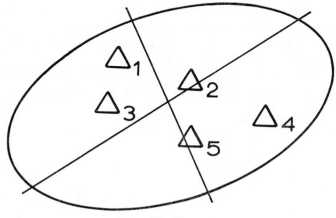

Fig. 18.

be indicated by a point outside the Venn diagram. A bench with children, or a table with children around it, is a self-evident picture of the set of children, from which all kinds of subsets and intersections can be formed. A set of books is represented on a shelf, where you can distinguish large and small ones, yellow and red ones, reading books and picture books, and so on.

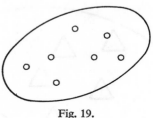

Fig. 19.

The pictures need not be photographically true to life; they should serve mathematics rather than design instruction. A set of apples can be represented as a pyramidal heap of circles, or like when apples are offered on a dish. If sketched, this indeed, leads to a Venn diagram, a circle with small circles in it, where the large circle represents the rim of the dish and the small circles the apples on it. That is entirely reasonable. Or, as an other example, take a breakfast table on which a set of breakfast utensils are exhibited, and where the subsets of all cups or of all objects at a certain place or of all edible objects can be formed. What I cannot understand, however, is delimiting a subset by laying a string on the table. I doubt whether an extra-logical delimitation of subsets can be recommended but if this should be done, it is more natural sawing the table, at least symbolically, apart.

I still understand a Venn diagram as in Figure 19, which suggests something like a set of counters on a table. If I look at Figures 20–21

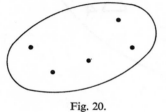

Fig. 20.   Fig. 21.

I am not sure if the designer meant five points in the plane though I am at a loss to explain the function of the closed curve picture. The letters in Figure 21 obviously do not belong to the picture but are the names of the points such as on a map the word "London" indicates the spot on the map where it is near. I am less sure what Figure 22 means

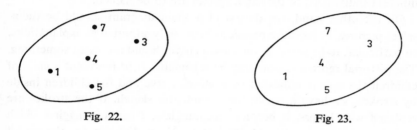

Fig. 22.   Fig. 23.

because of the strange numbers which may, or may not, be the names of the points.

Up till now, if a set is to be represented, the objects which were supposed to be its elements were still faithfully represented. In Figure 23 even this requirement ceases to be satisfied. Probably the author meant the set {1, 3, 4, 5, 7}. To indicate such a set it is correct to put the five figures into braces. But it is definitely wrong to put them in the picture of a closed curve. The components of a picture have to be pictures (of dishes, counters, points, etc.); names may be present as references or as verbal explanations of details. However, a curve surrounding names which are not references or verbal explanations suggests a set of names rather than the set {1, 3, 4, 5, 7}. Moreover, there is no indication about what brought the numbers, or in Figure 24 the letters, into the oval, and why they stand where they do rather than elsewhere. If one would ask the authors of the numerous Venn diagrams in school texts, I bet they could not tell it either. They probably never even thought about it. They simply copied it from each other*.

I related the story of a teacher reporting how he explained to his pupils that braces and Venn diagrams are the same. Of course, they are not the same. Braces are linguistic expressions whereas Venn diagrams

---

* I have been told that in some states of the German Federal Republic arithmetic textbooks are not officially approved unless they contain a large number of Venn diagrams. Thus authors have to comply with this.

are pictures. Inside the braces linguistic expressions are expected; pictures might be used therein as ideograms if this is done with a lucid understanding of the consequences. It should be clear whether an ideo-gram means a species or an individual, and if so which one; and it should be understood that this individualization can be a serious handicap if different individuals of the same species are to be named.

On the other hand, the details of a Venn diagram should be them-selves pictures, linguistic expressions being only admitted as explanations. In particular, to be sensible, the closed curve should represent something. The pictorial representation may be schematic. If to represent a class of children the wall is indicated by a closed curve and the children inside by strokes, we have a rough but meaningful sketch. If the strokes are replaced with letters, it becomes meaningless. I cannot imagine which urgent circumstances should motivate a Venn diagram for the set of the present presidents of the United States or for the set of the days of the week. I do not understand either why in a talk on parallel and inter-secting straight lines, the lines should be drawn as disjoint or intersecting ovals.

DIAGRAMMATIS VENNICA

Figure 25 is meant as a representation of the function that assigns to certain children their weight (in kg). The first closed curve contains

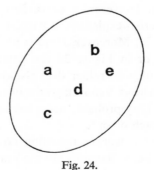

Fig. 24.

names rather than pictures of the children; the second contains numbers; the '29' has been doubled to make the mapping one-to-one (!). Of course a number line would have been much more natural if the author were not possessed by the idea that everything should be put into Venn diagrams, the *diagrammatis Vennica*.

I stress once more that other pictorial representations of sets can be much more efficient than Venn diagrams. The meaningless curve can almost always be dispensed with; more often than not it only proves that the designer was too lazy to think about how the represented elements could be bundled into a set. If the aim is not union and intersection relations but picturing the sets themselves, one should first consider what has to be attained by the picture and how it can be most efficiently attained. A set of vases and one of flowers are compared by putting the flowers into the vases rather than by Venn diagrams which would be ridiculous.

A few examples may show what is trusted to Venn diagrams. A class is introduced: Mary, John, and so on. Let Mary be named *a*, John be named *b*, and so on. (Notice the sophisticated turn: the child *is* Mary, but it is named *a*!) A Venn diagram like Figure 24 is drawn. Then

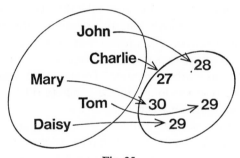

Fig. 25.

the question is asked whether Mary's nose is within the Venn diagram? Of course not. How could it, since Mary herself is not in the diagram! Mary's nose is to be represented by a dot outside the oval. And Mary herself? The author does not go as far as to ask this question. Though obviously Mary is sitting on her bench, rather than in the Venn diagram, she should in a sense stay in the Venn diagram, since she is named '*a*' and '*a*' is in the Venn diagram.

A set of potatoes – there the potatoes are inside the oval. To be sure, the potatoes are, but the set of potatoes is represented by a point outside, because it is not an element of itself.

I did not invent these examples, neither were they invented by some-one who wishes to ridicule Venn diagrams. The author is rather a proponent of Venn diagrams who firmly believes that such expositions are suited to inculcate 11–12 year-olds with a lasting love for mathe-matics. Clearly Venn diagrams are used here for aims for which they are entirely unsuitable. Pushing a once useful method into all kinds of cir-cumstances is simply dogmatic exaggeration, which is alas not unusual among mathematicians.

WHERE ARE SETS FOUND?

Where do you find numbers, circles, and sines? Not in the real world anyway. Yet numbers can be numerosities of real objects, there are circle-shaped things in reality, and the sine of the angle of a desk can be measured. There are things in the real world called numbers, circles, and sines, and they are in a sense related to that which bears the same name in mathematics, though I cannot take the liberty to identify them. It is generally accepted today that the relation between mathematics and reality is more subtle. The present way to express it is to say: to understand a piece of the real world I imitate it by a simplifying model, which is subjected to mathematization. To start with, such a model can be quite concrete. If in the long run the concrete ridges are ground off, it grows more and more abstract.

Take for instance natural numbers. The structure of the number sequence serves as a mathematical model wherever real things are counted. In the history of mankind this model starts its existence con-cretely: as fingers of the hand or the beads on the abacus. They are trustworthly models; they never belie $3+2=5$. Whether three cows and two cows are five together, however, depends on a lot of conditions. While I am counting, one cow can have run away or been stolen or have died, or the number could have increased due to the birth of a calf.

From concrete models it is a short step to more abstract models and to thought models. Addition usefully applies to cows, people and money; it is less appropriate for telephone numbers and altitudes. The linear function is a good model for the relations "price-weight" and "weight-content" though not for "numbers of workers – duration of work", "area-circumference", etc. In such cases people may speak of a failure of mathematics while it is the model that has been extended too widely.

Sets look more fundamental. For this reason it seems as though the set concept were directly, with no intermediate model, applied to reality. Indeed, if I envisage three objects and speak of the set of these objects, then it *is* the set of these three concrete objects; the set belongs to the real world rather than being imposed as a model concept on reality.

I agree that it may exceptionally look as if it were as simple as this. Yet this is a rare and unimportant exception. If the children find the picture of a set of three cherries in their book, are they actually three real cherries, and if so, which ones? "Three cherries", one child says, and the other, with the same book before his eyes knows which are meant. But are these real cherries? This doubt can be raised as early as the very beginning of set theory. I mentioned a television film where for a quarter of an hour pictures of objects were put between braces while a monotonous voice repeated "this is a set". In fact, set theory does not start until something is done with sets, sets are compared by mappings, sets of pairs are formed, sets of subsets found. To be sure, none of them, mappings, pairs sets, sets of subsets, are concrete phenomena. They are model concepts which are applied in one way or the other to reality.

This leads us to the question:

HOW ARE SET THEORY MODELS USED?

The question cannot possibly be answered by inventing artificial examples though the fact that today textbooks have plenty of them does not at all prove that it is as difficult to find good ones. Of course the point is not showing examples of sets but rather examples of what to do with sets.

I mentioned natural Venn diagrams. It is a natural problem to analyze such a concept as the common frontier of two countries. It is remarkable that the countries are usually not associated with something on the physical globe, but rather with two coloured areas on a map, which meet in something like a curve, which represents the common frontier. In mathematical terms, a country is a certain set on the map or on the globe, or on the earth itself, and the frontier of two neighbouring countries is the intersection of both point sets. I need not restrict the definition to neighbours, but then it can happen that countries have no common frontier, in other words, that the common frontier is void.

Of course, countries are not point sets on the globe. Near the frontier, or 12 nautical miles offshore it is difficult to tell whether a certain little spot belongs to a country or not; the Dutch enclave Baerle-Nassau in Belgium and the Dutch Embassy in Washington are other kinds of ambiguities. Further, countries have more than two dimensions; jurisdiction on mining and aviation extends them into a third dimension. In other situations a country would perhaps better be defined as the set of its cities, towns, and villages, or of its residents. Finally there are aspects of the country that are not fitted into any set theory models.

Let us, however, stick to the interpretation of a country as a set on the terrestrial surface. Then a statement like "the Netherlands is the union of its eleven provinces" is not too crazy. It also makes sense to consider the intersection of two or three provinces. A real or imaginary line would divide the country into a Northern and a Southern part, another into a Western and Eastern part, and it would be a reasonable question to ask how the North-East would be called in set theory. Or, how can the territory that Germany lost after World War II be expressed in terms of the former and present territories of other countries?

To move in another direction, let us divide the population of a country according to a number of characteristics: sex; adult or child; marital status; owner of a driver's licence A, B, C, D, E or not owner. Where in this pattern would you locate a female married bus driver? Suppose you have got the population of the Netherlands on punched cards, what would you do to find the card of such a person?

In a State lottery a prize of... is attributed to the lots ending with 3, a prize of... on the lots ending with 47, a prize of... on lots ending with 143, and so on. Which conclusion would you draw? Generalize this – consider the numbers from 000 to 999. The subset of numbers with n on the i-th place is denoted by N_i^n. Describe the number 123 in terms of such subsets. Imagine these numbers put in a natural way into the 1000 subdivision cubes of 1 dm^3 of a cube of 1 m^3. How do you describe the set N_i^n? Consider subsets described by certain equalities and inequalities (e.g. all digits equal).

Suppose space neatly subdivided into congruent cubes. Take the set of these cubes; consider subsets that could be called layers, columns, walls, and so on.

All these examples are of a very special type. If such a set is given you can tell immediately elements from non-elements – at least this is suggested by the model. The same is true of countries on a map. Mathematical examples may be more sophisticated. To find the points in the plane at a distance r from M you need a pair of compasses. The set of points as far from A as from B is found by a non-trivial construction. To find the set of x satisfying $x^2 - 3x + 2 = 0$ you should solve this equation. Obviously the student should also get acquainted with sets whose elements are not explicitly given. But this does not mean that every problem should be formulated as a question that asks for a solution set and that the solution of every problem should be written as a set. The set theory form should be chosen if it is relevant. "Who is afraid of the big bad wolf?" need not be formulated in searching for the set

$$\{x \mid x \text{ is afraid of the big bad wolf}\}$$

and the answer need not run like "the set is empty". When I was a university student the "set of the even prime numbers" was in our circle a familiar piece of facetious pretentiousness. I believe it is still pretentious but now people take it seriously. No doubt one can solve the equation $(?x)(x^2 - 3x + 2 = 0)$ according to the pattern:

$$\{x \mid x^2 - 3x + 2 = 0\} = \{x \mid x - 2 \cdot \tfrac{3}{2}x + \tfrac{9}{4} + 2 - \tfrac{9}{4} = 0\} =$$
$$= \{x \mid (x - \tfrac{3}{2})^2 = \tfrac{1}{4}\} = \{x \mid x - \tfrac{3}{2} = \tfrac{1}{2} \lor x - \tfrac{3}{2} = -\tfrac{1}{2}\} =$$
$$= \{x \mid x - \tfrac{3}{2} = \tfrac{1}{2}\} \cup \{x \mid x - \tfrac{3}{2} = -\tfrac{1}{2}\} =$$
$$= \{x \mid x = 2\} \cup \{x \mid x = 1\} = \{x \mid x = 2 \lor x = 1\}.$$

I do not see where the set concept becomes operational in this text. Every implication

$$\bigwedge_x (F(x) \to G(X))$$

can be written as

$$\{x \mid F(x)\} \subset \{x \mid G(x)\}$$

for instance "all men are mortal" as "the set of men is contained in the set of mortals". It is legitimate to say: "The set of the areas of the circles with radius 1 is the one-element-set $\{\pi\}$." When I say it is legitimate, I mean to say that it is a legitimate piece of sheer pretentiousness.

If, however, one says "the set of points in the plane with equal distances from A and B (formerly the locus) is the perpendicular bisector of AB", then the set theory model is operational. They are sets which are being compared and, moreover, they are sets that appear as such on the paper and in the sequel these kind of sets are subjected to set theory operations as intersecting.

I will not explain once again what purposes sets serve in mathematics. School didactics can profit from such knowledge but it does not suffice. Today at school, sets are introduced for purposes that are unknown in normal mathematics. This is not forbidden and it can even be didactically useful. The one thing, however, that is required is that sets are not introduced until one has thought about the specific purposes sets should serve, that is, how they should be related to lived-through reality and to the mathematical content. I have the impression that sets are more often introduced because it is fashionable, or because everybody does so, than after a conscious deliberation in any particular case.

In many methods sets, after having been introduced, serve to introduce or (on a higher level) to deduce natural numbers. I explained earlier that sets do not suffice to do this task, and I will not come back to this discussion. At the moment I would rather stress that once the natural numbers have been introduced or derived as cardinalities, the numerosity aspect of natural numbers soon fades away, and that deducing natural numbers is, in the nature of things, a *hapax legomenon*. This means that in both cases the set concept looses its operational character after a short delay. It is not any more needed, and as a consequence it does not occur for a long time. Or, what is even worse, the author makes a great effort to push the set concept forward in all contexts and to press everything he can into a set theory frame even if it is quite irrelevant or impossible – I earlier gave a few gruesome examples.

What else can be expected from the set concept? Some use it as a foundation of the function concept. I will show later that this is both a mathematical and a didactical misunderstanding. There is no need of sets as a precursor of functions, and even if sets come before functions they are hardly operational in developing functions.

As we saw earlier*, sets can be operational in combinational matter

* p. 190, 249

though with a stress on mappings rather than on pairs forming. Strangely enough they are rarely used in this domain.

STRUCTURED UNIVERSES – THE LITTLE WORLD

There is one context where set theory models are really relevant and can show their relevance from kindergarten onwards. I think up to now Dienes has been one of the few who have recognized and understood it. I mean the activity of dividing a universe with respect to several characteristics. The reader who looks back to the examples of the last section cannot but notice that all of them are of just this kind, and I bet that everybody who looks around for natural occurrences of the set theory model will hit upon such examples. Here the set theory relations and operations are, indeed, the adequate devices of structuring and formulating. Here inclusion, intersection, union, and complement are naturally related to lived-through reality, and this holds for the pair-forming too, provided it is not carried out by abstract pairing but by structuring a given set.

It is one more advantage of this context that operations rather than being applied to arbitrarily composed sets take place in a pre-established universe. This is important, especially with small children. From geometry teaching it is well known that closed shapes like parallelograms and cubes are more readily accessible than open ones as the angle and the straight line. The open universes, which in particular are at present being cultivated in the elementary schools, are, with their unpredictable wealth of objects and object classes, utterly confusing. As examples I recall the problem of the representation of Mary's nose and of the set of potatoes in the Venn diagram. If the universe of discourse is a school class or a heap of potatoes, such questions are irrelevant. Such open universes are accidentally met in non-mathematical problems, but then they are generally puns or traps like the one: "An American, a German, an Englishman, and a Frenchman jumped with parachutes from a plane. Who was the first on the earth?" – The answer: "Adam."

In the Dienes's material I had in mind, the universe is a box of blocks which have been divided according to criteria like colour, shape, length, and thickness. With such a universe logical games are played. There seem to be numerous editions of this excellent material. It is a pity that the one I know is combined by means of guidelines with a nonsensical use of Venn diagrams.

Though I estimate highly the Dienes material, I do not like one feature in it – namely that it offers the child an *a priori* sharply structured material. The child is given little opportunity to structure the universe self-reliantly. Of course, such universes with an easily perceivable and tight structure can boast of their own merits, but they should not be the only ones nor should they be exemplary. I find Dienes's material too mathematical. Mathematizing, which in the underlying case means structuring the universe according to certain characteristics is better learned with material which has not been so sharply structured in advance. Such material, though perhaps not as confortable, would be more realistic. With such a more general approach the chance diminishes that the subject matter is isolated and finally becomes reduced to a *hapax legomenon*.

For exercises with children of pre-school age I imagine a kind of universe, which I would call a "Little World", with contents something like the contents of a toybox. This "Little World" can be classified according to colour, shape, size, and function (mobile or immobile), meaning (carriages, automobiles, dolls, blocks), that is to say, the children should classify the "Little World". They can exercize refining and coarsing the structure, characterizing objects and kinds of objects by necessary and sufficient criteria. In such a Little World they can also learn what is necessary and what is contingent: if by chance in the Little World all red mobile things are cars, then this fact can be recognized as a theorem in the "Little World", which in other worlds ceases to be true. In the well-organized logical kit all criteria are independent; if the criteria are red-blue, angular-round, long-short, thick-thin, then every combination among the 16 combinations (such as red $\wedge$ angular $\wedge$ long $\wedge$ thick, etc.) is represented, and maybe even only once. In the toybox the criteria need not be independent; maybe all the red mobile objects are cars, whereas on the other hand not all the cars have to be red. There is a natural wealth of combinations.

The main thing, however, is the structuring activity, which is better exercized with this sort of material than with prestructured material. I stress pair forming once more in this context. If we introduce direct products in a group theory course at university, we would start with a given group G with two normal subgroups H and K, which have to be disjunct up to the 1-element, and would state remarkable properties of their product HK, viz., that HK is again a group, and that every element of HK can be represented in just one way as a product of an element of H and an element of K. Only after this concrete direct product is the abstract one defined: then we construct from two groups H and K, which have nothing to do with each other, the pairs $\ulcorner h, k \urcorner$ ($h \in H$, $k \in K$) and we relate them to each other by stipulating a multiplication: $\ulcorner h, k \urcorner \cdot \ulcorner h_1, k_1 \urcorner = \ulcorner hh_1, kk_1 \urcorner$. At school, if the pairs set $\ulcorner A, B \urcorner$ of two sets A, B is introduced, they do it the other way round: starting with abstractly combining the elements of A and B and arriving later, if at all, at the concrete creation of a pairs structure in a given set. From 5 boys and 4 girls the inscrutable set of pairs boy-girl is formed rather than structuring school time according the criteria of day and period to obtain a pairs set structured timetable.*

I discussed the "Little World" as a logical and set theory exercise for the kindergarten age group, but I would like to be a little more cautious for all that. I meant to say about the logical set theory material which has been proposed for small children that it is in my judgement too schematically and abstractly structured. I would rather replace it by freer material which would be more adaptable for active structuration by the child. I would rather not decide whether such exercises should really be done in kindergarten or the first grades of elementary school. Till now nobody has been able to tell me what the aim and use of this material is. Maybe working with such material is in itself a discipline of the mind – I mean that version of the material I proposed. Perhaps this could be tested in the future. If this were found not to be true, the material could at least be bottom level to something else although I am not sure what this should be. Up till now I saw this material only as bottom-level toys, a game that finishes the same way it began. I do not have the impression that much has been thought out as to how the play can be made to become serious, namely how these first beginnings are to be continued. If this question is not answered, these exercises can rightly be written off as a *hapax legomenon*.

I do not believe that this will be the conclusion. What matters is that

* See p. 190, 249.

the significance of the material is well understood and that it will become clear what can be attained with such material beyond local teaching successes in the global frame of mathematics teaching. The result would be crucial for the use of sets in elementary school. If sets are only used to explain what cardinalities are, they cannot be prevented from disappearing out of sight as fast as they have been introduced, because of the minor importance of the numerosity aspect of number. The set theory operations in structured universes would be a much more substantial use of sets. But we do not yet know what this subject means in the total educational context.

SETS OUT OF THE BLUE

I will repeat in mathematical terms what I mean by structured (or rather structurable) universes. The best way to explain it is by means of its admissible operations: singling out subsets by properties, and forming of intersections, unions, and complements. Mathematically viewed this is not much. If a universe of sets is meant in mathematics, it is always required to contain with any set V the set of its subsets $P(V)$. In the latter set one forms again subsets, e.g. the set of all finite subsets, and of course, the set $P(P(V))$ of all subsets of $P(V)$ cannot be missed.

These mathematically useful universes are intuitively confusing. Didactically they are impracticable. People seem to believe that infinity is the source of this confusion. Sets as those of the natural numbers, the integers, the even numbers, the decimal fractions are entirely accessible to intuitive understanding on a suitable level, but this can hardly be said about the set of the subsets of V, even if V is finite. With small finite cardinalities it can be a useful exercise to write down all of its subsets, but it is quite another thing to conceive these subsets together as elements of a new set and to apply the usual set theory operations on this new set. In textbooks I never found problems like "what is $P(V) \cap \cap P(W)$, $P(V) \cup P(W)$, $P(V) \backslash P(W)$ if V and W are given sets?" Such problems are required to test whether $P(V)$ has really been conceived as a set, but obviously the authors do not trust the pupils to take this test until they have reached a level of abstraction that is probably beyond school age.

In mathematical set universes the question can and must be asked whether some set is an element of another; this is a mathematically essential question. In the Little World it cannot be asked at all, since there elements of a set are palpable objects. On a higher level it cannot be avoided but this does not mean that it should be asked systematically and dogmatically. It should only be asked if the adherence of some object to another as an element of a set is clearly visible.

Once the concrete game with the Little World is finished, I would not try to avoid sets as elements of other sets at any price, but the abstraction that allows the set of all subsets of a set is an enormous step. I prefer other examples: the set Φ of all circles in the plane, where every circle is understood as the set of its points. Unlike the Little World these objects are not separately concretely realized; the elements of Φ cannot be laid out one beside the other, but still the set Φ is intuitively conceivable. Subsets of Φ and operations on them are naturally emerging, for instance the three sets of circles which are passing through three given points, and their intersection. The set of all subsets of the plane is an indigestible jelly because the general subset is anonymous, whereas each circle can, as it were, be called by its surname and first name, I mean by its centre and radius.

The number pairs of integers and their equivalence classes, which lead to the rational numbers are an analogous though more involved example. Departing, as several times mentioned, from the ring of integers $\mathbf{Z}$ the field $\mathbf{Q}$ of rational numbers arises by means of the equivalence classes of pairs $\ulcorner a, b \urcorner$ with $b \neq 0$ with respect to the equivalence relation $\sim$, defined by $\ulcorner a, b \urcorner \sim \ulcorner c, d \urcorner \leftrightarrow ad = bc$. The transition from the numbers to the pairs of numbers is not entirely unproblematic. Concretely, in the Little World, it would not be possible. There all ordered pairs of *different* objects can be formed though not the set of all of them, because to make one of them, one can be compelled to destroy another. Yet pairs with both components equal cannot at all be formed concretely. It seems that quite a few authors of textbooks did not recognize the consequences of this fact early enough. The set of the pairs thus requires a certain abstraction. The next step is class forming by equivalence, and finally the set of all classes must be considered, and in special situations subsets of this set. This seems to be an enormous abstracting effort, though in fact it is not as bad as one might have expected. Each equivalence class – or rational number – is a safe point of rest. Each equivalence class is completely determined by one of its members, and for this reason it is more concrete than the general subset. Since the equivalence classes are mutually disjoint the set of equivalence classes is more palpable than the set of all subsets. An equivalence class is fully represented by one of its members, and rather than the equivalence classes such representatives are used in practice. As we mentioned earlier* rather than working with the whole class of ¾ one behaves as though

$$\ldots \ulcorner -6, -8 \urcorner, \quad \ulcorner -3, -4 \urcorner, \quad \ulcorner 3, 4 \urcorner, \quad \ulcorner 6, 8 \urcorner, \ldots$$

were the same thing. In practice large subsets as elements of newly created sets are avoided. I do not assert that this is a must, but it is as little a must as to create sets out of the blue, in particular if they are rarely or never used.

LEVELS OF ABSTRACTION IN THE SET CONCEPT

If there is in the foregoing exposition one feature that should be stressed once more, then it is the rich didactical variety in the phenomenology of the set concept. What is, with a view to this variety, the meaning of such statements as that set theory can be taught at every level? At the bottom of the development of the set concept are the species of objects of the Little World which can be exposed one beside the other; on the top it is entirely axiomatized and formalized set theory, the objects of which only enjoy a formal existence; in between there is a broad spectrum.

The species of the Little World are followed by the sets drawn on a sheet of paper. Next come the mental sorts of the Little World, and the mental designs of sets. They can be operated on concretely or mentally. Still more advanced are sets the elements of which are sharply described and easily imaginable sets, such as certain sets of circles in the plane; they can be operated on by easily describable operations. The scope of purely formal cognition and reasoning is for a long while restricted to extremely simple facts like the transitivity of inclusion ($A \subset B \wedge B \subset C \rightarrow \rightarrow (A \subset C)$, and the injectivity of the product of injective mappings. Whenever sets are to be considered as elements of other sets, abstractive forces are heavily strained, since more often than not attempts at concretization

---

* See p. 227.

are due to fail or even to do harm. The unavoidable difficulties of abstraction can be characterized by a well-known example, the proof of the theorem that no set V can be equipotent with the set $\mathbf{P}(V)$ of its subsets. It runs as follows:

Take a mapping f of V upon $\mathbf{P}(V)$ to derive a contradiction. Every $x \in V$ has its $fx \in \mathbf{P}(V)$, and every $U \in \mathbf{P}(V)$ has its $u \in V$ with $fu = U$. The set

$$U = \{x \in V \mid x \notin fx\} \in P(V)$$

is constituted. Take u such that $fu \in U$. By definition

$$x \in U \leftrightarrow (x \in V \wedge x \notin fx).$$

In particular,

$$u \in U \leftrightarrow u \notin fu = U,$$

which is contradictory.

It is so simple a proof that there is not much in mathematics simpler than this. But anyone who once in his life taught this proof to first-year university students knows how difficult they find it, and anyone who has at all thought about it knows the reason why. It is not infinity. The proof has not anything to do with infinity; the theorem holds for finite sets, too, and independently of any infinity axiom. The real difficulty consists in that the relation of being an element of a set is accessible to concretizing intuition only in a perspicuous subject matter. In this respect operations like union and intersection are much easier. For this reason the proof of the above theorem is carried out abstractly and far from intuition. This should suffice to ban it from school mathematics, if it were not already to be rejected as a *hapax legomenon*.

It is worthwhile to compare this proof with that for the theorem that a line segment is not denumerable:

Let S_1 be a line segment. Suppose somebody asserts he can enumerate the points of S_1. He recites them as it were, say,

$$a_1, a_2, a_3, \ldots$$

I attempt to refute him. While he is reciting what he asserts to be the segment S_1, I am reconstructing a point of S_1 which he is due to forget. After he has chosen a_1, I choose a subsegment S_2 that excludes a_1.

After he has indicated a_2, I choose a subsegment S_3 of S_2 that excludes a_2, too, and so we continue. A sequence of segments S_i is produced such that

$$S_1 \supset S_2 \dots,$$

and always

$$a_i \notin S_{i+1}.$$

The S_i have in common a point c, which my opponent is due to miss. Indeed, $c = a_1$ is impossible, since $c \in S_2$ whereas $a_1 \notin S_2$. Likewise, $c = a_2$ is impossible, since $c \in S_3$ whereas $a_3 \notin S_3$. And so on: $c = a_p$ is impossible, since $c \in S_{p+1}$ whereas $a_p \notin S_{p+1}$. Thus c is lacking in the alleged enumeration.

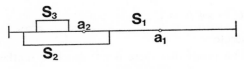

Fig. 26.

The proof is so perspicuous that it can be told to twelve year-olds (though I do not recommend it). In spite of the role of infinity it is easier than the preceding proof. Is it not even easier than the terrible proof using the diagonal procedure which as far as I know for no other reason than tradition has become so popular? The present one is not only simpler and more intuitive but it also shows exactly the essential feature of the number continuum: that the intersection of a decreasing sequence of line segments is non-empty.

I tried to indicate the variety of levels of abstraction of the set concept. I am not sure whether textbook authors are usually conscious of this. It is true they try to concretize as much as they can, but this is often just a source of disaster. These are essentially attempts with inappropriate means on an inappropriate subject. When dealing with fractions we discussed the limits of intuitive arithmetic; functions will be another example of less successful attempts on concretization. Venn diagrams which occasionally can be useful, are if overused a real danger. It is correct that the abstractive force of the students is an important factor to be seriously to be accounted for. Wrong concretizations are no use.

There is much, particularly in set theory, that resists attempts at concretization. If it is too abstract to be grasped by the student in its naked abstractness, the only thing to do is to renounce it.

I would like to mention another example of misleading concretization in set theory. It is a proof of the Schröder-Bernstein equivalence theorem for 11–12 year-olds.

Let us have A_1 equipotent with a subset A_2 by means of a one-to-one mapping f from A_1 on A_2. Let B between A_1 and A_2, thus $A_1 \supset B \supset A_2$. Then B is equipotent with A_1 (and A_2).

A Venn diagram (Figure 27) is drawn. The mapping f is iterated:

$$fA_1 = A_2, fA_2 = A_3, fA_3 = A_4, \ldots;$$

likewise

$$fB_1 = B_2, fB_2 = B_3, fB_3 = B_4, \ldots.$$

It is

$$A_1 \supset B_1 \supset A_2 \supset B_2 \supset A_3 \supset \ldots.$$

One notices the "rings" $A_i \backslash B_i$. Each of them is mapped by f upon the next, $A_i \backslash B_i$ on $A_{i+1} \backslash B_{i+1}$. A mapping g is defined as follows: On every ring $A_i \backslash B_i$ it agrees with f; elsewhere it is the identity. g maps A_1 upon B_1.

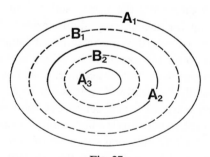

Fig. 27.

No doubt this is a simple and intuitive proof. Its intuitivity is even extremely relevant but it is so only for people with tremendous mathematical experience who understand the schematism of its concretization. It is meaningless for beginners who know Venn diagrams only as a background of sets of concrete objects. To understand this proof it is indispensable that one can forget about the plane as carrier of the sets $A_1, B_1, \ldots$, and that one can write down an abstract form of proof, free from intuition (which we did not do). Moreover to understand the theorem it is indispensable that the existence of different cardinalities is a well established and firmly integrated fact. Without this precondition the theorem is unmotivated.

SHAM SETS

Several times I have quoted didactically unfortunate examples of sets from all kinds of textbooks. I circumstantially discussed sets of letters; they can be admitted if precautions are observed though they are better avoided to avert disasters. Sets of meaningless symbols are nearly as dangerous. The set of the months with no letter 'r' seems to be an innocent pleasure; from here to the set of all the names of months with no 'r' in them is a small but particularly dangerous step. Indeed how many names can a month not be given? In something like a Little World the objects were individually represented on cards. Its author took the pleasure of speaking not only of the set of objects, but also of the set of cards to arrive at an example of a one-to-one mapping. I trust the reader will himself feel how dangerous this infringement on the well-defined complex of the Little World is.

It is striking how differently the word "set" is translated in different languages. Consulting various language dictionaries to find out what the word for 'set' means in everyday life in different languages, one begins to understand a bit better the examples by which sets are introduced in the teaching of mathematics in various countries. In Dutch the word used for "set" means usually "collection" so it is not to be wondered at that almost every Dutch textbook starts set theory with stamp collections. There is no need to explain why this is a bad example since stamp collectors have the habit of collecting only one specimen of every stamp. Together with misunderstanding of Venn diagrams this prepares the ground for a mistaken set concept.

In French the word used for "set" also means "together". This perhaps explains the immoderate use of Venn diagrams in French literature; togetherness is to be indicated by a closed curve that holds things together. In German the association of "set" with "quantity" leads to examples like "the set of five pounds of sugar". From the American literature I have already mentioned "the set of 5 dollars" represented by a 5-dollar note within braces, and "the set of the ten commandments", depicted by the stone tables, again within braces. Mainly in English-language textbooks I met a kind of example that I am going to analyze now. It is, for instance, the set of John's report grades, or the set of the average daily temperatures at Newport in 1960.

Of course such sets are perfectly legal, that is they are legal nonsense. What do the authors intend to do with such sets? Maybe calculate the average of John's grades or of the temperatures? But then these sets are of no use. Maybe all his grades were 50 and 60; then the set of his grades is {50, 60}, but from such data the average cannot be calculated; you ought to know how many times these numbers occurred in the list of the grades. Likewise, in the second example one cannot expect that all of the 366 daily temperature averages were different. The set of the temperatures is irrelevant; what matters is the total list. This, of course, is what the author means. But since in everyday English such a list of numbers, with equals among them, can be called a set, examples of "sets" with repetitions are quite usual in the English-American literature. I should say that wherever in the world I lectured about this subject, I was asked the nagging question how to deal with "sets with repetitions". It is strange that even textbooks that are unobjectionable on this point keep silent about this problem which, no doubt, cannot be all that unusual in the classroom.

The way out of this dilemma should properly be described under the subject "functions", but it is better to anticipate it. If I regard the list of John's grades, I notice not a set, but a more important feature – a function. I see a list of subjects and after each subject a grade. To each subject is a grade assigned, and such an assignment is called a function, in the present case a function that maps the set of subjects into the set of numbers $1, 2, \ldots$. It is the same with the list of temperatures at Newport: to each of the 366 days of 1960 there is a number assigned, namely the average temperature on that particular day. Such a function can, indeed, be useful. For instance, one can form its mean,

$$\frac{1}{n} \sum_{1}^{n} f(x_i),$$

where x_i are the various subjects or days.

Likewise I can work out the average weight of a basketful of eggs. I weigh them and note down: egg 1 ... oz, egg 2 ... oz, and so on. Usually such numbers are ordered in a monotonic sequence. Unintentionally I said "sequence". In fact a function from

$$\{1, ..., n\} \text{ to } V$$

is also called a sequence of n elements from V (and likewise, a mapping from $\mathbf{N}$ to V, an infinite sequence from V). In a sequence two elements can be equal; there are even constant sequences.

An analogous question that is often raised is whether such notations as $\{a, a, b\}$ are allowed. It characterizes the gap still existing between school and university mathematics that such questions can be raised. In higher mathematics expressions like $\{a\}$ are quite familiar, $\{a, b\}$ is not unusual, but $\{a, b, c\}$ is rare; and if expressions like $\{a, b\}$ are met at all, it would be in some sentence like "Let D be the set $\{0, 1\}$". Here $a \neq b$ by definition.

How can $\{a, b, c\}$ come in? Well, in a typical school mathematics context, namely to indicate the set of solutions of an equation, say of 3rd degree. Such an equation may degenerate into $x^2(x - 1) = 0$ say, where two roots coincide. Of course you would like to indicate that the root 0 counts for two. But $\{0, 0, 1\}$ does not help us. If it has any meaning, then it means the same as $\{0, 1\}$.

This example again shows which difficulties arise if a notation is used for purposes it was never intended to serve. In this case, too, sequences of roots would be the way out though it would be rather artificial. Why not do it the same way as in higher mathematics, that is, tell about a polynomial that its roots are α_i ($i = 1, ..., p$) with the multiplicities m_i respectively? Why invent special terminologies for school mathematics only to press everything in one set theory terminology?

DEDUCTIVITY IN SET THEORY

How much deductivity is introduced into set theory should depend on how far set theory is dealt with, and on how many connections are to be tied between the fundamental concepts of set theory. Logically all can be reduced to the $\in$-relation. By means of the $\in$, the $\subset$, $\cup$, $\cap$, $\backslash$ can be defined. I would like to know at what age a child can repeat, find,

SETS AND FUNCTIONS   367

and use deductively such definitions – obviously these are different levels.
The child may have understood a pattern like "if $a \in A$, then $a \in B$" though
it has not yet arrived at the deductive level. Such a statement may be
a valid description of "$A \subset B$" though no need whatsoever is felt to prove
$((A \subset B) \wedge (B \subset C)) \rightarrow (A \subset C)$ or the distributive or other laws.

A proof of the transitivity of "$\subset$" is, in fact, nothing but a translation
of the transitivity of "$\rightarrow$" into set language. I wonder here which statements are derived from which. Is the logical transitivity justified by that
of set theory, with the use of Venn diagrams, or is the set theory transitivity justified by an abstract argument in which logical transitivity is
hidden? Or are we going round in a circle?

We will come back in the chapter on logic to the connection between
set algebra and proposition logic. We will see that it is not as simple as
people usually think. On the contrary, it is so sophisticated that I would
not like to explain it to first-year undergraduates. I cannot see how a
deductive system of set algebra that does not look like a knot of vicious
circles could be possibly introduced in the lower or even in the higher
grades of secondary school.

This does not mean that deductivity should be avoided at this level.
Conscious reasoning should be stimulated at least to justify some termin-
ological conventions. For instance, the empty set can be justified by the
necessity of an unrestricted operation of intersection. The feature that the
empty set is contained in any set is closely connected to the usual interpretation of "$\rightarrow$". In fact since $p \rightarrow q$ is considered to be true as soon as
p is false, it follows that $(x \in A) \rightarrow (x \in B)$ is true as soon as A is empty;
but $(x \in A) \rightarrow (x \in B)$ is just a definition of $A \subset B$. However, it can hardly be
argued whether that interpretation of $p \rightarrow q$ should be justified by the
empty set being contained in every set, or whether it should be done the
other way round.

The foregoing is closely connected with the fact that the empty set,
though not gifted with an element, possesses a subset; this can be justified
by the expression 2^n for the number of subsets of a set of n elements,
which should be upheld for $n = 0$.

The difference between the element a and the set $\{a\}$ should be motivated though there is hardly anything to prove here. With all my examples
I never transgress the limits of local organization. I do not believe that
more is possible in the lower and even in the higher grades of secondary

school. Structuring the principles of set theory too much deductively is the same mistake as has prevailed for so long in geometry instruction: proving obvious-looking statements by circular-looking methods, and this on a level where the schoolchild does not feel the need for such sophistication. Of course, this does not exclude teaching of deductive connections at a higher level, and in applications of set theory.

One can readily understand why mathematicians are prone to teaching early set theory as a deductive system. Every mathematician is scared if he should sacrifice even a little bit of what he considers as absolute exactness. The usual solution of this dilemma is pouring the full load of deductiveness into the mathematics that is imposed on the pupil, and to leave the so-called problems to him as a field of his own activity. If you want to know what the author of every textbook hopes that the teachers and pupils who are supposed to use it, are able to do, you can draw quite a bit of information from the problem section. Does it match the theoretical part to the effect that the theory does not remain a *hapax legomenon*, or does it ask of the student no more but specializing correctly the parameters in the general theorems? In between there are, in fact, many intermediate stages. The problem section is especially important and informative as regards such methods that aim at teaching a system of mathematics; everything that does not fit too well into the system yet cannot be missed can fairly easily be moved into the problem section. If the main part asks for a high level of abstraction and deductivity, the problems can show how seriously this high level is taken by the author himself.

Perhaps it is asking too much to ask for an equivalence of theory and problems. It is not easy to invent adequate problems for set theory. To combine adequateness with didactical realizability asks for an even greater effort. Moreover, there is a dangerous temptation in this field – set algebra. I think it is clear what I mean: checking the distributive laws for union and intersection, finding another expression for $A\backslash(B\backslash C)$, calculating $(A \times B)\backslash(C \times D)$ if $A \supset C$ and $B \supset D$, and so on. They are not too bad, these problems; the danger lies in the "and so on". And you can be sure that it will go on so, once it is started. Set algebra is the right thing for people who would take it easy with teaching mathematics. In this field you can do marvels with drill; the drill rules are even easier than in ordinary algebra, in particular because in set algebra all needed brackets are made explicit, thus both $(A \cup B) \cap C$ and $(A \cap B) \cup C$ (rather than $(a + b)\, c$ though $ab + c$). But if, finally, set algebra is made too easy by drill, the field can be saved by all kind of complications. One can invent traps like in ordinary algebra that of tempting the solver to divide by 0. Though, properly said, an analogue does not exist in set algebra, you can build it in if you are clever. Define partitions $\{A_1, ..., A_n\}$ of a set V as follows:

$$V = A_1 \cup ... \cup A_n, \; A_i \cap A_j = \bigcirc \quad \text{for} \quad i \neq j, \, A_i \neq \bigcirc.$$

Then you can contrive quite a lot of problems on partitions which look so simple that the solver forgets about checking the third condition. For example: If $\{A_1, ..., A_p\}$ and $\{B_1, ..., B_q\}$ are partitions of the same set V, then is the set of the $A_i B_j$ a partition, too?

Within mathematics, set algebra is a trifling game; though I often interviewed mathematicians about it, I found none who uses rules of set algebra beyond intuition. I certainly know that set algebra together with logic admits of big applications – so big that to solve such problems you need computers. As soon, however, as this kind of application is tackled, the stress will no longer be on set algebra but on its relation to applications. Then it does not matter any more how to solve such set algebra problems but how to transform a realistic problem into one of set algebra. How to teach this is a problem that has hardly been tackled. I would like to take this opportunity to mention a type of problem that is quite normal in set theory, and which by its mere existence testifies to the didactic underdevelopment of this domain of teaching.

To come to this example let us first look at teaching arithmetic. There you meet problems like "John has 5 marbles, he gets 3 more, how many does he have now?" To solve such problems it does not suffice that children know how much $5 + 3$ is. Under given conditions they ought to be able to choose among several operations. This ability, which is exercised with such problems, guarantees the applicability of arithmetic.

Now a problem on sets: A is the set of adults, B the set of males, what is $A \cap B$?

Compare this with the first problem. Isn't it too bad? What good style is in set theory corresponds to the following version of the arithmetical problem:

John has 5 marbles, he gets 3 more, add 5 and 3.

Indeed it is too bad.

THE SET THEORY SYMBOLS

Quite a few times I have heard teachers complain about how difficult set theory symbols like $\in$, $\notin$, $\subset$, $\cup$, $\cap$, \ are for pupils. I used to shrug my shoulders. Now, after having thoroughly studied numerous textbooks, I can understand why. I would rather be astonished if the pupils did not have difficulties with the symbols. What can poor pupils and poor teachers do with problems like those in Figures 28–30? What if the union symbol is replaced by an intersection or difference symbol?

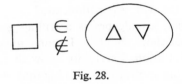

Fig. 28.

In fact, such difficulties can easily be avoided. Much more serious is the case of

$$\{x \in V \mid F(x)\}.$$

It is unbelievable how uncritically this is used, mostly because the user never thought about what it could mean. Blunders in the use of these notations are frequent, up to the highest levels of scientific literature. For this reason I will investigate it more closely.

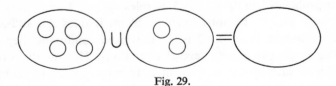

Fig. 29.

Firstly, cannot the first part, $x \in V$, be omitted? Why not confound the condition $x \in V$ with the condition that x possesses the property $F(x)$? In fact, '$x \in V$' is a property, too, and with

$$G(x) = F(x) \cap (x \in V)$$

the whole expression could be rewritten as

$$\{x \mid G(x)\}.$$

Well, it is a prescription that the first part is of the form $x \in V$, where 'x' is the variable subjected to binding, and V should be a set. What is the reason?

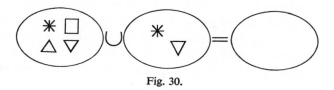

Fig. 30.

It is a subtle affair, and I am not sure whether I can make it entirely clear. Let us consider expressions like

$$\{x \mid \Phi(x)\}$$

to show that they will lead us into difficulty. $\Phi(x)$ should be a property of x (a predicate). Let us take the property $x \notin x$. It is a bit strange, but mathematicians should not shirk from strange things. We get the set

$$u = \{x \mid x \notin x\}$$

that is the set of all sets that are not elements of themselves. It leads to the famous paradox of Bertrand Russell: from $u \in u$ it follows that $u \notin u$, and from $u \notin u$ it follows $u \in u$.

This paradox can be avoided if $\{x \mid \Phi(x)\}$ is prohibited. It must be $\{x \in V \mid F(x)\}$, that is to select elements with the property $F(x)$ into a set, one has to choose within a given set V. By this measure the paradox can be avoided. If now we define

$$u = \{x \in V \mid x \notin x\},$$

we can still derive from $u \in u$ that $u \notin u$, but from $u \notin u$ we can only derive that $u \notin V$, wihch is not contradictory.

Maybe the reader wonders how to get enough sets if to define a set by a property, I have to draw on pre-existent sets. In an axiomatic build-up of set theory, this is achieved as follows. In a few cases set-building is not subjected to the above restriction, since experience shows that it does not lead to the above paradox; for instance it is assumed: the existence of the empty set; for every set a the existence of the set $\{a\}$ with a as its only element; the existence of the set of ordered pairs $\ulcorner x, y \urcorner$ with $x \in a$ and $y \in b$; to every set the existence of the set of its subsets; the existence of a certain infinite set; and a few more. In such an axiomatic system a satisfactory choice of sets is guaranteed.

This was to explain why it "must" be $\{x \in V \mid F(x)\}$. Is it fair to prescribe a certain notation without explaining its rationale? I think it is wicked. I set out to explain it to the reader but I do not expect him to be able to tell it to his pupils. But if he is not, he should not oblige his pupils to learn a notation they do not understand. In mathematics even notations have to be justified. Pupils should not be led to believe that mathematics is something like spelling where the authority of the teacher sets arbitrary rules.

Let us now turn to the second part of $\{x \in V \mid F(x)\}$. After the stroke a property should be indicated, and it should be done in such a way that the reader understands which one. In a simple case like $\{x \in \mathbf{R} \mid x < 3\}$ people succeed quite easily; but as soon as it becomes more involved, it goes wrong, not only in textbooks and exercise-books at school, but sometimes even in higher regions, because the author did not think about what the expression meant. How to write "the set of powers of 2"? Is it

$$\{x \in \mathbf{N} \mid x = 2^n, \quad n = 1, 2, ...\}?$$

How "the set of the 7-folds"? Is it

$$\{x \in \mathbf{N} \mid x = 7y, \ y \in \mathbf{N}\}?$$

This cannot be correct. Within the braces we notice a variable (n or y respectively) which is not bound or which does not show clearly the binding to which it should be subjected.

What is meant by "x is a multiple of 7" or by "x is divisible by 7"? Terminations like "ible" and "able" hide an existential quantifier; "x is divisible by 7" means the existence of a y with $x = 7y$. In the first formulation ("x is a multiple of 7") it is the indefinite article that hides the existential quantifier though under other circumstances the indefinite article may indicate a universal quantifier. (Compare the different meanings of the indefinite article in "I have a car", and "a car costs money".) Likewise "x is a power of 2" means "there is an n such that $x = 2^n$. The intended sets are thus correctly described by

$$\{x \in \mathbf{N} \mid \bigvee_{x \in \mathbf{N}} x = 2^n\},$$
$$\{x \in \mathbf{N} \mid \bigvee_{y \in \mathbf{N}} x = 7y\}.$$

To understand this, an advanced knowledge of mathematics is required. I do not believe this level can be reached by the average high school pupil. Is there not a way out? Some people say

$$\{2^n \mid n \in \mathbf{N}\},$$
$$\{7y \mid y \in \mathbf{N}\}.$$

But this is a new notation, in which all conventions on the use of the braces are ignored. Here the braces are to indicate the set of values of a function, viz. the function $\bigvee_{n \in \mathbf{N}} 2^n$, and $\bigvee_{y \in \mathbf{N}} 7y$ respectively. A good notation for the set of values of a function would be useful, but this is another question.

It goes from bad to worse. Once the above notation is admitted, all hell is let loose. You easily pass to notations like

$$\{ax^2 + bx + c \mid 2ax + b \geqslant 0\},$$
$$\{f(x) \in A \mid |f(x)| \in B \backslash A\},$$

where nobody can ascertain which variables are bound, a, b, c or x in the first example, f, x, A in the second. In the original notation you had to bind the variable to the domain which was described to the left of the stroke; in the extended notation nobody can tell the way of binding. It is a sad story, but it cannot be denied that such misuses of notation flourish even up to the highest regions of mathematical literature.

In a few school texts this problem has clearly been recognized. The above sets are there indicated by

$$\{x \mid x \text{ is a power of } 2\},$$
$$\{x \mid x \text{ is divisible by } 7\}.$$

But now it is doubtful why the expression "the set of all x with..." should be formalized and why not expressions like "x is a power of 2" or "x is divisible by 7".

Another abuse of the braces which is met with even in scientific literature is indicating a sequence $x_0, x_1, \ldots$ of real numbers by

$$\{x_i \mid i \in \mathbf{N}\}.$$

In the most liberal interpretation this means a set. The sequence should be indicated by something like

$$\Upsilon_{i\in\mathbf{N}}\, x_i\,.$$

We earlier explained the difference between sets and functions; this, in particular, becomes urgent as soon as sequences with equal members occur.

It is not difficult to tell what happens if at school the notation $\{x\in V \mid F(x)\}$ is introduced: at a very low level it is explained and applied with simple properties F but as soon as the properties get more involved, formalizing stops and sets are described in the vernacular. It should be seriously considered whether such a fragmentary use of $\{x\in V \mid F(x)\}$ really pays off. And first of all, it should be acknowledged that, except for such farces as

$$\{x \mid x \text{ is a planet}\},$$

the braces symbol does not become operational at all unless combined with the existential quantifier. Whether the braces should be used depends on how far formalizing of logic is to be pushed. We will come back to this question.*

INTUITIVE ILLUSTRATIONS OF FUNCTIONS AND MAPPINGS

In the most natural way, even before they have been defined, functions and mappings arise (I mostly use these terms synonymously). We have already met them. The mappings $3+$, $3-$, $3\cdot$ of the number line onto itself are most intuitive, and the intuitive character can be enhanced by a set of single arrows drawn from the original to the image. Instruments like slide rules and stretchers can be used to simulate addition, subtraction, and multiplication. Or rather than constructing them, we can imagine them and speak about slot machines and work in many ways with a function concept that springs most directly from reality, without saying what a function and a mapping is, and this "can" is even a "must". After the pupil has met with thousands of functions, has composed and invented them, it is a paradigm of mathematical activity to have him invent and formulate what a function is. Earlier I explained in general how important

---

* Bourbaki rejects the braces notations, probably for the same reasons explained above.

it is that the student consciously analyzes and organizes his own mathematical activity; in these proceedings the creation of new fundamental concepts like the function concept can excellently mark the transition to a higher level.

I have not yet taken up one particular kind of example of the function concept. It is just as natural and still closer to reality. I mean examples like price as a function of the quantity of a commodity, discount as a function of the amount, interest as a function of time, the path (of a car, train or plane) as a function of time, weight of a substance as a function of the volume, age as a function of the year number, temperature as a function of time – these are all examples of theoretical or empirical functions that are of multifarious use. To these classical examples many others can be added though they usually are absent – the volume or the surface of a box as a function of one or two or three linear dimensions, sines and cosines (though they are extremely simple, system superstitions do not allow them to be introduced before trigonometry starts): logarithmic functions (they, too, do not have to wait for a *theory* of the logarithmic function); light intensity as a function of the distance from the source; the height to which a fluid rises in a cylinder as a function of the quantity of fluid; the day-length as a function of the calendar date. You can pick and choose examples of functions, whereas examples of sets, if they are to be of some use, do not grow on trees.

The second group of examples is not as directly intuitive as the first, though they can be made intuitive in an indirect way, by graphics. In traditional school mathematics from the twenties until a few years back functions and graphics were nearly synonymous. Every university teacher was aware of the struggle first-year students had to fight to disconnect the function concept from its graphical illustration. It seems that graphics as part of the mathematical establishment are now considered a liability in some didactical circles. Some textbooks even abstain from mentioning them; in others they enter rather late, when functions have long since become a habit. This aversion to graphics is quite natural for people who set out to teach rather than mathematics, an unrelated system of mathematics. Then the numerous allusions to the function concept that would suggest the use of graphics, are simply absent, As a matter of fact all these examples can be introduced by natural problems which are as naturally solved by drawing graphic representations.

I stress the importance of graphics before I pass to such functions and mappings as cannot usefully be illustrated by graphics. Stress on one access to a mathematical concept is likely to be misinterpreted; it never means that the others are rejected. From a didactical point of view a many-sided approach is better than one-sidedness though those who are committed to a system can hardly appreciate the seeming chaos of a many-sided approach.

I mentioned concretization of mappings, namely by a set of arrows. The arrows can run from one Venn diagram to another as in Figure 31.

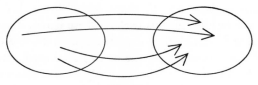

Fig. 31.

We also showed the functions $3+$, $3-$, $3\cdot$ visualized on the number line by arrows. The system of arrows serves in particular well to represent translations in the plane, and at the same time illustrates the vector concept. Curved arrows may be preferred to visualize rotations in

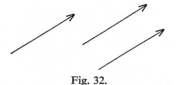

Fig. 32.

the plane; reflections require straight arrows of variable length. (Figures 33–34.) All this is hardly problematic, but it is not too important, either.

Fig. 33.

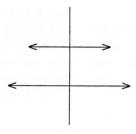

Fig. 34.

Difficulties arise if a number of mappings, for instance elements of a transformation group, are represented in one figure, or at least this is for some people a good opportunity to go astray. Translations in the plane are no problem. In Figure 35 it is easily seen which arrows belong to the same and which to different mappings.

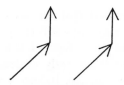

Fig. 35.

What the usual kind of difficulty is can be explained with an example that is most frequently found in the literature. It is the well-known group of four. As an abstract group it has the group table

e	a	b	c
a	e	c	b
b	c	e	a
c	b	a	e

Somewhat more concretely it is represented as a permutation group on the symbols 1, 2, 3, 4, if e, a, b, c are realized as mappings given by

$$e1 = 1, \quad e2 = 2, \quad e3 = 3, \quad e4 = 4,$$
$$a1 = 2, \quad a2 = 1, \quad a3 = 4, \quad a4 = 3,$$
$$b1 = 3, \quad b2 = 4, \quad b3 = 1, \quad b4 = 2,$$
$$c1 = 4, \quad c2 = 3, \quad c3 = 2, \quad c4 = 1.$$

A stronger concretization would be appreciated: 1, 2, 3, 4 are taken as the corners of a square (Figure 36). Now a is the reflection of the square at its vertical axis, b is the reflection at the horizontal axis, whereas c is the point reflection at the centre of the square, and e, of course, the identity mapping. It does not matter whether these mappings are supposed to act on the whole plane, the square, or its corners, though it should be clearly said what is meant.

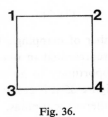

Fig. 36.

It can be readily understood that for some didacticians this is not yet concrete enough. The mappings still exist only in the imagination; one would rather prefer to show them. I saw pictures like Figure 37. It looks more concrete but is seriously misleading. It implies a strong suggestion of four different squares. Indeed, I saw it being taught by a teacher, who had understood it this way; he consistently spoke about four sets, and he did not realize that to combine one-to-one mappings into a group, they should act upon the same set.

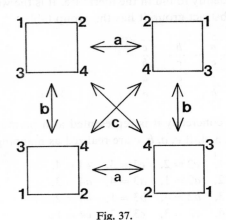

Fig. 37.

On the contrary, it is absolutely correct to draw one simple square (Figure 38) and to tell that under *a* the points exchange horizontally, under *b* vertically and under *c* diagonally. It can be shown by arrows

Fig. 38.

(Figure 39), and if colour is available, by colored arrows, one colour for the horizontal, one for the vertical and one for the diagonal arrows. In my opinion, this should be enough. But others judge that it is not

Fig. 39.

enough. They post as it were pupils in the corners (indicated by letters instead of figures) and describe the mappings as follows (Figure 40):

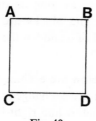

Fig. 40.

a: the pupils at *A* and *B* exchange their places and so do the pupils at *C* and *D*.

b: the pupils at *A* and *C* exchange their places, and so do the pupils at *B* and *D*.

c: the pupils at *A* and *D* exchange their places, and so do the pupils at *B* and *C*.

This is still correct but seemingly it is not yet concrete enough. The pupils get names: Arthur, Betty, Cecily, David, corresponding to the initials *A*, *B*, *C*, *D* to know who should stand in which corner. The marching orders are still formulated as above, but the more frequently they are applied to the pupils the greater is the temptation to say it in simpler terms, and finally it becomes

a: Arthur ↔ Betty, Cecily ↔ David,
b: Arthur ↔ Cecily, Betty ↔ David,
c: Arthur ↔ David, Betty ↔ Cecily.

These mappings (together with identity) form a group, too; it is again the group of four, though defined in an entirely different way. Of course this is allowed as well; but in any particular case one should know what is meant.

A variant of this theme is the following formulation. One is given four blocks, two triangular and two round ones, two blue and two red. The mappings are defined as follows:

a: exchange of shape,
b: exchange of colour,
c: exchange of both shape and colour.

Together with the identity they form the same abstract group. This is again an admissible example as long as one sticks to this definition. What, however, happens? The blocks are orderly and symmetrically arranged (Figure 41) and all of a sudden the colour- and shape-exchange transforms into:

a: above and below are exchanged,
b: right and left are exchanged,
c: both above-below and right-left are exchanged.

So we are back where we started.

It is worthwhile analyzing what happens here. To explain at a certain level what a function *f* is, it suffices to say that *f* assigns certain objects to certain others, but below this level such an assignment must be concretized to be understood. Concretizations are most useful in visual space. How can a mapping be concretized? A reflection in the plane is rather easy: you look into a mirror that stands orthogonal on the plane. To make it still more concrete, take a limited piece of paper to turn it.

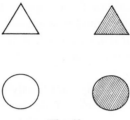

Fig. 41.

To concretize a translation, move the piece of paper over a pad. With drawn figures like our square *ABCD*, it is a bit more difficult. These difficulties led people to post objects at the points of the set to be moved under the transformation. The mapping f is now the prescription to displace the object at x to fx; it is a *displacement rule.*

Which kind of object should be chosen? It does not matter whether it is wood or lead, living or dead. Indeed, f is a displacement rule; it can be more or less easy to move lead or wood, living pawns can be commanded whereas dead ones must be moved by hand. That is the whole difference.

It does not matter what is moved, but would it be wise to do it with, say, white checkers only? Then before and after displacement everything would look the same. It is just the change that should be visualized. So what is posted in the points of the set under transformation, say in the corners of the square, must be clearly distinguishable objects. This is only done to recognize more easily what the effect of the displacement was. Meanwhile, what the displacement does effect does not depend on whether the object under displacement is wood or lead, red or green, round or triangular, living or dead. There should be no doubt: if f is the displacement rule, then what stands at x goes to fx.

Whatever stands at x, goes to fx. This is a little uncomfortable, because it is too abstract. "Whatever" hides a variable that is bound by generalization. Can it not be said more concretely? I give the pawns, or whatever else they may be, names: red, green, purple, yellow, or Arthur, Betty, Cecily, David. I post them; that is the "initial state". Then you can tell everything more easily: under a, Arthur and Betty change places as well as Cecily and David; and so it goes on.

This is a more comfortable formulation. But it only holds for the initial state. As soon as one of the mappings has been performed, the initial arrangement is changed, and what should happen now? It remains the same. But what does it mean? Does it remain

"a displaces the NE pawn to NW and the SE pawn to SW" or does it become

"a exchanges Arthur with Betty, and Cecily with David?"?

It is not the same. It is a change of viewpoint. It has been arrived at by steps but the decisive one was the "initial state". Up to this moment it did not matter what the pawns looked like and how they were named. But now everyone among them has got a "house" (this term is, in fact, used in the literature). Or in other words, each point of the set under transformation has got a permanent tenant, who, however, may travel around accidentally. The spots on which the mappings act, have now been supplemented by the qualities of the pawns that occupy them.

It can also be started from the other end. Mappings should be concretized. We just did it by interpreting the things to be mapped as spots in the plane. Now we start from a set of objects that may be lying or standing anywhere. Take: lion, elephant, camel; f transfigures cyclically lion into elephant, elephant into camel, camel into lion. Whether these three animals stay in Africa or in different zoos does not matter. Or, with another example: take four blocks, two triangular and two round, two red and two blue, and transfigure them by changing shape or colour, or both.

In general, in this concretization a set of clearly different objects is imagined, and then f is a *transfiguration rule*, which changes the object x into the object fx.

It is a decent concretization. But is it sufficient? Does it have enough concreteness if the objects are only imagined? Concrete objects are standing or lying somewhere rather than anywhere, and to put it more perspicously, it pays to arrange them in a meaningful way, as in Figure 42. To make it still more concrete, name the places above-right or NE,

and so on. So it begins, but the worst is still to come. It ends up as a
tragedy – a tragedy of errors.

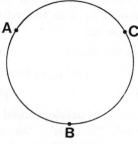

Fig. 42.

To avoid any confusion, one should clearly understand there are two
kinds of concretizing mappings (besides the earlier graphics and arrow
diagrams),

as displacements   as transfigurations.

The set in which the mappings take place is a

set of places   set of objects,

and the rule f tells that

the object at x the object x
is displaced to fx is transfigured into fx.

Both concretizations are acceptable, provided it is made clear that the

objects on the places   places of the objects

play an inessential part. It must be stressed that what happens with an
object under the influence of f

does not depend on its nature   does not depend on its
but only on its place   place but only on its
                                         nature.

It is utterly misleading to stipulate a preferential binding between objects
and places, such as

an initial state   a symmetric posting.

A complete concretization of the mapping concept, that is, with respect to both place and object is hardly possible (except maybe in graphics and arrow diagrams). The student who is expected to grasp the mapping concept, should be able to perform at least one of the following alternatives, to abstract

the place from the object   the object from the place,

that is, to imagine

objectless places   placeless objects.

There is little doubt that in developmental psychology the second precedes the first. "Stone", "triangle", "circle" are prior to "here", "there", "right", "left". Didacticians, however, who set out to concretize mappings according to both views, start with the first. This is not at all strange; the first kind is more familiar to mathematicians than the second, at least on account of geometry,

All attempts at group theory at school are highly unsatisfactory in this respect. Clear understanding is rare; a broad spectrum stretches from misleading statements to momentous blunders. The two views, which should be neatly separated, are intermixed, in formulations as well as in elaborations. Here is one example to show the grave errors that are fairly common:

The students Arthur, Betty, and Cecily are arranged in a circle. The mappings are:

i = identity

a = Betty and Cecily interchange,

b = Arthur and Cecily interchange,

c = Arthur and Betty interchange,

r = everybody moves one place to the right,

l = everybody moves one place to the left.

This shows how it is mixed up: a, b, c are transfigurations, r and l are displacements. What emerges from this confusion is not a group at all. Since the author put up a multiplication table without checking associativity he was not aware that it was not a group. (Here you get, for instance, $b(ra) = l$, $(br)\,a = i$.)

The author of this example intermixed both kinds of mappings. The mappings he actually defined, act upon the set of pairs ⌜person, place⌝, where the persons can be Arthur, Betty, Cecily and the places, as it were, 12 o'clock, 4 o'clock, 8 o'clock if all is projected upon a dial. The set which is acted on by the transformations has nine elements. If permutations of the first and second component separately are admitted as mappings, a group of $6 \cdot 6 = 36$ elements arises, the direct product of two symmetric groups of three permutands.*

Among the didacticians who have moved into this domain, there are not all that many who know its ambushes. I must explicitly stress that the pioneer in this field, Z. Dienes, behaves correctly as far as I can see**. Whoever observe him experimenting with children, admire this great artist leading his pupil on a tight rope safely over the abyss. Those pupils are active on the bottom level. Apparently such guidance is bound to fail if the ones guided are adults who are used to being active at higher levels. They undergo Dienes' group theory games much less instinctively, which explains the errors in their practice and in some explanations, influenced by Dienes – errors which extend from misleading formulations to quite fundamental blunders.

Already with Venn diagrams we noticed the pitfalls of concretization at any price which endanger the textbook author earlier than the teacher, and the teacher earlier than the pupil.

Their effect was formal in the case of Venn diagrams, whereas here they influence the content. To avoid such pitfalls a conscious analysis like ours is not indispensable. A few people clear these hurdles instinctively. Crystallographers are usually well acquainted with both concretizations of mappings. In a crystal certain atoms are found at certain places; the crystallographic symmetries can be interpreted as permutations of the atoms as well as of the places. Both are allowed, only mixing them up leads to errors. Crystallographers know which didactic difficulties this implies.

An analogous difficulty was earlier discussed in the case of cogredience and contragredience. It is what I called the coordinate interpretation where after choosing an origin and a gauge, coordinates are assigned to the points of the straight line, and addition and multiplication are described as coordinate transformations. If on the line the numbers are

* Readers familiar with group theory will notice that the above example comes from reducing this group with respect to a subset that is not a normal subgroup; this explains the lack of associativity.
** Not all the publications that bear his name or refer to him are his responsibility.

imagined as numbered pawns, then what happens under transformations are transfigurations rather than displacements. Transformations of the substratum, however, with the coordinate system fixed, can hardly be circumvented or excluded from consideration, but after the coordinate interpretation of addition and multiplication this leads straight into a veritable swamp of confusion. Therefore I proposed to attach the numbers firmly to the number line (the object interpretation). If the objects are not numbers but pawns, however, interpreting a mapping as a trans-figuration is so natural that it is indispensable to mention it, at least in order to warn against it.

Crystallographers and skilled mathematicians instinctively know how to avoid such pitfalls. If, however, textbook authors or teachers are to be influenced to avoid mistakes, an analysis like the above one is in-dispensable. One would say that it cannot be part of explicit teaching but this is only correct as long as instruction in mappings and group theory topics is restricted to the bottom level, and if no more is required than that children can recognize two groups, one of displacements and one of transfigurations, as isomorphic. (In fact they are not isomorphic but anti-isomorphic, and it is only with questionable conjuring tricks that the experimenter succeeds in convincing the subjects of the iso-morphy.) Should children experience this isomorphy as a miracle, or should we try to give them at least a feeling for the more profound con-nections?

All I have explained here points to limits on didactical efforts in this domain. To work on the bottom level, schoolchildren should at least be able to abstract sufficiently places from objects or objects from places. To progress to a higher level the pupil must be able to perform, though not formulate, an analysis like ours. And to teach such a topic, the teacher is required to master such an analysis perfectly.

I would mention some other complications in which Dienes has involved this topic. Dienes usually deals with groups G of one-to-one-mappings of a set V onto itself of a kind that is called simply transitive, that is, such that to any pair x, y out of V there is exactly one element f of G with $fx = y$. Then G itself can be interpreted as a group as follows:

An element x_0 of V is singled out to define a group operation in V which has x_0 as its one-element, viz. to given $x, y \in V$ find $f, g \in G$ such that

$$fx_0 = x, \quad gx_0 = y,$$

and put

$$xy = fg \, x_0.$$

To show that this is a group, associativity and other characteristic group properties have to be checked. Finally an isomorphism from G to V is stated by

$$\Upsilon_f f x_0.$$

In his applications of this principle, Dienes starts with no names for the elements of G though he has given names to the elements of V. Afterwards he indicates the mapping of G that carries x_0 into x, by x. He even identifies the mapping that carries x_0 into x, with x. It requires a tremendous amount of mathematical technique to follow this lead and to understand why it works.

There is a great danger of confusion if the identification is made too early.

If the above is applied to the group of four, and Arthur is singled out as we did above with x_0, then the identity mapping gets the name Arthur, the mapping that maps Arthur on Betty, and Cecily on David, is called Betty, the mapping carrying Arthur into Cecily, and Betty into David, is called Cecily, and finally that one mapping Arthur on David, and Betty on Cecily, is called David. This leads straight to the multiplication table

Arthur	Betty	Cecily	David
Betty	Arthur	David	Cecily
Cecily	David	Arthur	Betty
David	Cecily	Betty	Arthur

Once again, it is not at all easy to understand why this works, and I have not got the impression that the fairly considerable number of people working in this field didactically have understood it properly, though in my opinion tackling such a theme can only be justified by the aim of understanding it. The main thing I would stress, however, is that the transition from the operator to the operand view of such mappings (which, in fact, is only possible in simply transitive groups) is didactically unusually troublesome. I mentioned this earlier* in the special cases of the addition and multiplication groups of the rational numbers. I am afraid that only a small minority of teachers will be able to transform this topic into an acceptable subject in school mathematics.

THE DEFINITION OF THE FUNCTION CONCEPT

Later I will come back to function notations; at present I will restrict myself to the definition. I do not mean, of course, "definition" in a formalist sense. I rather mean the process of defining, the psychological and didactical preparation of the concept of function, and its operational definition, that is the way in which we actually use the concept. It looks safer to say function presentation instead of function definition.

Though the term function comes from Leibniz, our function concept will hardly be found in Leibniz's work, and any function notation is com-

* See p. 261.

pletely lacking therein. Newton, Leibniz and Leibniz's disciples worked with what one would call magnitudes. The magnitudes x, y, z can vary, not independently but in a certain interdependence. If a certain increment dx is attributed to x, then *ceteris paribus* y changes by dy, and the quotient of dy and dx is a new magnitude, which is added to the given stock. The relations between the $x, y, z, \ldots$ are never or almost never explicitly indicated. Analysis was operated in this way in the 18th century, and since analytical mechanics originated from that time, this is still the prevailing style of mechanics: *the path* is differentiated after *the* time, *the* velocity after *the* time, but if need be, also *the* velocity after *the* path, and *the* path after *the* velocity; and what is actually meant is the path covered by a certain material point, and the instantaneous velocity of that point at a certain, variable moment. This method which prevails in other fields of physics too (though not in all of them and certainly not in the most modern) is naive but extremely practical; mathematicians should pay more attention to it to analyze and to transform it into a consistent apparatus. It is a pity that in the past century, mainly by Jacobi's intervention, this method has been contaminated by the function concept. The result has been a mixed inconsistent jargon, which has become obsolete among mathematicians. Nevertheless imperfect language can be an excellent means of communication. With a figure and a finger on the blackboard indications like "this point" and "that point" are easily understood by the listener, and poorly-formulated mathematical arguments, in physics say, are clear enough to everybody who associates with them the same intuitive ideas as the speaker's. Yet more often a trustworthy formalism is to be preferred above such roundabout and vague intuitive language.

Function notations first occur in Euler's and D'Alembert's work, in the investigation of the vibrating string. As a matter of fact, this is the first case of a differential equation solved by means of "arbitrary" functions. These, however, are isolated cases. Not until the textbooks of the 19th century, do systematic expositions of the function concept occur such as: a function is a law which assigns a number to every number of a certain domain. In 19th-century geometry the same concept popped up under the name of mapping or transformation but not until the 20th century did it become clear that functions are special transformations, and today both terms are used almost synonymously.

In the above definition of function the word "law" occurs. What is a law? Well, let us say "assignment" though it does not change much. A function (mapping) of R into S is known as soon as I know for every element of R the corresponding element of S. Thus a function is nothing else but a set of pairs with the first member taken from R and the second from S, a subset of $\lceil R, S \rceil$ which, however, must satisfy certain conditions. Another way of expressing this is to say that a function from R to S is a special relation between R and S, since in general subsets of $\lceil R, S \rceil$ are just called relations between R and S.

A remark on "relation" is perhaps useful in this context. Not long ago a relation was something like "... older than...", that is, a pattern which assigned to a pair of subjects (such as John and Mary) a proposition (John is older than Mary). To such a "relation" in the logical sense corresponds one in the set theory sense as soon as the subjects are restricted to certain sets R and S; then the pairs which verify the logical relation, form a set theory relation, though of course logical and set theory relation are not the same thing. It is a pity that mathematicians have stolen the term relation from the logicians who need it so badly.

This remark was not a useless digression. What is intended by the above word "law" is just a logical relation which, if requested to be true, assigns to every member of R a member of S. It is merely a nicety to translate this logical relation into a set-theory one, and it is nothing more than a nicety. The set theory definition of function is by no means more exact than the original one, if "law" is understood as a logical relation with such and such a property.

Most people would not agree. They object that "law" and "assignment" are vague concepts whereas "subset" should be a precise one, but actually they are deceiving themselves. Subsets of a given set are obtained by assignments, viz. of the symbols "yes" and "no" to the elements of the given set. So in fact they are functions with at most two values. Actually nobody knows what subsets are. In Foundations of Mathematics it becomes clear that the concept of subset is the fundamental obscurity of set theory. The reason why people prefer the definition of functions via relations is a self-deception: they falsely believe that this approach better satisfies the extensionalistic demands of modern mathematics.

How can we present the function concept didactically – along the first way ("a law ...") or the second ("a subset of...")? Let us view a few functions which may serve as examples. The function "licence number of car..." – should I first form the set of all pairs ⌐car, licence number⌐ and then single out which belongs to which? That is, should I first attach all possible licence numbers to all possible cars and then take off the wrong ones? Or should I simply say that every car has a number assigned to it, and that this assignment is called the function "licence number of..."? The only argument against the second formula is that it is dead simple whereas mathematics according to an old adage should be the art of complicating simple things. "Mother of...", "three times...", "upper limit of..." – all these functions show the same intuitive structure of mapping, of assigning, which can only be obscured by a general relation concept, be it of logical or set-theory character.

This is my first point. Point two is the composition of functions. It can reasonably be motivated only by a mapping approach; in the realm of general relations it is an arbitrary unintelligible operation.

Point three is the most important. The relation definition of function is, both as regards content and notation, never applied. This I have verified with many books. Once introduced it may readily be forgotten, and it is not even recalled in such cases where it could successfully be applied. Well, there is one exception – certain school texts offer exercises to drill this definition, of course only to be buried when the exercises are finished.

This is a fatal consequence of bad didactics. Something that obviously cannot be put to any reasonable use develops, because it should be exercised, into an autonomous chapter of school mathematics which does not have anything to do with true mathematics. It is a sad fact that such a subject, once introduced, grows a tradition which can attain great longevity.

WHERE DO RELATIONS APPLY?

Because quite a few didacticians believe (wrongly) the relation concept to be more fundamental and more general than the function concept and because according to some teaching philosophies the more fundamental and the more general gets priority in teaching, they derive in teaching the function from the relation. Consequently they must offer an extensive treatment of relations first. Where are, in fact, relations encountered when the reality is organized by mathematical means? Examples do not grow on every tree. Indeed, relations differ from functions in that they do not play any role in applications. In a few languages relation means kinship*, and consequently textbook authors plunge into kinship relations, not in order to explain mathematical relations but rather to exploit pedigrees as a fertile field and an aim in itself. Clearly this is straying far from serious mathematics and from applying mathematics seriously. It has nothing to do with mathematical model building; it is a false pretence of mathematical structure. These are quite aimless exercises.

The reason why the relation hardly plays a role in applications is that, viewed from science, it has a mainly registering character. The father-son relation is a mere catalogue as is the <-relation in an ordered set. What matters in science are not descriptive catalogues, but connections, between lightning and thunder, between smoking and cancer, between the height of father and son (e.g. whether sons are taller than their fathers). It is not the relation father-son that matters, e.g. the catalogue of the father-son pairs, but rather the connection between two properties of the pair; in general, the connection between two or more aspects of a situation (smoking and cancer, sunspots and magnetic storms). This connection is not described by a relation but by what is usually called a correlation. This means, not registering *whether* but counting *how often* smoking or non-smoking is paired with cancer or non-cancer; not registering *whether* somebody is somebody's son but counting *how often* a certain height of fathers is paired with a certain height of sons. As the *function* testifies for the *causal* structure of the world, so does the *correlation* for its *stochastic* structure. In this realm the relation as such means nothing.

Should we start with relations early on? I agree that funny games can be played with kinship relations, but I do not see much connection between these games and mathematics. Certainly it is a good exercise to look why the brother relation is transitive and the half-brother relation is not, or to reduce the brother relation by means of quantifiers to the father and mother function. Certainly at a certain moment properties of relations such as reflexivity and transitivity must be analyzed, but this should not happen until such properties can be illustrated efficiently. In mathe-

* In Dutch the corresponding word means business connection. This is *our* peculiar difficulty if we must teach our children what relations are in mathematics.

matics many functions merit special attention and a proper name; very few relations are as important.

Of course there do occur relations in mathematics, but strangely enough the cases in which relations could really be useful are never used, as far as I know, to illustrate relations. I mean combinatorial problems, which earlier* have been mentioned in another context. For instance: How many diagonals does a n-gon have?

We are given an incidence relation between the set A of the n vertices, and the set B of the m diagonals. Each of the n elements of A is incident with $n - 3$ elements of B, each element of B with two elements of A. Therefore $(n - 3)\, n = 2m$, which delivers the value of m. Or:

The cube has 8 corners which form a set A, and 12 edges which form a set B. The incidence is a relation between A and B. Each of the 8 elements of A is incident with three of B, and each of the 12 elements of B is incident with two of A. One verifies $8 \cdot 3 = 12 \cdot 2$.

Here relations can be put into a meaningful and not *ad hoc* context. Of course, this can never be a reason for introducing relations early, and no argument at all to deal with them extensively in an early stage. To introduce the function concept, relations can be dismissed. In fact functions can even precede sets.

A SIDE-LEAP TO CATEGORIES

An important concept in set theory is the ordered pair – from two objects a, b one forms the ordered pair $\ulcorner a, b \urcorner$ that for $a \neq b$ is well-distinguished from $\ulcorner b, a \urcorner$. I considered it as so obvious that this concept must be introduced in the naive fashion that I would never have thought about mentioning it if I had not found a set theory sophistication on this point in a textbook.

What does this "ordered pair $\ulcorner a, b \urcorner$" mean? Clearly that one thinks of first a and then b in this order and communicates them accordingly. Well, "first-then" is no set theory concept. In set theory everything should be reduced to the $\in$-relation. There is, however, a secondary order relation, the inclusion, which for its part can be reduced to the $\in$-relation.

Somebody therefore contrived the trick of defining the ordered pair $\ulcorner a, b \urcorner$ as the set

* See p. 190, 249.

$$\{\{a\}, \ \{a, b\}\}.$$

Since then $\ulcorner c, d \urcorner$ becomes

$$\{\{c\}, \ \{c, d\}\},$$

we get $\ulcorner a, b \urcorner = \ulcorner c, d \urcorner$ if and only if

$$a = c \land b = d.$$

This is a clever artifice. It has one disadvantage, that is, you are allowed to forget it immediately because the only thing that counts for the ordered pair is

$$\ulcorner a, b \urcorner = \ulcorner c, d \urcorner \leftrightarrow [(a = c) \land (b = d)].$$

Do not worry. You can prevent your pupils from forgetting it: you can make them do three pages exercises on this trick and, to be safe, you can repeat these exercises periodically.

Something is wrong here, and not only from a didactical point of view. Definitions should be operational; fundamental definitions that can be immediately forgotten are simply wrong. This is, no doubt, one of the basic principles of modern mathematics. A thing must be defined by its directions of use. Maybe we do not always succeed in realizing this demand but we do consider every improvement in this respect as progress.

If the naive approach is not enough, the definition of the ordered pair can be formalized to a higher degree though it still expresses the operational task of the ordered pair: one postulates the existence of two universal functions ω_1, ω_2 (read: first member of..., second member of...), defined for some objects and such that it holds that

to any a, b there is one thing c such that $\omega_1 c = a$, $\omega_2 c = b$.
This c is denoted by $\ulcorner a, b \urcorner$.

Those who swear on the sets dogma may object that this introduction of ordered pair involves the concept of function, whereas a function should be introduced as a relation, that is a subset of a set of ordered pairs. They believe that is *dernier cri*. This is true, but unfortunately it is old-fashioned *dernier cri*. Though I already stressed this earlier, I will illustrate it in that context where people usually mutter or shout the word category.

If the direct product of two groups G_1 and G_2 must be defined, one first takes the set of pairs $\ulcorner G_1, G_2 \urcorner$, that is, the set of pairs $\ulcorner g, h \urcorner$ with $g \in G_1$, $h \in G_2$ and endows it with a group structure, to wit

$$\ulcorner g_1, h_1 \urcorner \cdot \ulcorner g_2, h_2 \urcorner = \ulcorner g_1 g_2, h_1 h_2 \urcorner.$$

If afterwards one asks what is really used about the direct product, it appears to be the following:

If in F one forgets about the second (first) factor, one just gets the structure of the group $G_1(G_2)$; forgetting the second (first) factor must be a homomorphism of $\ulcorner G_1, G_2 \urcorner$ on $G_1(G_2)$. Or, in a more formal wording:–

(0) *there are homomorphisms ω_i of F on G_i.*

Of course, this is not enough. If the group F' is homomorphically mapped by Φ upon F, then F' (instead of F) and the $\omega_i \Phi$ (instead of ω_i) also fulfill postulate (0).

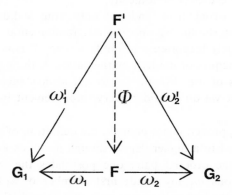

F must also fulfill a minimality condition:

(2) *If the ω_i' are homomorphisms of any F' upon the G_i, then there is a* unique homomorphism Φ of F' in F such that $\omega_i \Phi = \omega_i'$.

As soon as this is added (0) can be weakened to get

(1) *there are homomorphisms ω_i of F in the G_i.*

Of course the existence of such an F, that is, of the product, must again be proved, but then one proves more, namely the operational properties (1) and (2).

To this definition of direct product there exists what is called a dual, obtained by inverting all arrows. Let G_1, G_2 be groups. The *free product* of G_1, G_2 is a group F such that

(1') G_i is homomorphically mapped into F by means of an ω_i,

(2') to every group F' with homomorphisms ω_i' of G_i into F there is a unique homomorphism of F in F' with $\Phi\omega_i = \omega_i'$

This means that from G_1, G_2 a new group G must be combined without new relations; the new group should be, as it were, maximal.

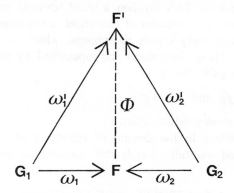

This defining by universal properties and of dualizing is a pattern which repeats itself with linear spaces, rings, algebras, and so on. In the theory of categories all these are generalized.

A category consists of *objects* and *morphisms* (e.g. groups and homomorphisms). To two objects A, B belongs a system $[B, A]$ of morphisms from A to B; to two morphisms

$$f \in [C, B], \quad g \in [B, A],$$

there is exactly one morphism

$$fg \in [C, A];$$

it is required that

$$(fg) h = f(gh)$$

as far as the expressions exist; further to every object A there is one morphism 1_A such that

$$f1_A = f, \quad 1_A g = g$$

as far as existent.

I will not enter into categories. They are not yet mature enough for school, even not for the first year of the university. At least, I do not know any representation of categories which does not presuppose a thorough understanding of mathematics. In particular, there is not the slightest indication how proofs of very simple facts from group theory and linear algebra can be made more conspicuous by means of categories. I mentioned categories here as an illustration of the trend towards operational definitions. This involves a trend towards mappings rather than sets. A typical embodiment of this trend is the object-free version of categories, which only knows morphisms, which can be multiplied with each other. There the objects are superseded by units, that is by those morphisms ε that fulfill

$$\varepsilon f = f \quad \text{and} \quad g\varepsilon = g$$

as far as the involved products exist.

Those who believe in the dogma of reduction of mathematics to set theory should carefully weigh this operational evidence against sets.

A CONTROVERSY ON FUNCTIONS

From higher mathematical literature I know the term function only as a synonym, or near-synonym, of the term mapping. The term function is usually preferred if the range of the mapping is a number set (maybe a vector set). Until recently I did not know any other terminology. I was greatly astonished at certain reactions to a short article I had written in a journal* because as I understood them, they were far off the mark. The explanation came much later, in a course of further teacher training. To my greatest surprise I learned in this course what the big problem is that pervades discussions on teaching sets and functions. It is the problem whether a function from A to B must be defined everywhere in A. The people who read my paper on functions tacitly assumed that I could not deal with any other problem on functions and consequently interpreted my article from this viewpoint, which came well-nigh close to a catastrophe.

The terminology in which a function from A to B is a relation that to

---

* *Euclides* **41** (1966), 299–304.

every element of A assigns *at most* one element of B seems to have been introduced by French or Belgian school texts. According to this definition a function from A to B may even be void. Until recently I had never even noticed this terminology. It was created by school mathematics to satisfy certain needs or pretended needs of school mathematics, I was told. How to formulate the task "draw the graphics of the function f with $f(x) = (1/x^2)$ $(x \in \mathbf{R})$"? I would reply – "precisely as I have done". But would pupils not be allowed to answer the problem by saying "there is no function from $\mathbf{R}$ to $\mathbf{R}$ with $f(x) = 1/x$"? No, because though the statement is correct, it does not answer the given problem. I did not ask "draw the graphics of the function f from $\mathbf{R}$ to $\mathbf{R}$ that satisfies $f(x) = 1/x^2$". A function f from A to B consists of three things: the sets A and B, and a certain part of $\ulcorner A, B \urcorner$. If you are asked to find a function, you must find out those three things. I agree that a lot of functions would be allowed as answers to the above question, namely any part of $\mathbf{R} \backslash \{0\}$ as a set A. To avoid this we could agree that *the* function with a certain property is that with the largest domain. There are ambiguities left with respect to B, which could be any set between $\{x \in \mathbf{R} \mid x > 0\}$ and $\mathbf{R}$. We could agree that we do not care about B or that we take B minimal.

In higher mathematics the usual terminology under such circumstances is: let f be the function with $f(x) = 1/x^2$ as far as meaningful $(x \in \mathbf{R})$.

Of course, the other interpretation, according to which the function from A to B need not be defined everywhere in A, is quite attractive, and it would have been a good thing if in an earlier stage of modern mathematics somebody had hit upon the idea to distinguish between functions and mappings. It did not happen, and I am not sure whether it would be wise to change the terminology now. Anyhow, this "big problem" is not even a little problem, and it is really too bad that by its mere existence it detracts the attention of educators from real problems.

THE FUNCTION NOTATION

In the last twenty-five years mathematical language has greatly changed – I mean both the language of formulas and the language around the formulas. As an afterthought one is surprised why this has taken so much time. However, even mathematicians do not throw old shoes away unless they are sure they already have new ones that do not pinch.

Familiar expressions and notations are preserved as long as possible, often even longer, and innovations are only accepted if they are overdue. Traditionally a function was indicated by $f(x)$ or by $y = f(x)$ or by $F(x, y) = 0$, and often it was not even clear which was a function of which.

This traditional notation was unproblematic as long as mathematicians studied one single function at a time. With functional analysis, with homotopy in topology, and gradually in more and more domains of research, single functions were superseded by sets, rings, ideals of functions. How can we express that a function belongs to a set A of functions? $f(x) \in A$ asserts something about the belonging to A, not of the function but of the function values, and $(y = f(x)) \in A$ or $(F(x, y) = 0) \in A$ would be sheer nonsense. The only solution is to indicate the intended function by f and its belonging to A by $f \in A$. This is one argument out of a host to show the inconsistency of certain badly-designed older function notations. The function, which assigns to every man his mother is now indicated by "mother of…" instead of "mother of x", the function, which assigns $f(x)$ to x, by f, the function which assigns log x to x, by log.

But what about the function which assigns $x^2 - 3x + 2$ to x? How can we express that the variable x in this expression should be bound? Sometimes it is done by circumlocution, e.g.

let f be the function defined by

$$(1) \qquad f(x) = x^2 - 3x + 2 \, .$$

This is a roundabout procedure which cannot be maintained in the long run.

Others prefer

$$(2) \qquad x \to x^2 - 3x + 2 \, ;$$

logicians are accustomed to Church's λ,

$$(3) \qquad (\lambda x)\,(x^2 - 3x + 2) \, .$$

I like better Russell's

$$(4) \qquad \check{x}(x^2 - 3x + 2) \, ,$$

though, afterwards, for typographical reasons, I put the ʏ upon a pole, thus writing

$$(5) \qquad \curlyvee_x(x^2 - 3x + 2) \, .$$

The domain of the variable can be easily indicated, e.g.

$$Y_{3 \leqslant x < 4}(x^2 - 3x + 2).$$

With the notation (2) this would not be possible. By (3) the otherwise indispensable letter λ is earmarked; this is a serious disadvantage. The symbol used in (4) is closer to the usual binding devices such as $\vee$ and $\wedge$, whereas (1) and (2) are quite abnormal and not flexible enough as follows from the next examples.

Let R be a vector space. Then

$$Y_x(x + a)$$

is the translation over the vector a.

$$Y_a Y_x(x + a)$$

is the, often required, mapping which assignes to a vector a the translation along a.

According to method (1) this should be formalized as follows:
Let T_a be defined by

$$T_a x = x + a \quad \text{for} \quad x \in R.$$

Then T is defined by

$$T a = T_a \quad \text{for all} \quad a \in R.$$

According to (2) the mapping should be defined by

$$a \rightarrow (x \rightarrow x + a),$$

which is difficult to read, in particular if the expressions are still more involved.

An analogous example, let G be a group. Then

$$Y_x \, a x a^{-1}$$

is an inner automorphism of G.

$$Y_a Y_x \, a x a^{-1}$$

then is an important homomorphism mapping G into its group of inner automorphisms.

Another example: f is a function of a real variable,

$$Y_x f(x - a)$$

the same function shifted over the distance a to the right,

$$Y_f Y_x f(x - a)$$

the shift over a, and

$$Y_a Y_f Y_x f(x - a)$$

the mapping which assigns to a the shift over a.

A notation for transforming an expression into a function symbol is badly needed. In the long run it simply cannot be dispensed with. I have made the above proposal; at present I am not acquainted with better solutions. Likewise, decent notations should be agreed on to terminate the present confusion on braces; on this, too, I have made proposals which, however, I will not discuss now.

What does this mean for teaching? Should the Y-sign be introduced at school? The answer is quite simple. I adduced three examples for the use of the Y-sign, in particular for its iterative use. These examples very well describe the advantages it has above other notations. Such or a similar sign should be introduced in school instruction when and where it becomes operational in the sense of these examples. Offering non-operational formal matter should be avoided everywhere.

CHAPTER XVI

THE CASE OF GEOMETRY*

First of all do not get bewitched by the diabolic charm of geometry; nothing can more extinguish in you the internal spirit of grace, of meditation and of mortification.

Oeuvres Complètes de Fénélon, VIII, 519 (ed. Paris 1852)

We see by experience that among equal minds and all other things being equal, he who possesses geometry, conquers and acquires an entirely new rigour.

B. Pascal, *Pensées et opuscules*, Hachette, p. 165, Note

The early study of Euclid made me a hater of Geometry, which I hope may plead my excuses if I have shocked the opinions of any in this room (and I know there are some who rank Euclid as second in sacredness to the Bible alone, and as one of the advanced outposts of the British Constitution) by the tone in which I have previously alluded to it as a schoolbook; and yet, in spite of this repugnance, which had become a second nature in me, whenever I went far enough into any mathematical question, I found I touched, at last, a geometrical bottom.

J. J. Sylvester, *The collected math. papers*, II, 660

During the last few years some determined efforts have been made to displace Euclid's Elements in our schools, but the majority of experienced teachers still regard it as the best foundation of geometrical thinking that has yet been published.

W. W. Rouse Ball, *A Short History of Mathematics*, 1888, p. 51

For a long time mathematics has been synonymous with geometry. In fact there have always existed other branches too, algebra, trigonometry, calculus, which, however, were not much more than collections of haphazard, badly founded rules, whereas geometry was a perfect conceptual system, where things rigorously followed from each other, and finally everything from definitions and axioms. Though other techniques were more proficient, geometry was genuine truth. But the high esteem in which geometry stood faded away. By their axiomatic systems Pasch and Hilbert revealed many gaps in classical geometry. On the other hand the Pasch-Hilbert style axiomatics were so complicated that you could just read them or do foundational research about them,

---

* Parts of this chapter were printed in *Educational Studies* **3** (1971) 413–435.

but you could not do geometry *within* them, and, in any case, could not teach geometry *with* them.

Once, geometry was not only an overpowering piece of deductive science; it was the oldest and most outspoken example of didactics. The first lesson on record was the experimental lesson Socrates taught Meno's slave before the eyes of his master, though Plato's report of this may be fictional. It is not by accident that the content of this Socratic lesson was geometry. Even today geometry would be an excellent theme of the Socratic method and of reinvention; in this respect it is equalled by probability only.

The deductive structure of traditional geometry has not just been a didactical success. People today believe geometry failed because it was not deductive enough. In my opinion, the reason was rather that this deductivity was not taught as reinvention, as Socrates did, but that it was imposed on the learner. Anyhow some people today preach and exhibit the abolition of geometry. Among those who should introduce youth to their cultural heritage, there are quite a few who would gladly thrust geometry in the cultural incinerator. The days of traditional geometry are counted, if at all it still survives in some places. What is destined to follow it? This urgent question stands behind the title of this chapter. The case of geometry – has it been sentenced to death, and did it get a fair trial? Has it rightfully been sentenced or on false evidence? Has the defendant been left without counsel? Should not the investigative procedures be reopened?

If today there is cause to be concerned about the future of geometry instruction and even to be afraid that geometry could disappear from the curriculum, then the first to be blamed are those who, actively or passively, have resisted the innovation of mathematical instruction. The voices of those who advocated renewal were not heard. The most dangerous group were those who believed they could save the old geometry by reinforcing its deductive structure; this was a hopeless task, indeed. Geometry is not only deductivity.

WHAT IS GEOMETRY?

Such questions can be answered on different levels. On the highest, geometry, somehow axiomatically organized is a certain part of mathematics that for some historical reason is called geometry. Mindful of the educational principles I have advocated, I would rather ask what geometry is on the lowest, the bottom level? There can be no doubt what I should then answer – geometry is grasping space. And since it is about the education of children, it is grasping that space in which the child lives, breathes and moves. The space that the child must learn to know, explore, conquer, in order to live, breathe and move better in it. Are we so accustomed to this space that we cannot imagine how important it is for us and for those we are educating? Well, let it be important – yet some may answer – but it is not important for geometry. Geometry, in fact, is mathematics, and as such it asks for more solid foundations than a living space which at least as an object of physical research is suspect to a genuine mathematician.

Geometry – science of space, of physical space. Does it not sound old-fashioned? You probably cannot believe that today a mathematician would dare to utter such claims. If physical space is that important, let the physicists take it up. Are we not mathematicians? Are we not the architects of mathematical structures, and if physicists or anybody else can use them, let them take what they want. The quicksand of reality is no basis to build a mathematical system; mathematics should be protected against any contamination with non-deductive germs. The mathematical system is paramount, and if the system requires that geometry starts with the affine plane, then physical space with its solids, its distances, its fittings can only be an obstacle on the road to good mathematics.

That is one philosophy, and in certain respects it can be a good philosophy. Those who are busy building deductive systems should be able to close their eyes to the seductions of reality, they should be able to forget what a triangle looks like in reality, that you can make a wooden triangle and move it all around. There are, however, other activities than building deductive systems. There are students who will never build deductive systems of their own or even rebuild those of others, though they must still learn mathematics. We cannot impose that philosophy on them.

Arbitrarily, just as they occurred to me, I have noted down a number of questions that may arise if one sets out to investigate space:

Why does a piece of paper fold along a straight line?

Why does a rolled piece of paper become rigid?

Why does a tied paper ribbon show a regular pentagon?

How do shadows originate?

What is the intersection of a plane and a sphere, of two spheres?

What kind of curve is the terminator on the moon?

Why can the radius of a circle be transferred six times around its periphery?

How come a beautiful star arises by this construction?

Why is the straight line the shortest?

Why do congruent triangles fit to cover the plane and why do congruent pentagons in general fail to do so?

How can people measure great distances on the earth, the diameter of the earth, and distances of celestial bodies?

What does a cube look like if viewed along a spatial diagonal?

What is larger, the superficies of a sphere cap, or that of the cylinder around it?

What is the shortest path for a light ray to travel from one point to another while touching a mirror?

How does a kaleidoscope work?

What is the biggest sphere in a tetrahedron?

Which kind of closed curves are equally as wide in all directions?

How does the liquid level in some vessel change if a certain quantity of liquid is added?

What is the relation between the real and apparent size of a body?

If a cube is split into six square pyramids with their vertices in the center and these pyramids are turned outside upon the corresponding faces, why does a rhombododecahedron arise?

How can you measure the inclination of a line and a plane, or of two planes?

Is there a horizontal (a vertical) line in every plane?

Which automorphisms are admitted by a square lattice in the plane?

How many points can a plane lattice possess on the unit circle if it has at most the origin within the unit circle?

What is the difference between a right and a left screw and why are they not equivalent under rigid motions?

What is a rigid motion on the sphere?

Why is a convex polyhedron rigid?

Why can a table with four legs wobble, and what is the difference with a table with three legs?

Why does a door need two hinges, and how can we add a third?

And finally the old question: why does a mirror interchange right and left though not above and below and what happens if I am not standing but lying in front of the mirror?

Notice that I did not ask any questions of practical use. My task would have been much simpler if I had done so. Notice, too, that there were no 'puzzles' in the list, but only questions of principal importance, which nevertheless can be answered with little ingenuity. They are meant to explain to those who do not know or do not believe it what grasping space by geometry involves. Earlier I insisted on how important it is that mathematics should be closely tied to reality when it is to be learned. No other approach can in general guarantee a lasting influence of mathematics on the learner. We mathematicians do not forget our mathematics because it is our principal business. What is unrelated to our living world fades away from memory. For the majority mathematics cannot be a goal; unrelatedly learned pieces of mathematics are forgotten and thus become uninfluential. If it starts of as grasping physical space, geometry is closely related to a reality that day by day presents itself to the mind. If understood in this way, geometry can be an excellent means to teach mathematics fraught with relations.

I would not claim that the interpretation of geometry as advocated here is new. On the contrary, there have long been mathematicians and didacticians who defended this approach to geometry against the deductive one. Clairaut's marvellous *Eléments de géométrie* of 1741 is witness to this. In the Netherlands from the nineteen-twenties onwards Tatiana Ehrenfest-Afanassjewa, wife and collaborator of the famous physicist Paul Ehrenfest, propagated this approach to geometry in papers and working groups. The *Übungensammlung zu einer geometrischen Propädeuse* (Den Haag 1931) has not yet been exhausted as a wealthy source of geometrical exercises. Tatiana Ehrenfest's influence, though primarily restricted to a small circle, has been a lasting one. One can imagine the contemporary objections against her propedeutic geometry – on the one hand the cry "that is experimental physics rather than mathematics", on the other "how can a teacher maintain discipline in a classroom where the children are walking around, counting paces, measuring distances, taking aims, and handling glue and scissors?" Her demand that geometry should start in space was hardly taken seriously at that time; today there is in my country hardly anyone left to deny it. "How can you dare speak about spheres to children who do not know a decent definition of a straight line?", was one of the objections. Her demand that in early geometry instruction one should not prove things that are obvious to the naked eye is as generally accepted today.

Tatiana Ehrenfest did not reject deductivity. She knew about mathematical axiomatics and cultivated it, but as a physicist she was as well acquainted with the strong interferences of space theories with physics. The goal of her geometry was a deductive system that had been influenced by Helmholtz's axiomatics. In this respect, too, she was more modern than most of her contemporaries. In fact, today such an approach would be preferred above the Pasch-Hilbert contraption.

WHY GEOMETRY INSTRUCTION?

The problem of use and aim in teaching geometry is not too much different from that in mathematics in general though some points would be stressed differently. Geometry on the one hand was always considered more as a discipline of mind than any other part of mathematics for it could boast of closer relations to logic. Genuine deductivity was the privilege of geometry whereas the business of algebra was substituting into, and transforming formulae. On the other hand, the criterion of use, though relevant in other parts of mathematics, entirely failed in geometry. A pragmatic programme for geometry could remain restricted to a small treasure of theorems like the Pythagorean, a few obvious theorems on similar figures and a few formulae for perimeters, areas and volumes. A pragmatic approach would not require a logical system of geometry as prescribed by the Euclidean tradition. Nevertheless, the abolition of geometry as a topic of instruction has not been demanded on the ground of pragmatic arguments. Whoever today is advocating abolishing geometry, would teach much more useless things; rather than blaming geometry for its logical system, he is dissatisfied with geometry because it is too weak a system.

If geometry as a logical system is to be imposed upon the student it would indeed be better abolished. There are more conclusive systems than any system of geometry that could be contrived. Geometry can only be meaningful if it exploits the relation of geometry to the experienced space. If the educator shirks this duty, he throws away an irretrievable chance. Geometry is one of the best opportunities that exists to learn how to mathematize reality. It is an opportunity to make discoveries, as examples will show. To be sure, numbers are also a realm open to investigation, thinking can be learned by computing, but discoveries made by one's own eyes and hands are more convincing and surprising. Until they can somehow be dispensed with, the shapes in space are an indispensable guide to investigation and discovery.

There is still more to it than that. In 1956 I expressed it as follows: geometry, as a logical system, is a means – perhaps even the most powerful means – to make children feel the strength of the human spirit, that is, of their own spirit.

I continued: if this really is our goal, teaching geometry is an unparalleled struggle between ideal and realization. I do not know whether a child engaged in his mathematical problems ever reached the conclusion that mathematics has been the work of outstanding human geniuses, but in any case, I am pretty certain that mathematics is rather than anything else a means to convince children of their own mental inferiority.

CONCRETE MATERIAL

I quote the van Hieles*:

The use of concrete material at the beginning of teaching geometry is often misinterpreted. People who advocate a concrete start, as well as others who object against it, often speak of an "experimental method". This means that they view the use of concrete material as a step from teaching geometry as a theoretical science to teaching geometry as an experimental science. But at the introductory stage geometry is not a science. If pupils try to pave a floor with congruent triangles, they do not attempt something which can be called an experiment in the sense of experimental technics. They will not check whether every part fits, they will finish building as soon as they grasp the total structure, and they will not repeat it with other triangles.

In fact, if experimental geometry means that the student makes experiments, then a great part of his mathematical activity should be experimental, as is the activity of the creative mathematician. If it should remind us of experimental physics, it is wholly mistaken. Maybe the

* In H. Freudenthal, *Report on Methods of Initiation into Geometry*, 1958, p. 76.

term "experimental geometry" evokes associations like putting a string around a circle or weighing a cut-out circle to determine its perimeter and area. For a certain period this dull pastime (which leads nowhere) was cultivated under the name of mensuration – its summit was a catalogue of formulae. However, the initiating into geometry meant here, is a bottom level activity to prepare the child for higher levels. The attitude of children toward the concrete material differs entirely from what would be expected in physics teaching, and from the realism of the physics laboratory. This is shown by the example mentioned in the above quotation. Just as typical is the following. In the first geometry lesson in Dina van Hiele's classroom, the children (12-year-olds) had to make drawings of sidewalks paved with square flagstones. One of the children drew stones with fissures and with sandgrains in the grooves between the stones. One word was enough to teach the child that such features did not belong to the context of geometry.

Since Tatiana Ehrenfest many kinds of concrete material have been designed to use in the introductory teaching of geometry. I have taken a closer look at those of the van Hieles and of van Albada*. Today the choice is much greater. Paperfolding, cutting, glueing, drawing, painting, measuring, paving, and fitting are all organized as geometrical activities.

What is most important is how the material is used. Indeed, it should not be mere playing. According to Dina van Hiele's formulation the aim of the concrete material is the thinking action of the child. Hand and brain work together in order to answer the question how a particular thing is made. If definitions are given at this stage, they will often be genetic ones, that is, telling how the thing to be defined is made. If later such definition is reformulated in a more formal way, the new definition should be connected to the old one. The later logical development should be rooted in the concrete material.

It is quite natural that geometry teaching with concrete material starts in space. I have already mentioned that this approach has now been generally accepted in my country. It is not in the classical tradition – for not until the 11th book does Euclid touch geometry in space (it is worthwhile noting the paradox that those who fight Euclid the most arduously are his most obedient imitators). Traditional geometry instruc-

---

* See the report quoted in the footnote on p. 407.

tion used to start with plane geometry in the 7th grade to reach space in the 10th or 11th. It was not unusual that students with a satisfactory performance in plane geometry failed in space. Their spacial imagination had been deadened by too much and too one-sided exercise of plane geometry.

How concrete material can be used is shown in the course reported in Dina van Hiele's thesis*, though the central part of this thesis was intended as a piece of didactical research.

DINA VAN HIELE'S EXPERIMENTS

The experiments took place with two parallel classes (the first form of the secondary school, i.e. 7th grade, twelve-year-olds).

The teacher showed the children cubes made of various material. With a meccano cube the children learned the notions of edge and corner. They counted the edges and the corners. They stated that the cube is bounded by six squares. They noticed how these squares have to be drawn in a connected pattern. They made such a cube. They became acquainted with the tools of geometry. How can one make a right angle? Double folding produces a right angle.

In a meccano cube string diagonals were tied. There are two kinds, which got names. On a cardboard cube the surface diagonals were drawn, counted and measured. How can one measure the space diagonals precisely? The top of the cardboard cube had not been fastened. In the teacher's cube a diagonal plane was fixed. It was a rectangle. The pupils understood how it could be constructed and how by this means the space diagonal could be measured. The rectangle was constructed. The children counted in how many ways it could be fitted into the cube.

They made a regular tetrahedron; in making it they learned how to get an equilateral triangle. Which kind of triangles are there in the square set? They found that these were not equilateral but right ones.

The teacher gave the students a network of a regular octahedron with a diagonal plane in it; the students made it.

Then symmetries were dealt with. The right half of a vase was drawn on

* Dina van Hiele-Geldof, *De didactiek van de meetkunde in de eerste klas van het V.H.M.O.*, 1957. See also the earlier quoted Report, Footnote on p. 407.

the blackboard. The children understood what this meant. They supplied the other half and then checked the drawing with a mirror. From the analysis of this procedure the children proceeded on to systematic constructions of symmetries in the plane. Then numerous other symmetric figures and bodies were dealt with. How can one find the centre of a circle?

Peripheries of circles were measured and compared. Precision of measuring, rounding off, and estimating were discussed. A regular hexagon was inscribed in the circle. The ratio of periphery and diameter must exceed 3. A circumscribed square showed that 4 was too much. Therefore some of the measurements must be wrong.

With four pencils of equal length they made a quadrangle that was not a square. Many examples of rhombs were found. Hinging models were shown. Paper rhombs were folded; they have two symmetry axes. Other properties of the rhomb were formulated.

The rhomb was the starting point for constructions. First the children drew arbitrary rhombs in their exercise books, then the position was prescribed (one corner given, and the two adjoining corners on a given line; the last corner is the mirror image of the first with respect to the line).

Mirror reflecting of plane figures was then systematically exercized. Beautiful figures were drawn and analyzed. Regular hexagonal prisms and regular octagonal pyramids were made. Notions as height and median were acquired. The kite figure was systematically used, in particular in constructions on a restricted drawing paper.

A few lessons were devoted to angles. Angles were shown by movements of the arms rather than defining what is an angle. A clock was used for examples. The protractor was introduced. Notions depending on angles were discussed.

This brought the first schoolterm to a close. What now follows is the main part of Dina van Hiele's thesis, a somewhat literal report on the second schoolterm. Instead of reproducing the highly informative didactical details, I shall restrict myself to a sketch of its contents. The second schoolterm was devoted to "Tiles".

The first lesson started with discussing congruence. The teacher's first examples were the congruent chairs in the class room. (Traditional school geometry knows congruent triangles only.) After a few wrong explanations ("equal areas") the students arrived at the understanding of congruence – "objects that cannot be distinguished."

A sidewalk has to be paved with congruent square tiles. All the pupils immediately drew long straight lines. Different patterns were discussed. In the patterns parallel lines were discovered; they need not be horizontal or vertical.

In the second lesson the teacher showed on the blackboard how to draw parallels. Starting from the star hexagon she drew a rhomb pattern and the children copied it. One child saw cubes in the pattern.

Third lesson: the teacher distributed sets of congruent regular cardboard polygons. The children were given the task of covering a plane with such congruent tiles. Is it possible with triangles, quadrangles, pentagons, hexagons, octagons? If so, they were to draw such a pavement. (To draw the pentagon they were allowed to use a protractor.)

Fourth lesson: sets of irregular cardboard polygons.

Fifth lesson: why does it not work with regular pentagons?

Sixth lesson: the pavement with triangles can be changed so as to contain only one system of parallel through lines. There are no through lines in the pavement with irregular quadrangles. The children discover all kind of structures in the triangular pavement. Equal angles are marked by the same colour. The sum of the angles of a triangle is discovered; in any corner the angle of 180° occurs in three ways. An analogous property of quadrangles. Would it have been possible to predict this property of the quadrangle? Why does it not work with regular pentagons?

Seventh lesson: the triangular pavement contains parallelograms – parallelograms are now discussed. Parallelograms of different size are discovered in the pavement. Enlargements are discussed and the trapezium. Paving with hexagons? The sum of the angles exceeds 360°. Sometimes it works – would it work with some kind of pentagons? Nonconvex quadrangles are considered.

In the eighth lesson the conclusions obtained till now with respect to the sums of angles and pavings are assembled in logical trees. (*Not with every* pentagon can the plane be paved.) The structures in pavements are considered anew. "Ladders" and "saws" are discovered in the pavements.

The ninth lesson treats "Ladder" and "saw" as organizing devices for the relations between angles at parallel lines.

The tenth lesson deals with logical organization of the relations between parallelism, "ladder" and "saw", sum of the angles of a triangle.

The eleventh to the seventeenth lesson includes enlargements in pavings, rotations, systematic counting of tiles, areas, similarity, and systematizing definitions.

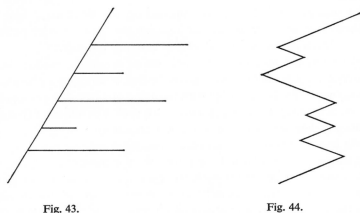

Fig. 43.   Fig. 44.

So far the teaching content of the second term. In the third term the children returned to the cube. The diagonal plane divided the cube into two prisms, and the pupils made models of such prisms. The teacher showed a regular pyramid with the face square of the cube as its basis and with half the edge of the cube as its height. How many of this pyramids fill the cube? How can these pyramids be made? How long are the side edges? The pyramids were then constructed by the children.

What about the volumes of these prisms and pyramids? One such pyramid was stuck upon every single face of the cube. What kind of body arises? What about the volume of the rhombododecahedron?

Regular bodies and halfregular bodies were also treated.

P. J. VAN ALBADA'S COURSE*

The first year (for 12-year-olds) was an introductory course, which will be described below in more detail. It was followed by three years syste-

* Cf. the Report mentioned in the footnote of p. 407.

matic geometrical instruction; plane geometry was always closely connected to space geometry. No obvious propositions were proved. In the fifth year the theory was repeated in a new organizatory scheme. The number of unproved propositions was strongly reduced. The system of lines and planes in a bundle was investigated as an example of non-Euclidean plane geometry, in order to make sure which theorems of the Euclidean geometry would remain valid and whether and how they could be proved in a general way.

The introductory course first tackled recognizing and constructing symmetries. Then simple problems of descriptive geometry followed, with further material of perspective character: From which level has a certain photograph been taken? What was the height of the sun? Telegraph poles. Constructions of third projections if two were given. Projections of regular solids. Shadow constructions. Regular polygons. Tiles. Making models. Shortest lines on cylinders and cones. Coloring maps. Running through graphs.

FITTING

Space with its solids is more concrete than the plane with its figures. In the plane the road to logical analysis is shorter; space is more intuitive and favours more creative activities. Plane figures are drawn, solids are built.

There is one exception in the plane – paving with tiles. The underlying psychological idea is here the same as in space, and it is at least as concretely realized. This idea is – fitting. It is a motor sensation. Psychologists can tell how strong the motor component is in young persons, and how important motor perception and motor memory is.

The edges of a network fit together. Prisms and pyramids fill the cube, the diagonal plane fits into the cube, the tetrahedron of the face diagonals fits into the cube; if turned outside the six pyramids filling the cube produce a rhombododecahedron. How marvellously the pieces of a mosaic pavement fit! The pavement contains through lines and straight angles, stars and parallel patterns.

Things fit, but do children ask why? With rare exceptions, they do not. All these miracles of space seem to leave no impression. Yet they grind slowly but efficiently. The greatest pedagogic virtue is patience. One day the child will ask why, and there is no use in starting systematic geometry earlier. It may even do harm to attempt it. The key to geometry is the word "why". Only killjoys will present it prematurely. The miracles of fitting are a preparation for systematic geometry, but even if this stage is reached, they cannot be dismissed. They remain the rough material of geometric thinking. The pupil should recall them and reconsider the old problems anew at every stage.

If fitting is the main idea, space should be recognized as the home of solid bodies. In the affine plane there are no problems of fitting. When I explained this to a teacher who had taught geometry for some time starting with the affine viewpoint, he was astonished. He confessed that he had never been aware of this feature. He had not realized how sophisticated the affine view was, how far it was from the space of solids. He had been misled by the textbook author though perhaps even the textbook author was not aware of it, and maybe had never even thought about it. How many deductive experiences are not needed to arrive at affine geometry? Affine geometry can never be the start of geometry instruction.

Between van Albada's and Dina van Hiele's introductory courses, there is a great difference though both are quite unclassical. In van Albada's course there is a rich variety of material which invites the child to think using his eyes and hands. The extensive descriptive geometry in the beginning is a characteristic feature. I think it is an important discovery by van Albada that the place of descriptive geometry, if it is accepted as a teaching subject, is the first rather than the last or the last but one grade of geometry instruction. At this young age students think with their hands and eyes. Our predecessors who judged that solid geometry must be preceded by plane geometry were not aware of the fact that descriptive geometry is more elementary than deductive plane geometry.

At every step Dina van Hiele's course shows attempts to detach deductivity from the visual-motoric adventure. In the triangles pattern the children see the sum of the angles of the triangle, in the quadrangles pattern that of the quadrangle. Then the question is asked whether on the basis of the sum of the angles of the triangle that of the quadrangle could be predicted. The first time this question is asked, it is a failure. The children do not understand what it means to make an inference from triangles to quadrangles. In the mosaic they can discover structures; structures are created, but there are no restructurations. Ten days later most of them have grasped it. To prove the equality of angles at parallel lines, they introduce the structure of ladder and saw. (Figure 45).

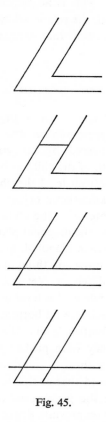

Fig. 45.

Counting corners and edges of a cube is a quite different thing. The cube has 8 vertices, with three edges parting from every vertex. Thus there are 24 edges. Just before they had counted the edges. There were 12. Thus 24 must be wrong. Yet nobody asks *what* is wrong. They have not yet grasped that not only a result but also a reasoning may be wrong. (Teachers told me that this idea may still be missing at an older age, if pupils have not yet reached the level where reasoning can be the subject of reasoning.) It is of no avail that the teacher explains the phenomenon of double counting; a supplementary exercise proves that there is no transfer at all. The relational structure between the vertices and edges of the cube is quite another kind than that of geometrical fittings; it requires another kind of abstraction. This is no structuring with auxiliary lines; to be structurally understood, the relational system of vertices and edges is to be viewed with an intuition that greatly differs from the attitude towards solid bodies in space.

DEDUCTION

The child's investigation of space can be organized in various ways. I sketched Dina van Hiele's approach because it has been analyzed most profoundly. The period covered by her course shows a permanent though discontinuous growth of the child's ability to organize its activity by logical means. At the bottom level the child is thinking, as it were, with its hands, eyes, and kinesthetic organ. The observer who knows what mathematics means interprets the child's activity as mathematics. As soon as the teacher shows the diagonal plane of the cube, the children succeed in constructing a space diagonal, and the observer can ascribe this success to the same course of thought that leads himself to the construction of the space diagonal. Yet it is still at the bottom level. The child can stay a long while at this level in geometry before it reaches the point where it will objectivate its bottom level activity. Quite a few manage excellently on this bottom level and never ascend to higher ones. Often the reason is that they were pushed to a higher level too early and aided by means of algorithms to simulate this higher level.

I have several times stressed that at this level the Socratic didactician would refuse to introduce the geometrical objects by definitions, but wherever the didactic inversion prevails, deductivity starts with definitions. (In traditional geometry they even define what is a definition – a still higher level in the learning process). The Socratic didactician rejects such a procedure. How can you define a thing before you know what you have to define? This is a general principle but it is particularly important in mathematics where "definition" has its special meaning. In mathematics a definition does not just serve to explain to people what is meant by a certain word. In mathematics definitions are links in deductive chains, but how can you forge such a link unless you know in which chain it should fit?

If Dina van Hiele showed her pupils a cube, a rhombus, a parallelogram or gave them examples of congruent figures, the pupils understood just as well what she meant as they would recognize in a chair, a bottle, or a doll their species though they had neither learnt a definition of these species nor had become familiar with all of their kind. Of course there may be uncertainties, for example to know whether a square belongs to the rhombi, or a rhombus to the parallelograms. The teacher can impose definitions to decide such controversies, but if he does so, he is degrading mathematics to something like spelling that is governed by arbitrary rules.

If the child knows what is a rhombus, what is a parallelogram, it can visually discover properties of these shapes. There are a lot of them; during the class discussion the children count them up. In the parallelogram opposite sides are parallel and equal, opposite angles are equal, adjacent angles sum up to 180°, the diagonals bisect each other, the parallelogram has a center of symmetry, it can be divided into congruent triangles, and the plane can be paved with congruent parallelograms. This is a collection of visual properties which asks for organization. I explained earlier how deductivity starts at this point; it is not imposed but unfolds itself from its local germs. The properties of the parallelogram are connected with each other; one among them can become the source from which the others spring. So does a definition arise, and now it becomes clear why a square shall be a rhombus and a rhombus be a parallelogram. In this course the student learns to define, and he experiences that defining is more than describing, that it is a means of the deductive organization of the properties of an object.

As I pointed out before this strategy does not match the intentions of those who believe in a system. How can you reason rigorously over something that has not been defined before, they ask? But this is just the thing that the creative mathematician is usually doing and which should be also allowed to learners. Indeed, most often definitions are not preconceived but the finishing touch of the organizing activity. The child should not be deprived of this privilege. Betraying a secret that could be discovered by the child itself is bad pedagogics; it is even a crime. Who has not yet observed six-year-olds discovering and inventing, and who does not know how angry they can be if the secret is betrayed too early? Twelve-year-olds are different, they have got used to imposed solutions and ask for the solution without trying. Good geometry instruction can mean much – learning to organize a subject matter and learning what is organizing, learning to conceptualize and what is conceptualizing, learning to define and what is a definition. It means leading pupils to understand why some organization, some concept, some definition is better than another. Traditional instruction is different. Rather than giving the child the opportunity to organize its spatial experiences, the subject matter is offered as a preorganized structure. All concepts, definitions, and deductions are preconceived by the teacher, who knows what is its use in every detail – or rather by the textbook author who has carefully built all his secrets into the structure.

EUCLID'S DEDUCTIVITY

What Socrates did with Meno's slave was bottom level activity, with concrete material, but nevertheless it was such an activity as holds in itself the germ of deductivity. Dina van Hiele's course even showed the first signs of logical organization. Later on I will illustrate local organizing with examples. I believe that there still exist many good didacticians who consider the learner's activity of local organization as indispensable and who favor it. In fact, in geometry it has a long tradition, which quite a few teachers must know from their own experience as pupils. It is not fair to measure Euclid's axiomatics with a modern yardstick. As a comprehensive work Euclid's Elements is a unique phenomenon in the mathematics of antiquity, but its method, rather than being uniform, is that of its components. Long before Euclid it seems to have become a habit to introduce a mathematical treatise with a number of principles, whether they were termed axioms, postulates, hypotheses, definitions, assumptions or something else. In any particular case it is a group of statements which are cut out on behalf of that special treatise in which they are being used, and it is quite normal that facts known from else-where are used without being reformulated. Such collections of principles existed before Euclid, at least since Hippocrates if not from the time of Thales, statements about the ratio of circular surfaces from which quadratures of lunulae were derived, simple symmetry statements from which the more complicated ones were deduced. At a later stage we find a celestial kinematics or computations on the sizes and the distances of celestial bodies, or a treatise on curve length, or one on the laws of the lever introduced by such special principles.

Euclid introduced the parts of mathematics he inserted into his Elements by the lists of principles he had found in the literature. By this procedure the Elements became a sum of logically organized parts of mathematics, rather than a logical organization of mathematics. The feasibility of a global organization may have lived at that time as a vague philosophical idea, but though Aristotle's contributions to this problem may not be underestimated, it should be recognized that this idea was never realized in antiquity. Even Eudoxos' theory of magnitude in Euclid's fifth to sixth book, which approaches modern axiomatics more than anything else in ancient mathematics, is incomplete as an axiomatic system of real numbers since it describes rather than autonomously creates magnitude.

To arrive at a global organization and at a modern style axiomatics, a more independent compiler than Euclid would have been required. The idea of completeness of an axiomatic system of geometry was probably far beyond the horizon of Greek mathematics. In fact, geometrical reality was described, rather than created by the definitions, postulates, and so on, and at any particular instant the description was restricted to those features that were considered as essential in that particular problem; if it appeared that some feature was lacking, recourse to reality would make sure how it had to be filled out. Though this was rigorous deductivity, its basis was adaptable rather than preconceived. From a psychological point of view this situation changed with Euclid's Elements; in antiquity an authoritative work like this was readily canonized. Euclid became the treasure of truth, and the organization of the Elements became the correct and definitive organization. There was no creative criticism of the Elements; all activity with respect to them was restricted to commentary. The Elements were a paragon of rigorous deductions from definitive principles, were they not? What was later taught in school texts as Euclid, was only a diluted form of Euclidean deductivity. But if there was anything to blame about the logic of this system, it was not the idea of local organization but rather the pretension that such a system (and Euclid himself) performed more than local organization.

TOWARDS LINEAR ALGEBRA

Meanwhile people had learned to found geometry algebraically. Disguised algebra already existed in Greek geometry, and even such seemingly genuine geometry as conics was of algebraic origin. From Descartes onwards algebra was admitted into geometry though the honorific title of true geometry was still reserved to the Euclidean method. However the more geometry proved unable to compete with the greater fertility of algebra and analysis, the more it was neglected, and the more its weaknesses became evident, the more people were inclined to rely on the so-called analytic geometry. Hilbert's *Grundlagen der Geometrie* could not turn back this trend. On the contrary, it showed even more clearly what was lacking in Euclid and how hard it was to fill the gaps. Moreover, was not the final result of Hilbert's approach the coordinatization and algebraization of geometry? What, then, was the use of his efforts and why not introduce geometry from the start as "analytic geometry"? This has the big advantage, too, that the full rigor of algebra is automatically transferred to geometry.

TOWARDS THE VECTOR SPACE OF LINEAR ALGEBRA

In "Analytic Geometry" since Descartes people had learned to use coordinate systems, to describe a point in space by a number triple, a plane by a linear equation between coordinates, a line by a pair of such equations, to express distances by means of the Pythagorean theorem and angles via the goniometric ratios as functions of the coordinates – a technique that had proved superbly useful in analysis and mechanics.

Was not it an obvious and welcome simplification to *define* points *a priori* by number triples – or if the n-dimensional approach is preferred, by number n-tuples – to give planes and hyperplanes by *definition* through linear equations, to put the distance of two points $\ulcorner \xi_1, ..., \xi_n \urcorner$, $\ulcorner \eta_1, ..., \eta_n \urcorner$ by *definition* as

$$\sqrt{\sum_i (\xi_i - n_i)^2},$$

and, in general to define geometrical figures and relations by equations between the coordinates?

The procedure became still more attractive after the geometrization of algebra by means of the vector concept. This created, unlike Euclidean geometry, an algebraic calculus adapted to geometry. As a geometric being indicated by one letter 'x', the vector got in a coordinate system coordinates $\xi_1, \ldots, \xi_n$, and was as readily identified with the ordered sequence of those coordinates. An ordered number n-tuple

$$x = \ulcorner \xi_1, \ldots, \xi_n \urcorner$$

was then termed a vector; vectors were multiplied by scalars,

$$\alpha x = \ulcorner a\xi_1, \ldots, \alpha\xi_n \urcorner$$

added to each other,

$$\ulcorner \xi_1, \ldots, \xi_n \urcorner + \ulcorner \eta_1, \ldots, \eta_n \urcorner = \ulcorner \xi_1 + \eta_1, \ldots, \xi_n + \eta_n \urcorner,$$

and multiplied by inner product,

$$x \cdot y = \sum \xi_i \eta_i,$$

and all these operations were geometrically credible.

Yet there was one weakness in this method. Unlike the points or vectors, the number n-tuples that represented them were not geometrical objects since they depended on a geometrically irrelevant coordinate system. This had to be accounted for; it should be specified how coordinates transform in the passage from an old coordinate system to a new one. This, then, was the unavoidable complement of the vector and tensor calculus. To make up for it a sophisticated technique had to be developed. In the twenties and thirties it degenerated into a festival of upper and lower subscripts, of raising and lowering subscripts, and so on; fossil relics of this period are still to be found in physics, which is proud of its conservatism.

The vector calculus was a great advance compared to old "analytic geometry"; to the university generation which started their studies in the twenties it came as a revelation. The impulse to approach vectors in still another way did not now come from geometry, or if it came from geometry, then it was in a roundabout way. It came rather from geometrized analysis, which for its own part had been influenced by abstract algebra. Since the beginning of the century analysis was penetrated by geometry – it started when certain sets of functions were named function spaces. These were infinite-dimensional spaces. Their elements could be interpreted as vectors, but the coordinate methods of vector geometry proved to be insufficient in this case. Axiomatics of vector space, therefore, takes its start with vector spaces of analytic origin; not before the mid-thirties is it transferred to geometry. This was the birth of a method that today is called linear algebra.

A vector space V over the real or the complex numbers or any field K whatsoever, is defined as an additively denoted group on which the elements of K act as homomorphisms, thus with the axioms:

$$\left.\begin{aligned}
(a + b) + c &= a + (b + c)\\
a + b &= b + a\\
a + o &= o + a\\
a + (-a) &= o
\end{aligned}\right\} \quad \text{for} \quad a, b \in V$$

$$\left.\begin{aligned}
\gamma(a + b) &= \gamma a + \gamma b\\
(\alpha + \beta) c &= \alpha c + \beta c\\
\alpha(\beta c) &= (\alpha\beta) c\\
1 \cdot a &= a
\end{aligned}\right\} \quad \text{for} \quad a, b, c \in V, \quad \alpha, \beta, \gamma \in K$$

Then linear dependence of subsets of V is defined, the concept of basis, dimension – maybe the exposition is restricted to 2- and 3-dimensional spaces; parallelism, linear manifolds, planes, half spaces, and so on, are defined.

This vector space is the substratum of what is usually called affine geometry, the fundamental concepts of which are incidence and parallelism. There is no concept of distance in this geometry; the maximum available in this sense is the ratio of *parallel* line segments. Though, one can determine in n-dimensional vector space the ratio of n-dimensional volumes, i.e. define axiomatically a volume function of vector n-tuples, determined up to a gauge factor. We will come back to this point.

No doubt it is not a hard thing writing down axioms like those of vector space and having the students drawing mechanically inferences from them. Our physicists will soon complain about this practice if it comes out that in the students' minds the concepts introduced in this way are not tied to any geometrical reality. It is incredible that tying these bonds is often badly neglected. It does not require much direct geometry, but for many even this is too much, it seems. They hurry to offer the student the *algebraic* model of n-dimensional vector space over K, formed by the n-tuples $\ulcorner \xi_1, ..., \xi_n \urcorner$ from K with the earlier mentioned operations, but meanwhile they forget about the much more important *realistic* model:

V consists of the arrows extended in ordinary space from a fixed point o. γa as an arrow is γ times as long as a, more precisely $|\gamma|$ as long in the same direction if $\gamma > 0$, and in the opposite direction, if $\gamma \leqslant 0$. $a + b$ is the arrow obtained if the arrow b is transported with its origin to the end of arrow a.

$$a + b = b + a$$

now expresses for independent a, b a well-known property of the paral-

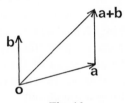

Fig. 46.

lelogram, whereas it is obvious for dependent a, b (Figure 46). From Figure 47 one reads that

$$(a + b) + c = a + (b + c)$$

tells something about the behaviour of a triangle under parallel transport,

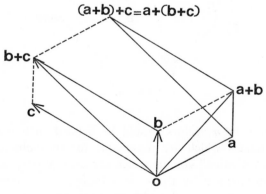

Fig. 47.

e.g. that if two sides are transported by parallelism over a vector a, the same happens with the third. The axioms of the second group, finally, are tied in an obvious way to similarity properties of elementary geometry.

The geometrically most important and first non-trivial consequence of the vector space axioms is the concept of volume. In an n-dimensional vector space a function of n vectors, called determinant, is explained, the value of which

$$\det(a_1, \ldots, a_n)$$

for the n vectors $a_1, \ldots, a_n$ is to give the "oriented" volume (after a certain norming) of the parallelotop spanned by $a_1, \ldots, a_n$. At least since Kronecker the relation between determinants and volumes has been fundamental in teaching determinants; quite a few modern textbooks, however, do not even mention the word volume when determinants are dealt with, and almost all of them introduce determinants without any geometrical motivation. For this reason I will consider the axiomatic definition of volume more closely.

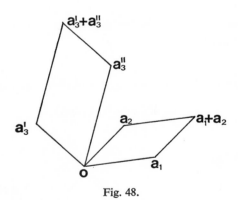

Fig. 48.

A function F of n vectors should be defined such that it satisfies intuitive postulates which are reasonable for the volume; in fact, it should be an "oriented" volume which can also become negative. Take a parallelotop spanned by the vectors a_1, a_2, a_3 of three-dimensional space; geometrically one is advised to compute the volume as the product of the "basis" parallelogram area and the "height"; the "heights" should be counted positive on one side of the "basis" and negative on the other.

Of course, height is not an affine concept, but however the height is defined, if a_1, a_2 span the "basis plane", then the height must be a linear function of a_3: if a_3 is replaced by γa_3, then the height is multiplied by γ; if a_3 is replaced by the sum $a_3' + a_3''$, then the same should happen with the corresponding "heights". (See Figure 48.) By these arguments we are advised to postulate:

(1) F is linear in each of its variables.

If two of the vectors $a_1, ..., a_n$ coincide, the parallelotop of these vectors collapses. Therefore it is postulated:

(2) $F(a_1, ..., a_n) = 0$ if for certain i, j with $i \neq j$ it happens that $a_i = a_j$.

From these two postulates it can be concluded:

If
$$b_i = a_i + a_j \quad \text{for certain } i, j \text{ with } i \neq j, \text{ and}$$
$$b_k = a_k \quad \text{for } k \neq i,$$

then
$$F(b_1, ..., b_n) = F(a_1, ..., a_n) + F(a_1, ..., a_j, ..., a_j, ..., a_n)$$
$$= F(a_1, ..., a_n).$$

And in an analogous way, if
$$c_j = b_j - b_i$$
$$c_k = b_k \quad \text{for} \quad k \neq j,$$

then
$$F(c_1, ..., c_n) = F(b_1, ..., b_n).$$

On the other hand
$$c_i = -a_j, \quad c_j = a_i,$$
$$c_k = a_k \quad \text{for} \quad k \neq i, j.$$

Hence
$$F(a_1, ..., a_j, ..., a_i, ..., a_n) = -F(a_1, ..., a_i, ..., a_j, ..., a_n),$$

from which it easily follows that:

(2') F is antisymmetric.

The postulates 1, 2 (or 1, 2') are complemented by a norming prescription: after the choice of an ordered basis $e_1, ..., e_n$ put:

(3) $F(e_1, ..., e_n) = 1.$

With the usual methods it is now shown that a function with the properties 1–3 exists and is uniquely determined; it is the determinant det. According to its introduction it may be interpreted as an oriented volume.

From the uniqueness of the function det satisfying 1–3, statements on the behaviour under linear mappings of V can be derived:

Up to a factor depending on A, $\det(Ax_1, ..., Ax_n)$ coincides with $\det(x_1, ..., x_n)$; this factor is called det A, thus

$$\det(Ax_1, ..., Ax_n) = \det A \cdot \det(x_1, ..., x_n),$$

where

$$\det A = \det(Ae_1, ..., Ae_n).$$

The linear mappings of V in itself with determinant 1 leave the n-volumes invariant. In a real vector space V the linear mappings with a positive determinant leave invariant the sign of the volume.

The last property is closely connected with what is called the orientation of n-space. Though we shall come back to this point, we anticipate the remark that real n-space is oriented by distinguishing some ordered n-tuple $\ulcorner a_1, ..., a_n \urcorner$ of independent vectors as positive; any n-tuple $\ulcorner b_1, ..., b_n \urcorner$ is then considered as positive or negative, respectively, according to whether there is a linear mapping A mapping a_i into b_i $(i = 1, ..., n)$ with a positive or negative determinant respectively (after the choice of a basis $e_1, ..., e_n$), in other words, n-tuples $\ulcorner b_1, ..., b_n \urcorner$ are defined as positive, if together with $\ulcorner a_1, ..., a_n \urcorner$ they have a positive volume.

Above we identified the n-dimensional vector space with the space of n-dimensional affine geometry. This is not wholly justified. We expect the space of affine geometry to be homogeneous; the vector space, however, possesses a distinguished point o. Quite complicated methods have been devised to wipe out this beauty spot; since the simple method to do this seems to be widely unknown, we will explain it here.

To every n-vectorspace V belongs an affine space E consisting of a set E and a set of one-to-one mappings $P +$ of V on E (that is one for every $P \in E$) such that

$$P + o = P$$
$$(P + x) + y = P + (x + y) \quad \text{for all} \quad x, y \in V.$$

($P +$ is as it were the attaching of vectors at P; the endpoint of the vector x attached at P is $P + x$).

By definition, for given $P, Q \in E$ there exists one $x \in V$ such that $P + x = Q$; this x is also indicated by $Q - P$.

A mapping F of affine E into E' is called *affine*, if $FP - FP_0$ is linear in $P - P_0$ (for fixed P_0; but then it even holds for any P_0).

Two affine spaces E, E' belonging to the same vector space V become affinely equivalent, if (after choosing $P_0 \in E, P_0' \in E'$) $P_0 + x$ and $P_0' + x$ are made to correspond to each other.

It must be observed that $Q - P$ is meaningful for $P, Q \in E$ though it is an element of V rather than of E. Though $P + Q$ has no meaning for $P, Q \in E$, it is still possible to grant certain linear combinations of the elements $P_0, \ldots, P_k$ of E a meaning, namely:

for $\qquad \sum_0^k \alpha_i = 0: \qquad \sum_0^k \alpha_i P_i = \sum_0^k \alpha_i (P_i - Q) \in V_i$

for $\qquad \sum_0^k \alpha_i = 1: \qquad \sum_0^k \alpha_i P_i = Q + \sum_0^k \alpha_i (P_i - Q) \in E.$

(One shows that these expressions do not depend on Q; finally one can put $Q = P_0$.)

In particular the second expression is geometrically significant: With $\sum \alpha_i = 1, \sum \alpha_i P_i$ is the center of gravity of the masses α_i in the points P_i.

Such a definition should not be offered as a definition of the center of gravity unless it has reasonably been motivated. This can be done as follows:

Let Σ be the system of

$$\ulcorner P_1, \ldots, P_k; \alpha_1, \ldots, \alpha_k \urcorner$$

with $P_1, \ldots, P_k \in E, \alpha_1, \ldots, \alpha_k$ real, and $\sum \alpha_i \neq 0$ ("α_i is a mass in P_i"). One defines

$$\ulcorner P_1, \ldots, P_k; \alpha_1, \ldots, \alpha_k \urcorner + \ulcorner Q_1, \ldots, Q_1; \beta_1, \ldots, \beta_1 \urcorner =$$
$$= \ulcorner P_1, \ldots, P_k, Q_1, \ldots, Q_1; \alpha_1, \ldots, \alpha_k, \beta_1, \ldots, \beta_1 \urcorner$$

as long as $\sum \alpha_i + \sum \beta_j \neq 0$.

An equivalence relation $\sim$ in Σ is postulated such that

$$(\varphi \sim \varphi') \wedge (\psi \sim \psi') \to \varphi + \psi \sim \varphi' + \psi'$$

as far as defined. Further:

$$\ulcorner P_0, P_1; \alpha_0, \alpha_1 \urcorner \sim \ulcorner \frac{\alpha_0}{\alpha_0 + \alpha_1} P_0 + \frac{\alpha_1}{\alpha_0 + \alpha_1} P_1, \alpha_0 + \alpha_1 \urcorner$$

which is again intuitively justified.

By induction it is shown that such an equivalence relation, if existent, is unique and that

$$\ulcorner P_0, ..., P_k; \alpha_0, ..., \alpha_k \urcorner \sim \ulcorner \frac{\alpha_0}{\alpha} P_0 + \cdots + \frac{\alpha_k}{\alpha} P_k; \alpha \urcorner$$

with

$$\alpha = \sum \alpha_i.$$

This relation, in fact, generates an equivalence.

Up to equivalence a mass system with mass sum $\neq 0$ can thus be replaced by one mass in a single point, the center of gravity of the system. The general replacement is brought back to that of two masses by one, which is well known from the law of the lever and easily motivated: the center of gravity of two masses divides the joining segment in the inverse ratio of the masses.

The theory of the gravity center is closely connected to that of convexity. The points

$$\alpha_0 P_0 + \alpha_1 P_1 \quad \text{with} \quad \alpha_0 + \alpha_1 = 1$$

form the *straight line* $P_0 P_1$; if moreover $\alpha_0, \alpha_1 \geqslant 0$, it is the *line segment* $P_0 P_1$. In general

$$\alpha_0 P_0 + \alpha_1 P_1 + ... + \alpha_k P_k \quad \text{with} \quad \sum \alpha_i = 1$$

gives the *linear variety* spanned by $P_0, P_1, ..., P_k$, while the restriction to non-negative masses delivers the *convex set* spanned by $P_0, P_1, ..., P_k$. Here a set is called convex, if with two points it contains the line segment joining them. Then, in fact, from $\sum \alpha_i P_i (\alpha_i \geqslant 0, \sum \alpha_i = 1)$ and $\sum \beta_i P_i (\beta_i \geqslant \geqslant 0, \sum \beta_i = 1)$ one gets

$$\lambda_0 \sum \alpha_i P_i + \lambda_1 \sum \beta_i P_i,$$

which for $\lambda_0 + \lambda_1 = 1$ and $0 \leqslant \lambda_0, \lambda_1 \leqslant 1$ has the same form

$$\sum \gamma_i P_i$$

with $\gamma_i \geqslant 0$ and $\sum \gamma_i = 1$. Furthermore, it is shown by induction that every convex set containing $P_0, P_1, \ldots, P_k$, also contains all

$$\alpha_0 P_0 + \alpha_1 P_1 + \ldots + \alpha_k P_k \quad \text{with} \quad \sum \alpha_i = 1, \alpha_i \geqslant 0.$$

TOWARDS THE INNER PRODUCT

The above exposition was meant to give the reader an idea of how much geometry is contained in affine space. Yet essential concepts of elementary geometry are still lacking – the concept of equality and the comparison of line-segments and angles (or rather the congruence of line segments and angles and the comparison of lengths of line segments and magnitude of angles). If these concepts are to be seized upon axiomatically, the structure of vector space must be complemented by an axiomatic, which historically again comes from analysis, namely from Hilbert space.

In the real vector space V a real-valued positive definite inner product $(\ldots, \ldots)$ is postulated, i.e. with the properties:

$$
\begin{aligned}
(\alpha x, y) &= \alpha(x, y) \\
(x + y, z) &= (x, z) + (y, z) \\
(x, y) &= (y, x) \\
|x|^2 &= (x, x) > 0 \quad \text{for} \quad x \neq 0.
\end{aligned}
$$

These postulates should again intuitively be motivated. This is not so simple; it requires quite a lot of geometrical knowledge.

It is agreed that intuitively the inner product (x, y) means: length of x times (oriented) projection of y upon x. Then the symmetry of the inner product is easily ascertained if one remembers how Euclid proved the Pythagorean theorem (Figure 49).

The rectangles APP_1B_1 (with $AB = AB_1$) and AQQ_1C_1 (with $AC = AC_1$) are of equal area because of the congruence of the triangles ABC_1 and AB_1C. It can, however, also be proved by the similarity of the triangles APC and AQB.

The second among the axioms on the inner product also requires a geometrical justification. Let us call $\pi(a)$ the projection of the vector a upon a fixed direction z; then

$$\pi(a + b) = \pi(a) + \pi(b)$$

has to be proved, or, equivalently,

$$\pi(\tfrac{1}{2}(a+b)) = \tfrac{1}{2}(\pi(a) + \pi(b)),$$

that is, if line segments are projected upon a straight line, then midpoints pass into midpoints. Or, more generally, if P moves uniformly on the line $P'P''$, then its projection upon the line $Q'Q''$ does so on this line.

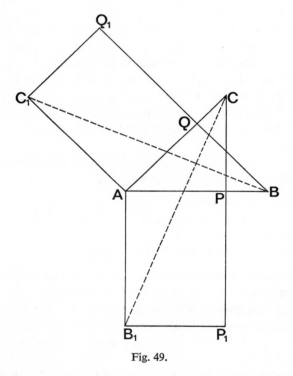

Fig. 49.

Or equivalently, two straight lines $P'P''$ and $Q'Q''$ are intersected proportionally by a pencil of parallel planes. With an auxiliary line intersecting $P'P''$ and $Q'Q''$ this is brought back to the special case of intersecting lines. (See Figure 50.)

Against the vector space with inner product as a substratum of Euclidean geometry the same objection can be raised as in the affine case: the unjustified exceptional role of the origin. As easily as in the affine case it can be removed – an affine space is attached to the vector space, and

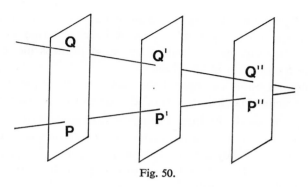

Fig. 50.

the result is called a Euclidean space. In this space distance is meaningful, namely $|P - Q|$ is by definition the distance P and Q; angles of straight lines can also be measured as will be explained later.

There is, however, a more serious objection against this "Euclidean space" as a substratum of Euclidean geometry. Euclidean geometry as understood from Euclid up to not long ago did not know such things as vector length and distance; no statements of Euclidean geometry tell about points having the distance 3. What matters in Euclidean geometry is equality and comparison of distances. Up to a few decades ago nobody would have considered as geometry a statement telling that some line segment has a certain numerical length, even if a measure unit had been added. With the vector space and the inner product it has become an uncontroversial habit to term a space with absolute inner products and lengths as Euclidean. Without doubt the inner product is a useful tool. What disturbs me is a certain lack of criticism if this tool is accepted as a means of describing Euclidean space. It should be recognized and students should understand that this algebraic apparatus involves an ageometrical element; that this so-called Euclidean space can be imposed upon physical space as a model only after a unit length has been chosen – in old Euclidean space this was not needed because it involved no absolute lengths. Moreover it should be made clear that the choice of the length unit does not prejudice to the effects of the model – the genuinely geometrical statements are always reflected in the same way in physical space however the length unit is chosen. This rests on the fact that the "true" Euclidean space admits as group of automorphisms that of similarities (that is of the mappings which conserve the ratio of distances), while in the "new" Euclidean space the autometrisms (that is the distance preserving mappings) are the only automorphisms. I do not object too much against the change of terminology; what disturbs me is that so few have been conscious of this change.

After this digression we turn to the geometric consequences of the axiomatic system. The axioms allow the definition of vector length $|x| = \sqrt{(x, x)}$, hence of distance, further of orthogonality, $(x, y) = 0$, of two vectors x, y. Two sets, in particular two linear subspaces of V are called orthogonal, if they are elementwise orthogonal. The orthogonal complement $W^{\perp}$ of W is the set of vectors orthogonal on W. The next facts are not wholly obvious:

A_m: Given a true linear subspace W of V of dimension m (finite) then $W^{\perp}$ consists of more than o.

B_m: A m-dimensional vector space V with inner product has an orthonormal basis $e_1, \ldots, e_m$, that is a basis with $(e_i, e_j) = \begin{matrix} 1 \\ 0 \end{matrix}$ for $\begin{matrix} i = j \\ i \neq j \end{matrix}$.

As long as one restricts oneself to three dimensions, the proofs do not cause difficulties. In the general case they require inductions, namely

$$B_m \to A_m \quad \text{and} \quad B_m \wedge A_m \to B_{m+1}.$$

To prove $B_m \to A_m$ it is supposed that B_m holds with respect to W, which delivers an orthonormal basis $e_1, \ldots, e_m$ of W. Outside W there is an $a \in V$ with which

$$b = a - (a, e_1) e_1 - \cdots - (a, e_m) e_m$$

is formed; since $(b, a_i) = 0$ for all $i = 1, \ldots, m$, it follows $b \in W^{\perp}$, while on the other hand $b \neq o$. To prove $B_m \wedge A_m \to B_{m+1}$ in a given V with dim $V = m + 1$, a subspace W with dim $W = m$ is assumed, and within W an orthonormal basis $e_1, \ldots, e_m$; moreover according to A_m a $b \neq 0$ is found in $W^{\perp}$; this is replaced by $e_{m+1} = (1/|b|) b$ and added to the basis of W.

If the n-dimensional vector space with inner product is coordinatized on an orthonormal basis $e_1, \ldots, e_n$, the connection with the older analytic geometry is restored: for the vectors

$$x = \sum \xi_i e_i, \quad y = \sum \eta_i e_i :$$
$$(x, y) = \sum \xi_i \eta_i$$
and
$$(x, x) = \sum \xi_i^2 .$$

In the vector space with inner product the absolute volume can be normed in a natural way: take an ordered orthonormal basis $\ulcorner e_1, ..., e_n \urcorner$ and set its volume equal to one. To justify this, it has to be shown that the choice of the basis does not play an essential role. Indeed, if one ordered orthonormal basis has the volume 1, then any other has the volume ± 1. This is not easily proved. It can be done as follows.

Let us first consider the autometrisms of Euclidean space, that is the distance preserving mappings. First, there are the translations T_a, defined by $T_a P = P + a$. Up to translations, every autometrism can be replaced with one leaving invariant a certain point P_0. The new autometrism can then be interpreted as one of the vector space V. Let A be this autometrism. Then $|Ax - Ay| = |x - y|$ for all $x, y \in V$, hence

$$(Ax - Ay, Ax - Ay) = (x - y, x - y),$$

and with $x = o$ or $y = o$ also

$$(Ax, Ax) = (x, x), (Ay, Ay) = (y, y).$$

From this follows

$$(Ax, Ay) = (x, y) \quad \text{for all} \quad x, y \in V,$$

hence the invariance of the inner product. A must be linear. Indeed, from

$$(A(x_1 + x_2), Ay) = (x_1 + x_2, y)$$
$$(Ax_1, Ay) \qquad = (x_1, y)$$
$$(Ax_2, Ay) \qquad = (x_2, y)$$

it follows

$$(A(x_1 + x_2) - Ax_1 - Ax_2, Ay) = 0$$

for all y; since Ay also runs through whole V,

$$A(x_1 + x_2) - Ax_1 - Ax_2$$

is orthogonal on V, thus vanishes.

The (linear) mappings of V that conserve the inner product, are called *orthogonal*. They map orthonormal bases on orthonormal bases; conversely, if two ordered orthonormal bases are given, there is an orthogonal mapping that carries the one into the other. The orthogonal mappings A are characterized by

$$AA' = 1,$$

where A' is the adjoint of A. To conclude that the determinant of ortho-gonal A is ± 1, it is needed that $\det A = \det A'$ (and this is not so simple for arbitrary n though for $n = 2,3$ it is easily verified). Anyhow, it appears that all orthonormal bases have the volume ± 1.

To settle the volume in V, one particular orthonormal basis has to be provided with a positive volume, in other words V, and consequently E, has to be oriented. Quite often oriented rather than unoriented Euclidean space is needed, in particular in physics. For instance the vector product of two vectors can only be defined in oriented (3-dimensional) Euclidean space. It can be done in the following way:

First it is proved:

Let f be a linear function in $V (\dim V = n)$; then there is exactly one $u \in V$ such that

$$f(x) = (u, x) \quad \text{for all} \quad x \in V.$$

The proof runs as follows: If $f(x) = 0$ for all $x \in V$, then take $u = o$. If not, define

$$W = \{ x \in V \mid f(x) = 0 \},$$

take $v \in W^{\perp}$, $v \neq o$; and put

$$u = (f(v)/(v, v))\, v.$$

Further, from $(u, x) = (u', x)$ for all x it follows $(u - u', x) = 0$, hence $u = u'$.

Now, in 3-dimensional oriented vector space V with inner product

$$\det (a, b, x)$$

is linear in x. Thus there is an $u \in V$ such that

$$\det (a, b, x) = (u, x) \quad \text{for all} \quad x \in V.$$

The vector u which is uniquely defined by a, b, is by definition the vector product of a and b,

$$[a, b].$$

Thus

$$\det (a, b, x) = ([a, b], x).$$

The following properties of $[a, b]$ are easily stated:

(1) $[a, b]$ is linear in a and b.
(2) $[a, b]$ is orthogonal on a and b.
(3) $[a, b] = o$ iff a, b are linearly dependent.
(4) $[a, b] + [b, a] = o$.
If above x is replaced with $[a, b]$, one gets

$$\det(a, b, [a, b]) = |[a, b]|^2.$$

If the first member is interpreted as the volume of a right prism with as a basis the parallelogram generated by a, b, and as a height the length $|[a, b]|$, then it is clear from this formula and geometry that the area of the basis parallelogram must be $|[a, b]|$. So in the frame of the theory we are developing, we are advised to *define* the area of the parallelogram a, b in the 3-dimensional oriented vector space V with inner product by

$$|[a, b]|.$$

If a, b are restricted to a plane in V, then $[\ldots, \ldots]$ is a scalar multiple γc of a fixed vector c, and the factor γ is in fact a volume function with the axiomatically postulated properties.

The dependence of the vector product on the orientation of space is obvious: if the orientation is changed, then $\det(a, b, x)$ and hence $[a, b]$ is multiplied by -1.

In coordinates on an orthonormal basis, if

$$a = \ulcorner \alpha_1, \alpha_2, \alpha_3 \urcorner$$
$$b = \ulcorner \beta_1, \beta_2, \beta_3 \urcorner$$
$$x = \ulcorner \xi_1, \xi_2, \xi_3 \urcorner$$

then from

$$\det(a, b, x) = \begin{vmatrix} \alpha_1 & \beta_1 & \xi_1 \\ \alpha_2 & \beta_2 & \xi_2 \\ \alpha_3 & \beta_3 & \xi_3 \end{vmatrix},$$

it follows

$$[a, b] = \ulcorner \begin{vmatrix} \alpha_2 & \beta_2 \\ \alpha_3 & \beta_3 \end{vmatrix}, \begin{vmatrix} \alpha_3 & \beta_3 \\ \alpha_1 & \beta_1 \end{vmatrix}, \begin{vmatrix} \alpha_1 & \beta_1 \\ \alpha_2 & \beta_2 \end{vmatrix} \urcorner.$$

In the older analytic geometry this was used to define the vector product. The advantages of the more abstract modern approach are obvious. They are, however, lost if the geometrical aspects are neglected.

THE ANGLE CONCEPT OF VECTOR SPACE

Among the essential concepts of elementary geometry we stressed those of line-segment and angle equality. In this exposition of linear algebra we did not yet mention angles. We now turn to this subject. We placed the inner product into elementary geometry by the relation (x, y) = length of x times oriented projection of y upon x. Within the frame of elementary geometry we can express this now symmetrically:

$$(x, y) = \text{length of } x \text{ times length of } y \text{ times } \cos \sphericalangle \ulcorner x, y \urcorner.$$

This justifies the definition

$$\cos \sphericalangle \ x, y = (x, y)/|x| \cdot |y|,$$

or if one restricts oneself to unit vectors x, y:

$$\cos \sphericalangle \ x, y = (x, y).$$

This defines the cosine of the angle $\sphericalangle x, y$ rather than the angle itself; to get the angle, the knowledge of the cosine function, e.g. from analysis, is required. Inverting it one gets

$$\sphericalangle \ x, y = \text{arc} \cos (x, y),$$

which should be normed such that

$$0 \leqslant \sphericalangle x, y \leqslant \pi.$$

This is in fact the angle concept of classical Euclidean geometry (though Euclid did not admit zero and straight angles). The angle concept of trigonometry is more refined (we will deal with angle in general later). Yet this refined angle concept is only possible in an oriented plane. There it is convened to compute the angle of an ordered vectors pair $\ulcorner x, y \urcorner$ by

$$\sphericalangle \ulcorner x, y \urcorner = \text{arc} \cos (x, y)$$
$$-\pi < \sphericalangle \ulcorner x, y \urcorner \leqslant \pi$$
$$\sphericalangle \ulcorner x, y \urcorner > 0 \quad \text{or} \quad < 0$$

according to whether $\ulcorner x, y \urcorner$ fits the positive or negative orientation of the plane.

Rather than as a number between $-\pi$ and π the angle is also understood as a real number mod 2π.

I have just supposed that the student knows the goniometric functions; they are beautiful examples of easily constructed graphics, and the sine function is early on used in physics. Maybe the student did not yet come across the addition theorems of the goniometric functions, but then they are now easily derived as follows:

Consider in the plane a rotation through the angle φ around the origin; from the images of the basis vectors, the matrix representation

$$D_\varphi = \begin{pmatrix} \cos\phi & -\sin\phi \\ \sin\phi & \cos\phi \end{pmatrix}$$

arises. If two rotations over φ_1 and φ_2 are performed in series, one over $\varphi_1 \varphi_2$ is obtained, thus

$$D_{\varphi_1} D_{\varphi_2} = D_{\varphi_1 + \varphi_2},$$

or

$$\begin{pmatrix} \cos\phi_1 & -\sin\phi_1 \\ \sin\phi_1 & \cos\phi_1 \end{pmatrix} \begin{pmatrix} \cos\phi_2 & -\sin\phi_2 \\ \sin\phi_2 & \cos\phi_2 \end{pmatrix} =$$

$$= \begin{pmatrix} \cos(\phi_1 + \phi_2) & -\sin(\phi_1 + \phi_2) \\ \sin(\phi_1 + \phi_2) & \cos(\phi_1 + \phi_2) \end{pmatrix}.$$

The rotations form a group Δ; in the matrix product the addition theorems of sines and cosines are exhibited, and others are easily derived from those.

If the student knows complex numbers, this can be made more perspicuous (or this matter is resumed, when complex numbers enter). As usual, the complex numbers are geometrically represented in the plane, with the absolute value as distance from the origin, according to the Pythagorean theorem, and the conjugation as the reflection on the axis of the reals. From $|\alpha|^2 = \alpha\bar{\alpha}$ and $|\beta|^2 = \beta\bar{\beta}$ it follows $|\alpha\beta| = |\alpha| \cdot |\beta|$. If the geometrical substratum of complex numbers is interpreted as a two-dimensional real linear space with basis 1, i, then the multiplication by $\alpha = \alpha' + i\alpha''$ is a linear mapping with the matrix

$$\begin{pmatrix} \alpha' & -\alpha'' \\ \alpha'' & \alpha' \end{pmatrix};$$

its determinant is $|\alpha|^2$. If $|\alpha| = 1$, then the multiplication conserves distances, and its determinant is 1. In this way the rotations around 0 can be interpreted as the multiplications by complex numbers of absolute value 1. The multiplicative group of these numbers, previously denoted by E, can consequently be identified with the rotations group Δ; more precisely, the rotation D_φ over the angle φ is identified with the multiplication by $\cos \varphi + i \sin \varphi$. The protractor axiom (see p. 329) gave us an isomorphism ω of the multiplicative group E of complex numbers of absolute value 1 on the additive group of real numbers mod 2π; we can now identify ω^{-1} with $\Upsilon_\varphi(\cos \varphi + i \sin \varphi)$, thus

$$\cos \varphi = \operatorname{Re} \omega^{-1}(\varphi), \quad \sin \varphi = \operatorname{J} \omega^{-1}(\varphi).$$

The addition rules for sines and cosines can now be derived from the homomorphism property of ω^{-1}

$$\omega^{-1}(\varphi_1 + \varphi_2) = \omega^{-1}(\varphi_1) \cdot \omega^{-1}(\varphi_2)$$

by calculating

$$\cos(\varphi_1 + \varphi_2) = \operatorname{Re} \omega^{-1}(\varphi_1 + \varphi_2) = \operatorname{Re}(\omega^{-1}(\varphi_1)\, \omega^{-1}(\varphi_2))$$
$$= \cos \varphi_1 \cos \varphi_2 - \sin \varphi_1 \sin \varphi_2.$$

REVISION OF THE ANGLE CONCEPT OF VECTOR SPACE

For this incorporation of the angle concept into linear algebra quite an amount of geometrical knowledge about angles is required, in particular the trigonometric angle concept and the goniometric functions are supposed. But once you have undertaken to mount geometry as linear algebra, it is swallowing a bitter pill if, to found angles, you have to pass along transcendent paths. The pill can be sweetened, however, and transcendence can be pushed into a corner. Though it is known that the plane rotations around the origin can be represented on an orthonormal basis by the matrices

$$\begin{pmatrix} \cos \phi & -\sin \phi \\ \sin \phi & \cos \phi \end{pmatrix},$$

it is now agreed to forget it and behave as though sines and cosines have never emerged. It is done as follows.

The group Δ of rotations around 0 is defined *a priori*, that is as that of the mappings that preserve distance, area, and origin. It is easily calculated that on an orthonormal basis they are the

$$\begin{pmatrix} \alpha' & -\alpha'' \\ \alpha'' & \alpha' \end{pmatrix} \quad \text{with} \quad \alpha'^2 + \alpha''^2 = 1.$$

Since the group Δ is commutative, it is decided to write it additively, that is Δ is isomorphically mapped upon an additive group W, which is purely formally defined. To every $\varphi \in W$ belongs in a one-to-one way a rotation D_φ and φ is called the rotation angle. Now, by definition

$$D_{\varphi_1} D_{\varphi_2} = D_{\varphi_1 + \varphi_2}.$$

In the matrix representation

$$D_\varphi = \begin{pmatrix} \alpha' & -\alpha'' \\ \alpha'' & \alpha' \end{pmatrix},$$

φ determines the numbers α', α'', which are also indicated by $\cos \varphi$ and $\sin \varphi$.

It follows from the matrix representation of D_φ that for every vector $\ulcorner \alpha', \alpha'' \urcorner$ of length 1, there exists a rotation, mapping $\ulcorner 1, 0 \urcorner$ onto $\ulcorner \alpha', \alpha'' \urcorner$, to wit

$$\begin{pmatrix} \alpha' & -\alpha'' \\ \alpha'' & \alpha' \end{pmatrix}.$$

Then for two arbitrary vectors a, b of length 1 there is also a rotation D_φ mapping a onto b; then by definition φ is the angle of a, b:

$$\varphi = \measuredangle \ulcorner a, b \urcorner$$

if

$$b = D_\varphi a.$$

Further with three unit vectors a, b, c and

$$\measuredangle (a, b) = \varphi \qquad \measuredangle (b, c) = \psi$$

by definition,

$$D_\varphi a = b, \quad D_\psi b = c,$$

hence

$$D_{\varphi + \psi} a = D_\varphi D_\psi a = c,$$

thus

$$\measuredangle (a, c) = \varphi + \psi,$$

that is the additivity of angles.

Or, the same in another more concrete guise: W is not formally defined as an additive group isomorphic with Δ, but instead the set of ordered pairs of unit vectors is introduced *with the equivalence* relation

$$\ulcorner a, b \urcorner \sim \ulcorner a', b' \urcorner$$

iff there is a rotation carrying a into a' and b into b', and with the addition

$$\ulcorner a, b \urcorner + \ulcorner b, c \urcorner = \ulcorner a, c \urcorner.$$

W is now the set of equivalence classes with the induced addition. It is shown that W and Δ are isomorphic.

From here a path leads to complex numbers. The unit vectors, considered as complex numbers of absolute value 1, form a multiplicative group isomorphic with E. No "transcendent" tool as the protractor axiom is introduced to justify E and its isomorphism with W, no specific mapping of E upon the additive group of reals mod 2π is introduced. Instead an additive group W isomorphic with the multiplicative group E is defined in a purely formal way and with no relation to real numbers.

Indeed transcendence is pushed into a corner. Angles are conceived algebraically – angles are rotations, which in computations are written additively instead of multiplicatively. Of course, this is not the elementary angle, which is measured by real numbers; an angle is not a number but an element of a vaguely known commutative group. If finally, for instance by means of the protractor axiom, the real angle measure is added to this theory, then in any case the "transcendent" step will have been delayed as long as possible.

The incorporation of the angle concept into linear algebra I started my sketch with presupposed an acquaintance with the angle concept and the goniometric functions; rotations were dealt with as a consequence and maybe complex numbers were used as a tool. After this I expounded how this would be reorganized by a mathematician who does not like the bitter taste of transcendence. This, in fact, is an elegant reorganization of the subject that opens wide perspectives. If the pupil can be persuaded to try this reorganization, it is a legitimate teaching subject (provided it is not taught to the detriment of more important subjects). Of course the student should be motivated to reorganizing. It is he who should feel the bitter taste of transcendent arguments (and before him the teacher who teaches this subject matter should have felt it also). He himself should have felt the need to push transcendence in a corner, and to do so he should have grasped transcendence. Logarithms, sines, and cosines are very concrete to him, at least if he has enjoyed good instruction, and though I, myself, do know that "concrete" and "transcendent" are not a pair of opposites, I cannot be sure that the learner does so. Reorganization is only possible and certainly only to be motivated if the learner can dispose of the means of reorganizing, and obviously some organization has to precede a reorganizing.

Then to be able to redefine them the learner is required to forget what are angles and goniometric functions. If the learner has already had experience of global organization, he may be able to understand this. If not, he will feel summoned to castrate himself. Of course this is a wrong view. Maybe "schizophrenia" fits better; as mathematicians we are used to, and perhaps even fond of, splitting our personality, forbidding the left hand knowing what the right hand is doing, though in actual fact it is simulated schizophrenia. Unfortunately we assume that this attitude is familiar to everybody who is going to learn mathematics, or at least, that everybody who is shown the trick learns and likes it. There are, indeed, quite a few textbook authors who assume this. In my experience this assumption is at most true of typical mathematicians (though not of all of them); many physics students who learn mathematics to use it, cannot appreciate this attitude.

I claimed that didactically it does not matter whether a transcendent angle concept in linear algebra is a bitter pill for the textbook author, what is more important is how the textbook user feels about it. I would approve the reorganization if the student is able to perform it. Of course, this is not the viewpoint of university mathematicians who demand that such things be taught by the school teacher. A teacher in the classroom can, in fact, command his students to experience a transcendent angle concept in linear algebra as a bitter pill or a sign of bad taste, to forget all about angles and goniometric functions, to write the multiplication group of the rotations additively and call the result angles, to form sines and cosines of these angles which he may by no means confuse with the sines and cosines he is acquainted with. An obedient pupil will generously be rewarded. After this game at blindman's buff, in which he has been led blindfold around so many corners and when the blindfold is removed, he is then allowed to be dazzled by the great miracle of the incorporation of the angle concept into linear algebra.

It is, however, a personally worthless mathematics, and it should not be wondered at that young students come to hate this kind of mathematics.

It is even worse with this kind of method. To satisfy a whim the angle concept is cut off from its origin and its applications, in particular if the "transcendent" step toward the real angle measure is not carried out. The real angle measure, as marked on a protractor and on a dial, belongs to the fundamental concepts of intuitive geometry, and to the indispensable tools of applied geometry, from drawings on paper, to surveying the universe, to using the table of goniometric functions. Modern textbook authors try to avoid it. This is said most strictly by Dieudonné*. The rotations group is written additively not because the usual angles are additive but only as a convenience, he says (p.111). And after having explained the addition rules and connected ones of trigonometry, he states (p. 114), "And that is all that can legitimately be known of what was formerly called trigonometry."

Of course Dieudonné knows better than anybody else that this is not true. The rotation group is written additively because angles have been, and for sound reasons still are, measured additively, and to consider sines and cosines as real functions contributes more to understanding and applying mathematics than all the fleas a mathematician can catch to put in another's ear. Of course Dieudonné knows that trigonometric functions are met with at every step in analysis, science, and technical science (p. 161), but nevertheless he claims that this only regards astronomers, surveyers, and authors of trigonometry text books.

Dieudonné however, can, even justify his claim that "this is all that can legit mately be known of what was formerly called trigonometry", because he has based his own geometry expressively upon axioms that "do not allow to prove the existence of this measure" (the additive angle measure) (p. 19). Would you believe that with such abuses axiomatics can be popularized?

LINEAR ALGEBRA AS GEOMETRY

I have shown how in order to get rid of geometry, people more and more got used to approaching geometry "analytically", and how this led to

---

* J. Dieudonné, *Algèbre linéaire et Géométrie élémentaire*, Paris, Hermann, 1964.

vector calculus and finally via the geometrization of analysis and algebra to linear algebra. Today it is a familiar idea that geometry has become obsolete by linear algebra, or that geometry is identical with linear algebra *. This is a ridiculous interpretation as is clearly proved by every textbook on this subject. I showed with many details how much geometry is involved in linear algebra and how to use it to motivate teaching linear algebra. Though I did not expound how important linear algebra is, I would like to mention subjects to which it should at least be related, namely linear differential equations and stochastic processes. Many textbook authors, up to university level, are unfamiliar, so it seems, with these obvious relations. They do not know how linear algebra is applied, and in order to apply linear algebra anyhow, they condemn geometry to be the victim. The only task, however, that would fit geometry in this context, namely as a means of motivation, is dismissed as too loose an obligation.

Some time ago I participated in a conference on teaching geometry. If now I analyze its results, I am struck by the fact that there was very little said about teaching geometry and very much on teaching foundations of geometry, that is, about the global axiomatic organization, and then of course prefabricated ones. Only a small minority promoted the idea that teaching geometry could be worthwhile and that any instruction in the foundations of geometry should be preceded by one in geometry itself. It probably never occurred to most of those present that geometry could and should be taught in a less sophisticated way – so they simply did not bother about such approaches.

No doubt linear algebra is an appropriate method to provide a system of geometry how ever restricted this system may be. This, then, is usually the form in which linear algebra is offered as geometry. It is a pious fraud. As far as linear algebra is offered as geometry, it is imposed upon the learner, and as far as the learner may be active in linear algebra (that is in problems), it is a unsavoury broth in which float coagulated lumps which are a far cry of geometry. Geometry is permitted as far as the

---

* Linear algebra is often called geometry today. An extreme example is a book entitled *Topological Geometry*. Guess what this means! Why, it is linear algebra though – how old-fashioned – over the field of real and complex numbers. Clearly the author was ashamed of it, and as a fig leaf he invented the name topological geometry; indeed, the mentioned fields are topological fields.

method of linear algebra extends, and this little bit is milled and washed out indefinitely. The old triangle constructions were certainly silly; the so-called geometry problems of linear algebra are not less so; moreover they are nauseating.

The fundamental mistake is that geometry is subordinated to a system of mathematics. The only place where it can be fitted in is in linear algebra, and there it is only welcome since this is a way to make people believe that the linear algebra being taught has some use. How much geometry is taught and in which way depends only on whether and how it fits into the system. This means that it starts with affine geometry, and that the most conspicuous feature of space, I mean fitting, is neglected. Worse still, with such a rigid approach no opportunity is left to the children to explore space and the solids in it, to organize the subject matter, or to invent definitions and deductions. On the list of problems I ventured to display there is not any which can meaningfully fit into such a system. Maybe you can compute the intersection of a sphere and a plane or of two spheres by linear algebra, but to discover whether the result is a circle you have to know what is a real sphere in real space. Of course you can work out that the radius of a circle equals the side of the in-scribed regular hexagon by an analytic proof if you prefer proofs that obscure all essentials. Linear algebra is entirely unsuitable for *discovering* whether congruent triangles can cover the plane, or whether pentagons in general can not, and at the same time it is not even suitable for *proving* such facts. I could continue in this way with one example after another on my list, to show how impotent linear algebra is in such a domain. The geometry allowed by linear algebra is a dreary product. Its "high-lights" are to prove that two different straight lines can have none or one intersection, and that for circles these numbers are 0, 1, 2. Maybe vector algebra could even provide an insipid proof that the three per-pendicular bisectors of the sides of a triangle pass through one point. The only geometrical subjects that could adequately be tackled by vector space, I mean barycenter and convex bodies, are generally dis-regarded because they do not fit into the system of mathematics.

Foundations of geometry is more fit to be tackled by linear algebra, but than it should be foundations developed by a pupil who is acquain-ted with geometry. The reader will have noticed that with linear algebra one gets rather artificial foundations of geometry, artificial because angles are absent among the fundamentals and it takes enormous trouble to reconstruct them. The angle concept is one of the precious gifts of geometry, a gift which should not be refused, a "transcendent" tool by which extraordinary results are easily obtained, much more easily than by algebraic-analytic methods. It is true every proof can be translated into analysis, but before doing so one has to possess a proof, and to find a proof geometry is needed.

It is even worse as regards the angle concept. With linear algebra it cannot be proved that the sum of angles of a rectangle is π. It costs a lot of trouble to get the result "congruent π mod 2π" because linear algebra does not yield any more than angles mod 2π. For some people this has been a reason to forbid angles other than those mod 2π. To Euclid the heptagon had an angle sum of 10 right angles; with the angle concept of trigonometry it is π mod 2π. This does not imply that the one is right and the other wrong but rather that there are various angle concepts, as will be explained more fully latter.

It would not be fair to claim that all who try to incorporate geometry into algebra do so because they hate geometry. On the contrary they often undertook to "save geometry". They themselves learned geometry according to a system which as they now know was counterfeit. "Saving geometry" meant that it had to be incorporated into a sound system of mathematics; they cannot help it if everything that cannot fit into the system must be dropped. If geometry is to maintain a place in mathematical instruction, it must be rigorous. System builders know only one level of rigour, that of the system; everything below this level they consider as fake, and all above as high-brow. According to them geometry must be adapted to this level.

In fact, as we exposed earlier, the pretentions of the system-builders are hardly justified. Usually such a system of mathematics is not any less ramshackle than the old geometry, but modern authors have learned how to more successfully hide these deficiencies. This, however, is not the feature for which I blame them. It is rather that they reason from the system downwards without realizing that to be able to reason *from* the system you should first have reasoned *towards* the system. To be able to interpret geometry as linear algebra, the learner – and not only the textbook author – should first have become acquainted with geometry.

"SAVING GEOMETRY" BY AXIOMATICS

There are yet other people anxious to save geometry. There are people that fear the denaturation of geometry by linear algebra, but rather than speaking on behalf of teaching geometry, they would compete with the rigour of algebra. As an antidote they recommend foundations of geometry, that is, a Pasch-Hilbert style system of geometry, maybe modernized according to Artin, or in some other way – for no other subject than geometry can so many different axiomatic systems be contrived, but so long as their authors do not divulge their line of thought, it is hard to say why one should be any better or any worse as a teaching subject.

In fact, linear algebra already presents an axiomatic system of geometry. Why are they not satisfied with this system? It is not clear what has led the axiomatic "rescuer" of geometry to object against linear algebra. It cannot be because it starts with the affine view, neither because it does not do justice to the angle concept, nor that linear algebra is not appropriate to discovering geometrical truth, nor even because proofs of geometrical truth by linear algebra are insipid.

None of these points can have been decisive because in the axiomatic system they recommend it is more or less the same. Those who believe in linear algebra as a surrogate for geometry are right if they object against the axiomaticians that linear algebra performs the same in geometry and, moreover, is a universal tool, one which is not designed for geometry alone and not only the whim of its particular author. What do the "rescuers" of geometry really mean?

If I am not mistaken it is the fact that linear algebra presupposes real numbers, which would be a blemish in geometry. I would not be a mathematician if I could not understand such scruples. But the pupils who are supposed to have the same kind of scruples are not mathematicians, and most of them will never become mathematicians. Of course geometry can be performed without numbers – the Greeks did so and for this reason we still say "square" rather than "second power". Of course, geometry can be *founded* without numbers, since von Staudt, Pasch, and Hilbert showed how to derive the field axioms from geometrical axioms. But because something *can* be done does not imply that it *should* be done.

The axiomaticians of geometry, too, are steering towards linear algebra as a goal. Once the axioms have been formulated, their goal is not a treasure of geometrical facts, but the algebraization of geometry, that is, showing that such an axiomatic geometry can be described by linear algebra over a field fixed by the geometry (maybe that of the reals); this field is constructed within geometry. The way from the geometrical axioms to linear algebra, then, is the only thing added. One starts earlier, the field is not presupposed but constructed from the geometrical axioms – affine axioms provide a vector addition for independent vectors (Figure 51), and indirectly for dependent ones (Figure 52); the

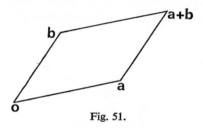

Fig. 51.

vectors form a group; the endomorphism that maps 1 into a (Figure 53) is interpreted as a left multiplication by a; by this definition the straight line 01 becomes a skew field if an axiom like Desargues' is assumed. Another geometric axiom, Pappus-Pascal's, makes the skew field become a field, and if geometrical order axioms are added, an ordered skew field. A final step, a topological axiom, leads to the field of reals.

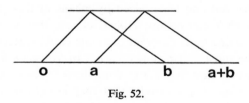

Fig. 52.

Isn't it wonderful? I love it so much that during the last 35 years I often come back to it in my courses; but perhaps I do not love it enough, in any case not to become crazy about it. For I object to calling this geometry and offering it 11–12 year olds. I teach it to students who knows what geometry is, in a course which offers my listeners quite a lot

of substantial geometry that is new to them and in which it forms a tiny
segment. But what can this scrap of foundations of geometry mean
within school mathematics? What task can it fulfill there? Students at
University have acquired the field of reals in an operative way, maybe
with in the background the number line. If they can feel the need of
refounding the field of real numbers, this should be satisfied in a clear
and distinct way. They should be led frankly and honestly to the axioms
of ordered field (archimedically ordered field) rather than aside into the
thicket, where as in the tropical rain forest the geometrical axioms
flourish, ten or twenty in number, where finally, at the end of the excur-
sion at the edge of the thicket, the field axioms emerge like a fata morgana.

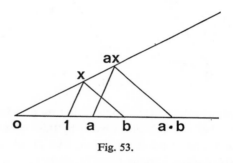

Fig. 53.

Hilbert's axiomatics is a classic. People who do not know much about
geometry seem to believe that his axioms are in some way obligatory,
that they allow no deviation. Hilbert, they say, proved that geometry
can be coordinatized and algebraized by means of the field of reals. It
is a misleading characterization; Hilbert choose the axioms to get this
result, but employing quite different ones one could reach the same goal.

No doubt the most conspicuous feature of Hilbert's axiomatics and
many newer ones is that they are so complicated. They comprise a large
number of axioms, some so trivial that they are easily forgotten in an
enumeration, others so involved (in particular order axioms) that they
are hard to memorize. The whole is so impenetrable that nobody would
try working within the axiomatic system; no discoveries can be made
within the axiomatic system, and proving propositions is a difficult thing
to do. For the sake of rigorous deductivity one has moved into the axiomatic system but the deductive structure remains utterly sketchy. Again

and again it is repeated that "it is easily shown that..." and "we omit the proof which though quite long would not open new perspectives." These are honest confessions, which are even true for reasoning in such an axiomatic system is a dreary business.

This is not to blame Hilbert or other people who made similar efforts. Such axiomatic systems were not created to have people moving within them. There are axiomatic systems of the latter kind, too, simple perspicuous ones like those of group, field, projective plane. Those of Euclidean geometry, however, used to serve other aims. Euclidean geometry is acted out unaxiomatically by all reasonable people. If the axiomatic systems of Euclidean geometry are considered, the business that matters is to reason *about* the axioms, to explore their mutual relations, their dependence and independence, their completeness. Axiomatic systems of Euclidean geometry are not created for exercises in Euclidean geometry but for metageometric explorations, for research into the foundations of geometry. Of course, every adult mathematician knows these facts. If he imposes on the student an axiomatics in order to let him execute geometry *within* the axiomatic frame, he is professing a double-standard morality like that of Jupiter and the oxen. As a full-fledged mathematician I am allowed to exercise geometry unaxiomatically because this is the indispensable preliminary stage of the axiomatic organization of the subject matter. Once this is reached, it is the turn of the learner. He is allowed to draw more or less mechanical conclusions within the system – an activity which the adult mathematician has honestly dismissed as irrelevant by such phrases as "it is easily shown that...", "the proof is omitted because...". Certainly there are more human axiomaticians who do not demand such stupifying exercises, who are satisfied if the student can repeat the phrases "it is easily shown that..." and so on – but then, of course, he should do it at the place where they belong.

The essential function of such an axiomatics is reserved to its author: organizing the subject matter to arrive at the axiomatic system, detaching it from the subject matter to be organized to arrive at a logically independent axiomatics, and finally restoring the bonds if it must be shown that the axiomatic system actually completely describes the subject matter under organization. If geometrical axiomatics is to be a meaningful teaching subject, the student must be allowed to perform it as an activity of his own. But this is not what the author means. Either the author of an axiomatics for use in the school classroom is convinced that axiomatizing is a business of Jupiter rather than of the oxen, or he has ascertained by thought experiment that it would be too difficult a thing to be left to the pupil. A learner who has never exercized organizing a subject matter locally will probably not be able to do it globally. Prefabricated axiomatic systems have a value all their own. They can be a useful subject matter to people who are experienced in axiomatizing. If a pupil has learned axiomatizing with simple material, he will rediscover in more complicated axiomatic systems well-known features; he will be able to disentangle and to understand the system as though he built it himself. For someone who has never exercized axiomatizing, an axiomatic system of geometry can only be an indigestable lump of mathematics added to so many others.

AXIOMATICS OF GEOMETRY IN TEACHING

Later I shall say something on axiomatics in general but some points can be anticipated right now. Axiomatics can have a practical and a forming value. In the case of geometry practical values can be excluded. Through an axiomatic system the pupil can be introduced to *rigour of expression* and to *deductivity without gaps*. Yet as to linguistic expression the modern axiomatics of geometry is hardly further developed than Euclid's; its language is still badly formalized; in all designs I know it is entirely determined by the idiom and the syntax of the vernacular. I do not stress this to disprove it; at the axiomatic level this is admissible rigour. Moreover, deductivity without gaps is a far cry from these systems; instead we again get such phrases as "it is easily shown that..."

Another thing that can be learned, not in axiomatics but in axiomatizing, is cutting the ontological bonds, *anontologization*, which is expressed in a classic way by Hilbert when he says "We imagine...". The objects of the axiomatic system become undefined thought-objects, which, restricted by undefined relations, are implicitly defined. In this context the relativity of geometry can be understood, that is the fact that instead of Euclidean geometry one could propose quite different geometries – an idea of great formal value. But I repeat again – the pupil should not learn such facts verbally but by developing himself such a deviating geometry.

How an axiomatic system like that of Euclidean geometry is translated into algebra and what is a model of an axiomatic system is also be learned in axiomatics.

I will now scrutinize from another viewpoint whether and how an axiomatics of geometry can lead to such results, which would indeed be welcome, in order to answer the question whether and how axiomatics can and should be taught.

It should be clear that to do so I cannot restrict myself to the axiomatics of *geometry*, and that I do not consider axiomatics as a crown to decorate mathematical instruction in its classical form. On the other hand, as mathematicians we know what the axiomatic method is worth, how it has contributed to the growth of mathematics in our century and how it has penetrated mathematics. Should axiomatics be taught in schools? If it is taught in the form it has been in the majority of projects in the last few years, I say "no". Prefabricated axiomatics is no more a teaching matter in school instruction than is prefabricated mathematics in general. But what is judged to be essential in axiomatics by the adult mathematician, I mean *axiomatizing*, may be a teaching matter. After local organization the pupil should also learn organizing globally and finally cutting the ontological bonds. But to do so, he must be acquainted with the domain that is to be organized, and the bonds that are to be cut should exist and should be vigorous. This is an exacting demand. The pupil who has never been self-reliant in organizing, will overlook connections only if the number of links is small, and the bonds with reality usually are little cultivated and weak. Of course, all these demands can be dismissed if the student is confronted with a ready-made axiomatic system from which he may obediently draw a few conclusions. He can be drilled in this art, but this can hardly contribute to understanding axiomatics. The only result would be to enlarge again the stock of denatured school mathematics.

All available examples of geometrical axiomatics in school mathematics are extremely complicated. Without going deeper into the didactical merits of such geometrical axiomatics, one can adduce this as an argument against the postulate that geometry should be learned axiomatically. But as an argument it does not suffice to condemn these efforts. Maybe one day somebody will design a simple axiomatic system for school instruction in geometry. This is not at all impossible. Till now tradition has been a heavy yoke. I myself can imagine a solution in the spirit of the Helmholtz-Lie space problem, but this does not matter here.

An axiomatic system of such a degree of complication as the usual ones of geometry cannot be properly understood by a learner who does not already know the internal connections. He cannot grasp the aim of the single axioms, their interrelatedness and their relations to the consequences which are due to be drawn. After such experiences in axiomatics, the pupil will leave the school with the idea that axiomatics serves to complicate simple things. It seems to me that we cannot afford as mathematicians to add fresh fuel to popular misconceptions on mathematics.

Till now I have not even considered the usual projects on geometrical axiomatics from the didactical viewpoint. Though I am not responsible for the dogmatic presentation and the lack of any didactic motivation, I am not entitled to decline them on these grounds. I cannot recognize didactically what the author calls a successful experiment with this project, but this does not exempt me from the duty to attempt a thought experiment to determine how someone could construct such an axiomatic system. After a short inspection, however, it appears that constructing such an axiomatic system requires such deep insight into the geometrical connections as cannot be expected at school even with the most gifted pupils. At some places in these projects this fact is explicitly admitted, in particular at places where the author built in esoteric knowledge which is obviously not possible at the schoolchild's level. Such facts are honestly admitted by the author because the master-idea of such a project is not to lead the pupil by axiomatizing to an axiomatic system, but to confront him with a ready-made system, a system with built-in surprises that should function as self-igniting gadgets. (It is a pity that with no guarantee supplied, this offer lacks all kind of attractivness that characterizes most industrial devices.)

The proper aim of geometric axiomatics, by which I mean the cutting of the ontological bonds, can be written off, since this kind of axiomatics presupposes that this goal was reached. The pupil is asked to forget all about points and lines that can be seen with the naked eye or that which was proved in the past. He has to restrict himself to statements that are laid down in the axioms and to use them as a basis. Why? Such changes of policy were well-motivated wherever they were taken in the history of mathematics. The modern geometrical axiomatics arose after the success of non-Euclidean geometry, after people had dared to doubt Euclidean geometry; the axiomatics of real number was incited by the paradoxes of the limit concept – not to mention more examples. Which doubts should be nurtured in the pupil to convert him to a new attitude? He can be told that something was wrong with the old approach, but can he be brought into the state of experiencing it? Perhaps this question can be answered positively. To work at this answer would be more decisive than to present a ready-made axiomatic system of geometry.

It is a familiar solution to tell the pupil that we are playing a game with the axioms as its rules. The schoolchild knows what a game is and what rules are. He likes playing games and he accepts it is sportsmanlike to submit himself to rules. It is a pity that geometry is the worst example to which this argument can be applied. Why play such an involved game if there are much simpler ones? But there is more to it than that. This argument is a declaration of educational bankruptcy – a fairy tale instead of the truth which would be too much for pupils' intelligence. The schoolchild may believe that school is a meaningless game which is rewarded with good marks and finally with a diploma if it is played well, though perhaps up till now he has excepted mathematics, which under the badly understood cover of unrelenting rigour may conceal deeper truths than ablative absolutes and the dates of kings and battles. Must we deprive him of this last belief? Certainly in some respects mathematics *is* a game. But this sounds quite different and has quite another effect if it is said by somebody who has experienced it than merely from the parroting of others who do not really know what such metaphors mean.

Something of what is said here about full axiomatic systems of geometry still holds if the view is restricted to partial ones, say of affine geometry. Other arguments fail. Affine axiom systems are usually simpler. But in any case it cannot be avoided that the learner knows affine geometry before he passes to affine axiomatics. It is not possible to organize a field that is unknown. Knowledge of affine geometry, however, is not implied by that of Euclidean geometry. It is not enough to advise the pupils that "now we do it without compasses". The student must have himself done it without compasses to know what this means. In fact, it is not easy to have him accept this restriction. It is hardly possible to explain to pupils what it means to restrict to ruler and compasses – in any case I could not find any book where it was attempted. Maybe it is easier to sell him the otherwise forbidden tool for drawing parallels. But what affine geometry really is, cannot be properly learned by a verbal explanation but rather by using such an instrument, and I would like to stress that it is better learned in space than in the plane.

The step that leads to cutting the ontological bonds is not easier in affine geometry than it is in the Euclidean version. To lead the pupil in this direction a different orientation is required.

But why insist on *geometrical* axiomatics? Nobody doubts that axiomatics is possible in school mathematics – axiomatics of group, measure, linear order, cyclic order, angle concept, but in any case axiomatics as an activity of axiomatizing. From the first mathematics lesson onwards the schoolchild can meet with groups, measures, ordered sets, operations with angles. It is by no means more difficult to discover the common element in the numerous models of such an axiomatic system and the internal relations of these models than it is to discover complete induction in the examples of complete induction. And it is perhaps even easier than to isolate a formal definition of the parallelogram in the confusing variety of properties of the parallelogram. A pupil who discovers and formulates the common elements in such models and chooses from this variety a few features from which he derives the others is engaged in a pronouncedly mathematical activity with lasting and widely transferable effects. He learns the global organization, that is organizing not a system internally, but a category of systems by looking from outside – he learns to axiomatize. Cutting the ontological bond, then, is no new problem. Axiomatizing by abstraction makes the bonds that should disappear, fade away (as in arithmetics the marbles or chairs or flowers subjected to arithmetical operations fade away). Afterwards the pupil can be made to become conscious of this process, but then it is certain that the process has taken place; whereas in teaching geometrical axiomatics there is not the slightest guarantee that the student has performed the cutting of the ontological bond.

It is a pity that in the numerous publications on axiomatics at school the formal value of axiomatizing is not even mentioned. I think this is due to a lack of faith in mathematics and in the personality structure of the adolescent. Mathematics as an activity should be reserved for the adult mathematician, the man who possesses the tools and knows how to use them. Axiomatizing is the privilege of the masters. The pupils must learn axiomatics, the master knows what is good for them.

There are many fields in which to learn axiomatics; geometry does not just belong to them. But once the schoolchild is familiar with axiomatics, would it not be possible to lead him to geometrical axiomatics? Before answering this question, one should ask what is the aim envisaged. I reject the answer that without axiomatics there is no rigour in geometry. It depends on the context what rigour means, and whosoever would justify geometrical axiomatics by the need for rigour should be obliged to indicate a context which cannot be adequately covered by local organization. Such contexts exist but the usual axiomatic programmes do not fit them. It is not true that the pupil "must" learn something (say axiomatic-geometry rigour) unless the "must" is caused by the need of the learner rather than the teacher. It should be shown by a thought experiment how such a need can arise; the last link in this experiment would be doubting the trustworthiness of geometry as exercized before. I cannot tell where in instruction today such doubts are nurtured.

One argument in support of geometrical axiomatics is the fact that cutting the ontological bond cannot be completely learned in abstracting axiomatics, because there it is too easy, as we have seen. It is much more difficult with geometrical axiomatics, which is not merely abstracting, and which is tied to reality by very strong intuitions. Therefore it makes sense to exercize axiomatics anew in geometry.

This would be an argument though not a compelling one. In my opinion geometrical axiomatics is not a compelling need at school level as long as axiomatics itself is merely a curiosity. Nevertheless I will explain what at this moment I would consider example of geometrical axiomatics at school level, the Dutch experiments of P. J. van Albada.

Within spatial Euclidean geometry one turns to geometry on the sphere, which can even be transformed into the elliptic plane by identifying diametral points. One tries to prove in elliptic geometry theorems which are well-known from the Euclidean plane. Those for which this is possible are listed while another list contains the obvious failures. One tries to derive theorems of elliptic geometry from each other in order to get familiar with elliptic geometry, and to find common proofs for those which hold in both geometries, that is without referring explicitly to one particular of these geometries. This leads to the problem that the pupil may know from abstracting axiomatics – finding common foundations of Euclidean and elliptic geometry. How this task can be mastered at school level I have not investigated in detail; as I mentioned earlier I would prefer to be guided by the Helmholtz-Lie space problem.

(In this programme the elliptic geometry could not possibly be replaced by hyperbolic geometry. The usual model of hyperbolic geometry is artificial and hardly accessible in a synthetic way, and doing it without a model, as Bolyai and Lobačevski did, would be too great an effort for school instruction.)

I have examined this method because it yields axiomatizing geometry as a natural problem, the same which instigated the 19th century axiomatic efforts. It is fortunate that we can revise history by referring in comparative investigations to elliptic geometry, which for historical reasons had long been overlooked.

But I would stress again that I do not claim that geometric axiomatics is a "must" at school. On the other hand this does not mean that I completely write off geometry in primary and secondary education. On the contrary, geometry penetrated top to bottom by group theory *is* a school subject, and I am convinced that more and better geometry can be taught by a teacher who in mathematical rigour follows his own conscience rather than having his scruples prescribed by the frowning axiomatician.

AXIOMATICS AND TRADITIONAL DEDUCTIVITY

It is a familiar objection by the axiomaticians to say – traditional deductive geometry is also axiomatics though it is the bad one of the juggler who is hiding his axioms in his top hat and sleeves. What is the use of this patchwork? Isn't honesty the best policy?

The assertion that traditional deductivity and axiomatics are not essentially different is paradoxically both right and wrong. It is right in so far as there is little to justify the axiomaticians's claim to complete honesty; it is not true that he is concealing nothing and depises conjuring tricks. Axiomatics from Pasch and Hilbert onwards pre-supposes the syntax and semantics of the vernacular; without any further justification, one defines "lines are parallel" and continues speaking of parallel lines, parallel projection, parallelism, and so on; one defines intersecting

lines and continues with "lines that meet each other". Of course that is
perfectly legitimate at this level. But there are other levels. There is one
where offence is taken at the alarming looseness of the vernacular, and
axioms and other statements are formalized. Formalization, too, knows
more than one level; on a supreme level even deductions can be formalized.
Axiomatizing is not the summit of honesty and rigour; there are levels
above as well as below. Axiomatics has not monopolized honesty. To
every level of learning corresponds a level of honesty and rigour. The
honesty and rigour belonging to a certain level cannot be enforced if
the pupil is not on this level, though again and again it is attempted, and
of course with no real success. Geometrical axiomatics is particularly
dangerous. Higher level tricks are so easy and captious to be built in;
thanks to the automatism of axiomatics they are supposed to function
automatically, that is even if the pupil lacks any insight. I admit that this
is good style in our educational system, but conscientious educators
never liked it. Axiomatics can lead us deeper into this swamp.

From a didactical point of view there is a big difference between
axiomatics and traditional deductivity. I characterized it earlier by the
terms "local" and "global organization". Everybody knows that it takes
some time till average pupils are able to oversee a proof as a whole.
Looking beyond a particular theorem to see the connections with other
statements takes even more time. Even if he has barely reached this
level, he is pressed toward the next, that is global organization – it *is*
pressure if it is not made certain whether the pupil has reached this
point and if the axiomatic system is imposed on him.

There is still another respect in which traditional deductivity differs
from axiomatics: the status of definitions. In the course of his mathematical experience the student has got acquainted with two kinds of
definition, the describing definition which outlines a known object by
singling out a few characteristic properties, and the algorithmically
constructive and creative definition which models new objects out of
familiar ones. The implicit definition by axioms, however, which plays
an important part in modern mathematics, is both describing and creative
though it is not so algorithmically. In this objectively and didactically
new feature the axiomatic method is well distinguished from traditional
deductivity. Traditional deductivity means local organization, up to an
uncertain vague horizon. In axiomatics this horizon is fixed, or rather

people claim that they can, and even do, fix the horizon. I have explained why this claim is unfounded.

LOCAL ORGANIZATION—THE PERPENDICULAR BISECTORS

How can we save geometry if both linear algebra and axiomatics are not fitted to do the job?

It is a strange question. Nobody would dare to ask how to save physics or zoology, which, however, have never been axiomatized. Or rather if somebody did ask this question, he would probably mean how could physics or zoology be saved from the claws of, rather than for, mathematics.

Children learn to work out how much three pounds of sugar cost if the price of one pound is given, and what the area of a rectangle is if the sides are known, though the greater part of these notions have never been fitted into an axiomatic system. Never, when mathematics is applied, does the applier move within an axiomatic system. Applied mathematics, too, would rather be saved from, than for, pure mathematics. Not only those domains are to be protected against axiomatic dogmatism, learners, too, are endangered. Didacticians who instill pupils with a well-honed formalized axiomatic apparatus, are generally proud of their experience that those pupils like nothing more than operating within the well-defined limits of a system. This is hothouse mathematics, which is no match for the stresses of reality. An outstanding example of living mathematics that can be killed by axiomatics is probability. Geometry cannot be saved unless the pupil is allowed to experience it as an activity, prefabricated it will die by suffocation.

I revealed earlier how in introductory geometry the student can be led to learn to organize shapes and phenomena in space by means of geometrical concepts and their properties. At a higher level he should organize these concepts and their properties by means of logical relations. Above this level this relational system can become a subject of investigation.

Let us consider an example. The crucial childhood experience of quite a few mathematicians who have written autobiographies was the theorem on the perpendicular bisectors of a triangle passing through one point. This is a beautiful theorem. Children can easily discover it, provided it is formulated in a less symmetrical way: "Draw the bisectors of AB and BC, which intersect at M; look where the bisector of AC passes." Let us analyze the proof in the same way as the learner should do after he found it.

The proof rests on the property of the bisector of XY being the set of all points equidistant from X and Y, which may have been recognized by symmetry arguments. M is on the perpendicular bisector of AB, whence

$$MA = MB;$$

M is on the perpendicular bisector of BC, whence

$$MB = MC.$$

From both follows

$$MA = MC,$$

whence M is on the perpendicular bisector of AC.

The proof is a combination of a few surprises. The first and second equalities are found by applying the bisector property one way, the third is a consequence of applying it the other way. First and second, M is on the bisector, thus M is equidistant, third M is equidistant, thus M is on the bisector. I think this is the first psychologically convincing occurrence of the logical complex characterized by such concepts as inversion, necessary and sufficient, if and only if.

The next surprise is the transitivity of the equality of line segments. The seemingly trivial property of transitivity should be made explicit to understand the proof. Again I think it is the first possible approach to the transitivity property and the first example of its productivity.

The third surprise is that such a symmetric statement as that about the three perpendicular bisectors must be tackled in an asymmetric way to prove it. It is an important step to learn that "three lines pass through the same point" means the same as "one line passes through the intersection of the two others". It is the first example of a methodological paradigm which is useful up to the highest levels of mathematics.

The fourth and maybe the greatest surprise is that an incidence theorem (three lines passing through one point) is proved by metric arguments. It requires a not so easy analysis to understand the profound reason of this feature.

Finally it may be mentioned that the theorem leads to the fascinating construction of the circumcircle.

The proof of the theorem on the perpendicular bisectors is not only a marvellous piece of geometry, and a rich source of didactical ideas, it is also a good example in geometry of what I have called local organization. It can be treated as soon as children have understood the perpendicular bisector as a locus of equidistance. They need not be able to prove this crucial property of the perpendicular bisector. A proof of the locus property of the bisector cannot contribute anything to the understanding of the circumcircle theorem. I even doubt whether a proof of such an obvious fact as the locus property of the bisector can be recommended at an early stage. At a more advanced stage, it would make more sense to ask why the perpendicular bisector of XY is the locus of points equidistant from X and Y; then one may even ask why equality is transitive, which comes down to understanding what equality means. One can ask why the bisectors of different sides of the triangle intersect, and why straight lines have at most one intersection. Of course such an arrangement contradicts the philosophy of mathematics as a prefabricated system. It is the way of exploration, in mathematics as well as any other science whatsoever, which is *the* way to understand and explain phenomena. The question as to why the bisectors are concurrent is much alike to why an electric bell rings or why it does not, why the stomach digests food and not digests itself; why comets have a tail, and who has committed the murder, two questions "why", asking for a reason or a cause. And all of them have in common the feature that no answer is definitive. You can continue asking: "But why is the bisector a locus of equidistance?". "Why is equality transitive?". "Why does the current activate the electromagnet?". The answer to any question contains the germ of fresh ones. It is an apparently infinite chain, although Aristoteles believed it could be suspended on the principles as the first reason and on God as the first cause. But does it really matter whether the chain is infinite or not, if at least I am able to avoid vicious circles? The practice of everyday knowledge as well as of science, indeed, is at a certain moment, to stop asking why. To repair the bell, I do not need Maxwell's theory, and if I study Maxwell's theory, I can dismiss field quantization.

I admit from this point onwards mathematics is a bit different. Mathematicians invented the axiomatic trick, that is accepting the vice of vicious circles as a virtue. You stop asking what points and lines are; instead of an explicit definition you tell what you are allowed to do with them. Actually every science behaves in this way, every science is based on implicit definition, but mathematics is the only one in which this is cultivated as the summum of deductivity, and even more: after a system has been axiomatized, its bonds with reality can be cut; by anontologization it becomes a self-contained field.

We are again back at axiomatics, but I think we can now more clearly distinguish what axiomatics means. A mathematical text may start with axioms because it is ready-made mathematics. Mathematics as an activity never does so. In general, what we do if we create and if we apply mathematics is an activity of local organization. Beginners in mathematics cannot do more than that. Every teacher knows that most pupils can only produce and understand short deduction chains. They cannot grasp long proofs as a whole, and still less can they view a substantial part of mathematics as a deductive system. We are lucky if they can learn to organize locally a mathematizable field of reality or a piece of mathematics itself, because this is just what they will need in everyday life and in their profession.

Organizing locally is not a deficient or illicit or dishonest activity in mathematics. It is a generally accepted attitude of the grown-up mathematician in pure and applied mathematics even though he would never publish such exercises. None of the various axiom systems of geometry has ever been used to find or to prove geometrical statements if they are needed in algebra of analysis. It is much too complicated and the road from the axioms to important theorems is much too long. The proof is superseded by the firm conviction that it can be done but that it is hardly worthwhile. One is satisfied with the local organization up to a changing horizon of evidence. No less a mathematician than Hilbert, the father of modern axiomatics, cultivated the art of local organisation in his geometry courses.* Coxeter's *Introduction to Geometry*** is a marvellous demonstration of this attitude. The author knows in any case exactly where this horizon lies, and which kind of rigour is adapted to the subject matter; for instance, no recourse to the axioms is needed for Morley's theorem on the trisectrices, whereas a theorem like Sylvester's on collinear

---

* D. Hilbert and Cohn-Vossen, *Anschauliche Geometrie*, Berlin-Leipzig 1932.
** New York 1961, 1969.

points which essentially depends on order properties, needs an axiomatic background.

LOCAL ORGANIZATION–STEREOGRAPHIC PROJECTION

To illustrate once more what is geometry and local organization in geometry, I take a more involved example. One knows that stereographic projection carries circles into circles (or straight lines) and leaves angles invariant. How can we prove this?

The sphere σ touches the plane ε in the South pole S; from the North pole N we project σ onto ε; P, Q, R on σ are mapped into P', Q', R' on ε; PP', QQ', RR' pass through N. First we prove:

$PQP'Q'$ are on a circle.

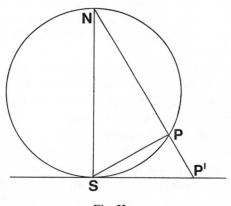

Fig. 53a.

Indeed, in the right triangle NSP' the perpendicular on the hypotenuse is SP, whence

$$\overline{NS^2} = \overline{NP} \cdot \overline{NP'}.$$

With Q instead of P it is

$$\overline{NS^2} = \overline{NQ} \cdot \overline{NQ'},$$

whence

$$NP \cdot \overline{NP'} = NQ \cdot \overline{NQ'},$$

from which follows that P, Q, P', Q' are on a circle r.

For the same reason Q, R, Q', R' are on a circle p.

The circles p and r intersect in two points; thus through p and r a sphere π passes. Hence: three points of σ are lying on one sphere with their images.

Let c be a circle on σ and c' its image in ε. Choose points P, Q, R on c. Through P, Q, R, Q' a sphere τ passes; τ also contains Q', R'. τ intersects ε in a circle c^*, which contains Q', too. This holds for any point Q of c. Thus c' is contained in c^*. If now the stereographic projection is inverted, it appears that $c^* = c'$. Thus c' is a circle. Circles are mapped into circles.

Now the invariance of angles. What does this mean? The angle of two curves through a point P is defined as the angle of their tangents at P. Take on σ through P two curves κ_1, κ_2; their images under stereographic projection are κ'_1, κ'_2. The angle of κ_1, κ_2 at P shall come out to be equal to that of κ'_1, κ'_2 at P'.

κ_1, κ_2 may be replaced by any other pair of curves that touch κ_1, κ_2 at P. In particular, κ_1, κ_2 can be taken as circles through S. Now κ_1, κ_2 intersect each other under equal angles at P and at S; likewise κ'_1, κ'_2 intersect under equal angles at P' and S; finally κ_1, κ'_1 are tangent to each other at S, and so are κ_2, κ'_2. Hence κ_1, κ_2 intersect each other under the same angle as κ'_1, κ'_2. Thus κ_1, κ_2 intersect at P under the same angle as κ'_1, κ'_2 at P'.

Is this not a beautiful proof? Of course there are more involved ones*. It can be turned in another way: you can interpret the stereographic projection as an inversion at the sphere with centre N and radius NS. One can prove it algebraically, too, and if it is done in a clever way it need not be complicated and it can lead to new insights.

Now our criticism, which should be to the point.

First of all, particular situations of points and circles should be considered. If P happens to coincide with N, its image will be a newly-invented point at infinity. If a circle on σ passes through P, its image is a straight line.

* D. Hilbert und S. Cohn-Vossen, *Anschauliche Geometrie*, Berlin 1932, pp. 218–221.

A circle on σ can happen to lie in one plane with its image.

If at the end of the proof, the point P happens to coincide with S, the equality of the angles is proved by a short cut. Already at an earlier stage one has to be careful with a circle passing through S if it is shown that it is lying on a sphere with its image.

Further, why does a straight line through N, which is not parallel to ε, meet the sphere once more? Why are the tangents of σ at N parallel to ε? Why is NS perpendicular on ε? Why does the sphere τ intersect the plane ε in a circle? Why are the two angles of two circles intersecting at two points equal?

Ridiculous questions – everybody can see this! Though, if you do not yet believe it, we will prove it for you. For instance, the last statement; I use the reflection at the symmetry plane π of AB; it interchanges A and B and leaves the circles through A and B invariant. Reflections conserve the angle measure.

Why, then, is a circle κ through A, B invariant under the reflection at π? Why, a circle obviously passes into a circle; its intersection C with π is invariant, A, B are interchanged; three points determine a circle.

Why is it obvious that under reflections circles pass into circles? Because spheres pass into spheres and planes into planes and circles are intersections of spheres and planes. Why do spheres pass into spheres? Because they are defined by distance properties and distances are preserved under reflections. Why are distances preserved? I answer this with the congruence theorems. At long last the questions will stop. Or else, I will stop answering. I need not be ashamed. Everywhere in everyday life and science this is good sport.

Why is SP perpendicular on NP'? How did you move to the 9th grade? This is the angle in the semicircle*. It is a pity, before long this answer will no longer be relevant, even if changed into "how did you ever pass the final school examinations?" Neither in linear algebra nor in any axiomatics of geometry you come across anything like the theorem on the angle in the semicircle. I am not complaining about it; there are so many interesting things about this theorem that even at university it would not be an unworthy topic.

---

* In the German text I continued: "Das ist doch der Thales." This cannot be translated, since every nation attributes different theorems to Thales.

Why is $\overline{NS}^2 = \overline{NP} \cdot \overline{NP'}$? In Euclid this is a preparation for the Pythagorean theorem, but today there are better proofs of this theorem. The relation can be proved by similar triangles.

A more serious question – how is it reasoned from $\overline{NP} \cdot \overline{NP'} = \overline{NQ} \cdot \overline{NQ'}$ that P, Q, P', Q' are on a circle? The converse statement is more familiar, but the proof, again with similar triangles, is analogous.

Further, why are two circles κ_1, κ_2 intersecting in two points A, B lying on a sphere? Take beside A and B points C and D on κ_1, κ_2 respectively. There is a sphere through A, B, C, D; with three points a sphere contains the circle through these points.

Again and again it is the same thing over again : "Ask me a question." There are people who cram into a proof all you can ask about it or prepare it by lemmas. This is again a method to kill geometry.

I must mention one more point. I spoke of invariance of angles. Which angle concept was I looking at? As I formulated it, it could have been the old Euclidean angle, and in fact it holds for this concept. But this is not enough. Instead of curves, one can take oriented curves, instead of a pair of curves an ordered pair. Then the angle is that of an ordered pair of vectors. In the plane this is an angle mod 2π. But how about space? There by a motion any angle can be moved into its opposite. Well, angles of tangent vectors at a sphere σ are not angles of arbitrary vectors in space; they, too, make sense mod 2π, and they are preserved under rotations of the sphere. But now, one has to observe (twice) that the angles of κ_1, κ_2 at the intersections are not equal but opposite.

After these examples of locally restricted organization I turn to what I earlier called organizing a field.

ORGANIZING A FIELD–THE IDEAS OF ORIENTATION

The method of geometry should be applied wherever it is superior to the algebraic method. But every virtue of geometry has, Janus-like, a weakness on its other face.

The most conspicuous weakness is that a figure drawn or imagined to lead the course of thought may be misleading. A special figure will serve as though it was the general case, and to be a safe guide, it is drawn as general as possible, it must not be an isosceles triangle if I mean a triangle, it must not be a rectangle if it is about parallelograms, and of course different points may not coincide. Then it becomes intuitively clear what would not be seen as easy algebraically – that the angles of the triangles are as general as the sides, that a general parallelogram is also general with respect to the diagonals, that if two points of a figure are different, then certain other points and certain straight lines differ, and that if some data coincides, others will coincide, too.

Though it must be admitted that even a "general" triangle once it has been drawn, is acute or obtuse, and the sight of only one kind can seduce us to make more general statements than are strictly correct. It can also happen that some property of the general figure does not apply to the special one, for instance if by the coincidence of certain points some auxiliary line becomes indeterminate. Maybe the generality of the "general" figure is spurious, for instance if it matters whether the point C on the line AB is lying between A, B or outside. The following are points of superiority but at the same time points of weakness
in the geometrical method,
        mastering degenerations,
        the intuitivity of the orientation properties,
and as a third,
        operating with angles.

To translate this from geometry into algebra, tedious and useless hair-splitting is required if it works at all. On the other hand the geometric method invites the most generous slovenliness. (As a curiosity I must mention that before Hajos proved it, geometers tacitly assumed that a parabola has a unique focus.)

Let us turn to orientation properties. In the triangle ABC the bisector from A intersects the opposite side in D; the incircle of ABC touches AB in E. What is the mutual situation of D and E on AB? (Figure 54.)

Of course if need be, it is easily worked out by analytic geometry, but to get more insight, you have to deal with it more fundamentally. Suppose $AC > BC$. The triangle MDE has a right angle at E, so the angle MDE must be acute, hence less than its adjacent angle. Since $\angle CAB < \angle CBA$, $\angle ACD = \angle BCD$, thus $\angle ADC > \angle BDC$, this is the case if and only if $\angle EDC = \angle BDC$, hence if E is on BD.

Decisions like the preceding are often required in proofs in geometry; more often than not they are not too difficult because the figure shows what happens, though this does not exclude accidental mistakes.

It is, however, desirable that more attention is paid to the orientation properties in plane and space; I earlier explained why this is important, and I shall come back to this point. I would not, however, urge that a complete, maybe even axiomatically based, theory of orientation is developed in school instruction. On the contrary, what really matters is bringing intuitive though unconscious facts to pupils' consciousness rather than making long-winded deductions. Though I have expounded this matter at several different places, I must now come back to this point, but I will try not to repeat myself too much.*

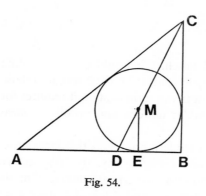

Fig. 54.

What Euclid mentioned on orientation concepts was restricted to the order concept in magnitudes (length, angle, measure, areas). By distinguishing extensions of line segments over the one or the other endpoint, Euclid implicitly admits the possibility of orientation on the straight line, but no axiom, no postulate, no definition tells anything about this difference. There is not any indication of the orientation of the plane in Euclid, though the astronomer who applies the geometry of the sphere has to take all such subtleties into account. In an early stage of geometry it was of great merit to consider figures such as Figures 55–56, which are only distinguished by orientation properties, as equivalent; at Pasch's age, on the contrary, it was a progress to bid farewell to the Euclidean tradition and to make orientation conscious.

* Hans Freudenthal und Arnold Bauer: "Geometrie – phänomenologisch", in: Grundzüge der Mathematik II, edited by H. Behnke, Göttingen, 1960.
Hans Freudenthal, Observing Mathematics, London 1967, pp. 199–247.

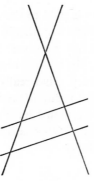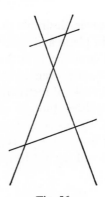

Fig. 55.   Fig. 56.

Hilbert followed Pasch. We would do it a bit different today. Pasch and Hilbert used betweenness. This is a ternary relation (B is between A and C); the first non-trivial statement on it requires four variables, which is quite uncomfortable; notions and proofs by means of betweenness are tedious.

More adapted to modern notions is the linear order, the before-afterness or, as we would prefer to say, the left- and right-ness, a binary relation, which allows a non-trivial statement in three variables, viz. transitivity: if A is left of B and B left of C then A is left of C.

On a straight line, say in the affine plane, two (mutually opposite) orientations are distinguished by intuition. A straight line with such an orientation is called "oriented" or "directed"; to every straight line belongs two directed ones. From this concept those of halfline and line segment can be derived; any point A on a directed line determines the "halfline of points right of A"; the line segment AB consists of the points between A and B, that is, right of A and left of B, or right of B and left of A. A subset of the plane is called convex if with two points it contains all points in between.

To interconnect the orientations of the various lines, it is postulated:

Parallel projection of one line onto another maps an oriented onto an oriented line. (Thus in Figure 57 if in one orientation of g holds A left of B left of C left of D,..., then in one orientation of g' does hold A' left of B' left of C' left of D',...) This postulate replaces the complicated Pasch axiom.

Intuition tells that a straight line g divides the plane into two parts. With the means available this is shown as follows. (Figure 58.) Take an oriented auxiliary line h that intersects g, say at D. Let h^- and h^+ be the set of points left and right of D respectively. The projection parallel to g is called π_g; the π_g-originals of h^- and h^+ are the sets into which the plane is divided by g.

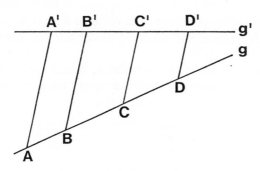

Fig. 57.

Now, this division of the plane seems to depend on the choice of the auxiliary line h, but the dependence is inessential, as follows from the fact that the parallel projection π_g maps oriented on oriented lines. It is also easily seen that two points not in g are in different halfplanes determined by g if and only if the joining line segment intersects g. Every halfplane is convex but ceases to be so as soon as any point of the other halfplane is added.

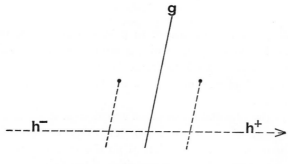

Fig. 58.

Standing on a straight line g and orienting it by my stretched arms from left to right I am also determining one of the halfplanes of g in the plane as the front side and the other as the back side. By this qualification the plane is oriented. The plane, too, admits two orientations; placing oneself in space on the other side of the plane, one gets back side and front side of a line in the plane interchanged. But to define the orientation of the plane its embedding into space can be dispensed with: the plane is oriented if for everyone of its oriented lines it is settled which of its halfplanes is its front and which its back provided that the following holds:

If g is pierced by h from back to front, then h is pierced by g from front to back. (See Figure 59, where the "eyes" are to indicate the front.)

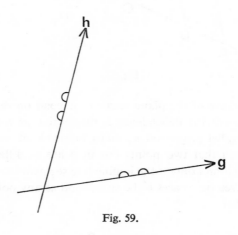

Fig. 59.

The affine plane can be shown to possess exactly two orientations, that is, if it is known of one pair of intersecting oriented lines, which one pierces the other from back to front, the same can be ascertained for any other pair of lines. This can be shown by geometry though here algebra is easier.

Assume in the oriented affine plane an origin o. If suffices to consider lines through o. Every vector $a \neq o$ determines a line oriented from $-a$ towards a, on which αa is left of βa if $\alpha < \beta$. The ordered pair of independent vectors a, b is called positive if the line oriented from $-b$

towards b pierces that from $- a$ towards a from back to front, otherwise it is called negative. Then obviously

if $\ulcorner a, b \urcorner > 0$ and $\alpha > 0$
then $\ulcorner \alpha a, b \urcorner > 0, \ulcorner a, \alpha b \urcorner > 0, \ulcorner - a, b \urcorner < 0, \ulcorner a, - b \urcorner < 0,$
$$\ulcorner b, a \urcorner < 0.$$

Further, since b and $b + \alpha a$ are on the same side of the line oriented from $- a$ towards a:

if $\ulcorner a, b \urcorner > 0$ then $\ulcorner a, b + \alpha a \urcorner > 0.$

This reminds the definition of area. Choose a basis e_1, e_2, number its elements such that $\ulcorner e_1, e_2 \urcorner > 0$ and put area $\ulcorner e_1, e_2 \urcorner = 1$. Then it follows from the preceding:

$\ulcorner a, b \urcorner > 0$ iff area $\ulcorner a, b \urcorner > 0.$

Thus the orientation of the plane is settled, if it is known which one of a pair of oriented lines (eventually the pair of that from $- e_1$ towards e_1 and that from $- e_2$ towards e_2) pierces the other from back to front. Conversely, the existence of such an orientation is shown by putting

$\ulcorner a, b \urcorner > 0$ iff area $\ulcorner a, b \urcorner > 0.$

as a definition.

Further it has resulted that the affine mappings which preserve the area, preserve the orientation, too, and conversely.

I will be brief on orientation in space. Again it is postulated: on every straight line two opposite orientations are distinguished; a pencil of parallel planes maps two straight lines, intersecting the pencil planes, such that orientation passes into orientation.

Again it can be shown that every plane divides space into two halfspaces. Space is oriented if of every plane in space it is settled which of its halfspaces is its lower and which its upperside. Again these dispositions should agree with each other; this requirement can be formulated as follows:

Let a_1, a_2, a_3 be three independent vectors; a_1, a_2 span a plane π, which is oriented such that $\ulcorner a_1, a_2 \urcorner > 0$ in π; let g be the line oriented from $- a_3$ to a_3. It is defined

$\ulcorner a_1, a_2, a_3 \urcorner > 0$ if π is pierced by g from below to above.

One now has to postulate that the sign of
$\ulcorner a_1, a_2, a_3 \urcorner$ is invariant under even permutations.

Then again $\ulcorner a_1, a_2, a_3 \urcorner > 0$ can be reduced to vol $\ulcorner a_1, a_2, a_3 \urcorner > 0$.
Invariance of orientation and of the sign of the volume are again
equivalent properties of affine mappings.

ORGANIZING A FIELD–CYCLIC ORIENTATION

The oriented line is characterized by a linear order. In the pencil of
halflines (or oriented lines) from a point 0, another kind of orientation
prevails; it is called cyclic, and it is well known from the dial and the
annual cycle. It makes sense to ask whether Castor was born before or
after Pollux. It is not meaningful to ask whether in the halfday cycle
3 o'clock comes before or after 9 o'clock, in the year cycle Easter before
or after Whitsunday. It does made sense to say that the sequence 3 o'clock,
6 o'clock, 9 o'clock is correct, and likewise Easter, Whitsunday, Christmas
rather than the inverse. But 6 o'clock, 9 o'clock, 3 o'clock, is also correct, and so is Christmas, Easter, Whitsunday.

Among the $n!$ arrangements of n things $a_1, ..., a_n$,

$$a_{i_1}, ..., a_{i_p}, a_{i_{p+1}}, ..., a_{i_n}$$

and

$$a_{i_{p+1}}, ..., a_n, a_{i_1}, ..., a_{i_p}$$

are called cyclically equivalent. With this equivalence notion cyclic
equivalence classes are formed.

Orienting a finite set cyclically means choosing one among the cyclic
equivalence classes of its elements.

Orienting an arbitrary set Z cyclically means orienting everyone among
its finite sets cyclically such that if $V \subset W \subset Z$ (V, W finite), the cyclic
orientation of W extends that of V.

A triple a, b, c allows two cyclic orientations $abc = bca = cab$ and
$acb = cba = bac$. The cyclic orientation of a set Z is completely known
as soon as it is known on all triples of Z. It cannot, however, be arbitrarily
prescribed on the triples. There is a compatibility condition:

(∗) If abd and bcd are in the cyclic orientation, then acd (and abc) are also. (The bracketed statement can be derived from the preceding, since *abd* and *bcd* can also be written as *dab* and *cdb*.)

A cyclically-oriented set Z can be transformed into an ordered set Z_u by ripping, as it were, Z at u. It is defined

$$x \text{ left of } u \text{ for all } x \neq u,$$

and

$$x \text{ left of } y \text{ iff } xyu \text{ in the cyclic orientation.}$$

The property (*) then corresponds to transitivity in Z_u.

The cyclic orientation can also be analyzed as follows:

Two linear orders in Z are called cyclically equivalent if Z can be divided in two sets X and Y such that

both orders coincide in X,
both orders coincide in Y,
in one of both every element of X comes before every element
of Y,
in the other every element of Y comes before every element
of X.

It is easily checked that this is a decent equivalence relation. An equivalence class of linear orders is called a cyclic orientation of Z.

Of a cyclically oriented set Z a *n-fold covering* can be formed (it is again cyclically oriented): rip Z at u, take n copies of the ripped Z_u and sew them cyclically together. More precisely:

Consider the pairs set $\hat{Z} = \ulcorner Z, I \urcorner$ where I is the set of integers mod n, in an obvious cyclic orientation. The cyclic orientation of $\hat{Z}$ is fixed as follows:

In the cyclic orientation of $\hat{Z}$,

$$\ulcorner x, i \urcorner \ulcorner y, i \urcorner \ulcorner z, i \urcorner \quad \text{if} \quad xyz,$$
$$\ulcorner x, i \urcorner \ulcorner y, i \urcorner \ulcorner z, j \urcorner \quad \text{if} \quad i \neq j \quad \text{and} \quad xyu,$$
$$\ulcorner x, i \urcorner \ulcorner y, j \urcorner \ulcorner z, k \urcorner \quad \text{if} \quad ijk \quad \text{in the cyclic orientation of } I.$$

∞-fold covering of Z is also possible, but then a linearly ordered set $\tilde{Z}$ arises:

Consider the pairs set $\tilde{Z} = \ulcorner Z, I \urcorner$ where I is now the ordered set of integers, and put

$$\ulcorner x, i \urcorner \text{ left of } \ulcorner y, i \urcorner \quad \text{if} \quad xyu,$$

⌜x, i⌝ left of ⌜y, j⌝ if $i < j$.

The covering does not depend essentially on u.

A natural cyclic orientation already exists in the pencil of unoriented lines through the origin o of the oriented plane:

Let g_1, g_2, g_3 be three of these straight lines. Choose a vector $a_1 (\neq o)$ on g_1; then a_2, a_3 can be chosen on g_2, g_3 respectively such that ⌜a_1, a_2⌝ > 0 and ⌜a_1, a_3⌝ > 0. If now ⌜a_2, a_3⌝ > 0, then put $a_1 a_2 a_3$ in the cyclic orientation of the pencil.

In other words,

$g_1 g_2 g_3$ in the cyclic orientation if the g_i can be oriented such that g_1 is pierced by g_2 and g_3 from back to front and g_2 is so by g_3, or;

$g_1 g_2 g_3$ in the cyclic orientation if vectors a_i can be found on $g_i (i = 1, 2, 3)$ such that

$$⌜a_1, a_2⌝ > 0, \quad ⌜a_1, a_3⌝ > 0, \quad ⌜a_2, a_3⌝ > 0.$$

It can be checked that this definition fulfills the condition (*) though again it is easier by algebra than by geometry. It follows from the following

REMARK: If ⌜a, b⌝ > 0, ⌜b, c⌝ > 0, ⌜c, a⌝ > 0, then no x exists with ⌜a, x⌝ > 0, ⌜b, x⌝ > 0, ⌜c, x⌝ > 0.

It is proved as follows: a, b, c are linearly dependent, thus $\lambda a + \mu b + vc = o$ with certain λ, μ, v (not all of them 0). From $0 = $ area ⌜$a, \lambda a + \mu b + vc$⌝ $= \mu \cdot$ area ⌜a, b⌝ $+ v \cdot$ area ⌜a, c⌝ it follows that μ, v have the same sign, and finally with a replaced by b and c, that λ, μ, v have the same sign, say, are all $\geqslant 0$. Then with an x as above,

$$0 = \text{area} ⌜\lambda a + \mu b + vc, x⌝ > 0,$$

which is a contradiction.

After this remark it can be shown that $a_1 a_2 a_3$ and $a_2 a_3 a_4$ in the cyclic orientation imply that $a_1 a_3 a_4$ is so, as required by (*).

That is, from

$$⌜a_1, a_2⌝ > 0, \quad ⌜a_1, a_4⌝ > 0, \quad ⌜a_2, a_4⌝ > 0,$$
$$⌜a_2, a_3⌝ > 0, \quad ⌜a_2, a_4⌝ > 0, \quad ⌜a_3, a_4⌝ > 0,$$

it must follow

$$⌜a_1, a_3⌝ > 0, \quad ⌜a_1, a_4⌝ > 0, \quad ⌜a_3, a_4⌝ > 0.$$

The only thing to be proved is that $\ulcorner a_1, a_3 \urcorner > 0$ follows. If it were not so, then $\ulcorner a_3, a_1 \urcorner > 0$ and this would lead to the contradictory

$$\ulcorner a_1, a_2 \urcorner > 0, \quad \ulcorner a_2, a_3 \urcorner > 0, \quad \ulcorner a_3, a_1 \urcorner > 0,$$
$$\ulcorner a_1, a_4 \urcorner > 0, \quad \ulcorner a_2, a_4 \urcorner > 0, \quad \ulcorner a_3, a_4 \urcorner > 0.$$

The double covering of the oriented pencil of lines can intuitively be obtained by replacing every line by an oriented line. This is the orientation of the pencil of oriented lines (or of halflines). A direct definition runs as follows. Again an oriented line is represented by a vector a ($\neq o$) on it such that the line is oriented from $-a$ towards a; the line will be indicated simply by the vector a. If the lines a and b intersect each other, $\ulcorner a, b \urcorner$ is defined as above; for lines a, b, however, with opposite orientation we put $\ulcorner a, b \urcorner = 0$, which is in agreement with "area $\ulcorner a, b \urcorner = 0$".

Let a, b, c be different oriented lines. Then in

$$\ulcorner a, b \urcorner \gtreqless 0, \quad \ulcorner b, c \urcorner \gtreqless 0, \quad \ulcorner c, a \urcorner \gtreqless 0$$

at least a pair of $>$-signs or a pair of $<$-signs appears; we prescribe abc to belong to the cyclic orientation of the pencil if the $>$-sign occurs at least twice. As above the validity of (∗) can be checked; again the *Remark* plays a role.

It is easily seen that linear mappings that preserve the sign of the area also preserve the orientation in the lines pencil and in the halflines pencil.

Moreover it is clear that the orientation of the plane is determined by that of the lines pencil or of the halflines pencil. In this way the orientation of the plane can be interpreted as a sense of turning around. Of course this has nothing to do with rotations in the sense of Euclidean geometry; our substratum is still the affine plane. It is the cyclic travel through the pencil. We oriented the plane on which we move by first orienting a line in the plane with our stretched arms from left to right and then considering the direction of our eyes as its front side. By definition the turning sense is moving the right hand to the front. In everyday life it is called a left turn (anti-clockwise). This is in the concrete plane the orientation of the pencil.

In space the orientation was given by an oriented plane and its back side. This can now be viewed as follows. In the plane a turning sense is given by which the plane is oriented; moreover an arrow that pierces the plane from back to front. (Figure 60.) The combination of both of them, the turning and the forward sense is a characteristic property of screws and corkscrews. Therefore the orientation of space is also called its "screw-sense". The living space usually is oriented such that the horizontal plane is given the left turn and the piercing arrow is directed from below

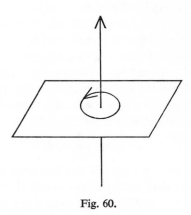

Fig. 60.

to above. This corresponds to the screw motion "left turn-out" or "right turn-in". It is the screw sense of ordinary right screws and corkscrews.

ORGANIZING A FIELD–THE ANGLE CONCEPTS

As has been stressed several times, there is more than one angle concept. Some didacticians claim that there is only one which is correct. Love of order is fine unless it goes as far as to forbid important concepts because they do not fit into the system. Properly said such would be a bad mathematical attitude. It has cost a great deal of trouble to get mathematicians used to the fact that there are various number concepts, which are now carefully distinguished from each other. If rather than being distinguished all angle concepts but one are forbidden, pupils will never learn to distinguish them – forbidding rules never work.

Euclid defines the angle as an inclination of lines (even curves were admitted); he meant halflines, because otherwise he would not be able to distinguish adjacent angles from each other. He is not consistent, however;

in the next definition he speaks of straight lines, comprising the angle, which fits better the view on an angle as part of the plane.

Euclid does not know zero angles, nor straight and bigger than straight angles. If the angle is to be part of the plane the latter should be admitted. If, however, an angle is only an unordered pair of halflines, it does not make sense to distinguish *two* angles in *one* pair of halflines.

Euclid compares, adds and subtracts angles. One speaks of equality of angles as one does of line segments; if the angle is a part of the plane, congruence would be a better term. Euclid takes the liberty of adding angles beyond two and even four right angles; the results cannot be angles according to the original definitions. The lack of angles beyond two right angles causes complications, e.g. in the theorem of centre and periphery angles at the circle, as soon as the periphery angle is right or obtuse. Nevertheless one feels that Euclid's angle concept is consistent.

In trigonometry another angle concept is familiar; the angle is viewed on as a centre angle of a circle (say with radius one); there arcs and angles correspond to each other; angles are measured by arcs, such that 360° and 2π correspond to each other. Unlike line segments, there is for angles a natural gauge, the full circle, which is measured by 360° or 2π; angle measures are numbers with no measure unit. With self-overlapping arcs on the unit circle one gets arc lengths exceeding 2π. Angles, however, are generally dealt with as numbers mod 2π.

This angle definition is more refined than that of Euclid with pairs of halflines. With a pair of halflines we cannot tell the difference between $\frac{1}{2}\pi$ and $\frac{3}{2}\pi$ because nobody tells us whether the arc should be drawn inside or outside. To decide this, we must take an *ordered* pair of halflines; some convention must be agreed upon, say that the measuring arc starts left of a and finishes right of b. But we can tell left from right only in the *oriented* plane. Goniometric angles are possible only in the oriented plane, and they are measured on the unit circle by the arc that runs from a to b in the sense of the cyclic orientation of the pencil. Thus the goniometric angle is a function of ordered pairs of halflines in an oriented plane. If the orientation is inverted, the angle of $\frac{1}{2}\pi$ is changed into one of $\frac{3}{2}\pi$ or $-\frac{1}{2}\pi$.

If the plane is not oriented or if the space rather than the plane are under discussion, such angles cannot be distinguished; then α and $2\pi - \alpha$ would be the same, but it is better then to count angles from 0 to π.

Thus Euclid was quite consistent when he did not allow for angles above two right angles; otherwise he would have been obliged to orient the plane – an arbitrary and somewhat artificial procedure. How do we do it in everyday life? Whether a driver deviates from his direction to the left or to the right, it is always a right angle, but with the usual orientation of the plane we move on, the left turn should be called 90° and the right turn 270° – sailors who like mathematicians speak a private language, call it backing and veering, terms which I would not recommend to take over. For the same reason I would not tell a person who asks the way, to turn 270° or $-90°$ at the traffic light. Moreover the whole system is due to fail in three dimensions.

In so-called analytic geometry another angle concept prevails. There one speaks of the angle of two straight lines, but this is not what is actually meant. If it were the angle of a *non-ordered* pair of lines, an angle would not be distinguished from its adjacent angle. It is rather the angle of an *ordered* pair of lines. To the angle of an ordered pair of halflines it can be brought back as follows: on the lines g and h through 0, the point 0 determines the opposite halflines g^+, g^- and h^+, h^-, respectively. All (goniometric) angles $\measuredangle(g^+, h^+)$, $\measuredangle(g^+, h^-)$, $\measuredangle(g^-, h^+)$, $\measuredangle(g^-, h^-)$ are meaningful and equal up to π. So an ordered pair of lines determines an angle mod π.

This also follows from the formula by which the angle φ of two lines, say

$$y = ax$$

and

$$y = bx,$$

is computed:

$$\operatorname{tg}\varphi = \frac{b-a}{1+ab}.$$

Here the tangent intervenes; since it has the period π, we can determine φ only mod π. If the two lines are interchanged, the tangent and consequently the angle is replaced by its opposite.

School geometry in space knows still another angle concept, the angle of a non-ordered pair of lines, thus properly with angles from 0° to 90°.

A survey on these angle concepts looks as follows*:

Goniometry	Elementary Geometry	Analytic Geometry	Space Geometry
	Angle concept: the angle of		
an ordered	a non-ordered	an ordered	a non-ordered
	pair of		
halflines	halflines	lines	lines
	in the		
oriented	non-oriented	oriented	non-oriented
	plane, determined		
mod 2π	between 0° and 180°	mod π	between 0° and 90°

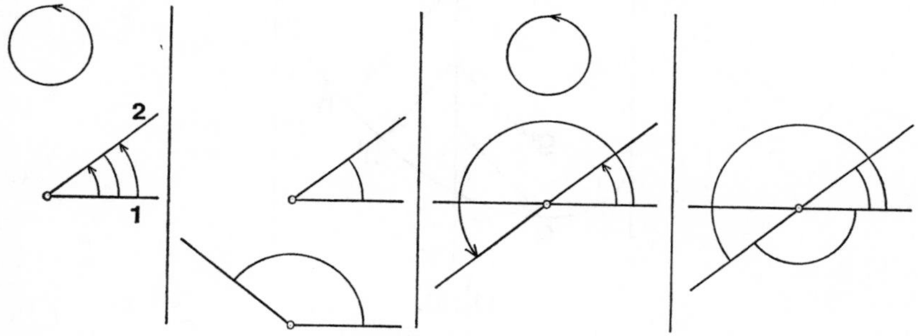

Fig. 61.

The terms "Goniometry" etc., must be taken with a pinch of salt. For instance space would allow the angle of unordered pairs of halflines, and if the space is oriented, an angle mod 2π would even be possible for ordered pairs of *skew* halflines g, h. If g and h are in a plane this cannot succeed, even if the pair is given as ordered, since the orientation of space does not determine an orientation in the plane. If g, h are skew, however, one is advised to consider among the screw motions that carry g into h those which correspond to the screw-sense of the space, and to define that screw angle as angle of g and h. More precisely (Figure 62): connect the origin of g with that of h by a line k oriented from g to h and move g and h parallel along k to a fixed point of k;

* From H. Freudenthal und A. Bauer, "Geometrie – phänomenologisch", in *Grundzüge der Mathematik*, IIA, Göttingen 1967.

there new halflines g', h' are obtained. g', h' may be supposed on different lines; the plane ε through g' h' is oriented such as to yield together with k the orientation of the space. The angle of g and h is by definition the angle of g' and h' in the oriented plane ε.

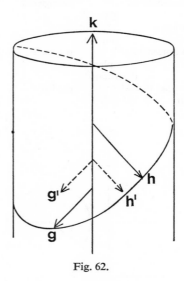

Fig. 62.

Observe that this is an angle of a non-oriented pair of halflines (or oriented lines) in the oriented space. If g and h are interchanged, k as well as ε are re-oriented in the opposite sense, and g', h' are interchanged; both changes cancel each other out. It is now better understood why the two halflines must be skew to get this kind of angle.

According to the table the Elementary Geometry angle was meant between 0° and 180°. Euclid, however, adds beyond 180° if, for instance, he speaks about four right angles. If somebody has turned two and a half times round his axis he has covered 900°. This is an angle that measures turns; it belongs properly to kinematics. But not only to kinematics. If sine and cosine are considered as analytic functions, they are defined for any real argument and are periodical mod 2π. If these arguments are viewed on as angles, we must allow angles from $-\infty$ to ∞. Let us call them *analytic angles* because their role is in analysis, as arguments of the goniometric functions. We will come back to their connection with elementary geometry and goniometry angles; finally we will see that properly said the analytic angles do not depend on analysis.

Three angle concepts are particularly important. We first indicate how they are instrumentally measured. The Elementary Geometry angle is measured with the semicircle protractor; the directions for use are that one side passes through 0 and the angle measure is read at the other side; this procedure is unique. The Goniometry angle is measured with a full circle protractor; again one side must pass through 0 and the angle measure is read at the other side. But now an *ordered* pair of sides is to be considered and it is decreed that the first side passes through 0. The orientation of the plane also plays a part; the protractor shall be laid down such that the turning sense from 0° via 90° to 180° matches the orientation of the plane (that is, anti-clockwise). The procedure is self-explanatory, since the protractor shows certain figures and the good position is that where the "two" appears as 2 rather than as its mirror image.

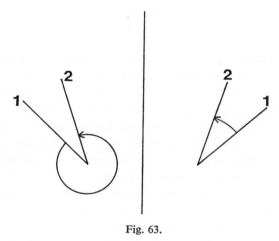

Fig. 63.

A protractor for "analytic" angles is any instrument that counts turns such as an electricity meter or a hodometer, which registers the whole or fractional turns of a certain disk.

Finally a few remarks on the behaviour of angles under motions and symmetries of the plane or the space. No problem arises if it is about angles defined in non-oriented plane or space; motions and symmetries are automorphisms; both lengths and angles are an invariant under all automorphisms, thus under motions and symmetries. The oriented plane and the oriented space enjoy a smaller automorphism group; it consists of the motions, since the symmetries, with negative determinant, do not preserve the orientation. Angles that depend on orientation pass into their opposites under symmetries.

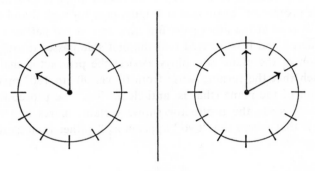

Fig. 64.

In lectures I used to illustrate this by two pictures (Figures 63–64); one shows how an angle under reflection behaves, the other how a dial does: 2 o'clock passes into 10 o'clock. With the second figure I caused a useful confusion; the discussion showed the logical difficulties which are inherent in these notions. (I am astonished that such problems are nowhere mentioned in the literature; anybody who has thought about them must have stumbled upon the same difficulties. But silence is typical behaviour from those who have neatly organized a subject matter – objectivating the result and wiping out all traces of mathematics as an activity.)

The mirror image of the clock caused the following objection: "You have omitted the figures on the dial. If you had added them, it would have been obvious that 2 o'clock does not pass into 10 o'clock but again into 2 o'clock though on the mirror image dial; thus angles are preserved under symmetry." Another member of the audience objected: "The image angle is 30° like the original; you could have done better to draw the mirror image of the little arc with the arrow, rather than the big arc; with the new orientation of the plane it again means 30°." A third objector made this more intuitive by also reflecting a protractor in the mirror (Figure 65), but this then was the most direct way of detecting what is wrong with these objections. We had agreed, indeed, on laying down the full circle protractor upon the drawing plane such as to show a two as a 2 rather than as its mirror image. By this procedure we made sure that the turning sense of the protractor matches the conventional orientation of the plane; moreover the digit 0 should appear on the first

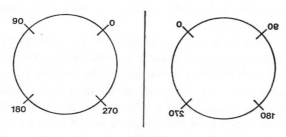

Fig. 65.

side of the angle whilst the angle measure should be read on the second side. The first condition is violated if the mirror reflection is also exerted upon the protractor: the mirror image of a protractor is no admitted tool (in this respect it is distinguished from a ruler). If before and after the transformation the same protractor is used, it comes out that the angle is changed by the transformation. True, a reflection can be interpreted as a mapping of the oriented plane onto the oppositely oriented plane (thus as an isomorphism instead of an automorphism); then the angles remain invariant. Yet this is not the point here. It was our viewpoint that the oriented plane is mapped upon itself; this mapping is not an automorphism.

I am going to illustrate this by another example. Let us consider the Euclidean plane as a metric space, thus with a distance notion (not only a congruence notion for line segments). Then a homothety with the factor 2 is not an automorphism, it multiplies all line segment lengths by 2. Somebody objects: "The ruler which measures the lengths, too, undergoes the homothety; measured with the new ruler all lengths are preserved, thus homothety preserves distance."

This example shows even more clearly what was wrong in the former objections. Agreeing upon the Euclidean plane being a metric space means concretely that a well-defined ruler has been adopted, and this instrument, of course, may not be falsified. If the homothety is interpreted as transforming the ruler, too, then rather than a mapping of a plane on itself, it is one of the plane on another plane with another gauge, with another ruler. On the contrary, in a Euclidean plane with a notion of congruence rather than of distance a homothety *is* an automorphism; there rulers with scales are allowed to transfer line segments by congruence, though the scale unit has no numerical meaning. So far the analysis of a paradox.

Let us now come back to the question what the adding of Elementary Geometry angles beyond 180° means. The Elementary Geometry angles form a set in which addition is restricted. The twofold covering of the system of angles mod 180° yields the angles mod 360°; Euclid's system in which angles are unrestrictedly added reminds the infinite covering of the system of angles mod 360°; there it makes sense to state that the heptagon has the sum of angles 5π. Yet it is not exactly Euclid's system because it also allows unrestricted subtraction of angles, which is not possible in Euclid's system. After the following analysis we will come back to this point.

Let us consider the cyclically oriented pencil of halflines through the origin; in this set a fixed halfline o is assumed. Let a function ϕ be defined by $\phi(g) = \measuredangle\,(o, g)$; then ϕ maps the halflines pencil on the set W of the angles. If W is cyclically oriented as the halflines pencil, it becomes a cyclically oriented set. Moreover W is an addition group with the property that

addition preserves the orientation, that is if $\alpha\beta\gamma$ are in the cyclic orientation so are $(\alpha + \xi)\,(\beta + \xi)\,(\gamma + \xi)$;

negation inverts the orientation, that is if $\alpha\beta\gamma$ are in the cyclic orientation $(-\alpha)\,(-\beta)\,(-\gamma)$ are not.

From this results that:

If $0\alpha\beta$ are in the cyclic orientation so are $\alpha\beta(\alpha + \beta)$.

For then $0(-\alpha)\,(-\beta)$ are not, so $0(-\beta)\,(-\alpha)$ are, and so are $(\alpha + \beta)\,\alpha\beta$.

Let us now form the infinitely-fold cover $\hat{W}$ after having ripped W at 0. As formerly the elements of $\hat{W}$ are the pairs

$$\ulcorner\alpha, i\urcorner \quad \text{with} \quad \alpha \in W \quad \text{and } i \text{ an integer;}$$

$\hat{W}$ is oriented as formerly, to wit:

⌐α, i⌐ left of ⌐β, i⌐ if $0\alpha\beta$ in the cyclic orientation,
⌐α, i⌐ left of ⌐β, j⌐ if $i < j$.

The group structure, too, can be lifted upon $\hat{W}$; put

$$\ulcorner\alpha, i\urcorner + \ulcorner\beta, j\urcorner = \ulcorner\alpha + \beta, i + j\urcorner \quad \text{if} \quad 0\alpha(\alpha + \beta)$$
$$= \ulcorner\alpha + \beta, i + j + 1\urcorner \quad \text{if} \quad 0(\alpha + \beta)\alpha$$

in the cyclic orientation. This is again an abelian group, which is an ordered group, too; addition preserves the orientation, that is, "α left of β" implies "$\alpha + \xi$ left of $\beta + \xi$".

Let us call the system $\hat{W}$ that of the analytic angles, on the one hand as a contrast to "geometric", on the other hand because often if sines and cosines are considered as analytic functions, it becomes habitual to consider the real arguments of these functions as angles that are varying between $-\infty$ and ∞.

The preceding construction is not yet sufficient. *A priori* we do not know whether the "analytic" angles can be measured by real numbers. $\hat{W}$ is simply an ordered additive group. For instance, to halve such angles the basic field of the geometry must allow for square roots, as is shown by the formula

$$\cos\tfrac{1}{2}\alpha = \sqrt{\tfrac{1}{2}(1 + \cos\alpha)}.$$

The protractor shows how angles are measured. It is, as it were, a curved ruler; angles are measured by the same kind of numbers as line segments. If we accept the set of numbers as the number line, there is no reason why we should refuse this to analytic angles however the set of reals has been introduced. If the real numbers have intuitively been accepted to measure line segments, then angles can as intuitively be measured by them. If real numbers are infinite decimal fractions, then the same measuring procedure that assigns decimal fractions to line-segments can be applied to angles. And all this is true even in the most profound mathematics. The following holds:

Let G be a Dedekind ordered group (that is an ordered group such that for any partition of G into a lower and an upper class, G_+, G_- (with $a \in G_+ \land b \in G_- \to a < b$), either the lower class has a largest and the upper class no smallest element, or the upper class has a smallest and the lower class no largest element). Then *G* is isomorphic to the addition group of reals.

If it is supposed that line segments are measured by real numbers, it is an easy consequence that the analytic angles form a Dedekind ordered group and thus can be measured by real numbers too.

But as was earlier explained when the organization of algebra was discussed, rather than requiring a formal theory of real numbers, one can postulate by means of a "protractor axiom" that algebraic operations take place in such a field as allows the measuring of angles by elements of the field.

However that may be, fundamentally these analytic angles have not too much to do with analysis. Departing from the Goniometric angle, analytic angles can be obtained by an infinite covering of the system, and this is an elementary procedure which has nothing to do with limits, differentiating, and integrating. If on the other hand real numbers have been accepted to measure line segments, there is not the slightest reason why they should be banned when angles are to be measured. The same measuring procedures that lead to the measuring of line segments by real numbers yield angle measures too, whether this measuring has been mathematized by decimal fractions or Dedekind cuts; and finally if reals should be avoided at all, there is still the way out left assuming the protractor axiom.

I stress this so much because it seems that this matter is governed by misunderstandings which I will come back to later. Meanwhile, after this disgression I turn again to the Euclid's Elementary Geometry angle. I already warned against identifying it with the analytic angle. It is not as simple as that, however. Euclid does not know negative angles, so he can do with angles of non-ordered pairs of halflines and he need not orient the plane. Euclid starts with angles between 0° and 180° and extends this system in *one* direction. The result is one half of the system of analytic angles; whether it is the positive or negative half cannot be decided without an orientation, but then we may evaluate the angular measures according to their absolute values.

Anyhow the system of analytic angles fulfills the important function that one half of it, say the positive one, yields Euclid's Elementary Geometry angles. Here the analytic angles up to 180° are directly visualized as inclination measures between halflines (unordered pairs in a non-oriented plane); larger angles emerge as abstract sums of such angles. It is as though line segments would not be concretely available beyond the lengths of 100 cm and larger ones had to imagined as sums of the smaller kind. In this system of Elementary Geometry angles, addition is unrestricted though not subtraction; subtraction cannot be interpreted as the addition of a negative magnitude since no negative magnitudes exist.

In Euclid's system the absence of angles between 180° and 360° as original magnitudes is a bit annoying. I mentioned earlier the theorem on center and periphery angles. Other examples are non-convex polygons; if the theorem on the sum of the angles should extend to this case, a measure of re-entrant angles must be admitted. To define such angles ordered pairs of halflines are required; this implies that to speak of the sum of angles of a polygon one has to tell in which sense it is travelled; then a triangle can yield 180° or − 180° according to whether it is travelled with the orientation of the plane or against it. If angles of ordered pairs of halflines in the oriented plane are added (as Euclid does with angles, of non-ordered pairs of halflines) the system of analytic angles arises with values from − ∞ to − ∞ and unrestricted additions, and with an unrestricted subtraction, too, which can be interpreted as an addition of the opposite magnitude. As we saw, this system of analytic angles is the infinite covering of that of Goniometry angles.

At least three angle concepts are practically, and thus didactically, important. Systematizing mathematicians are prone to restrict themselves to one and to eliminate the others. It is the same mentality that led the Greeks to restrict themselves to integers and to ban fractions. Of course, in everyday life and in numerical mathematics one used fractions though in pure mathematics they were forbidden. It is the same schizophrenic attitude as that of a mathematician who recognizes the goniometric angle concept only, but of necessity speaks of the visual angle under which he sees an object and who knows very well that a half turn and a turn and a half is not the same when he turns a key in a keyhole. I admit there are people who are not convinced by such arguments. To their view the existence of instruments to measure angles is rather an argument against angles in mathematical instruction. Their suspicion is in particular aroused by the cyclic orientation of the halflines pencil and that angle concept I termed analytic. Dieudonné brands these notions with such terms as inconsistent, transcendent, and ridiculous – three adjectives which in any case contradict each other. As we have often enough stressed, however, cyclic orientation is quite reasonable provided the plane has been oriented, which is indispensable to various uses; I cannot understand why it should be regarded as ridiculous or transcendent. The analytic angles are obtained as an infinite covering of the system of Goniometry angles. This is a natural procedure and in no way ridiculous or inconsistent, and is moreover neither kinematic nor analytic, whichever field is accepted. If Dieudonné* avoids the field of reals to make such angles impossible, as he says, then in any case this is a wrong way to reach such a goal. In the affine plane over *any ordered field* the halflines pencil is reigned by the earlier dealt with cyclic orientation; turning around is a meaningful notion, and the infinite covering of the cyclic orientation can be formed; this produces what I called analytic angles. Whether the analytic angles should be relegated to analysis or to kinematics, as Dieudonné puts it, depends on how the subject matter is to be arranged; whether it is allowed to name them angles is a matter of terminology. To be restricted in geometry to those methods that in some system of mathematics belong to algebra is an unreasonable prohibition. Of course, one could argue that the subject is *elementary* geometry, and that the integers, which are needed to form the infinite cover, are not elementary. This is how the term "elementary" is used in foundations of mathematics. In this sense elementary arithmetics would not be elementary but I think we had better look for what is elementary in the sense of didactics. If we do so, we certainly cannot decide by dogmatic standards what belongs to elementary or to more advanced geometry instruction.

We now turn to just this question. What I have explained till now about orientation and angles was rather the mathematical background. It is quite another question which details out of this background picture must be pushed into the foreground, and any attempt to answer it with with no regard to the learning process should be opposed.

I stressed that the *Elementary Geometry angle*, the *Goniometry angle* and the *analytic angle*, concretized by measuring processes, are very natural concepts. None of these three concepts can be dispensed with.

---

* J. Dieudonné, *Algèbre linéaire et géométrie élémentaire*, Paris 1964. In particular, the Introduction.

They should be introduced early, and I believe, at about the same time. This has the supplementary advantage that the student learns from the beginning that there *are* three angle concepts. Should they be distinguished terminologically, then *absolute angles*, *angles*, and *turn around angles* would be the recommended terminology. As symbols one could use ⊰ for the absolute angles, and ⊰ for the "angles"; in the second symbol the turning sense of the plane is put upon the paper. It should be stressed that angles deal with pairs of oriented lines or halflines, and that without an orientation of the plane, mutual inclinations of halflines cannot be counted beyond 180° though they can be added with no limit. This is as unproblematic as adding lengths of line segments that are not on the same line, and of time intervals that are not contiguous, or if you wish, as adding weights of eggs. Though the union of eggs is not an egg, their weights may be added.

Introducing "angles" should be preceded by orienting the plane in the simplest way, by the turning sense which is familiar from the clock and other instruments. Operating with such angles would be easier if students are familiar with arithmetics modulo an integer. Addition should be experienced as a functional procedure; interpreting the addition on the number line as a translation should be sided by interpreting the addition in the halfline pencil as a rotation; likewise subtracting from a fixed angle should be seen as a reflection. Rather than on the whole plane these operations are then seen as acting on the pencil or the border of the protractor. The angle should also be discovered in the deviation from rectilinear motion; it should be clear that when running around a polygon, one turns at every corner through the *exterior* angle. If I characterized this kind of angle as a "Goniometry" one, I would not say that at this early stage goniometric functions should be introduced though there is no need to delay their introduction too long. They are most beautiful examples of mechanically produced functions, which can easily be put into graphics and which are early used in such applications as optics. Of course complicated goniometric formulae like the addition theorems should not be dealt with until they are really needed and accessible to easy proofs.

The "angle" should unambiguously be defined as a Goniometry angle, that is, as a measure which in addition and subtraction behaves modulo the full angle (360°). Light is shed on this concept if it is clearly contrasted with that of the "turn around angle". This angle, which is so important in many applications must be expressively mentioned and dealt with aside of the "angle" to prevent misunderstandings. To avoid the "turn around angle" would be ostrich-like behaviour.

The turn around angle is most strikingly demonstrated if the goniometric functions are graphically set out (Figure 66). A point is moving

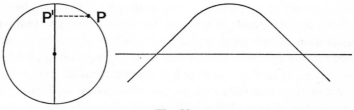

Fig. 66.

uniformly on the unit circle; its projection on a perpendicular line performs a harmonic vibration, the amplitude of which can be graphically set out as a function of the angle (or of time). What can be more advisable than extending the function, that is to have the point running indefinitely forwards and backwards over the circle? Mathematizing our intuition we get as a domain of the argument of the function exactly what we have described as the infinite cover of the circle.

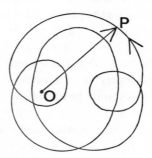

Fig. 67.

The turn around angle allows for many applications; it also describes how many times a closed oriented polygon or a closed oriented curve in the oriented plane turn around a point o (Figure 67); it is the turn around angle that is described by a vector OP if P runs on the curve. (The analogue with surfaces in space is much more involved because there the wonderful tool of the angle is lacking.) It is another important feature that the sums of Elementary Geometry angles beyond 180° can be concretized by means of the turn around angle.

Furthermore, the three angle concepts should be fundamentally compared with regard to the operations performed with them, how they are added and subtracted; that it does not make sense multiplying angles with each other; that "angles" can be doubled, tripled, multiplied by n, under which operations the images cover the halflines pencil or the circle twice, thrice, n-fold; that "angle"-division is a multivalued operation; that, on the contrary, turn around angles can uniquely be halved, and divided into three or more equal parts; what happens with angles under motions and symmetries. There is an abundance of geometric analysis which can be carried out at the lowest level. The theorem on periphery and centre angles leads to a mechanism which transforms one motion into a motion of double velocity. Can the same be done with other factors? Which kind of angles play a part if transmission is to be understood geometrically? How are circle arcs measured by angles?

This may be enough on the angle concept in an early stage of geometry; the orientation of the plane enters the exposition as the turning sense; orientation of space, however, is hardly meaningfully accessible at this stage. If the algebraization of geometry by means of vector algebra starts, it should happen in a naive non-axiomatic way rather than by linear algebra, and of course not as affine geometry, but on an orthonormal basis. The plane is simply described by vectorial means. The student should already be familiar with motions and reflections so that their representation by matrices with goniometric functions, in the coefficients,

$$D_\varphi = \begin{pmatrix} \cos\phi & -\sin\phi \\ \sin\phi & \cos\phi \end{pmatrix}$$

does not meet any difficulty. From the product of such matrices

$$D_\varphi D_\psi = D_{\varphi+\psi}$$

the addition theorems for the goniometric functions are obtained such as has earlier been exposed.

Here the orientation of the plane expresses itself as a turning sense, as the circulation in the halflines pencil or on the unit circle according to the increase of the angular coordinate. On the other hand, detaching this mathematical turning sense from the conventional turning sense of the concrete plane (the left turn) can be attempted. In fact, the turning sense is already fixed by the mutual situation of the basis vectors e_1, e_2, and simply by assuming this pair of vectors the plane can arbitrarily be oriented. The angle of the ordered pair e_1, e_2 is to be fixed at 90°, that is, the turning sense is the one that carries e_1 into e_2 most directly. The possible bases fall into two sets, corresponding to the two possible turning senses.

Detaching the turning sense from the concrete left turn is not a subject to speak lightheartedly about. I cannot say where such a subject could be dealt with. In the traditional literature such subtleties are trampled down regardless.

If possible, one should go farther. The orientation of the plane should be formulated like we introduced it here: the lines oriented "from left to right"; their front and back sides; the ordered pair of oriented lines or halflines, the first of which is pierced by the second from back to front (there lines need no longer be orthogonal).

It is quite another question whether at this stage the area of parallelograms would allow for algebraization. An argument against is that the area formula cannot be understood unless it arises from an axiomatic area definition, in particular, that the sign of the area is hardly intelligible in an non-axiomatic context. But as soon as the area with sign is available, its relation to orientation should be elucidated.

In any case this should be done as soon as linear algebra is approached and constructed axiomatically. I have already analyzed the part played by geometry in this process, and I showed how the principles of geometry can be subjected to a renewed criticism, with a foundational twist. The new point of view would be to consider all one knows about points, lines, lengths, angles, areas as mere guide-lines for the deductive build-up from axioms to deductions to theorems. This means an ontological detachment, which makes an independent build-up possible. Anew the question can be raised, when and with what kind of pupils this would be possible. I cannot answer this, since the methods I am acquainted with presuppose a detachment which took place in the mind of their authors and is expected to manifest itself as a telepathic force in the minds of the pupils.

If this detachment is possible, one could continue in a way I sketched earlier when dealing with linear algebra. It starts with affine geometry and passes to an axiomatic definition of the volume function of ordered pairs and triples of vectors. To this the orientation of the plane, and maybe of space, may be connected. We noticed that the cyclic orientation in the halflines pencil of the plane can be approached by affine geometry; we explained what cyclic orientation means abstractly and how it is described algebraically in the halflines pencil. Two of the numbers

$$\text{area } \ulcorner a, b \urcorner, \quad \text{area } \ulcorner b, c \urcorner, \quad \text{area } \ulcorner c, a \urcorner$$

must be positive if abc is to be in the cyclic orientation. I do not venture a judgement on whether an abstract formulation of the concept of cyclic orientation is possible at school level, and whether the above criterion for the cyclic orientation of a, b, c in the halflines pencil can be conveyed.

Independently, after an axiomatic definition of the oriented Euclidean plane, angles can be introduced in the way I sketched earlier. The group Δ of the rotations around the origin is considered. It acts simply transitively on the halflines pencil; theoretically one may define the angle of an ordered pair of halflines by the rotation carrying the first into the second. This is the most beautiful abstract mathematics, but keep away from this pious fraud. As little you should tell your pupils the fairy tale that all we did is assign in a purely formal way to the multiplicative group Δ of the rotations an isomorphic additive group, called angles. It would be sheer deception. The student has known for long that angles are measured by numbers; if he should be offered an axiomatic approach he is entitled to one that accounts for this knowledge. What is precisely the aim of this schizophrenic behaviour where he is expected to theoretically understand angles as elements of a vague Abelian group while practically he reads their sines and cosines in a table? Can he understand the real meaning of this schizophrenia, is he expected to simulate it, or is he intentionally being taught a theory that is divorced from practice?

The multiplication group Δ should factually be mapped upon an additive modulo group of *reals*. To stay within the axiomatic frame one can use the protractor axioms. First the rotation around the origin that carries $\ulcorner 1, 0 \urcorner$ into $\ulcorner a, b \urcorner$ is replaced by the complex number $a + bi$ of absolute value 1, which implies Δ to be replaced by the multiplicative group of complex numbers of value 1. Then the protractor axiom is applied to get the wanted isomorphism on the reals mod 2π.

If the student is axiomatically acquainted with the entire field of reals as an ordered field with an extra axiom (lowest upper bound, or Dedekind cut), this familiarity should be fully used to pass from the cyclically ordered group Δ to its infinite cover and to ascertain that it is a Dedekind ordered group, thus isomorphic to the addition group of the reals.

GROUPS IN GEOMETRY. CRITICAL ANALYSIS

In my ICMI report* of 1958 I stated that since the beginning of the century when F. Klein advocated groups, this subject – or even mappings – had not influenced school instruction in a substantial way. I indicated the usual mistakes which showed that didactics of mappings was still poorly developed. Finally I indicated which way of introducing the group of motions in my opinion was the most advisable.

With regard to the first point much has changed in the last ten years – groups became a fashion, which as is the fashion with all fashions has been a bit exaggerated. As to the second point I should confess that my warning against mistakes had no useful effect and in any case new ones emerged. Third, the positive proposals seem indeed to have been adopted in the meantime.

How can one explain why F. Klein's hopes were fulfilled so late, even in Germany where Klein was almost worshipped? I already mentioned that what Klein defined as Elementary Mathematics from a Higher Point of View was taught from a height where elementary mathematics was no longer visible; not until the most recent period did school and higher mathematics grow to meet each other. F. Klein had formulated his *Erlanger Programm* in general terms, but he carried it out in much too narrow a framework, that is, as a theory of algebraic invariants of certain subgroups of the projective group; from Cayley's metric to pentacyclic coordinates this is even at the lowest level too far from school mathematics. In Klein's own interpretation of the *Erlanger Programm* stress is laid on the mutual relations of the geometries, which are elucidated

* H. Freudenthal, "Report on a Comparative Study of Methods of Initiation into Geometry", *Enseignement Mathématique* 5 (1959), 119–139.

by invariant theory, transfer principles, adjunctions; Klein hardly admits that there is some use of groups within one geometry, in particular if it is so pedestrian as ordinary Euclidean geometry. At least in Germany the badly understood authority of Hilbert's *Grundlagen der Geometrie* worked also against groups and transformations in school geometry. In a certain sense Hilbert's work was conservative; it contributed to lengthen the life of Euclid's methods for half a century. (Yet Hilbert was not a dogmatist; in the Appendices to his work he showed quite different paths to foundations of geometry, namely via group theory.)

What was needed was a rethinking of the subject matter, and of the methods of school geometry independently. Tradition prevailed, even if some people tried to introduce mappings. In 1958 I noticed that no systematic course of elementary geometry based on the transformation concept had been developed, and that even important problems in teaching transformations had not been recognized. According to my analysis the main problem was the following. There is a danger that the learner might understand transformation as simply picking up a figure and laying it down elsewhere, without changing its shape or while applying some similarity or affinity. Of course, this is a serious misapprehension; the result would not be a group of mappings, but at most a groupoid. This "free mobility" of figures *in the plane* is quite a different notion from mappings of *the whole plane* on itself. If mappings are to be composed to a group, there must be *one* substratum set, say the plane, which in each of those mappings is mapped one-to-one upon itself. Picking up a square from the place Q_1 and laying it down at Q_2 is a mapping f of Q_1 on Q_2; it can be composed with a mapping g that lays Q_3 down at Q_4, to a mapping gf only if $Q_2 = Q_3$ so the essential characteristics of a group, unrestricted composition, is here lacking. The result would be a set of mappings some of which can be composed while others cannot – a groupoid (or category). In the present case the mappings though restricted to squares can be extended to the whole plane, which means that the groupoid arises from a group by restriction, but this is not what happens with groupoids in general.

Of course if people express themselves as though the mappings of the group displace just one square, they mean something else; what is picked up and laid down elsewhere is not a particular figure but the whole plane, and in this formulation it is correct. But people consider the whole plane as being too abstract an object; they prefer the much more palpable square as a substratum and are not aware how dangerous this restriction is. Displacing a single figure is indeed more intuitive, and the less intuitive notion is very likely blocked by the more intuitive one. Moving models, though in some respects useful, can be extremely dangerous in this respect. However transformations are concretized, it should be absolutely clear on which set they are acting. Of course the mapping of the substratum may be exemplified by means of a subset, a rotation of space around a vertical axis by turning a chair around this axis, which by chance may just pass through the centre of the chair, but if one does so, extending the motion to other objects is indispensable; for instance, to have a nearby chair turning around the same axis, rather than around its own. This is to avoid the misapprehension that rotations are composed with axes fixed within the object rather than in space. I have already analyzed the confusion between displacement and transfiguration*. Numerous mistakes of this kind have been made in the last few years. Already in 1958 I had complained about the misapprehension that mappings of plane figures in *others* are believed to form a group. This mistake has likewise spread, maybe under the influence of Piaget's work, where it is quite usual.

A frequent example is standing up and sitting down as inverse operations that are said to generate a transformation group. What in this example is the set that is being transformed? Obviously it consists of two states of one person – standing and sitting. The mapping "sitting down", however, is only defined for the standing state, and the mapping "standing up" only for the sitting state. Or, if the mapping "sitting down" ("standing up") is considered to leave the sitting (standing) state invariant, the two mappings cease to be one-to-one; there is a binary operation between two elements a (standing up) and b (sitting down), with $a^2 = a$, $b^2 = b$, $ab = a$, $ba = b$, but this is not a group.

A frequent variant is opening and shutting a door, sometimes refined with half opening or shutting.

The same mistake may creep in if a figure is to be mapped upon itself and the different stages of the figure are shown one beside the other; teachers and students who use such a text are easily misled to believe

* p. 383.

they are different figures, which are mapped one upon the other. Earlier I dealt with an example of this representation (Figure 37).

Certainly, groups of mappings of *one figure* upon itself (rather than the whole plane) are admissible, for instance, (Figure 68) the eight autometries of a square (reflections with respect to horizontal, vertical,

Fig. 68.

and oblique axes; rotations over 0°, 90°, 180°, 270°). If this is what is meant, it should be said. It should be absolutely clear whether such a mapping extends to the entire plane, whether it is restricted to the square, or perhaps, to its corners. Restricting it to the square may be advantageous. Upon the drawn square a moveable one can be laid and turned around and back to face. The corners or four partial squares can be indicated by letters to give a clear view on what happens with them under mapping; then the letters must also be put on the back side. In actual fact, this is not a good procedure. What happens with the letters? Do they undergo the reflection, or are they unchanged? Different colours in the corners of the square are better.

If geometry is the aim, stressing of transformation groups like that of the square is objectionable. Certainly, many things become easier if a finite figure rather than the whole plane is the substratum; the finiteness of the figure is a real advantage. The big disadvantage is that such comfortable approaches can block less comfortable ones. The mappings undergone by such a figure are extendable to the whole plane (or the whole space) in a natural way, and these global mappings have to be tackled later in geometry. If, however, the student's attention is drawn too forcefully and too often to the restrictions of these mappings to special figures, there is a real danger that the global mappings are blocked or do not function such as they would have done if the restrictions had never been allowed. In any case, if finally the global mappings shall be dealt with, the teacher must make sure that they are not blocked, or he must make efforts to clear the blockage. It is an analogous situation to the traditional teaching of geometry, where insight in geometry in space is seriously hampered by the priority for many years of plane geometry.

Groups have become a fashion in school teaching, or at least are becoming a fashion. But fashions in teaching are not as easily adopted as in women's clothing. If a new look in dress is propagated there are always enough girls who adopt it, whereas teaching is usually dominated by an older generation which is not as susceptible to new fashions. There is more to it than that: a garment somehow betrays how it is put on, whereas if a teacher is given new teaching matter, it is often not clear what is up and what is down, what is front and what is back, how to get into it, and where the buttonhole is for some particular button. To be sure, some of it is the kind of manufacture that, were it a garment, you would be ashamed to wear.

In fact, the case of group theory is relatively harmless if compared with elementary arithmetics that can be made entirely impossible by Venn diagrams. Groups are generally dealt with by people who know what groups are; what they do with groups is usually sound. Their imitators, however, are less reliable.

There is a rich variety of material in this field, mostly staged as a game, and then serviceable from early childhood onwards. In multifarious ways games can be based on the symmetric group of three permutands, which in every disguise betrays its abstract structure. If I say they are games, it is not meant in a derogatory sense. It is an important kind of game. It is, as we put it, bottom level and important as such if it leads to a higher level. I cannot decide whether it does so since it is always presented as bottom level; the level of which it should be the prelevel is not indicated. I do not say that this is wrong. Experiments are indispensable though they should serve some further aim.

Experimenters claim that with this subject matter children learn mathematizing, but so far as I can see, what actually happens in such experiments is a far cry from mathematizing. What is in practice done is putting the game into formulae – it is *formalizing* rather than *mathematizing*. In many situations formalizing is easier than mathematizing with the consequence that a stream of formulae supersedes mathematics. Formalizing instead of mathematizing is a real danger even at the bottom level.

Can recognition of isomorphisms be exercized with this kind of game? In principle one would reply yes, though much more experience is needed in order to organize the material so carefully that this goal can be reached. All I have seen to date is chaotic (this is not censure) – the chaos of the experiment, but I would prefer a better organized chaos.

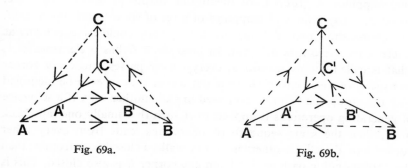

Fig. 69a.   Fig. 69b.

What happens is that isomorphisms are *suggested* to the children on unsatisfactory grounds, or that they are *shown* to the children in the most palpable way, then formalized by means of group tables, whereas the only real way to conceive them and to make them conceivable is conceptualization. Isomorphisms should be understood conceptually rather than algorithmically – this is where mathematics starts.

An author who in order to please the pupils stays on the bottom level is threatened by the danger of wrong concretization. From a booklet that belongs to the best literature in this field, I take what I think is an exemplary derailment. There are two street networks (Figures 69a–b), the dotted lines are one-way streets, the full lines are both way streets. The dotted lines, oriented according to the arrows, represent the same group element (of order 3), the full lines represent another group element (of order 2). More precisely, these group elements act as mappings upon the six corners in such a way that every corner passes into the next according to the driving direction. If the two generating operations are composed arbitrarily, a group arises, which for both networks has the order 6, though the one is 6-cyclic whereas the other is isomorphic to the symmetric group of three permutands.

But why should it be a group? This question is not answered, or rather the answer is delayed till after formalization. What must be known to conclude that it is a group? The mappings defined by the driving directions are one-to-one, because each among the three driving directions once reaches, and once departs from, every corner. The generators are one-to-one mappings of the corner set upon itself, and the same is true of all mappings generated by composing them. So in any case a set of one-to-one mappings, a group G of one-to-one mappings arises. There are, however, many groups of mappings of a set of six elements upon itself. The figures show two of them, but such a group could have as many as 6! elements. Here it is different. In both cases G has 6 elements. G is what is called simply transitive; every corner passes into every corner by exactly one element of G. Thus the corner set can even be identified with the group. This can be expressed in still another way. If a sequence of generating operations is applied to A such that finally one falls back ot A, then the same sequence of operations leads from every other corner X to X itself. Or otherwise, if one walks a closed path from A, then the corresponding path issuing from any corner X is also closed. This is equivalent to the statement that every element of G that fixes A, fixes every corner, thus with the property of simple transitivity.

But why is this so? Of course, one can convince oneself that it is correct, by working out all the particular cases. This is not elegant and it is not mathematics. In fact, in Figure 69a you can see it with your own bare eyes. There G is also an automorphism group of the pattern (not the total one, which would contain reflections too, but only that of the rotations), and as such it is immediately recognized as a group. In Figure 69a this reasoning, as I see it, permits the assertion that the figure defines a group. It is now suggested to the learner that in the case of Figure 69b this holds true also. But this case is entirely different because here the group G is not commutative. Appealing to the automorphism group would be a failure here; it is hardly recognizable in the drawing. It does not coincide with G as a transformation group either; if G is interpreted as a group of left multiplications, the automorphism group consists of the right multiplications. Figure 69a leads to a commutative group and there G and its automorphism group are identical as transformation groups. In Figure 69b this is different since the automorphism group is badly recognizable, it fails as a means of seeing that a path that closes once always closes.

I am going to explain this more technically. Figures 69a-b are what is called group images *. Take a group G; its elements are mapped as corners of a graph; two pairs $\ulcorner a, b \urcorner$ and $\ulcorner c, d \urcorner$ are joined by the same kind of arrow (e.g. of a certain colour), if

$$a^{-1}b = c^{-1}d,$$

in other words, if it is in both cases the same right multiplication (to wit by $a^{-1}b = c^{-1}d$) that maps the first element of the pair into the second. (In fact arrows for a system of *generators* suffice to describe the group. In the Figures 69a-b this simplification, among others, was adopted.) This defines a graphic structure. The group elements operate as right multiplications along the arrows. What are now automorphisms of this structure? Left multiplications leave the structure invariant since the relation defining the structure,

$$a^{-1}b = c^{-1}d,$$

keeps holding if a, b, c, d are simultaneously multiplied by an $x \in G$ at the *left*. The left multiplications form a group isomorphic with G. In fact the isomorphism consists in having a left multiplication by x correspond to a right multiplication by x^{-1}.

If now a figure is given which *looks like a group image*, how can we see that it *is* a group image? It is not at all an easy task to answer this question. One way is simply working it out. Once you wish to *see* it, you will instinctively try to reason by automorphisms. This works very well in the commutative case and it fails under non-commutativity. Inferring by analogy from the commutative to the non-commutative case is hardly justified. The method suffers from an obvious lack of insight; it is blindman's buff at the bottom level.

This is a sore point in Dienes' sublime performance. I touched on it earlier. A certain group is obtained as a simply transitive transformation group of a certain set V; afterwards the set V is identified with the group in an obvious way; as soon as one element of V has been distinguished as the unit, V and G become identical. The reader or listener does not feel comfortable; after that premature identification he feels unsure about how in heaven's name the simple transitivity has been recognized, whether it was well motivated or surreptitiously. Probably all was correct but since one doubts one's own conviction, there is reason to doubt whether the subjects were rightly convinced.

* "Gruppenbilder" in German.

The means of obtaining groups in these and analogous methods differs greatly from what is the usage in mathematics. Group images serve in group theory as means of *illustration* rather than *definition*. To use group images to define groups would be a dubious method because you cannot read in such an image whether it is the image of a group. It is also quite unusual to construct groups as simply transitive transformation groups since – not unlike the property of group image – the simple transitivity is not easily verified. Why should the school (and even the kindergarten) claim *other* methods than are usual in normal mathematics? It reminds one of the words of J. S. Brunner I quoted earlier* and those of Bärbel Inhelder on which it was based. I have never been convinced by those arguments. If high level mathematics is tailored to a lower level, why should it be a stork version? Are not we going to create a new autonomous school mathematics, now embellished with terms like group, field, cardinality? If the higher level can be tailored to the lower one only by transforming it in something completely different, it would be better dropped. Nothing will be lost. For since when have we adapted Rabelais for the kindergarten and Beethoven for the mouth organ?

If at the bottom level groups are introduced as games, it is tempting to stress one feature of groups that may be an end but never a start and that in any case has no right on exclusiveness – I mean the group as a set with a binary operation. It is tempting because this algorithmic feature meets the needs of the play instinct, and this is the main reason why textbook authors may succumb to the temptation. No doubt over-stressing this feature means a distortion of the group concept. How far this can go, is shown by the example of M. A. Jeeves'** work, which as a psychological investigation may be highly remarkable. In those experiments a little machine is used which if adjusted performs a certain binary operation. The experimenter and the subject each dial one element of a finite set of symbols, to which the machine produces and makes visible a third. The binary operation is always a group operation though this is not told to the subjects; of course they are not told either what a group is. The groups in question are little groups, cyclic ones, the group of four, and dihedral groups. The subject is expected to

* p. 128.
** Z. P. Dienes and M. A. Jeeves, *Thinking in Structures*, London 1965 – Z. P. Dienes and M. A. Jeeves, The *Effects of Structural Relations upon Transfer*, London 1970.

guess the structure of the group in question; whether he can is tested by asking him to make predictions. The subject makes his choice after the experimenter so he has the power to try factors he feels are crucial. It is not clear from the description how many times he may try, but in any case probably less than what would be needed for full information, which in fact would easily surpass the capacity of the subject's memory. The subject is rather expected to draw inductive inferences. If several times under the binary operation Δ showed to behave as a neutral element ($\Delta \cdot x = x$), the subject should infer that Δ behaves in every product as a neutral element; if several times products of symbols with itself yielded the element Δ, the subject should infer that this is true of all elements; if a number of products were commutative, the subject should conclude that all of them are commutative; if several times the product of symbols of equal colour was a yellow symbol and the product of symbols of different colours was a red symbol, the subject should conclude that this is a general rule. With such keys the subject is expected to structure the data to arrive at a complete catalog of the binary operation.

These highly interesting experiments have nothing to do with group theory. It is not investigated whether some shadow of the associative law is cast into the subject's mind, whether he feels the existence of a neutral element or the inverse as a vague necessity. The experiments could have been done with any kind of binary operation. It is a bottom level exercise in structuring data, which may be useful as such, but groups come into it nowhere. It is the closest kind of a well-known type of problem: "Continue the sequence "2, 8, 14, 20" or "which word does not fit in the sequence "pincers, violin, saw, file". It has nothing to do with groups because the stress is on the binary operation, and it has nothing to do with mathematics because it is bottom level with no perspective on a higher one. (This does not exclude that it may contribute in some way to the knowledge of the learning process.)

Till now I have only said what groups are *not*. The essential thing in the group concept is not the binary operation – if it were why do we not allow other kinds of binary operations? It is not at all characteristic of groups and they do not derive their importance from the fact that they are systems with binary operations. Maybe you would object that at least associativity is so natural a law that it is accepted with no ado by every learner; it allows one to forget about brackets which is a benefit for which the user may congratulate himself. This, however, is a fraudulent argument, first because it does not justify considering binary operations at all, and second because it gives the formalism the right to dictate dogmas. It is the view that anticipates formalizing; the student should work according to rules settled by an anonymous authority and imposed on behalf of that authority by the teacher. Formalizing which is one of the farthest aims, is presupposed; instead, the start is a formal apparatus that could be one of the results. This is the only context that is fitted by a justification of the associative law as a matter of convenience, which, in fact, is nothing but a "stork" tale in the realm of mathematics.

Why are groups so enormously important in mathematics? The answer can be very short: groups are important because the automorphisms of any structure whatsoever form a group, the automorphism group of that structure, and because so much can be learned from its automorphisms about the structure itself. This is the principle of groups, and it is this principle that makes groups so universally useful in all of mathematics. It is an important principle, it is great in its simplicity, and if students are to learn anything about groups, then this principle is the first and last of all wisdom.

WHAT IS A STRUCTURE?

EXAMPLES: – A set M with its elements and subsets and with the base set structure of $x \in X$ or $x \notin X$; four things a, b, c, d with the neighbourhood relation "a, b are neighbours, b, c are neighbours, c, d are neighbours, d, a are neighbours"; a square in the plane with the distance relation; a point lattice; the Euclidean plane as a metric space; the Euclidean plane with the congruence relation for line segments; the affine plane with collinearity as a relation; an ordered set with the order relation; an algebraic field with the sum and product relations; a crystal with the distance relation among its atoms. I could continue for quite a while, and in any case I could ask for the automorphisms of the structure S.

Let us consider a structure S, that is a set M with a relation R or a system ϕ of relations. An automorphism of S is a one-to-one mapping f of S onto itself with the property that for any relation R of ϕ

$$R(x, y, z, ...) \leftrightarrow R(fx, fy, fz, ...)$$

holds, in other words, f is required to preserve every relation of ϕ, and its negation; the relation should be fulfilled by $x, y, z, \ldots$ if and only if it is so by $fx, fy, fz, \ldots$.

An example shows that the "if and only if" or the preservation of both R and non-R is a reasonable requirement. Take the set M of natural numbers with a unary relation R, where $R(x)$ means "x is even". The one-to-one mapping f of M onto itself with

$$f1 = 2, \quad f2 = 4, \quad f3 = 1, \quad f4 = 6, \quad f5 = 3, \ldots$$

leaves the relation R invariant though it carries also some elements that do not have the property R into elements that do have it. It is reasonable to require of an automorphism that it does not create new fulfillments. For this reason it is postulated that both R and non-R are preserved, or that the validity of $R(x, y, z, \ldots)$ is necessary and sufficient for that of $R(fx, fy, fz, \ldots)$.

Let S be a structure and G the set of its automorphisms. Then obviously the identity belongs to G, with any f its inverse, and with f and g the composed fg. The automorphisms form a group with the composition as the group operation.

If groups are introduced, it are mostly automorphism groups of certain structures. This way of introduction guarantees that the thing defined *is* a group; rather than working it out, this result is obtained conceptually, and this is a great advantage. Preferring conceptual to algorithmic approaches is in fact one of the most conspicuous features of what we like to call modern mathematics.

The conceptual introduction of a group G as an automorphism group of a structure S partly means a shift of the problem. Now one has to make sure whether the defined group G really is that group G that should be defined. But to check what is the automorphism group of the proposed structure, one can again proceed conceptually and according to great principles. How this is done, I prefer to show by means of an example.

Let S be the square lattice in the plane (points with integral coordinates). What is the group G of congruencies that leave S invariant? The translation t_a over a vector a belongs to G and so do the rotations d_i over $i \cdot (\pi/2)$ ($i = 0, 1, 2, 3$) around the origin, and the reflection s at the horizontal axis. How do we find all elements of G?

Let $f \in G$. Then f carries the origin into some lattice point a, thus $f \ulcorner 0, 0 \urcorner = a$. The translation t_a does likewise so $f_1 = t_a^{-1} f$ fixes $\ulcorner 0, 0 \urcorner$. Now f_1 maps $\ulcorner 1, 0 \urcorner$ into a lattice point that is a neighbour of $\ulcorner 0, 0 \urcorner$ that is, into $\ulcorner 1, 0 \urcorner$, $\ulcorner 0, 1 \urcorner$, $\ulcorner -1, 0 \urcorner$, $\ulcorner 0, -1 \urcorner$. The same is done by d_0, d_1, d_2, d_3 respectively. So if i is properly chosen, $f_2 = d_i^{-1} f_1$ fixes both

$\ulcorner 0, 0 \urcorner$ and $\ulcorner 1, 0 \urcorner$, and consequently the entire horizontal axis. Then f_2 is the identity or the reflection s. Working back to f, one gets

$$f = t_a d_i \quad \text{or} \quad t_a d_i s.$$

This is the most general element of G. The integral translations, the rotations over $i \cdot (\pi/2)$ ($i = 0, 1, 2, 3$), and the reflection s together generate G.

I illustrated this general principle to compute automorphism groups by an example which, I believe, reflects very well the general situation. I could have espoused the same policy with regard to the theorem that states that the automorphisms form a group, and at school it would not, indeed, be wise to deal with structures in general, or to do so early. One would take a very special structure to recognize that the automorphisms form a group; next time if automorphisms of a structure are to be found, the pupil will remember the first example and transfer its method. If this has happened often enough, a pupil who has been educated in this spirit may feel the need to generalize this pattern and to arrive at the concept of structure and its automorphism group.

Generating groups as automorphism groups and computing them systematically is genuine group theory, that is, if offered to the student, it is a bottom level activity that prepares higher level activities. These are quite different perspectives but introducing groups by means of group images or as systems with a binary operation, whether they are bluntly imposed, or arrived at by steering right ahead to the system with the binary operation and its algorithmic formalization. Not a few do call this formalization mathematizing or axiomatizing, which is utterly misleading.

Of course there are groups that are a priori given as systems with a binary operation such as the additive group of the integers and the multiplication group of the positive numbers. But even these can be seen as remarkable instances showing how far the idea of automorphism has penetrated into modern mathematics; it is not unusual that even these groups are introduced as automorphism groups: the addition group of the integers as the automorphism group of a minimal ordered set in which every element has one predecessor and one successor; the multiplication group of the positive numbers as an automorphism group of the ordered addition group of the reals. I do not say that it should be done in this way; it is bad to stick to one single method. Adding and multiplying of numbers can be interpreted as group operations, and this should not be neglected. But numbers have to serve so many other aims that the group theory interpretation is not allowed to prevail.

Both of the groups we mentioned right now are met in a simply transitive representation. This may have been the reason why in general Dienes is steering straight to simply transitive representations of the groups he deals with. Maybe the need for concretizing was also instrumental. If the symmetric group of three permutands is dealt with, the need may be felt to handle its six elements not as permutations (i.e. mappings) but as genuine objects and to concretize them. I am not sure whether this is a fortunate idea. In any case it does not contribute at all to understanding geometrical groups (such as that of the automorphisms of the plane); I am rather afraid these notions will be blocked. If the subject matter is infinite groups, or even relatively large groups, the original idea of the automorphism group of a structure is much clearer than the derived one of its simply transitive representation. I cannot agree with people who try to avoid mappings as group elements because they feel mappings ar too abstract, and who thus steer straight ahead to concretizations in order to finally land in the safe harbour of the algorithm. If mappings as group elements are too abstract, group theory itself is better avoided. Deforming or denaturing group theory is too high a price.

To be sure, there are many mathematical investigations in which groups are just sets with binary operations with certain properties, in particular many such investigations where groups have become aims themselves. Wherever group theory serves other aims, which is its main task in school instruction, it can do so because groups are automorphism groups of structures, and this is the feature which with due stress should be made clear.

THE DIDACTICS OF THE CONGRUENCE GROUP

The chapter "Sets and Functions" contains a fundamental analysis of the didactics of groups, which has been continued here in the Chapter entitled "Geometry". I could have dedicated one special chapter to groups, but everything is so closely connected, in particular in good teaching, that every delimitation is arbitrary. Since this is well known to almost all who propagate group theory in school mathematics, it is a pity that they are so easily tempted to stroll in a field where groups become an aim in itself. In all attempts I had in view the connection with geometry teaching is stressed, and this is the reason why the present chapter invites dealing with groups. It is a progress that F. Klein's old ideal of the penetration of geometry by group theory is now being realized; conversely I think many innovators are convinced that groups are to be dealt with in a close connection with geometry. I mentioned in passing that it is not always a success. I could even say that some of the methods used to teach groups are such that they may indeed be detrimental to the penetration of geometry by group theory and prejudicial to the understanding of groups in geometry. If to concretize the group elements, the group is replaced by a simply transitive representation, the geometrical concreteness of the group itself is destroyed in most cases; the shift of stress to the formalized algorithm obscures all geometric understanding. Even more dangerous is the restriction of the constituting mappings of the group to a part of the plane or even to finite sets. It has often been noticed that beginners have difficulty in seeing a mapping as acting upon the whole plane or the whole space. Textbooks betray that this is not easy even for textbook authors, while Piaget and his collaborators never achieved it. In the earlier quoted report*, I analyzed these difficulties. There is one mapping, however, that is seen immediately by everybody over the whole plane: the axial symmetry or reflection. Central symmetries and rotations are less easy; translations is the most difficult case. If it starts with axial reflections, and if rotations and translations are introduced as products of axial reflections, there is a real chance that the child will understand such mappings as acting upon the whole plane.

In that report I mentioned a Polish scheme where this sequence was followed, that is, first reflections, then rotations and translations as products. However, there the global view was neglected far too much; reflections were too often applied to figures rather than to the plane, and their global character was too little used. The reason why the start from the reflection was preferred was that reflections do not depend on a theory of parallels. In fact, in the way it was represented there it was not correct, though this is perhaps not so important.

* p. 407.

A German scheme which was submitted proceeded quite differently. The situation had carefully been analyzed, and the difficulty was clearly indicated, but nevertheless the synthesis started with translations, which were concretized by translations of a square lattice of transparent material on a fixed under-layer. It is true the square lattice is a natural infinite figure – it may be even as such unique – and its movements can suggest translations and rotations of the whole plane and prevent the dangerous reduction to parts of the plane.

There are, however, more arguments in favour of reflections. Reflections are more interesting than rotations and translations. To beginners in geometry congruent shapes are the same. Nothing seems to have happened when a figure has been displaced from one spot to another. In this respect rotations are a bit more operative than translations. If a cube is displaced, it looks as if nothing has happened; if it is turned and put on an edge or a corner, something has changed. Mirror reflection gives the strongest feeling of an important event. As transformations reflections are more attractive, more copious, and less problematic than rotations and translations. In all the national reports on which the quoted report was based, reflections were stressed.

At that time they were already been widely utilized in the Netherlands; there existed a multifarious literature on the didactics of reflections, in particular in the earlier mentioned work of van Albada* and the van Hieles*. Today the reflection as a starting point to geometry is generally accepted. One Dutch course** may be mentioned. It passes from reflections to congruences in the plane; from the beginning the behaviour of line segments and "angles" (rather than absolute angles) is considered; later equiform and affine mappings are dealt with. Without mentioning groups it is the spirit of group theory. The classification of congruences in the plane and in the space, such as performed in the earlier mentioned book of mine is an attractive subject and a paragon of local organization with group theory means; there it is demonstrated what exactness of operating means in a non-axiomatic medium.

* p. 407.
** M. G. Kuipers, J. Siepelinga, R. Troelstra and G. Tromp, *Gemoderniseerde meetkunde op basis van afbeeldingen*, Groningen 1968. Compare, on a higher level, the earlier-mentioned booklet: H. Freudenthal, *Observing Mathematics*, London, New York, 1967.

GEOMETRIC AXIOMATICS BY GROUP THEORY

To terminate this chapter I come back to the question of axiomatics. Group theory should pervade geometry even in the axiomatic approach. If geometry is to be axiomatized, one should look for a group theory structure. It is not too far-fetched to consider a reflection geometry like F. Bachmann's though the Bachmann approaches themselves would be too abstract. It is indispensable that equality of line segments and of angles belong to the fundamental concepts rather than being obtained a posteriori from the axiomatic system by devious detours, as it often happens with the equality of angles. Moreover it should be required that the axiomatics is linked to the ordinary procedures in geometry such that reasoning *within*, and not only about, the axiomatic system, is a feasible feature. The main difficulties, which up to now have never been conquered, are properties where orientation plays a part.

In my view, a group theory axiomatics of geometry can be found in the Helmholtz space problem rather than via the Hilbert approach. I shall shortly indicate what this entails.

Let R be a metric space with the metric ρ. An autometry of R is a mapping f of R upon itself that preserves the metric, thus

$$\delta(fa, fb) = \delta(a, b) \quad \text{for} \quad a, b \in R.$$

Point triples $\ulcorner a_1, a_2, a_3 \urcorner$ and $\ulcorner a_1', a_2', a_3' \urcorner$ are called congruent if

$$\rho(a_i, a_j) = \rho(a_i', a_j').$$

In Euclidean spaces of arbitrary dimension it is true that

(∗) Congruent point triples can be mapped into each other by autometries of the whole space.

This still holds in hyperbolic and spheric spaces. In elliptic spaces (∗) is not necessarily true for triples with large distances, though even there it is true that

(∗∗) sufficiently small congruent point triples can be mapped into each other by an autometry of the whole space.

An a priori weaker statement would be:

(∗∗) There is a small equilateral triple of points which by autometries can be mapped into any congruent one.

This property suffices to characterize Euclidean and non-Euclidean spaces within a certain large class of metric spaces if certain *inessential* changes of the metric are allowed: If R is a space with the metric ρ, then ρ is changed into ρ' by means of a continuous function ϕ such that $\rho'(a, b) = \phi(\rho(a, b))$ for $a, b \in R$.

More precisely:

Let R be a locally compact connected metric space with property (∗∗). Then R is essentially a Euclidean or non-Euclidean space*.

This is an extremely simple group theory characterization of these spaces. Afterwards one can define what are lines, planes, and so on: the line through a, b is the set of all points fixed together with a and b under autometries, and likewise for planes. Finally the Euclidean geometries can be distinguished from the others, e.g. by the existence of a simply transitive subgroup (that of the translations).

The proof of the quoted theorem requires tools from very sophisticated mathematics. Moreover, this axiomatic characterization would not fulfill the desiderata I formulated above; even straight lines are lacking among the fundamental concepts of the system. Nevertheless it seems to me that for a school axiomatics of Euclidean geometry one should look in this direction. It is a suggestion I have made many times and a very apt one to stress in concluding the present chapter.

---

* Cf. e.g. H. Freudenthal, "Lie Groups in the Foundations of Geometry", in: *Advances in Mathematics* **1** (1954), 145–190.

CHAPTER XVII

ANALYSIS

From his early childhood Chasles drank water only... A famous mathematician was pleased to remark: If Chasles would drink wine, he would possibly work on integral calculus.

J. Bertrand, *Eloges acad.*, n.s. 1902, p. 40

Freshmen are still allowed to believe in irrational numbers, thankfully and with no criticism to view the complex domain as an indispensable tool, to naïvely enjoy limit processes, and to accept infinity as the multiplication table.

E. Netto, *Elementare Algebra*, 1904, Vorwort

Should we discuss the indispensable fundamental concept in the introduction to higher analysis with due thoroughness... it seems to me that the well-known saying "a bad bargain is dear at a farthing" applies here too. I am convinced that the effort that is indispensable to learn mathematics, is not increased by the logical reinforcement of the method of proof.

A. Pringsheim, *Jahresb. D.M.V.*, 7 (1897–8), 142–143

STARTING ANALYSIS

Teaching the techniques of differentiating and integrating and of developing functions in series, will not be discussed in the present chapter. Neither do I intend to relegate analysis into a little corner of a larger room, which under the name of "Topology" or "Mixed Structures" would fit better into a system of mathematics. Even less than in other fields will analysis be treated as a structure that ought to inspire deferential adoration, but rather as a tool which is badly needed by those who learn to handle it, and handled efficiently if need be. This requires other abilities than knowing elegant linguistic expressions that define what an open set is, or a limit, a differential quotient* or an integral; it is more important to have undergone these notions geometrically and numerically even if they cannot be fitted into a definition that is above reproach.

Is there really a need to tell in all details how multifariously a learner

---

* Quite a few may be frightened by my preference for the plastic and instructive term "differential quotient" against the colourless "derivative".

can undergo the fundamental notions of analysis? There should not be any, but if I look into various textbooks, I begin to wonder whether many authors ever experienced them, or in any case so consciously that that they could express it in their methods. A few of them deal with applications of analysis as though it were an appendix; I am afraid that these examples have no effect since as applications they come much too late in the educational process. Once I listened to someone who enthusiastically advocated introducing the differential quotient as a velocity; he was proud of this approach close to reality. But it was not as close as he believed. He saw reality through a narrow crack, and it does not really matter very much whether this one crack is a little wider than the others. Would a lot of cracks be of more help? Learning to pierce through a lot of cracks is just not an educational aim. Why should one not prefer an approach along a broad front which has proved so successful in elementary arithmetics? Again we are as close to reality as we have been then.

What the differential quotient and the integral of a function mean depends on what the function means, and this can be many different things.

THE NUMERICAL APPROACH

A function can be given numerically, e.g. by a table. From this table can be formed the difference table*, which is a meaningful procedure in interpolation. If tables of the same function with wide and narrow mesh are compared, the difference obviously depends on the mesh. This dependence can be eliminated. If the difference is divided by the mesh, and thus the difference replaced by the difference quotient, the result will be to a reasonable degree independent of the mesh (Cf. in a table like that on page 514 the difference forming in the whole table with that in the first column). Finally the question arises what happens if the mesh tends to 0, which is answered by the differential quotient. Yet another question is how the original table can be recovered from the difference quotient table. The sum table is formed or rather the table of the sums multiplied by the mesh. This can also be done with original tables, and not only with tables which have originated as difference quotient tables. By a limit procedure the integral table is found.

* The table of the differences between one number in the table and the preceding.

		0	1	2	3	4	5	6	7	8	9
9·00	2.1	97225	97336	97447	97558	97669	97780	97891	98002	98113	98224
·01	2.1	98335	98446	98557	98668	98779	98890	99001	99112	99223	99333
·02	2.1	99444	99555	99666	99777	99888	99999	00109	00220	00331	00442
·03	2.2	00552	00663	00774	00885	00995	01106	01217	01327	01438	01549
·04	2.2	01659	01770	01880	01991	02102	02212	02323	02433	02544	02654
9·05	2.2	02765	02875	02986	03096	03207	03317	03428	03538	03648	03759
·06	2.2	03869	03979	04090	04200	04311	04421	04531	04641	04752	04862
·07	2.2	04972	05083	05193	05303	05413	05523	05634	05744	05854	05964
·08	2.2	06074	06184	06294	06405	06515	06625	06735	06845	06955	07065
·09	2.2	07175	07285	07395	07505	07615	07725	07835	07945	08055	08165
9·10	2.2	08274	08384	08494	08604	08714	08824	08934	09043	09153	09263
·11	2.2	09373	09482	09592	09702	09812	09921	10031	10141	10250	10360
·12	2.2	10470	10579	10689	10799	10908	11018	11127	11237	11347	11456
·13	2.2	11566	11675	11785	11894	12004	12113	12223	12332	12442	12551
·14	2.2	12660	12770	12879	12989	13098	13207	13317	13426	13535	13645
9·15	2.2	13754	13863	13972	14082	14191	14300	14409	14519	14628	14737
·16	2.2	14846	14955	15064	15174	15283	15392	15501	15610	15719	15828
·17	2.2	15937	16046	16155	16264	16373	16482	16591	16700	16809	16918
·18	2.2	17027	17136	17245	17354	17463	17572	17681	17789	17898	18007
·19	2.2	18116	18225	18334	18442	18551	18660	18769	18877	18986	19095
9·20	2.2	19203	19312	19421	19530	19638	19747	19855	19964	20073	20181
·21	2.2	20290	20398	20507	20616	20724	20833	20941	21050	21158	21267
·22	2.2	21375	21483	21592	21700	21809	21917	22026	22134	22242	22351
·23	2.2	22459	22567	22676	22784	22892	23001	23109	23217	23325	23434
·24	2.2	23542	23650	23758	23867	23975	24083	24191	24299	24407	24515
9·25	2.2	24624	24732	24840	24948	25056	25164	25272	25380	25488	25596
·26	2.2	25704	25812	25920	26028	26136	26244	26352	26460	26568	26675
·27	2.2	26783	26891	26999	27107	27215	27323	27430	27538	27646	27754
·28	2.2	27862	27969	28077	28185	28292	28400	28508	28616	28723	28831
·29	2.2	28939	29046	29154	29261	29369	29477	29584	29692	29799	29907
9·30	2.2	30014	30122	30229	30337	30444	30552	30659	30767	30874	30982
·31	2.2	31089	31196	31304	31411	31519	31626	31733	31841	31948	32055
·32	2.2	32163	32270	32377	32484	32592	32699	32806	32913	33021	33128
·33	2.2	33235	33342	33449	33557	33664	33771	33878	33985	34092	34199
·34	2.2	34306	34413	34520	34627	34734	34841	34948	35055	35162	35269
9·35	2.2	35376	35483	35590	35697	35804	35911	36018	36125	36232	36338
·36	2.2	36445	36552	36659	36766	36873	36979	37086	37193	37300	37406
·37	2.2	37513	37620	37727	37833	37940	38047	38153	38260	38367	38473
·38	2.2	38580	38686	38793	38900	39006	39113	39219	39326	39432	39539
·39	2.2	39645	39752	39858	39965	40071	40178	40284	40390	40497	40603
9·40	2.2	40710	40816	40922	41029	41135	41241	41348	41454	41560	41667
·41	2.2	41773	41879	41985	42092	42198	42304	42410	42517	42623	42729
·42	2.2	42835	42941	43047	43154	43260	43366	43472	43578	43684	43790
·43	2.2	43896	44002	44108	44214	44320	44426	44532	44638	44744	44850
·44	2.2	44956	45062	45168	45274	45380	45486	45591	45697	45803	45909
9·45	2.2	46015	46121	46226	46332	46438	46544	46649	46755	46861	46967
·46	2.2	47072	47178	47284	47389	47495	47601	47706	47812	47918	48023
·47	2.2	48129	48234	48340	48446	48551	48657	48762	48868	48973	49079
·48	2.2	49184	49290	49395	49501	49606	49712	49817	49922	50028	50133
·49	2.2	50239	50344	50449	50555	50660	50765	50871	50976	51081	51187
9·50	2.2	51292	51397	51502	51608	51713	51818	51923	52028	52134	52239

To demonstrate these procedures appropriate functions should be chosen – logarithms, squares, sines – to discover interesting laws, and also functions which have arisen from a concrete problem, if the problem itself requires forming differential quotients or integrals. Of course, such a numerical approach should be real rather than simulated. This requires at least a table computer, though more extensive table constructions should be performed with electronic computers, thus providing also an opportunity for the student to exercize programming. This can be supplemented by an introduction into more sophisticated methods of interpolation.

THE GRAPHIC APPROACH

If the function is graphically represented, the graphic correlates of differential quotient and integral are slope and area (below the graphic image). Whereas in the numerical approach these concepts dawned as vague limits, they strike one at first sight as ready made objects in the graphical approach; only in due course is the learner compelled to analyze them and to understand them to be limits – an instructive example of mathematizing intuitive matter. The slope of the graphic is understood as the slope of the tangent and the tangent as limit of secants. In other words, the slope of the graphic at a point is the limit of the average slopes in intervals which are contracting on that point. The area of a curvilinearly bounded plane surface is the limit of the area of approximating polygons. They are oriented areas; the parts below the axis, that is, negative function values produce a negative contribution, and under an inversion of the integration path the signs are inverted also. According to this convention the formula

$$\int_a^b + \int_b^c = \int_a^c$$

is meaningful and valid even if a, b, c do not fulfill $a < b < c$. The approximating polygons can be chosen as stair polygons or as graphics of piecewise linear functions (Figures 70a–b).

It can be shown in two different ways that differentiating and integrating are inverse operations; both efforts should be exacted from students, since both proofs are paradigmatic for numerous applications of differential quotient and integral. On one hand differentiating of the integral function is shown to lead back to the original function, on the other hand integrating the differential quotient appears to reproduce the original function up to a constant.

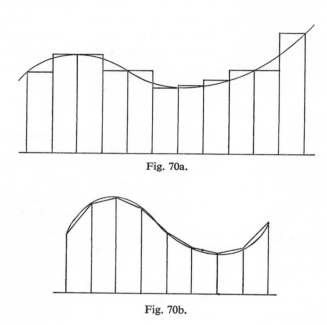

Fig. 70a.

Fig. 70b.

Let f be the given function; the increase of

$$\int_a f(\xi)\, d\xi$$

between x and $x + \Delta x$ is the area below f between x and $x + \Delta x$,

$$\int_x^{x+\Delta x} f(\xi)\, d\xi\;;$$

divided by Δx it is approximately the values of f between x and Δx, which in the limit for $\Delta x = 0$ becomes $f(x)$. (Cf. Figure 71.)

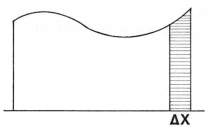

Fig. 71.

Conversely, the differential quotient $f'(x)$ of f at x is approximately

$$f'(x) \sim \frac{f(x + \varDelta x) - f(x)}{\varDelta x}$$

thus

$$f'(x)\, \varDelta x \sim f(x + \varDelta x) - f(x),$$

thus integrating from a to b,

$$\int_a^b f'(x)\, dx = f(b) - f(a).$$

(Cf. Figure 72.)

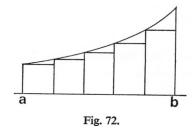

Fig. 72.

Rules like

$$\frac{dy}{dx} = 1 \bigg/ \frac{dy}{dx}$$

in the case of strictly monotonic dependence, and

$$\frac{dz}{dx} = \frac{dz}{dy} \cdot \frac{dy}{dx}$$

are intuitively obvious. Almost as obvious is the partial integration in the case of monotonic dependence (cf. Figure 73).

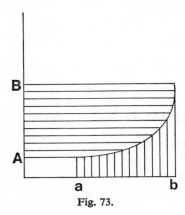

Fig. 73.

$$\int\limits_{a}^{b} y\,dx + \int\limits_{A}^{B} x\,dy = bB - aA.$$

It was explained earlier* how to show that

$$\int\limits_{1}^{x} \frac{d\xi}{\xi}$$

is a logarithmic function log; the basis of these logarithms is denoted by e, thus $\log e = 1$. Now with $\log x = y$

$$\frac{dy}{dx} = \frac{1}{x},$$

thus with $x = e^y$,

$$\frac{dx}{dy} = e^y,$$

which means that the exponential function with basis e is reproduced under differentiation. More generally, with

* p. 327.

$$x = a^y, \quad y = {}^a\log x,$$

one gets

$$y = \log x / \log a$$

$$\frac{dy}{dx} = 1/x \log a,$$

$$\frac{dx}{dy} = x \log a$$

$$= a^y \cdot \log a.$$

To integrate a linear function, it suffices to look at its graphic picture.

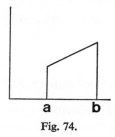

Fig. 74.

(Fig. 74.) For $y = cx$

$$\int_a^b y \, dx$$

becomes the area of a trapezoid, $\frac{1}{2}(b - a) c$, thus for instance,

$$\int_0^x \xi \, d\xi = \frac{1}{2}x^2.$$

From this it follows

$$\frac{dx^2}{dx} = 2x,$$

which can also be proved directly. From here, by means of partial integration, inverse and chain rule the functions

$$\curlyvee_x x^\alpha$$

with rational α can be attacked, and even with real α if the logarithm is used, though I would prefer first using intuitive means to understand that (for $\alpha > -1$)

$$F(x) = \int_0^x \xi^\alpha d\xi$$

is in any case a fixed multiple of $x^{\alpha+1}$: The graphic defined by $y = x^\alpha$ is invariant under the linear mapping that takes x into ρx and y into $\rho^\alpha y$ and consequently multiplies the area by $\rho^{\alpha+1}$; thus

$$F(\rho x) = \rho^{\alpha+1} F(x),$$

and in particular with $x = 1$ and ρ replaced by x:

$$F(x) = F(1) x^{\alpha+1}.$$

THE GRAPHIC APPROACH IN A BROADER SENSE

In the graphic definition of differential quotient and integral it can be useful if the graphic is visualized in a broader sense than as a curve in the plane. In

$$\int_0^a \xi^2 \, d\xi$$

the ξ^2 should also be interpreted as the area of a square of side $|\xi|$ so that the integral becomes the volume of a quadratic pyramid of side a and height a. (Figure 75.) Likewise one can imagine a more general body, which stretches along the horizontal axis. (Figure 76.) Let the area of the vertical cross-section at x be $f(x)$, and $F(x)$ the volume between fixed a and a variable x. Then

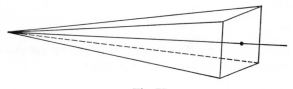

Fig. 75.

$$F(x) = \int_a^x f(\xi)\, d\xi \,,$$

and

$$F'(x) = f(x).$$

This applies to many situations, for instance to solids with a rotational symmetry. If the profile of such a revolution solid with horizontal axis

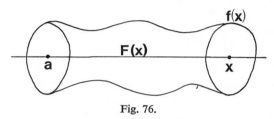

Fig. 76.

is given by the function f, then the vertical cross-section at x has the area $\pi f(x)^2$, the volume from a to x becomes

$$\pi \int_0^x f(\xi)^2\, d\xi \,;$$

for a cone, f is a linear function, say $f(x) = \alpha x$, thus the volume of a cone with height x and basic radius αx is

$$\pi \int_0^x (\alpha\xi)^2\, d\xi = \tfrac{1}{3}\pi\alpha^2 x^3\,.$$

By the same method the superficies $S(x)$ and the volume $V(x)$ of a sphere with the radius x can be related to each other: $V(x + \Delta x) - V(x)$ is the volume of the spheric shell with interior radius x and exterior radius $x + \Delta x$. Divided by Δx this is approximately the superficies of the sphere with radius x, whence

$$\frac{dV}{dx}(x) = S(x)\,;$$

in fact

$$\frac{d\left(\tfrac{4}{3}\pi x^3\right)}{dx} = 4\pi x^2\,.$$

Or conversely, imagine the sphere divided into shells of thickness Δx; one with interior radius x and exterior radius $x + \Delta x$ has approximately the volume $S(x)\, \Delta x$; summing up these volumes from 0 or r yields the volume of the sphere of radius r, and at the limit for $\Delta x = 0$:

$$\int_0^x S(\xi)\, d\xi = V(x) ;$$

in fact

$$\int_0^x 4\pi\xi^2\, d\xi = \tfrac{4}{3}\pi x^3 .$$

An analogous relation is that between the superficies $S(x)$ and the volume $V(x)$ of homothetic cubes with the edge length $2x$. I do not believe that by quoting these examples I am forcing open doors. But there are many textbooks, even university textbooks, which do not mention such facts as, for example, that under certain conditions the superficies function can be obtained from the volume function by differentiation – purely formal, non-intuitive analysis has become a good habit.

A beautiful classical, or rather preclassical, example of intuitive integration is Torricelli's computation of the volume inside the surface that arises from rotating the orthogonal hyperbola around an asymptote. If the rotation axis is taken vertically (third axis in $\ulcorner x_1, x_2, x_3 \urcorner$-space), the equation of the surface is (Figure 77)

$$\{\ulcorner x_1, x_2, x_3 \urcorner \mid x_3 \sqrt{x_1^2 + x_2^2} = c^2\} .$$

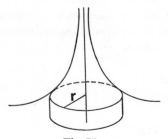

Fig. 77.

The volume $V(r)$ below this surface and above the circular disk

$$\{\ulcorner x_1, x_2, x_3 \urcorner \mid x_3 = 0 \wedge x_1^2 + x_2^2 \leqq r^2\}$$

is to be determined. $V(r)$ is closely connected to the superficies $S(r)$ of the convex part of the cylinder above the circle

$$\{\ulcorner x_1, x_2, x_3 \urcorner \mid x_3 = 0 \wedge x_1^2 + x_2^2 = r^2\};$$

again S is the differential quotient of V, and V is the integral function of S. On the other hand, it is easily seen that

$$S(r) = 2\pi c^2,$$

from which follows

$$V(r) = 2\pi c^2 r.$$

Another preclassical example is the superficies of the spherical calotte. In a sphere of radius r let $K(h)$ be a calotte of height h and $S(h)$ be its area. The difference between the calottes $K(h + \Delta h)$ and $K(h)$ is approximately the convex part of the frustrum of a cone with the side line Δs and the radius ρ, thus

$$S(h + \Delta h) - S(h) \sim 2\pi\rho\Delta s.$$

Now in similar triangles (Figure 78)

$$\Delta s : \Delta h \sim R : \rho,$$

thus

$$\frac{S(h + \Delta h) - S(h)}{\Delta h} \sim 2\pi R,$$

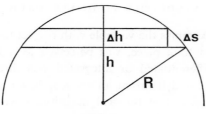

Fig. 78.

thus

$$\frac{dS}{dh} = 2\pi R$$

and consequently

$$S = 2\pi Rh.$$

Just as intuitively the superficies of general revolution surfaces can be computed. If the axis is horizontal and the profile of such a surface is given by the function f then the layer from x to $x + \varDelta x$ is again approximately the convex surface of the frustrum of a cone with the side line $\sqrt{(\varDelta x)^2 + (\varDelta y)^2}$ and the radius y, thus with the area (Figure 79)

$$2\pi y \sqrt{1 + \left(\frac{\varDelta y}{\varDelta x}\right)^2} \varDelta x,$$

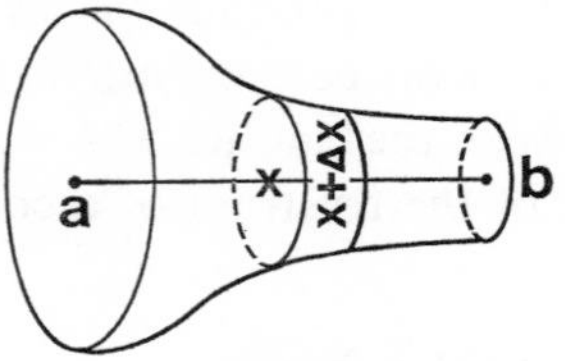

Fig. 79.

which by integration yields

$$2\pi \int_a^b f(x) \sqrt{1 + f'(x)^2}\, dx.$$

VELOCITIES AS AN APPROACH

In the preceding examples the variable with respect to which differentiation or integration took place, was perceived as a line segment. The function to be differentiated or integrated was directly or indirectly given as a graphic, and it meant an arc length, an area, or a volume. If a function connects two physical magnitudes with each other, the differential quotient and the integral may have some physical meaning.

The best known in this respect is the velocity of a movement as the differential quotient of the path with respect to the time; the inverse problem, however, namely to obtain the distance travelled by a car from its velocity graphic, is almost never raised in textbooks. The velocity differentiated with respect to the time yields the acceleration, that is, the velocity of change of velocity. There are quite a lot of other processes besides the local movement for which the velocity is meaningful, e.g. the velocity of influx or efflux of a liquid into or out of a vessel, the velocity of electricity flux from a condenser, the velocity of increase of a population or a capital, and the velocity of radioactive decay of some substance. Conversely, for many of these processes one has counting or computing instruments, which cumulatively register the consumption or the increase, and so on, as if it were analogue integrators.

An important example is mechanical work as the integral of the force along the path. If the force imparts the mass point m at x the acceleration $(d^2x)/(dt^2)$, work is converted into kinetic energy. If the mass point moves from x_0 to x_1 during the time from t_0 to t_1 where its velocities are v_0 and v_1, respectively, the kinetic energy accumulated is

$$\int_{x_0}^{x_1} m \frac{d^2x}{dt^2}\, dx.$$

The integrand can also be written as

$$m \frac{d^2x}{dt^2} \frac{dx}{dt}\, dt = \tfrac{1}{2} m d \left(\frac{dx}{dt}\right)^2.$$

Thus the integral becomes

$$\tfrac{1}{2} m (v_1^2 - v_0^2),$$

which is the amount by which the kinetic energy is increased. If it is put 0 for $v_0 = 0$, one gets the well-known value

$$\tfrac{1}{2} m v^2$$

for the kinetic energy of a mass m with the velocity v.

This reflection is highly paradigmatic and fraught with relations with other subjects; it should not be missed out in any instruction of analysis at school. Or must we leave it to the physics teacher to somehow conjure up the expression $\frac{1}{2}mv^2$ using some counterfeit proof?

Work as inner product of force and path is closely connected to linear algebra. We will come back to this point later when we deal with gradients.

DENSITIES AS AN APPROACH

In the last examples the magnitude with respect to which differentation and integration took place, was time. If a continuous mass distribution along a line (the x-axis) is given, the mass density can be asked for; if it is $f(x)$ in the point x, then the interval Δx at x contains the mass $f(x)\,\Delta x$; between a and b one finds the mass

$$\int_a^b f(x)\,dx.$$

Rather than with mass, one can charge the line with any other magnitude of density $f(x)$ at x. If $F(x)$ is the fraction of the population at age $\leqq x$, it can be considered as the integral function of a certain function f, such that $f(x)\,\Delta x$ is the fraction of people in the age bracket x to $x + \Delta x$. Then $F(x)$ is also called the probability that a person from the population is of age $\leqq x$, and $f(x)$ is the density of probability of the age x. In general with stochastic magnitudes one is led to consider the distribution and the frequency function, where the first is the integral of the second (Figure 80). If beyond continuous masses and probabilities discontinuous ones are

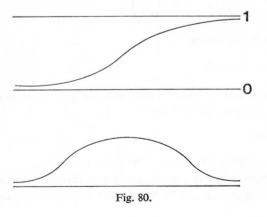

Fig. 80.

admitted, the way to the extension of the integral concept towards the Stieltjes integral is open. The point of departure is the cumulative function F, which need not be everywhere continuous and differentiable; a mass point on the line, where the mass density would be infinite is reflected by a jump of the distribution function.

There are few illustrations of the integral concept as attractive as those by densities, in particular in the form of probabilities; the required knowledge of probability usually does not go beyond what is suggested by common sense. To show this, I anticipate one of those numerous examples. A person has the habit of dropping into a restaurant for dinner between 6 p.m. and 8 p.m. to stay there 45 minutes. What is the probability at any instant that he is in there? A second person has the same habit. What is the probability that both of them meet there? How long, on average, do they stay there together? One arrives at $6 + 2x$ hours, the other at $6 + 2y$ hours. In Figure 81 the shaded area shows the pairs

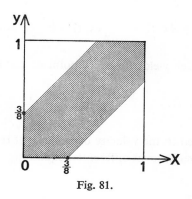

Fig. 81.

$\ulcorner x, y \urcorner$ when both of them meet; the surface is $1 - \frac{25}{64}$, and that is the probability that they meet. The time they stay together is under the same conditions $\frac{3}{4} - 2|x - y|$ hours. This function must be integrated over the shaded area to get the average time of them being together, but it can also be computed as a volume by elementary geometry. The solid consists of two frustra of triangular prisms lying on the two trapezoids into which the diagonal of the square divides the shaded domain; the volume of such a frustrum is the product of the cross-section area and the average height. The result is $\frac{63}{256}$ hours.

GRADIENTS AS AN APPROACH

If along the axis a variable temperature, $f(x)$ at x, is given, then df/dx is the temperature gradient; its importance rests in the fact that heat flows against the gradient with a velocity proportional to the gradient. If for the temperature $f(x, t)$ we strike the balance at the time t over the interval from x to $x + \Delta x$, we find at x an efflux velocity of

$$k \frac{\partial f}{\partial x} (x, t)$$

and at $x + \Delta x$ an influx velocity

$$k \frac{\partial f}{\partial x} (x + \Delta x, t),$$

thus a balance influx velocity

$$k \frac{\partial f}{\partial x} (x + \Delta x, t) - k \frac{\partial f}{\partial x} (x, t) \sim k \frac{\partial^2 f}{\partial x^2} (x, t) \, \Delta x$$

for the interval, which yields for every point of that interval

$$k \frac{\partial^2 f}{\partial x^2} (x, t).$$

This is to be equated to the velocity of increase of the temperature at x; thus one gets the well-known differential equation

$$\frac{\partial f}{\partial t} = k \frac{\partial^2 f}{\partial x^2}$$

for the heat conduction, which applies to other diffusion processes as well.

In two and three dimensions the gradient of a function F is obtained by partial derivation,

$$\text{grad } F = \left\lceil \frac{\partial F}{\partial x_1}, \frac{\partial F}{\partial x_2} \right\rceil ,$$

$$= \left\lceil \frac{\partial F}{\partial x_1}, \frac{\partial F}{\partial x_2}, \frac{\partial F}{\partial x_3} \right\rceil ,$$

respectively. It is a vector field, which at every single point indicates the direction and strength of the strongest increase. In fact

$$dF = \sum \frac{\partial F}{\partial x_i} dx_i,$$

that is, dF is the inner product of grad F and the vectorial path dx,

$$dF = (\text{grad } F, dx)$$

$$F(x) - F(x^0) = \int (\text{grad } F, dx),$$

where the integral is to be taken along a path from x^0 to x. If grad F is interpreted as a field of force, then (grad F, dx) is the work it performs along the path from x^0 to x, thus $F(x) - F(x^0)$ is the work performed along the path from x^0 to x; it is also the difference of potential energy between x^0 and x.

This is important for *physics* at school. Thus with the greatest pleasure the mathematician leaves the belonging mathematics to the physicist, since anyhow school analysis is restricted to functions of one variable. There is not the slightest argument in favour of this restriction if intuitive analysis rather than algorithmic analysis is the aim. In fact, the gradient can be an aim and a point of departure for quite attractive reflections. For intuitivity's sake we restrict ourselves to the case of two dimensions.

We imagine the function F of two variables graphically or rather geographically as a mountain over the plane of the pair of variables, in which it is represented by its isohypses (curves of equal height). (Figure 82.) In every single point there is a direction of biggest slope (the slope

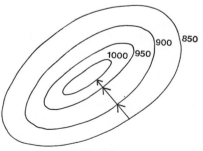

Fig. 82.

direction); it is indicated by a vector, the length of which is proportional to the slope. (On a real mountain the water would flow against the slope directions.)

This image can be simplified by considering first a linear function F^*, thus giving an oblique plane instead of the crooked mountain. Then the isohypses (Figure 83) are parallel lines; the value of the slope is every-

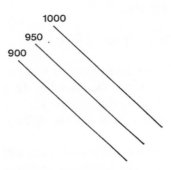

Fig. 83.

where the same and the slope direction is orthogonal to the isohypses. Let

$$F^*(x_1, x_2) = a_0 + a_1 x_1 + a_2 x_2,$$

thus

$$\Delta F^* = (a, \Delta x)$$

where a is the vector $\ulcorner a_1, a_2 \urcorner$, Δx the vector $\ulcorner \Delta x_1, \Delta x_2 \urcorner$ and ΔF^* the increase of F^* along this vectorial path. If Δx is orthogonal to a, the inner product vanishes, which means a direction of constant height. On this direction a is orthogonal so a is the direction of strongest increase. If Δx is a unit vector in the direction a, then one gets $\Delta F^* = |a|$ so according to its length a yields the value of the strongest increase. According to our former difinition of grad we can also say

$$\Delta F^* = (\text{grad } F^*, \Delta x),$$

An arbitrary function is approximated in $x^0 = \ulcorner x_1^0, x_2^0 \urcorner$ by a linear function F^*; the curved mountain is replaced by its tangential plane. grad F and grad F^* are the same at x^0, but now F^* changes from point to point, and consequently grad F^*, too.

A path in the plane from x^0 to x is divided into small pieces. The increase along the path is built up by summands

$$\Delta F = (\text{grad } F, \Delta x).$$

In the limit this becomes the integral from x^0 to x,

$$F(x) - F(x^0) = \int (\text{grad } F, dx),$$

the integral being taken along the path.

To add an attractive idea to this subject, one can study the various kinds of point with a vanishing gradient; compare in Figure 84 the iso-

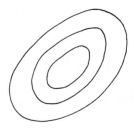

Fig. 84.

hypses around a minimum or maximum, in Figure 85 around a saddle point. From here one can go as far as to offer an introduction into the Morse theory on the number of maxima, minima and saddle points of a function within a domain. A film which has been made on this subject shows convincingly how far analysis can progress with intuitive methods.

Fig. 85.

CAPACITIES AS AN APPROACH

Another application of analytical concepts is capacities, occurring in physics under various names. The capacity of a condenser is the relative influx of electric charge needed to increase the potential of the condenser, thus

$$C = \frac{de}{dV},$$

where V is the potential of the condenser, e the accumulated charge and C its capacity, which may depend on V. A flow of electric charge

$$I = \frac{de}{dt}$$

causes via

$$\frac{dV}{de} = \frac{1}{C}$$

a change of potential, given by

$$\frac{dV}{dt} = \frac{dV}{de} \cdot \frac{de}{dt},$$

thus

$$V(t_1) - V(t_0) = \int_{t_0}^{t_1} \frac{1}{C} I \, dt.$$

The intuitive background of the capacity concept can be described as follows. Imagine a vessel of variable cross-section, $f(x)$ at the height x. How much liquid must be added to increase the liquid level from x to $x + \Delta x$? The quotient of added liquid and level increase produced (at the limit $\Delta x = 0$) is the capacity. It is the limit of

$$\int_{x}^{x+\Delta x} f(x) \, dx / \Delta x,$$

which is

$$f(x).$$

Analogously the heat capacity is defined as the limit ratio of the imparted quantity of heat and the increase of temperature (in this case it does matter how the process took place, for instance with constant pressure or constant volume, if it is about gases); the heat capacity per unit mass is known as specific heat.

A particularly interesting example of this sort is the work needed to increase the velocity. Let v be the velocity and E the kinetic energy of a mass m. Then

$$E = \tfrac{1}{2}mv^2,$$

thus

$$\frac{dE}{dv} = mv.$$

People are so accustomed to approximately constant capacities that they rarely realize that with increasing v more work is needed to increase the velocity by the same amount. (It is better known that the braking path of a car is a quadratic function of the velocity.)

Here the occurrence of logarithmic differential quotients must be mentioned. If the length l of a bar depends on the temperature T, an informative magnitude is the dilatation coefficient

$$\frac{1}{l}\frac{dl}{dT}.$$

Likewise the elasticity modulus of a bar of length l subjected to a stress σ is defined by

$$\frac{1}{l}\frac{dl}{d\sigma}.$$

"Elasticity" in economics means a characteristic of the dependence between the price p of a product and the sale s. If

$$\frac{ds}{dp}$$

is large, then small changes of the price require large adaptations of the sale; it is called high elasticity. The prime necessities of life show little elasticity.

FRAMEWORKS AND LINKAGES AS AN APPROACH

We now turn to a widespread occurrence of differential quotients: comparing changes of two magnitudes in a geometrical figure, which depend on each other in a way that is more or less kinematically motivated. The first example that comes to mind is differentiating the sine neither in the graphic of the function, nor while using the addition rules of this function, but directly at the circle that defines the sine. (Figure 86.)

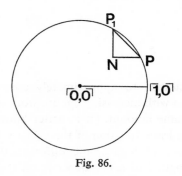

Fig. 86.

By definition the point P, which on the unit circle has the arc distance s from $\ulcorner 1, 0 \urcorner$, possesses the coordinate representation

$$\ulcorner \cos s, \sin s \urcorner.$$

If the point P moves with unit velocity on the unit circle, the velocity vector is orthogonal to the radius vector; consequently

$$\frac{d}{ds} \ulcorner \cos s, \sin s \urcorner$$

is a scalar, to wit constant, multiple of

$$\ulcorner - \sin s, \cos s \urcorner,$$

say

$$\frac{d}{ds} \cos s = - \rho \sin s,$$

$$\frac{d}{ds} \sin s = \rho \cos s.$$

The only thing lacking is the constant ρ. It can be computed at $s = 0$, thus

$$\rho = \lim_{s=0} \frac{\sin s}{s}$$

must be determined. However,

$$s = 2 \cdot \text{circle sector } OAB,$$
$$\sin s = 2 \cdot \text{triangle } OAB.$$

It can be shown in various ways* that the limit ratio is 1. Thus $\rho = 1$. (Figure 87.)

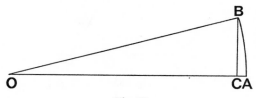

Fig. 87.

What happens with the arc length under stereographic projection? (Figure 88.) The limit of the ratio $PQ : P'Q'$ is to be evaluated if Q moves to P; in the limit the arc length PQ may be replaced with the right distance PQ. The similar triangles PNQ, $Q'NP'$ show that

$$PQ : Q'P' = NP : NQ'.$$

In the limit this ratio becomes

$$NP : NP'.$$

Thus for the arc lengths s and s' of original and image curve at P and P' respectively, one obtains

$$\frac{ds}{ds'} = \frac{NP}{NP'}.$$

For the areas σ, σ' the limit ratio becomes

$$\frac{d\sigma}{d\sigma'} = \left(\frac{NP}{NP'} \right)^2.$$

* We will come back to this point later.

Of course these results can also be obtained by more formal differential calculus if an unintelligible proof is preferred. This is again a beautiful example to show how important it is to be guided by geometrical intuition. (This should be remembered by those who would bury geometry.)

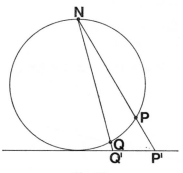

Fig. 88.

Let us consider a moving plane upon a fixed one. It should be a motion composed of a uniform clockwise rotation around the point O of the fixed plane and a uniform horizontal translation. The image of a point $P = \ulcorner x_1(0), x_2(0) \urcorner$ at the time t is a point $P(t) = \ulcorner x_1(0), x_2(t) \urcorner$, such that

$$x_1(t) = \alpha t + x_1(0) \cos t + x_2(0) \sin t,$$
$$x_2(t) = \quad - x_1(0) \sin t + x_2(0) \cos t.$$

It is useful to have a clear image of the field of velocity vectors at time t and of the orbits of different points. Near the horizontal line through O it are simple curves (with no self-intersection) which are close to the horizontal axis; points far from this axis describe paths with more and more dense self-intersections. The transitions between both kinds are paths with stationary points. For a point, say, $\ulcorner 0, x_2 \urcorner$, being stationary at the time t it is required that the translation and rotation velocities cancel each other. It is as if a circle with radius α is rolling on the straight line $x_2 = -\alpha$; the point $\ulcorner 0, -\alpha \urcorner$ then moves along a line that has been long known as the cycloid.

By no means would I advocate that in analysis instruction a walk is taken through the classical curves panopticum. The only thing I had in mind was to indicate how an old seemingly dead subject can be reanimated if examined from a modern viewpoint. A most instructive special subject is the classical construction of the tangent of the cycloid (Figure 89): the

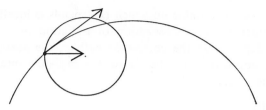

Fig. 89.

tangent is halving the angle of the translation and the rotation velocity. (The angle varies from $-\pi$ through 0 to $-\pi$ in the negative sense; its half does so from $\tfrac{1}{2}\pi$ to $-\tfrac{1}{2}\pi$ to jump from $-\tfrac{1}{2}\pi$ to $\tfrac{1}{2}\pi$.)

THE SO-CALLED APPLICATIONS

Insofar as analysis is taught related to non-mathematical fields of knowledge, the usual method is to define the differential quotient and the integral within mathematics and to mention at most the relation between differential quotient and velocity. The so-called applications are dealt with later, in differential equations. It is clear from the general exposition why I reject this method. Such applications are much too late; from the introduction onwards analysis should be fraught with relations; already the fundamental concepts should be learned in this larger context. Of course, this does not mean that I would skip those applications; on the contrary, I would broaden and deepen them.

The simplest application is that on the uniformly accelerated motion of falling bodies, of a mass point moving on an inclined plane, and on the parabola of projection. Then come the numerous framings of the problem which leads to the differential equation of the exponential function. The most perspicuous framing is to consider a magnitude, say a population, or a capital, or a radioactive substance, which increases or decreases at a rate, approximately proportional to the available quantity, $\Delta Q \sim \alpha Q \Delta t$, thus

$$\frac{dQ}{dt} = \alpha Q,$$

which is solved by

$$Q(t) = Q(0) e^{\alpha t}.$$

A case where the variable on which Q depends is locally rather than temporally interpreted, is absorption of radiation in a medium; the intensity Q depends on the completed path x, the absorbed quantity ΔQ depends approximately linearly on the available intensity and the path Δx, thus

$$\frac{dQ}{dx} = \alpha Q,$$

$$Q(x) = Q(0) e^{\alpha x},$$

where now α is negative.

The connection is less directly made in the example of heat conduction. The velocity of heat transfer is proportional to the temperature difference with the surroundings; by the loss of a heat quantity ΔQ the temperature difference diminishes by $\Delta \vartheta$, which is proportional with ΔQ, thus

$$\Delta \vartheta \sim - \kappa \Delta Q,$$

and

$$\Delta Q \sim \alpha \vartheta \Delta t,$$

thus

$$\Delta \vartheta \sim - \alpha \kappa \vartheta \Delta t,$$

and in the limit

$$\frac{d\vartheta}{dt} = - \alpha \kappa \vartheta,$$

thus

$$\vartheta(t) = \vartheta(0) e^{-\alpha \kappa t}.$$

A classical example is the barometric height formula. Its derivation exhibits a new complication. Let the air pressure in an air column of cross-section 1 be given by $p(x)$ as a function of the height x. The specific weight of the air is proportional with the pressure, say $\kappa p(x)$ at the height x. From x to $x + \Delta x$ the pressure diminishes by the weight of the air contained in this segment, that is by $- \kappa p \Delta x$, thus

$$\Delta p \sim - \kappa p \Delta x.$$

In the limit

$$\frac{dp}{dx} = -\kappa p,$$

$$p(x) = p(0) e^{-\kappa x}.$$

If the height is to be obtained as a function of the pressure, one gets

$$x = \frac{1}{\kappa} \log(p(0)/p(x)).$$

An analogous problem is the charged column with the total height h and the cross-section $Q(x)$ at the height x, which should be constructed to yield the same pressure p at any height. Then the cross-section at the height x is charged by $pQ(x)$. From x to $x + \Delta x$ the charge decreases by $p\Delta Q$, which must be equal to the weight of the column layer from x to $x + \Delta x$, that is to $\rho Q\Delta x$, where ρ is the specific weight of the material. Thus

$$p\Delta Q \sim -\rho Q\Delta x,$$

thus

$$p\frac{dQ}{dx} = -\rho Q,$$

thus

$$Q(x) = C \cdot e^{-(\rho/p)x}.$$

Another quite involved example is the tension of a driving belt stretching over a cylinder. (Figure 90.) The tension increases from A to B,

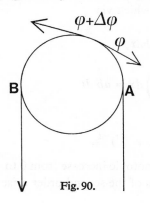

Fig. 90.

where the stress is applied. The increase equals the friction that the belt undergoes on the cylinder. On the cylinder we use the angular coordinate φ; let the tension of the belt at φ be $S(\varphi)$. From φ to $\varphi + \Delta\varphi$ the belt undergoes a friction force proportional to the normal component of the tension, that is

$$\mu S \sin \Delta\varphi\,.$$

On the other hand this expression equals the difference of the tension at $\varphi + \Delta\varphi$ and φ, thus

$$\Delta S \sim \mu S \sin \Delta\varphi\,,$$

thus

$$\frac{dS}{d\varphi} = \mu S\,,$$

$$S(\varphi) = e^{\mu\varphi} S(0)\,.$$

So the tension increases along the cylinder exponentially with the angle (independently of the radius of the cylinder).

We started with the exponential function as a law of growth. Exponential growth is obviously an ideal limit case. If the magnitude x should show ''saturated'' growth, dx/dt cannot be proportional to x but rather to a function of x that vanishes twice, say at 0 and a. The simplest function to do so is a quadratic one. One gets

$$\frac{dx}{dt} = bx(a - x)\,,$$

a differential equation, which via

$$\frac{dx}{x(a - x)} = b\,dt\,,$$

$$\left(\frac{1}{a - x} + \frac{1}{x}\right) dx = ab\,dt$$

is solved by

$$x = a(1 - C\,e^{-abt})^{-1}\,.$$

The solution shows monotonic increase from 0 to a (for positive a and b).

Differential equations of the second order arise in vibration problems.

A point of the mass m with one degree of freedom is elastically tied to the origin, that is by a force proportional to its amplitude x; moreover it is submitted to a damping force (friction) which is proportional to its velocity, and finally an exterior force K depending on time (e.g. periodically) is acting on it. This leads to a linear differential equation

$$m \frac{d^2x}{dt^2} + \rho \frac{dx}{dt} + \mu x = K.$$

The lefthand member is the sum of the inertial force, the damping force and the elastic force, while the term on the right is the exterior force.

If ρ and K vanish, the solutions are free vibrations

$$e^{\pm i\sqrt{\mu/m}\,t}$$

with the period $2\pi/\sqrt{\mu/m}$. Positive ρ yields solutions that die out exponentially; a periodically acting exterior force, however, can incite vibrations of the same period. However we shall not enter into the details of that particular theory.

The same differential equation is obtained for small vibrations of a pendulum. Then x is the angular amplitude; in the differential equation, however, we meet the angular acceleration and velocities multiplied by L, which is the length of the pendulum; μx should be replaced with the tangential component of the gravitational force, which is $mg \sin x$, but as long as the vibrations are small, $\sin x$ may be readily replaced with x. Then the differential equation becomes

$$m \left(\frac{d^2x}{dt^2} + \frac{\rho}{m} \frac{dx}{dt} + \frac{g}{L} x \right) = K;$$

for free vibrations this implies the well-known expression for the period

$$2\pi \sqrt{\frac{L}{g}}.$$

In an electric circuit with the current I the potential drops along a resistance R by RI, along the self-induction L by $L\,(dI/dt)$, and through the condenser with capacity C by $(1/C)\int_0^t I\,dt$. This total potential difference is to be provided by the electromotoric force E, such that

$$L\frac{dI}{dt} + RI + \frac{1}{C}\int_0^t I\,dt = E$$

or

$$L\frac{d^2I}{dt^2} + R\frac{dI}{dt} + \frac{1}{C}I = \frac{dE}{dt},$$

which is again a second order differential equation. There are many more examples of the occurrence of such equations.

The second order differential equation can also be hidden in a system of first order differential equations

(*)
$$\frac{dx_1}{dt} = \alpha_{11}x_1 + \alpha_{12}x_2 + \alpha_{13}$$
$$\frac{dx_2}{dt} = \alpha_{21}x_1 + \alpha_{22}x_2 + \alpha_{23}$$

or briefly,

$$\frac{dx}{dt} = Ax + c.$$

Indeed

$$\frac{d^2x}{dt^2} + a\frac{dx}{dt} + bx + c$$

can be replaced by

$$\frac{dx_1}{dt} = x_2$$

$$\frac{dx_2}{dt} = -bx_1 - ax_2 + c,$$

where $x_1 = x$. Conversely, after a second differentiation (*) can be replaced by a second order differential equation for a suitable linear combination of x_1 and x_2.

The system (*) possesses a beautiful graphic interpretation. At the point x in the plane the vector $Ax + c$ is attached to produce a vector field. Solving the differential equation

$$\frac{dx}{dt} = Ax + c$$

means finding curves such that in any of its points the tangent has the field direction. (Figure 91.) The classification of vector fields according to the character of its zeroes, is an attractive subject. (Figure 92a–c.) Algebraically this classification depends on the eigenvalues of A (real, positive, negative, mutally equal, complex of absolute value 1, and so on). This is in fact a relevant application of linear algebra and perhaps

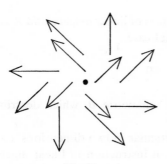

Fig. 91.

the most important, which of course applies in more than two dimensions, too. It is hardly credible but it does happen that linear algebra is sometimes taught in university mathematics instruction without mentioning its application to systems of linear differential equations. Another relation that cetainly ought to be included in teaching linear algebra at university level, is that on one parameter linear groups:

$$\frac{dx}{dt} = Ax$$

is solved by

$$x = e^{tA}x_0;$$

the e^{tA} form a group of linear mappings, which maps the addition group of the reals t homomorphically.

I also mention the systems of second order differential equations

$$\frac{d^2x}{dt^2} + A\frac{dx}{dt} + Bx = C$$

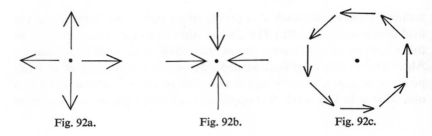

Fig. 92a. Fig. 92b. Fig. 92c.

(where x and c are vectors of linear n-space and A and B linear mappings), in particular the special case

$$\frac{d^2x}{dt^2} + Bx = 0$$

with positive definite symmetric B, which describes general undamped vibrations.

Parts of this, in particular in two dimensions, could without too much difficulty fit into school instruction in linear algebra. There are quite a few realistic interpretations of the differential equations (*), to which we will now turn. All of them follow a certain pattern. There are two physically defined magnitudes, for instance two commodities or two chemical substances x_1, x_2 with laws of growth which depend linearly on x_1, x_2, themselves, that is x_i produces in the time Δt a quantity $\alpha_{1i}x_1\Delta t$ of the first and $\alpha_{2i}x_2\Delta t$ of the second; a negative contribution, of course, means consumption rather than production.

In particular the system

$$\frac{dx_1}{dt} = -\alpha x_1 + \beta x_2,$$

$$\frac{dx_2}{dt} = \alpha x_1 - \beta x_2$$

has a probabilistic interpretation, as a stochastic process: a system is capable of two states; at the time t it is in these states with probabilities x_1, x_2 respectively $(x_1 + x_2 = 1)$ to pass in the time interval Δt from state 1 into state 2 with probability $\alpha\Delta t$ and with probability $\beta\Delta t$ from state 2 into state 1. The development of the probabilities is described by the differential equation.

Another kind of application, though hardly suitable for school instruction is the catenary. A mass homogeneous, flexible plane curve is suspended while fixed in its endpoints; which shape does it assume? The basis vector e_1 is chosen horizontal, the basis vector e_2 vertical against the direction of gravity. The curve length from a fixed point is taken as a parameter on the curve; the vector of tension in the sense of increasing s is $T(s)$. The piece from s to $s + \Delta s$ is subjected to the forces

Thus
$$- T(s), \quad T(s + \Delta s), \quad - \mu g \Delta s \cdot e_2.$$

$$\frac{dT}{ds} = \mu g \, e_2$$

$$T = \mu g s \cdot e_2 + a$$

where a is a fixed vector $\ulcorner a_1, a_2 \urcorner$. T is a scalar multiple of the tangent-vector dx/ds,

$$\frac{dx_1}{ds} = \rho T_1, \quad \frac{dx_2}{ds} = \rho T_2,$$

$$\frac{dx_2}{dx_1} = \frac{T_2}{T_1} = \frac{\mu g s + a_2}{a_1},$$

or briefly

$$\frac{dx_2}{dx_1} = \alpha s + \beta.$$

Put

$$p = \frac{dx_2}{dx_1}$$

and differentiate once more with respect to x_1:

$$\frac{dp}{dx_1} = \alpha \frac{ds}{dx_1} = \alpha \sqrt{1 + p^2}.$$

$$\frac{dp}{\sqrt{1 + p^2}} = \alpha \, dx_1.$$

$$p = \sinh \alpha x_1 + c_1.$$

$$x_2 = \frac{1}{\alpha} \cosh \alpha x_1 + c_1 x_1 + c_2.$$

A subject that easily fits into school instruction, is the *suspension bridge.* (Figure 93.) On a flexible plane curve (a cable) a homogeneous bridge is

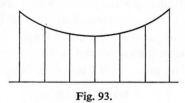

Fig. 93.

suspended; the bridge is heavy enough to have the weight of the cable neglected. In the balance of forces the gravity now counts as

$$- \mu g \Delta x_1 \cdot e_2 \,,$$

where μ is the bridge mass per length unit. With the former notations the differential equation is simplified to

$$\frac{dT}{dx} = \mu g \, e_2 \,.$$

Thus

$$T = \mu g x_1 e_2 + a \,,$$

where a is again a fixed vector $\ulcorner a_1, a_2 \urcorner$. Now T is a scalar multiple of the tangential vector, thus

$$\frac{dx_2}{dx_1} = \frac{T_2}{T_1} = \frac{\mu g x_1 + a_2}{a_1} \,.$$

The solution becomes

$$x_2 = \tfrac{1}{2} \frac{\mu g}{a_1} x_1^2 + \frac{a_2}{a_1} x_1 + c \,,$$

a parabolic curve. The coefficient of x_1^2 has now a physical meaning; it involves the elasticity constant.

ORDER OF MAGNITUDE

As easily as the physicist speaks of order of magnitude, so just as carefully does the mathematician avoid it. In teaching analysis it will hardly be mentioned. In analytic number theory something like order of magnitude is well-known. I mean Landau's O and o, but people grown up in, and accustomed to, modern linguistic habits in mathematics tend to shiver if they see this symbolism with its wrong use of the equality sign, wrongly indicated functions and mysterious variables. $(f(x) =$ $= O(g(x))$ does not mean that $f(x)$ equals the value of the function O for the argument $g(x)$, but rather that $f(x)/g(x)$ is bounded for large x.)

Of course the pupil should understand that x^3 increases more rapidly than x^2 and e^x more rapidly than any power of x, but what I want to discuss here is something quite different. For the intuitive understanding of differential quotient and integral the intuitive understanding of order is an indispensable presupposition. The definition of differential quotient involves that f at x_0 is approximated by a linear function f^* such that

$$f(x) - f^*(x)$$

tends more rapidly to 0 than $x - x_0$. Indeed since

$$\frac{f(x) - f(x_0)}{x - x_0} - f'(x_0)$$

tends to 0,

$$f(x) - f(x_0) - f'(x)(x - x_0)$$

tends more rapidly to 0 than $(x - x_0)$, and if the existence of the second derivative is supposed, even such that divided by $(x - x_0)^2$ it is still bounded. The student should recognize this not only in the formula but also in the graphic of the function and its tangent. An analogous remark is to be made about higher derivatives: if f is k-times differentiable at x_0, it can be approximated near x_0 by a polynomial f^* of k-th degree, such that

$$f(x) - f^*(x)$$

tends more rapidly to 0 than $(x - x_0)^k$. Not long ago this important feature was lacking in almost all university texts on analysis while much attention was paid to the most sophisticated "remainder terms".

How well is the integral of a smooth function f approximated by lower or upper stair functions or by piecewise linear functions? (Figures 94–95). Let h be the mesh of the subdivision; the variation of f in an interval of length h is at most of the same order as h; the error committed in the integral by replacing f with a constant function in an interval of length h is at most of the order h^2; added over all partial intervals, it becomes of the order h at most.

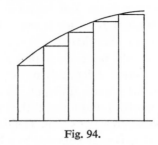

Fig. 94.

But what happens with piecewise linear approximation? Which error is committed if the function f is replaced in the interval of length h by a linear one, that is, if the graphic is replaced with its chord? The chord is parallel to a tangent in the interval; after what has been said in the last but one paragraph the error committed is of an order smaller than h, and if f is once more differentiable, of order h^2; in the integral this is an error of order h^3 in an interval of length h, and of order h^2 in the whole.

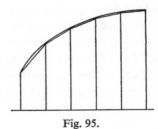

Fig. 95.

The accuracy of the approximation is astonishingly improved by an order of magnitude, if the lower and upper Riemann sums are replaced by approximating polygons. This is illustrated by applying it to the integration of special functions, say x^2. An obvious question arises – can we not improve the result still more by using approximating polygons of higher degree? The answer leads to interpolation theory. An analogous question: could we not use similar procedures to improve the accuracy if we differentiate numerically a function given by a table?

How well is sin x approximated by x at 0? It can be seen in Figure 96 by comparing the circle sector AOP with the triangle POP'. The error is of the order x^3. Which order if $P'A$? The similar triangles APB and $AP'P$ show that $P'A$ is of the order PP'^2 (thus x^2).

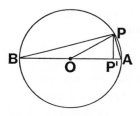

Fig. 96.

DIFFERENTIALS

When deriving for instance the differential equation that leads to the barometric formula we said that from the height x to the height $x + \Delta x$ the pressure decreases by the weight of the air contained in this layer,

that is by $\kappa p \Delta x$. Here the pressure in this layer has to be substituted for p. This pressure, however, is not a constant; it varies between p and $p + \Delta p$. What should we substitute for p when putting

$$(**) \qquad \Delta p \sim - \kappa p \, \Delta x?$$

Well, it does not really matter. The variation of p between x and $x + \Delta x$ is at most of the same order as Δx; whichever value from p to $p + \Delta p$ is substituted makes a difference which is of order $(\Delta x)^2$. Divided by Δx the error in

$$\frac{\Delta p}{\Delta x} \sim - \kappa p$$

becomes of order Δx, which vanishes in the limit to yield

$$\frac{dp}{dx} = - \kappa p.$$

It is the same pattern in all cases where we departed from realistic data to get a differential equation. A formula like (**) means an equality up to a remainder of higher order. Another way to write it down is

$$\Delta p = - \kappa p \Delta x + \cdots,$$

or

$$\Delta p = - \kappa p \Delta x + o(\Delta x),$$

where the dots or $o(\Delta x)$ mean something that tends faster to 0 than Δx. The classical notation is

$$p = - \kappa p \, dx.$$

Then one speaks of the infinitesimal interval from x to $x + dx$, which contains the air weight $- \kappa p dx$; the equation tells that this equals the change dp of the pressure p. Division by dx finally leads to the differential equation

$$\frac{dp}{dx} = - \kappa p.$$

The question whether and how differentials should be introduced in school mathematics has been extensively discussed, indeed the literature on it is enormous. The discussion is irrelevant if the preliminary question, namely which aim the differentials have to serve is not answered. Useless differentials can readily be dismissed. If dy and dx occur only in the combination dy/dx or under the integral sign after the integrand, the question as to what dx and dy mean individually is as meaningful as to ask what the 'l', 'o', 'g' in 'log' mean. To be sure one can tell that the differential notation is useful with a view to the chain and the substitution rules,

$$\frac{dz}{dx} = \frac{dz}{dy} \cdot \frac{dy}{dx}$$

$$\int_{\varphi(a)}^{\varphi(b)} f(x) \, dx = \int_a^b f(\varphi(u)) \frac{dx}{du} \, du,$$

if $x = \varphi(u)$. Moreover computations with differentials are comfortable if differential equations like

$$\frac{dy}{dx} = \frac{f(x)}{g(y)}$$

are solved via

$$f(x)\,dx = g(y)\,dy,$$

$$\int f(x)\,dx = \int g(y)\,dy,$$

by establishing with

$$F(x) = \int_a^x f(\xi)\,d\xi \quad \text{and} \quad G(y) = \int_b^y g(y)\,dy$$

the relation

$$F(x) = G(y)$$

between x and y, as we did when solving the differential equation of the catenary. It is easy to justify this without differentials by means of the substitution rule:

$$g(y)\frac{dy}{dx} = f(x),$$

$$\int g(y)\,dy = \int g(y)\frac{dy}{dx}\,dx = \int f(x)\,dx,$$

which, however, hardly contributes to understanding better the procedures involved.

Differentials are an essential part of the so-called differential forms. An expression like $v\,du$ gets a numerical value, namely

$$\int_\omega v\,du$$

if for u and v functions are substituted and integration is performed over a path ω. If they are functions of, say, k variables, then ω will be a path in k-dimensional space,

$$\int_0^1 v(\omega_1(t), ..., \omega_k(t))\frac{d}{dt}u(\omega_1(t), ..., \omega_k(t))\,dt.$$

Then vdu is a functional that in a prescribed way assigns a number to a pair of functions and a path. We will come back to this point later.

In didactic discussions on differentials such applications do not count, if any application ever counts and the discussion is not entirely restricted to the linguistic phenomenon of the differential. How does it come then that the discussion on differentials never dies? The thorn in the flesh is physics, where people are happy with infinitesimal paths, times, work, and happily divide such things by each other while neglecting higher order terms.

I think I have made it clear enough that the reason is not physics as such. If realistic data are mathematized by analysis, the differentials crop up. Two magnitudes are varying in dependence on each other; rather than telling that the small increases Δx and Δy correspond to each other and $\Delta y/\Delta x$ converges to dy/dx, one speaks of the infinitesimal changes dx, dy and their quotient dy/dx. Instead of

$$\Delta p \sim - \kappa p \Delta x$$

where p is to be taken somewhere in the interval x to $x + \Delta x$, one says directly

$$dp = - \kappa p dx .$$

The intuitive idea is that the infinitesimal change of p is expressed linearly by that of x. This is the way a physicist expresses himself, and I trust that in his private life no mathematician who has to solve such problems will spurn differentials. This is the way a physicist teaches physics, either fully conscious that it is his good right to do so, or feeling somewhat guilty – depending on whether he is a sovereign master of mathematics or whether he is frustrated by mathematics. Among those mathematicians, however, who would be able to teach the students the mathematics applied by the physicist, there are only a few who would appreciate that students get acquainted with it, and still fewer who would dare to teach it. The teaching in secondary schools is under strong pressure from abstract university mathematics, which is far from that mathematics that people apply. Multirelated analysis at school and university can be approached in many ways; all the approaches we have indicated have in common the idea of differential as an intuitive element. If multirelated analysis is to be taught intuitively, there is no need to raise the question whether differentials should be dealt with; on such a ground they will grow like wild plants. At this level there isn't any need either to explain what differentials are; we do not explain axiomatically or by other means how a geometrical drawing has to be read, do we? I know that mathematics teachers have difficulty in teaching a subject that is not clearly dissected into definitions, suppositions, assertions, and proofs, but they can learn from the physicist how it should be done.

In my examples I have avoided differentials because I have already behaved in a quite unorthodox way, and I was afraid of upsetting the reader even more than I have up to now, before I had time to explain what differentials mean in the didactics I advocate. It does not matter whether a *small* piece of the catenary from s to $s + \Delta s$ or an *infinitesimal* one from $s + ds$ is considered, whether instead of the relation

$$T(s + \Delta s) - T(s) \sim \mu g \Delta s \cdot e_2$$

an equation

$$T(s + ds) - T(s) = \mu g ds \cdot e_2$$

is written, but the second version is more honest. The university student should learn it from the mathematician in order to understand the language of the physicst, and at school he should have already been prepared to accept this method. It is an impossible situation that the mathematician teaches a mathematics that cannot be applied and the physicist applies a mathematics that has not been taught by the mathematician.

MAGNITUDES AND FUNCTIONS

This schizophrenia is more deeply rooted. The rift developed at the end of last century and it has broadened ever since, under the influence of the modern development of mathematics, and in particular as a consequence of the penetration of mathematics by set theory and the continuous linguistic reshaping of mathematics. If we continue to teach mathematics in a more and more purified style and more and more devoid of heuristics, the appliers of mathematics will give their students the mathematics they believe their students need, without relying on the mathematicians at all.

I already claimed that the reasons are more profound; it is not just that the one uses ε and δ and exact limit definitions, while the other speaks of infinitesimals and differentials. It starts as early as the concept of function in its set theory frame and as the more and more adapted function notation. Perhaps the reader has noticed that the notation of my examples did little justice to the spirit by which I had earlier characterized modern mathematics. Nevertheless I can assure him that I retract nothing of the praise I bestowed on the modern function concept. Rather I wish to show how dangerous those dogmatic attempts are to squeeze everything into one system, and how many objective and didactic values may be lost by such attempts.

My examples abounded with such differential quotients as dp/dx, where the pressure is differentiated with respect to the height, ds/ds' where one arc length is differentiated with respect to another, even $d\sigma/d\sigma'$ with a differentiation of one surface area with respect to another, dT/ds, where the tension is differentiated with respect to the arc length, the work with respect to the path (but it could also be done with respect to velocity); in de/dV the charge was differentiated with respect to the potential, in dV/de the potential with respect to the charge. This is the mathematics and the mathematical terminology of the physicst, and often it is an extremely advantageous one. In mathematics things like dV/de tend to become obsolete. V' is preferred, which means differentiation of V with respect to its variable whatever its name may be; indeed by proposing a function V we do not stipulate anything about the letter that may be put behind the V in brackets. de/dV and dV/de together are not possible; indeed, can be take 'V' on the one hand as a function symbol and on the other as a variable (what ever this may be) and then invert things?

Well, $V, e, p, x, s, s', \sigma, \sigma'$ as they occur in the examples are not functions, and the whole terminology of functions is not suited to this context. They are rather what we will call magnitudes. It is like a black box. There are dials outside which can be adjusted; let us call magnitude what is communicated by such a dial. Adjustments of the dials are not independent of each other. If I change one, others in consequence will change also while still others remain independent. By means of such black boxes the functioning of machines is described. Some people will be prone to consider the physical world, too, as such a black box.

To the magnitudes of the black box other, dependent ones can be added, the sum and product of two magnitudes, the square, or the logarithm of one magnitude. If we look how a change dx of a magnitude x influences a magnitude y to change by dy (all other things unchanged) and divide dy by dx, we get a magnitude dy/dx which perhaps is also registered by the black box and which with respect to others may be called a velocity, a capacity, an elasticity and so on. If u and v are such magnitudes $\int v\,du$ can be registered, which may perhaps depend on the path which the system – the black box – has followed.

Certainly functional dependences play a part here but they are not made explicit and are not accounted for in the notations. If x changes, y will change but no function that tells how y depends on x, is explicitly mentioned. If dy/dx is formed, it does not mean that 'y' is a functional symbol and 'x' a variable. To be sure we can form dx/dy as well (which is the reciprocal of dy/dx). The symbols for magnitudes are not interchangeable; x is the path, t the time, dx/dt the velocity or rather the path, time, velocity of the system under consideration (for example of a mass point). Even dx/dm can be formed if the system admits varying the mass m of the mass point. Here x is as little a function of t as of m. If need be, one can introduce functions to make these dependencies explicit. Let p, V, T be respectively the pressure, volume, and temperature, of a gas; p can be differentiated with respect to V while T is fixed, or with respect to T while p is fixed. It is not made explicit how the one depends on the other except under special circumstances.

But why did this method fall into disrepute among mathematicians? The reason is the mixing up of two views and notations, the magnitude and the functional method. How should we express the way x depends on t or p, V, T depend on each other? Physicists write $p(V)$ and $p(T)$, which means p as a function of V if T is fixed, and p as a function of T if V is fixed, respectively. This is in flat contradiction to the modern development of the notion of function. There 'p' is the functional symbol and p is a well-defined mathematical function, whereas the argument symbol between the brackets after 'f' means nothing; it is a mere place filler.

This in itself would not be too serious a conflict. One could resign oneself to this contradiction between the old magnitude and the new functional interpretation and apply either though not intermix them. It is unfortunate, however, that the old notation which is still used by physicists lacks consistency. They call p the pressure, $p(V)$ the pressure at volume V, $p(T)$ the pressure at temperature T. But what to do if as it may happen the volume depends functionally on the temperature? Is the pressure then denoted by $p(V)$ or by $p(T)$ or by $p(V(T))$? Any mathematician who has worked in thermodynamics knows this confusion, and the mere recollection may give him the creeps. Of course, there are no functions at issue. The physicist who is viewing the real situation behind the formulae, knows exactly what he means; it is the same attitude as that of a geometer who trusts the figure to tell its story and therefore can express himself in a more realistic way than one who is anxious to avoid any connnection with reality.

To quote an example from geometry, let us look how a curve in space is defined as a space vector function of a real variable. In old geometry, and even today in mechanics the variable curve point is named x, and then $x(s)$ can denote its dependence on one parameter s, and $x(t)$ that on another parameter t; if a parameter change is applied from s to t by means of φ, one gets beside $x(s)$ the notation $x(\varphi(s))$, which means the same. The poor student who takes a mathematics course from 9–10 and a physics course from 10–11, has just a quarter of an hour to rearrange his mind, because up till now the lecturers that embody this university schizophrenia did not have the time to come together to discuss the question.

It is tempting, indeed, but it cannot be justified any more that in one and the same context the letter 'x' means two separate things, first, a magnitude and second, the way the magnitude depends on another which is indicated between the brackets that follow – simply because it is wrong to indicate two different things using the same symbol. It may sometimes be adequate to indicate the way the magnitude x depends on the magnitude x by $x(s)$ and the way it depends on t by $x(t)$, but it is badly adapted to the function notation. If we have to tell how the pressure depends on the volume or on the temperature, we would be better advised to use the functional symbols φ and ψ, respectively, to write $p = \varphi(V)$, $p = \psi(T)$, or, still more generally $p = \chi(V, T)$. But this need not mean casting away the good with the bad. We should allow the physicists and ourselves to indicate magnitudes by letters, thus granting them (and us) the extraordinarily helpful differentiation of one magnitude with respect to another and the implied differential quotient notation. Thus, if x and t are place and time, dx/dt would mean the velocity. If moreover the dependence of the place with respect to the time, is given by

$$x = f(t),$$

the dependence of the velocity with respect to the time is told by

$$\frac{dx}{dt} = f'(t).$$

But this is not enough. The old notation, where p can mean both a magnitude and a functional symbol (namely to indicate the way one depends on another), has in any case one great advantage in that it assigns algorithmically a function to a magnitude. The procedure I explained above to introduce a new letter for any function that tells how some magnitude depends on some other, is utterly circumstantial and impracticable. Is there not a more expedient method?

I recall the devices by which expressions involving x are transformed into functional expressions.

$$x \to x^2$$

is a usual notation for the function "square of ...". Instead of this I proposed

$$\Upsilon_x x^2.$$

Can we not use this trick here? If x and t are magnitudes, say x the place of a point at time t, then

$$t \to x$$

could be the function f that expresses x by t, that is

$$x = f(t).$$

In my own notation I would use

$$\Upsilon_t x.$$

This is not a direct consequence of the principle according to which expressions are to be transformed into functions, because x is not an expression that involves t. The connection between t and x is not indeed explicit; it is hidden in the black box. My proposal leads beyond the formal transformation of expressions into functions, but the step is rather small and quite natural.

Thus the pressure as a function of the temperature would be

$$\curlyvee_T p,$$

as a function of the volume,

$$\curlyvee_V p,$$

as a function of both

$$\curlyvee_{\ulcorner T, V \urcorner} p.$$

(Obviously $\curlyvee_T P$ is not one function, but one for each V; but this is not a new feature.)

We now get for example,

$$\curlyvee_t \frac{dx}{dt} = (\curlyvee_t x)'.$$

$$\curlyvee_t x = \curlyvee_s x \curlyvee_t s.$$

It looks a strange notation until one gets accustomed to it.* Meanwhile one can use yet others which are more familiar. In general, substituting some values into the functions under discussion means that some of the dials of the black box have to be adjusted, or that magnitudes have to be replaced with numerical or vectorial values. Now the value of x at the time with the value t_0 can be indicated by

$$x_{t=t_0}.$$

This is an old usage with velocities, where one writes

$$\left(\frac{dx}{dt}\right)_{t=t_0}.$$

Examples of the use of these symbols are

$$(\curlyvee_t x)(t_0) = x_{t=t_0},$$

$$(\curlyvee_t x)'(t_0) = \left(\frac{dx}{dt}\right)_{t=t_0}.$$

Such artifices can probably serve to clear up partial derivatives – a notoriously delicate matter.

* I did not live up to my own proposals in this exposition.

I do not claim that this is the final solution. Rather it should be understood as a challenge. It would be healthy if competent and interested people would radically ponder this matter. The calculus of magnitudes, method and notation of differentials and differential quotients are precious devices, and we are not entitled to exact from the physicist that he barters away good old shoes for new ones that pinch. We should rather do what in the past has proved to be good policy, that is, reinterpreting a formalism in such a way that it becomes wholeheartedly acceptable.

However sophisticated the result may be, what counts in school teaching is that we teach the pupils analysis with the most expedient tools he can use. The differentials, the geometric, mechanic, and physical magnitudes and their differential quotients are most efficient devices of intuitive analysis; we cannot afford to withhold them from learners. Purism inspired by set theory can only lead to catastrophic blockages of understanding.

CONTINUITY AND CONVERGENCE

Properly said it is not right to conjure continuity and convergence in one breath – I mean it is wrong didactically. Logically they are a close kin but this idea can only be the result of analysis and formalization; the kinship of these concepts can be the goal of a learning process rather than its basis. The convergence of a sequence, a series, even a function can be proved with no previous definition of what is convergence. Though the idea of continuity forces itself upon the learner, it can be a hard thing to prove continuities unless the concept of continuity has sufficiently been analyzed. Convergence proofs at not too high a level are performed on special sequences and such that the limit is, as it were, computed and it is even estimated how far to go to pass beneath a given error bound. With the continuity of functions one could try the same, but it would only remain a preparatory stage to take linear or quadratic functions to show that they are continuous, preceding a general definition of continuity. It is as a *general* property that continuity plays a role, that is because from continuity other properties such as integrability can be derived.

Our exposition leaves little doubt that one can advance a long way in analysis with an intuitive notion of continuity. Thus it is a quite natural question to ask whether higher level sophistications are desirable. Is there any use of continuity in analysis as taught at school? It is readily seen that continuity and differentiability are entirely irrelevant. What matters is *uniform* continuity and differentiability. To show that a continuous function is integrable, it is instrumental to know that a small difference in the arguments makes the differences of the function values uniformly small; this is required to conclude that the difference of area between the stairs polygon and the curve (Figure 70) becomes arbitrarily small if the mesh tends to zero. To be sure, by Heine-Borel or Bolzano-Weierstrass it can be shown that every continuous function in a closed bounded interval is uniformly continuous, but I doubt whether up till now anybody has nurtured an ambition to prove or even to mention this theorem at school. If, however, integrability of continuous functions is the only aim that is intended with the fixation of the concept of continuity, it should be honestly realized that this aim is not attainable. It would then make much more sense to formulate at once the uniform continuity, which in fact is easier than formulating simple continuity.

Differentiability is an analogous case. What matters is uniform differentiability, which means that

$$\left| \frac{f(x+h) - f(x)}{h} - f'(x) \right|$$

becomes arbitrarily small, uniformly in x, if h becomes small, that is, for every $\varepsilon > 0$ there is a $\delta > 0$ such that the above expression becomes $< \varepsilon$ as soon as $|h| < \delta$, or otherwise that

$$\frac{f(x_1) - f(x_2)}{x_1 - x_2}$$

converges uniformly to $f'(x)$, if x_1, x_2 tend to x. We used this again and again, when we replaced differential by difference quotients (for instance when we proved that the integral of the derivative is, up to an additive constant, the original function*, and in many applications and analogies of this theorem, as well as in all that has been said about order of magnitude**.

* p. 517.
** p. 546.

No doubt the uniform differentiability of f follows from the continuity of the derivative f', which is usually assumed in the suppositions of such proofs, but this is again a property which has to be proved by Heine-Borel. Here, too, it is to be recommended to assume at once uniform differentiability. In this sector even university teaching is unsatisfactory, but I will not dwell too long on such sophistications.

If for some reason it is decided that continuity or uniform continuity should be taught at school, the most direct way is to slap the ε-δ-definition in the student's face. Even at university such a policy does not enable the majority of the students to check in a particular case whether the condition is fulfilled. On the other hand I cannot but regret that up to this moment no didactics of the continuity notion has been developed. In particular, any logical analysis of the didactic situation is still lacking.

The difficulties implicit in the continuity concept are quantifiers and the order of quantifiers of different kinds. To explain this I have to anticipate what should properly be left till Chapter XIX, which is about logic.

Continuity of f means intuitively: small changes of x correspond with small changes of $f(x)$. Or: if x changes little, $f(x)$, also changes little. Words like "small", "big", "little", "much", "short", "long", may hide a quantifier, but formal linguistic criteria are often insufficient to know which kind. Always, sometimes, everywhere, somewhere – exhibit clearly the universal or existential quantifier, but the linguistic formulation does not unveil that in the continuity definition the second small (or little) hides a universal, and the first an existential, quantifier. To grasp it, a logical analysis is badly needed. The meaning of the quantifiers in "small" or "little" is better indicated in the more exact formulation: to sufficiently small changes of x correspond arbitrarily small ones of $f(x)$. Or: if x changes sufficiently little, $f(x)$ changes arbitrarily little. Still from this formulation it is a long step to understand that first the "arbitrarily little" must be prescribed before the "sufficiently little" is to be determined.

The intuitive continuity definition involves two difficulties of formalizing – first, decoding of hidden quantifiers, second, settling the order of quantifiers of different kinds. Good didactics should at least separate these difficulties from each other. It is not unlikely that the continuity definition is where the students meet essential quantifiers for the first time. Universal ones as in

$$a + b = b + a \quad \text{for all} \quad a, b$$

are inessential. Even the changing quantifier pair in

for any a there is an x such that $a + x = b$

is inessential, because here, as most often at school mathematics level, the existential quantifier is of an algorithmic kind; the "there is" can be eliminated since the thing that is said to exist, can explicitly be shown – in the case at issue it is called "$b - a$".* Non-algorithmic quantifiers are more likely to be met in non-mathematical than in mathematical contexts. In school mathematics an existential statement usually rests on a construction of the object in question, whereas numerous examples in everyday life remind one of the proverbial needle in a haystack, which, though it exists, cannot in fact be found.

Before the student can progress to logical (and even more to psychological) intricacies such as the continuity concept, the teacher (or the textbook author) must grasp the inherent difficulties of quantifiers. The student should have passed the stages of experiencing:

> *quantifiers*, and in particular
> *non-algorithmic quantifiers* with their negations,

he should have learned

> *decoding hidden quantifiers*

and he should have grasped

> the *essentiality of the order* of quantifiers.

I have already suggested that it is a long road, which should not be started at the end where most of the difficulties are accumulated.

If I speak of quantifiers, I obviously do not mean pieces of a wel

---

* Algorithmicity should not here be understood in the way the logician defines algorithms. In the theorem on the intermediate zero of a continuous function between a positive and a negative function value, the graphic image of a continuous function is persuasive enough to build up the belief in the algorithmic existence of the zero; only after a thorough analysis of the continuity concept can one grasp that it allows for much more general functions than can properly be reflected by a simple graphic image, and that the graphically suggested existence of such an algorithm is an illusion. On the other hand, to the naive perception the existence of an infinity of prime numbers would not be algorithmic, though it is guaranteed by an algorithm.

formalized logical language. It is the vernacular that the learner must know to formalize, if he has to reshape the continuity definition into a more exact one. The quantifiers he has to experience are named "every", "all", "everywhere", "always", "a certain", "some", "somewhere", "sometimes", and so on, but even in the unassuming indefinite article "a" he should detect the universal or existential quantifier. With the hidden quantifiers he must first be confronted where they occur simply or, in any case, with no order complications. In

> good work takes time

he would discover the existential quantifier hidden in "time" (there is a time limit beyond which it becomes good).
In

> from times immemorial...

or

> for ages...

he would notice the universal quantifier (however long I can remember).
In

> the deepest secrets will come to light.

he will recognize that the superlative is asserting something about all secrets, in

> it is beyond my stoutest hopes

about all hopes whatsoever. In

> many hounds soon catch the hare

the "many" will suggest to him the existence of a big enough pack that the hare cannot escape, but in

> as many as

he recognizes the universal quantifier.

These have been examples of one, though hidden, quantifier. If more quantifiers are at issue, the student should be aware of the importance of order first in those cases where the quantifiers are overt. For example in

> Always somebody was here

and
> Somebody was always here

(for every t there is an x, such that person x was here at time t – there is an x, such that for all t the person x was here). Or in

> Once everyone believed in God,

and

> Everybody once believed in God

(there is a t such that at time t every x believed in God – for every x there is a t such that x at time t believed in God). Or with partly hidden quantifiers:

> Every man has a mother,

and

> All (together) have a mother

(for every x there is an y such that y is mother of x – there is an y such that y is mother of x for every x.)

Of all such examples the student should be able to form the negation. Both quantifiers are hidden in

> The fleetest and strongest must perish at last

(for every x there is a time t where he must perish).

Essential simple quantifiers which, moreover, are hidden, are not frequent in school mathematics. Examples are:

> $\sqrt{2}$ is irrational

(there are no integers p, q such that $p^2 = 2q^2$);

> x is divisible by 5

(there is an integer y such that $x = 5y$);

> x is a power of 2

(there is an integer y such that $x = 2^y$). As we mentioned earlier* even above school level the ability is sometimes lacking to recognize the quantifiers in these structures, though this is still a far cry from the

---

* p. 372.

complications of the definition of continuity. But even among the constructions with two or more quantifiers in succession there are some which are conceptually easier than the definition of continuity. For instance,

> the function f is positive for large arguments.

Clearly "large" is hiding a quantifier, but which one is meant, or is it more than one? Which kind of functions does this statement aim at? Something like the function $\curlyvee_x x^2$ or like the sine? Is it an assertion about all large x or about some of them? It should be made more precise:

> the function f is positive for all large arguments,

or

> the function f is positive for some arbitrarily large arguments.

These are two different quantifier successions.
First,

> there is an a, such that for all $b > a$ it holds $f(b) > 0$.

Second,

> to every a there is a $b > a$ with $f(b) > 0$.

Still more involved are the statements:

> the function f becomes large for all large arguments,

and

> the function f becomes large for some large arguments.

In the first case one also says

> f grows beyond all limits,

in the second

> f becomes larger and larger.

For the first case $\curlyvee_x x^2$ is a paradigm, for the second $\curlyvee_x x \sin x$. Compared with the preceding pair, a quantifier "for every M" is to be added in the beginning, whereas at the end 0 is to be replaced by M in $f(b) > 0$, thus

> for every M there is an a such that for all $b > 0$ it holds that $f(b) > M$

and

> for every M and every a there is a b such that $f(b) > M$.

It is also useful to form the negations of all these statements.

The preceding was to indicate the kind of exercises that could prepare the analysis of the continuity notion; examples outside mathematics should not be forgotten. For example the mutual relation of the hidden quantifiers in

> in a great choice many can find what they want,

or

> you can fool all of the people some of the time, and some of the people all of the time, but you cannot fool all of the people all of the time.

Or the famous definition:

> a specialist is somebody who knows more and more about less and less, and finally knows all about nothing.

A particularly nice example is

> many a little makes a mickle,

which is a somewhat informal wording of the Archimedean axiom: for given a and b there is a natural n such that n times a exceeds b.

An illustrative example is also the proverbial

> little causes produce great effects.

It is clearly a denial of the continuity in causal processes, and as a consequence as shows the theory of quanta, the denial of causality itself. The statement can be interpreted in several ways. Which quantifier is contained in "great", "arbitrarily great" or "some great"? In the first case it would mean

> there are arbitrarily large effects that are due to little causes,

in the second

> there are effects the magnitude of which exceeds a positive measure and which are due to arbitrarily small causes.

If this is mathematically interpreted in the way that the cause assails a magnitude x, and the effect manifests itself in a magnitude y, while the function f tells which value of y corresponds to a value of x, then the above saying reads to a small change of x can correspond an arbitrary large one of y

or

to a small change of x can correspond one of y that lies above a fixed positive bound ε.

If f is to be continuous the first is certainly forbidden, but even the second is so, and this is one prohibition for every positive ε, which with increasing ε becomes more and more severe. The "small change" of x is here understood arbitrarily small, that is smaller than any $\delta > 0$:

to every $\delta > 0$ there are changes of x by less than δ to which correspond changes of y by ε or more.

This is forbidden for every $\varepsilon > 0$ if f is to be continuous:

there is a $\delta > 0$ such that to every change of x by less than δ corresponds a change of y by less than ε.

At this point it is required that the student is already acquainted with the way quantifiers behave under negation.

Discontinuities should be visualized by graphics, for instance by that of a postage or a tax tariff, but also by mappings of a more general kind. All kind of causal connections between magnitudes can serve to visualize continuity. Take, for instance, target practice, that is, to a small change in aiming corresponds a small change in hitting, and compare it with effects which depend discontinuously on the cause. If the student has advanced far enough to be familiar with quantifier symbolism*, it should be used as much as possible. In particular the negation of quantifiers is then more clearly exhibited, in the present case with respect to the transition from

$$\neg \bigwedge_{\delta>0} \bigvee_{\ulcorner x_1, x_2 \urcorner} (|x_1 - x_2| < \delta \wedge |f(x_1) - f(x_2)| \geqslant \varepsilon),$$

to

$$\bigvee_{\delta>0} \neg \bigvee_{\ulcorner x_1, x_2 \urcorner} (|x_1 - x_2| < \delta \wedge |f(x_1) - f(x_2)| \geqslant \varepsilon)$$

to

$$\bigvee_{\delta>0} \bigwedge_{\ulcorner x_1, x_2 \urcorner} \neg (|x_1 = x_2| < \delta \wedge |f(x_1) - f(x_2)| \geqslant \varepsilon)$$

to

$$\bigvee_{\delta>0} \bigwedge_{\ulcorner x_1, x_2 \urcorner} (\neg (|x_1 - x_2| < \delta) \vee \neg |f(x_1) - f(x_2)| \geqslant \varepsilon)$$

* This will be tackled in Chapter XIX.

to

$$\bigvee_{\delta>0} \bigwedge_{[x_1, x_2]} (|x_1 - x_2| < \delta) \to |f(x_1) - f(x_2)| < \varepsilon).$$

It is, however, not sufficient that the student learns to work in the formalized language. He should also learn the many ambiguous translation rules:

For small u it is $F(u)$

can mean

for all sufficiently small u it is $F(u)$

or

for some arbitrarily small u it is $F(u)$, and correspondingly formalized,

$$\bigvee_a \bigwedge_{u<a} F(u)$$

or

$$\bigwedge_a \bigvee_{u<a} F(u).$$

And again, more precisely,

$$\bigwedge_{u<a} \cdots \quad \text{means} \quad \bigwedge_u (u < a) \to \cdots,$$
$$\bigvee_{u<a} \cdots \quad \text{means} \quad \bigvee_u (u < a) \wedge \ldots$$

It is the concept of uniform continuity that has been obtained here. I already explained that this is the form in which the concept is applied. It must not be forgotten that this continuity concept depends on the definition domain, that

$$\curlyvee_x x^2 \quad \text{and} \quad \curlyvee_x x^{-1}$$

are continuous as functions in finite intervals and in $x > \alpha$ (for $\alpha > 0$), respectively, though they cease to be continuous in this sense if x is not restricted or if all $x > 0$ are admitted, respectively. As a new sophistication one can introduce the continuity in a single point x_1. The quantification over x_1, x_2 together is then reduced to one over x_2 alone. If continuity is required in *every* point, a new quantifier $\bigwedge_{x_1}$ is to be added at the head of the expression rather than somewhere in between. This illustrates anew the part played by order in the use of quantifiers.

What of all these things should be taught at school? How far should the teacher pass beyond the intuitive non-analyzed notion of continuity? Our discussions were to show that the logically analyzed and more or or less formalized concept of continuity belongs in another context than that of analysis. If at all, it should be exercized on the basis of logic, in connection with logic and as a means to deeper logical insight. For analysis, as exercized at school, the formalized continuity concept is irrelevant; the degree of formalization of the continuity concept depends on the depth that the student has to attain in logic, and it is in this connection that continuity should be viewed. The yes or no with respect to the formalized continuity concept can, however, be pronounced with a great many gradations. If mathematics is taught in a way adapted to the character of the student, logic can play a great or, if any, a small part; corresponding to these extremes continuity can be formalized with the use of logical symbols, or the intuitive concept of continuity may be just enough. But whatever happens, the intuitive continuity concept will be the starting point and the rough material of any projected sophistication.

But even after sophistication the intuitive continuity concept should be used wherever it is sufficient and useful. This applies in particular to the teacher and textbooks author who in order to be able to help the pupil should be acquainted with all shades of formalizing.

In the subtitle I mentioned convergence too, though I already remarked that in analysis at school convergence is rather an algorithmic notion. The limit of a sequence and the degree to which it is approached, is explicitly given by the sequence. It is simply stated that a is the limit of the sequence a_n, and it is proved by making $|a - a_n|$ small. There is hardly any need to define in general what is the limit of a sequence. The need of a definition, which then must be non-algorithmic, is much more felt with continuity. Once, however, continuity has more or less been formalized, a revision of the limit notion is well motivated. Then one gets the same logical structure; $|a - a_n|$ is to be made small for all sufficiently larg n:

for every $\varepsilon > 0$ there is an N such that for $n \geq N$ all $|a - a_n|$ become $< \varepsilon$.

It is well known that continuity of f at x_0 can also be formalized by means of the limit concept,

if $\lim x_n = x_0$, then $\lim f(x_n) = f(x_0)$,

that is, for any sequence x_n converging to x_0 the sequence of $f(x_n)$ converges to $f(x_0)$.

This quantification over all sequences converging to x_0 is not a trifle. On the contrary, it is profound, as it is difficult, to prove the equivalence of the ε–δ-definition and the limit-definition of continuity. The best approach is to prove:

ε–δ-continuity $\to$ lim-continuity,

$\neg$ (ε–δ-continuity) $\to$ $\neg$ (lim-continuity).

THE DEVELOPMENT OF ANALYSIS
AT SCHOOL – FUNDAMENTALS

In which way and to what extent can the teaching of analysis at school be systematized? To explain what is required to answer these questions, I will stress the following example,

$$\int_a^b \frac{dx}{x}.$$

As mentioned earlier* this integral can serve to introduce the logarithmic function before analysis proper has started. This introduction would rest on three suppositions:

(1) the existence of the area between the hyperbola and the horizontal axis and between two ordinates,

(2) the usual additivity of area.

(3) the behaviour of this area under special affine transformations (multiplication in one axis direction by ρ and in the other by ρ^{-1}) as it is found in parallelograms (that is invariance in the underlying case).

From these assumptions it follows that the area from a fixed to a variable ordinate is a logarithmic function.

The next step, now within analysis, is introducing approximating polygons. Condition 1 is preserved:

(1') The existence of the areas at issue.

But now (2) and (3) can be proved if it is assumed:

* p. 327.

(2′) The areas of the approximating polygons converge towards the area of the curvilinearly bounded domain.

The next step would be to acknowledge the intuitively obvious property (2′) as a consequence of the (uniform) continuity of the integrand. The postulates are now:

(1″) The existence of the areas at issue.

(2″) Continuous f can be approximated up to $\varepsilon > 0$ by a stair function (or a piecewise linear function).

(3″) If $g(x) \leq f(x)$ for all x, then $\displaystyle\int_a^b g(x)\,dx \leq \int_a^b f(x)\,dx$.

Indeed, as soon as f is approximated by f_ε up to ε,

$$f_\varepsilon(x) - \varepsilon \leq f(x) \leq f_\varepsilon(x) + \varepsilon$$

leads to

$$\int_a^b f_\varepsilon(x) - \varepsilon(b - a) \leq \int_a^b f(x)\,dx \leq \int_a^b f_\varepsilon(x)\,dx + \varepsilon(b - a)$$

thus to the convergence

$$\lim_{\varepsilon = 0} \int_a^b f_\varepsilon(x)\,dx = \int_a^b f(x)\,dx.$$

Up to now it was always supposed that the integral of given f exists; from this assumption its value and properties could be derived, and the integral could be obtained as a limit. To assure the existence of the integral under sufficiently general conditions, say for continuous functions, a fundamentally new method must be envisaged. The limit is no longer pre-existent; it must be created, and this is done by the artifice of the Cauchy sequence. The sequence of areas of approximating polygons is to be regarded as a Cauchy sequence and the convergence of any Cauchy sequence must be admitted. The second can be postulated axiomatically, but already the proof of the first requires a quite complicated apparatus. Estimating the areas of the approximating polygons is not the difficulty, provided uniform continuity of the integrand is assumed. What is really annoying is that the approximating polygons do not form a sequence in the usual sense; they are not indexed by natural numbers, they are a non-countable infinity.

This difficulty can be avoided if rather than arbitrary polygons only two kinds are admitted, lower and upper stair polygons. With them the lower and upper sums are formed; the first have a lowest upper bound, the others a greatest lower bound, which by uniform continuity must coincide; their common value is by definition the integral of the function. As a characteristic property of real numbers the convergence of Cauchy sequences is then replaced by the existence of the lowest upper and greatest lower bound of sets bounded from above and below, respectively. The restriction, however, which is then imposed on the approximating polynomials, is quite artificial and causes annoying difficulties at other places, for instance if the transformation rule for integrals is to be proved. There are, however, devices by which one can avoid these difficulties. If one looks into university texts and analyzes the way it is done, one cannot but admire the authors' proficiency in inventing sophistications, which the learner does not notice, and of course does not understand. For these reasons I do not believe that at school it would be wise to go further than accepting the existence of the integral of a continuous function without a formal proof.

It is much the same with the theorem that allows to compute integrals as primitives. If it is known $f(x) = F'(x)$, one can obtain the integral of f by

$$\int_a^b f(x)\, dx = F(b) - F(a).$$

The intuitive proof* of this theorem uses the fact that the difference quotients of a function F converge *uniformly* to the differential quotient; with no restrictions this would not be true, but it is true if the differential quotient $F' = f$ is continuous. I indicated already that the "correct" differentiability notion is uniform differentiability; it is just what is most often used. The equivalence, however, of continuous and uniform differentiability is not easily proved, and, in any case, the proof cannot be a subject of teaching at school.

* p. 516.

Yet there is a way out. Let

$$f(x) = F'(x) \quad \text{and } f \text{ continuous.}$$

If again one takes the liberty to suppose that

$$G(x) = \int_a^x f(x)\, dx$$

exists, one can prove without difficulties by differentiation that

$$G'(x) = f(x),$$

thus

$$(F - G)' = 0.$$

The only thing still needed to conclude that F and G are equal up to an additive constant, is that a function H with vanishing differential quotient H' is constant. Then indeed

$$\int_a^b f(x)\, dx = F(b) - F(a).$$

Here we needed the fundamental theorem:

A function the derivative of which vanishes (in the interval a, b) *is constant* (in this interval).

Anyone who has taught analysis knows that this theorem is the crux of the theory. It is intuitively so clear that the only thing one does not understand is why its proof presupposes so much. It is usually proved via the mean value theorem, which is by itself a freak, since it is always applied in a way that the position of the mean value does not matter. The mean value theorem can be avoided, but this is not the place to show how this can be done*.

The reason why the theorem on the constancy of functions with vanishing derivative needs such a complicated proof, is as follows. In some way we must use the fact that the function is defined in a whole interval; as soon as there is one point in the interval where the function is not defined, the theorem ceases to apply. Thus the topological property that dis-

---

* Cf. H. Freudenthal und H. Wäsche in: *Grundzüge der Mathematik* (ed. by H. Behnke *et al.*), Göttingen, 1962, III, 25–55.

tinguishes the real number field from others must be used; at some place the convergence of Cauchy sequences or the existence of the lowest upper bound must enter the proof.

Life is made much easier if one employs a principle which I have used on several occasions. I proposed that continuity should always be understood as uniform continuity, and differentiability as uniform differentiability. If f is differentiable in this sense from a to b, and if its derivative vanishes, it follows that to every $\varepsilon > 0$ there is a $\delta > 0$ such that

$$\left| \frac{f(x+h) - f(x)}{h} \right| < \varepsilon \quad \text{for all } h \text{ with } 0 < h < \delta$$

and all x in the interval from a to $b - h$. If now n is so chosen as to make $h = (1/n)(b-a) < \delta$ and the interval is divided into n equal parts by the sequence $a = x_0 < x_1 < ... < x_n = b$, one gets

$$\left| \frac{f(x_{i+1}) - f(x_i)}{h} \right| < \varepsilon,$$

whence

$$|f(x_{i+1}) - f(x_i)| < h\varepsilon = \frac{1}{n}(b-a)\varepsilon,$$

and after summation over i,

$$|f(b) - f(a)| < \sum_i |f(x_{i+1}) - f(x_i)| = (b-a)\varepsilon,$$

which is true for any (arbitrarily small) ε, thus

$$f(b) = f(a).$$

This holds for the ends of all partial intervals also, which proves f to be constant.

The theorem of the constancy of a function f with vanishing derivative was proved under the condition of *uniform* differentiability of f; in fact, this is no restriction since if $f' = 0$, then f is continuously differentiable, hence by a theorem mentioned earlier uniformly differentiable.

How important the uniform differentiability is and how influential in intuitive analysis is shown by one more example.

One sees with the naked eye that a function f with differential quotient always positive is monotonically increasing. How can we prove it? From $f'(x) > 0$ it only follows that for small positive h

$$f(x_0 - h) < f(x_0) < f(x_0 + h);$$

by no means does it that near x_0,

$$f(x_1) < f(x_2) \quad \text{for} \quad x_1 < x_2.$$

And even $f'(x) > 0$ for all x does not imply trivially the monotonic character. It can be proved by the mean value theorem or similar devices. Again it becomes easy as soon as the differentiability is understood in the uniform sense; the proof is very like the preceding one.

To sum up I would propose: if in school instruction the subject matter should be organized globally beyond the reach of intuitive analysis, the most ambitious goal should be the following: continuity and differentiability are always interpreted in the uniform sense, or respectively the uniform continuity or differentiability of a continuous or continuously differentiable function are assumed without proof; then the theorems on the integrability of a continuous function and the mutual relation between differentiation and integration are derived without any difficulty. If the continuity notion is to be formalized, it should be done in a logical and preferably in a *symbolically* logical context.

THE DEVELOPMENT OF ANALYSIS
AT SCHOOL – GONIOMETRIC FUNCTIONS

In our introduction of the logarithm its differential quotient is given as it were by definition. Following the inversion rule this settles the differential quotients of the exponential functions. The differential quotient of

$$x^\alpha = e^{\alpha \log x}$$

can be obtained by the rule on composed functions. This fits nicely into a system of analysis.

Goniometric functions are a different case. Since sine and cosine were expressively defined by geometry, they can hardly be expected to fit as nicely into the system. Sines and cosines could be read in the figure of an angle, and what an angle meant could be *seen*. It is true these notions can be axiomatized, as we have already shown. A protractor is postulated, that is a function ω that maps the multiplication group of complex number of unit absolute value (or the group of rotations around the origin) homomorphically upon the addition group of reals mod 2π.

Why 2π and, more to the point, what is 2π? Till now it was just a measure of the full angle. In the practice of goniometric tables it is rather $360°$. It would not have been too mad to make the measure of the full angle 1; then the protractor function would have mapped upon the reals mod 1. Why 2π? Because it is useful to measure angles by the

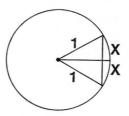

Fig. 97.

corresponding arcs on the unit circle and 2π is by definition the circumference of the unit circle. The arc length of curves is defined by integrals, though this is not the reason why I am dealing with this subject in the present chapter. In a short moment, however, it will become clear what measuring angles by arcs and the number 2π have to do with analysis. Up to now we only know through geometry what the arc length is, but no matter how the act length is formally defined it is pretty certain that the ratio "chord to arc" must tend to 1 if the chord decreases to 0. This means (see Figure 97)

$$\lim_{x=0} \frac{\sin 2x}{2x} = 1,$$

whence

$$\left(\frac{d \sin x}{dx}\right)_{x=0} = 1.$$

Measuring angles by unit circle arcs has the consequence that the derivative of the sine at $x = 0$ gets the value 1. This is the more profound reason in analysis for measuring angles by arcs on the unit circle. (It is similar to what has happened with the "natural" logarithm: $d \log x/dx = 1/x$.)

The inversion f of the protractor function ω is given by

$$f(t) = \cos t + i \sin t.$$

f can even be interpreted as a homomorphic mapping of the addition group of the reals (rather than the reals mod 2π) on the multiplication group of complex numbers of absolute value 1; then the real numbers are to be understood as "turn around" angles. The question now arises whether f is really such that the arc length on the unit circle measured from 1 to $f(t)$ in the positive sense is t. Till now we have satisfied a necessary condition, namely that the ratio chord to arc converges to 1.

To answer this, one must first tell what is the arc length of a curve. One inscribes polygons with sides converging to 0 and defines the limit

Fig. 98.

of their lengths on the arc length of the curve (Figure 98). Rather than adding up the lengths of the chords one can in the limit integrate the length of the tangent vectors. If the plane curve is given by

$$x_1 = f_1(t), \quad x_2 = f_2(t),$$

the arc length from τ_0 to τ_1 becomes

$$\int_{\tau_0}^{\tau_1} \left(\sqrt{\frac{dx_1}{dt}} \right) + \left(\frac{dx_2}{dt} \right)^2 \, dt.$$

If this is applied to

$$f_1(t) = \cos t, \quad f_2(t) = \sin t, \quad \tau_0 = 0, \quad \tau_1 = t,$$

the integrand becomes 1, which in fact makes the arc length from 0 to t assume the value t.

Now the goniometric functions have been detached from their geometrical origin, though they are not yet expressed algorithmically. To get an algorithmic hold on them, one needs more profound considerations*.

f, which maps an addition group homomorphically in a multiplication group, behaves in this respect as an exponential function though it takes complex values (on the unit circle) for real arguments. We connect it to the well-known function

$$\curlyvee_t e^t .$$

This function coincides with all of its derivatives. This fact leads to the development

$$e^t = \sum_{n=0}^{\infty} \frac{t^n}{n!}$$

which is meaningful for complex t, too. Moreover the homomorphism property extends to complex arguments. Thus the function maps the addition group of complex numbers into the multiplication group of complex numbers without 0, the real upon the positive axis; if in

$$e^{t+\bar{t}} = e^t e^{\bar{t}} = e^t \overline{e^t} = |e^t|^2$$

one takes t imaginary, then $t + \bar{t} = 0$, thus $|e^t|^2 = 1$, which means that the imaginary axis is mapped into the unit circle. So

$$g(t) = e^{it}$$

defines a function g that maps the addition group of reals into the multiplication group of complex numbers of absolute value 1. Such homomorphisms are determined up to an order preserving automorphism of the addition group of the reals. The f that was defined by

$$f(t) = \cos t + i \sin t$$

is such an homomorphism. In 0 both have the same derivative, namely i, which implies that they coincide, thus

$$e^{it} = \cos t + i \sin t$$

By this formula the sine and cosine are algorithmically fixed, that is, not as functions which map arcs on lengths as we obtained them geo-

* See footnote on p. 572.

metrically and developed them conceptually by the precise arc length definition, but by means of infinite series.

This is just an outline sketch. To prove that t *is* the arc length from 1 to $f(t)$ is certainly the most difficult part; the remainder is not beyond the reach of an intelligent 11–12th grade pupil. It deepens the angle concept and with respect to matter and method it looks more valuable than many other things that are accepted subjects in mathematics teaching.

THE DEVELOPMENT OF ANALYSIS AT SCHOOL – BEYOND SYSTEMATICS

I have proposed quite a few subjects in analysis which are meaningful and valuable at school and could globally be organized, and I sketched how this could be realized. But whether it should be done depends of course on the aims of the actual instruction. I will now turn to those subjects that do not fit into any system that can be realized at school. All the subjects I included under the subtitle "The graphic approach in a broader sense" are examples: volume computations via integration of cross-section areas (in particular of revolution solids), the surface area as differential quotient of the volume, and the surface of revolution solids. Volumes and areas of curved surfaces were computed before the notions themselves were defined, or rather something about these notions was proved after a (well motivated) *ad hoc* definition. This is nevertheless a valid method of working. Why shouldn't we compute the superficies of the sphere calotte without having defined superficies in general? Archimedes did so, and why shouldn't we? This is, indeed, local organization. It is the same with all these examples I collected as velocities, densities, gradients, and with the kinematical and mechanical examples. Again and again theorems are asserted and proofs given about notions which, if at all, were defined *ad hoc*. Motion, force, pressure, tension, vibration, current, catenary – they do not fit into any *mathematical* system, and fitting them into systems of physics would be an enormous task which has not yet been properly attempted. The catenary is produced by an infinitely thin thread, which is suspended at two points. The thread should be flexible though not extensible. What does this mean? If you refuse to believe the equilibrium conditions of a little piece of the catenary, I lack all mathematical means to convince you, not to mention the lack of any axiomatic approach. But this is true of any application of mathematics. If axiomatics is the only thing you place your trust in, you cannot even use mathematics to calculate what 10 eggs cost, if the price of one egg is given. The examples I gave are of this kind – mathematized reality. Some time ago I read about efforts to improve the teaching of analysis by raising standards of rigour. I believe that analysis at school can be improved only by relating it closer to reality. If more abstraction is not counterbalanced by a closer proximity to reality, it will only yield more unrelated and thus worthless stuff.

CHAPTER XVIII

PROBABILITY AND STATISTICS*

Je vois bien que la vérité est la même à Toulouse et à Paris.

Lettre de Pascal à Fermat, 29 juillet 1654

Calcul des Probabilités. Première Leçon. 1. L'on ne peut guère donner une définition satisfaisante de la Probabilité...

. . . .

Le calcul des probabilités offre une contradiction dans les termes qui servent à le désigner, et, si je ne craignais de rappeler ici un mot trop souvent répété, je dirais qu'il nous enseigne surtout une chose: c'est de savoir que nous ne savons rien. Fin.

H. Poincaré, *Calcul des Probabilites*, 1896, p. 1, p. 274

They say that Understanding ought to work by the rules of right reason. These rules are, or ought to be, contained in Logic; but the actual science of logic is conversant at present only with things either certain, impossible, or entirely doubtful, none of which (fortunately) we have to reason on. Therefore the true logic for this world is the calculus of Probabilities, which takes account of the magnitude of the probability which is, or ought to be, in a reasonable man's mind.

J. Clerk Maxwell

Eudoxe – Cet argument me touche; je me déciderai peut-être à écrire un jour l'*Eloge du Jeu.*

E. Borel, *Traité du Calcul des Probabilités et de ses Applications* **IV**, fasc. 3, 2nd ed., 1952

In my original draft this chapter was called "Applications", but I have already said so much about applications in various contexts earlier on in the book, that an attempt at completeness would mean a lot of repetition. I would not claim, however, that I have exhausted the subject. I mentioned linear programming only briefly, while numerical methods have only been tackled now and then. Computers alone would have merited a chapter, but this would have been better written by my colleagues on the lower floors who have experimented with computers at school, than by the present author who has never visited a class working in this field.

There is, however, one broad area left where my own experience may

---

* An extract of this chapter has already been published in: *The Teaching of Probability and Statistics*, Stockholm 1970, Almqvist & Wicksell.

be of some value, and this became the subject and title of the present chapter. I consider probability a paragon of applied mathematics, and whatever is understood under applications, it can only be mathematics close to reality and charged with relations. There are quite a few who do not approve of this and even fear reality as a menace to mathematics. Such an aseptic course for highly motivated 14–16 year-olds is on my desk. Its author says:

Textbooks in probability all refer to "non-mathematical creatures" like tacks, dice, roulettes, arrivals of customers, coin tossings, gambling, occurrences, indistinguishable objects (!), and so on. Many students of probability are attracted (so I have always been) by these creatures and this terminology (How to gamble if you must!) but for others they cause confusion. Sometimes these creatures are found not only in examples and problems but also in theorems and proofs. Of course this is not at all incorrect (and it contributes to the charm of probability theory) as these creatures can easily be made part of the mathematical object language, for instance, by naming special finite probability spaces (or more general probability spaces) with these names.
    For the beginner, however, it may be helpful if the mathematical theory of probability and the real world are clearly distinguishable. For instance, with a phrase like "a symmetric die is tossed" it should be made clear whether the intention is to describe a real world activity or a specific finite probability space.

I have at length discussed the postulate that the student should learn separating mathematics and reality from each other. Yes, I said, certainly he should learn this, and certainly it helps the understanding both of mathematics and reality. Yet they should not be offered to him separately. He should learn to separate them himself as soon as their interrelations have grown strong enough to prevent the separation from damaging either part. In any case separation at the start, which is advocated in the quotation, is wrong. It is precisely the beginner who should *not* learn an unrelated mathematics which serves no function in reality. These are principles that have proved enormously useful in elementary arithmetics and they extend to probability, too. The quoted author maintains that some people are confused by the relations to reality. But for others it is also confusing that one is not allowed to divide by 0, that multiplying starts at the right and dividing at the left, that not all functions are linear, that $(ab)^n = a^n b^n$ though $a^m a^n = a^{m+n}$. We don't abolish something for all just because a few have difficulties with it, or do we? There can be little doubt that students educated in a well-oiled unrelated mathematics will dislike nothing more than a mathematics charged with relations, which they cannot master by formal rules but which instead requires them to develop their own activity. It is bad teaching to yield to those who are confused by relating to reality, and it is even worse to let the others pay for it by getting an instruction more appropriate for those who are easily confused by this.

To be perfectly honest, I believe it is neither the principle of separation of mathematics and reality nor regard for the particular difficulties of one group of students that cause a pedagogue to write, teach, and generally recommend calculus of probability cut off from reality; rather it is badly understood rigour and the fear of losing one's footing at the first deviation from the path of pure formalism. Most mathematicians suffer from this frustration as long as they teach. And in one respect the cited author is right – in many textbooks on probability the world of non-mathematical creatures is only a figleaf to cover the nakedness of pure mathematics. After a realistic motivation one flies as fast as one can into the safe harbour of mathematical formalism and relegates reality into the quarantine of examples and problems. The cited author is more honest; he performed a radical separation of mathematics and reality, so complete that reality is not admitted under any guise. But then one question must be asked. Why for heaven's sake teach probability if there are so many other interesting fields of mathematics?

It should be made clear that the demand for technically formalized mathematics in probability is very low. Once you have mastered fractions, you can advance quite far in probability; a bit of algebra suffices to formulate the principles of probability in a general way; real numbers and analysis can be dispensed with for quite a while, but as soon as you can afford a little bit of this theory, you can reach quite profound notions in probability, more profound ones than would be ever attempted at school. If probability is to be axiomatized, it can be done with an axiomatic system that is the simplest that in mathematics exists. To apply probability one need not insert profound physical theories between mathematics and reality; probability can be applied to reality as directly as elementary arithmetic, that is, by means of models that everybody can immediately understand. The fact that so much and such a variety of results can be obtained in probability by such simple mathematics, is a strong argument in favour of mathematics (and in favour of probability). To explain to people what mathematics really means, one finds the most convincing examples in probability.

I would like to do this using the questions probability in history started with (except for unavoidable forerunners) – the two problems which are said to have been posed by Chevalier de Méré to Pascal.

De Méré knew that it was advantageous to bet on the occurrence of at least one six in a series of four throws of a die – maybe this was an old experience! He argued that it must be as advantageous to bet on the occurrence of at least one double-six in a 24 toss series with a pair of dice. As Fortune disappointed him, he complained to his friend Pascal about the preposterous mathematics which had so deceived him.

You know Pascal's answer. *The probability of one six in one toss is $\frac{1}{6}$, the probability of no sixes in one toss is $\frac{5}{6}$, the probability of no sixes in four tosses is $(\frac{5}{6})^4$; at least one six in four tosses is the negation of no sixes in four tosses, hence the probability is $1 - (\frac{5}{6})^4 \approx 0.516$ which is a little more than one half. Analogously, the probability of no double sixes, when tossing a pair of dice is $\frac{35}{36}$, and finally the probability of at least one double-six in 24 tosses is $1 - (\frac{35}{36})^{24} \approx 0.491$, which is less than one half. So de Méré had lost his money according to the rules of, and in perfect argeement with, mathematics. So shall be punished all those who call down curses on mathematics!

De Méré's other query was the "problème des partis". A and B have contracted to play a set of games with equal chances for both of them. The person who first reaches five points takes the stakes. Owing to circumstances beyond their control they are compelled to stop playing at a point where A has won 4 games and B has won 3 games. How should the stakes be divided? Some people said 4 : 3 was fair, others were in favour of $(5 - 3) : (5 - 4)$. Who was right? Neither, said Pascal as an arbiter. Suppose that two more games were played. There are four possibilities:

A wins, A wins
A wins, B wins
B wins, A wins
B wins, B wins.

* When I wrote this I believed that Pascal was the person who had taught Méré this computation. B. L. van der Waerden has now convinced me that de Méré had himself already found a computation (either similar or this very one); from his violent reaction against deceptive arithmetic one may still assume that he undertook this computation after first having trusted in the double six in 24 throws and having acted correspondingly.

In three of these cases A takes the stakes, while B wins only in one case. A has three chances against one of B. The stakes should be divided in the ratio of $3:1$.

There are a lot of examples to explain to people with a general education what mathematics is, but for many reasons I prefer these two queries which de Méré posed to his friend Pascal. The irrationality of $\sqrt{2}$, the cardinality of the continuum, the complete induction, the existence of an infinity of prime numbers, the theorem on the bisectors of the sides of a triangle – these are excellent examples but they are all, with the exception of the last, too remote from reality and too abstract. They fail to show that mathematics, though a transcendent kind of thought, is immanent in the real world. But there is another, still more important reason: de Méré's problems shed a sudden, unexpected light on the great problem of mathematics teaching. Chevalier de Méré certainly was an educated man, and doubtless he had learned mathematics, yet as soon as he was dropped in a situation where he had to apply it, he was not able to do so. He applied the mathematics he knew, the kind of mathematics which in my childhood was called the rule of three – if I bet on one specific result out of *six* in *four* tosses, I am betting on one specific result out of *thirty-six* in *twenty-four* tosses, because $6:4 = 36:24$. And in the second problem, since the data 3, 4, 5, and something has to be distributed among two persons, one concludes that it must be done in a ratio like $4:3$ or $(5-3):(5-4)$. Poor de Méré, like a faithful student he had applied the mathematics he had learned but in spite of this he was punished. Maybe he would have performed better if he had never learned mathematics at all! Then there would have been some chance that he would have applied not the mathematics he had learned but a mathematics that he would have to create himself.

De Méré is not so much a historical figure, as a paradigm, an ancestor of the prolific offspring of the present day, of all the poor de Mérés of today who have learned a mathematics they cannot apply. Each of us will perhaps at least once have played the part of Pascal when he was consulted by people confronted with mathematics they did not understand.

I like the two de Méré problems, not only because they are mathematical jewels and highlights in the history of mathematics, but even more because they illuminate profound and characteristic features of teaching and learning mathematics. From olden times the rule of three, or in modern terminology, the linear function has been an important mathematical tool of explaining and mastering phenomena in physics, chemistry, astronomy, economics, and in other fields of human activity. It is a cheap procedure in experimental science to fit observational data to a linear function, and even before any experimentation has taken place, the linear function is the cheapest mathematical model. Using it dispenses with rethinking a situation, and such a dispensation is usually gladly accepted. Of course, from antiquity people knew about inverse proportionality, but even Plato uttered at least thrice the surprise of the common man that not all functions are linear, namely in the example of the area of a circle as function of the circumference, the hypotenuse as a function of the other sides of a right triangle, the geometric mean as a function of its terms. Though today everybody would consider it as a matter of evidence that the luminosity caused by a light source of distance r is proportional to r^{-2}, Oresme still assumed a piecewise linear function, which vanished at a certain distance, depending on the strength of the source.

We have already compared the traditions in teaching elementary arithmetic with those in mathematics from fractions onwards. We noticed a sudden switch from mathematics oriented to reality towards the learning of techniques, techniques of the linear function, of the quadratic function, of solving triangles, of trigonometry, of differentiating and integrating. New subject matter did not improve didactics: sets, relations, and logic are already taught as a formal technique. Teaching new mathematics can be worse than teaching the old one.

What is most essential, mathematically and educationally, in our two examples? It is not the ready-made mathematics that is needed to solve them, but the rediscovered or re-invented mathematics that is needed to arrive at the solution; the novelty without precedent of the problem. To be sure, in history they were solved by Pascal, but history isn't old hat, is it? Every man has his own history, in which such problems may have a place, not as three centuries old memorabilia, not as pieces of a well-organized probability theory with a ready-made analysis and synthesis, but as though they were new, unheard of and unsolved problems.

The most beautiful deductive system of probability does not guarantee its applicability. The usual mistakes in this field differ greatly from mistakes in mathematical techniques. Those who never had the opportunity of making these mistakes, also did not either get the opportunity to *unlearn* them. How can he know that the probability of having one's birthday on 12 July and the probability of two people having the same birthday are not only equal but even due to, as it were, isomorphic patterns? What was the use of someone learning probability if, like the people who did not learn it, he still believes that the second is much less probable than the first? If in a gathering of 50 people one asks how probable it is that there are two people with the same birthday in the room, it is nearly always the case that this probability is grossly underestimated. The mathematician who stages this can count on a success such as only magicians can boast of, if several pairs, maybe even a triple, can be found with the same birthdays.

When estimating probabilities even experienced probabilists and statisticians can err. A most astonishing case is the traditional condemnation of Mendel on statistical evidence. In his famous genetic experiments with peas Mendel considered seven pairs of characteristics, a dominant and a recessive one, indicated as usual by A, B, C, D, E, F, G and a, b, c, d, e, f, g, respectively. Chance saw to it that among 33 different varieties he had bought from seed merchants there was to every one of the seven characteristics (at least) one pair the members of which deviated in this characteristic and in no other. It would be a strange accident that produces such an improbable event, the statistical critics claimed. Thus Mendel cheated – this, indeed, is the statistical conclusion if somebody claims something has happened which according to probability theory is quite improbable. This judgment on Mendel was underwritten by prominent statisticians, and today it is found in many books on Mendel. Just recently B. L. van der Waerden asked how small is this probability that among 33 varieties there is for every pair of characteristics a pair of varieties the members of which deviate in exactly the given pair of characteristics. The result was $97\frac{1}{2}\%$. What Mendel claimed to have happened, was not at all improbable. On the contrary it was even highly probable. This probability can be computed by the most elementary methods; it was v. d. Waerden's idea to compute it rather than merely parrot what others said about it. That prominent statisticians can make grave errors like this shows that probability is a most peculiar phenomenon. Where the stress is on relations to reality, rigour must also be viewed in a less formal way.

From the genesis of probability there have always existed controversial problems, that is, problems which were solved in different ways until a more careful analysis showed who was right. Those who were wrong were not necessarily second class mathematicians. Pure mathematics does not know analogies to this phenomenon. There was, for instance, the drawers problem of Bertrand. There are three drawers, each with two sections. The first drawer has in each section a gold coin, the second has a gold coin in one section and a silver coin in the other; the third has silver coins in both. First one drawer, and then one of its sections is opened at random; what is the probability that the other section contains a coin of the same metal? If, for instance, the visible coin is a gold one, the drawer with silver coins only is excluded and the choice is reduced to two drawers. So it seems that the probability of a mixed drawer, which originally was $\frac{1}{3}$, has now increased to $\frac{1}{2}$. How can the probability be changed by opening one drawer? This question, however, is not relevant. Nevertheless, the probability remained $\frac{1}{3}$ and whoever does not believe it, may make a wager and lose his money. This is a remarkable kind of punishment, quite different from the usual one of punishing by bad marks.

Let the drawers be named A, B, C and their sections be indicated by subscripts 1, 2, such that A_1, A_2, B_1 contain gold and B_2, C_1, C_2 silver. There are six cases, and in two only, namely in B_1 and B_2 does the other section contain the other metal. If after drawing and opening silver was found, it is one of the cases B_2, C_1, C_2 no more than a third of which (namely B_2) is a mixed case. This is so obvious that one can hardly understand how anyone could disagree. Nevertheless the problem emerges again and again in other disguises with the wrong solutions.

One variant is the following – it is a lottery among twenty persons, two of whom will receive a prize. So every participant knows that among the others at least one must win a prize. The situation arises that the lottery has taken place but the result has not yet been disclosed. One of the participants, say A, goes to the organizer of the lottery and asks him: "You need not tell me whether I have won a prize nor whether B or C or any other particular person has won a prize. I know anyhow that at least one of the others got a prize; please tell me the name of one of them, and be sure I will not abuse the sign of confidence". The organizer complies with his wish so A now knows the name of one of the others who received a prize. Has his own chance of getting a prize now decreased from $\frac{1}{10}$ to $\frac{1}{19}$? He knew for certain that one of the others must get a prize so what has been changed by the new information? The doubt is justified though not the argument by which it is motivated. A's chances did not change. In fact, after the first lottery a second took place: in the case where A did not win, the organizer had to choose at random one person among the winners and disclose his name. Let us consider the cases where B is among the winners and his name is given. The probability that A and B win is $1/\binom{20}{2}$; the probability that B wins together with another, is $18/\binom{20}{2}$, the probability that, moreover, his name is chosen, is $9/\binom{20}{2}$. The conditional probability that A wins while B has been designed as a winner, is

$$1/\binom{20}{2} : (1 + 9)/\binom{20}{2},$$

which, indeed, is $\frac{1}{10}$.

To understand this and similar paradoxes, it is instrumental to grasp that besides the explicit an implicit lottery took place and also how they are related to one another. If probability is cut off from reality, if "realistic creatures" are forbidden, this is no matter of concern; but it becomes so as soon as probability should be applied. If one prefers to be spared of these troubles or to spare others, the question arises to which aim probability is to be learned and taught.

These examples were meant to show how difficult probability is, but this does not mean that we shall make it difficult for others. Isn't mathematics the art of making things easy? To do this we develop general thinking patterns in mathematics and try to organize them axiomatically. Often we have not yet succeeded in doing so; we work unconsciously with most of these patterns without ever recognizing them (we shall return to this point in the next chapter). Such thinking patterns exist also for the mathematization of real situations, and nobody ever thought how to axiomatize and formalize them. Such patterns we called tactics and strategies. It looks a hopeless undertaking to catalogue them in pure mathematics, not to mention applications. They are learned by rediscovery, by imitation, by use and by explaining them to others. Of course, one can warn people to watch out for incompletely described lotteries in probability problems; beside the explicit one there may be an implicit lottery. This can be useful, but before warning somebody, we must first have experienced the error ourselves, and these warnings are more effective if the person I warn has made the error himself. Errors in probability are possible on many levels. Later we will meet other instances.

Again and again the attempt is made to block errors by recipes and memotechnic rules. Probability has its own theory how it is applied – I mean mathematical statistics, which tells how probabilities can be estimated by samples. It is frightening to see this domain of mathematics, the paragon of free thinking activity, being turned into its opposite, into a system of rigid rules. It is, indeed, just a little step from freedom to slavery if people are not trusted to use and not misuse their freedom. Those who try to justify dogmatic didactics with the argument that pupils like the system and just wish to remain within the system, can draw on their own experience because they taught probability and statistics in this way.

Textbooks on mathematical statistics for the use of students in the natural and social sciences are most often of this recipe character; baldy understood methods and formulae are drubbed into the heads of the students. Fortunately, heads are more indulgent than stomachs. A misunderstood cooking recipe is not likely to be repeated, but for a wrongly applied, unrelated mathematics there is more often than not no retaliation except a disapproving mark, and even this is a measure that is no longer applicable after the student has left college.

The applications of mathematics I allude to are often mere sham applications, where it is believed that around undecidable or irrelevant problems numerical material can be collected to be processed by mathematical methods. This is not unusual in social sciences, in psychology and pedagogics. Experiments with subjects are designed without considering whether the parameters at issue are relevant and whether neglected parameters would not be more important; as a consequence small variants of entirely worthless teaching methods are extensively investigated and compared. A striking example of this kind was discovered by Suppes *et al.** This was an investigation into which factors are instrumental in

* P. Suppes, Elizabeth F. Loftus, and M. Jerman, "Problem-Solving on a Computer-Based Teletype', *Educational Studies in Mathematics* 2 (1969), 1–15.

solving word problems (for instance a key word, change of units, number of operations, and so on). Following a suggestion from L. Henkin the repetition factor was taken into consideration, that is whether one problem and the next require the same arithmetical operations. The statistical factor analysis showed that the last-mentioned factor was the dominating one and the most significant. If this factor had been neglected, the factor analysis would have led to entirely wrong conclusions. The discovery of this factor produced in any case a most valuable result in that the whole method was found to be irrelevant.

I am convinced that with many psychological and pedagogical experiments the same situation applies. Experiments which are theoretically poorly founded and poorly organized in practice are processed by means of a mathematics which is irrelevant if not totally false. Obviously, the "cooking books" used in processing the numerical material contain many recipes which do not allow cooking without understanding the underlying mathematics, and sometimes even a few recipes which applied literally can only produce rubbish. It is distressing that even mathematicians who turn to pedagogical experiments sometimes forget that they are mathematicians and as such should be able, entitled, and obliged to check and understand the mathematics they apply. They then have to suffer for having never experienced applications closely connected with mathematics. Possibly mathematics in their minds is separated from the rest, and can only act thereon through predesigned and predescribed channels.

We have given here a rough sketch of two kinds of teaching degeneration: probability as an abstract system cut off from reality, and on the other hand a system of patterns of computations to be filled out by numerical data. They look like opposites of each other but they are complementary in a most natural way. If applications are to be taught *in addition to* an abstract theory, there is no way to do it, except the recipe system. Or is there? It even fits marvellously in one textbook, the theory and the problems alternating with each other – the problems for actual use and the theory for conscience's sake. The skilled teacher will skip the theory and solve examples to show how the trick works.

I have often enough pointed out how important it is for the student to learn to mathematize. It is a pity that even some people who fundamentally agree with this pay mere lip service to it if probability is involved, not to mention those who see probability only in the context of set and measure theory. Because probability is a beautiful example of applying set and measure theory, it is taught as set and measure theory, though then it ceases to be beautiful. And those who teach it this way believe that they are being ultra-modern! In fact, it is as old-fashioned as teaching spherical trigonometry because it is a battleground of trigonometric formulae. Adequately understood, probability provides the best opportunity of showing students how to mathematize, how to apply mathematics – not only the best, but perhaps even the next and last opportunity after elementary arithmetic, since the rage for formalism seems to have spoiled all other teaching material. I like probability and I teach it to college freshmen, but I must say that I would hate it to be introduced into high school teaching because I fear it too will be spoiled, as it has been in quite a few experiments which have actually been carried out. I know that many probabilists and statisticians share my view.

I will tell you something about my experiences with a chapter on probability. For many years I have been teaching it to college freshmen (mathematicians and phyicists): the course comprises about 10–12 lessons, each three-quarters of an hour, with about the same number of two-hour periods devoted to exercises. I do not teach it as a part of measure theory, but as generally useful mathematics, in the hope that students will be able to apply what they have learned in these lessons a little better than what they have learned in other courses. I shall not describe to you the content of this course. Instead I would prefer to tell you about my own teaching experiences, which, though obtained at college level, may also apply to pre-college education.

Of course, I never start by telling the students what probability is. In fact, there is as little need to do this as there is in explaining what a point is in a course on geometry. The reason, however, why there is no need to do so is even more profound in probability than in geometry. It is logical in probability rather than ontological as it is in geometry. Any question on probabilities can be replaced by one on betting rates. Instead of asking somebody whether he estimates one probability larger than the other, or how large he estimates some probability, I can propose a wager to him. Behavioristic definitions instead of logical ones are completely valid and trustworthy in elementary probability, since every deviation from what is the logical background would be severely punished by material losses. This was, in fact, the argument which convinced de Méré even before he consulted Pascal. I will come back to this point later on.

If I did not start with a definition of probability, I must confess that I always started with examples of probabilities, but now I know that even this is wrong. I realised this when, during a weekend conference on primary education in mathematics, the participants were asked to sit together in groups of four and to elaborate a primary mathematics lesson from a choice of forty subjects. The group I belonged to chose "Toto". I am not sure whether Americans know what the word "Toto" means in Europe, but most European children of primary school level are acquainted with it. "Toto" is an abbreviation of "totalizator", the tote board or betting office of classical horse-racing, which now handles organized betting on soccer contests. The gambler fills out a form with 13 lines corresponding to 13 soccer games and three columns which mean win, lose, and tie. According to a fixed pattern the betting total is divided among the correct guessers, those who have missed one, and those who have missed two answers.

Our group chose Toto and decided to elaborate a lesson for 10–11 year-olds. The lesson should be started by asking the children what Toto means. But then, what should the next question be? To ask how large the probability (or the chance) is of having one's form filled out at random and nevertheless correctly, as somebody proposed? No. After a few not so successful attempts we decided not to use the expressions "probability", "chance", or "at random" at all. The teacher would ask the children to draw-out Toto forms and fill them in. Then the forms would be compared with one filled in by the teacher; forms which agree with the teacher's would be considered winners. Of course it is more than likely that nobody will win (there might be identical ones among the children's forms, and if this happens it is worth discussing). The next question will be – would there possibly have been a winner if we had played this with a class of 100 students? 1000 students? 10,000 students? And so on. Teachers in our group claimed that 10–11 year-olds are so well acquainted with Toto that they would, correctly, wait for the million bracket to give a positive answer. The next step would be in a more mathematical setting and would deal with a Toto of one contest, of two contests, and so on, to find what finally could be called the probability of guessing correctly the result of 13 contests.

This experiment has been a very valuable lesson for me. If I teach probability in the next academic year, I will start in an analogous way, that is by letting the students guess some probabilities. Actually I will start with de Méré's first problem or rather with the experience which provoked the problem. My first question will be: how many times must a die be thrown to get an equal chance of at least one six? I have always asked this question, but this used to happen at the end of the first lesson. The students always answered: three. Next year if they again answer "three", I will perform the experiment of tossing a die thrice and I will repeat it a few times. We will record from those series of three the favourable cases though actually there is no need to do so. Within a few attempts we will get a series with a six first or second. I will ask whether we should continue such a series of three or not. This is a first indication against the guess that three throws are sufficient for an equal chance of at least one six. If this indication is accepted, we would start computing the probability of at least one six in 1, 2, 3, ... throws in the crude natural way, which leads to the expression

$$\frac{1}{6} + \frac{5}{6} \cdot \frac{1}{6} + \left(\frac{5}{6}\right)^2 \cdot \frac{1}{6} + \cdots$$

To arrive at a more intelligent method of computation we would consider the square and cube pattern representing the possible and the favourable dice results x, y and x, y, z. This undoubtedly leads to the insight that "at least one six" is better replaced with its equivalent "not without six". I think it is the first profound and convincing example, not of the equivalence of "there is an x with the property..." and "not all x lack the property...", but of the fertility of this equivalence of "sometimes" and "not never" which in logic should be mentioned along with others such as "somewhere" and "not nowhere", "somebody" and "not nobody", and so on. As you know, in probability, interpreting "at least one..." via its negation is an important technique. It should be taught by leading the student to re-invent it instead of deriving it in a measure theoretical context. After these preparations, de Méré's proper question on the two dice is merely a routine problem. A nice example I would add is the advertising (quoted by de Moivre) of a gambling club which for an event with a probability $\frac{1}{32}$ paid only 28 times the stakes; they justified the claim that this was fair by offering a bet that the event would occur at least once in 28 trials.

One query I usually raise in this context is whether, instead of throwing one die four times as is needed in the solution of the previous problem, I would be allowed to throw four dice together. Of course, I ask what "at least one six" now means. Too little attention is paid in traditional courses to the fact that probability problems can be often formulated in many similar yet equivalent ways. To get an idea how probability is applied the student should become acquainted with the variety of disguises under which a problem can be hidden. In mathematics the isomorphism of *problems* is as important a teaching subject as that of *mathematical entities* and this notion is not acquired by formal definitions but by confronting the student with such isomorphisms.

As a simple and illustrative example consider the following. Ask someone to compare the chance that a person chosen at random has his birthday on a given day, with the chance that two people chosen at random have the same birthday. Those without mathematical experience will tell you that the latter chance is much smaller. Strangely enough, if afterwards you ask them to compare the chance of throwing a six with one die and the chance of throwing doublets with a pair of dice, they will not hesitate to estimate them as equal. It will cost you some trouble to make it clear to them that these problems are isomorphic as soon as their numerical differences are disregarded.

I have personally observed the following many times. You will often be told that in the usual system of phone numbers the figure 0 has a larger frequency than other numbers owing to the fact that so many redundant zeroes are added in the vacant places on the left. In contrast, in the usual system of numbering pages of a book they consider the distribution uniform. Even quite a few freshmen do not realize what is wrong with these statements. It is useful to have them compute the probabilities of a digit 0 and of a digit 1 in the usual system of writing down the integers from 1 to 100 or from 1 to 100,000.

One of the first problems I deal with in my freshman course is that of the probability of the different outcomes of the sum of points of three dice. It is a tremendously useful exercise in showing students how to write down systematically the possible combinations. If the computation has been done, it strikes us that 10 and 11 have the same probability

$(\frac{1}{8})$ as 9 and $12(\frac{25}{216})$, and so on. How can we understand this symmetry? After a few attempts to explain it a solution is proposed. If you turn a die upside down, the result x is changed into $7 - x$, so if all dice are turned, the sum s is changed into $21 - s$ which consequently arises with the same probability as s. Fine, I agree, it is a fact that our dice carry the pairs of numbers 1 and 6, 2 and 5, 3 and 4 on opposite sides. It is possible, however, to imagine the numbers 1 to 6 distributed over the sides of the die in a different way. Old Etruscan dice have been found showing 1 and 2, 3 and 4, 5 and 6 on opposite sides. Which such dice, would the result be the same? I mean by this, would 10 and 11, 9 and 12, and so on, show the same probability?

The reaction to this question is the same every year. A few students smile, a few laugh, and a vote taken shows a vast majority in favour of equality of the results. Nevertheless, closer interrogation proves that all of the students are severely disoriented, as disoriented as the poor boy who in a high school examination was asked whether the Trojan war was before or after the Flood. When I posed the question on the three dice to a group of mathematics teachers the consternation was as great but here nobody dared to answer. There is indeed good reason for this disorientation. Everybody feels that the distribution of the numbers 1 to 6 over the sides of the die should not matter, but it is not easy to understand how it influences the former argument of turning the dice upside down. I think it is extremely useful to analyze this situation. The argument of turning the dice upside down is as correct as, for instance, the argument if $x^2 - 3x + 2 = 0$ and the earth is round, then $x = 1$ or $x = 2$. It is correct in formal logic but not if arguments are required to reveal the very essentials. The former argument should run: since with one die x and $7 - x$ have the same probability, with three dice the probability of s and $21 - s$ is the same. It does not matter whether the transition from x to $7 - x$ in every die is performed by turning it upside down, and therefore relying on this realisation of the function $x \rightarrow 7 - x$ is operationally wrong. It would not be difficult to find more examples of such "wrong" proofs but I think that this one is particularly illustrative.

Simple combinatorics is the backbone of elementary probability and our teaching of probability should take account of this fact. Serious mistakes in simple combinatorial problems are very common, maybe as common with our freshmen who have been taught a lot of mathematics at high school as with American undergraduates who have learned less. It is a characteristic of combinatorial problems that the mathematics they require is extremely simple. The essential thing to be done is to mathematize the problems since they are not usually encountered with mathematized wording. This mathematizing is something which is taught as little in our high schools as in high schools abroad. The main point of difficulty is the strange and multifarious disguises in which isomorphic problems can present themselves.

The number of ordered pairs (a, b) taken from two finite subsets A, B of cardinalities m and n is of course $m \cdot n$. The union of such subsets, if disjoint, has $m + n$ elements. This is as simple as it can be but it is an utterly worthless abstract theory if forming and recognizing products and unions have not been systematically exercised.

Take the following example. There are three rooms with two beds in each and three married couples to be assigned to these six beds such that husband and wife sleep in different beds in the same room. In how many ways can this be arranged? The students will rightly argue that first there are $3! = 6$ ways of putting the three couples into the three rooms, then there remain two ways to assign the couple in the first room to the two beds, two ways in the second room, two ways in the third, and finally $6 + 2 + 2 + 2 = 12$, so there are 12 solutions to the problem. If such answers are given at college level, something, or rather a great deal, is wrong with mathematics teaching at the high school level. I must confess in this respect I do not expect much improvement from new mathematics if it is interpreted as it has been in quite a number of texts I have seen. The educational problem of acquiring simple combinatorial techniques is not solved by teaching set theory but by having the student disentangle complex situations in which such combinatorics play an essential part. Such situations are usually found within probability but there are enough outside it too. Finite groups often require such techniques. For instance, to find the automorphisms of the symmetric group of four permutands, one would consider that an automorphism is known by its action upon the six 2-cycles (ij), that (12) can pass onto everyone among them, that after fixing (12), (34) is also fixed, and (13) can still pass into (13), (14), (23), (24), which data fix the automorphism. After all these steps have been done correctly, students will still conclude that there are $6 + 4$ instead of $6 \cdot 4$ automorphisms.

In my first year university course on probability I deal with various occurrences of combinations in a systematic and logically connected way. I start with the well-known Galton board, a vertical isosceles right triangle of pins which are numbered as follows: one pin in the highest, 0th row; two pins numbered 0, 1 from the left in the next, 1st row; three pins numbered 0, 1, 2 from the left in the 2nd row, and so on. Balls are introduced through a slot to fall upon the topmost pin on which they rebound and are deflected to arrive with equal probabilities at the two pins in the first row where they are again deflected to the pins in the 2nd row, and so on. After a zig-zag path the balls come to rest between partitions under the bottom row. I do not show a concrete Galton board, but students readily understand that most of the balls will accumulate near the centre of the bottom row and that only a few of them will fill the cells in the wings. I suggest the distribution of the balls by sketching the well-known de Moivre curve which will be dealt with at the end of the course.

To find the distribution of the balls mathematically, we imagine that one ball is introduced into the slot and that instead of rebounding at every pin it divides into two balls which go to the next pins in the next row to be divided again. At every pin the number of passing balls is noted. This leads to the Pascal triangle which is numerically exhibited. Its generation is described recursively: the number of balls passing at the k-th pin of the n-th row is called $\binom{n}{k}$. Then the Pascal triangle is defined by

$$\binom{n+1}{k+1} = \binom{n}{k} + \binom{n}{k+1}$$

and a few boundary conditions. From these definitions the expression

$$\binom{n}{k} = \frac{n!}{k!(n-k)!}$$

is easily derived.

The numbers $\binom{n}{k}$ are afterwards easily identified with the binomial coefficients in the binominal formula. The equality

$$\sum_{i=1}^{n} \binom{n}{i} = 2^n$$

is also noted.

The number of zig-zag paths from the top to the k-th place in the n-th row is $\binom{n}{k}$. But what is a zig-zag path? To describe a zig-zag path of length n, the ball makes n choices of "right" or "left". A zig-zag path is a mapping Φ of the number set $\{1, ..., n\}$ into the set $\{\text{right, left}\}$, indicating the two possible choices. The path Φ ends at the kth element of the n-th row after n choices among which k are "right", in other words if the Φ-original of "right" has cardinal k. Hence

$$\binom{n}{k} = \frac{\text{number of mappings of } \{1, ... n\} \text{ into } \{\text{right, left}\} \text{ with}}{k \ \Phi\text{-orginals of "right".}}$$

A zig-zag path Φ is completely known if the Φ-original set of "right" is given, because the others are necessarily the Φ-originals of "left". Consequently,

$$\binom{n}{k} = \text{number of subsets of } k \text{ elements out of } \{1, ..., n\}.$$

A traditional term for such a subset is "combination of k out of n"; this term has to be mentioned but its use is perhaps better avoided.

Blackening k out of n circles or drawing k cards out of a deck of n cards may or may not be examples of forming a subset of k out of the given set of n things. If I get the task to blacken k circles or to draw k cards, I can ask whether the order of executing the task matters or not. If the order does not matter, the mathematical description of this procedure is: take a subset of k elements. If the order does matter, then I should say: take a sequence of k elements avoiding repetitions, that is, make a one-to-one mapping ϑ of the set $\{1, ..., k\}$ into the given set of n elements. Obviously the number of such mappings is $k!$ larger than the number of subsets of k out of a set of n. (The traditional term for a k-sequence out of n is "variation of k out of n".)

The task of seating k persons upon n chairs is the same kind of problem. Indeed, it is performed by mapping the set of people one-to-one into the set of chairs. However, if I am only interested in whether a chair is occupied though not by which person, then I have to look for subsets of k rather than for sequences of k out of n. It depends on the problem whether a choice of k out of n is to be considered as a subset or as a subsequence. Often it does not matter. The probability of finding at least three of a kind among five cards taken at random from a deck of 52 cards is the quotient of the favorable and of all cases. It does not matter whether a "case" is interpreted as a sub*set* or as a sub*sequence* of five cards; the second interpretation would mean an extra factor 5! both in numerator and in denominator, which finally cancels out. This is paradigmatic for what usually happens in such problems.

This should not only be experienced in examples but should also be analyzed in a more abstract way. Let V be a finite set, P_k the set of sub*sets* of k elements of V and S_k the set of sub*sequences* of k elements of V; let Φ be the "forget-mapping" that assigns to a sub*sequence* of V the sub*set* of its elements. Φ always maps $k!$ elements of S_k upon one element of P_k. We assume that the elements of S_k are produced by drawing k times from the urn V while putting back the drawn element after every drawing. Let A be a subset of S_k; the probability of getting an element of A is

number of A/number of S_k.

Let B be the Φ-image of A. If the set A is now such that with any sequence it also contains any of its permutations, then the Φ-original of B is again A. Then A has $k!$ times as many elements as B and the above quotient can also be computed from

number of B/number of P_k.

In which combinatorial computations can S_k be replaced with P_k? This can occur if from the onset only such sets of sequences are admitted which with any sequence contain the permuted ones. This is the exact translation of "the order does not matter". This was the case in the example of three of a kind; there every hand with three of a kind is counted as favorable, with no regard to the order in which the five cards have been received.

To explain the difference between what are traditionally called combinations and variations, the language of sets and mappings, such as I have used here, may be of great help. In fact, I believe combinatorics can be one of the first convincing and profound examples for the use of mappings in school mathematics. Its place in teaching comes before any systematic course on probability in the higher grades.

For instance, dividing a set S of n elements into a set of k_1 elements, a set of k_2 elements, ..., a set of k_p elements, all disjoint but with $k_1 + k_2 + \cdots + k_p = n$, is more clearly formulated as mapping S onto $\{1, ..., p\}$ such that the original of $i(=1, ..., p)$ consists of k_i elements. It is well known that the number of these mappings is

$$\frac{n!}{k_1! k_2! ... k_p!}.$$

It is proved by choosing inductively the original set of 1, from the remainder that of 2, and so on, and finally that of $p - 1$. It is worthwhile to analyze what actually happens if a deck of 52 cards is divided into four piles of thirteen. According to our previous definition I should take a function Φ which assigns to every $x = 1, ..., 52$ one of the numbers 1, 2, 3, 4 (or N, E, S, W) such that $\Phi(x) = i$ $(i \in \{1, 2, 3, 4\})$ for exactly thirteen x. Usually the cards are dealt according to a fixed function Φ_0, e.g., defined by $\Phi_0(x) = x$ (mod 4), but before dealing the cards have been shuffled, i.e., subjected to a random permutation π. Consequently the actual Φ is the product $\Phi_0 \pi$ of the two mappings. It is easily proved but not trivial that as a means of randomization Φ and Φ_0 are equivalent.

Leaving combinatorics and turning to probability proper, the first important concepts are stochastic dependence and independence and conditional probability. In my experience their implementation is an easy enterprise because they can be introduced and illustrated by numerous and multifarious examples. This experience, though well established, is met with serious doubts by people who are committed to an axiomatic approach; it shows one of the didactic reasons why the axiomatic approach has to be rejected. I am in the habit of introducing a bag assumed to be filled with the numbers 1, ..., 1000, and the subsets of multiples of 4, 5, 10, 20 in order to investigate dependence and independence. What is the information that the drawn number is divisible by 4 worth if I would like to have it divisible by 10 (20)? How does the probability of x belonging to A change if I restrict myself to those x that belong to B? If the conditional probability equals the original one,

$$\mathscr{P}(x \in A \mid x \in B) = \mathscr{P}(x \in A),$$

A is by definition independent of B. On the other hand the conditional probability is computed by

$$\mathscr{P}(x \in A \mid x \in B) = \frac{\mathscr{P}(x \in A \cap B)}{\mathscr{P}(x \in B)}.$$

The criterion of independence now appears in the form

$$\mathscr{P}(x \in A \cap B) = \mathscr{P}(x \in A) \cdot \mathscr{P}(x \in B).$$

So independence can also be defined by the validity of the product rule. This is meaningful for $\mathscr{P}(x = B) = 0$, too, and it shows the symmetry of the independence relation with respect to A and B.

This is but one approach out of a host. In my experience the close connection between independence and conditional probability is beneficial to quick understanding. Lovers of systematics would prefer to separate them and to start with independence; the connection then will come to the learner later as a surprising fact. I prefer as usual the broad approach. I admit, however, in my courses I did not illustrate conditional probability by really complicated examples, whereas independence, of course, is mentioned again and again.

If A and B are independent, thus

$$\mathscr{P}(x \in A \cap B) = \mathscr{P}(x \in A)\, \mathscr{P}(x \in B),$$

then also

$$\mathscr{P}(x \in \bar{A} \cap B) = \mathscr{P}(x \in \bar{A})\, \mathscr{P}(x \in B),$$

and so on, thus both A and its complement $\bar{A}$ are independent of B and of its complement $\bar{B}$. If

$$\mathscr{P}(x \in A) = \alpha, \quad \mathscr{P}(x \in B) = \beta,$$

then in the case of independence the table

	A	$\bar{A}$
B	$\alpha\beta$	$(1 - \alpha)\,\beta$
$\bar{B}$	$\alpha(1 - \beta)$	$(1 - \alpha)\,(1 - \beta)$

shows the probabilities of $A \cap B$, and so on. I used to illustrate this with the pair ⌜rain, rain forecast⌝, which can assume the values ⌜yes, yes⌝, ⌜yes, no⌝, ⌜no, yes⌝, ⌜no, no⌝. Here one would like to have all probability concentrated in the main diagonal; right above and left below there should be zeros. This would be a case of total dependence, which can hardly be realized. Meanwhile one would try to get these numbers small rather than zero. The other extreme is total independence, where in the table above the probabilities behave according to the product rule. Then the forecast is not worth anything; the probability of rain is the same whether rain is forecast or not.

From here one can advance to patterns with more than two lines and columns and to formulating dependence and independence for stochastic variables, say u and v with the values $1, \ldots, k$ and $1, \ldots, l$, respectively. They split my set in subsets $A_i (i = 1, \ldots, k)$ where u takes the value i, respectively, and B_j $(j = 1, \ldots, l)$ where v takes the value j, respectively. Independence of u and v means that u and v take all their values independently, that is

$$\mathcal{P}(z \in A_i \cap B_j) = \mathcal{P}(z \in A_i)\, \mathcal{P}(z \in A_j).$$

Now one can start from the other end, I mean, with two sets A and B from which the pairs set $\ulcorner A, B \urcorner$ is formed; in A and B there are subsets X, Y, respectively, for which probabilities are defined. In $\ulcorner A, B \urcorner$ probabilities are explained by

$$\mathcal{P}(\ulcorner x, y \urcorner \in \ulcorner X, Y \urcorner) = \mathcal{P}(x \in X)\, \mathcal{P}(y \in Y).$$

If again $\ulcorner A, B \urcorner$ is split with respect to the first and second factors, one gets sets $\ulcorner A_i, B \urcorner$ and $\ulcorner A, B_j \urcorner$ and from

$$\begin{aligned}
\mathcal{P}(\ulcorner x, y \urcorner \in \ulcorner A_i, B \urcorner \cap \ulcorner A, B_j \urcorner) &= \mathcal{P}(\ulcorner x, y \urcorner \in \ulcorner A_i, B_j \urcorner) \\
&= \mathcal{P}(x \in A_i)\, \mathcal{P}(y \in B_j) \\
&= \mathcal{P}(\ulcorner x, y \urcorner \in \ulcorner A_i, B \urcorner)\, \mathcal{P}(\ulcorner x, y \urcorner \in \ulcorner A, B_j \urcorner),
\end{aligned}$$

their independence follows.

Whereas first a given set was structured according to a double division, the new starting point is two sets and their product which is structured according to a double division induced by the product; if originally in the given pattern independence was discovered as a *particular fact*, the product pattern is now built up according to the *postulate* of stochastic independence. Both ways should be employed but as I pointed out earlier, the didactic start is analysis, that is, structuring the data, which later is followed by synthesis, building a structure. One is given the data of weather and weather forecast and one starts structuring the pairs such as they are formed by the daily observations, on the one hand with respect to the weather and on the other hand with respect to the forecast.

Or the fathers and sons are given with respect to their body lengths and the data are structured once with respect to the fathers and then again with respect to the sons. This is a quite natural procedure. It is not as natural to structure the results of a pair of dice once with respect to one die and then with respect to the other, because the situation is so simple and perspicuous that the student is inclined to pass immediately to synthesis: he combines every result of one die with every result of the other and applies the product rule consciously or unconsciously; he exercizes directly joining two probability fields before they have arisen by analysis. Of course, this is quite valid and only system fanatics would object to it, but it should not remain an instinctive activity. The student should be led to consider a game with two dice that are connected by a short or long string. Now the elements of the pair are not detached from each other; one has to start with the pairs set and to structure it according to the first and second die, to observe the probabilities and to look whether the product rule is still valid.

This is a particularly illustrative example and worth discussing seriously. Nobody would doubt that two dice which are connected by a very long string or are cast separately in different rooms will show independent results, and that the results become more and more dependent if the string is gradually shortened. The reason why probability theory can be applied so efficiently, is the a priori notions we have formed, and are entitled to have formed on the independence of sets or stochastic variables. We need not check whether two dice cast in Utrecht and Amsterdam, respectively, produce independent results. Of course these are not innate ideas but at some point of our mental development we stepped from the magic into the scientific stage and acquired those indispensable prejudges on stochastic independence. This means that should the dice at Utrecht and at Amsterdam even once behave against our expectation and show dependence, we would try all we could to save the rule; we would search for secret connections, for fraud or falsification of the data. In former times philosophers puzzled over why nature has pleased to be organized according to the causal principle. It is, however, even more astonishing why there are so many opportunities to apply a mathematically fertile rule like the product rule of probability.

If probability is to be somehow related to reality, the enormous usefulness of independence must clearly be outlined. To realize this the student must know what is independence, not in an axiomatic context, not in a mathematized formulation of this notion, but rather in any possible relation to reality. As pointed out before, it is quite understandable that this notion, if not dealt with close enough to reality, will cause difficulties.

To be honest I should mention another kind of difficulty. There is one in particular which disappoints me every academic year. It is the following problem. A bag contains the four numbers 1, 2, 3, 4 which are drawn in random order (permutation), every number in the correct place being paid \$1. Compute the expectation of this promise. Students always answer the question by working out all permutations x_1, x_2, x_3, x_4 of 1, 2, 3, 4 with the corresponding payments:

$$
\begin{array}{llll}
1\ 2\ 3\ 4; 4 & 2\ 1\ 3\ 4; 2 & 3\ 1\ 2\ 4; 1 & 4\ 1\ 2\ 3; 0 \\
1\ 2\ 4\ 3; 2 & 2\ 1\ 4\ 3; 0 & 3\ 1\ 4\ 2; 0 & 4\ 1\ 3\ 2; 1 \\
1\ 3\ 2\ 4; 2 & 2\ 3\ 1\ 4; 1 & 3\ 2\ 1\ 4; 2 & 4\ 2\ 1\ 3; 1 \\
1\ 3\ 4\ 2; 1 & 2\ 3\ 4\ 1; 0 & 3\ 2\ 4\ 1; 1 & 4\ 2\ 3\ 1; 2 \\
1\ 4\ 2\ 3; 1 & 2\ 4\ 1\ 3; 0 & 3\ 4\ 1\ 2; 0 & 4\ 3\ 1\ 2; 0 \\
1\ 4\ 3\ 2; 2 & 2\ 4\ 3\ 1; 1 & 3\ 4\ 2\ 1; 0 & 4\ 3\ 2\ 1; 0
\end{array}
$$

(I always ask why there are no payments of 3.) The sum of the payments is 24, the expectation is \$1 – a curious result.

Is there an easier way to find it? Of course, among the 24 permutations you must have 1 in the first place 6 times ($x_1 = 1$), 6 times a 2 in the second ($x_2 = 2$), a 3 in the third ($x_3 = 3$), a 4 in the fourth ($x_4 = 4$), though these coincidences can occur in combinations.

Note that I have proved the general theorem on the expectation of a sum of random variables before

$$
\mathscr{E}\left(\sum_1^n x_i\right) = \sum_1^n \mathscr{E}(x_i)
$$

and when I proved it I stressed that it holds with no regard to questions of dependence and independence of the involved variables. But no-one has hit on the idea that this can be applied to the four variables x_1, x_2, x_3, x_4 which take the values 1, 2, 3, 4 with equal though dependent probabilities, or rather to the payments

$$
y_i = \begin{cases} 0 \\ 1 \end{cases} \text{ for } x_i \begin{cases} \neq i \\ = i \end{cases}
$$

to compute the desired

$$\mathscr{E}(y_1 + y_2 + y_3 + y_4).$$

If I draw attention to this general theorem, students object that the variables are dependent. If I recall to them the generality of the theorem and its proof they agree but in their hearts they do not believe that this "trick" is in fact sound.

The next problem of this kind should be separated from the first by at least one week. Given a bag containing two quarters, two dimes, two nickels, you are allowed to draw at random three coins out of this bag. What should you pay for this opportunity? Again they start working out the 20 cases of drawing three coins out of six and the corresponding incomes to arrive at the expectation $20 + 10 + 5$ which would not have been different if the bag had contained just one of every kind of coin. They recognize that their method was wrong again but I am convinced that in their hearts the majority still do not believe what logic tells them – these are reasons of the brain which the heart does not know (to invert a famous saying of Pascal's).

Something was wrong with my teaching and experience has taught me what. I should not have started with the general theorem but with one example or even with both and proved the theorem first in the special case of the example and then in general. By summing up the permutations it becomes obvious that the 1 occurs six times at the first place, the 2 six times at the second, the 3 six times at the third, the 4 six times at the fourth, and this, slightly generalized is the entire proof. In the example it is obvious that the dependence does not matter; the letters and formulae of the general proof serve only to obscure this fact. I do it now in another way and it has been a complete success. The example is more convincing than the general proof; beyond formal issues the general proof can only be understood by people who understood the example. Nevertheless my former approach is the classical method and that of traditional teaching philosophy from the first classes of mathematics upwards. Possession of a general theorem almost never guarantees its application and the fact that one learned it too early may even frustrate easy applicability. (I should tell you, but please note that this is a secret – that quite a few people working professionally in probability and statistics can apply the addition law only in abstract and not in concrete contexts.)

Of course to apply the addition law to *variances* one has to suppose independence. The foregoing examples can be used to make this clear. I usually like to state this law a bit differently. I speak about dispersion (square root of the variance), saying that dispersions are added according to "Pythagoras". This is not just a nice formulation, but touches on the very profound reason for the usual behaviour of the dispersion. In fact, it is an idiosyncrasy of statisticians to overstress the variance for technical reasons while in all applications in natural sciences the dispersion is the natural and useful concept. Dispersion and its addition according to Pythagoras fits into the conceptual world of the practitioner of natural sciences. He is familiar with the fact that of n independent copies $x_1, ..., x_n$ of a stochastic variable x the dispersion of the sum

$$\mathscr{D}\left(\sum_1^n x_i\right) = \sqrt{n}\,\mathscr{D}(x)$$

is $\sqrt{n}$ times that of x and that the dispersion of the average

$$\mathscr{D}\left(\frac{1}{n}\sum_1^n x_i\right) = \frac{1}{\sqrt{n}}\,\mathscr{D}(x)$$

is $\sqrt{n}$ times smaller than that of x.

The $\sqrt{n}$-law is a striking feature wherever probability is applied in nature. There are textbook writers who have never noticed this fact. In my opinion, students have to learn and understand this law in a mathematical course and not have to wait to learn it from some theoretical physicist or some experimental physics instruction book in order to get acquainted with it. Many mathematicians would not agree. They object that expectation and dispersion are only two parameters of a distribution and they would pass as quickly as possible to higher moments, Fourier transforms, or to special families of distributions with indeed no more than two parameters. People applying probability in statistics or in science know that in many cases these two parameters carry all useful, and often even all relevant, information. I would like to stress the use of expectation and dispersion and how one can make do as long as possible with these simple tools.

One of the most important applications of the $\sqrt{n}$-law is absent in almost all textbooks on probability. The daily number N of responses of a geigercounter per second, the number N of molecules in a cubic millimeter of gas, the number N of electrons passing a milliampere current in a second is dispersed around its average $\bar{N}$ with the dispersion $\sqrt{\bar{N}}$ (as soon as $N \gg 1$). The probabilistic reason of this phenomenon should be explained in any college freshman course on probability, maybe even in high school courses. As mathematicians we simply cannot afford to leave such fundamantals to physicists. Therefore, it is a sad fact that in almost all modern textbooks on probability applications in physics are never mentioned. Even error theory is usually neglected or passed over. There is no need to connect it to the normal distribution. In observational data the dispersion is a suitable measure of the error even if the distribution is not normal. Error calculus is still the most important and most frequent application of probability. It should figure in any course on probability, even at high school level. Again we cannot afford to leave error theory to the instruction pamphlets of the physics laboratory. I will give an example what can actually happen if we allow this.

One of the prescriptions of such an instruction booklet is to draw 400 times a card from a deck of 52 cards and to count the spades. Such a series of 400 has to be taken ten times. Though many thousands of students have worked with this booklet, a series with less than 75 or more than 125 spades never occurred in the reports because according to the instructions, observational data out of the 3σ-bounds are to be rejected. Worse still, even the variance of the ten results of the ten series of 400 had to fit into bounds prescribed by this booklet and since these bounds were badly chosen some students had to waste their time with 40,000 instead of 4000 drawings. When these probabilistic experiments were discussed with the physicists they finally admitted that while it was not very sound mathematics, it was just the mathematics experimental physicists had to learn rather than the high-brow mathematics of mathematicians.

No doubt the weak law of large numbers, proved under the condition of finite dispersion, belongs to the fundamentals of slightly advanced probability. The law is easily proved, it shows again the importance of the expectation and the dispersion, and it is the best departure to arrive at the principles of statistical inference. It is better than the more efficient, but rather clumsy, central limit theorem. Only when the law of large numbers has been understood are the normal distribution and the central limit theorem didactically justified, though of course their proof can be omitted. To explain the subject I go back to the Galton board. It exhibits the sum of n independent copies x_i of a stochastic variable x which takes the values 0, 1 with equal probabilities. The arrangement of the Galton board suggests the variable $\sum x_i$ to be diminished by its expectation $n/2$, which means that the centre of the basis is accepted as the origin of the scale. To make things converge it is natural to divide $\sum x_i - n/2$ by its dispersion $\frac{1}{2}\sqrt{n}$, that is to reduce the scale by a factor $\frac{1}{2}\sqrt{n}$. The stochastic convergence of the variables $(\sum x_i - n/2)/\frac{1}{2}\sqrt{n}$ is now suggested by the normal curve drawn in the picture of the Galton board.

Afterwards students may be told that the normal law applies, not only to the Galton board, but under broad conditions, to any sum of a large number of stochastic variables. A closer analysis shows three kinds of occurrences of the normal law: first, as a law for computing the distribution of sums of stochastic variables such as are formed in processing observational data; second, as an error law thanks to the unconscious summing of elementary error sources in the process of observation, and third, as a natural law applying in cases where extra-human nature has already formed such kinds of sums, as in the length of maple leaves or in the velocity of molecules in a gas.

Among the subjects I would add to my freshman course if enough time were available are games theory and stochastic processes. They would also fit into a high school course on probability. Both fields are a tremendous treasure-house of beautiful examples. As an example of games theory, take the following. A writes down one of the numbers 1, 2, 3, 4, 5 and B must guess the number. If the number that A has written down is i and B has guessed correctly, B receives i cents from A. If B makes a wrong guess, he receives nothing. Of course, B must also put a stake in the game, but the main question at this stage concerns the strategies that A and B should follow. You know what the problem is. If A writes down many fives he will have to pay out many fives. If he shuns fives, B, if he notices it, will name no fives; he will confine himself to 1, 2, 3, 4 and increase the chance of a good guess. Such dilemmas were known in probability from the beginning of the 18th century. They were solved by von Neumann's discovery of the minimax principle: A can, and should, play so that B's maximal gain expectation is minimized. It is rather easy to explain this principle in the underlying example, simple arithmetic suffices to understand it.

The principles of stochastic processes can be explained by simple games, in fact the "problème des partis" is an example of a stochastic process. Stochastic processes as a teaching subject has the advantage of providing valuable opportunity to practice matrix operations.

Probability is so close to its applications that it can even boast a theory how it is applied, I mean mathematical statistics. Should we deal with statistics in a college freshman course or in a high school course on probability? The principle of statistical inference is easily demonstrated with nice, simple examples which do not require sophisticated techniques of probability. Sign test, or double dichotomy, are sufficient material to explain the two hypotheses pattern and to analyze it profoundly. There is little need and it would be rather misleading to tie the principles of statistical inference to the normal distribution.

If more complications are wanted, an example like the following may be chosen: Two kinds of urns are considered, one filled with $\frac{3}{4}$ white and $\frac{1}{4}$ black balls, the other with $\frac{1}{4}$ white and $\frac{3}{4}$ black ones. The first is called white and the other black though outside they look alike. I am offered one urn and must guess which kind it is. I may draw 10 times (with putting back) and look for the colour. It is clear that from many white balls in the sample I will conclude that the urn is white, and from many black ones that it is black. But how much is many? The probability of drawing from a white urn x white balls among 10 is

$$x = 0, 1, 2 \quad 3 \quad\quad 4 \quad\quad 5 \quad\quad 6 \quad\quad 7 \quad\quad 8 \quad\quad 9 \quad\quad 10$$
$$0,000 \quad 0,003 \quad 0,016 \quad 0,050 \quad 0,146 \quad 0,250 \quad 0,286 \quad 0,188 \quad 0,056$$

If, for instance, I decide to consider the urn as white as soon as I found 7 or more white balls among 10, and as black if it were 6 or less, then the

probability of calling a	black urn	white urn
black	99,7 %	22 %
white	0,3 %	78 %

equals the percentage indicated in the table.

The decision which strategy I choose, depends on the consequence of the choice. Assume, for instance, that I have been offered the urn for $ 100 and can sell it, if it is white, with a profit of $ 10, while if it is black, I will suffer a total loss; assume moreover that the sample costs 10 ¢ a ball.

Then a balance can be struck. With the above strategy I lose $ 100 if the urn is black, thus with a 0,3% probability; the expected loss is 30 ¢ plus the cost of the sample. I earn $ 10 if the urn is white, that is with 78% probability; the expected gain is $ 7.80 minus the cost of the sample. Finally a gain expectation of $ 6.80 and a loss expectation of $ 1.30 are confronted with each other. My policy will depend on the a priori probability, that is the frequence ratio of good (white) and fake (black) urns on the market.*

These examples admit of many variations. I would not, however, recommend teaching any technique of mathematical statistics to college freshmen of high school students. All the textbooks including statistics that I know of are written as if to train future statisticians and indeed it often seems as if everybody who has learned a few statistical formulae believes he is a statistician. No part of mathematics is applied with less judgment than is statistics. Statistics as it is usually taught is the worst source of misinterpretation of mathematics. Mathematical statistics, though invented to handle numerical data with a critical mind, is often used to substitute mechanics for criticism. If we teach statistics to people who are not supposed to become statisticians, we are advised to educate their critical mind by showing them principles rather than mislead them with superfical techniques. Of course this is a general principle in mathematics teaching to which everyone will at least pay lip service. For these reasons, therefore, I simply do not understand the philosophy of those who propose the teach high school children a lot of statistical techniques, and I consider this kind of philosophy a most dangerous menace to teaching meaningful mathematics.

Though in my teaching I use set theory concepts and terminology as much as possible and where necessary, the probability field for me is always concretized by an urn with tickets or coloured balls. Every problem is translated into an urn problem. In the urn sorts are formed, and from sorts partial urns are obtained. When multiplying probability fields the two urns serve to build up the urn of pairs. Drawing from an urn n times and putting back is interpreted as drawing one ball from each of n copies of the given urn, or drawing one piece from the hyperurn

* For more details: Hans Freudenthal, *Probability and Statistics*, Amsterdam, Elsevier, 1968, p. 79–83.

that arises from multiplying the n copies. In fact, it does not matter whether finite or infinite probability fields are considered; what is drawn from an urn containing real numbers are not exact numbers, but as in physical observations, numbers within certain bounds; it is the probability of the drawing result lying between certain bounds x_1, x_2 that is determined; in some cases it can be represented by an integral

$$\int_{x_1}^{x_2} f(x)\, dx.$$

To understand this no Lebesgue integrals are required.

In my course I do not deal with axiomatics of probability though for obvious reasons I must tackle this here. With respect to axiomatics the question "whether?" is answered by the other question "which kind of?" A measure theory one like Kolmogorov's? But as Kolmogorov rightly pointed out, probability theory is more than measure theory. For probability theory the measure theory pattern is no more than a void case. According to Kolmogorov "the independence of trials and stochastic magnitudes is that notion that lends probability theory its characteristic appearance"; in these notions he discovers "at least the first germs of the characteristic problematic of probability". To combining independent magnitudes corresponds in set theory the Cartesian multiplication of measures. Probability is not some measure theory, but measure theory in which attention is paid to measures of multiplicative origin. Or more generally, what matters in probability is almost never one single probability field, but rather interrelatedness of many probability fields, the fact that one is part of another, that one has arisen from others by multiplication or mapping. An adequate axiomatics of a domain shall account for its essential ideas (for this reason angles must not be absent as a fundamental concept in an axiomatics of elementary geometry). In an axiomatics of probability the relations between probability fields should be exhibited; in modern terms it should be formulated in categorical language. This, however, can hardly be realized at school. The least that should be required from an axiomatic system of probability is the occurrence of the concept of independence among its fundamentals and the multiplication of independent probabilities among its axioms. I cannot grasp the meaning of an axiomatics of the probability concept where this is lacking. Of course, an axiomatic formulation of stochastic independence could only be understood if the students have already learned that stochastic independence is defined by the validity of the multiplication law. Moreover students must be quite experienced in axiomatizing. The naive approach is to say: "If events are independent, the multiplication law applies to them". On the next level the learner must be accustomed to calling events independent if the multiplication law applies to them. In axiomatics, it is again the old version: "If probability fields are independent, the multiplication law applies". But now independence, which originally was rooted in the naive experiences, has become an undefined fundamental concept as are points and lines in geometry. This cannot be understood by people inexperienced in mathematics.

I doubt whether so much logical sophistication fits into the teaching at school of probability. Around a probability theory taught through its applications, axiomatics is not much more than a meaningless ornament. On a higher level, where linear functionals tend to supersede old measure theory, a Huygens-style axiomatics based on expectations or stakes looks more adequate than Kolmogorov's set theory-based axiomatics, and an axiomatics in the categorical sense is more adequate than a pure measure theory.

There is little chance left that incorporating probability into school programmes can be prevented. Must this lead to spoiling the last oasis of reality-related mathematics? I am afraid this is inevitable if probability is considered as a subject that is worth devoting two hours a week in some of the higher grade. I can, however, entirely accept A. Engel's ideas*, that is, to pervade all mathematics by probability at an early stage – as soon as the children get to know about fractions, not just because it is useful for future probability teaching but because this penetration brings mathematics nearer to reality. In Engel's approach probabilities are not the subject of arid theorems and formulae. They are acted out in the classroom, initially with dice and roulette-wheels, but soon stylized or simulated (that is the technical term) by the use of tables of random numbers. Stochastic processes with their multifarious

---

* A. Engel, in: *Les répercussions de la récherche mathématique sur l'enseignement*, Conférences CIEM, Echternach 1965. – A. Engel, in: *The Teaching of Probability and Statistics* (ed. by L. Råde), Almqvist and Wicksell, Stockholm 1970, 87–150.

relations to reality play a big part. In this abundance of concrete problems probability is experienced as a part of life.

Engel's example is the most impressive among many excellent attempts to tackle the teaching of probability at an early stage in mathematics education. Most of the others I know, however, peter out after ten or twenty lessons, which means that in spite of their quality they accomplish little. Engel's approach is an attempt at continuity. I believe that a student who experienced probability concepts early on and intensively, can better experience, and even assimilate, mathematizations far from reality on a higher level. Probability at a higher level can also take advantage of descriptive statistics at a lower level. Descriptive statistics is useful anyhow, and it is an educational riddle why it has not been part of the curriculum for many years. It is simply incredible that even today many so-called educated people cannot read a statistical graph. Earlier on I mentioned an excellent textbook in this field.*

---

* U. Pampallona & L. Ragusa Gilli, *Che cos'à la statistica*, Torino, Loescher, no date.

CHAPTER XIX

LOGIC

Quadragenarian seeks substitute for daily walks prescribed by the doctor. High reward.

Advertisement in a Swiss newspaper

First I thought it was your brother. When you came nearer I thought it was you. But now you are your brother.

Overheard

Why does the dog wag the tail? Because the tail cannot wag the dog. It's too heavy isn't it?

It is not incest to marry one's own widow.

From a course on Criminal Law

Before Christ years were counted backwards.

From a history lesson.

How large is the radius of a circle of 22 cm perimeter if π is allowed to be taken $3\frac{1}{7}$?

From a mathematics textbook.

One cat has four legs, no cat has five legs, thus one cat has nine legs.

Three boys + two girls = five children = two boys + three girls

WHAT IS LOGIC?

Nobody would really deny that above examples are somehow related to logic. On the contrary, if we hear them, are we not inclined to exclaim "that is illogical", and do we not try to uncover the "countersense" by logical means? These examples do not have, however, much to do with what is called logic in mathematical texts. Note that I did not quote examples like

> No emperor is a chimney-sweep,
> all chimney-sweeps bring luck,
> thus no emperor brings luck.

Such examples would have at least something, or even quite a bit, to do with what has been the subject of textbooks on logic from classical times onwards. But these examples were created to justify the existence of old logic. These collections of problems, which were obligatory learning for a successful pass in logic examinations, constitute frightening evidence as to what happens when a subject is cut off from other disciplines and from reality. Formal logic has changed enormously in the last century, but the examples it still uses as illustrations have not improved much. There are good reasons why they could not.

Logic is somehow related to thinking; it is logic if we make thinking an object of thinking. Do not worry about me, I know this is old fashioned. Formal logicians will want to devour me, or at least pity me. Logic is the discipline of formal systems, they say. Nevertheless, I will chance it. I will take the chance and call logic that which everybody calls so, even a formal logician once he has left the room where he studies formal logic.

SCHEMATIZING AND FORMALIZING

The external expression of thinking is language, while thinking itself is to a certain extent a "speaking to oneself". Nevertheless unlike many formalists and behaviorists we will not identify thought with its linguistic expression. In fact, the same thought can be expressed in multifarious ways, in the same language, or in other languages. There is, of course, a close tie between thought and its linguistic expression. If we make thinking the object of our thinking, we are exercising logic, and then we can hardly avoid thinking about the linguistic expression of our thinking, and finally we express our thoughts on thinking linguistically. We can, however, stress the one or the other. On several occasions we have analyzed concepts and proofs (e.g. our analysis of the proof on the perpendicular bisectors) to discover their logical structure and the underlying thinking patterns without bothering about the consequences for mathematical language. On the other hand we have analyzed linguistic structures (e.g. the different kind of adjectives with the noun "group"), with consequences of mainly a linguistic character. All this belongs to logic. It is, however, useful to distinguish both ideas, in particular with a view to didactics. Where thinking in the narrow sense is the object of thinking, I would like to use the word "*schematizing*"; where linguistic formulating takes a mathematical character, and in particular, a mathematically irreproachable language is aspired to, I will speak of *"formal-izing"*.

I would like to clearly distinguish between them and in my exposition it should be clear what I speak about since it is impossible to neatly deal with first the one and then the other. There is a schematizing activity in which the linguistic expression is a means rather than an end, and there is formalizing, where a language is mathematically analyzed, by mathematical devices, which may belong to the same or to another language. This extends to teaching: logic does not necessarily mean symbolic logic, and the use of linguistic symbols does not necessarily mean that one is studying logic.

LOGICAL PATTERNS*

What can be considered today as a well-established stock of logical patterns rests on an analysis of the thinking process by which this process has been dissolved, as it were, into its atoms. Traditional logic departed from the simple examples of everyday thinking; strongly biased by certain languages, one discovered certain patterns in it. In more recent times logic underwent a strong influence from the more specialized language that has been developed to express mathematical thought. Of course it was always idealized rather than real thinking that was analyzed. But this is not a strange feature. Mathematics has, indeed, always been applied to idealizing models of reality. If, however, the results of this analysis should be applied in teaching, as is our intention, then it is relevant to ask whether what we have learned by analyzing the idealized thinking process is instrumental in stimulating and improving real thinking processes. By thought experiments it can be investigated to which degree the idealized thinking process is exemplary. Obviously the most sophisticated analysis and synthesis of the thinking process would be didactically worthless if it acted against the real thinking process. Even it it is not as bad, the results of the schematizing activity could be didactically ineffective if the active mind works more comfortably with thinking patterns that have escaped to the attention of the logician. This would not mean that the logician's work has been useless.

---

* I will call the forms to which schematization leads patterns rather than schemes.

If people would not think according to these patterns, it can still pay to teach them to machines. I mean this seriously. In the background, and sometimes even in the foreground of schematizing activity for the last century, we find the idea of giving mathematics a form in which it can be handled by machines. It is not at all certain that this should also be the best form in which to teach mathematics to people; on the contrary it is quite improbable. Compare, for instance, how differently a man and a computer should be programmed to tend a gas-station. If we teach students rather than computers, it can only be helpful to profit to a high degree from the fact that our students are people rather than computers. We already pointed out that for a long time teaching the atomic result of a field analysis has been considered as most profound didactic wisdom, though now many believe that the importance of the analyzed elements depends on whether they have been found by the pupil himself.

Whatever the logical patterns found by analysis look like, two questions must be raised:

> whether the patterns are sufficient,

and if they are sufficient,

> whether the patterns are useful.

Maybe other complexes, larger units, other fundamental concepts are further reaching. But even these are not the main questions. The patterns should be applied and to this end one should know, teach, and learn and know how to teach

> how the non-schematic is to be schematized.

Thinking patterns as offered us by formal logic could be sufficient in the following sense: a mathematical course of thought, if at all valid, could be subjected to these patterns to check whether it is valid, that is to say whether it can be fitted into the patterns. We can hardly expect more than this from the patterns of formal logic. They are certainly not sufficient to fill the gaps in a non-conclusive course of thought, to solve a given mathematical problem, or to find problems to propound to oneself or others. The patterns of formal logic may be sufficient to check whether a definition is constructed according to the rules, but they do not contribute to deciding which definitions are most fitted to organizing a certain field. Maybe very simple mathematical facts can be analyzed or proved by submitting them to the formal logical patterns in an arbitrary order, but no global organization can be obtained by such a haphazard procedure.

Up to now little has been done beyond the realm of atomic logical patterns. They are easily formalized and, no doubt, the main tendency of mathematical logic is formalizing. The logical patterns that are really used are not the atomic ones that formal logic has isolated; if they were so, thinking would perish in prolixity. What is really operative, are larger complexes of logical experience, which are much more difficult to formalize, and the more dominating the global view becomes, the more logical tactics yield their place to logical strategies. I would not dare to claim that in the future, too, logical strategies will resist formalization. For the time being, however, well-known and formalized logical patterns are restricted to handling atomic units, or rather, such material which according to a general belief is the final result of farthest analysis.

What was strategy at a lower level can become mere tactics at a higher one. Advices like "to prove something start assuming it is wrong", or "put the unknown quantity x" are (prior to the organization of logic or algebra) strategies which prepare the organization of the field which afterwards gets the name "propositional logic" and "elementary algebra" respectively. Once these organizations have taken place, the globally effective strategies get the status of tactics. With a view to this level-dependence of the frontier between strategies and tactics, it may be useful to produce examples of strategies at a high level, which may, moreover, show how little formalization has advanced in this matter.

Let us consider the well-known proof of the existence of the greatest common divisor of two integers, n_1, n_2. From ancient times one knows the so-called Euclidean algorithm; one number is divided by the other with remainder,

$$n_1 = q_1 n_2 + n_3 ,$$

which is repeated with n_2 and n_3,

$$n_2 = q_2 n_3 + n_4 ,$$

and so it continues; the last non-zero remainder is the greatest common divisor, which is verified by backward substitution; this leads at the same time to a representation

$$d = x_1 n_1 + x_2 n_2$$

of the greatest common divisor. With such linear combinations one moves within the additive group H of integers generated by n_1, n_2; of this group d is the smallest positive element. The proof is now remodelled according to a general strategy in the way that the additive group H generated by n_1, n_2 is introduced at one blow and in H the smallest positive element d is sought for. By its way of generation d is of the form $x_1 n_1 + x_2 n_2$; thus every divisor e of n_1, n_2 is a divisor of d. The only thing left to prove is that d itself is divisor of n_1, n_2. Strangely enough it is easier to show that d is divisor of *all* elements of H – this is again a typical feature. Now we can say, divide given $y \in H$ with remainder by d

$$y = qd + r;$$

then $y \in H$, $d \in H$, $qd \in H$, $r = y - qd \in H$, where as a remainder r should be smaller than d, whence $r = 0$. This, however, can be turned more elegantly. If not every $y \in H$ is divisible by d, one should look for the least positive offender k (this is the official terminology). Thus $k \in H$, not divisible by d, and positive minimal. Then also $k - d \in H$ and not divisible by d, while $k - d < k$. On the other hand $k \geq d$ because d was minimal positive in H, which would prove $k - d$ to be a lesser offender.

Three strategies, which are of much more general use, are instrumental in this proof. Notice that the numerically important Euclidean algorithm and finally even division with remainder have vanished as demonstrative devices. This is a serious drawback; certainly in teaching both methods have to be put forward, the conceptual one along with the constructive one.

Minimum principles are important strategies in number theory. Such principles are useful for instance, for putting quadratic forms with integral coefficients into a normal form or for constructing bases of abelian groups. There is an equivalence concept and there are certain operations transforming certain objects (say quadratic forms) into equivalent ones. One characterizes representatives of the equivalence classes (normal forms) by certain equations and inequalities between parameters (coefficients of the form). One shows that every object is equivalent to one of these representatives by reducing the deviations from the normal form stepwise by means of the equivalence operations, making them finally vanish. That is the old procedure. Today one says: replace the object by an equivalent one such that its deviations from the normal form are minimal, and show that possible positive deviations could be further reduced yet. Or, alternatively, if the object with the least deviation from the normal form were not itself in the normal form, one would seize the least offender and continue by reasoning like we did above. Here the case is a bit different, however, because the objects unlike the integers are not presented with a given order relation; one must be satisfied with suitable partial orders – again a paradigmatic idea.

To prove that a monotonic mapping of the number line upon itself is necessarily continuous a laborious concourse of epsilons and deltas can be conjured. Today another approach is preferred. The topological structure of the set of real numbers is determined by its order structure since the intervals defined by the order form a basis of the topology; by definition monotonic mappings leave invariant the order structure, and consequently the topology, which proves such mappings to be continuous.

The strategy that manifests itself here, that is, to proceed from the logical dependence of two structures to derive certain properties of auto-morphisms of these structures is of the greatest importance. If, for instance, it is to be proved that the automorphisms of a projective space R over a skew field K are necessarily of algebraic nature (that is, generated by linear mappings over K and automorphisms of K), one is advised to reconstruct K from the data of the projective space R; if the analogue is to be proved for the automorphism of a quadric Q, the K is to be re-constructed from the data of the quadric. If it is to be shown that in certain classes of topological groups every (algebraic) automorphism is continuous, then one is advised to reconstruct the topology from the algebra of the group.

Zorn's Lemma, which today may be counted among the tactical devices, needs strategic ideas in order to be applied. To prove, for instance, that the union of a set Ω of subgroups of a group E, if completely ordered according to inclusion, is again a group, one reasons as follows: let $a, b \in \bigcup_{F \in \Omega} F$. Then there are $G, H \in \Omega$ with $a \in G, b \in H$. Because of the order in Ω, it is $G \subset H$ or $H \subset G$, say $G \subset H$. Then $a, b \in H$, whence $a^{-1}b \in H$, thus $a^{-1}b \in \bigcup_{F \in \Omega} F$, which proves the union to be a group. Everybody skilled in applications of Zorn's Lemma has experienced this method of reasoning hundreds of times. One day it will be formalized, which in this case would not be too difficult.

I could continue with such examples for quite a while, but I would have preferred to quote examples from axiomatizing to uncover the strategies that are instrumental to this activity. From Archimedes' theory of the lever to Riemann's axiomatic comprehension of hypergeometric functions to von Neumann-Stone's axiomatic of Hilbert space to categories, coercive ideas of axiomatization are felt, as coercive as words on the tip of the tongue which shy away from being pronounced. I really cannot say a reasonable word about the strategies of axiomatizing, and I am afraid that if I did try, I would only stutter a few silly remarks.

I hope that the present examples are sufficient to make credible the argument that it is not enough in the analysis of thinking patterns to have reached certain atomic patterns; only the blinkered or prejudiced can maintain that. In a very restricted sense they may suffice but certainly not according to usefulness, which can only be tested in practice. This does not mean that these atomic patterns are useless. I will later investigate what they can mean in instruction. But they are not the whole truth. Of course I cannot require a teacher to teach a logic which has not yet been made explicit by the logicians, and which is still mostly an unconscious activity of those who exercize it. This would be an impossible demand even if addressed to textbook authors. What I am entitled to and willing to do, is to draw the attention to these problems – which strategies do we possess, and can we make them conscious to ourselves to such a degree that it influences our teaching? Can we even formulate them to make them available to others to benefit their instruction?

SCHEMATIZING

As we explained earlier, more important than patterns is, didactically viewed, schematizing, that is making patterns. It is a pity we do not consciously know most of our patterns. This looks didactically a disadvantage, or does it? Is it not rather an advantage because what we do not know consciously, we cannot consciously transmit? And is it not

LOGIC 623

indeed fortunate that we cannot transmit, as a ready-made subject, patterns that exist only implicitly in our schematizing? What can be taught explicitly is just schematizing rather than patterns. In fact, this only holds true at a certain level, and it explains why research instruction can be effective – the learner must keep an eye upon how the teacher works because the teacher does not know it himself. But it does not hold true any more after due account to the levels. A thinking pattern can be formalized to such a degree that it becomes pure routine while it is accessible to the student only through the experience of a strategy. I will explain this by examples. From antiquity onwards logic has been exercized in mathematics teaching, whether as schematizing or formalizing. Every teacher will now and then teach some logic. It can be done more or less systematically, but whatever happens there is no didactically sound path to logical concepts than logical exploration – that is, the analysis of situations which in this case must be thinking situations. Thinking situations in everyday life usually are too simple, and as we pointed out before, it is better not to try to mathematize too simple situations. More involved ones are generally accessible with more ease because they show more mathematizable features.

In examples we repeatedly met with such instances, and then we showed a logical analysis of the kind the student should be expected to perform. I mention the theorem on the perpendicular bisectors with its abondance of opportunities of logical analysis. What couldn't we learn from this example,

> the "necessary-sufficient" pair: if $MA = MB$, then M on the perpendicular bisector of AB, if M on the perpendicular bisector of AB, then $MA = MB$;
> the meaning of transitivity of a relation,
> asymmetrizing of symmetric statements,
> proving incidences by metric means.

The "necessary-sufficient" and the transitivity, once formulated, develop by many-sided use into tactics, though to the teacher, working at a higher level, they have been so for a long time. Yet this does not entitle him to impose these patterns on his students. On the contrary, it is by departing from such situations that the student should acquire the thinking patterns of the "necessary-sufficient" and of the transitivity, and finally formalize them, if necessary. Many other patterns will remain unformalized for a long time or perhaps for ever. Examples of these are the third and fourth of the above strategies, which are hardly formalizable at school level.

I could quote here quite a number of former examples*, but rather than repeating old examples I will introduce a few new ones. The first is a kind of riddle which is quite popular today. A knight has been sentenced to be punished for some reason, but afterwards has been conditionally pardoned and given the option of opening one of two doors. Behind one there is a tiger which will devour him, behind the other a princess whom he may marry. Each of the doors is watched over by a guard, who knows what lies behind his respective door. One of the guards always tells the truth, while the other always lies, and each knows the other's character. The knight, of course, does not know who is telling the truth and who is lying, but he is allowed to ask the guards a "yes–no" type of question, to find out which door he should open. What question should he ask?

The problem can be simplified. This time take one guard who either always tells the truth or always lies. The knight asks him the following question "What would you answer if I asked you whether the princess is behind that door?" If the guard is a liar and behind the door is the princess (or the tiger), his answer to the question whether the princess is behind the door would be "no" ("yes"). If, however, he is asked what he would answer to that question if he must, he is by virtue of his being a liar obliged to say "yess" ("no"). The final result is the truth, thanks to the double negation. The consequent liar is a reliable witness provided we know he is always lying; we simply assume the contrary of what he tells us. But even if we do not know whether he is an obdurate liar or a lover of truth, he can still be a trustworthy source of information, provided he is asked a well-designed question.

We can reformulate this as follows. We are given a black box. It may be one whose output precisely reproduces an input p ("the one telling the truth") or one that transforms p into non-p ("the liar"). In both cases the black box can be transformed into a source of truth by feeding

---

* In particular p. 84 et seq., though most of them are of a linguistic kind which is dealt with later.

back every message once from the output to the input. The result will necessarily be *p* or non-non-*p*, which in fact are equivalent.

From classical times onwards the best-known thinking pattern in school instruction was provided by geometry. Geometrical reasonings are structured according to definition, proposition, supposition, statement, and proof; in constructions some more links are traditionally required. For the same reason geometry has been since antiquity the paradigm of malfunctioning of imposed patterns. Though these are important and exemplary patterns for all of mathematics they are worthless for the learner who has not felt the need for schematizing and therefore does not grasp its necessity. Moreover, it is quite useless to dictate organizing patterns for a subject matter which is still non-existent for the learner or which in the eyes of the learner needs no organization. Often traditional didactics goes even further than this; by attempting formalization one tries to define what is a definition, a proposition, a supposition, a statement, a proof, or a construction.

THE INDIRECT PROOF

There is one thinking pattern I shall deal with in more detail – indirect proof. Along with contraposition the indirect proof is a traditional logical subject matter in geometry teaching. This may appear amazing. With a view to the logically elementary character of school geometry, one would imagine that indirect proofs can be dispensed with at school level. If textbooks are consulted, this suspicion seems to be confirmed. Often proofs that look indirect are not actually so. Let us consider an example.

It is to be proved that through three non-collinear points A, B, C there passes at most one plane. Let us assume that there were two of them, α and β. Some axiom has to be accepted, for instance, that two planes with two different points P and Q in common, have also the whole straight line PQ in common. In the present case this implies that AB, BC, CA are wholly contained in both α and β. Now take an arbitrary point D in α, not on those lines. At least one of the lines DA, DB, DC is not parallel with BC, CA, AB, respectively. Let us suppose, for instance, that DA and BC intersect in E, different from D. Thus E is on AB, thus in β, and so is A, and AE. Since D is on AE, it is in β. Consequently, every point of α is in β, and by converting the argument, every point of β is in α. So α and β coincide.

Is this an indirect proof? Of course not! But it usually is formulated as an indirect proof. It starts by saying: "Let α and β be different planes through A, B, C." It is a quite natural tendency to formulate it this way. But in fact the supposition $\alpha \neq \beta$ is nowhere used in the proof. We can make in any proof whatsoever the additional assumption that the thing to be proved is wrong, without using it. This does not transform a proof into an indirect one.

(The proof contained a distinction of cases according to whether DA or DB or DC is not parallel to the opposite side of A, B, C, respectively. This looks like an indirect argument, though it can be readily eliminated. To be sure, there are geometries where this statement is not true. We here observed ordinary geometry.)

To take another example – to prove that certain lines in the plane are parallel, one supposes they were not and derives a contradiction. Is this an indirect proof? I would answer, no. Parallels are negatively defined, as non-intersecting lines. The direct way to prove that something does not happen is to assume it does happen. Therefore I would not call it a genuine indirect proof. A similar case – to prove $\sqrt{2}$ is irrational, it is assumed that $\sqrt{2} = p/q$ with integral p, q.

It is not an indirect proof either if from "if $PA = PB$, then P on the perpendicular bisector of AB" is derived "if P is not on the perpendicular bisector of AB, then $PA \neq PB$". The transition from one statement to the other is performed by contraposition (if $p \to q$, then $\neg q \to \neg p$.), and though this principle is the basis of the method of indirect proof, it is in itself not an indirect proof. $p \to q$ tells us in any case that the truth of p involves that of q. But then it is clear without any sophistication that the falsehood of q involves that of p. Of course, like all elementary things in the world this can be complicated by a chain of conclusions: Given $p \to q$. Suppose $\neg q$. To be proved $\neg p$. Assume $\neg \neg p$, hence p. Then since $p \to q$ is given. This contradicts the supposition $\neg q$. Thus $\neg p$. To imitate the indirect proof, a lot of words are wasted on something that is more elementary than the indirect proof. It is strange that often when textbooks deal with indirect proof, they forget to mention the pattern of contraposition.

In one textbook I found the following explanation. In an indirect proof one starts enumerating all cases that are possible with respect to the statement; all of them are investigated one after the other. According to the author it would be an indirect proof if some theorem on triangles would be proved by checking it first for acute, then for right, and finally for obtuse triangles. Of course this is no indirect proof though an indirect proof can indeed be hidden under the case distinction. In an indirect proof *one* assumption is made, namely, that the statement is wrong. The indirect proof is logically based on the contraposition, that is, the equivalence of

$$p \to q \quad \text{and} \quad \neg q \to \neg p.$$

The method meant in the quotation rests on the equivalence of

$$[(p \vee q) \to r] \quad \text{and} \quad [(p \to r) \wedge (q \to r)].$$

It is not an indirect proof either – it is on the contrary a blunder – if in order to prove something, it is already assumed to be right. I need not explain that if you want to prove something to be true, you are not allowed to presuppose it. If I allowed this, then I could prove $1 = 2$ by first presupposing it, multiplying it by 0, and stating that the result $0 = 0$ is true. "Stop, you have multiplied by 0, and this is forbidden" – is the cry. No, the only thing not allowed is division by 0. Indeed multiplication by 0 is an irreversible step. If one starts with the statement to be proved, p, and step by step replaces it by equivalent q, r, s, that is such that $p \leftrightarrow q$, $q \leftrightarrow r$, $r \leftrightarrow s$, and if the truth of s is obvious, then you have proved the truth of p. But actually you have worked too hard. To attain this result, $p \to q$, $q \to r$, $r \to s$ would have sufficed.

If I assume something though it is wrong, the mistake will come home to roost; sooner or later I will be confronted with a contradiction. If parting from p, I never meet a contradiction, p would be consistent anyway and could also be assumed to be true. But consistency has not been proved if I have not met a contradiction after only one trial. To prove it I should have to take any chain of conclusions from p and show that none leads to a contradiction; in fact only one has been checked.

What is the origin of the phrase "suppose it were true". I think it is the analysis figure of geometrical constructions, which is introduced by saying – "suppose ABC is the triangle asked for". Or perhaps it is the text problem – "suppose the unknown number of marbles is x".

The text gives you an equation $f(x) = 0$ for the unknown. You draw a conclusion from $f(x) = 0$, $x = 13$, say. Usually this proves nothing more than that if there is a solution, it is 13. Whether 13 does in fact solve the problem should be verified. Even if the mathematical arguments were reversible, you do not know whether all text data have been excavated and translated into mathematical conditions (suppose the result were $12\frac{1}{2}$ and the text does not allow halves).

What is really an indirect proof? This question is even harder to answer than what is a proof. It can only be properly explained within a fully formalized proof theory, and the answer would be different from what would be reasonably expected because of the rigid formalization. To tell what is an indirect proof, one had better follow one's own intuition in this respect, at the same time being careful. Case distinctions can conceal an indirect proof. Pure existence proofs are genuinely indirect; to prove the existence of an x with the property $F(x)$, it is supposed there were no such x, $\neg \bigvee_x F(x)$, in other words $\bigwedge_x \neg F(x)$, and a contradiction is derived from $F(x)$ being false for every x. If a function f is continuous between 0 and 1, positive at 0 and negative at 1, its vanishing somewhere between 0 and 1 is obtained by such an existence proof, which does not produce an actual zero of the function.

Since there are no genuine existence proofs in elementary geometry, textbook authors used to make great efforts to invent such examples. I am not sure whether they were satisfied with the results. It is usually some theorem, which has already been proved directly, and for which an indirect proof is constructed. The place where an indirect proof is exhibited, is easily located if one turns over the leaves and looks where in a figure a dotted line appears very close to a full line. The accompanying text will contain some passages like "let us assume the line did not pass through P..." while to visualize this assumption the author tried with the right ear on the drawing paper to see and draw a wrong line. In the stage where the student is desperately struggling with the relationship between logic and intuition, this is a questionable illustration of the idea of indirect proof.

As has been outlined, all indirect proofs can be eliminated from elementary geometry. Should they be eliminated from teaching geogeometry, too?

Not at all! You would not even succeed if you tried. Like the many-headed Hydra of Greek mythology the indirect proof grows seven new heads for every one cut off. The role of the indirect proof is quite different from what textbooks suggest it to be. The indirect proof is and shall be an expression of the unhampered activity of the learner. The indirect proof is a very common activity ("Peter is at home since otherwise the door would not be locked"). A child who is left to himself with a problem, starts to reason spontaneously "... if it were not so, it would happen that...".

The indirect proof is first of all a heuristic device. I shall show this with an example. I draw a square lattice in the plane (that is the set of points with integral coordinates). Around which points of the plane are there non-trivial rotations of the plane that leave the lattice invariant? The answer is obvious: the corners of the lattice, the midpoints of the sides, and the centres of the meshes. But how does one prove that this is all? Instinctively one starts reasoning "were it...". If P were such a point on the side AB and closer to A than to B, then P is closer to A than to any other lattice point and there is no other lattice point into which A could pass under the rotation around P. If P were in the interior of the mesh $ABCD$ though not on the perpendicular bisector of AB, then...

Afterwards, of course, one would try to cut off the detours and avoid indirect reasoning. Indirect proofs are, as it were, written in rough-copy. A textbook or a lesson on geometry is a fair copy where no indirect proof is admitted. If the teacher would tell the student what is an indirect proof, he is advised not to contrive examples but to catch a student performing an indirect proof and let him understand consciously what he did unconsciously. By first transforming every indirect proof into a direct one according to a seasoned pattern, in order to purge geometry of any blame, and then contriving unmotivated indirect proofs because students should have at least seen one, is simply nonsense. Before the indirect proof is exhibited, it should have been experienced by the pupil.

BETWEEN SCHEMATIZING AND FORMALIZING

The last-mentioned examples were thinking patterns where language played a subordinated role. Earlier examples* just stressed the linguistic

* p. 84 et seq.

component. "The greatest poet among the painters, and the greatest painter among the poets" or the talks on Black and White show logical features hidden in the linguistic expression; the language of these examples is still wholly unmathematical, and understanding it properly means formalizing it in a mathematical direction. Not until this has been done, can it become clear where the definitions are hidden and what is the course of the reasoning. To be sure, what is told in conventional mathematical language can be formalized to a higher degree, too, and sometimes this can be useful; but starting from unmathematical matter it is a much longer way to formalization.

I must stress again and again that it does not make sense to teach a logical formalism detached from the subject matter which it is supposed to formalize. This principle holds true for any formalism though logical formalism is particularly dangerous in this respect. Pupils can be trained to such a measure that they solve the most difficult problems of such a formalism and the reliability and the enthusiasm of these pupils could ever be adduced as proof of successful teaching. I said that you can teach children this. Actually it has already happened, not once but often. It is the most barren mathematics imaginable though perhaps mathematics is the wrong name for such a stupid activity, one which is much better performed by computers. When I mentioned the frightening collections of problems of old-fashioned logic, I should have added that these old records of horror are seriously challenged by the problem collections of the new logic.

It is the old curse of isolation again. Logic can be useful if it is not logic for logic's sake. Logic as an aim in itself is better left to the logicians. The child must learn to discover the logical patterns in proofs and theorems and to use these forms in his formulations. But above all, he must learn to profit from this logic in non-mathematical linguistic situations. It was not by accident that the numerous examples of logical-linguistic situations emerged when I dealt with mathematics as a *disciplina mentis*.

Traditionally, logic was the art of syllogisms, and during the centuries very few became aware of the fact that one cannot go very far with mere syllogisms. In fact, the syllogism is just enough to formalize the subject-predicate structure. It does not allow inferences like

> A horse is an animal,
> thus the head of a horse is the head of an animal.

The old logicians knew that there were relations but for philosophical reasons they rejected them. To formalize inferences like the one above, functions and predicates of several variables are needed.

By tradition logic was married to geometry; closer scrutiny might have betrayed the fact that even in geometry syllogisms are poor devices, but no-one hit on the idea to effectuate this marriage and to adapt logic to geometry rather than the other way round. Geometry was considered as the training ground of logic, but then logic was that activity that everybody, except logicians, called logic. It was that implicit logic that is so hard to formalize, and certainly not the little part that had been formalized. Up to the beginning of the nineteen-sixties textbooks and teaching books on geometry did not express the slightest doubt about whether geometry is the training ground of logic, while algebra books kept silent on logic. In algebra the pupil was handed over a well-functioning system of rules to transform given expressions in a well-prescribed direction. Geometry did not know such reliable patterns. Traps in algebra (for instance, dividing by 0 and multiplying inequalities by negative numbers) were not eliminated by logical analysis but blocked by extra-rules.

In traditional school practice the term algebra can be translated by "directions for completing patterns" or, in stronger terms, filling out printed forms. The printed text is engraved in the learner's memory, and it is his task to fill out the gaps in the text. The result looks like what you would overhear if you listened to a participant in a telephone conversation: "Yes... yes... no... ye-e-s... three... no". With much acuteness one can perhaps discover in the inflections of the voice and the facial expression of the speaker what the other participant is saying. Each year when I looked over the final examination papers of our grammar schools I could not but help admire the teacher who knows which form the pupil had in mind when filling it in. This, in fact, is the curse of algebra, that there are several, nay many printed forms, and it does not benefit understanding if the one thinks it was a tax return while the other had a money order in mind.

In geometry, too, there are preprinted forms, but there they cannot be filled out as mechanically; they also do not lead the way as far as those of algebra. This is one of the reasons why geometry is better renowned as a school of logic than algebra. A geometrical proof, if it is good, is a conclusive discussion. An algebra problem is a filling in exercise with the printed text omitted. If the pupil logical education is to profit as much from algebra as from geometry, it is indispensable that the teacher maintains in algebra problems the formal requirements he is used to in geometrical proofs – this is not an unreasonable demand since solving an algebra problem is proving something. Of course it would be annoying for the pupil to reproduce literally the form imprinted in his memory (and for the teacher to read it). But there is no need to do so, because just as we possess an algebra symbolism from Viëta (about 1600) onwards, so from Peano (about 1900) we have the same for logic. Fortunately symbolic logic is making headway. Using it does not mean applying logic, but it can be a means to make logical discussions easier.

It is highly informative to look for the forms students have in mind when solving an algebraic problem. I have borrowed two examples from J. van Dormolen*. These are two solutions of the problem:

To prove that $3x^2 + 12x$ has a minimum and to determine the x where it is reached.
(I) $3x^2 + 12x = 3(x + 2)^2 + 4$ has a minimum, which is assumed for $x = -2$. Reason: $(x + 2)^2$ must become $0 \rightarrow x = -2$ if this is 0 it is multiplied by $3 \rightarrow$ still 0 then 4 added and one gets the minimum which is assumed: 4.
(II) The expression $3x^2 + 12x$ is a quadratic equation. If in both parts 3 is put outside brackets the expression does not change. Then inside the brackets is $(x^2 + 4x)$, that does not equal $(x + 2)^2$ for we have added 4. To make it correct, -4 must be subtracted. The -4 must be multiplied by 3. Then we get $3(x + 2)^2 - 12$ and this is entirely equal to $3x^2 + 12x$. The expression has a minimum of -12 since a square is always positive or zero. It must be multiplied by 3, thus it is at least 0, namely if $x = -2$ one gets $3(-2 + 2) - 12$, and this is -12. The value of the square is always positive, $\times 3$ remains positive thus the minimum is -12.

These are, indeed, informative examples. The logical course of thought is interrupted by a behaviouristic one. Arguments are not logical but taken from computing prescriptions – this is a natural method in algebra. Forms have been instilled in the student, which means that often formalizing has started too early, not as the last stage of the learning process but before he reached the level of the material which had to be formalized.

In geometry it is not as easy. If logic is identified with schematizing, geometry is closer to logic than algebra. Algebra is by tradition more formalized than geometry; in geometry one depends more on thinking patterns, while mastering a language goes a long way in algebra. This, indeed, is the reason why today people tend to turn away from the more

* Cf. J. S. ten Brinke, *Euclides* **45** (1970), 327–336.

exacting geometry, which with its thinking patterns poses difficult teaching problems, and try to algebraicize geometry in order to as easily master it as algebra by mere linguistic means. It is this love of ease that will come home to roost when the student finds he must apply mathematics after having experienced it as a meaningless language.

If geometry is prone to schematizing and algebra to formalizing, the close connection between geometry and logic can be understood as long as formalizing has not yet been experienced as a mathematically valuable activity. With the rise of symbolic logic the moment where the logical status of algebra was acknowledged drew nearer. Nevertheless no-one will be surprised that we take our examples of schematizing mostly from geometry while those of formalizing come from algebra.

FORMALIZING IN THE REALM OF PROPOSITIONS

If an equation like

$$x^2 - 3x + 2 = 0$$

is given, pupils are prone to react with

$$x = 1 \quad \text{and} \quad x = 2.$$

where the "and" is spoken but not written. An exacting teacher then remarks: "$x=1$ and $x=2$ are not compatible." The well-trained pupil now would give the answer that he meant:

$$x = 1 \quad \text{or} \quad x = 2.$$

Such an incident is closed with the teacher's injunction to the student: "If you mean '*or*' write it down".

I would ask the teacher – why would you have him write "or" since for many decades we have got the symbol $\vee$? You do not require him to write down "square root of bracket open a plus b bracket closed square", do you? But there is more to it than that. "$x = 1$ *and* $x = 2$" is a good answer, too, as long as you know what it is an answer to. In geometry teaching the teacher considers it as his duty to take over the task of the mother tongue teacher. There questions are raised and answers given in whole sentences. In algebra, however, any disconnected sequence of words – or should I say of cries – is sufficient, because in algebra filling out forms is the order of the day. If the teacher writes $x^3 - 3x + 2 = 0$ the student knows that he has to find the x that satisfy it, and if the equation is $x^2 - 3ax + 2a^2 = 0$, the pupil does not bother to compute a rather than x. If this is so, the pupil is entitled to deal with the teacher as a wise man who has enough of one word. "$x=1$ *and* $x=2$" is correct for the pupil and means: "$x=1$ is a solution *and* $x=2$ is a solution". In other words,

$$[(x = 1) \rightarrow (x^2 - 3x + 2 = 0)] \wedge [(x = 2) \rightarrow (x^2 - 3x + 2 = 0)]$$

which is equivalent to

$$[(x = 1) \vee (x = 2)] \rightarrow (x^2 - 3x + 2 = 0).$$

The only thing the teacher could answer, and which would be relevant, is – "and are there no other solutions?" It is this which expresses

$$(x^2 - 3x + 2 = 0) \rightarrow [(x = 1) \vee (x = 2)].$$

The preceding was to explain what logical symbols can do. I do not demand that every algebraic computation is written down with logical and set theory symbols. Behind your desk you do not do so, do you? But the least one may require is that the text clearly shows what follows from what, and whether a variable is bound existentially or universally or interrogatively. There is no need to specify at every step the logical rules or mathematical axioms and lemmas that justify it, no need to repeat at every step all the suppositions, or to represent solving an equation as a chain of equalities between sets in brace notation. A discussion as the one above on "and" and "or", however, can be made easier, or even possible, by the use of logical symbols.

In traditional algebra instruction equations are solved according to a pattern where equations are replaced step by step by equivalent ones. It is an artificial method invented by school teachers to keep their pupils from making mistakes. It works only in very simple cases and even then it may be too complicated. The natural procedure is to derive from the proposed equation, say

$$\sqrt{x + 1} + \sqrt{x + 4} = \sqrt{x + 9},$$

consequences, which bring the equations nearer to an explicitly solvable one, say to

$$(3x + 28)\, x = 0;$$

such a procedure does not pass through a chain of equivalences, but the given equation is provisionally only used as a necessary condition, thus

$$\sqrt{x + 1} + \sqrt{x + 4} = \sqrt{x + 9} \to (3x + 28)\, x = 0.$$

Then follows the "verification"; the obtained values are substituted for x to check whether they satisfy the equation and which ones do; it is checked for which values the arrow may be inverted.

To be sure, in the case of a numerical quadratic equation the verification can be omitted since by a general theorem it is known that all solutions of such an equation can be represented by a certain formula. But this is an exceptional case. Everybody knows that it is advantageous to consider an equation first as a mere necessary condition. This is a most natural procedure if the equation has arisen from a realistic problem, that is, by mathematizing a realistic situation. Often under such circumstances one does not know for certain whether any condition has been forgotten; it is quite normal that afterwards some mathematically admissible solution is rejected as physically useless, which only means that the mathematical translation of the problem was incomplete. It is a matter of course that in solving such problems the student should be accustomed to scrutinizing the mathematically obtained solutions.

If equations are solved by stepwise equivalences, an intermediate text is perhaps dispensable. But in any case it should be indicated what is the unknown that the student should work out. Why must it always be x? (The x-epidemic has now spread from the old equations symbolism to modern set theory symbols; in 999 out of 1000 cases it is "the set of x such that...".) The text should also clearly show which are the solutions; if there is more than one, the "and" and "or" should explicitly be indicated.

If an equation is not solved by the rigid method of equivalences, one needs even more. It should be clearly indicated what follows from what, whether an equation has been replaced with a conjunction or a disjunction of two equations, etc. All this can briefly and adequately be indicated with logical symbols.

This, however, does not mean that the logical-symbolic apparatus becomes autonomous. While using the symbols one understands what they mean. There is no need to formulate generally that from $p \to q$ and $q \to r$ one may conclude $p \to r$, and to perform such inferences there is no need to appeal to general rules, since the arrows have a definite meaning. To negate conjunctions and disjunctions no general rules are required since they are meaningful operations. This, too, should not be exaggerated. Certain rules will crop up while using the symbols, and then one will not spurn the opportunity to formulate them in general terms. On the other hand one would not go as far as detaching the logical symbolism from its meaningful context. Later I will explain why this would not even be possible.

Meanwhile I give a few more examples for the use of logical symbols as a means of mathematical expression. As long as logic stands in a meaningful context, propositions are not meaningless symbols, but are meaningful in the usual sense that they represent a content, and also in the more formal sense that a truth value can be ascribed to them. Everybody knows the truth tables, where two propositions with their disjunction, conjunction, and so on, are the entries of a catalogue of compatible truth values (0 for false, and 1 for true):

p	q	$\neg p$	$p \vee q$	$p \wedge q$	$p \to q$	$p \leftrightarrow q$
0	0	1	0	0	1	1
0	1		1	0	1	0
1	0	0	1	0	0	0
1	1		1	1	1	1

There is, however, another more elementary and more natural use of truth tables, which I would prefer to start with; that is, not comparing a few abstract syntactical combinations of propositions but rather surveying the mutual relations of certain special propositions. This is full of meaning, and is just what is really used. I will give two examples.

There are well-known theorems in geometry with a multiple supposition and a multiple assertion which can be converted in many ways. With respect to a quadrangle $ABCD$ consider the following statements:

$$p: AB//CD, \qquad r: AB = CD,$$
$$q: AD//BC, \qquad s: AD = BC.$$

With the symbols $\wedge$, $\vee$ for "and" and "or" it is

$$(p \wedge q) \leftrightarrow (r \wedge s),$$
$$(p \wedge r) \leftrightarrow (q \wedge s),$$

But $q \wedge r$ can be true while neither p nor s is so, as examples show. All possibilities with respect to p, q, r, s are exhausted by the pattern

$$
\begin{array}{lccccccccc}
p & 1 & 1 & 0 & 1 & 0 & 0 & 0 & 0 \\
q & 1 & 0 & 1 & 0 & 1 & 0 & 0 & 0 \\
r & 1 & 0 & 1 & 0 & 0 & 1 & 0 & 0 \\
s & 1 & 1 & 0 & 0 & 0 & 0 & 1 & 0
\end{array}
$$

Next, an example from another domain to show that in spite of traditionally different terminology logic is everywhere the same. Let us consider twice differentiable functions f at a point a (an interior point of the definition interval), and the statements

$$p: f'(a) = 0,$$
$$q: f''(a) > 0,$$
$$r: f''(a) < 0,$$

$s:$ f has a maximum at a,
$t:$ f has a minimum at a.

Then $(s \vee t) \rightarrow p$, $(p \wedge q) \rightarrow t$, $(p \wedge r) \rightarrow s$ and nothing else. For p, q, r, s, t the following combinations

$$
\begin{array}{lccccc}
p & 0 & 0 & 1 & 1 & 1 \\
q & & & 1 & 1 & 1 \\
r & & & & 1 & 1 \\
s & 1 & & & & 1 \\
t & & 1 & 0 & &
\end{array}
$$

are excluded (where in the blank places zeros and ones can arbitrarily be put). All remaining combinations (there are eight) are admissible.

Of course, instead of with the statements p, q, r, s, t, this can also be formulated with the set of quadrangles or the set of functions P, Q, R, S, T, that fulfill the conditions p, q, r, s, t, respectively; then one would speak about equalities, inclusions, and non-inclusions between unions and intersection of these sets and their complements. This is absolutely legitimate, that is, it is a legitimate hobby. In spite of their equivalence there are cases where the logical formalism and there are cases where the set theory formalism is more adequate.

I have announced that I would explain why I do not believe in detaching logic from the meaningful contents it covers. I should say, in the first that I do not know of any successful attempt at such a detachment (except logic taught from the start isolated from any content). I doubt whether the proper teaching problem of this subject has ever been tackled or even noticed. The problem is that symbolic logic entails a sharp rupture with the logical habits of the vernacular. It is well known that mathematicians interpret "or" in a more concise way than it is interpreted in the vernacular – they did so even before symbolic logic. It is always the including "or", and never the excluding one. It is also well known that mathematicians have taken the liberty of considering the statement "all elements x of V have the property $F(x)$" already as true if V is void. It is known, too, that in everyday terminology a statement is considered as false if it asserts less about a subject than one knows or should know ("$8 + 4 = 11$ or 12" is considered wrong and is marked as such though formally it is true).

THE IMPLICATION

The gist of the matter, however, is the implication "if... then...", indicated by an arrow. From two propositions p, q composite propositions $p \vee q, p \wedge q$ can be formed, and with the use of the negations, $\neg p \vee q$, $\neg(p \vee q)$, and so on. The meaning of ' $\vee$ ' (or), ' $\wedge$ ' (and) is quite clear. The ' $\rightarrow$ ' is a different case. One would like to interpret '$p \rightarrow q$' along with p and q as a proposition. With '$p =$ it rains' and '$q =$ the streets are wet' it is not difficult; one gets the clear sentence "if it rains, the streets are wet". With '$p =$ it rains' and '$q = (2 \cdot 2 = 4)$' it is not as easy; the statement does not look truly meaningful, and the same can be stated if $p = (2 \cdot 2 = 5)$ and $q = (2 \cdot 2 = 4)$ or $q = (2 \cdot 2 = 6)$. If in the vernacular or even in mathematical everyday language the "if... then..." pattern is used, the background idea is not something like an "or" or "and" combination. The idea is rather: if I know this is the case, I can infer that something else also holds. This, however, is much too vague an idea to be accounted for in formalizing. Moreover, there is a real need to consider a "if-then" sentence as the equal of an "or" or an "and" sentence. Very often mathematical definitions involve the validity of a "if-then" sentence as a criterion. For instance:

> $A \subset B$ means by definition that every element of A is an element of B – formalized
> $A \subset B$ means by definition $\bigwedge_x[(x \in A) \to (x \in B)]$.

Or, more involved:

> R is called compact if every infinite subset of R has an accumulation point – formalized
> $C(R)$ means by definition $\bigwedge_{X \subset R}(\infty(X) \to A(X))$,

where C, ∞, A are the predicates of compactness, infinity and having an accumulation point.

How should '$\to$' be understood? Formally this can only be answered by means of a truth table for '$\to$'. The meaning of '$p \to q$' must be settled for non-specified p, q, as a function of p and q though without considering their contents. This is, indeed, quite a formal view. Certainly I cannot settle the meaning of 'p before q' or 'p after q' or 'p lest q' unless I know p and q as to their contents; if this condition is not fulfilled I do not even know whether they are meaningful. (To this you could object that this does not matter since "if it rains then $2 \cdot 2 = 4$" is accepted though properly said it is meaningless, and I must confess I cannot refute this objection convincingly.) If the contents of p, q are waived, all that remains and cannot be waived is their truth values. Disjunction and conjunction can satisfactorily be explained by means of their truth tables. Why should it not be done in the same way with '$\to$'? It has been agreed that '$p \to q$' is false if and only if p is true and (nevertheless) q is false. In other words: $(p \to q)$ equivalent with $\neg p \vee q$. This is quite reasonable though there are some awkward consequences such as that

> if the earth is a planet, then $2 \cdot 2 = 4$,
> if the sun is a planet, then $2 \cdot 2 = 4$,
> if the sun is a planet, then $2 \cdot 2 = 5$

are considered as true. It is not too bad, one is inclined to say; if this is a truth, it is an infertile truth, since antecedens and consequens are singular statements which were already settled to be false or true. It is a bit different if p and q themselves depend on variables. There is a well-known connection between sets and propositions: there belongs to a set V the proposition involving a variable x

$$p_V : x \in V$$

which is considered to be true if and only if $x \in V$; x should move in a fixed universe U. It is easily seen how the $\cap$, $\cup$,\, and $\wedge$, $\vee$, $\neg$ correspond to each other, respectively:

$$(p_A \wedge p_B) \leftrightarrow p_{A \cap B},$$
$$(p_A \vee p_B) \leftrightarrow p_{A \cup B},$$
$$(\neg p_A) \leftrightarrow p_{U \backslash A}.$$

This can also be illustrated by Venn diagrams though attempts to prove anything in this context as some textbook authors have undertaken, must necessarily lead into a labyrinth of vicious circles.

The '$\rightarrow$' must not be forgotten; to

$$p_A \rightarrow p_B,$$

or

$$(x \in A) \rightarrow (x \in B)$$

must correspond a set, that is the set of those x for which this proposition is true. Now the implication is true if either the antecedens is false or the consequens true; thus the set at issue consists of the $x \notin A$ and the $x \in B$, which is the set $U \backslash (A \backslash B)$. Thus

$$(p_A \rightarrow p_B) \leftrightarrow p_{U \backslash (A \backslash B)}.$$

It is irritating that with

$$(x \in A) \rightarrow (x \in B)$$

nobody associates the crazy set of x that fulfill this condition but rather the situation where all x fulfill the condition

$$\wedge_x [(x \in A) \rightarrow (x \in B)].$$

This yields a relation between A and B, which is also known as

$$A \subset B.$$

This is more naturally connected to $(x \in A) \rightarrow (x \in B)$ than the set $U \backslash (A \backslash B)$. If a similar interpretation is tried with $\wedge$, $\vee$, $\neg$, one gets the list

$$\bigwedge_x [(x \in A) \wedge (x \in B)] \leftrightarrow A \cap B = U,$$
$$\bigwedge_x [(x \in A) \vee (x \in B)] \leftrightarrow A \cup B = U,$$
$$\bigwedge_x \neg (x \in A) \leftrightarrow A = \bigcirc,$$
$$\bigwedge_x [(x \in A) \rightarrow (x \in B)] \leftrightarrow A \subset B.$$

A similar thing could be done with the existential quantifier:

$$\bigvee_x [(x \in A) \wedge (x \in B)] \leftrightarrow A \cap B \neq \bigcirc,$$
$$\bigvee_x (x \in A) \vee (x \in B) \leftrightarrow A \cup B \neq \bigcirc,$$
$$\bigvee_x \neg (x \in A) \leftrightarrow A \neq U,$$
$$\bigvee_x [(x \in A) \rightarrow (x \in B)] \leftrightarrow A \backslash B \neq U.$$

The set, however, with the properties at issue is

$$\{x \mid (x \in A) \wedge (x \in B)\} = A \cap B,$$
$$\{x \mid (x \in A) \vee (x \in B)\} = A \cup B,$$
$$\{x \mid \neg (x \in A)\} = U \backslash A,$$
$$\{x \mid (x \in A) \rightarrow (x \in B)\} = U \backslash (A \backslash B).$$

It is logically correct and nicely symmetric but psychologically it is all wrong. It is difficult to get accustomed to translating '$\rightarrow$' like $\vee$, $\wedge$, $\neg$ into set theory terms, that is, as a set rather than a relation between sets. The reason is the inescapable non-static operational character of the "if-then". Compare:

A horse is an animal,
thus the head of a horse is the head of an animal.
Put $x = 3$. Then $2x = 6$.

"Thus" and "then" are not written '$\rightarrow$' but '$\vdash$'. The $p \rightarrow q$ is read "if p, then q"; it is a sentence from the same language to which p and q belong. Using the '$\vdash$' means standing above that language; $p \vdash q$ can mean that if p is supposed to be true, then q comes out to be true, or even, that q can be derived from p.

It is true if $p \vdash q$ then it is allowed to maintain $p \rightarrow q$; if q holds under the condition p, it can be shown that $p \rightarrow q$ holds with no precondition. But $p \rightarrow q$ fulfills more tasks than granting the inference from p to q. If p is false, it does not make much sense to write down $p \vdash q$. On the other hand, $p \rightarrow q$ is still meaningful if p happens to be false, it is even true in this case. Moreover, it may be useful. An example was the definition of compactness. If in

$$C(R) \leftrightarrow \bigwedge_{X \subset R} [\infty (X) \rightarrow A(X)]$$

the R happens to be finite, then $\infty(X)$ holds for no admissible X, whence $\infty(X) \to A(X)$ becomes true for any $X \subset R$; thus the condition on compactness is fulfilled and R is compact. Finite spaces are always compact – that is the consequence of our view on ' $\to$ ', and it is a highly useful consequence.

Another example, which we dealt with earlier, is even simpler:

$$(A \subset B) \leftrightarrow \wedge_x [x \in A) \to (x \in B)].$$

If A is empty, then $x \in A$ is always false, thus $(x \in A) \to (x \in B)$ is always true, thus $A \subset B$ is true. The empty set is a subset of any set. This is again a highly useful arrangement. That is to say, it forces itself upon us as soon as we admit the empty set as such. Aristotle's logical terminology, if interpreted in set theory, involves there being no empty set; thus to him "all quirxes are quorxes" can at most be true if there is at least one quirx and the same holds even for "all quirxes are quirxes". To us the second statement is true anyway however a quirx may be defined and the first is true as soon as there are no quirxes at all.

All flying elephants lay eggs

is considered as trivially true by the modern logician because there are no flying elephants; Aristotle would not agree. Not until there is at least one flying elephant, would we agree with Aristotle; then the statement would not be trivially true, but we would then have to check whether those flying elephants lay eggs. But as long as the set of flying elephants is empty, we are entitled to ascribe them all properties we want.

People who go to the doctor if they have a headache

form a set to which belong even those who never have headache;

Those who blush when they lie

comprise even those who never lie.

People who do not stop if challenged by the guard are shot

threatens with death those, too, who were not challenged at all.

"The temperature of the water is 20°C" means that if a thermometer is dipped into the water, after a while the mercury column adjusts itself to scale point 20" states that the temperature is 20°C anyhow if nobody puts a thermometer into the water.

Of course, it is not obligatory to decide that way. The vernacular has its own rules, and these rules can also be justified, though not within a strictly formalized system. The statements of the vernacular cannot be replaced with truth values, and the relations between statements cannot be read in truth tables. There things are much more difficult than in a heavily formalized artificial language, which, however, is insufficient even for the needs of a mathematics considered as an activity.

It is sad that with respect to implication the formal logical use deviates so greatly from the vernacular. As a consequence mistakes around the implication are the rule even at the highest level of mathematical activity. Mistakes with implications in a subordinated clause, e.g. as a definition, are quite common, even such obvious errors as that the assertion

$$x^2 + x + 5 = 0 \rightarrow x = 1$$

be false (in the domain of real numbers). A more sophisticated occurrence is

$$\wedge_{a,b}([\wedge_x\{(x^2 + ax + b = 0) \rightarrow [x = 1 \vee x = 2]\}] \rightarrow$$
$$\rightarrow [(a = -3) \wedge (b = 2)].$$

If $x^2 + ax + b = 0$ implies $x = 1$ or $x = 2$, then $a = -3$ and $b = 2$. This is wrong because for instance

$$x^2 + 1 = 0 \rightarrow [(x = 1) \vee (x = 2)]$$

is true*. I already pointed out the errors made in textbook literature and beyond while using braces to describe the set of x such that... The implication in subordinated clauses is a similar case. Such abuses as with "the set of all x..." are harmless if committed in a non-formalized language. It does not, however, go together with the exacting pretences of a formalized language. Pretending to express all in a formalized language one does not master is mere ostentatious pseudo-learning.

I have dealt with these things in detail because many textbooks authors do not seem to understand how difficult they are and how carefully things have to be considered before one can start teaching this subject. Something like the symbolism of implication will work well only in

* Cf. H. Freudenthal, *The Language of Logic*, Amsterdam, Elsevier, 1966, p. 52–3.

very simple contexts, that is, where deviation from the vernacular is not too wide. As long as such restrictions are imposed on the free use of the formal implication, it does not make sense to detach the logical formalism from the content matter to operate on it in a meaningless way. I must make it clear that I do not claim it is impossible to teach pupils this. I only say that it would mean teaching the pupils a formal technique that remains formal and does not tolerate any content lest it cease to function. Nobody then knows why such a technique should be taught.

I do not object to letting the pupil become acquainted with the truth table of $p \to q$, with the logical equivalence of $p \to q$ and $\neg p \lor q$, but do not urge that they are also psychologically equivalent to him because they are not so for ourselves either as long as we are active in mathematics. Consider, for example, the definition of $A \subset B$ by $x \in A \to x \in B$. It is a reasonable definition. Why should I say $\neg (x \in A) \lor (x \in B)$ instead? This would mean explaining $A \subset B$ by (Complement of A) $\cup B =$ universe. This is legitimate, but is it wise?

If the different logical combinations are concretized by switching models, $p \to q$ should not be forgotten. It is not easy to find a nice model for $p \to q$. The $p \to q$ is considered false if and only if p is true and nevertheless q is false. Then a red light should flash. Take the following example.

Outside an elevator a green light shows that the elevator is working. If through some deficiency the elevator does not answer my call, the light turns red to tell me that I had better use the stairs. Thus as long as I do not press for the lift, the light is green. If I press and it comes, the light remains green. Only if I press and the elevator does not move, does the light turn red. If the contraption is to show a green light for truth and a red one for falsehood, then it concretizes the value of the proposition "if I press for the elevator, it comes".

(I was told about a fishing rod which shows a red light if one tries to pull it up when there is nothing on the line. Try to invent more examples.)

FORMALIZING – THE STRUCTURE OF MATHEMATICAL LANGUAGE

I have dealt with the syntax of algebraic language* in detail because it

* Chapter XIII.

must be detrimental to teaching algebra that even the mere existence of something like a syntax of algebraic language seems to be a hardly known fact. I did not say that this syntax should be taught or even that teaching algebra has to start with teaching its syntax; the teacher, however, should master it consciously.

The situation regarding the mathematical language around formulae is not much better. What is offered as a syntax of mathematical language in all attempts at formalizing is entirely unsatisfactory. On several occasions I took the opportunity of dealing with the mutual relations between the vernacular, mathematical language, and formalized language. I do not understand what could be the use of complicated pieces of formalized language if these relations are not brought into relief during teaching.

I have many times indicated points of difference between the vernacular, the language of formulae, mathematical language around the formulae, and formalized language. I have shown why the definition of a group as "a set in which a multiplication is defined" is unsatisfactory, why in the definition of a group the multiplication is better incorporated explicitly, and the group understood as a pair consisting of a set and a multiplication, or even a quadruple consisting of a set, a multiplication, a one and an inversion. I pointed out that a commutative group is a special group while an ordered group is not a group but a pair consisting of a group and an order. "Galois group", moreover, is not a group at all but a functor that assigns a group to a pair of fields. I repeat these examples of conscious formalizing, of conscious linguistic creativity. Such subtleties can be imposed on the learner; because it is language, it will function without much difficulty but from this procedure one cannot expect much transfer. If the pupil is expected to learn formalizing – and I believe formalizing will be one of the important activities of mathematicians in the future – he should experience these examples of formalizing in their "coming into being" and as an urgent need, rather than being confronted with the final result. Moreover, manipulating a language consciously must contribute substantially to linguistic education in general.

As a striking feature of the language of algebraic formulae I mentioned bracketing. Few consciously know its characteristics. If we should believe algebra textbooks, it is the task of brackets to be dissolved and reintroduced. In the often quite primitive fragments of formalized language there are few signs of understanding that brackets can have some structuring task in formalizing; there is not much more than the braces of "the set of x such that...", which unfortunately is the worst example, where a punctuation tool was casually selected to indicate some kind of binding. I pointed out that the vernacular knows quite a few other means of syntactic structure, flexions, prepositions, conjunctions, subordinate clauses, and (sometimes somewhat arbitrary) punctuation. More often the syntactic structure must be derived from the material meaning. The material meaning rather than the syntactic structure shows that brackets are differently to be put in "ripe apples and pears" and "hot dogs and icecream". In mathematics one cannot afford to omit brackets, trusting that the contents will show where they should be. Mathematics requires more formality. $4 \cdot (5 + 3)$ is as meaningful as $4 \cdot 5 + 3$, and it can matter to know precisely what is meant.

The vernacular and mathematical language have quite different techniques of handling variables, that is, ambiguous names. It is clearly a hopeless task to assign to every object a proper name. For this reason in an early stage in language man invented beside proper names so-called appellatives; using the term "stone" one can name any stone, the term "mouse" every mouse, and where it matters "this stone" can be distinguished from "that stone", "this mouse" from "that mouse". The first geometers must have taught this way – connect this point to that one, intersect this line with that circle. Then they invented naming points by letters and gave lines, parallelograms, circles, algorithmically derived names. In algebra symbols for the unknown and its powers were invented; from geometry was borrowed the method of indicating indeterminates by letters. In mathematics variables are exchangeable. While the variable "stone" can indicate stones only, and the variable "mouse" only mice, the variables $a, b, c, ..., x, y, z, ..., A, B, C, ...,$ $\alpha, \beta, \gamma, ...$ are of general use and only incidentally restricted. (To be sure there are *a priori* restricted variables: the variable ' $+$ ' is only used to mean an addition, the variable ' $<$ ' always means an order relation.)

The techniques of indicating the binding of variables are even more divergent. In the phrases "in a triangle the sum of the angles is $180°$" and "draw a triangle", "a triangle" aims on the one hand at all triangles and on the other at "there is a triangle". This sloppiness of the vernacular cannot be cured by numerals. With "two triangles are congruent if…" and "draw two triangles" it is the same dilemma: "all pairs of triangles" or "there is a pair".

In mathematics it becomes more and more a habit to account for the kind of binding. As means of binding are known:

$\bigwedge_x F(x)$, the universal quantifier: for all x is $F(x)$,

$\bigvee_x F(x)$, the existential quantifier: there is an x such that $F(x)$,

$\{x \mid F(x)\}$, the set forming binding: the set of all x such that $F(x)$,*

$\curlyvee_x F(x)$, the function forming binding: $F(x)$ as a function of x,

$\downarrow_x F(x)$, the article binding: the x such that $F(x)$.

$?_x F(x)$, the interrogative binding: asked for the x such that $F(x)$.

Not belonging to mathematics and non-formalizable is the demonstrative binding: this (that) x.

Translation of symbols into the vernacular is marred by the usual problems of interlinear version. '$\neg$' and '$\rightarrow$' were similar cases. I do not know of any language in which a sentence can be negated by simply prefixing a negation particle (even in English this would at least require inversion). To read '$\neg$' as "it is false that" would be off the mark, since "it is false that" represents a super-ordinated view where to statements are assigned truth values. The '$\rightarrow$' cannot be rendered by interlinear version, in all the languages I know it stands as an "if" at the beginning, maybe completed by a "then" halfway. Some people read '$\rightarrow$' as "implies"; to others this sounds as a superordinating clause, which tells of the expressions of the language which "follows" from which. If $F(x)$ is to be read "x is a flying elephant", then the interlinear version "there is an x such that x is a flying elephant" of $\bigvee_x F(x)$ sounds unnecessarily clumsy compared with the easy "there are flying elephants". The crux of interlinear version is the universal quantifier. Let us consider the statement "all men are mortal". The set H of men is introduced and the predicate M of being mortal; $M(x)$ is agreed on to be read as "x is mortal". Now it is written

* Instead of the braces I proposed the symbol ↑.

$$\bigwedge_{x \in H} M(x),$$

"for all x in the set H of men, x is mortal". Or

$$\bigwedge_x (x \in H \to M(x)),$$

"for all x, if x is in the set of men, then x is mortal". By their sheer clumsiness both phrases are quite unlike the phrase "all men are mortal" which was our subject of formalizing. If formalized language shall be a teaching matter, this kind of translation will be a useful and, in any case, indispensable exercise. The foregoing can still be complicated by replacing the predicate M by the set J of mortals. It becomes

$$\bigwedge_{x \in H} x \in J, \quad \text{or} \quad \bigwedge_x [(x \in H) \to (x \in J)],$$

or

$$H \subset J.$$

For $\bigwedge_x F(x)$ one often hears or reads the semi-formalized explanation "for all x, $F(x)$"; I do not like separating two mathematical expressions by a linguistic (non-algorithmic) comma, which cannot be pronounced. People are inclined to read it "for all x holds $F(x)$", where unfortunately the "holds" represents superordination. I had recourse to "for all x is $F(x)$", which does not look too bad.

We have already noticed that the vernacular operates a quite involved system of binding devices. There are varieties to indicate one kind of binding, but often the same devices serve to indicate quite different bindings. Texts around mathematical formulae are usually edited in the vernacular though symbolic editing becomes more and more frequent. Sophistications in the vernacular are tried to make the kind of binding explicit and overt. It is no longer simply "$f(x)$ vanishes" but "$f(x)$ vanishes for all x" or "always" or "identically"; or, if existential binding is aimed at, "$f(x)$ vanishes for appropriate x", "for some x", "sometimes". We noticed earlier* how a naive definition of continuity "if x changes little, $f(x)$ changes little" can be raised stepwise to higher precision; the first "little" becomes "sufficiently little", the second "arbitrarily little", which shows that the first involves an existential, the second a universal quantifier, whose order is a matter of attention. All this is inferred not on the ground of formal criteria but because the

* p. 561 et seq.

description of what is meant by continuity can evoke correct associations even in its less precise version. If finally the definition of continuity is fully formalized, then any doubt as to the quality and the order of the quantifier is excluded.

There are three languages involved in this activity, the vernacular, a version of the vernacular adapted to the needs of mathematics, and a wholly formalized language. Translating from one language into the other should be learned and mastered; interlinear versions are of little use. If a text is to be translated from a less into a more formalized language, the text must be understood; for the inverse procedure it is at least required that the language into which it is translated is sufficiently mastered to obtain smooth translations.

The half formalized intermediate version of the adapted vernacular has made great progress in the last few decades; the majority of mathematicians now master it quite well, and young college students learn it with a relative ease if the teacher is conscious of the fact that his students do not yet know the language, takes pains to teach it, and gives the students the opportunity to exercise it. It is different with formalized language. I do not believe that an appreciable number of mathematicians, except logicians, are really familiar with this language; at least they lack training (and I do not exclude myself in this respect). Among mathematicians it has become quite a habit to write after the existential quantifier an appellative rather than a mathematical variable and to continue with a "such that", for instance,

$$\exists \text{ group } G \text{ such } \forall \text{ true subgroups } H \subset G \ldots$$

So is it written on the blackboard – though it is rarely printed like this. More subtle errors are made if quantifiers are overlooked which are not explicitly indicated in the vernacular and in the intermediate version. "The set of all number sequences with positive members" is written down in an interlinear version,

$$\{\{a_n\} \mid a_n > 0\},$$

"the set of polynomials with positive coefficients" becomes

$$\{a_0 + a_1 x + \cdots + a_n x^n \mid a_i > 0, \quad i = 0, \ldots, n\};$$

I could continue with this kind of example for quite a while. Liberties that can be taken in the vernacular with its restricted means of expression, are mere sloppiness if imitated in formalized language. In expressing oneself in formalized language one becomes committed to do it in the spirit of that language.

This holds true for still more cogent reasons at school level. The use of logistics is often merely pretentious. It is a way of making oneself (and others) believe in one's high standard of learning, but as soon as essential quantifiers are needed, it breaks down or one retires to the safer vernacular. Binding in every algebraic formula all universal quantifiers explicitly, as for instance in

$$\bigwedge_{a,b,c} [(a + b) c = ac + bc],$$

is ridiculous if it stands along with

$$\{x \in N \mid x \text{ is divisible by } 7\}.$$

A fully formalized language is not everywhere to be preferred. I dared to predict earlier on that though the formalized language will make headway, a vernacular that is more and more adapted to mathematics will flourish alongside the formalized language. The atomic character of the formalized language has definite advantages as long as details are stressed; the bigger and cruder structures of the adapted vernacular serve better the global understanding.

For the learner the stress should be on formalizing, rather than on formalism, that is, on creating new means of expression in a more or less formalized language. With a few examples I showed that this is not so simple because of the difficulties arising from quantifiers and other binders. Much attention must be paid to linguistic complexes which hide a variable along with its binding, which I mentioned earlier*. In "somebody", "nobody", "sometimes", "always", "somewhere", "everywhere" the variable and its binding are overt; one has to look out with "little", "much", "small", "big", "long ago", "finally" and notice that they hide quantifiers and it costs effort to know which ones and in which order they follow each other. Possessives like "the function has a zero" hide existential quantifiers, and so do endings like the "ible" in "divisible" and the 'able' of "composable" and "countable". For centuries as a paradigm of a subject-predicate-structure with an all-quantifier the

* p. 562 et seq.

sentence "All men are mortal" was repeated, up to a few years ago when somebody discovered that this structure is one quantifier richer than hitherto believed: "x is mortal", in fact, means "there is a moment t such that x dies at time t". Thus "all men are mortal" means "for every x, if x is a man, there is a t such that t is a moment and x dies at t".

As I was compelled to deal with quantifiers intensively in analysis* there is little point in coming back to them but it would be useful to add a few remarks of a general character. It depends on the level of instruction how far quantifiers should be dealt with and how far they are formalized. But if this is done, the part played by quantifiers should be clear.

In an introduction to logic I wrote about the universal and the existential quantifier in something like the following terms:

"For all x is $F(x)$" means

$$F(a) \wedge F(b) \wedge F(c) \wedge \ldots,$$

which is shortened to

$$\wedge_x (F(x)).$$

"There is an x such that $F(x)$" means

$$F(a) \vee F(b) \vee F(c) \vee \ldots,$$

which is shortened to

$$\vee_x F(x).$$

Professional logicians are scandalized when confronted with this. They will not allow you to interpret the "all" and the "there is" as an unrestricted conjunction or disjunction with as many factors as there are subjects because such infinite expressions were not properly defined. They compare it with the awkward procedure of passing from finite to infinite sums without explaining what an infinite sum can mean. This comparison, however, is off the mark. It is at best comparable with the "and so on" with which the child interrupts counting, or with the dots in

$$\tfrac{1}{3} = 0,333\ldots$$

or, in general, with the naive notions of a decimal fraction.

* p. 562 et seq.

But the logicians' objection can also be answered in another way. Even for *two* summands the conjunction and disjunction symbols were not properly defined; they were introduced as a comfortable way of writing. The objection would be right if proposition logic had axiomatically been founded, and after its finite conjunctions and disjunctions one would have behaved as though infinite ones were also meaningful. We are not, however, moving within an axiomatic system; we are speaking an open language, capable of modifications and additions.

If I intend to tell somebody who does not know mathematics that

$$\sum_{i=1}^{n} (2i - 1) = n^2,$$

I show him that

$$1 + 3 = 4, \quad 1 + 3 + 5 = 9, \quad 1 + 3 + 5 + 7 = 16, \quad \text{and so on}$$

and I hope that after the "and so on" he will understand how things continue. Or in order to convince him that after 10^6 there is still a prime number, which unfortunately I do not know, I would let him try the next numbers to find one.

It is the same in logic. In order to explain what it means that $F(x)$ holds for all x, I tell him it holds for a, for b, for c, and so on. That $F(x)$ should hold for *some* x, I express by enumerating it holds for a or b or c, and so on. This is as natural as it can be. But to write it down or to print it is forbidden – *anathema sit*. There seems to be, indeed, after the Holy Writ, a "Holy Print"*. But if such a procedure is anathema, how can I convince my listeners or readers that "not all" means the same as "some not" and "there is no" means the same as "for all not". How can I have them operate with quantifiers and observe their laws if this interpretation is not present in the background? Are there people who understand

$$\sum_{i=1}^{n} (2i - 1) = n^2$$

though they never noticed that

$$1 + 3 = 4, \quad 1 + 3 + 5 = 9, \quad 1 + 3 + 5 + 7 = 16, \dots ?$$

* p.54.

Are there among logicians people who can understand $\bigwedge_x$ and $\bigvee_x$ only axiomatically and who are not any more affected by the intuitive experience that led to these symbols? But even if they existed, they would be wrong to presuppose this state of mind to be that of the learner.

In introducing $\bigwedge_x$ I stress departing from

$$F(a) \wedge F(b) \wedge F(c) \wedge \ldots,$$

and in introducing $\bigvee_x$, that from

$$F(a) \vee F(b) \vee F(c) \vee \ldots,$$

because this facilitates understanding the rules for $\wedge$ and $\vee$, and because this is an opportunity for neat and entirely sound applications of experiences acquired in working with disjunctions and conjunctions. Thus, for instance, from

$$\neg \bigwedge_x F(x)$$

to

$$\neg (F(a) \wedge F(b) \wedge F(c) \wedge \ldots)$$

to

$$\neg F(a) \vee \neg F(b) \vee \neg F(c) \vee \ldots$$

to

$$\bigvee_x \neg F(c).$$

Moreover, it is a natural justification of the notation

$$\bigwedge_x F(x), \ \bigvee_x F(x),$$

which for obvious reasons I prefer above

$$\forall_x F(x), \ \exists_x F(x).$$

Often the subscript of $\bigwedge$ and $\bigvee$ (the variable subjected to binding) is not an absolutely free occurrence but rather restricted to a set, say V, for instance,

$$\bigwedge_{x \in V} F(x), \quad \text{for all } x \text{ from } V \text{ is } F(x),$$
$$\bigvee_{x \in V} F(x), \quad \text{there is an } x \text{ from } V \text{ such that } F(x).$$

It is important to know how this is written with a freely variable x. In the second case '$x \in V$' is a supplementary condition imposed on x, along with $F(x)$, in the first case $F(x)$ is only urged of those x that already fulfill $x \in V$ rather than of those with $x \notin V$, too. This leads to writing

$$\bigwedge_x [(x \in V) \to F(x)],$$
$$\bigvee_x [(x \in V) \land F(x)].$$

Attentive students always ask why the $x \in V$ from the subscript reappears in one case with a ' $\to$ ' and in the other with a ' $\land$ '. The reason is clear from what we said, but it is instructive to negate both expressions. To do this we replace the first by

$$\bigwedge_x [\neg (x \in V) \lor F(x)]$$

in other words,

$$\bigwedge_x [(x \notin V) \lor F(x)],$$

which negated becomes

$$\bigvee_x \neg [(x \notin V) \lor F(x)]$$

or

$$\bigvee_x [(x \in V) \land \neg F(x)].$$

Now the $\neg$ has duly appeared; chasing the $x \in V$ back into the subscript one gets

$$\bigvee_{x \in V} \neg F(x)$$

as a negation of

$$\bigwedge_{x \in V} F(x).$$

In a similar way as a negation of

$$\bigvee_{x \in V} F(x)$$

one would expect

$$\bigwedge_{x \in V} \neg F(x).$$

Indeed, it goes through

$$\neg \bigvee_x [(x \in V) \land F(x)],$$
$$\bigwedge_x \neg [(x \in V) \land F(x)],$$
$$\bigwedge_x [\neg (x \in V) \lor \neg F(x)],$$
$$\bigwedge_x [(x \in V) \to \neg F(x)].$$

What quantifiers mean cannot be appreciated until quantifiers of a different kind are alternating; this must have become clear when we analyzed the notion of continuity. If quantifiers are studied at all the succession of quantifiers should be exercised. This can be done with numerous examples such as I introduced elsewhere*. An expression with several quantifiers involves at least two variables which can be overt or hidden, algorithmic or essential. Let us consider a relation K, where xKy is read "x is a child of y". (For the variables human examples are substituted.)

$$\bigvee_x \bigvee_y xKy \quad : \text{ somebody is a child,}$$
$$\bigvee_y \bigvee_x xKy \quad : \text{ there is somebody with a child,}$$
$$\bigvee_x \bigwedge_y xKy \quad : \text{ somebody is a child of everybody,}$$
$$\bigvee_y \bigwedge_x xKy \quad : \text{ somebody has everybody as his child,}$$
$$\bigwedge_x \bigvee_y xKy \quad : \text{ everybody is a child of somebody,}$$
$$\bigwedge_x \bigvee_x xKy \quad : \text{ everybody has a child,}$$
$$\bigwedge_x \bigwedge_y xKy \quad : \text{ everybody is a child of everybody,}$$
$$\bigwedge_y \bigwedge_x xKy \quad : \text{ everybody has everybody as a child.}$$

Another example:

$G(x, t)$ means: I seize the thing x at instant t,
$S(x, t)$ means: I see the thing x at instant t,
$t < t'$ means: instant t precedes instant t'.

Then we write down

I always see something.
Sometimes I see nothing.
Everything is seen by me sometime.
If I see something, I seize it immediately.
I do not seize a thing unless I have seen it before.

Solutions:

$$\bigwedge_t \bigvee_x S(x, t),$$
$$\bigvee_t \neg \bigvee_x S(x, t) \quad \text{or equivalently} \quad \bigvee_t \bigwedge_x \neg S(x, t),$$
$$\bigwedge_x \bigvee_t S(x, t),$$
$$\bigwedge_t \bigwedge_x [S(x, t) \rightarrow G(x, t)]$$
$$\bigwedge_t \bigwedge_x \{\neg G(x, t) \vee \bigvee_{t'} [(t' < t) \wedge S(x, t')]\}.$$

* H. Freudenthal, *The Language of Logic*, Amsterdam, Elsevier, 1966, p. 45–54.

The last could also be interpreted as

$$\bigwedge_t \bigwedge_x \{G(x, t) \leftrightarrow \bigvee_{t'} [(t' < t) \wedge S(x, t')]\}.$$

It looks like a meaningless concoction but whoever has struggled with the continuity notion will agree that it has something to do with mathematics. Formalizing statements with hidden quantifiers must be exercized if continuity is to be made a precise concept. I exhibited this analysis earlier. f is called continuous at x_0 if for every $\varepsilon > 0$ there is a $\delta > 0$ such that for all x it follows from $|x - x_0| < \delta$ that $|f(x) - f(x_0)| < \varepsilon$. Thus

$$\bigwedge_\varepsilon (\varepsilon > 0) \to \bigvee_\delta \{(\delta > 0) \wedge \bigwedge_x [(|x - x_0| < \delta) \to$$
$$\to (|f(x) - f(x_0)| < \varepsilon)]\}.$$

Continuity everywhere and uniform continuity require one more quantifier $\bigwedge_{x_0}$ to be placed at the head of the expression or aside of $\bigwedge_x$, respectively.

These quantifiers are the reason why continuity is a difficult notion; the blame is often laid on the inequalities, which can be refuted by experience. In our country where inequalities have been exercized from the start of algebra lessons, students at university often run ashore over continuity.

Continuity is one of those complicated logical structures which cannot be missed in modern mathematics, and in particular, in analysis. I already discussed whether and how far this is subject matter for school mathematics. The mathematics student at university should in any case be accustomed to quantifiers as early as possible. Nothing is to be gained by delaying it. The earlier the student is vaccinated with quantifiers the better will he stand the quantifier fever.

Some years ago I asked how school mathematics can manage it without towering quantifiers upon each other. When I tried to answer it, I was surprised. What was the matter? School mathematics knew of these dangerous towers of quantifiers, and strangely enough in algebra (at least in the Netherlands) which is renowned to be logically simpler than geometry. I took my examples from an exemplary collection of 250 problems*. In our textbooks even more involved material is found. I quote a few of those cascade problems:

* *Euclides* 32, 97–152 (1956/7).

No. 49: (a) Which condition must a and b fulfill if

$$- x^2 + ax + a + b = 0$$

shall be negative for all x?

(b) Which condition must b fulfill if there shall be values of a that fulfill the foregoing condition?

Symbolically,

$$?_b \bigvee_a \bigwedge_x (- x^2 + ax + a + b < 0).$$

Another example:

No. 69: (a) Prove that the minimum of $x^2 + px + q$ is for no pair of p and q larger than $p + q + 1$.

(b) For which value of p and q does the minimum equal $p + q + 1$?

$$\neg \bigvee_{p,q} \bigwedge_y \{[\bigvee_x (x^2 + px + q = y) \wedge \neg \bigvee_x (x^2 + px$$
$$+ q < y)] \to (y > p + q + 1)\},$$
$$?_{p,q} \bigwedge_y \{[\bigvee_x (x^2 + px + q = y) \wedge \neg \bigvee_x (x^2 + px + q) < y)]$$
$$\to (y = p + q + 1)\}.$$

There is, however, a huge difference between these examples and that of continuity. The dangerous quantifiers in these examples are paper tigers. The teeth of the quantor $\bigwedge_x$ in

$$\bigwedge_x (- x^2 + ax + a + b < 0)$$

are pulled out by the discriminant. Our students know by routine that the above expression is equivalent to

$$a^2 + 4(a + b) < 0;$$

by this the problem is reduced to

$$?_b \bigvee_a [a^2 + 4(a + b) < 0].$$

But the next quantifier, $\bigvee_a$, is as senile as the preceding. The discriminant reduces the problem to

$$?_b (16 - 16b > 0),$$

and now the first possibility for the candidate to flounder arises because after so much training in quadratic and fractional inequalities, he will certainly not know what to do with linear ones.

The second example is much similar. Between the square brackets is the statement "y is the minimum of $x^2 + pq + q$", which involves two canned "existential quantifiers". Fortunately the candidate is not compelled to open the can to take them out because he has a recipe at his disposal to expurgate them. He writes down the minimum of the function and all complications gently dissolve in the problem

$$?_{p,q}(- q^2 + q = p + q + 1).$$

How difficult such problems can become if the usual quadratic functions are replaced, say, by the much simpler linear ones, comes to light if for fun you think about the truth of the propositions

$$\bigvee_z \bigwedge_y \bigvee_x (xy = z),$$
$$\bigwedge_z \bigvee_y \bigwedge_x (xy = z),$$
$$\bigwedge_x \bigvee_y \bigwedge_z (xy = z).$$

In both examples we quoted, it was algorithmic quantifiers we met with, that is, algorithmically we could reduce a proposition $\bigwedge_x F(x)$ to one without a quantifier $\bigwedge_x$, and in the case of $\bigvee_x F(x)$ we could indicate immediately all x for which the statement holds.

In the definition of continuity, however, any indication is lacking which would aim at an algorithm which to every $\varepsilon > 0$ delivers a $\delta > 0$ with the well-known properties, and the all-quantifiers cannot be eliminated by algorithmic means either (unless special function classes are at issue).

It is non-algorithmic quantifiers that can escape the comprehension of the beginner. They pile up by hundreds but even the skilled mathematician cannot grasp quantifier towers of more than three or four storeys in one view. He knows how to get a better picture by taking once in a while a little tower of three or four storeys, rolling it like a collared herring and sticking it with a "definition" label. For instance, the definition of continuity involves that of function. A function is a set G of number pairs $\ulcorner x, y \urcorner$ (the graphic) such that to every x there is one and only one y with $\ulcorner x, y \urcorner \in G$. The universal and the existential quantifier are overt but the "only one" hides one more universal quantifier. Symbolically the function definition reads

$$\bigwedge_x \bigvee_y \{(\ulcorner x, y \urcorner \in G) \wedge \bigwedge_{y'} [(\ulcorner x, y' \urcorner \in G) \to (y' = y)]\}.$$

This complicated structure with non-algorithmic quantifiers is hidden behind the innocent word "function" which occurs in the continuity definition. Moreover, that definition presupposes the concept of real number which has a logical depth of certainly a few dozens of quantifiers in series. To work with such concepts one should be able to unroll every single collared herring of quantifiers, with no prospect of algorithmical elimination.

Of course, the skilled teacher both at school and at university will help his students to understand the structure by effective canning and algorithmizing of quantifiers. How this can be done, I once expounded in a book review. In a modern textbook on analytic geometry I found after an axiomatic introduction of vector space the following:

"DEFINITION: The n-dimensional affine space V^n is a set of objects, named points, with an atlas K, that is a system of maps $k, k', \ldots : V^n \to A^n$, one-to-one mappings on the n-dimensional vector space A^n, with the following properties:

(I) To two maps $k, k' \in K$ there is a vector $d \in A^n$ such that, if a and a' are images of the same point of V^n on the maps k and k', respectively, then

(1) $a' = a + d$,

in other words, if k^{-1} is the inverse of k, then

(2) $a' = k'k^{-1}a = a + d$ for every $a \in A^n$.

(II) Conversely, to every $k \in K$ and $d \in A^n$ there is a map $k' \in K$ for which (2) holds."

We notice here a double towering of four quantifiers, the first "*there is* an atlas with the property: *for every* pair of maps of the atlas *there is* a d such that *for every* pair $a, a', \ldots$ it holds that $a' = a + d$. A second tower is found in (II). Obviously these quantifiers have artificially been put into this structure. How can we eliminate them?

First, one notices that in (I) the author avoided the obvious term "translation". "For all a, a' with... it holds that $a' = a + d$" is an unnecessarily complicated expression for "$a \to a'$ is a translation over the vector d". By this simpler expression we have canned one quantifier. "There is a d such that for all a, a' it holds that $a' = a + d$" now becomes "$a \to a'$ is a translation". The second quantifier has disappeared. (This is a typical method: one defines d-translation first, and then tacitly omits the d.) But we have not yet finished. The quantifiers over the maps are due to negligence. We forgot to number the maps. The indication "maps $k, k', ...$" is inefficient. Can we not give every map an algorithmic name? Yes, we can. We simply add to k as a subscript the point which is mapped by k on the origin, thus $k_p p = 0$. The definition now reads:

The affine space V^n is a set with an atlas K of maps $k_p ...$, such that

(1) $k_p p = 0$,

(2) $k_{p_1} q - k_{p_2} q$ constant (that is, independent of q).

But it can be done even better. Take it as a rule that an algorithm should not contain useless complications. Why should we write the p in k_p as a subscript? Can we not read $k_p q$ as a function of two variables? Then of course we write it as a difference $q - p$ (instead of $k_p q$). Now the ugly atlas is burned! The definition now reads:

The affine space V^n is a set with the following structure. A mapping of $V^n \times V^n$ on the vector space A^n is distinguished, it is called the subtraction of points of V^n; the image of $p, q \in V^n \times V^n$ is denoted by $q - p$, which is an element of A^n (a vector). For fixed p the mapping $q \to q - p$ is "one-to-one" and "upon"; $p - p = 0$, $(q - p_1) - (q - p_2)$ is constant, thus equals $p_2 - p_1$.

The last three postulates can be simplified:

(1) $(q - p) + (r - q) = r - p$,

(2) $q - p = 0$ implies $q = p$,

(3)   the equation $q - p = x$ has for given $x \in A^n$ and $p \in V^n$ one solution. This unique solution is denoted by $p + x$.

Of course this definition of affine space can be obtained more directly. If one starts with a phenomenological analysis rather than with axiomatics, one is lead with certainty to this or a similar definition – essentially the same definition we arrived at in our analysis of affine space in Chapter XII.

After this digression I return to the cascade problems. The above definition of affine space was an example of ineffective complications. The cascade problems were an example of ineffective facilitations. Too low a level can be as dangerous as too high a level. The quantifier towers of the cascade problems are humbug, an illusion of logical depth, where there is in fact only shallowness. Such exercises can easily be played down, "if it does not do any good, it does no harm either". But it is the question whether this is true. It is the question whether the difficulties students experience with mathematical problems, and in particular those met in the transition from school to university and in any direct application of school mathematics, are not the consequence of training in feigned logical depth. Could the permanent drill with algorithmic quantifierc not have the effect of blocking the understanding of non-algorithmic ones? With a view to similar phenomena the answer, I fear, could be "yes". A double fear comes over me, the fear of a double blocking. By this kind of exercise something is blocked both in the pupil and in the teacher, and the teacher's blocking is perhaps even worse, since young people may still hope to break through this blockade.

It is an axiom of teachers' training that the teacher should know more than merely what he teaches. This "more" does not only aim at the subject matter. The teacher has to know the things he knows in a form different from that in which he is teaching them. He shall not only stand above the subject matter which he teaches but also above its logical form. To reach this goal he shall be able to fathom the logical depth of subject matter. Logic can help him to do so if it is more than indirect proof, conversion of theorems, equivalence, and so on. Rather than teaching logic, the mathematics teacher shall use logic and he shall make conscious to the learner that logic the learner is using.

The teacher should be able to do more. He should also stand above the method he has chosen of presenting subject matter, and be able to make this method conscious to himself. In this task, too, logical analysis can be helpful. Not in the trivial sense that it is the logical structure that determines the method, but rather because by logical analysis one can discover the level of understanding and its logical relation. How much can be learned from mathematics in this respect, has been unveiled by the analysis of the van Hieles: according to them every new level is the metatheory of the preceding.

APPENDIX I

PIAGET AND THE PIAGET SCHOOL'S INVESTIGATIONS
ON THE DEVELOPMENT OF MATHEMATICAL NOTIONS

The somewhat summary criticism I administered on several occasions to Piaget's work demands more detailed argument. Before going into this I would like to stress the wealth of ideas in his work, his originality, not to say genius, while not excluding the negative undertones which often reverberates this word.

It is not Piaget's fault that didacticians and textbook authors have misused Piaget's name as a sacred anointment of their work. But on the other hand, it is a hardly excusable fault of mathematicians in general that they never used to voice their adverse criticism of Piaget's work loud enough. Piaget could have learned from their criticism, and maybe he would have even liked to. Such criticism would have at any rate contributed to make clear the proper importance of Piaget's work.

The criticism of mathematicians should not only be restricted to the purely mathematical (or rather pseudo-mathematical) aspects of Piaget's work. A mathematician should be able to indicate in Piaget's problems what is adequate and what is distorted, and with a bit of common sense he could be the person best placed to uncover the numerous errors in Piaget's experiments and interpretations.

In my analysis I restricted myself to four works by Piaget and his collaborators.[1] There is an extensive literature of continuations of Piaget's work. While much of it contains the same kind of mistakes, others are quite critical. I cannot deal with this matter here.

On reading Piaget, mathematicians are troubled by many details which I will scarcely touch on here, especially Piaget's habit of borrowing mathematical terminology and applying it with quite divergent meanings.

---

[1] N: J. Piaget & Aline Szeminska, *La génèse du nombre chez l'enfant*, Neuchâtel-Paris 1941.

G: J. Piaget, Bärbel Inhelder & Alina Szeminska, *La géométrie spontanée de l'enfant*, Paris 1948.

E: J. Piaget & Bärbel Inhelder, *La représentation de l'espace chez l'enfant*, Paris 1948.

L: J. Piaget & Bärbel Inhelder, *La génèse des structures logiques élémentaires*, Neuchâtel 1959.

If a mathematician speaks about topological space, projective space, and Euclidean space, he is refering to well-defined concepts. "Topological, projective, and Euclidean methods" are perhaps vaguer terms but can hardly be misunderstood and, if need be, can be made more precise, e.g. by group theory arguments. If Piaget uses such terms in a yet vaguer sense still and often far removed from their mathematical meaning, he can hardly be blamed. If the didacticians and textbook authors who refer to Piaget do not notice that Piaget's notions do not match the homonymous mathematical notions, they share responsibility for this disturbing confusion. Piaget's misunderstanding of mathematical notions such as cardinal number, ordinal number, mapping, and transformation group is worse because they all decisively influence in one way or another some of his experimental approaches. The worst of these are genuine blunders such as believing that a cylinder keeps the same content if its diameter is halved and its height is doubled.

PIAGET'S ATTITUDE TO MATHEMATICS

As I have already said, I will not deal with such details. I would rather like to characterize Piaget's attitude to mathematics in its totality. Discussions of a mathematical character are in general dispersed over all his books. **E**, however, is distinguished from most of his other books, not only by its much higher standard, but also by a concentration of the more mathematical subject matter into a final chapter. Whereas in his other works one is inclined to jump over the hardly intelligible discussions of mathematical character, in **E** one is bluntly confronted with this concentration of them when one reaches the final chapter of this book. I have taken over a section from this chapter to let it speak for itself. I offer it in translation, which may be somewhat lacking in smoothness, since I am not a professional translator who is obliged to translate things he does not understand. The following specimen comes from **E**, p.566–570. It deals with what Piaget calls the eight infralogical operations that constitute Euclidean space:

I. ADDITION AND SUBTRACTION OF ELEMENTS

Let us take an object (of one or more dimensions) occupying a placement [2] with respect

---

[2] Translation of *emplacement*.

to other objects: it thus determines a figure, which can be interpreted either as the shape of the object or of its placement, that is, as a "figure of space" or a bounded part of the system of placements. These placements are nothing else but certain connections[3] between the objects which will be dealt with from the operations II onwards; since, however, psychologically the operations I are regarding the shape of the object rather than that of its placement, it would be useless to invert the order of the operations. Operations I simply consist of uniting and dissociating the parts of the shape being considered: $A + A' = B$; $B + B' = C$, and so on, which guarantees the conservations of the whole both with respect to the placement and the shape of the object itself.

II. PLACEMENTS AND DISPLACEMENTS

Let us now consider several separated objects and order them either with respect to an arbitrary arrangement or along a straight line. Then one gets $A \to B \to C$, and so on. These objects are called "placed" with respect to each other. In the system of the operations constituting Euclidean space, however, the inverse operation is not simply traversing the sequence in the inverse sense $\to C \to B \to A$; it is the change of placement, that is the "displacement", which can invert the whole sequence or simply one element with respect to one or more others, e.g. $A \to C \to B$ by inverting $B \to C$. As we showed in detail elsewhere, this displacement introduces a distinction between the order of the elements and that of the placements, as well as between two correlative operations of the same kind, depending on whether the order is applied to moveable objects and their possible displacements or to fixed placements which can be traversed by those movements. The notion of displacement is restricted to these qualitative (or intensive) notions before it is integrated into the metric "group" of six parameters which is known as the "group of displacements".[4]

III. RECIPROCITY[5] OF REFERENCES

Let us now suppose two neighboring figures (constituted by the shapes of the objects or of their placements) added up according to type I while departing from A_1 as a reference. Then one gets for instance $A_1 + A'_1 = B_1$ and $B_1 + B'_1 = C$. One can always come to the same union C while departing from A'_1 or B'_1 as a reference and calling it A_2, whence $A_2 + A'_2 + B_2 = C$. Together with the groupings of higher dimension

---

[3] French: *rapports*. I avoided the translation "relations" because *relation* will be used in a more technical sense.

[4] Groupe des déplacements. – Whereas the operations of the first kind were dividing and composing, those of the second kind are displacement of figures in space or of parts of space, for instance interchanging two pieces of a straight line. In *groupe des déplacements*, however, *déplacement* does not mean displacement of a figure but motion of the whole space. I did not translate "group of motions" in order to show how Piaget arrives at this identification. In Piaget's work the transformation group is never properly understood. Displacements need not form a group and those displacements considered by Piaget cannot even be extended to constitute a group, and anyhow do not have anything to do with the group of motions.

[5] I did not translate *réciprocité* by a more suitable term; réciprocité is already wrong according to French mathematical terminology. The authors mean something like equivalence.

(VI) this operation III leads to the reciprocity of coordinate systems, where A_1 or A_2 or A'_2 are considered as the "origins" of each of the systems at issue.

IV. NESTING[6] OF INTERVALS AND DISTANCES

The interval between two points arranged along a straight line is a distance. The conservation of distances is guaranteed by the fact that their points and the straight line belong to the fixed placements though they can be traversed by a moving object. The relation between X and Y that is constituted by its displacement, is an asymmetric relation[7]; the distance constitutes the corresponding symmetric interval relation; it is symmetric because it is the same distance from X to Y as from Y to X, that is $X \leftrightarrow Y = Y \leftrightarrow X$.

V. BI-UNIVALENT[8] MULTIPLICATION OF ELEMENTS

A linear sequence of elements $A_1 + A'_1 = B_1$, $B_1 + B'_1 = C_1$, and so on, multiplied by another $A_2 + A'_2 + B'_2$, and so on, constitutes a surface; both of them multiplied by a third generate a volume.

VI. BI-UNIVALENT MULTIPLICATION OF THE RELATIONS OF PLACEMENT AND DISPLACEMENT

These are the same operations, now expressed in terms of asymmetric relations (order of placement and displacement) which generate precisely a coordinate system. Such a system is nothing else but a placements lattice ordered as a function of reference points[9] or of objects considered as fixed, where these placements are ordered according to two or three dimensions simultaneously; while one of the ordered sequences constitutes an axis of the system, the second ordered according to another dimension constitutes a second axis. The intervals between the ordered placements as such consist of invariant distances with respect to operation IV. As we showed in Chapters XII–XIV, such a coordinate system need not be metric[10]. To understand this it suffices

[6] This subtitle is probably erroneous. Instead of *emboîtements* (nestings) it should be *relations symétriques* (symmetric relations); *emboîtements* was probably meant to stand in a parallel place on p. 551, where it is meaningful; it seems to be slipped in here by mistake during proof-reading.

[7] In classical philosophical terminology "relation" is a property that admits of more and less; "big" and "small" are relations, and the distance of two points is a relation. This terminology is still influential in Piaget, but there are more "modern" undertones, too; for instance, two cities may be said to be related by a railway; this relation is asymmetric because it makes a difference to travel from X to Y or vice versa; their distance, however, is the same; that is the "conservation of distances".

[8] French: *bi-univoque*. I did not translate it by "one-to-one", because otherwise I would not have known how to translate *co-univoque* in VII.

[9] Uncertain translation. Because of grammatical incongruence (singular-plural construction) the text cannot be properly translated. It is not clear whether the lattice or the placements are ordered, though the one is as unintelligible as the other.

[10] In the sequel it becomes somewhat clearer what the authors mean by this, but in Chapters XIII–XIV this has not even been mentioned. The problems posed in those chapters to the subjects could be solved without using a metric, and this was even the easiest way to solve them. Probably the authors meant to say: In Chapters XII–XIV we did not investigate whether such a coordinate system is already felt as a metric one.

to analyse the structure of this groupment of relation VI more explicitly than we did in § 3–4. Let us have a set of pointwise placements ordered according to two dimensions departing from 0 (and represented in the table by fat points connected to each other by dotted lines) and let a_1; a'_1 and b'_1[11] or a a_2; a'_2 and b'_2 be the relations uniting them (that is the dotted lines), which can be interpreted either asymmetrically or symmetrically according to whether they are expressed in terms of order or of distance. Then one gets:

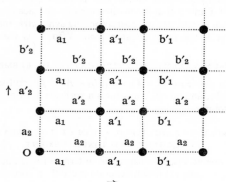

It is seen that each of both sequences of placement or distance relations $a_1 + a'_1 = b_1$; $b_1 + b'_1 = c_1$, and so on, and $a_2 + a'_2 = b_2$; $b_2 + b'_2 = c_2$ remains intensive, because there is neither a common unit nor a definite connection[12] between the successive parts a, a' and b'. Yet these intervals a_1; a'_1 and b'_1 or a_2; a'_2 and b'_2 come out as being identical with themselves by bi-univalent correspondence (with respect to each of both dimensions), where this qualitative equality is easily assured by the parallelism of the lines along which the points are arranged.[13]

Such a multiplicative table of placement relations, then, exactly translates how children of level III B (Chapters XIII–XIV) construct their systems of reference. From the point of view of distances and because of the lack of a metric the subject can only draw the conclusion $a_1 < b_1$ or $a'_1 < b_1$ (if $a_1 + a'_1 = b_1$) as well as the constant equality of the intervals between the parallels.[14] But it is easily seen that the introduction of the

---

[11] The semi-colons are better replaced by commas.

[12] Rapport; see footnote 3 of Appendix.

[13] "Identical" and "equal" are used as synonyms. If it is said that intervals are identical with themselves, it is not meant as a tautology; the authors mean the equality of those intervals which in the figure have been prematurely designated by the same symbol; on the other hand there is no quantitative relation stipulated between intervals that have been indicated by different symbols: "the relations remain intensive".

[14] The connection of perpendicularity is not a necessary element of the theory, but it is given by the maximal opposition of the corresponding directions in two dimensions. Original footnote. – Remark by the present author: according to the authors, children at this level cannot compare intervals in different directions though they can arrive at the notion of perpendicularity by comparing intervals in different directions.

measure (that is that a' or b is metrically reported to a) suffices to transform such a grouping into a mathematical coordinate system.[15]

VII. CO-UNIVALENT MULTIPLICATION OF THE ELEMENTS

Other than the bi-univalent correspondences which are proper to the two preceding systems, the multiplication by co-univalent correspondence generates the notion of triangle in two, and tetrahedron in three dimensions.[16]

VIII. CO-UNIVALENT MULTIPLICATION OF THE RELATIONS

The pattern of this grouping is that of an increasing symmetric interval which is generated by two asymmetric connections[17] of progressive value[18], that is (Figure 99).

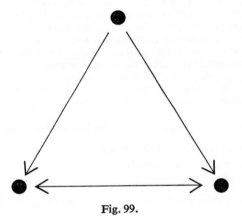

Fig. 99.

As has been shown in Chapter XII this operative system gives rise to the qualitative evaluation of the angles before the introduction of a measure.

These have been the eight operative groupings which we have observed in the infralogical construction of Euclidean space; obviously they reproduce as to the form the eight systems described in § 3–4 with the topological and projective notions though,

[15] It is the same wrong formulation which we corrected in footnote 10 to the Appendix. The authors made the subjects design a map of a landscape by means of a coordinate system by putting the landscape into a rectangular frame; they did not at all investigate whether the children would have been able to proceed by comparing lengths because according to the authors this ability belongs to the higher level of "schematizing".

[16] The authors mean here parallel lines mapped onto each other by central rather than by parallel projection, such as drawings in perspective.

[17] Rapports.

[18] "Increasing" and "progressive" mean that in the perspective view the distance increases in the direction of the viewer.

from every total systematisation onwards[19], with a new meaning that integrates the topological connections while adding definite specifications. It is the point to ask oneself what this number eight means and why it is not more nor less. First of all, this depends on the close parallelism between the infralogical and the logical operations: uniting, putting into relation, and multiplying according to neighborhoods and spatial differences, or, in general, according to resemblances and qualitative differences, boils down to the same from the groupings as from the relations point of view however different the respective meanings of these set structures may be[20]. This is why we get back the eight forms of groupings we described earlier in the field of logical operations[21]; this convergence is quite interesting from the viewpoint of the unity of the functioning of the operative mind. In this course of thought the number eight rather than being arbitrary represents the product of the following combinations, which seem to be the only possible ones according to qualitative intensive connections: one can add in simple sequences of elements or classes (I) and of relations (II); one can add them in different possible senses, from which results the reciprocity of class and element systems (III), and the construction of symmetric relations (IV). Finally one can multiply them, that is uniting two or more additive sequences into tables with double or multiple entries by means of bi-univalent correspondence of the classes and elements (V) or of the relations (VI), or by co-univalent correspondence of the classes and elements (VII) or of the relations (VIII). Since the last distinctions of the bi-univalent and the co-univalent correspondences result from the opposition of asymmetries and symmetries, one gets the following combinations: 2 (elements or relations) × 2 (asymmetries or symmetries) × 2 (additions or multiplications) = 8.

This is Piaget's crucial idea. It is worthwhile making the system explicit:

(1)   elements (sets) – relations,
(2)   asymmetric – symmetric.
(3)   addition – multiplication.

We describe this in the dyadic system by 0,1 at the 1st, 2nd, 3rd place from the right. Then we get:

000 (I) Elements, asymmetric, addition: the addition of intervals which, however, is *symmetrically* interpreted.

001 (II) Relations, asymmetric, addition: the linear displacement, though however *no addition* of relations was ever mentioned; the distinction between I and II was not "elements – relation under addition" but "placement – displacement".

010 (III) Elements, symmetric, addition: the equivalence of linear reference systems with different origins, called reciprocity.

[19] Here I did not understand the text.
[20] The translation is entirely uncertain.
[21] Classes, relations et nombres. Études sur les «groupements» de la logistique et la réversibilité de la pensée. Virin (1942). Original footnote.

011 (IV) Relations, symmetric, addition: the distance notion.
100 (V) Elements, asymmetric, multiplication, and
101 (VI) Relations, asymmetric, multiplication: the construction of coordinate systems, with however no visible difference between V and VI, that is, neither that of (I) and (II) between placement and displacement, nor that between 000 and 001 between element and relation.
110 (VII) Element, symmetric, multiplication.
111 (VIII) Relation, symmetric, multiplication.

According to this pattern the pair "asymmetric-symmetric" is reflected by the pair "bi-univalent – co-univalent" (parallel projection–central projection). The authors stress this expressedly since anybody else would have done it (if at all) the other way round, and the figures in both cases clearly show that the authors also originally meant it the other way round.

After our short analysis this extract speaks so loud for itself that there is no need to add a criticism. It is, however, not too far-fetched to ask whether such ideas have influenced Piaget's work in a decisive way. They did influence it, but I doubt whether they were in any way decisive influences. They are the least felt in **E**. The psychological experiments in **E** focus around physically testable statements on the phenomenological world rather than on the linguistic expressions of phenomena. Yet even in **E** there are traces of these ideas, in particular in the aforementioned Chapter XIV. By a suggestive design of the experiments it is achieved that the subjects reconstruct a landscape according to the Piaget theory of multiplication of relations, that is by means of a Cartesian coordinate system. There is little reason to take such mistakes seriously. But it *is* a serious mistake if, to justify a particular kind of didactics, people tell you Piaget proved Euclidean geometry to start psychologically with Cartesian coordinates.

THE ROLE OF LANGUAGE IN PIAGET'S EXPERIMENTS

The verbal element in Piaget's experiments is quite noticeable. Even in experiments where children are active with their hands, the description of the experiment reads like a question-and-answer game. Anybody who studies Piaget asks spontaneously whether the subjects understood the questions of the experimenter, or even whether the children knew what it means to answer context-free questions. In some cases, it even seems doubtful whether the experimenter understood the answers of the children.

Quite a few times Piaget and his collaborators must have been concerned about the problem whether their subjects understood the questions. Several times, indeed, they asked questions like the following (N, p. 12):

> In fact, one could ask oneself sometimes whether he has grasped the question: does he understand that it aims at the total quantity, or does he simply think that he is being asked about the change in the number of the glasses, or about the level or the width of the glasses. Yet the problem is just to know whether the child is able to view the quantity as a whole that results from the coordination of the different connexions[22] perceived: the fact that one of those aspects is isolated, as happened with the children just mentioned[23], can thus be caused by a misunderstanding of the notions at issue as well as of the verbal question itself.

One would expect that the authors would try to exclude the second possibility, but nothing like this happens. They are entirely satisfied by the opportunity of explaining the subjects' failure by a misunderstanding of the notions rather than of the language, and they continue their analysis as though this were the correct explanation. At other places the discussion about whether the subjects understood the essential questions of the experimenter is closed in the same abrupt manner before it has really been opened. A strange case is in N, p. 55–56:

> But could one not object that this is due to misunderstanding of the words: even though the child admits that the number of bottles and glasses remains the same when one of the two collections is gathered into a heap, he would answer "there are more there"[24], simply to express the idea that the shape of the collection has changed and that the space claimed has increased. It is just because of this objection and because it is difficult to eliminate a verbal misunderstanding by words, that we multiply the situations and the examples in the course of these two chapters. The more we investigate new facts the more we can choose between the two interpretations.[25]

But even averaging over a large number of observations involving a systematic error does not bring us nearer to the truth. In fact, in many cases it is as clear as day that the questions were not understood; sometimes this is even expressly so stated by the children; moreover a whole

[22] Rapports.
[23] The French text is corrupt.
[24] Doubtful translation.
[25] Text unintelligible.

sequence is so misleading that they may be considered as *a priori* unintelligible.

The authors have recognized or at least should have recognized the importance of the linguistic formulation of their questions, since the questions are mostly differently worded according to the age or level of the subjects. With the little ones questions are vaguely formulated, sometimes even in "baby" language; with increasing age the precision of formulation is increased, too, so it is not to be wondered at that the answers are improving. But what is really being investigated then, is not a development of the notions at issue, but skill in communicating. Of course, this criticism does not mean that there has been no development of the notions but rather that it has not been properly isolated in a domain of perturbing factors.

N starts with investigating whether and to which degree children understand that pouring a fluid from one vessel into another or into a number of vessels does not influence the quantity; the subjects are asked whether this is more or less than that or as much as that. According to the authors' intention the question aims at the quantity rather than at the number of vessels or the height of the level of the fluid. This fact, however, is not included in the information provided to the children[26]; the experimenters' questions are sometimes even misleading, to which contributes the linguistic circumstance that in French both "is this more?" and "are there more?" can be translated by the same phrase "y en a-t-il plus?" There is even more to it than that. I could not tell from my own experience whether children of a certain age know certain words; I can tell this of French-speaking children even less than of Dutch- or German-speaking ones. I would say it ought to be a preliminary requirement that such experiments are preceded by making sure of the essentials of the dictionary. This has been systematically neglected. On the contrary it is rather obvious that the little ones did not know the words *plus* and *moins* (more and less), or in any case they were not familiar with them in a context like that of the experiments; in fact, they replace *plus* by *beaucoup* (much) and *moins* by *peu* (little); sometimes the experi-

---

[26] It is hard to explain why this information is provided in exceptional cases; e.g. in N,11 it is expressedly explained to Kac that "less" is to aim at the quantity of fluid rather than at the number of the vessels. So it is not to be wondered at that his results are better than those of others.

menters take over this terminology. (Some children know the words *plus* and *moins* in "plus grand", "moins grand", and in similar combinations, but a *plus* and *moins* with no complement that aims at numerosity seems to be unknown to them.)[27]

It is still worse with the word for "equal". In talks with the subjects even the experimenters do not use the word "autant que", even with older children; maybe because it seems to be thought high-brow. It is always *"la même chose"* (the same). So the children are asked: "Y a-t-il la même chose dans les deux verres?" (N, 10), "est-ce qu'il y a la même chose de perles?" (N, 34), "y a-t-il la même chose d'oeufs et de coquetiers?" (N, 61), "c'est encore la même chose?" (N, 64). To this question "is this the same?", an adult would answer: "What do you mean? The same shape, the same quantity, or the same number?" Children obviously do not dare to do so; even when they are in doubt, they think that they must answer anyhow, though in fact they sometimes say "I do not know". (N, 85.) This, however, does not at all cause the experimenter to explain what "the same" means in this particular case. If he did, he would be laying his cards on the table, would he not? A number of coins or beans is put on the table to form a certain configuration, and the children are asked to reproduce "the same". The children interpret this as "the same figure" and nobody tries to explain to them what is actually meant. (N, 80 sq.) They are asked to form with matches "the same" figure as is given with the coins; if they protest, nothing is explained (N, 85). The subject is supposed to understand "the same" in any particular case in the sense meant by the experimenters. With the older children they are more successful, which is interpreted as proof that the notions "equal number", "equal quantity", "equal content", "equal shape" develop in such and such a way. Actually the only thing that has been investigated is how children of different ages manage to adjust to imprecise ways of adult expression.

The question of linguistic communication is even more urgent in the sequence of experiments that starts in N, 202, and continues in a broader

[27] There are, however, strange divergences. The subjects of N, Chapters I, II, and IV do not know *plus* and *moins* except in comparatives, but those of Chapter III of the same age are quite familiar with these words, though they are less so with comparatives. What is the reason for this? Has the second group been trained in the use of *plus* and *moins*, or is this due to editorial divergences, to be ascribed to the various experimenters?

stream in **L**. The subject is shown a number of wooden beads most of which are brown, while a few are white; the subjects are asked whether there are more wooden or more brown beads. Little children usually answer: "More brown beads". This experiment is repeated with many variations (**L** 104 sq.): the subject is given 20 coloured pictures, among which 16 display flowers; of the flower pictures 8 show primroses, and among the primroses there are 4 yellow ones. The questions posed are for instance: "Are there more flowers than primroses? Are there more yellow primroses than primroses?" In a similar experiment flowers are replaced by animals. From the results Piaget concludes that the children do not master the inclusion. This conclusion is at least wrong for the reason that the experiments combine two difficulties: first the inclusion, and secondly numerical comparing of two non-disjoint sets. Indeed, typical questions are: "can you make a longer string with the brown beads or with the wooden beads?" It should have been the first task of the investigation to make sure whether comparing two sets that cannot simultaneously be formed is not too difficult an assignment. But this is not the main point. The essential thing is again the linguistic misunderstanding.

If an adult is asked whether there are more brown or more wooden beads (where all brown beads are of wood), he would answer: "You mean *other* wooden beads, do you not?" And likewise with flowers: "You mean whether there are more primroses than other flowers, more yellow ones than of other colours?" Such juxtapositions like wooden beads and brown beads, flowers and primroses are considered as flatly wrong in everyday language, though they will sometimes be used to make a joke or to express malice, such as "the tail is longer than the dog", or "men and negroes". The experimenters avail themselves of such wrong constructions to play tricks on the children. But if children take the same liberty in this respect, for instance, by speaking about "flowers and primroses", the authors make the comment that the children behave "as though primroses were not flowers" (**L**, 136). Why are the children not allowed to commit the same linguistic "mistakes" as shown them by the adults? Why not extend to the children the right to think "as though primroses were not flowers" after a wrong question of the experimenter, and then to answer the question as if the experimenter had meant "other flowers". There is not the slightest indication that these experiments test the mastership of inclusion; they are rather tests of linguistic behaviour. An investigation by G. A. Kohnstamm[28] has shown that after a brief linguistic training of this subject matter most of the subjects give the desired answers. Other investigations[29] show that more general linguistic exercises suffice to improve the reactions of children to Piaget-style questions.

Another sequence of experiments in which Piaget is led to state the failure of little children with regard to inclusion, looks like this (L, 65 sq): the subject is shown, for instance, blue circles and blue squares, and also red squares. If asked questions like "are all the round ones blue?", "are all the squares red?", younger children generally give "wrong answers". The children motivate these "wrong answers", and the explanations show that they do not know that the position of "all" in the sentence decides its meaning. Indeed, how can linguistically un-skilled little children find their way through a thicket of questions like "are all the round ones blue?", "are all the blue ones round?", "are the round ones all blue ones?", "are the blue ones all round ones?", "are these all red ones?", "are all these red?" This can be even difficult for adults (see L, 105). In their excellent analysis (L, 73–78) the authors come very near to the conclusion that all the difficulties the children experience are linguistic difficulties with the position of "all", only to terminate with the unexpected declaration that the whole trouble is the lack of mastery over the inclusion.

The answers, however, show another feature which has permanently been neglected by Piaget and his collaborators, I mean that the children have no idea what a formal answer is. If I enter a meeting room and ask "are all chairs occupied" and somebody answers "no, you can sit on a bench", then this is an answer, not to the formal question, but to the intentional question "where can I sit?" This is the way Piaget's subjects are reacting. They are used to answering questions meaningfully rather than formally. But now they are confronted with questions which must appear meaningless to them because they do not know that they fit into a system to be published as a book. They are not suspicious

[28] *Acta Psychologica* **21** (1963), 313.
[29] I. E. Sigel, Annemarie Roeper, and F. H. Hopper, *British Journal of Educational Psychology* **36** (1966), 301–311.

because they have not yet experienced how to deal with people who
ask questions like: "have you stopped beating your wife?"

The same thicket of questions around "all" is built around "some"
(L, 79 sq., in particular 97–98). The children must willy-nilly find their
way with this vague concept. "Give me some tulips"[30] may not be answered by giving one or all the tulips. One asks: Are all tulips flowers?",
"are some tulips flowers?", "are some flowers tulips?", "are all flowers
tulips?", "are all tulips some flowers?".

ONE-ELEMENT SETS AND THE EMPTY SET

Piaget claims that little children do not yet recognize a one-element
set as a set. This may be true since these children have not yet got any
formal set notion at all. It is, however, interesting how Piaget proves it
by experiment (L, 124):

We have made use of a material consisting of three or six triangles; the subjects had to
guess which one had a cross on the back; this card could be distinguished by the fact
that it was unique in its colour (e.g. a blue one between two yellow ones)...

Notice that the children are not told that this card is also unique with
respect to its upper side. It comes out that the older children score even
worse than the youngest, viz. 5–7 years 50% success, 7–9 years 75%,
10–12 years 33%. The authors explain this retrogression by the fact

that the subject artificially complicates a problem that has become too simple for him

No comment. The experiment has, in fact, nothing to do with the one-
element set.

It is much the same with the empty set. I quote from L, 149:

The experiment was made in the most natural form of square, round, and triangular
cards bearing pictures of trees, fruits, houses, and so on, and others with no picture.
Since this should be classified, first arbitrarily, later by dichotomy, it is easy to observe
the reactions of the subject, whether he is struck by the absence of pictures on certain
cards, or whether he restricts himself to transferring to all elements positive characters,
say of shape.

In classifying the subjects neglect the set of empty cards:

... the child refuses to construct the empty set.

[30] Quelques tulipes – French does not have two different words corresponding to
"some" and "a few".

The set of empty cards is, according to Piaget, an empty set. After what we have quoted from **E** this is not shocking any more.

THE DESIGN OF EXPERIMENTS

Most of the experiments are surcharged. Rather than being given a simple task the children are given a combination of several tasks. Such a simple problem as whether the children are able to put two sets in a one-to-one relation is never isolated by itself, but only appears in very complicated contexts. In the course of the transfusion experiments only a few subjects are asked to predict what happens with the fluid level in a narrower cylinder (which is answered correctly by all of them) but rather than investigating this systematically, the children are nagged with linguistic unintelligibilities.

Several times the general description of an experiment and its execution with the single subject do not agree with one another (**N**, 53). The discussion of the experiments sometimes involves other subjects than the account of the experiments (**N**, 162: Tis does not exist), and other facts are discussed than those which have been reported before (**N**, 162: Dit). Often the answers of the children are understood badly. A curious example is the following (**G**, 101): Two similar dolls are placed at different heights; the child is asked whether it is farther from A to B or from B to A.[31] The subject explains:

it is not the same distance, because the little man below looks to the feet of the man above, and the man above looks to the eyes of the man below... it is farther for the man below because it is higher.

It is a pity that after this nice remark in the beginning the child confuses above and below, but it is even more regrettable that the experimenter did not understand this remark.

I conclude with a more fundamental point: In **E**, 537 we read:

... the young subjects do not arrive at imagining themselves the results of such actions, even the simplest, unless they have actually performed them...

This is, indeed, an important principle, which has been observed in **E** more often than in other places. Too often, however, in his talks with

---

[31] According to Piaget little children cannot conceive the symmetry of distance.

the subjects the experimenter sticks to thought-experiments. This not only provokes mistakes from the children, but it has the still worse effect of leading the experimenters propose experiments to the children which cannot be performed in the intended way, or even experiments whose results would greatly surprise the experimenters if they were actually performed.

APPENDIX II

PAPERS OF THE AUTHOR ON MATHEMATICAL INSTRUCTION

[1] De algebraische en de analytische visie op het getalbegrip in de elementaire wiskunde, *Euclides* **24** (1948), 106–121.

[2] Kan het wiskundeonderwijs tot de opvoeding van het denkvermogen bijdragen. Discussie tussen T. Ehrenfest-Afanassjewa en H. Freudenthal (Publicatie Wiskunde Werkgroep van de V.W.O.), Purmerend, 1951.

Partial translation of 2:

[2a] Erziehung des Denkvermögens (Diskussionsbeitrag), *Archimedes* Heft 6 (1954), 87–89.

[3] De begrippen axioma en axiomatiek in de wis- en natuurkunde, *Simon Stevin* **30** (1955), 156–175.

[3a] Axiom und Axiomatik, *Mathem. Phys. Semesterberichte* **5** (1956), 4–19.

[4] Initiation into Geometry, *The Mathematics Student* **24** (1956), 83–97.

[5] Relations entre l'enseignement secondaire et l'enseignement universitaire en Hollande, *Enseignement mathématique* (2) (1956), 238–249.

[6] De Leraarsopleiding, *Vernieuwing* **133** (1956), 173–180.

[7] Traditie en opvoeding, *Rekenschap* **4** (1957), 95–103.

[8] *Report on Methods of Initiation into Geometry*, ed. by H. Freudenthal (Publ. Nederl. Onderwijscommissie voor Wiskunde), Groningen, 1958.

[9] Einige Züge aus der Entwicklung des mathematischen Formalismus, I, *Nieuw Archief v. Wiskunde* (3) **7** (1959), 1–19.

[10] Report on a Comparative Study of Methods of Initiation into Geometry, *Euclides* **34** (1959), 289–306.

[10a] A Comparative Study of Methods of Initiation into Geometry, *Enseignement mathématique* (2) **5** (1959), 119–139.

[11] Logica als Methode en als Onderwerp, *Euclides* **35** (1960), 241–255.

[11a] Logik als Gegenstand und als Methode, *Der Mathematikunterricht* **13**, 5 (1967), 7–22.

[12] Trends in Modern Mathematics, *ICSU Review* **4** (1962), 54–61.

[12a] Tendenzen in der modernen Mathematik, *Der math. und naturw. Unterricht* **16** (1963), 301–306.

[13] *Report on the Relations Between Arithmetic and Algebra*, ed. by H. Freudenthal (Publ. Nederl. Onderwijscommissie voor Wiskunde), Groningen, 1962.

[14] Enseignement des mathématiques modernes ou enseignement moderne des mathématiques? *Enseignement Mathématique* (2) **9** (1963), 28–44.

[15] Was ist Axiomatik, und welchen Bildungswert kann sie haben?, *Der Mathematikunterricht* **9**, 4 (1963), 5–29.

[16] The Role of Geometrical Intuition in Modern Mathematics, *ICSU Review* **6** (1964), 206–209.

[16a] Die Geometrie in der modernen Mathematik, *Physikalische Blätter* **20** (1964), 352–356.

[17] Bemerkungen zur axiomatischen Methode im Unterricht, *Der Mathematikunterricht* **12**, 3 (1966), 61–65.

[18] Functies en functie-notaties, *Euclides* **41** (1966), 299–304.

[19] Why to Teach Mathematics so as to be Useful?, *Educational Studies in Mathematics* **1** (1968), 3–8.

[20] Panel Discussion, *Educational Studies in Mathematics* **1** (1968), 61–93.

[21] L'intégration après coup ou à la source, *Educational Studies in Mathematics* **1** (1968–1969), 327–337.

[22] The Concept of Integration at the Varna Congress, *Educational Studies in Mathematics* **1** (1968–1969), 338–339.

[23] Braces and Venn Diagrams, *Educational Studies in Mathematics* **1** (1968–1969), 408–414.

[23a] Geschweifte Klammern und Venn-Diagramme, *Der Mathematikunterricht* (1971), 84–90.

[24] Further Training of Mathematics Teachers in the Netherlands, *Educational Studies in Mathematics* **1** (1968–1969), 484–492.

[25] A Teachers Course Colloquium on Sets and Logic, *Educational Studies in Mathematics* **2** (1969–1970), 32–58.

[26] ICMI Report on Mathematical Contests in Secondary Education

(Olympiads), ed. by H. Freudenthal, *Educational Studies in Mathematics* **2** (1969–1970), 80–114.

[27] Allocution au Premier Congrès International de l'Enseignement Mathématique, Lyon 24–31 août 1969, *Educational Studies in Mathematics* **2** (1969–1970), 135–138.

[28] Les Tendances Nouvelles de l'Enseignement Mathématique, *Revue de l'enseignement supérieur* **46–47** (1969), 23–29.

[28a] Die neuen Tendenzen im Mathematik-Unterricht. *Neue Sammlung* **11** (1971), 146–153.

[29] Verzamelingen in het onderwijs, *Euclides* **45** (1970), 321–326.

[30] The Aims of Teaching Probability, in *The Teaching of Probability & Statistics*, ed. L. Råde, Stockholm, Almqvist and Wiksell, 1970, p. 151–167.

[31] Introduction, in *New Trends in Mathematics Teaching*, Vol. II, Unesco (1970).

[32] Un cours de Géométrie, in *New Trends in Mathematics Teaching*, Vol, II Unesco (1970), 309–314.

[33] Le Language Mathématique, Premier Sém. Intern. E. Galion, Royaumont 13–20 août 1970, OCDL, Paris, 1971.

[34] Geometry Between the Devil and the Deep Sea, *Educational Studies in Mathematics* **3** (1971), 413–435.

[35] Kanttekeningen bij de nomenclatuur, *Euclides* **47** (1971), 138–140.